WHO TO CALL

WHO TO CALL

THE PARENT'S SOURCE BOOK

☎

DANIEL STARER

QUILL

WILLIAM MORROW
NEW YORK

It is the policy of William Morrow and Company, Inc., and its imprints and affiliates, recognizing the importance of preserving what has been written, to print the books we publish on acid-free paper, and we exert our best efforts to that end.

WHO TO CALL: THE PARENT'S SOURCE BOOK

ISBN 0-688-11729-5

Library of Congress Cataloging-in-Publication Data has been requested

Library of Congress Number: 91-28612

Printed in the United States of America

First Quill Edition

1 2 3 4 5 6 7 8 9 10

BOOK DESIGN BY M 'N O PRODUCTION SERVICES, INC.   /   MICHAEL MENDELSOHN

To my parents,
Johanna and Robert Starer,
with all my love

ACKNOWLEDGMENTS

My thanks to Nick Ellison, my agent, who found an excellent home for this book. Thanks also to Liza Dawson, my editor, whose enthusiasm and suggestions were vital in shaping *Who to Call*. I especially appreciate the hard work by Wendy Bellerman, Liza's assistant, who helped reorganize the manuscript. Finally, I would like to thank my wife, Maggie, for her help at all stages of this book.

CONTENTS

CONTENTS

CONTENTS

CONTENTS

INTRODUCTION

Parents have a never-ending need for reliable information on unfamiliar subjects. After our first child was born three years ago, my wife and I had a surprising number of questions that could not be easily answered by child-care books or our pediatrician. Our daughter, Katie, was born with a mild birth defect requiring an operation. The pediatrician recommended a surgeon at the hospital where he is affiliated. Naturally, we wanted both a second opinion and an independent evaluation of the surgeon's credentials.

Like all parents, we also had many other questions on a great variety of subjects. I wanted to call the manufacturer of a baby monitor that was making bizarre noises. My wife wondered if an older model crib at her mother's house had ever been recalled for safety problems. We needed information about car seats, a prescription drug, child care, and sources to buy disposable, biodegradable diapers by mail.

Fortunately for us, I'm an information researcher with twelve years experience using New York City's libraries, access to fifteen hundred computerized databases, and a small collection of reference books on my desk. I could easily identify the organizations that would provide accurate answers over the phone and send us helpful brochures.

Katie not only had a highly successful operation but all our other questions were answered quickly and intelligently. I realized then that all parents have questions best answered by telephone. Experts, phone hotlines, and other sources gladly help—if we ask. However, most parents don't know these sources exist and have no idea how to reach them.

This book directs you to the thousands of organizations that can make you an "instant expert" on virtually every unfamiliar subject that might arise as your children grow. Often, the answers you seek will be found in the first phone call you make or in the free brochures you request. Other times, you may need to call a group's national headquarters or a state office for a referral to a local organization. Using this book, you are rarely more than one, two, or three calls away from the answer you need.

CHAPTER 1

HOW TO FIND INSTANT INFORMATION BY PHONE

The advantages of talking with an expert by phone are many. An expert's advice usually costs nothing. A conversation between the two of you allows the expert to address your situation specifically. If you don't understand something, the expert can explain it differently. Frequently, an expert offers vital information you didn't even know to ask for or information unavailable in printed form. Using the phone allows you to remain anonymous if the subject (like teenage sex) embarrasses you. Best of all, answers are instantaneous. The phone is more convenient than seeking help at the local library or traveling to an expert's office to talk in person. Finally, it is one of the least expensive ways to get information. Even if you call coast-to-coast with daytime rates in effect, most short calls cost less than a dollar.

Everyone can gather information by phone. As part of my research business I am well paid for telephone research and I needed no formal training in phone techniques.

Most of the phone numbers in this book are for use by the public. The experts you reach are happy to hear from you. Not only is it their *job* to help you but they also welcome the opportunity to share their years of experience with the public. As a courtesy, however, it is a good idea to prepare for your calls ahead of time.

Organize Your Questions Beforehand

Even if you only call an organization for copies of their free brochures, it makes sense to decide first exactly what you wish to know and exactly what information you'd like to receive. Some organizations have dozens or even hundreds of brochures. It would be a shame if they sent you material that didn't address your specific needs.

Ask yourself: "If one perfect brochure could answer my questions what would it be called?" Jotting down the title of this ideal, imaginary brochure helps you focus on your query and the answers you need. If your family is going on vacation and you want advice about the dangers of Lyme disease in the Catskill Mountains during August, ask for exactly that. Don't ask the Lyme Borreliosis Foundation simply to send their standard brochures on avoiding deer ticks.

When calling an expert for advice, always prepare your questions in advance. If your queries are concise and specific, most experts willingly take the time to talk. Introduce yourself, explain why you need the information, and state exactly what you wish to know. The expert can then tailor an answer to your needs and nobody's time is wasted.

Experts Want to Help

Getting and using the best possible information for your family is your right as a parent and consumer. If at any time you feel awkward about calling a stranger for help, remember your rights. Also remember that most of these organizations exist to help you. Experts who devote themselves to gifted children, drug prevention, and summer camp referrals care deeply about their work. In most cases, the people who answer the phone at these organizations are dedicated to public service. They *enjoy* helping you—the public.

Rarely, an organization may prove unwilling or too busy to help. Don't be discouraged. Ask for an alternate source of information or ask when it would be better to call. If you strike out, refer again to this book. In most cases you'll find more than one organization specializes in each subject.

Reducing Phone Costs

The telephone is one of the cheapest, and certainly the fastest, ways to get information. A two-minute daytime call anywhere in the continental United States to request brochures costs less than fifty cents (slightly more to Hawaii and Alaska). A ten-minute conversation with an expert costs a few dollars. It could take you hours to locate the same information in the library. Writing a letter may be cheaper but you must take the time to write it, and a response may take weeks.

Phone costs can be controlled in several ways. Obviously, if the organization has a toll-free 800 number, make use of it. I've tried to include virtually all 800 numbers useful to parents. If you suspect an organization has an 800 number not listed in this book, call toll-free directory assistance at 1 (800) 555-1212.

You can also call an organization when it's closed and leave a message on its answering machine. If you hope to reach a specific person, call prior to normal working hours, after hours, or when he or she is likely to be at lunch. The person will probably call you back. This may sound sneaky, but if you expect a lengthy conversation and wish to save on phone costs, the method works. In most cases the organization, not the expert, pays for the call. To increase the likelihood of a return call, always leave a concise message explaining why you are calling and what you need to know.

Who to Call First

A rule of thumb in information research is to *start* with the most specific or targeted source of information available. For example, if you wish to find a local support group for parents raising a child with a cleft palate, call the Cleft Palate Parents' Council, not the American Academy of Pediatrics.

This book contains a wide variety of information sources. If the national organizations that seem appropriate to your topic can't help, call the state offices listed in many chapters. Also, check Chapter 13, "Information on Any Topic," for a list of national, state, and local referral agencies covering virtually any subject.

Once you decide which organization seems most appropriate, call and talk to one or two staff members, perhaps a public affairs officer or a knowledgable assistant. If you don't need an immediate answer, ask for the publications department and request literature on the subject. Only after reading the brochures and acquiring a better understanding of the topic are you ready to talk with an organization's executive director or top expert. These experts gladly help you if you use their time intelligently.

At larger organizations, the library and the education department are also valuable sources of information. An organization's reference librarian usually possesses a thorough knowledge of its areas of expertise. These professionals spend all day answering questions about the subject, identifying and photocopying published articles, and even running computer database searches. If the information you need is not readily available in an association's brochures or by talking with their experts, the association's librarian is your next logical source. Remember, however, librarians are busy people. If they cannot answer your question quickly by checking a few handy reference books, they will probably suggest you send a letter outlining what you need to know. You can often expect a response within two to three weeks.

Note-Taking Versus Tape Recording

Should you tape record a conversation with an expert or simply take notes? Most of the time, you won't need a tape recorder. If you take careful notes and write them up immediately after your conversation, the information should be complete and correct. I can't emphasize enough the importance of writing up your notes right away. More than once I've allowed myself to become distracted and later struggled to make sense of my scratchings on the note pad.

If you expect a lengthy discussion about a technical or confusing subject, you may decide to record it. Electronics stores sell inexpensive couplers or microphones that allow most cassette players to record a telephone conversation. It is considered polite to inform the other party that you will be recording them. Be aware that some people decline to be recorded or become less helpful if they are being taped.

IF YOU WRITE A LETTER

Never send a letter before calling. Although every effort has been made to ensure the addresses in this book are up-to-date, organizations do move or go out of existence. Before writing, you should confirm the address and determine the person or department that should receive your letter. If answering your questions requires substantial research or photocopying, you may be charged. In addition, some organizations charge for brochures or require a self-addressed, stamped envelope (SASE). Ask about the cost in advance so you can enclose a check or SASE with your letter and expedite your request. (A very small percentage of organizations in this book do not list their phone numbers. You must write rather than call these groups.)

If you write a letter, make it short and very specific. The recipient is not likely to respond quickly, if at all, to a three-page tome containing ten detailed questions. Try to keep the letter simple, to the point, and no more than one page. If you have a lot of questions, ask the less important ones at another time. Some organizations request a letter because they are bureaucracies which tend to generate paperwork. Other groups, often the understaffed ones, try to control their work load by assuming only the most serious inquirers will take the time to put their requests in writing. In either case, once you have a letter on file, these organizations may be happy to answer all your future questions over the phone.

If at all possible, send a typed letter free of spelling and grammatical mistakes. If your request for information is urgent, say so in your letter. I often cite a date by which I need a response. Aside from the return address, make sure your phone number appears on the letter. The recipient may want to call you to clarify a question.

Twelve Ways to Get the Best Results Over the Phone

1) *Identify yourself first.* Most people like to know to whom they are speaking. Unless you wish to remain anonymous because the subject (such as venereal disease) makes you uncomfortable, it is best to identify yourself fully. For example: "Good morning. My name is Mary Johnson. I'm a parent from Teaneck, New Jersey. Could you please help me find day-care centers in my community?"

2) *Be polite.* Just because it is the expert's job to help the public doesn't mean they should be taken for granted. You would be amazed how grumpy and demanding callers can sound. If your tone is polite and respectful, you get better information more quickly.

3) *Be positive.* Never phrase a question negatively: "You don't have any information on this, do you?" That invites the negative response: "No, I don't have any information." Always assume the person you call can help. If he or she can't, ask for a referral to another source.

4) *Be prepared.* If you have several questions, write them all down ahead of time. You can then concentrate on what the expert is saying rather than on what you should ask next. Also, if you have a list, you can check off the questions as you go without worrying you might forget one.

5) *Be specific and explain why you need the information.* Knowing how you will use the information helps an expert provide more effective answers. The question "What do you have on preventing missing children?" is much too broad. You will get much better results by asking, "Can you supply information that would help a parent teach a five-year-old girl how to avoid being kidnapped?" Give the expert as much help as possible in targeting his or her response.

6) *If you know what you want, ask for it, not for what you assume the organization has.* In the interest of space, I have limited the description of each organization in this book to no more than a few sentences. That does not mean an organization limits itself to the services or publications I mention. When you call, ask for exactly what you wish to find.

7) *If you're unsure of what you need, ask for help formulating your questions.* If a subject is technical or complex, let the expert guide you. Briefly describe what you've

learned on the subject, then admit you do not yet know the types of information you need. Encourage the expert to take the initiative. A smart and willing expert helps you to ask the appropriate questions, answers those questions, and opens doors to other sources of information.

8) *Ask for specific brochures.* I am occasionally amazed by the brochures I am sent. After a conversation in which I thought I conveyed what I needed, the mail carrier arrives with something totally off the subject or inappropriate.

If you are not in a hurry, first ask to be sent a list of publications and audiovisuals. Then, look over the list at your leisure and select the ones you'd like. If you are in a hurry, ask the publications department to describe the brochures on your subject. You can save a step by ordering them right away. Organizations with a lengthy list of publications may be unwilling to describe them over the phone, but it doesn't hurt to ask.

Whenever possible, ask for brochures by title. You will have better luck than if you leave the choice up to the telephone staff. Only after you request the obviously useful titles should you ask the person to suggest other materials.

9) *Ask for a sample newsletter.* Organizations do not automatically send a copy of their newsletter when you request brochures. Yet, newsletters can be a terrific source of information. Some have a Questions-and-Answers section for the public. Others describe activities, products, and services you might find useful.

10) *Be persistent.* Usually, the person who first answers the phone is a telephone operator or the least experienced staff member. That person may be untrained or unwilling to help you properly. Don't get discouraged. If you believe this organization is the best one for your needs, politely rephrase your question. If that doesn't work, ask to speak with a superior or to be transferred to a different department, such as public relations, education, or publications. In the worst case, call back at another time and hope a different person answers the phone.

If you leave a message and no one calls you back, try again in a few days. When an expert fails to return your call, it probably means that person is busy rather than unable or unwilling to help. Sometimes only persistence helps find the information you need.

11) *Consider calling more than one organization.* Not every person who sounds knowledgable over the phone is really an expert. Sometimes an assistant tries to relieve the boss's work load by fielding difficult questions. Although meaning well, these assistants may provide inappropriate or incorrect information.

Some organizations have biases or vested interests that may influence their point of view. For example, a pharmaceutical firm's opinion about the safety of a drug they manufacture may differ sharply from that of a public interest group. Sometimes, experts from different organizations offer contradictory opinions without any hidden motives. For example, three different experts may advise three very different approaches to handling a child who is not reaching its potential in school.

If the subject you are researching is important enough, call *at least* two organizations to see if their suggestions jibe. I find it best to ask my questions anew each time rather than ask one expert to confirm what another has said. In the interest of "professional courtesy," some experts would rather not disagree with their colleagues before the public.

12) *Say thank you.* If someone has been helpful to you in answering questions or sending information, tell him so. You will smooth the path for the parents who follow you. If someone has been unusually generous with her time, send her a thank-you note. It takes only a minute, creates goodwill, and may even further that person's career. If you ever need additional help, that expert will probably remember your kindness and gladly answer your future questions.

Four Questions with Which to End Every Phone Conversation

No matter who you call, you'll get better results if you ask these questions before hanging up.

1) "Is there anything else I should have asked concerning my problem?"
2) "Is there any published material on the subject that your office could send me?"
3) "Are there any particularly good brochures or books I should obtain from other sources?"
4) "Who else should I speak with for additional help at other national, state, or local organizations?"

Remember: Always call an organization before you write to it. Confirm the address, and ask which person or department should receive your letter. If requesting printed materials, ask if there is a fee and if a self-addressed, stamped envelope is required.

CHAPTER 2

FERTILITY, PREGNANCY, CHILDBIRTH, AND INFANT CARE

Pregnancy, childbirth, and infant care require new parents to learn about a wide range of subjects. The year that starts once you learn you are pregnant, and ends when your newborn is comfortably settled into a routine, is a year filled with many decisions.

How can I protect the fetus from environmental dangers? Which childbirth method is best for me? How can I avoid a cesarean or postpartum depression? How can I best care for my infant?

Aside from the physicians or other health-care professionals you choose, many organizations are available to answer your questions and send free brochures during and after your pregnancy. The sections of this chapter are organized in the approximate order you may need them.

If you experience difficulty getting or staying pregnant, the organizations listed in the FERTILITY section will help you find the most advanced treatments. Once you are pregnant, see the PREGNANCY AND CHILDBIRTH section for groups offering information on childbirth methods (including Lamaze and Bradley) and groups promoting birth in the home, in birthing centers, or in hospitals. You will also find organizations with information on high-risk pregnancies, preventing birth defects, cesareans, postpartum depression, and abortion.

A month before your baby arrives, refer to the INFANT CARE section for help with perinatal care (just before and after birth), premature babies, breastfeeding, circumcision, and diapers.

SEE ALSO

Chapter 5 if your baby has a medical disorder or you need further information on a health-related issue. The last section of Chapter 5, STATE CHILD AND MATERNITY HEALTH DEPARTMENTS, lists state offices that make referrals to state and local programs for expectant or new parents. Under the DISEASES AND DISORDERS section of Chapter 5, Sleep Disorders may also be of particular interest to new parents.

The SUDDEN INFANT DEATH SYNDROME (SIDS) section of Chapter 7 lists organizations that work to prevent this tragedy.

The MAIL ORDER CATALOGS section of Chapter 12 lists mail order merchants who supply virtually everything the expectant and new parent needs. See particularly Books, Baby Supplies, Furniture and Furnishings, and Maternity and Nursing Clothes.

FERTILITY

American Fertility Society (AFS)
2140 11th Avenue S., Suite 200
Birmingham, AL 35205
(205) 933-8494
The Society refers the public to local fertility specialists and sends pamphlets on ovulation, endometriosis, male infertility, recurrent miscarriage, and new technologies for assisting couples with fertility problems. A list of publications is available.

Donors' Offspring
P.O. Box 33
Sarcoxie, MO 64862
(417) 548-3679
Donors' Offspring offers information to persons involved in artificial insemination, including the infertile, donor insemination families, donor families, surrogates, and professional personnel. A list of publications and audiovisuals is available.

Fertility Institute

9339 Genesee Avenue, Suite 220
San Diego, CA   92121
(619) 455-7520
The Institute offers diagnostic and treatment services by board certified obstetricians/gynecologists. The Institute sponsors programs on unexplained infertility, makes referrals for counseling, and researches new treatments. It publishes a free newsletter and supplies informational pamphlets on in vitro fertilization, sex preselection, sperm washing, and artificial insemination.

Fertility Research Foundation

1430 2nd Avenue, Suite 103
New York, NY   10021
(212) 744-5500
The Foundation conducts surveys on all aspects of infertility, researches genetic defects, counsels childless couples, and offers medical services.

National Infertility Network Exchange (NINE)

55 Dunbar Avenue
Piscataway, NJ   08854
(201) 699-0414
NINE is a mutual-help group for infertile people. It offers a referral service, conducts educational programs, and maintains a speakers' bureau. It publishes a newsletter six times a year.

Resolve, Inc.

5 Water Street
Arlington, MA   02174
(617) 643-2424
Resolve offers counseling, makes referrals, supplies literature on the emotional and medical issues of infertility, provides contact with other members, distributes adoption information, and gives emotional support for infertile couples. It publishes a newsletter five times a year.

PREGNANCY AND CHILDBIRTH

GENERAL ORGANIZATIONS

SEE ALSO

the SEX section of Chapter 9 under Pregnancy for organizations devoted primarily to teenage pregnancy.

American College of Nurse-Midwives
1522 K Street, N.W., Suite 1120
Washington, DC   20005
(202) 289-0171
The College is a professional organization that will answer inquiries and make referrals regarding midwifery.

American College of Obstetricians & Gynecologists (ACOG)
409 12th Street, S.W.
Washington, DC   20024
(202) 863-2518
This professional society acts as an information clearinghouse for both professionals and consumers. The College offers free booklets to the public on childbirth, menopause, infertility, sex education, and contraception. Audiotapes and films are also available.

Couple to Couple League, International (CCL)
P.O. Box 111184
Cincinnati, OH   45211-1180
(513) 661-7612
The League helps couples interested in natural family planning by using the sympto-thermal method (STM). STM lets couples determine periods of fertility and infertility by recording basal body temperatures. Among CCL's publications are *The Art of Natural Family Planning,* an audiovisual entitled *The Springtime of Your Life,* and a bimonthly newsletter.

Healthy Mothers, Healthy Babies Coalition (HMHB)
409 12th Street, S.W.
Washington, DC   20024-2188
(202) 863-2458
(800) 533-8811
HMHB, an informal association of ninety-five national professional, voluntary, and governmental organizations, helps educate pregnant women. The Coalition answers questions from the public, distributes the *Maternal and Child Health Publications Catalog,* and publishes a newsletter, *Healthy Mothers, Healthy Babies.*

Info-Grossesse/The Pregnancy Healthline
Department of Epidemiology & Biostatistics
McGill University
1020 Pine Avenue W.
Montreal, QU   H3A 1A2
Canada
(514) 933-8776 (Monday through Friday 1:00 P.M. to 5:00 P.M.)
A telephone service which provides information about pregnancy and reproductive risks to both professionals and the public.

Maternity Center Association
48 E. 92nd Street
New York, NY   10128
(212) 369-7300
This birthing center is operated by mid-wives under the supervision of doctors. It offers classes for expectant parents, runs a large reference library, makes referrals, and sells a variety of books, pamphlets, and videotapes.

Midwives' Alliance of North America
P.O. Box 1121
Bristol, VA   24203-1121
(615) 764-5561
The Alliance offers referrals and information about midwifery and publishes a newsletter.

Mothers' Center Development Project
336 Fulton Avenue
Hempstead, NY   11550
(516) 486-6614
(800) 645-3828
The more than one hundred chapters of the Mothers' Center provide support groups in which pregnant woman and recent mothers can share their experiences with one another and with health-care providers. Free consultations are available. The Center publishes a newsletter, a manual, and several free booklets.

National Center for Education in
    Maternal & Child Health (NCEMCH)
38th and R Streets, N.W.
Washington, DC   20057
(202) 625-8400
NCEMCH answers questions about pregnancy and childbirth, child and adolescent health, nutrition, high-risk infants, genetics, women's health, and maternal and child health services and programs. They produce newsletters, bibliographies, referral lists, booklets, resource guides, and other educational materials. Most are free. Their free guide, *Maternal and Child Health Publications Catalog,* lists hundreds of publications.

National Institute of Child Health &
    Human Development
Office of Research Reporting
Building 31, Room 2A-32
9000 Rockville Pike
Bethesda, MD   20892
(301) 496-5133
NICHHD performs and promotes basic and clinical research in maternal and child health. It answers inquiries on such topics as developmental disabilities, fertility and infertility, developmental biology and nutrition, mental retardation, and pediatric and maternal AIDS. Single copies of publications are available. Topics include Down Syndrome, oral contraception, precocious puberty, smoking and pregnancy, vasec-

tomy, childhood hyperactivity, child health, sudden infant death syndrome, and developmental disabilities.

National Women's Health Network
1325 G Street, N.W.
Washington, DC   20005
(202) 347-1140
Although mainly involved with lobbying for health-related legislation to protect women's rights, the Network offers referrals and publications to consumers on a wide range of health issues including diseases, pharmaceuticals, and maternity subjects.

**Planned Parenthood Federation of
   America, Inc.**
810 7th Avenue
New York, NY   10019
(212) 541-7800
The eight hundred centers associated with the Federation offer education, counseling, and medical services in the areas of contraception, abortion, fertility, and family planning. Check your area telephone directory for a local center or call the national headquarters for a referral. Ask for their publications catalog.

**Positive Pregnancy & Parenting Fitness
   Be Healthy, Inc.**
51 Saltrock Road
Baltic, CT   06330
(203) 822-8573
(800) 822-8573

A national organization offering workshops, publications, and materials on prenatal and postpartum exercise and stress management, making pregnancy and parenting a more joyful and fulfilling experience. It publishes a biannual newsletter and a catalog listing books, tapes, and other products for pregnancy and parenting.

CHILDBIRTH PREPARATION

**American Academy of Husband
   Coached Childbirth**
P.O. Box 5224
Sherman Oaks, CA   91413-5224
(818) 788-6662
(800) 423-2397
(800) 42-BIRTH (422-4784) (in
   California)
The Academy trains childbirth coaches in the Bradley method.

**American Society for Psychoprophylaxis
   in Obstetrics (ASPO/Lamaze)**
1840 Wilson Boulevard, Suite 204
Arlington, VA   22201
(703) 524-7802
(800) 368-4404
ASPO/Lamaze is made up of nearly seven thousand physicians, health professionals, and parents, supports the Lamaze method of childbirth and family-oriented maternity care. ASPO/

Lamaze trains and certifies teachers, runs prenatal classes for expectant parents, and maintains a registry of certified teachers and supportive physicians. In addition to a film on prepared childbirth, the organization offers printed materials on prepared childbirth, parenting, and family-centered maternity care. Among its publications are a directory of members, and two magazines, *Genesis* and *Lamaze Parents' Magazine.*

Childbirth Education Foundation
P.O. Box 5
Richboro, PA   18954
(215) 357-2792
The Foundation promotes alternatives to traditional hospital births. It provides advice and referrals regarding home births, birthing centers, infant bonding, and breastfeeding. Films and videotapes are available for rental.

**Childbirth Without Pain Education
   Association (CWPEA)**
20134 Snowden
Detroit, MI   48235
(313) 341-3816
CWPEA supplies the public with information about childbirth and the Lamaze method, monitors teachers, and provides numerous educational materials dealing with Lamaze.

**Informed Homebirth/Informed Birth &
   Parenting (IH/IBP)**
P.O. Box 3675
Ann Arbor, MI   48106
(313) 662-6857
IH/IBP offers information about safe alternatives to traditional in-hospital delivery, general information on parenting, and alternatives in education. In addition, it trains childbirth educators and birth assistants. Books on these topics are available for purchase.

**International Association for Childbirth
   at Home**
P.O. Box 430
Glendale, CA   91209
(213) 663-4996
This association of parents and childbirth professionals provides support and current information for parents wishing to deliver safely at home or in the hospital. The Association offers education programs and makes referrals.

**International Association of Parents &
   Professionals for Safe Alternatives in
   Childbirth (NAPSAC)**
Route 1, Box 646
Marble Hill, MO   63764
(314) 238-2010
The Association trains childbirth professionals and parents in the methods of natural childbirth. It publishes books on such issues as compulsory hospitalization, freedom of choice in childbirth,

breastfeeding, infant care, parenting, and nutrition. It also publishes a *Directory* of alternative birth programs and a newsletter, *NAPSAC News*.

International Childbirth Education Association (ICEA)

P.O. Box 20048
Minneapolis, MN   55420
(612) 854-8660
ICEA answers questions and makes referrals regarding family-centered maternity care, childbearing, and breastfeeding. It publishes the *International Journal of Childbirth Education,* the *ICEA Membership Directory,* videos and materials for teacher education, and a catalog of specially selected books on childbirth.

National Association of Childbearing Centers

3123 Gottschall Road
Perkiomenville, PA   18074
(215) 234-8068
Will refer parents to childbearing centers across the United States, and publishes a slide series on birth centers.

Read Natural Childbirth Foundation

P.O. Box 956
San Rafael, CA   94915
(415) 456-8462
Promotes the Read method of labor and delivery pioneered by Grantly Dick-Read. The method teaches breathing patterns and relieves fear through education.

HIGH-RISK PREGNANCY

SEE ALSO

the Premature Babies section of this chapter.

Center for Study of Multiple Birth

333 E. Superior Street, Suite 463-S
Chicago, IL   60611
(312) 266-9093
The Center hosts conferences on the scientific nature of multiple births and distributes information on medical risks involved.

Confinement Line

Childbirth Education Association, Inc.
P.O. Box 1609
Springfield, VA   22151
(703) 941-7183
The Confinement Line offers information and telephone support for women confined to bed because of medical

complications of pregnancy. Trained volunteers, previously on bedrest themselves, staff the organization.

High-Risk Pregnancy Support Group
Georgetown University Hospital
3800 Reservoir Road, N.W.
Washington, DC   20007-2197
(202) 784-3750

For Georgetown University high-risk inpatients and outpatients whose pregnancy is affected by such symptoms as psychosocial stress, prenatal diagnosis of anomalies, premature labor, and previous losses, this group seeks to relieve anxiety and stress, and reduces the sense of isolation through peer support.

PREVENTING BIRTH DEFECTS

SEE ALSO

the ENVIRONMENTAL SAFETY section in Chapter 6 for additional organizations that offer information on environmental hazards.

Arizona Teratogen Information Service
Arizona Health Sciences Center
Department of Pediatrics
1501 N. Campbell Avenue
Tucson, AZ   85724
(602) 626-6016
(800) 362-0101 (in Arizona)
Primarily for Arizona residents, this free, confidential telephone counseling service supplies health-care personnel and pregnant women with up-to-date information on potential environmental hazards. If requested, a written summary will be sent to the caller and a copy to the primary health-care provider. Individuals considered at risk

are referred to genetic counselors. Follow-up counseling at birth and at one year will be done after exposure to certain agents.

Association of Birth Defect Children
3526 Emerywood Lane
Orlando, FL   32806
(407) 859-2821
Offering information and support to families of children with birth defects caused by in utero exposure to environmental contaminants such as drugs, chemicals, and radiation, this association has an ongoing registry that contains demographic data and medical

histories of member families in the United States and Canada. It responds to questions on topics such as drug use during pregnancy and the care and rehabilitation of birth defect children. It publishes two newsletters.

Biomedical Research Institute
Saint Paul Children's Hospital
1345 N. Smith Avenue
Saint Paul, MN   55102
(612) 298-8835
The Institute's goal is to educate everyone about the clinical significance and public health implications of cytomegalovirus (CMV) infection. It publishes a brochure that answers common questions about CMV and a newsletter for families who have children with congenital CMV.

California Teratogen Registry
University of California Medical Center
   at San Diego
225 W. Dickinson Street
Room H8124B
San Diego, CA   92103-1990
(619) 294-6084
(800) 532-3749 (in California)
The registry distributes information on potential teratogens in an effort to prevent birth defects. For women in the San Diego area and California residents who will travel to San Diego, a free pediatric dysmorphologic examination is offered after the delivery.

Connecticut Pregnancy Exposure
   Information Service & Risk-Line
University of Connecticut Health
   Center
Department of Pediatrics Division of
   Medical Genetics
Farmington, CT   06032
(203) 674-1465
(800) 325-5391 (in Connecticut)
This free hotline offers current information about possible risks to a fetus if the mother is exposed to a particular medication or substance during pregnancy. The service is available for pregnant women, those planning a pregnancy, and health-care workers. The service provides telephone consultation and a written follow-up.

DES Action USA
2845 24th Street
San Francisco, CA   94110
(415) 826-5060
DES Action USA offers free information for and about diethylstilbestrol and DES-exposed persons. Among its publications are *DES Exposure: Questions and Answers for Daughters, Mothers and Sons* and *Fertility and Pregnancy Guide for DES Daughters and Sons.*

Iowa Teratogen Information Service
Department of Pediatrics
Division of Medical Genetics 2 JCP
Iowa City, IA   52242
(319) 356-2674

This service responds to in-state and out-of-state inquiries from both health professionals and the general public on birth defects.

Magee-Women's Hospital
Department of Reproductive Genetics
Forbes Avenue and Halket Street
Pittsburgh, PA   15213
(412) 647-4168
This service answers questions from both health-care professionals and the general public on reproductive issues and dangers.

March of Dimes Birth Defects Foundation
1275 Mamaroneck Avenue
White Plains, NY   10605
(914) 428-7100
Dedicated to preventing birth defects, the March of Dimes provides educational programs on maternal and newborn health to professionals and the public. Check your telephone directory to find a local office or call the national office for a referral.

Montana Pregnancy Riskline
Shodair Hospital
840 Helena Avenue
Helena, MT   59601
(406) 444-7500
(800) 521-2229
The Riskline offers information about the possible effects on a fetus when the mother is exposed to certain drugs or substances during pregnancy. It provides up-to-date references and a critical review of available literature to anyone needing information, education, or counseling.

National Clearinghouse for Alcohol & Drug Information
P.O. Box 2345
Rockville, MD   20847-2345
(301) 468-2600
(800) 729-6686
(800) 662-HELP (4357)
The Clearinghouse publishes several free pamphlets, including *Should I Drink? Think First of Your Unborn Child* (offered in both English and Spanish) and *Preventing Fetal Alcohol Effects*.

National Institute of Environmental Health Sciences
Public Affairs Office
Research Triangle Park, NC   27709
(919) 541-3345
Experts will answer questions about the effects of toxic substances on reproduction and an unborn fetus. Free publications are also available.

Pregnancy Healthline
Pennsylvania Hospital
Division of Obstetrics & Gynecology
8th and Spruce Streets
Philadelphia, PA   15213
(215) 829-KIDS (5437)

The Healthline responds to inquiries from both professionals and lay persons. It will assess risk to a fetus from exposure to medicines, drugs, industrial chemicals, or other toxic agents. A written summary of information is sent to the caller.

Teratology Hotline
Children's Hospital of Wisconsin
Birth Defects Center
P.O. Box 1997
Milwaukee, WI   53201
(414) 931-4172
This hotline primarily serves southeast Wisconsin but will accept out-of-state calls. The majority of inquiries are answered over the phone; however, in more serious cases, clients may be asked to visit the center for counseling. Follow-up material is sent to the client's health-care provider.

Teratology Information Network
University of Medicine & Dentistry of
   New Jersey
Department of Pediatrics
Division of Human Genetics
401 Haddon Avenue
Camden, NJ   08103
(609) 757-7869
The Network provides information to both health-care personnel and the general public. A service fee may be required for inquiries needing extensive follow-up.

CESAREAN BIRTH

Cesarean Prevention Movement (CPM)
P.O. Box 152
Syracuse, NY   13210
(315) 424-1942
CPM's goal is to lower the rate of cesarean deliveries and to create a support network for women recovering from cesarean deliveries. CPM provides free information and brochures on cesarean prevention and vaginal birth after a cesarean delivery.

Cesareans/Support Education &
   Concern (C/SEC)
22 Forest Road
Framingham, MA   01701
(617) 877-8266
C/SEC offers information on cesarean delivery, prevention, and vaginal birth following a cesarean. The group provides emotional support for cesarean-delivery families and publishes brochures on a variety of related topics.

C-Section Experience
P.O. Box 1186
Palatine, IL   60078-1186
(312) 934-4147
This organization provides emotional support and childbirth education to parents of babies born by cesarean section. The group runs a telephone helpline, produces several pamphlets on cesarean birth, and publishes the newsletter, *C-Section Experience.*

POSTPARTUM DEPRESSION

Depression After Delivery
P.O. Box 1282
Morrisville, PA 19067
(215) 295-3994
If you suffer from postpartum depression or psychosis, this organization is a clearinghouse for information and referrals.

International Postpartum Support
927 N. Kellogg Avenue
Santa Barbara, CA   93111
(805) 967-7636

ABORTION

Pro-choice

Offers technical help in starting self-help groups for women having postpartum depression. The organization also sponsors research and offers educational programs for both lay people and professional health-care providers.

Mothers are People Too
c/o ASPO/LAMAZE
1840 Wilson Avenue, Suite 204
Arlington, VA   22201
(703) 524-7802
An informal support group of mothers who help other mothers during the postpartum period.

SEE ALSO

Planned Parenthood above in the PREGNANCY AND CHILDBIRTH section under General Organizations.

National Abortion Federation
1436 U Street, N.W., Suite 103
Washington, DC   20009
(202) 667-5881
(800) 772-9100
This Federation serves as an information clearinghouse and hotline on abortion services. It publishes *The Consumer's Guide to Abortion Services* and a quarterly newsletter.

National Abortion Rights Action League
1101 14th Street, N.W., 5th Floor
Washington, DC   20005
(202) 408-4600
Offers brochures on the pro-choice point of view.

Pro-Life

American Life League
c/o America's Family Center
P.O. Box 1350
Stafford, VA   22554
(703) 659-4171
Provides referrals and educational materials espousing the right-to-life point of view.

National Right to Life Committee (NRLC)
419 Seventh Street, N.W., Suite 500
Washington, DC   20004
(202) 626-8800
NRLC offers referrals and brochures on the alternatives to abortion.

INFANT CARE

GENERAL ORGANIZATIONS

Association for Infant Massage
c/o Leslie Day
79th Street Boat Basin, Box 9
New York, NY   10024
(212) 877-1268
This association of child-care professionals distributes information about the physical and psychological benefits of infant massage. It runs workshops, gives demonstrations, offers teacher training, and sells cassettes and article reprints.

Center for Infant Study
University of Maryland School of
   Medicine
Department of Psychiatry
Howard Hall, Room 132
660 W. Redwood Street
Baltimore, MD   21201
(301) 328-2485 or 2486
The Center studies infant mental health and will answer inquiries, provide counseling, and make referrals to parents with children under three years old at risk for mental illness.

Infant-Parent Institute
328 N. Neil Street
Champaign, IL   61820
(217) 352-4060
This private teaching and clinical service focuses on problems of attachment in infants and adults. It will answer questions and make referrals on a limited basis.

National Center for Clinical Infant Programs (NCCIP)
2000 14th Street N., Suite 380
Arlington, VA   22201-2500
(703) 528-4300

This association of mental health and health-care professionals, though concerned mainly with policy matters, does offer referrals to the public on health topics relating to children under age three.

National Center for Education in Maternal & Child Health
See above in the PREGNANCY AND CHILD-BIRTH section of this chapter.

Newborn Rights Society
P.O. Box 48
St. Peters, PA   19470
(215) 323-6061
The Society provides information about the rights of newborns and is against unnecessary medical procedures such as automatic circumcision and silver nitrate drops. It offers children's services, conducts research, hosts educational seminars, and maintains a library and speakers' bureau.

Reginald S. Lourie Center for Infants and Young Children
11710 Hunters Lane
Rockville, MD   20852
(301) 984-4444

A private, nonprofit center focusing on early diagnosis, treatment, and prevention of emotional and developmental problems in children from birth to age five. Through early intervention programs, consultation, research, and training, the center gives children and their families a healthy emotional start in life.

World Association for Infant Psychiatry & Allied Disciplines
Division of Child Psychiatry
LSU Medical Center
1542 Tulane Avenue
New Orleans, LA   70112-2822
(504) 568-3997
Though primarily for child development professionals, the Association will answer questions and make referrals on a limited basis.

PERINATAL CARE

National Perinatal Association (NPA)
101-1/2 S. Union Street
Alexandria, VA   22314-3323
(703) 549-5523
NPA educates health-care professionals and parents about health care for infants shortly before and after birth. Though primarily interested in legislative matters, NPA answers questions and makes referrals to the public.

National Perinatal Information Center
  (NPIC)
1 State Road, Suite 102
Providence, RI   02908
(401) 274-0650
NPIC makes referrals regarding perinatal care and publishes a monthly magazine, *Perinatal Press.*

Parent Care, Inc.
101-1/2 S. Union Street
Alexandria, VA   22314-3323
(703) 836-4678
Parent Care provides information to perinatal professionals and parents of high-risk infants. It helps create mutual support groups, hosts conferences, and publishes a quarterly newsletter, *Parent Care,* with information on premature infant care.

PREMATURE BABIES

SEE ALSO

the Perinatal Care section above.

Intensive Caring Unlimited (ICU)
910 Bent Lane
Philadelphia, PA   19118
(215) 233-4723
A self-help group for parents experiencing a high-risk pregnancy, caring for a premature or sick baby, or suffering from the loss of an infant. The group offers meetings, education, counseling, a variety of resources, and referrals to other sources of help.

IVH Parents
P.O Box 56-1111
Miami, FL   33256-1111
(305) 232-0381
For parents of and professionals who care for children having suffered an intraventricular hemorrhage following a premature or traumatic birth. Intraventricular hemorrhage can result in such conditions as cerebral palsy, hydrocephalus, mental retardation, and seizures. This group conducts research, exchanges information, and offers emo-

tional support and telephone counseling. It publishes a newsletter and a members list.

Parents of Preemies, Inc.
23020 Wild Hunt Drive
Gaithersburg, MD   20879
(301) 253-6534
A self-help support group.

Parents of Prematures
P.O. Box 3046
Kirkland, WA   98083
(206) 283-7466
The organization offers self-help for parents whose infant has been hospitalized or born prematurely. There is a monthly newsletter, guidelines for establishing a group, and meetings offering education and emotional support.

BREASTFEEDING AND INFANT NUTRITION

SEE ALSO

the NUTRITION section of Chapter 5.

American Pediatric Gastroesophageal
  Reflux Association
23 Acton Street
Watertown, MA   02172
(617) 926-3586
Chronic gastroesophageal reflux (GER) manifests itself in vomiting, poor weight gain, respiratory problems, and crankiness. The Association, for parents and concerned professionals, provides emotional support and medical information, gathers data on GER and the families of GER babies, and maintains an advisory board and registry.

Concerned Formula Mothers
P.O. Box 14025
St. Louis, MO   63155
(314) 469-7886
An organization for parents of "Neo-Mull-Soy Babies," whose children suffer learning disabilities resulting from their infant formula. These severe disabilities could be confused with retardation, autism, cerebral palsy, or Tourette syndrome.

Formula
P.O. Box 39051
Washington, DC   20016
(703) 527-7171
Offers information and referrals regarding the safety and nutritional soundness of infant formulas. In addition, Formula collects data on children suffering disabilities from being fed non-chloride formula (Neo-Mull-Soy and Cho-Free). This group helped put the Infant Formula Act into effect.

Human Lactation Center
666 Sturges Highway
Westport, CT   06880
(203) 259-5995
The Center conducts research, promotes education on breastfeeding and its effects, and provides supportive care and consultation for mothers. It publishes books on maternal and infant nutrition, feeding practices, and a monthly journal, *Lactation Review*.

Infant Formula Council (IFC)
5775 Peachtree-Dunwoody Road
Suite 500-D
Atlanta, GA   30342
(404) 252-3663
Though membership is for manufacturers and vendors of infant formula, the Council provides information to the public on scientific research on infant

formula. It publishes a number of brochures and papers, including *Infant Formula: Questions and Answers* and *Infant Feeding and Nutrition.*

Lact-Aid International
P.O. Box 1066
Athens, TN   37303
(615) 744-9090
Lact-Aid makes nursing trainers, other breastfeeding aids, and neonatal and pediatric home-care products. It also offers seminars and workshops. For a fee, parents can receive breastfeeding information.

La Leche League International
9616 Minneapolis Avenue
P.O. Box 1209
Franklin Park, IL   60131-8209
(708) 455-7730
(800) LA LECHE (525-3243)
For women who want to breastfeed their babies, La Leche offers counseling, information, encouragement, and referrals to local groups nationwide. Call the 800 number for a referral to the La Leche group nearest you. Publications include pamphlets and such books as *The Womanly Art of Breastfeeding* and *Nightime Parenting*. La Leche also provides information on where to rent breast pumps.

Wellstart, San Diego Lactation Program
4062 1st Avenue
P.O. Box 87549
San Diego, CA   92138
(619) 295-5193
Though primarily for San Diego residents, Wellstart's helpline will answer questions about breastfeeding, nutrition, and perinatal and postpartum health.

CIRCUMCISION

National Organization of Circumcision Information Centers (NOCIRC)
P.O. Box 2512
San Anselmo, CA   94960
(415) 488-9883
NOCIRC works to end routine circumcision. It publishes a newsletter, *No Circ*, and offers videotapes, pamphlets, books, and reports on the medical aspects of circumcision.

Non-Circumcision Educational Foundation
P.O. Box 5
Richboro, PA   18954
(215) 357-2792

The Foundation provides parents with brochures and videotapes supporting the view that routine circumcision is unnecessary.

DIAPERS

National Association of Diaper Services
2017 Walnut Street
Philadelphia, PA   19103
(215) 569-3650
An association for industry professionals that conducts research, performs laboratory tests, and runs an information service. Will answer questions and make referrals on a limited basis.

Textile Laundry Council
316 Chestnut Street
Moorestown, NJ   08057
(609) 722-1182
Though primarily for members of the diaper service industry, the Council will answer questions and make referrals on a limited basis.

CHAPTER 3

PARENTING

Being a good parent is one of life's most important responsibilities. Luckily, many organizations are available to help. The first part of this chapter describes organizations that offer information, services, support, and referrals to all parents. These groups can help make parents more effective in raising happy, well-adjusted children. The remainder of this chapter describes groups that serve SINGLE PARENTS, STEPPARENTS AND FOSTER PARENTS, those interested in ADOPTION, and information for GAY PARENTS, and the parents of TWINS AND TRIPLETS.

SEE ALSO

Chapter 9, Adolescence, if you need help with a troubled teenager.

The CHILD ABUSE AND NEGLECT section of Chapter 10 lists groups that help if you or someone you know is in danger of harming a child.

The LEGAL MATTERS section of Chapter 10 describes organizations concerned with divorce, child custody, children's rights, and other legal concerns.

The MAIL ORDER CATALOGS section of Chapter 12 under Books lists merchants who supply numerous books with parenting advice.

The SELF-HELP CLEARINGHOUSES section of Chapter 13 lists referral services if you wish to find a local support group to help with an emotional or parenting problem.

☎ ☎

GENERAL ORGANIZATIONS

Active Parenting, Inc. (AP)
810 Franklin Court, Suite B
Marietta, GA   30067
(404) 429-0565
(800) 826-0060
AP is a commercial publisher and distributor of a video-based parenting education program designed to provide parents with the information and skills necessary to raise cooperative, responsible, and courageous children. They also provide free advisory and information services. Their products include *Active Parenting: The Newsletter of Video-Based Parenting Education* and *The Active Parenting Handbook.*

Catalyst Information Center
250 Park Avenue S.
New York, NY   10003
(212) 777-8900
Catalyst works with corporations and individuals to develop career and family options. It is a national resource for issues in the workplace such as maternity/parental leave, child care, relocation, benefits, and leadership development for women. Catalyst answers inquiries and distributes publications on all aspects of parents in the workplace.

Center for the Study of Parent Involvement (CSPI)
303 Van Buren Avenue
Oakland, CA   94610
(415) 465-3507
CSPI helps increase and improve the involvement of parents in the education of children. The group advises and consults parents, community workers, and educators.

Effectiveness Training, Inc.
531 Stevens Avenue
Solana Beach, CA   92075-2093
(619) 481-8121
This for-profit company offers training programs for parents, youth, teachers, and leaders in effective communication techniques and problem-solving methods. Publications include *P.E.T.: Parent Effectiveness Training.*

Family Resource Coalition
230 N. Michigan Avenue, Suite 1625
Chicago, IL   60601
(312) 726-4750
Parents can call for information and referrals to two thousand local groups within the Coalition that provide support to strengthen the family. Guidelines for starting a group are

also available. Among its publications are *Programs to Strengthen Families: A Resource Guide* and *Family Resource Program Builder: Blueprints for Designing and Operating Programs for Parents,* and a short videotape.

Fatherhood Project
c/o Bank Street College of Education
610 W. 12th Street
New York, NY   10025
(212) 222-6700
This national clearinghouse provides information on father-participation programs. It works to increase the role of fathers as nurturers involved in rearing children.

Formerly Employed Mothers at Loose Ends (FEMALE)
P.O. Box 31
Elmhurst, IL   60126
(312) 279-8862
FEMALE's newsletter and group meetings help women move from the paid workforce to at-home mothering. In addition, the affiliated groups operate as an advocate for family and work issues.

Lollipop Power, Inc.
P.O. Box 277
Carrboro, NC   27510
(919) 560-2738
Lollipop is a feminist collective working to overcome sex-role stereotypes in the

lives of children. They will send a publications list of their books and brochures on request.

Minnesota Early Learning Design (MELD)
123 N. 3rd Street, Suite 804
Minneapolis, MN   55401
(612) 332-7563
An association of more than sixty discussion groups nationwide for parents of children through age two, MELD also offers programs for Hispanic families, teenage mothers, handicapped parents, and for parents of older children.

Mothers at Home
P.O. Box 2208
Merrifield, VA   22116
(703) 352-2292
This organization helps mothers who prefer to stay at home and raise their children themselves. They publish *Welcome Home,* a monthly magazine.

Mother's Connection
468 Rosedale Avenue
White Plains, NY   10605
(914) 946-5757
This network for at-home mothers of young children provides mother's groups, play groups, and baby-sitting exchanges to lessen the sense of isolation.

Mothers Matter
171 Wood Street
Rutherford, NJ   07070
(201) 933-8191
This small group offers educational materials that help with parenting skills and increase the enjoyment of parenting.

National Center for Family Studies
Catholic University of America
620 Michigan Avenue, N.E.
Washington, DC   20064
(202) 635-5996 or 5431
The Center conducts research projects on all aspects of the family. Offers information, referral, and advisory services.

National Forum of Catholic Parent
   Organizations (NFCPO)
National Catholic Educational
   Association
1077 30th Street, N.W., Suite 100
Washington, DC   20007-3852
(202) 293-5954
NFCPO offers information on how parents can increase their influence in the educational process within and beyond the Catholic Church. Publishes *The Catholic Parent* (quarterly) and the *Catholic Parent Organizations Starter Kit.*

One and Only
P.O. Box 35351
Station E
Vancouver, BC   V6M 462
Canada
(604) 222-2931
One and Only will refer you to local groups that provide emotional support, information, and networking for parents of an only child or of children more than five years apart.

Parental Stress Services
600 S. Federal, Suite 205
Chicago, IL   60605
(312) 427-1161
An organization for both parents and children in stressful family situations, participants meet separately in groups run by volunteers to understand themselves and family members. A newsletter is published bimonthly. The service offers group start-up guidelines and educational films and videos.

Parents' Resources, Inc.
P.O. Box 107, Planetarium Station
New York, NY   10024
(212) 873-0609
Supports groups for parents to help each other. Offers referrals if you are looking for a group and technical assistance if you wish to start one.

SINGLE PARENTS

Parents Without Partners
8807 Colesville Road
Silver Spring, MD   20910
(301) 588-9354
With over eight hundred chapters, this
is by far the largest parenting organization in the United States. It provides
information and support services to
anyone raising children alone. The
group publishes a bimonthly magazine,
The Single Parent.

Single Mothers by Choice
P.O. Box 1642, Gracie Square Station
New York, NY   10028
(212) 988-0993
A national network of forty-eight chapters prints a newsletter and other literature and runs group meetings for
women who choose to have a child
outside of a permanent relationship
with a man.

Single Parent Resource Center
1165 Broadway, Room 504
New York, NY   10001
(212) 213-0047
A network of self-help groups provides
information and referrals on many subjects concerning single parents. It runs
seminars, a resource library, and publishes a newsletter.

Single Parents Society
527 Cinnaminson Avenue
Palmyra, NJ   08065
(609) 424-8872
The Society's discussion groups,
newsletter, events, and instructional
programs work to improve the circum-
stances and support the interests of
once-married parents.

**The Sisterhood of Black Single
    Mothers, Inc.**
1360 Fulton Street, Room 413
Brooklyn, NY   11216
(718) 638-0413
The Sisterhood provides a network of
support for single, black mothers and
runs a youth awareness project designed to strengthen the black family.
It publishes a quarterly newsletter.

Women on Their Own, Inc. (W.O.T.O.)
P.O. Box 1026
Willingboro, NJ   08046
(609) 871-1499
Through networking, financial aid, advocacy, and an increase in public
awareness, W.O.T.O. provides support
for women raising children without a
partner.

STEPPARENTS AND FOSTER PARENTS

SEE ALSO
the ADOPTION section of this chapter for groups assisting foster parents.

The LEGAL MATTERS section of Chapter 10 lists groups aiding stepparents and foster parents concerned with legal problems.

Foster Grandparent Program
ACTION
806 Connecticut Avenue, N.W.
Room M-1006
Washington, DC   20525
(202) 634-9349
The Foster Grandparent Program enrolls low-income volunteers age sixty or over to assist children who have special needs in health and education. The Program offers advisory and information services and distributes brochures.

Grandparents Raising Grandchildren
3851 Centraloma Drive
San Diego, CA   92107
(619) 223-0344

This organization is for grandparents or other relatives bringing up a child or worried about a possibly abusive situation a child may be in.

National Foster Parent Association
Information & Services Office
226 Kilts Drive
Houston, TX   77024
(713) 467-1850
The nation's largest group promoting the care of children in foster homes. Offers foster parents information on their legal rights. Publishes *National Foster Parent Association—National Advocate*.

Stepfamily Association of America, Inc.
   (SAA)
602 E. Joppa Road
Baltimore, MD   21204
(301) 823-7570

SAA acts as a support network and national advocate for stepparents, remarried parents, and their children. It has local chapters across the country. Publications include *Stepfamily Bulletin, Stepping Ahead Program Manual* (with Leaders Manual), and materials on how to start a local chapter.

ADOPTION

Adoptee/Natural Parent
   Locators-International
P.O. Box 1283
Canyon Country, CA   91351
(805) 251-4477
This organization helps adoptees, natural parents, and adoptive parents locate each other through a computer-based registry of adoptees and parents. Publications include a newsletter, *In Search of Identity,* books, reports, journal articles, directories, and educational videos.

Adoptees in Search, Inc. (AIS)
P.O. Box 41016
Bethesda, MD   20814
(301) 656-8555
AIS is composed of adult adoptees, adoptive parents, birth parents, and others. AIS maintains a computerized search registry for the Middle Atlantic states, provides search consultations, and distributes publications about finding one's parents.

Adoptive Families of America, Inc.
3333 Highway 100 N.
Minneapolis, MN   55422
(612) 535-4829
This national organization of 250 groups provides information for present and prospective adopting families, and helps place children in homes. It publishes a magazine bimonthly.

Adoptive Parents Committee, Inc.
   (APC)
210 5th Avenue
New York, NY   10010
(212) 683-9221
APC is dedicated to the improvement of adoption and foster care laws. It educates the public and adoptive parents about all matters involving adoption and foster care. APC advises prospective adoptive parents on methods and sources of adoption, and publishes a newsletter, *Adoptalk,* and pamphlets: *How Parents Tell Their Children They are Adopted, Guide to Independent*

Placement, and *The 10 Most Asked Questions.*

Aid to Adoption of Special Kids (AASK)
450 Sansome Street
San Francisco, CA   94111
(415) 434-2275
A nonprofit, California-licensed adoption agency with branch offices nationwide, AASK helps place older children, sibling groups, minority children, and emotionally, mentally, and physically disabled children in permanent homes. Publishes the *AASK Newsletter.*

Committee for Single Adoptive Parents
P.O. Box 15084
Chevy Chase, MD   20815
No phone number listed.
The Committee acts as an information service to current and prospective single adoptive parents of both sexes. It supports the rights of children to an adoptive family regardless of any handicap or any difference in race, creed, color, religion, or national origin. Committee publications include the *Handbook for Single Adoptive Parents* and a list of sources of available children.

Concerned United Birthparents, Inc. (CUB)
2000 Walker Street
Des Moines, IA   50317
(515) 263-9558
(800) 822-2777

CUB is a national support and advocacy group for parents who have surrendered their children for adoption. It has members in all states and branches and representatives in more than twenty-four states. CUB offers peer support for parents whose children are missing as a result of adoption and provides information on laws and legislation impacting the relationship of parents with children adopted by others. Publications include pamphlets and brochures.

Edna Gladney Center (EGC)
2300 Hemphill
Fort Worth, TX   76110
(800) GLADNEY (452-3639)
(800) 772-2740 (in Texas)
EGC provides supportive and caring services for those involved in adoption. It offers a licensed adoption agency, including a placement division for special needs infants, plus medical care, education, and residential facilities, and post-adoption programs for families, birthparents, and adoptees.

Families Adopting Children Everywhere (F.A.C.E.), Inc.
P.O. Box 28058
Northwood Station
Baltimore, MD   21239
(301) 488-2656
F.A.C.E. is a nonprofit organization that answers inquiries, provides advisory and

reference services, conducts a six-week course on adoption, and distributes a newsletter, *F.A.C.E. Facts.*

International Families
P.O. Box 1352
St. Charles, MO   63302
(314) 423-6788
An organization and support service for families interested in foreign adoption, this group publishes a newsletter, provides information, and makes referrals.

Latin America Parents Association (LAPA)
P.O. Box 339
Brooklyn, NY   11234
(718) 236-8689
A nonprofit volunteer association of adoptive parents that helps people who want to adopt children from Latin America; publishes a newsletter, *Quetal.*

National Adoption Exchange
1218 Chestnut Street, Suite 204
Philadelphia, PA   19107
(215) 925-0200
The Exchange is a national network that brings children waiting for adoption together with parents who want to adopt them. Publications include: *Adoption Resource Directory, Adoption Resources for Children and Families of Minority Cultures,* and *Directory of Adoption Exchanges Serving the United States.*

National Committee for Adoption
1930 17th Street, N.W.
Washington, DC   20009-6207
(202) 328-1200
The Committee focuses on children needing to be adopted by supporting local adoption agencies and running the National Adoption Hotline. Pregnant women and teenagers can call collect.

National Organization for Birthfathers & Adoption Reform (NOBAR)
P.O. Box 1993
Baltimore, MD   21203
(301) 243-3986
NOBAR is an advocacy and support group for fathers who have given their children up for adoption or risk losing them through adoption. It publishes a newsletter, supplies information, and makes referrals.

North American Council on Adoptable Children, Inc. (NACAC)
1810 University Avenue, Suite S275
St. Paul, MN   55104
(612) 644-3036
NACAC works on behalf of special-needs children, those with physical or mental handicaps, older children, sibling groups, and minority children. NACAC

believes that every child has the right to a permanent, loving family through adoption. The Council offers referral services and publishes several books and brochures.

Operation Identity
13101 Black Stone Road, N.E.
Albuquerque, NM   87111
(505) 293-3144
Through its newsletter and referrals, Operation Identity provides emotional support for all those involved in the adoption process. Additionally, it helps adults search for their natural families.

Orphan Voyage
2141 Road 2300
Cedaredge, CO   81413
(303) 856-3937
Provides information, education, and networking for adults separated from their natural families by adoption. Also makes referrals to groups and individuals for counseling.

Surrogate Parent Program
11110 Ohio Avenue, Suite 202
Los Angeles, CA   90025
(213) 473-8961
The Surrogate Parent Program helps infertile adoptive couples. It arranges surrogate parent contacts including interviewing and selecting both adoptive couples and surrogate mothers, arranging their meeting, and finalizing adoption.

Yesterday's Children
P.O. Box 1554
Evanston, IL   60204
(312) 545-6900
The group provides counseling and assistance for adoptees in search of their biological families.

GAY PARENTS

SEE ALSO

Gay & Lesbian Advocates & Defenders (GLAD) and Custody Action for Lesbian Mothers Inc. (CALM) in the LEGAL MATTERS section of Chapter 10.

Federation of Parents & Friends of
   Lesbians & Gays (FLAG)
P.O. Box 20308
Denver, CO   80220
(303) 321-2270

A national organization comprising two hundred chapters for families with gay members. It is dedicated to increasing understanding within families and educating the public as a whole.

TWINS AND TRIPLETS

National Organization of Mothers of
   Twins Clubs, Inc. (NOMOTC)
12404 Princess Jeanne, N.E.
Albuquerque, NM   87112-4640
(505) 275-0955
NOMOTC sponsors research and education to encourage the individuality of each twin and helps expectant and new parents of twins find educational materials and support. Publishes *MOTC's Notebook* (a quarterly newspaper) and two brochures: *Your Twins and You* and *How to Organize a Mothers of Twins Club.*

Triplet Connection
P.O. Box 99571
Stockton, CA   95209
(209) 474-3073
A national support group for families expecting and raising triplets (quintuplets, etc.). The Connection provides prebirth information and publishes a newsletter.

☎

CHILD CARE

Choosing an appropriate, affordable, convenient, safe, and enriching place or person to care for their preschool children is one of the most difficult decisions parents make. In most communities, three basic types of care exist. The most expensive choice is a private baby-sitter or nanny who comes to your home each day or lives in. With the second choice, family day-care, your child stays in someone else's home. Family day-care providers are usually mothers who take care of their own children too. The final choice, a day-care center, may be located in a community center, church, synagogue, or business.

The many factors that help determine which option is best for you include cost, the hours needed, the flexibility of the provider should your schedule suddenly change, the location, the length of time you plan to use the service, the number and ages of your children, and when you wish to start. Other considerations include the training, experience, and educational philosophy of the caregiver(s).

Some parents never need to look far to find care for their child. These lucky parents usually hear about the ideal arrangement from a friend. Other parents visit dozens of day-care centers, family day-care homes, or interview a dozen nannies. Fortunately, several hundred referral agencies and associations of local providers advise parents and make recommendations.

This chapter has three sections. The first two, NATIONAL ORGANIZATIONS and AU PAIR AGENCIES, offer nationwide referrals or placement services. The third section, STATEWIDE, COUNTYWIDE, AND LOCAL REFERRAL SERVICES, lists agencies and associations that direct parents to all types of child care.

With so many information sources, where do you start? Turn to the section of this chapter that covers your state. In most cases, your best bet is first to call the *countywide* office nearest you. If a countywide office is not available or not helpful, call the *statewide* office, if one is listed. If neither of these options works, try one of the *local child-care-provider associations.* These local associations can be wonderfully helpful if you remember two things: First, these associations exist primarily to support and promote family day-care providers, who are paid to care for children in the provider's home; second, some associations are run by a working child-care provider who may try to interest you in her service. Nevertheless, many parents find these associations excellent sources of referrals.

Child Care in Your Home

To find a babysitter or nanny, you should ask friends and your pediatrician for referrals. Some parents place notices on bulletin boards in their neighborhood. You should also call the statewide and countywide referral agencies listed in this chapter for help. These sources may recommend employment agencies that specialize in babysitters as well as other organizations that list individual sitters. Many of the countywide referral offices are familiar with the reputations of specific employment agencies. If you want to avoid paying an employment agency's fee, ask the statewide or countywide referral offices about nonprofit groups that list baby-sitters. These offices also offer information on the current pay scales typical in your area.

Some parents prefer to answer advertisements in newspapers under Situation Wanted or place their own ad in the Help Wanted section. Most major metropolitan areas have at least one newspaper containing numerous such ads. For example, the best such paper in New York, *The Irish Echo,* is used by baby-sitters and nannies from Ireland, the Caribbean, and other parts of the world. Ask any working baby-sitter, or one of the referral offices in this book, which newspapers are best in your area. If you place an ad, be prepared for a deluge of calls. Stories about a hundred inquiries the first morning are common.

If you wish to hire a nanny with formal training in child care, consider calling the American Council of Nanny Schools, listed in the NATIONAL ORGANIZATIONS section that follows. The Council makes referrals to schools which help find employment for their trained graduates. If you would like to hire an au pair—a European eighteen-to-twenty-five-year-old who lives in and has child-care experience—call the offices listed below under AU PAIR AGENCIES.

As the employer of a baby-sitter or nanny, you must pay social security, unemployment insurance, and possibly collect taxes. Talk to your tax advisor for help. Otherwise, call your local and state offices of taxation to learn their requirements. The IRS can be reached at (800) 829-3676. Be sure to request IRS publication 503, *Child and Dependent Care Expenses,* and ask what other forms are required as an employer of household help.

Family Day Care

Approximately two hundred thousand of the homes used to care for other people's children are regulated by state governments. Approximately another one million are not regulated. To find providers of family day care, call the countywide referral agencies and the local child-care-provider associations listed for your state. Remember that some of the local associations are run by providers who will make referrals to others but who may also try to promote their own service if you live nearby.

If none of the countywide referral agencies or local associations prove helpful, call the National Association of Child Care Resource and Referral Agencies and the National Association for Family Day Care. Both groups are listed in the NATIONAL ORGANIZATIONS section below and both make referrals to local sources of information about family day care.

Day Care Centers

To find group day care not being offered in someone's home, call the countywide and statewide referral agencies listed for your state. If none of them are helpful or close enough, call the National Association of Child Care Resource and Referral Agencies, listed in the NATIONAL ORGANIZATIONS section below. They may know of new or additional referral agencies. You should also contact local churches, community centers, YMCAs, and local public and private schools for referrals to day-care centers. Your local yellow pages may list centers under Day Care, Nursery Schools, or Child Care.

NATIONAL ORGANIZATIONS

American Council of Nanny Schools
(ACNS)
Delta College
University Center, MI   48710
(517) 686-9417
ACNS represents approximately twenty-five schools nationwide that train nannies. If you wish to employ a nanny, the Council will advise which schools in your area offer an employment service for their graduates.

Child Care Action Campaign
99 Hudson Street, Room 1233
New York, NY   10013
(212) 334-9595
Although primarily a lobbying group, this organization publishes a newsletter, *Childcare ActioNews,* which follows trends in child care for working parents.

National Association for Family Day
Care (NAFDC)
725 Fifteenth Street, N.W., Suite 505
Washington, DC   20005
(202) 347-3356
(800) 359-3817
If none of the associations of local child care providers listed in this chapter are close enough to you, call NAFDC to see if other groups exist in your area.

National Association of Child Care
Resource and Referral Agencies
(NACCRRA)
2116 Campus Drive, S.E.
Rochester, MN   55904
(507) 287-2220
NACCRRA will direct parents to local child-care referral agencies nationwide. If you call the statewide or countywide agencies in this chapter and are not satisfied, call NACCRRA to see if other local agencies exist.

AU PAIR AGENCIES

The federal government has authorized these agencies to place au pairs in American homes.

Au Pair Care
1 Post Street, Suite 700
San Francisco, CA   94104
(800) 288-7786

AuPair/Homestay USA
1015 15th Street, N.W., Suite 7521
Washington, DC   20005
(202) 628-7134

Au Pair in America
102 Greenwich Avenue
Greenwich, CT   06836
(800) 727-2437

Au Pair Intercultural
Flavia Hall
Marylhurst College Campus
P.O. Box 147
Marylhurst, OR   97036
(503) 635-3702
For Western locations only.

Au Pair Programme USA
36 S. State, Suite 3000
Salt Lake City, UT   84111
(801) 943-7788

EF AuPair
1 Memorial Drive
Cambridge, MA   02142
(800) 333-6056

EurAuPair
228 N. Pacific Coast Highway
Laguna Beach, CA   92651
(800) 333-3804

InterExchange
356 W. 34th Street
New York, NY   10001
(212) 947-9533

STATEWIDE, COUNTYWIDE, AND LOCAL REFERRAL SERVICES

Within each section, the agencies and associations are organized alphabetically by town. Note that some countywide offices handle several counties. Call the one nearest you, even if it is not in your county.

Alabama

Statewide Referral Agency

Alabama Association for Child Care
   Resource & Referral Agencies
309 N. 23rd Street
Birmingham, AL   35203
(205) 252-1991

Countywide Referral Agencies

Child Care Resource Center, Inc.
P.O. Box 348
Auburn, AL   36831-0348
(205) 749-0426

Child Care Options
457 Conti Street
Mobile, AL   35502
(205) 433-1312

**Family Guidance Center of
  Montgomery, Inc.**
925 Forest Avenue
Montgomery, AL   36106
(205) 262-6660

**Coosa Valley Child Care Resource &
  Referral Agency**
P.O. Drawer 1
Talladega, AL   35150
(205) 362-3852

Local Child Care Provider Associations

**Jefferson County Child Development
  Council**
1608 13th Avenue S., Suite 221
Birmingham, AL   35205
(205) 933-1095

Mobile Family Day Care Association
146 University Boulevard
Mobile, AL   36608
No phone number listed.

FOCAL
3703 Cleveland Avenue
Montgomery, AL   36101
(205) 262-3456

L.C.C.P.'s of Montgomery
485 Dunbarton Road
Montgomery, AL   36117
No phone number listed.

Alaska

Statewide Referral Agency

**Alaska Child Care Resource & Referral
  Alliance**
P.O. Box 103394
Anchorage, AK   99510
(907) 279-5024

Countywide Referral Agency

Child Care Connection
P.O. Box 103394
Anchorage, AK   99510
(907) 278-2273

Local Child Care Provider Associations

Alaska FCC Society
1013 E. Dimond Boulevard, Suite 377
Anchorage, AK   99515
(907) 344 KIDS (5437)

AFCCS—Interior Chapter
P.O. Box 82424
Fairbanks, AK   99708
No phone number listed.

AFCCS—Kodiak Chapter
P.O. Box 2146
Kodiak, AK   99615
No phone number listed.

AFCCS—Sitka Chapter
P.O. Box 2453
Sitka, AK 99835
No phone number listed.

Arizona

Countywide Referral Agencies

Family Service Agency
1530 E. Flower Street
Phoenix, AZ   85014
(602) 264-9891

Association for Supportive Child Care
2510 S. Rural Road, Suite J
Tempe, AZ   85282
(602) 829-0500

Tucson Association for Child Care, Inc.
1030 N. Alvernon Way
Tucson, AZ   85711
(602) 881-8940

Local Child Care Provider Associations

Family Connection
1530 E. Flower Street
Phoenix, AZ   85014
(602) 264-9891

Arizona Association of FDC Providers
1631 E. Guadalupe, Suite 201
Tempe, AZ   85283
(602) 345-9388

SAFCA
7941 E. Birwood
Tucson, AZ   85715
(602) 721-0067

Arkansas

Countywide Referral Agency

Arkansas Child Care Resource &
   Referral Center
5 Statehouse Plaza
Little Rock, AR   72201
(501) 375-3690

Local Child Care Provider Association

Washington County FDCHA
P.O. Box 1522
Fayetteville, AR   72702
No phone number listed.

California

Statewide Referral Agency

California Child Care Resource &
   Referral Network
809 Lincoln Way
San Francisco, CA   94122
(415) 661-1714

Countywide Referral Agencies

Community Connection for Child Care
420 8th Street
Bakersfield, CA   93301
(805) 322-7633

Child Care Coordinating Council of San Mateo County, Inc.
1838 El Camino Real, Suite 214
Burlingame, CA   94010
(415) 692-6645

Child Development Resource Center
809 H Bay Avenue
Capitola, CA   95010
(408) 476-8585

Valley Oak Children's Services
1024 Esplanade
Chico, CA   95926
(916) 895-3572

Contra Costa Child Care
3020 Grant Street
Concord, CA   94520
(415) 676-KIDS (5437)

City of Davis Child Care Services
23 Russell Boulevard
Davis, CA   95616
(916) 756-3747

Humboldt Child Care Council
805 7th Street
Eureka, CA   95501
(707) 444-8293

Solano Family & Children's Services
2750 N. Texas Street, Suite 450-G
Fairfield, CA   94533
(707) 422-2881

Sierra Nevada Community Services Council
256 Buena Vista, Suite 210
Grass Valley, CA   95945
(916) 272-8866

River Child Care, Inc.
P.O. Box 1060
Guerneville, CA   95446
(707) 887-1809

Growth & Opportunity, Inc.
321 San Felipe Road, Suite 14
Hollister, CA   95023
(408) 637-9205

Resources for Family Development
1520 Catalina Court
Livermore, CA   94550
(415) 455-5111

Child & Family Services
2406 Kent Street
Los Angeles, CA   90038
(213) 413-0777

Crystal Stairs, Inc.
5105 W. Goldleaf Circle, Suite 200
Los Angeles, CA   90056
(213) 299-0199

Children's Services Network of Merced
  County, Inc.
1701 N Street
Merced, CA   95340
(209) 722-3804

Community Resources for Children
1754 2nd Street, Suite A
Napa, CA   94559
(707) 253-0366

Child Care Resource Center
5077 Lankershim Boulevard, Suite 600
North Hollywood, CA   91601
(818) 762-0905

Child Care Connection
8314 Rathburn Avenue
Northridge, CA   91325
(818) 349-1815

Bananas, Inc.
6501 Telegraph Avenue
Oakland, CA   94609
(415) 658-0381

Plumas Rural Services Child Care
  Resource & Referral
P.O. Box 1079
Quincy, CA   95971
(916) 283-4453

Options
3505 N. Hart Avenue, Suite 230
Rosemead, CA   91770
(818) 280-0777

Child Action, Inc.
2103 Stockton Boulevard, Suite 8
Sacramento, CA   95817
(916) 453-0713

Moutain Family Service
P.O. Box 919
San Andreas, CA   95249
(209) 754-1075

YMCA Childcare Resource Services
1033 Cudahy Place
San Diego, CA   92110
(619) 275-4800

Children's Council of San Francisco
1435 Market Street
San Francisco, CA   94103
(415) 864-1234

Community Coordinated Child
  Development Council/Santa Clara
  County
160 E. Virginia, Suite 200
San Jose, CA   95112-5888
(408) 998-4900

Marin Child Care Council
828 Mission Avenue
San Rafael, CA   94901
(415) 454-7951

Connections for Children
612 Colorado Avenue, Suite 104
Santa Monica, CA   90401
(213) 452-3202

Community Child Care Council of
  Sonoma County, Inc.
2227 Capricorn Way, Suite 105
Santa Rosa, CA   95407
(707) 544-3084

Infant/Child Enrichment Services
14326 Tuolumne Road
Sonora, CA   95370
(209) 533-0377

CDI-Choices for Children
P.O. Box 18295
South Lake Tahoe, CA   95706
(916) 541-5848

Family Resource & Referral Center
1149 N. El Dorado, Suite C
Stockton, CA   95202
(209) 948-1553

Human Response Network
P.O. Box 2370
Weaverville, CA   96093
(916) 623-KIDS (5437)

Local Child Care Provider Associations

FDC Providers, Inc.
1789 Terrace Drive
Belmont, CA   94002
(415) 592-1088

Benicia Day Care Association
Solano County Licensed DCA
407 Larkin Drive
Benicia, CA   94510
(707) 747-6420

California Federation of FDC
362 Midori Lane
Calimesa, CA   92320
(714) 795-1351

Kings County Community Action
  Organization
1222 W. Lacey Boulevard
Hanford, CA   93230
(209) 582-4386

San Joaquin FDCA
1827 E. Eight Mile Road
Lodi, CA   95240
(209) 463-1158

Greater Long Beach/Lakewood FDC
  Association
5449 Fairbrook Street
Long Beach, CA   90815
(213) 494-4679

Fresno County FDCA
P.O. Box 3603
Pinedale, CA   93650-3603
(209) 432-6343

Family Service Agency of San Mateo
35 Renato Court
Redwood, CA   94061
(415) 365-2284

Family Day Care Providers, Inc.
P.O. Box 15733
Sacramento, CA   95852
(916) 424-0699

Sacramento FDCP
P.O. Box 15733
Sacramento, CA   94585
(916) 362-4453

Monterey County FDC Association
P.O. Box 4122
Salinas, CA   93912
(408) 449-7017

California Child Care R&R Network
809 Lincoln Way
San Francisco, CA   94122
(415) 661-1714

San Francisco FDCA, Inc.
90 Paradise Avenue
San Francisco, CA   94131
(415) 333-9169

Santa Clara FDCA
P.O. Box 7472
San Jose, CA   95121
(408) 998-8379

Marin FDCA
P.O. Box 83
San Rafael, CA   94915
(415) 453-0346

San Diego County FDCA
P.O. Box 2595
Spring Valley, CA   92077
(619) 741-2383

Solano FDCA
2014 Marshall Road
Vacaville, CA   95688
(707) 446-9489

Whole Child Services
P.O. Box 7382
Vallejo, CA   94591
(707) 552-1290

Colorado

Statewide Referral Agency

**Colorado Child Care Resource &
    Referral Network**
5675 S. Academy Boulevard
Colorado Springs, CO   80906
(719) 540-7252

Countywide Referral Agencies

Boulder Children's Services
P.O. Box 791
Boulder, CO   80306
(303) 441-3180

**Mile High United Way Child Care
    Resource & Referral**
2505 18th Street
Denver, CO   80211-3907
(303) 433-8900

The Women's Center
424 Pine Street, Suite 104
Ft. Collins, CO   80524
(303) 484-1902

Child Care Clearinghouse
1129 Colorado Avenue
Grand Junction, CO   81501
(303) 241-0190

Family First Resource & Referral—Red
  Rocks Community College
13300 W. 6th Avenue, Box 22
Lakewood, CO   80401-5398
(303) 969-9500

Local Child Care Provider Associations

Jefferson County CCA
5900 Dudley Street
Arvada, CO   80004
(303) 432-6503

Boulder CC Support Center
2160 Spruce Street
Boulder, CO   80302
(303) 441-3180

Colorado Family Day Care Association
999 18th Street
North Tower, Suite 1615
Denver, CO   80202
(303) 292-2764

Work and Family Consortium
999 18th Street
North Tower, Suite 1615
Denver, CO   80202
(303) 293-2444

Wildwood Resources, Inc.
6143 S. Willow Drive, Room 320
Englewood, CO   80111
(303) 850-7700

FDCH Association of Gunnison &
  Hinsdale Counties
373 Mesa Loop
Gunnison, CO   81230
No phone number listed.

Colorado Association of FCC
P.O. Box 594
Wheatridge, CO   80034-0594
(303) 761-3138

Connecticut

Countywide Referral Agencies

Child Care Connections of Western
  Connecticut
70 North Street
Danbury, CT   06810
(203) 794-1180

North Central Child Care Info Line
Region 4
900 Asylum Avenue
Hartford, CT   06105
(203) 482-9471

South Central Child Care Info Line
Region 2
1 State Street
New Haven, CT   06511
(203) 624-4143

Southwest Child Care Info Line
Region 1
83 East Avenue, Room 107
Norwalk, CT   06851
(203) 333-7555

Southeast Child Care Info Line
Region 3
74 W. Main Street
Norwich, CT   06360
(203) 346-6691

Northwest Child Care Info Line
Region 5
232 N. Elm Street
Waterbury, CT   06702
(203) 482-9471

Northeast Child Care Info Line
Region 6
948 Main Street
Willimantic, CT   06226
(203) 456-8886

Local Child Care Provider Associations

Greater Hartford DCPA
8 Jackson Road
Bloomfield, CT   06002
(203) 242-9553

Greater Bridgeport FDCA
105 Williamsburg Drive
Bridgeport, CT   06606
(203) 374-3608

Child Care Resource of Connecticut
862 Farmington Avenue, Box 278
Bristol, CT   06010-3923
(203) 583-5393

Supplemental Child Care Services
800 Federal Road
Brookfield, CT   06804
(203) 775-8971

Groton Navy Housing
FDC Support Group
13 Monroe Lane
Groton, CT   06340
(203) 455-1235

Killington Group
579 N. Roast Meat Hill Road
Killingworth, CT   06417
(203) 663-1801

Madison Day Care Association
18 Cornfield Lane
Madison, CT   06443
(203) 421-3338

Child Care Providers Association
25 Lockwood Street
Meriden, CT   06450
(203) 634-8857

Middletown Day Care Association
171 Eastern Drive
Middletown, CT   06457
(203) 346-0005

Greater New Haven Providers Exchange
  Group
71 Barnett Street
New Haven, CT   06515
(203) 389-9753

Connecticut Homes in Licensed
  Daycare Association (CHILD)
60 Fitch Avenue
New London, CT   06320
(203) 443-4707

Association of FDC Providers
50 Oakwood Street
Norwalk, CT   06850
(203) 847-3170

Child Care Info Line
7 Academy Street
Norwalk, CT   06890
(203) 853-2525

TVCCA—Homes
2 Cliff Street
Norwich, CT   06360
(203) 889-1365

Southington Day Care Providers
  Association
359 Old Turnpike Road
Plantsville, CT   06479
(203) 528-2981

Lower Naugatuck Valley FDCA
26 Laurel Lane
Seymour, CT   06483-2216
(203) 735-5972

Greater Stamford FDCA
162 Berrian Road
Stamford, CT   06905
(203) 329-8982

Waterbury DC Association
35 White Oak Lane
Waterbury, CT   06705
(203) 757-7379

West Hartford DC Providers Association
14 Hugh Street
West Hartford, CT   06119
(203) 232-9086

Association of FDCP
19 Hickory Drive
Westport, CT   06880
(203) 227-9298

Family Day Care Training Program
599 Matianuck Avenue
Windsor, CT   06095
(203) 688-7333

Northwest C.A.R.E.
P.O. Box 655
Winsted, CT   06098
(203) 496-1575

Delaware

Countywide Referral Agency

Child Care Connection
3411 Silverside Road
Baynard #100
Wilmington, DE   19810
(302) 479-1660

Local Child Care Provider Associations

**FDC Support Group for New Castle
   County**
3050 Court Avenue
Claymont, DE   19703
(302) 792-2615
(302) 573-2716

**Delaware Association of Family Child
   Care Providers**
P.O. Box 926
Newark, DE   19714-9261
(302) 453-8435

Dover Provider Association
346 Paul Drive
Smyrna, DE   19977
(302) 653-4753

District of Columbia

Countywide Referral Agency

Washington Child Development Council
2121 Decatur Place, N.W.
Washington, DC   20008
(202) 387-0002

Local Child Care Provider Associations

United Planning Organization
Family Day Care Homes
810 Potomac Avenue, S.E.
Washington, DC   20003
(202) 546-7300 (ext. 277)

Washington Association for FDC
2338 13th Place, N.E
Washington, DC   20018
(202) 529-8558

Florida

Statewide Referral Agency

**Florida Child Care Resource & Referral
   Network**
1282 Paul Russel Road
Tallahassee, FL   32301
(904) 656-2272

Countywide Referral Agencies

**Child Care Association of Brevard
   County, Inc.**
18 Harrison Street
Cocoa, FL   32922
(407) 636-4634

Child Care Resource & Referral, Inc.
551 S.E. 8th Street, Suite 500
Delray Beach, FL   33483
(407) 832-0844

Child Care Connection of Broward
County
4740 N. Street
Rd 7 Building C, Suite 200
Ft. Lauderdale, FL   33319
(305) 486-3900

Child Care of Southwest Florida, Inc.
3625 Fowler Street
Ft. Myers, FL   33901
(813) 278-4114

Alachua Community Coordinate Child
Care
P.O. Box 12334
Gainesville, FL   32604
(904) 373-8426

Child Care Central
421 W. Church Street
Jacksonville, FL   32202
(904) 630-3698

Suwannee Valley Community
Coordinated Child Care
P.O. Box 2637
Lake City, FL   32056
(800) 542-5456

Child Care Options/Latchkey Services
1715 E. Bay Drive, Suite H
Largo, FL   34698
(813) 584-7462

Child Care Connection
366 Goodlette Road S.
Naples, FL   33940
(813) 649-4816

Childhood Development Services, Inc.
3230 S.E. Maricamp Road
Ocala, FL   32671
(800) 635-5437

Community Coordinated Child Care for
Central Florida, Inc.
1612 E. Colonial Drive
Orlando, FL   32803
(407) 894-8393

United Child Care, Inc.
801 S. Yonge Street
Ormond Beach, FL   32174
(904) 673-3730

Early Childhood Services, Inc.
1241 N. East Avenue
Panama City, FL   32401
(904) 785-0988

West Florida Child Care & Education
Services, Inc.
P.O. Box 12242
Pensacola, FL   32581-2242
(904) 438-7422

Child Care of Southwest Florida, Inc.
1750 17th Street
Unit B-2
Sarasota, FL   34234
(813) 366-2149

Coordinated Child Care of Pinellas, Inc.
4140 49th Street, N.
St. Petersburg, FL   33709
(813) 521-1853

YMCA Child Care Resource & Referral
4326 El Prado, Suite 10
Tampa, FL   33629
(813) 831-5515

Local Child Care Provider Associations

Florence Fuller Child Development
   Center
200 N.E. 14th Street
Boca Raton, FL   33432
(407) 391-7274

Child Home DCP for Children &
   Infants of Orlando
P.O. Box 481
Clarcona, FL   32710
(305) 298-3877

Bay Area Child Care Association
P.O. Box 4896
Clearwater, FL   34618
(813) 449-0259

Providers Support Group
Eglin Air Force Family Day Care
c/o 21-A Choctaw Road
Eglin Air Force Base, FL   32542
(904) 651-2149

Tri-County Child Care
P.O. Box 1068
Lakeland, FL   33802
(813) 688-6952

Childhood Development Services
306 N.W. 7th Avenue
Ocala, FL   32675
(904) 629-6405

Seminole County FDC
213 Citrus Drive
Sanford, FL   32771
(407) 321-6674

4-C Association
406 Dupont Drive
Tallahassee, FL   32304
(904) 576-5694

Child Care Services
School Board of Palm Beach County
3323 Belvedere Road, Room 501-A
West Palm Beach, FL   33406
(407) 684-5123

Georgia

Countywide Referral Agencies

Care Connection
850 College Station Road, Suite 332
Athens, GA   30610
(404) 353-1313

Care Solutions, Inc.
5 Concourse Parkway, Suite 810
Atlanta, GA   30328
(404) 393-7366

Save the Children/Child Care Solutions
1340 Spring Street, N.W., Suite 200
Atlanta, GA   30309
(404) 885-1585

Child Care Solutions of North Georgia
Gainesville College
Gainesville, GA   30503
(404) 535-6383

Local Child Care Provider Associations

Federation of 7 Cooperatives
FDC Provider Program
100 Edgewood Avenue, N.E.
Room 1228
Atlanta, GA   30303
(404) 534-6882

Family Day Care Providers
3730 Sulene Drive
College Park, GA   30349
(404) 761-7298

**Gwinnett County Child Care Network &
   FDCA**
1381 Reddington Lane
Norcross, GA   30093
(404) 242-2077

South Georgia Association of Family
   Day Care
4027 Lantern Lane
Valdosta, GA   31602
(912) 247-9789

Georgia FDC Providers Association
Route 1, Box 226B
Wrightsville, GA   31096
(404) 524-6882

Hawaii

Countywide Referral Agency

**Parents Attentive To Children
   (PATCH)**
810 N. Vineyard Boulevard
Honolulu, HI   96717
(808) 842-3874

Local Child Care Provider Association

People Attentive to Children (PATC)
419 Waiakamilo Road, Room 203A
Honolulu, HI   96817
(808) 842-3965

Idaho

Countywide Referral Agencies

Child Care Connections
P.O. Box 6756
Boise, ID   83707
(208) 343-KIDS (5437)

Child Care Choices, Inc.
1000 W. Garden
Coeur d'Alene, ID   83814
(208) 765-6296

Human Services Center, Inc.
3100 Rollandet
Idaho Falls, ID   83403
(208) 525-7281

Southeast Idaho Community Action
   Agency
P.O. Box 940
Pocatello, ID   83204
(208) 232-1114

Local Child Care Provider Associations

ADA County CC Association, Inc.
1821 S. Phillippi
Boise, ID   83705
(208) 322-8833

Illinois

Statewide Referral Agency

Illinois Child Care Resource & Referral
   System
100 W. Randolph, Suite 16-206
Chicago, IL   60601
(312) 814-5524

Countywide Referral Agencies

Aurora YWCA Child Care Resource &
   Referral
201 N. River
Aurora, IL   60506
(708) 897-1363

Child Care Resource & Referral
John A. Logan College
Carterville, IL   62918
(618) 985-6384

Day Care Action Council
4753 N. Broadway, Suite 726
Chicago, IL   60640
(312) 769-8000

Jane Addams Child Care
3212 N. Broadway
Chicago, IL   60657
(312) 769-8100

Dekalb County Community Coordinated
   Child Care
145 Fisk Avenue
Dekalb, IL   60115
(800) 848-8727

The Child Care Connection
Illinois Central College
East Peoria, IL   61635
(309) 694-5553

YWCA Child Care Resource & Referral
739 Roosevelt Road
Building 8, Suite 210
Glen Ellyn, IL   60137
(708) 790-6600

Child Care Resource & Referral of
  Marion North
Rend Lake College
Route 1
Ina, IL   62806
(618) 437-5321

Association for Child Development
P.O. Box 1370
Lagrange Park, IL   60525
(708) 354-0450

Illinois Child Care Bureau
P.O. Box 2290
Lagrange, IL   60525
(708) 579-9880

YWCA
220 S. Madison
Rockford, IL   61104
(815) 968-9681

Community Child Care Connection,
  Inc.
730 E. Vine Street, Room 209
Springfield, IL   62703
(217) 525-2805

Child Care Resource Service
274 Bevier Hall
9055 S. Goodwin
Urbana, IL   61801
(217) 333-3252

YWCA of Lake County
1900 Grand Avenue
Waukegan, IL   60085-3402
(708) 662-4247

Local Child Care Provider Associations

Belleville DCA
313 N. 4th Street
Belleville, IL   62220
(618) 234-3552

Tri-Village FDCA
30 51st Avenue
Bellwood, IL   60104
(312) 547-7202

McHenry County DCP Association
67 Fairfield Lane
Cary, IL   60013
(312) 639-7590

Champaign County DCA
1213 Julie Drive
Champaign, IL   61821
(217) 359-1700

Charleston HDC Providers
709 20th Street
Charleston, IL   61920
(217) 348-0258

C.A.E.Y.C.
410 S. Michigan Avenue, Suite 525
Chicago, IL   60605
(312) 427-5399

Chicago City Wide College FDC
3901 S. State Street, Room 244
Chicago, IL   60609
(312) 624-7300

Erie Neighborhood House
1347 W. Erie
Chicago, IL   60622
(312) 666-3430

Family Support Services of Englewood
3120 W. Arlington
Chicago, IL   60624
(312) 265-9058

Far Southside Home DC Association
11026 S. Indiana Avenue
Chicago, IL   60628
(312) 468-4664

North Side FDC Association
1917 W. Belle Plaine
Chicago, IL   60613
(312) 549-3658

West Side DC Providers Association
5475 W. Hirsch
Chicago, IL   60651
(312) 379-7319

Judy's Child Care Referral Service
1142 Tampico
Edwardsville, IL   62025
(618) 656-8763

K.I.D.S.
640 Parkside
Elmhurst, IL   60126
(312) 941-3247

Evanston HDC Program
1840 Asbury Avenue
Evanston, IL   60201
(312) 864-5610

Fort Sheridan CC Program
Building 205
Fort Sheridan, IL   60037
(312) 926-2602

North Suburban DC Support Group
2231 Swainwood Drive
Glenview, IL   60025
(312) 998-0726

Association for Saline County DCP
612 W. Perish
Harrisburg, IL   62946
(618) 252-3650

S.S.A.E.Y.C./Basics FDC Support
1736 Cedar Road
Homewood, IL   60430
(312) 755-8109

Joliet Area HCCPA
818 Glenwood Avenue
Joliet, IL   60435
(815) 726-7915

Professional DCP
924 Rolling
Lisle, IL   60532
(312) 968-3701

South Suburban Area Association
16516 S. Ashland
Markham, IL   60426
(312) 333-3721

Illinois DCH Operators Association
6832 Beckwith Road
Morton Grove, IL   60053
(312) 966-4657

Mount Carmel HDCP Association
c/o Donna's Tot Spot
218 E. 5th Street
Mount Carmel, IL   62863
(618) 262-8260

Association of Second Mothers
P.O. Box 542
Mount Prospect, IL   60056
(312) 253-7667

Naperville FDCA
1034 Snowden Court
Naperville, IL   60540
(312) 961-9179

Illinois State HCCA, Inc.
710 N. Grove
Oak Park, IL   60302
(312) 524-0696

Basics—Child Care Services
   Information
P.O. Box 604
Park Forest, IL   60466-0604
(312) 754-0938
(312) 748-2378

Peoria Area HDCA
1929 W. Daytona
Peoria, IL   61614
(309) 685-8164
(309) 692-3265

Illinois Valley DCA
904 Putnam Street
Peru, IL   61354
(815) 223-3704

Rockford Day Care Homes
1219 Auburn Court
Rockford, IL   61103
(815) 962-5451

For Kids Sake
1309 Elmhurst Lane
Schaumburg, IL   60194
(312) 885-3976

Warrenville FDCA
29-W-271 Batavia
Warrenville, IL   60555
(312) 393-1279

Wheaton Area Support Group
1700 Kay Road
Wheaton, IL   60187
(312) 653-0497

Indiana

Statewide Referral Agency

Indiana Association for Child Care
   Resource & Referral
4460 Guion Road
Indianapolis, IN   46254
(317) 299-2750

Countywide Referral Agencies

Day Care Resources/Human Resources
   Department
P.O. Box 100
Bloomington, IN   47402
(812) 331-6430

YWCA
2000 Wells Street
Fort Wayne, IN   46808
(219) 424-4908

Day Nursery Association
615 N. Alabama, Suite 108
Indianapolis, IN   46204
(317) 631-4643

YWCA Child Care Resource & Referral
   Program
4460 Guion Road
Indianapolis, IN   46254
(317) 299-0626

Tippecanoe County Child Care, Inc.
P.O. Box 749
Lafayette, IN   47902
(317) 742-4033

Community Coordinated Child
   Care, Inc.
802 N. Lafayette Boulevard
South Bend, IN   46601
(219) 289-7815

Community Coordinated Child Care for
   the Wabash Valley, Inc.
619 Washington Avenue
Terre Haute, IN   47802
(812) 232-3952

Local Child Care Provider Associations

FDC Providers Association
Child Care Services
City of Bloomington H.R.D.
P.O. Box 100
Bloomington, IN   47402
(812) 339-2261 (ext. 37)

Heartline, Inc.
21 W. Main Street
Brownsburg, IN   46112
(317) 852-7872

Children, Inc.
715 McClure Road
Columbus, IN   47201-6610
(812) 379-2319

Southwestern Indiana CCA
3014 Eastbrook Drive
Evansville, IN   47711
(812) 476-6231

University of Evansville Children's
  Center
200 S. Alvord
Evansville, IN   47714
(812) 477-4803

Child Care of Allen County
Family Day Care Providers
1021 W. Wayne Street
Fort Wayne, IN   46804
(219) 426-5428

Family Day Care Providers
1021 W. Wayne Street
Fort Wayne, IN   46804
(219) 426-4528

Fort Wayne Area FDCPA
4902 Southwood Avenue
Fort Wayne, IN   46807
(219) 745-4380

Gary Neighborhood Services
300 W. 21st Avenue
Gary, IN   46407
(219) 883-0431

A Rainbow House DCC
3849 Alsace Place
Indianapolis, IN   46226
(317) 897 4915

Care Connectors
P.O. Box 36152
Indianapolis, IN   46236
(317) 899-3463

Day Nursery Association of
  Indianapolis, Inc.
615 N. Alabama Street, Suite 104
Indianapolis, IN   46204
(317) 636-5727

New Beginnings, Inc.
2075 Suffolk Lane
Indianapolis, IN   46260
(317) 876-3067

T.J. FDC Homes, Inc.
6518 E. 52nd Place
Indianapolis, IN   46226
(317) 547-3551

Tomorrow's Child
4850 Barlow Drive
Indianapolis, IN   46226
(317) 546-4374

Hoosier Valley Economic Opportunity
  Center
P.O. Box 843
Jeffersonville, IN   47130
(812) 283-4128

Saint Joseph County FDCA
234 W. Colfax
Misawaka, IN   46545
(219) 259-6725

United DCC of Delaware County
312 S. Vine Street
Muncie, IN 47305
(317) 282-1742

Children's League of LaPorte County
211 Hickory Street
P.O. Box 104
Otis, IN   46367
(219) 785-2366

Iowa

Statewide Referral Agency

Iowa Commission on Children, Youth &
    Families
Department of Human Rights
Lucas Building
Des Moines, IA   50319
(515) 281-3974

Countywide Referral Agencies

Child Care Resource & Referral Center
P.O. Box 464
Carroll, IA   51401
(712) 792-6440

Community Child Care Resource &
    Referral Center
2804 Eastern Avenue
Davenport, IA   52803
(319) 324-3236

Polk County Child Care Resource
    Center
1200 University, Suite F
Des Moines, IA   50314
(515) 286-3536

Project Concern/Phone A Friend, Inc.
2013 Central Avenue
Dubuque, IA   52001
(319) 557-1628

Community Coordinated Child Care
202 S. Linn, P.O. Box 2876
Iowa City, IA   52244
(319) 338-7684

Mid-Sioux Opportunity, Inc.
418 Marion Street
Remsen, IA   51050
(712) 786-2001

Child Care Resource Center
2700 Leech Avenue
Sioux City, IA   51106
(712) 274-2212

Child Care Coordination
P.O. Box 4090
Waterloo, IA   50704
(319) 233-0804

Child Care Resource & Referral
117 N. 1st Street
Winterset, IA   50273
(515) 462-1509

Local Child Care Provider Associations

Cedar Rapids Area Family Home Child
    Care Association
700 43rd Street, N.E.
Cedar Rapids, IA   52402
(319) 393-8356

Home Child Care Association
3103 Fair Avenue
Davenport, IA   52803
(319) 324-4662

CC Providers Association
1436 32nd Street
Des Moines, IA   50311
(515) 227-2033

Child Care Resource Center
1200 University City View, Suite F
Des Moines, IA   50314
(515) 286-2004

Family Child Care Providers
   Co-operative Association
P.O. Box 398
Hills, IA   52235
(319) 679-2401

Family Day Care Association
2317 Cae Drive
Iowa City, IA   52240
(319) 351-8600

Mid-Iowa FDCA
7 S. 13th Street
Marshalltown, IA   50158
(515) 752-7287

Family Day Care Association
820 S. Harrison
Mason City, IA   50401
(515) 424-1331

Black Hawk County FDC Homes
   Association
732 Stephan Avenue
Waterloo, IA   50701
(319) 234-4077

Child Care Coordination & Referral
   Service
2530 University Avenue
Waterloo, IA   50701
(319) 233-0804

Iowa FCC Association
P.O. Box 65816
West Des Moines, IA   50265
(515) 225-3654

Tri-County CCPA
Route 4, Box 167
Winterset, Iowa   50273
(515) 462-4195

Kansas

Countywide Referral Agencies

Heart of America Family Services
8047 Parallel Parkway
Kansas City, KS   66112
(913) 753-5280

Everywoman's Resource Center
1002 S.W. Garfield, Suite 109
Topeka, KS   66604
(913) 357-5171

CHILD CARE

Child Care Association
1069 Parklane Office Park
Wichita, KS 67218
(316) 682-1853

Local Child Care Provider Associations

Fredonia Child Care, Inc.
632 N. 7th, P.O. Box 69
Fredonia, KS 66736
(316) 378-4362

NE Kansas Community Action
Route 4, Box 187
Hiawatha, KS 66434
(913) 742-2222

Reno County CCA
103 S. Walnut Street
Hutchinson, KS 67501
(316) 669-0291

Douglas County Child Development
  Association
P.O. Box 1373
Lawrence, KS 66044
(913) 842-9679

Day Care Connection
7763 Quivira
Lenexa, KS 66216
(913) 962-2020

Johnson County CCA
5750 W. 95th, Apartment 140
Overland Park, KS 66207-2969
(913) 341-6200

Martin Luther King CC Program
1214 N. Santa Fe
Salina, KS 67401
(913) 827-5808

CC Providers of Kansas
P.O. Box 164
Topeka, KS 66601
(913) 232-2008

Family CDCA
217 N. Fern Street
Wichita, KS 67203
(316) 264-5817

Kentucky

Countywide Referral Agencies

Kentucky Coalition for School Age
  Child Care
200 High Street
Bowling Green, KY 42101
(502) 842-4281

Child Care Council of Kentucky
800 Sparta Court, Suite 100
Lexington, KY 40504
(606) 254-9176

Community Coordinated Child Care
1215 S. 3rd Street
Louisville, KY 40203
(502) 636-1358

Local Child Care Provider Associations

Northern Kentucky FDCA
1125 Madison Avenue
Covington, KY   41011
(606) 431-2075

Louisiana

Countywide Referral Agencies

Child Care Information, Inc.
P.O. Box 45212, D.223
Baton Rouge, LA   70895
(504) 293-8523

Child Care Resources
P.O. Box 51837
New Orleans, LA   70151
(504) 586-8509

Child Care Services of NW Louisiana
209 Milam, Suite C
Shreveport, LA   71101-7728
(318) 227-1812

Local Child Care Provider Associations

Louisiana Housing Assistance Corp.
3400 Jackson Street, Suite A
Alexandria, LA   71301
(318) 487-5646

Day Care Home Section
Louisiana Department of Education
P.O. Box 94064
Baton Rouge, LA   70804
(504) 342-3707

Evangeline CAA
403 W. Magnolia Street
Ville Platte, LA   70586
(318) 363-0090

Maine

Statewide Referral Agency

**Maine Association of Child Care
    Resource & Referral Agencies**
P.O. Box 280
Milbridge, ME   04658
(207) 546-7544

Countywide Referral Agencies

**Penquis Child Care Resource
    Development Center**
120 Cleveland Street
Bangor, ME   04401
(207) 941-2843

Child Care Resources of Waldo County
Route 1, Box 2511
Brooks, ME   04921
(800) 445-0127

Bath Brunswick Child Care Services
44 Water Street
Brunswick, ME   04011
(207) 725-6506

Child Care Opportunities
P.O. Box 1093
Ellsworth, ME   04605
(207) 667-2467

Child Care Connections
87 High Street
Portland, ME   04106
(207) 871-7449

Careline Resource Development Center
55 Bowdoin Street, P.O. Box 512
Sanford, ME   04083
(207) 324-0735

Finders/Seekers
P.O. Box 278
South Paris, ME   04281
(800) 543-7008

Local Child Care Provider Associations

DHRS, Inc. FDC Network
87 High Street
Portland, ME   04101
(207) 871-7443

Bangor Area Child Care Providers
5 Epworth Street
Presque Isle, ME   04769
No phone number listed.

FDCA of Mid-Coast Maine
P.O. Box 124
Rockport, ME   04865
(207) 236-2403

The Maine FDC Association
95 Scamman Street
South Portland, ME   04106
(207) 799-7204

York County Family Day Care
5 John Street
Springdale, ME   04083
(207) 324-0337

Maryland

Statewide Referral Agency

Maryland Child Care Resource Network
608 Water Street
Baltimore, MD   21202
(301) 752-7588

Countywide Referral Agencies

Maryland Committee for Children
608 Water Street
Baltimore, MD   21202
(301) 625-1111

Child Care Consortium
22 S. Market Street
Frederick, MD   21701
(301) 695-4508

Western Maryland Child Care Resource
   Center
Bryan Centre, 6th Floor
82 W. Washington Street
Hagerstown, MD   21740
(301) 733-6914

Child Care Connection, Inc.
101 Monroe Street
Rockville, MD   20850
(301) 217-1773

Local Child Care Provider Associations

Harford County FDCA
144 Post Road
Aberdeen, MD   21001
(301) 272-5817

Baltimore City FDCA
1922 E. 30th Street
Baltimore, MD   21218
(301) 889-7654

Baltimore City Providers Association
5403 Moravia Road
Baltimore, MD   21206
(301) 485-5656

Worchester County FDCA
Route 1, Box 82B
Bishopsville, MD   21813
(301) 352-5246

Calvert County SMDCPA
7435 Dakota Avenue
Chesapeake Beach, MD   20732
(301) 855-4983

**Prince Georges County Quality CC
   Network**
9801 Brandywine Road
Clinton, MD   20735
(301) 868-9128

Howard County FDCA
6649 Dovecoat Road
Columbia, MD   21044
(301) 997-0392

Allegany County FDCA
123 W. 2nd Street
Cumberland, MD   21502
(301) 724-4450

Anne Arundel County FDCA
P.O. Box 376
Gambrills, MD   21054
(301) 647-3961

Washington County FDCA
1173 Green Lane
Hagerstown, MD   21740
(301) 733-6230

Garrett County FDCA
304 D Street
Mount Lake Park, MD   21550
(301) 334-9590

Maryland State FDCA
3726 Dance Mill Road
Phoenix, MD   21131
(301) 592-6347

Charles County FDCA
1104 G Chapel Point Road
Port Tobacco, MD   20677
(301) 934-9234

Cecil County FDCA
2127 Principio Road
Rising Sun, MD   21911
(301) 658-6603

Prince Georges County FDCA
6001 Taylor Road
Riverdale, MD   20737
(301) 927-8422

Kent County & Queen Anne's
   County FDCA
Liberty Street, P.O. Box 188
Rockhall, MD   21661
(301) 778-6047

Montgomery County FDCA
9907 Markham Street
Silver Spring, MD   20901
(301) 681-5367

Baltimore County FDCA
702 Providence Road
Towson, MD   21204
(301) 339-7199

Massachusetts

Statewide Referral Agency

Massachusetts Office for Children
10 West Street, 5th Floor
Boston, MA   02111
(617) 727-8900

Countywide Referral Agencies

Home/Health & Child Care, Inc.
Box 296
Avon, MA   02322
(800) 222-5609

Child Care Resource Center, Inc.
552 Massachusetts Avenue
Cambridge, MA   02139
(617) 547-1063

Child Care Resources of Children's Aid
   & Family Service, Inc.
344 Main Street
Fitchburg, MA   01420
(508) 343-7395

Preschool Enrichment Team, Inc.
276 High Street
Holyoke, MA   01040
(413) 536-3900

Child Care Circuit
190 Hampshire Street
Lawrence, MA   01840
(508) 686-4288

Child Care Resource Exchange
Box D-626, 4 Park Place
New Bedford, MA   02742
(800) 338-1717

Child Care Focus
56 Vernon Street
Northampton, MA   01060
(413) 586-3404

Resources for Child Care
311 North Street
Pittsfield, MA   01201
(413) 499-7982

Quincy Community Action Program
1509 Hancock Street
Quincy, MA   02169
(617) 479-8181

Childcare Resource Connection
17 Tremont Street
Taunton, MA   02780
(508) 823-9118

Child Care Search
60 Turner Street
Waltham, MA   02154
(617) 891-4557

PHPCC/Child Care Resource & Referral
   Consortium
200 5th Avenue
Waltham, MA   02154
(617) 890-8781

Warmlines
492 Waltham Street
West Newton, MA   02165
(617) 244-6843

Child Care Connection
UWCM—484 Main Street, Suite 300
Worcester, MA   01608
(508) 757-3880

Local Child Care Provider Associations

Massachusetts Association for FDC
   Providers
961 Old Keene Road
Athol, MA   01331
(508) 249-6792

Attleboro Area DC Support Group
(508) 285-3290

Beverly Area Support Group
(508) 922-0824

Brockton Support Group
(508) 583-8552

Brookline Support Group
(617) 385-8118

Family Day Care Program, Inc.
29 Harvard Street
Brookline, MA   02146
(617) 738-0703

Associated Day Care Service FDC
302 Broadway
Chelsea, MA   02150
(617) 889-4884

Valley Cap FDC
P.O. Box 417
Chicopee, MA   01014
(413) 592-4168

Day Care, Inc.
Referral Services
260 Cochituate Road, Room 210
Framingham, MA   01701
(508) 877-7696

Greater Haverhill FDCA
(508) 372-2800

Medford Support Group
(617) 396-6652

Needham Support Group
(617) 444-2007

Norwood Association of Home
  Providers
289 Prospect Street
Norwood, MA   02062
(617) 769-5362

Pittsfield Support Group
(413) 442-0753

South Shore Council for Children
  Support Group
(508) 696-2323

Taunton Support Group
(508) 822-1053

Massachusetts Support Group
21 Chrome Street
Worcester, MA   01604
(508) 754-1028

Network of Licensed Day Care
  Providers
5 Hadley Road
Westboro, MA   01581
(508) 366-9859

Michigan

Statewide Referral Agency

Michigan Community Coordinated
  Child Care Association
2875 Northwind Drive, Room 200
East Lansing, MI   48823
(517) 351-4171

Countywide Referral Agencies

Child Advocacy Community
  Coordinated Child Care
150 W. Center Street
Alma, MI   48801
(517) 463-1422

Child Care Coordinating & Referral
  Service
2454 E. Stadium Boulevard
Ann Arbor, MI   48104
(313) 971-5460

Community Coordinated Child Care of
  Detroit/Wayne County, Inc.
5031 Grandy
Detroit, MI   48211
(313) 579-2777

Flint Genesee Community Coordinated
  Child Care
310 E. 3rd Street, 5th Floor
Flint, MI   48502
(313) 232-0145

Saginaw Valley Regional Community
Coordinated Child Care
305 3rd Street
Freeland, MI   48623
(517) 695-5080

Kent Regional Community Coordinated
Child Care
233 E. Fulton, Suite 107
Grand Rapids, MI   49503
(616) 451-8281

Ottawa County Community Coordinated
Child Care
529 E. 16th Street
Holland, MI   49423
(616) 396-8151

Child Care Resource and Referral
268-B E. Kilgore
Kalamazoo, MI   49001
(616) 346-3296

Office for Young Children
P.O. Box 30161
Lansing, MI   48909
(517) 887-6996

Community Coordinated Child Care of
the Upper Penisula
125 W. Washington, Suite F
Marquette, MI   49855
(906) 228-3362

Macomb County Community
Coordinated Child Care
21885 Dunham
Mt. Clemens, MI   48043
(313) 469-6993

Grand Traverse Community
Coordinated Child Care Council
1701 E. Front Street
Traverse City, MI   49684
(800) 678-4951

Oakland County Community
Coordinated Child Care Council
255 N. Telegraph Road, Suite 206
Waterford, MI   48328
(313) 858-5140

Local Child Care Provider Associations

Michigan FCC Providers Alliance
251 Sunset
Ann Arbor, MI   48103
(313) 663-0154

Oakland County CC Association
328 Bird
Birmingham, MI   48009
(313) 645-2588

Genesee County FDCA
7265 Davison Road
Davison, MI   48423
(313) 653-4289

Wayne County Professional Caregivers
  Association
14082 Cloverlawn
Detroit, MI 48238
(313) 931-4177

Ottawa County FDC Association
75 E. 22nd Street
Holland, MI 49423
(616) 396-7548

Ottawa County 4C/SCAN
529 E. 16th Street
Holland, MI 49423
(616) 396-8151

Capital Area FDC Association
1701 Lenore Avenue
Lansing, MI 48910
(517) 372-3753

Minnesota

Statewide Referral Agency

Minnesota Child Care Resource &
  Referral Network
2116 Campus Drive, S.E.
Rochester, MN 55904
(507) 287-2497

Countywide Referral Agencies

Parenting Resource Center, Inc.
Box 505
Austin, MN 55912
(507) 433-0692

Community Action Council Child Care
  Resource & Referral
14451 County Road 11
Burnsville, MN 55337
(612) 431-7752

Minnesota Child Care Innovations, Inc.
12700 Nicollet Avenue, S., Suite 204
Burnsville, MN 55337
(612) 894-0727

Tri Valley Child Care Resource &
  Referral, Inc.
Box 607
Crookston, MN 56716
(218) 281-6672

The Family Resource Center
P.O. Box 836
Lindstrom, MN 55045
(612) 257-2400

Child Care Resource Center
3602 4th Avenue, S.
Minneapolis, MN 55409
(612) 823-5261

Greater Minneapolis Day Care
  Association
1628 Elliot Avenue, S.
Minneapolis, MN 55404
(612) 341-2066

Prairie Five Community Action Council
P.O. Box 695
Montevideo, MN 56265
(507) 269-6578

Lakes & Prairies Child Care Resource
& Referral
P.O. Box 919
Moorhead, MN   56560
(507) 233-7514

East Central Regional Development
Commission
100 S. Park Street
Mora, MN   55051
(800) 323-7126

Child Care Resource & Referral
1610 Commerce Drive
N. Mankato, MN   56001
(507) 389-5087

Scope Resource Center
122 E. McKinley
Owatonna, MN   55060
(507) 455-2560

Child Care Resource & Referral, Inc.
2116 Campus Drive, S.E.
Rochester, MN   55904
(800) 462-1660

Central Minnesota Child Care, Inc.
P.O. Box 1797
St. Cloud, MN 56302
(612) 251-5081

Resources for Child Caring
450 N. Syndicate, Suite 5
St. Paul, MN   55119
(612) 641-0332

Washington County Child Care
Resource & Referral
14900 61st Street, N.
Stillwater, MN   55082
(612) 779-5023

Heartland Community Action
Agency, Inc.
P.O. Box 1359
Willmar, MN   56201
(612) 235-0850

Local Child Care Provider Associations

Mower County FDCA
1200 2nd Avenue, S.W.
Austin, MN   55912
No phone number listed.

Carver County FDCA
515 Westwood Lane
Chaska, MN   55318
(612) 448-5761

Meeker County CCA
Route 2, Box 741
Dassel, MN   55325
No phone number listed.

Dodge County FDCA
1021 4th Avenue, N.E.
Dodge Center, MN   55927
No phone number listed.

Saint Louis County Professional FDCA
2119 W. 5th Street
Duluth, MN   55812
No phone number listed.

Fairbault FDCA
144 Fairview
Fairmont, MN   56031
No phone number listed.

Itasca FDCA
709 4th Avenue, S.E.
Grand Rapids, MN   55744
No phone number listed.

McLeod County Association
731 California Street
Hutchinson, MN   55350
No phone number listed.

Morrison FDCA
700 Florence Avenue
Little Falls, MN   56345
No phone number listed.

Watanwan CCA
40 Route #3
Madison, MN   56256
No phone number listed.

Child Care Professionals
234 Clark Street
Mankato, MN   56001
No phone number listed.

Lyon County FDCA
302 S. 4th
Marshall, MN   56258
No phone number listed.

Clay County FDCA
P.O. Box 94
Moorhead, MN   56560
No phone number listed.

Scott County LFDCA
16347 Mandan Avenue, S.E.
Prior Lake, MN   55372
(612) 447-4932

Goodhue County FDCA
744 Pioneer Road
Red Wing, MN   55066
No phone number listed.

Family Child Care Inc.
P.O. Box 7012
Rochester, MN   55903
(507) 282-3432

Minnesota Licensed FCCA
1910 W. County Road B, Suite 103
Roseville, MN   55113
(612) 427-3775

Stearns County Child Care
916 S. 11th Avenue
St. Cloud, MN   56301
No phone number listed.

Association of Minnesota Family Day
  Care Licensors
P.O. Box 65033
St. Paul, MN 55165
No phone number listed.

Wilder Ramsey CCA
Wilder FCC Network
911 Lafond Avenue
St. Paul, MN 55104
(612) 642-2094

Dakota County FDCA
136 E. Annapolis Street
West St. Paul, MN 55118
No phone number listed.

Nobles County FDCA
1815 Eleanor
Worthington, MN 56187
(507) 372-2116

Mississippi

Local Child Care Provider Association

Mashulaville Community Day Care
  Center
Route 4, Box 33-AA
Macon, MS 39341
(601) 726-5680

Missouri

Countywide Referral Agencies

Heart of America Family Services
3217 Broadway, Suite 500
Kansas City, MO 64111
(816) 753-5280

Child Day Care Association
915 Olive, Suite 913
St. Louis, MO 63101
(314) 241-3161

Local Child Care Provider Associations

Blue Springs CCA
3013 S.E. 6th Street
Blue Springs, MO 64015
(816) 228-5442

KCMC Child Development Corp.
1800 E. 84th Terrace
Kansas City, MO 64127
(816) 474-3751

Missouri Family Day Care, Inc.
3916 San Francisco Court
St. Louis, MO 63115
(314) 385-8245

Montana

Countywide Referral Agencies

Human Resources Development
   Council
P.O. Box 2016
Billings, MT   59103
(406) 248-1477

Child Care Connections
321 E. Main, Suite 423
Bozeman, MT   59715
(406) 587-7786

Local Child Care Provider Associations

Billings Child Care Association
420 Clark Avenue
Billings, MT   59101
(406) 248-6039

Butte Child Care Association
110 Milky Way
Butte, MT   59701
(406) 494-8341

Great Falls DCA
4307 North Star Boulevard
Great Falls, MT   95401
(406) 761-7678

Montana CCA
1623 12th Avenue S.
Great Falls, MT   59405
(406) 452-8427

Nebraska

Countywide Referral Agency

Midwest Child Care Association
5015 Dodge, Suite 2
Omaha, NE   68132
(402) 551-2379

Local Child Care Provider Associations

Nebraska Family Day Care Association
P.O. Box 297
Grand Island, NE   68802
(308) 384-1682

Building Tomorrow Thru FDC
2202 S. 11th Street
Lincoln, NE   68502
(402) 474-7949

Family Service Child Care Resource
   Center
2202 S. 11th Street
Lincoln, NE   68502
(402) 474-7949

PRIDE
1708 Urbana Lane
Lincoln, NE   68505
(402) 466-0669

Nevada

Countywide Referral Agency

Child Care Resource Council
1090 S. Rock Boulevard
Reno, NV   89502
(702) 785-4200

Local Child Care Provider Associations

Carson City CCA
401 E. John Street
Carson City, NV   89701
No phone number listed.

Clark County CCA
P.O. Box 15372
Las Vegas, NV   89114
No phone number listed.

Home Sweet Home CCPA
5170 E. Hacienda Avenue
Las Vegas, NV   89122
No phone number listed.

Las Vegas Valley CCA
236 S. Rainbow Boulevard, Room 153
Las Vegas, NV   89128
(702) 363-3428

Nevada State CCPA
1951 S. Rainbow Boulevard
Las Vegas, NV   89102
No phone number listed.

Family Day Care Home Program
554 CSG/SSRC
Nellis AFB, NV   89191
(702) 652-2909

North Nevada CCA
3880 Picadilly Drive
Reno, NV   89509
No phone number listed.

New Hampshire

Statewide Referral Agency

New Hampshire Association of Child
   Care Resource and Referral Network
99 Hanover Street, P.O. Box 448
Manchester, NH   03105
(603) 668-1920

Countywide Referral Agencies

University of New Hampshire, O'Kane
   House Child Care Resource and
   Referral
Durham, NH   03824
(603) 862-2895

Child & Family Services of New
   Hampshire
99 Hanover Street
Manchester, NH   03105
(603) 668-1920

Rockingham County Child Care
  Services
287 Lawrence Road
Salem, NH   03079
(603) 893-8413

Local Child Care Provider Associations

Concord FDCA
(603) 224-3912

New Hampshire FDCA
RFD 1, Box 305
Epping, NH   03042
(603) 679-8200

Organization of DCP
370 Laxon Avenue
Manchester, NH   03103
No phone number listed.

Rockingham FDC
287 Lawrence Road
Salem, NH   03079
(603) 893-9172

New Jersey

Statewide Referral Agency

Statewide Clearinghouse
Division of Youth & Family Services
CN 717
Trenton, NJ   08625
(609) 292-8408

Countywide Referral Agencies

Camden County Division for Children
1300 Admiral Wilson Boulevard
Camden, NJ   08101
(609) 968-4260

Community Coordinated Child Care
60 Prince Street
Elizabeth, NJ   07208
(201) 353-1621

United Way of Monmouth County
1415 Wycoff Road
Farmingdale, NJ   07727
(908) 938-2250

The Work-Family Consortium, Inc.
P.O. Box 881
Flemington, NJ   08822
(908) 788-8600

Bergen County Office for Children
21 Main Street
Hackensack, NJ   07601
(201) 646-3694

Atlantic County Women's Center
P.O. Box 311
Northfield, NJ   08225
(609) 646-1180

**Passaic County Child Care Coordinating
  Agency, Inc.**
262 Main Street, 5th Floor
Paterson, NJ   07505
(201) 684-1904

Child Care Channels
700 Sayre Avenue
Phillipsburg, NJ   08865
(201) 454-2074

Children's Services of Morris County
855 Route 10 East, Suite 114
Randolph, NJ   07869
(201) 927-6060

Southern Regional Child Care Resource
   Center
700 Hollydell Court
Sewell, NJ   08080
(609) 582-8282

The Child Care Connection, Inc.
2425 Pennington Road
Trenton, NJ   08638
(609) 737-2418

Children's Home Society Child Care
929 Parkside Avenue
Trenton, NJ   08618
(908) 505-1133

Programs for Parents, Inc.
56 Grove Avenue
Verona, NJ   07042
(201) 857-5171

Local Child Care Provider Associations

Family Tree, FDC
197 Jackson Road
Atco, NJ   08004
(609) 768-8190

Visiting Homemakers Services of
   Hudson County
561 Broadway
Bayonne, NJ   07002
(201) 823-1004

Monday Morning, Inc.
276 White Oak Ridge Road
Bridgewater, NJ   08807
(201) 526-4884

Burlington County Community
   Action—REACH
718 Route 130
Burlington, NJ   08016
(609) 386-5800

Camden County Division for Children
2101 Ferry Avenue
1800 Pavilion, Room 513
Camden, NJ   08104
(609) 757-6869

FDC Provider Network
1169 Kenwood Avenue
Camden, NJ   08103
(609) 342-1615

New Jersey FDCPA
P.O. Box 4147
Cherry Hill, NJ   08034
(609) 428-1249

Monmouth City Board of Social
   Services
P.O. Box 3000
Freehold, NJ   07728-9990
(201) 431-6167

Bergen County Office for Children
Administration Building
Court Plaza S.
21 Main Street, Room 114W
Hackensack, NJ   07001-7000
(201) 646-3694

Child Care Connection
P.O. Box 6325
Lawrenceville, NJ   08648
(609) 896-2171
(609) 896-8160

Association for Montclair FDC
68 Hawthorn Place
Montclair, NJ   07042
(201) 783-5683

Day Nurseries, Inc./FDC
54 Orange Road
Montclair, NJ   07042
(201) 783-6846

Children's Services of Morris County
P.O. Box 173
Mount Freedom, NJ   07970
(201) 895-2676

FDC Network of Middlesex County
181 How Lane
New Brunswick, NJ   08902
(201) 745-3616

Monday Morning, Inc.
568 Parkview Avenue
North Plainfield, NJ   07063
(201) 668-4884

Old Firth School
Prospect Street
Phillipsburg, NJ   08865
(201) 454-7000
(201) 782-0612

Monday Morning, Inc.
31 Hereford Drive
Princeton Junction, NJ   08550-1507
(609) 799-5588

Family Day Care Organization of New
    Jersey
Children's Home Society
929 Parkside Avenue
Trenton, NJ   08618
(609) 695-6274

FDC of Gloucester County
Inter-boro Plaza, Unit 2
Hurffville-Cross Keys Road
Turnersville, NJ   08012
(609) 853-9089

Union County DC Program
219 47th Street
Union City, NJ   07087
(201) 348-2750

Programs for Parents, Inc.
Montclair State College
16 Waterbury Road
Upper Montclair, NJ   07043
(201) 857-5171

New Mexico

Countywide Referral Agencies

Las Cruces Child Care Resource &
  Referral
Box 30001
Dept. 3R
Las Cruces, NM   88003
(505) 646-1165

Roswell Child Care Resource &
  Referral, Inc.
P.O. Box 3038
Roswell, NM   88202
(505) 622-9000

Child Care Resource & Referral
  Project/Santa Fe Community College
P.O. Box 4187
Santa Fe, NM   87502-4187
(505) 438-1344

Local Child Care Provider Associations

New Mexico FDCA
2721 Texas, N.E.
Albuquerque, NM   87110
No phone number listed.

Niños HDCA
P.O. Box 5661
Santa Fe, NM   87501
(505) 982-1070

Sante Fe HDCA
P.O. Box 5661
Santa Fe, NM   87501
(505) 473-0246

New York

Statewide Referral Agency

New York State Child Care
  Coordinating Council
237 Bradford Street
Albany, NY   12206
(518) 463-8663

Countywide Referral Agencies

Capital District Child Care Coordinating
  Council, Inc.
352 Central Avenue
Albany, NY   12206
(518) 426-7181

Steuben Day Care Project/SCEOP
P.O. Box 352
Bath, NY   14810
(607) 776-2125

Broome County Child Development
  Council, Inc.
29 Fayette Street, P.O. Box 880
Binghamton, NY   13902-0880
(607) 723-8313

Child Development Support
    Corporation
P.O. Box 474258
Brooklyn, NY   11247
(718) 398-2050

Child Care Coalition of Niagara
    Frontier, Inc.
656 Elmwood Avenue
Buffalo, NY   14222
(716) 882-6544

Putnam County Child Care Council
73 Gleneida Avenue
Carmel, NY   10512
(914) 228-1994

Cortland Area Child Care Council, Inc.
111 Port Watson Street
Cortland, NY   13059
(607) 753-0106

Delaware Opportunities, Inc.
47 Main Street
Delhi, NY   13753
(607) 746-2165

EOP Child Care Resource Development
    Program
Elmira College
Box 855
Elmira, NY   14901
(607) 734-3941

Day Care Council of Nassau
    County, Inc.
54 Washington Street
Hempstead, NY   11550
(516) 538-1362

Child Care Council of Suffolk
    County, Inc.
145 Pidgeon Hill Road
Huntington Station, NY   11746
(516) 427-1206

Day Care & Child Development Council
    of Tompkins County, Inc.
609 W. Clinton Street
Ithaca, NY   14850
(607) 273-0259

Sullivan County Child Care Council
P.O. Box 864
Liberty, NY   12754
(914) 292-7166

Child Care, Inc.
275 7th Avenue
New York, NY   10001
(212) 929-4999

Parent Resource Center
165 Charles Street
Painted Post, NY   14870
(607) 936-3704

Dutchess County Child Development
    Council, Inc.
53 Academy Street
Poughkeepsie, NY   12601
(914) 473-4141

Western New York Child Care
  Council, Inc.
1344 University Avenue
Rochester, NY   14607
(800) 333-0825

Rockland Council for Young Children
185 N. Main Street
Spring Valley, NY   10977
(914) 425-0572

Onondaga County Child Care Council
215 Bassett Street
Syracuse, NY   13210
(315) 472-6919

Child Care Council of Westchester, Inc.
470 Mamaroneck Avenue
White Plains, NY   10605
(914) 761-3456

Local Child Care Provider Associations

Steuben County FDC
309 W. Morris Street
Bath, NY   14810
(607) 776-2125

Bronx Child Care Network
Bronx Community College
2205 Sedgwick Avenue
Bronx, NY   10453
(212) 367-8882

Citywide FDC Provider, Teacher, Parent
  Association
750 E. 216th Street
Bronx, NY   10467
(212) 655-6343

Davidson Provider Association
160 W. 174th Street
Bronx, NY   10453
(212) 299-9264

Highbridge Provider Association
1055 University Avenue, Room 3P
Bronx, NY   10452
(212) 588-3307

Saint Peter's CC Network
741 E. 219th Street
Bronx, NY   10467
(212) 515-5065

Brockwood Child Care Association
363 Adelphi Street
Brooklyn, NY   10025
(718) 783-2610

Erasmus Child Care Network
814 Rogers Avenue
Brooklyn, NY   11226
(718) 462-7700

National Congress of Neighborhood
  Women
249 Manhattan Avenue
Brooklyn, NY   11211
(718) 388-6666

Salvation Army
464 Bristol Street
Brooklyn, NY   11212
(718) 342-0350

Erie County FDC
190 Franklin Street
Buffalo, NY   14202
(716) 852-6124

Chemung County FDC
318 Madison Avenue
Elmira, NY   14901
(607) 734-6174

Orange County FDCA
95 Country Club Drive
Florida, NY   10921
(914) 651-7447

Twelve Towns YMCA FDC
69–02 64th Street
Glendale, NY   10921
(718) 821-6271

Hilltop CC Network
86-70 Francis Lewis Boulevard
Holliswood, NY   11427
(718) 465-2000

Certified FDC Providers of Westchester
   County, Inc.
138 S. 9th Avenue
Mount Vernon, NY   10550
(914) 699-3859

BMCC Child Care Network
199 Chambers Street, Room N310
New York, NY   10007
(212) 618-1123

Child Care, Inc.
275 7th Avenue
New York, NY   10001
(212) 929-7604

Children's Health Services
690 Amsterdam Avenue
New York, NY   10025
(212) 865-3741

Fort Washington Toddler Care Network
720 Fort Washington Avenue, Room 6C
New York, NY   10040
(212) 785-7863

Henry Street Settlement Urban Family
   Center
128 Baruch Place
New York, NY   10002
(212) 475-6400

Hudson Guild Provider Association
427 W. 26th Street
New York, NY   10001
(212) 947-2372

Jewish CCA
575 Lexington Avenue, 3rd Floor
New York, NY   10022-6102
(212) 490-9160

Jewish FDC Network
92nd Street Y
1395 Lexington Avenue
New York, NY   10128
(212) 427-6000

Lower East Side Family Resource
137 E. 2nd Street
New York, NY   10009
(212) 677-6602

Salem FDCPA
1305 Amsterdam Avenue
New York, NY   10027
(212) 663-5927

Talbot Perkins CC Network
116 W. 32nd Street
New York, NY   10001
(212) 736-2510

Queens CC Network
108-25 62nd Drive
Queens, NY   11375
(212) 271-3098

Licensed FDCA of New York State
346 LaGrange Avenue
Rochester, NY   14615
(716) 647-1615

Monroe County FDCA
670 Empire Boulevard
Rochester, NY   14609
(716) 482-4006

Capital District FDC
263 Lisha Kill Road
Schenectady, NY   12309
(518) 786-1205

Silver Lake FDCPA
12 Markham Drive
Staten Island, NY   10310
(718) 981-9452

North Carolina

Statewide Referral Agency

North Carolina Child Care Resouce &
    Referral Network
700 Kenilworth Avenue
Charlotte, NC   28204
(704) 376-6697

Countywide Referral Agencies

Child Care Networks
222 Carr Mill
Carrboro, NC   27510
(919) 942-0184

Child Care Connections of Moore
    County, Inc.
P.O. Box 938
Carthage, NC   28327
(919) 947-2687

Child Care Resources, Inc.
700 Kenilworth Avenue
Charlotte, NC   28204
(704) 376-6697

Durham Day Care Council
119 Orange Street
Durham, NC   27701
(919) 688-9550

Child Care Information Program
1200 Arlington Street
Greensboro, NC   27406
(919) 378-7700

Child Care Directions
P.O. Box 911
Laurinburg, NC   28353
(919) 276-3367

Child Care Resource & Referral of
   Wake County
103 Enterprise Street, Suite 209
Raleigh, NC   27607
(919) 821-0482

SE Community College Child Care
   Resource & Referral
P.O. Box 151
Whiteville, NC   28472
(919) 642-7141

Local Child Care Provider Associations

Buncombe County CD
50 S. French Broad Avenue
Asheville, NC   28801
(704) 255-5259

Orange, Chatham, Alamance
   Counties FDCA
c/o Child Care Networks
Carr Mill Mall, Suite 217
Carrboro, NC   27510

Infant Care Project
Frank Porter Graham
Box 8180
Chapel Hill, NC   27599
(919) 966-7187

North Dakota

Countywide Referral Agency

Early Childhood Training Center
North Dakota State University
P.O. Box 5057
State University Station
Fargo, ND   58105
(701) 237-8040

Local Child Care Provider Associations

Pembina/Walsh County DCA
P.O. Box 553
Cavalier, ND   58220
(701) 265-3315

North Dakota Providers Association
620 9th Avenue S.
Grand Forks, ND   58201
(701) 775-4523

North Dakota Child Care Providers, Inc.
625 2nd Avenue E.
West Fargo, ND   58102
(701) 282-6353

Ohio

Statewide Referral Agency

Ohio Child Care Resource & Referral
   Association
92 Jefferson Avenue
Columbus, OH   42315
(614) 224-0222

Countywide Referral Agencies

Info Line
474 Grant Street
Akron, OH   44311
(216) 376-7706

Community Coordinated Child Care
1225 E. McMillan
Cincinnati, OH   45206
(513) 221-0033

Child Care Resource Center
3135 Euclid, Suite 302
Cleveland, OH   44115
(216) 431-1818

Child Care Clearinghouse
414 Valley Street
Dayton, OH   45404
(513) 461-0600

Northwestern Ohio Community Action
   Commission
1933 E. 2nd Street
Defiance, OH   43512
(419) 784-2150

Child Care Resource Center
385 Midway Boulevard, Suite 312
Elyria, OH   44035
(216) 324-7187

Center for Alternative Resources
P.O. Box 77
Newark, OH   43055
(614) 345-6166

Child Care Insights, Inc.
19111 Detroit Road
Rocky River, OH   44116
(216) 356-2900

YW Child Care Connections
1018 Jefferson Avenue
Toledo, OH   43624
(419) 255-5519

Local Child Care Provider Associations

Child Care Association
2657 Highland Avenue
Cincinnati, OH   45219
(513) 861-1248

Comprehensive Community Child Care
2400 Reading Road
Cincinnati, OH   45202
(513) 621-8585

Hamilton County FDCA
5026 Oberlin Boulevard
Cincinnati, OH   45237
(513) 242-8635

Center for Human Services
1240 Huron Road, 5th Floor
Cleveland, OH   44115
(216) 861-3395

Franklin County FDCPA
1443 E. 19th Street
Columbus, OH   43211
(614) 291-0608

North West Ohio CAA—FDCA
9924 W. Washington
Napoleon, OH   43545
(419) 784-2150

Lucas County Professional DCPA
1743 Freeman Street
Toledo, OH   43606
(419) 537-9579

WPAFB Child Development
2750 ABW/SSRC
Wright Patterson AFB, OH   45433
(513) 257-4919

Oklahoma

Countywide Referral Agencies

Child Care Connection
3014 Paseo
Oklahoma City, OK   73103
(405) 525-3111

Child Care Resource Center
1430 S. Boulder
Tulsa, OK   74119
(918) 587-CARE (2273)

Local Child Care Provider Associations

Broken Arrow Licensed FDCHA
1311 W. Hot Springs Street
Broken Arrow, OK   74011
No phone number listed.

Norman FDCA
1520 Windsor Way
Norman, OK   73069
(405) 364-0932

Oklahoma City Association of FDC
8328 N.W. 112th Terrace
Oklahoma City, OK   73162
(405) 721-0981

Rainbow Fleet, Inc.
3016 Paseo
Oklahoma City, OK   73103
(405) 521-1426

Oregon

Statewide Referral Agency

Oregon Child Care Resource & Referral
   Network
325 13th Street, N.E., Room 206
Salem, OR   97301
(503) 585-6232

Countywide Referral Agencies

Linn & Benton Child Care Resource & Referral
6500 S.W. Pacific Boulevard
Albany, OR   97321
(503) 967-6501

West Tuality Child Care Services, Inc.
2813 Pacific Avenue, Suite C
Forest Grove, OR   97116
(503) 357-4994

Metro Child Care Resource & Referral
P.O. Box 16521
Portland, OR   97216
(503) 256-5484

UCAN's Child Care Resource & Referral
2448 W. Harvard Boulevard
Roseburg, OR   97470
(503) 672-7004

Mid Willamette Child Care Information Service
325 13th Street, N.E., Suite 206
Salem, OR   97301
(503) 585-2491

Local Child Care Provider Associations

Rogue Valley HDCPA
312 Helman Street
Ashland, OR   97520
(503) 482-9253

Lane Country Red Cross
150 E. 18th Street
Eugene, OR   97401
(502) 344-5244

LaGrande PRO
903 North Avenue
LaGrande, OR   97830
(503) 963-2594

Child Care Connections
1046 Lozier Lane
Medford, OR   97501
(503) 779-6483

Child Care Unlimited Association
1057 Court Street
Medford, OR   97501
(503) 770-5893

Albina Ministerial Alliance
P.O. Box 11243
Portland, OR   97211
(503) 285-0493

Provider Resource Organization
P.O. Box 42677
Portland, OR   97242
(503) 235-3169

Salem PRO
2860 Wiggles Court, N.E.
Salem, OR   97030
(503) 585-9435

Pennsylvania

Countywide Referral Agencies

Community Services for Children, Inc.
431 E. Locust Street
Bethlehem, PA   18018
(215) TOT-INFO (868-4636)

Probe
3400 Trindle Road
Camp Hill, PA   17011
(717) 737-2584

International Institute for Erie
P.O. Box 486
Erie, PA   16512
(814) 452-3935

Delaware Valley Child Care Resource &
  Referral Center
840 W. Main Street
3rd Floor
Lansdale, PA   19446
(800) VIP-KIDS (847-5437)

Child Placement Network, Inc.
2720 Potshop Road
Norristown, PA   19403
(215) 584-0960

Child Care Choices
125 S. 9th Street, Suite 603
Philadelphia, PA   19107
(215) 592-7644

United Way's Child Care Network
200 Ross Street
Suite 600, 5th Floor
Pittsburgh, PA   15219
(412) 392-3131

Child Care Consultants, Inc.
376 E. Market Street
York, PA   17403
(717) 854-CARE (2273)

Local Child Care Provider Associations

Suburban FDC, Delaware County
143 Willowbrook Drive
Clifton Heights, PA   19018
(215) 284-7768

FDC Associates of Lehigh Valley
450 Arlington Street
Easton, PA   18042
(215) 253-7721

Montgomery County FDCA
365 Heritage Lane
King of Prussia, PA   19406
No phone number listed.

Lancaster County FDC Support Group
3 Inglewood Court
Lancaster, PA   17603
(717) 394-3470

Tri-State CCPA
P.O. Box 1978
Media, PA   19063
(215) 499-7410

Associated Day Care Service/FDC
710 Jackson Street
Philadelphia, PA   19148
(215) 389-8500

United FDCA of Philadelphia
2112 W. Chew Avenue
Philadelphia, PA   19138
(215) 842-3924

Pennsylvania FDCPA
327 E. 12th Street
Pittsburgh, PA   15120
No phone number listed.

Substitute Mothers for Loving
1702 Washburn Avenue
Scranton, PA   18504
(717) 344-0799

Tri-County CCA
510 Steinhour Road
York Haven, PA   17370
(717) 938-3340

Rhode Island

Countywide Referral Agency

Options for Working Parents
30 Exchange Terrace
Providence, RI   02903
(401) 272-7510

Local Child Care Provider Associations

FCCH of Rhode Island, Inc.
16 Woodland Street
Lincoln, RI   02865
(401) 724-3464

Kent County FCC Support Group
139 Brentwood Avenue
Warrick, RI   02886
(401) 737-1066

South Carolina

Statewide Referral Agency

South Carolina Child Care Resource &
   Referral Network
2129 Santee Avenue
Columbia, SC   29205
(803) 254-9263

Countywide Referral Agencies

Child Care Options, Inc.
1521 Wappoo Road
Charleston, SC   29407
(803) 556-5706

Childcare & Seniorcare Solutions
P.O. Box 24617
Columbia, SC   29224
(803) 736-7652

Greenville's Child, Inc.
P.O. Box 8821
Greenville, SC   29604
(803) 242-8320

Local Child Care Provider Associations

**Interfaith Community Service/South
  Carolina**
1401 Washington Street
Columbia, SC   29201
(803) 252-8390

South Dakota

Countywide Referral Agencies

Child Development & Family Relations
Box 2218
South Dakota State University
Brookings, SD   57007
(605) 688-5730

Positive Parent Network
P.O. Box 2792
Rapid City, SD   57709
(605) 348-9276

Tennessee

Countywide Referral Agency

**Tennessee Child Care Resource &
  Referral Services**
TN DHS/Day Care Services
Nashville, TN   37248-9600
(615) 741-0290

Local Child Care Provider Associations

**Knoxville Association of Family &
  Group DCH**
2124 Ohio Avenue
Knoxville, TN   37921
No phone number listed.

**Tennessee Association of Family &
  Group Day Care**
4916 Oakbrook Court
Knoxville, TN   37918
(615) 689-2144
(615) 689-2799

**Memphis Family & Group Home
  Association**
1811 Meadow Hills
Memphis, TN   38107
No phone number listed.

Porter Leath Day Care Homes
2171 Heard Street
Memphis, TN   38108
No phone number listed.

Middle Tennessee DC Association
4956 Briarwood Drive
Nashville, TN   37211
(615) 833-2239

Nashville Association of DCP
522 Russell Street
Nashville, TN   37204
(615) 383-7336

Texas

Statewide Referral Agency

Texas Association of Child Care
  Resources & Referral Agencies
4029 Capital of Texas Highway S.
Suite 102
Austin, TX   78704
(512) 440-8555

Countywide Referral Agencies

Austin Families, Inc.
3305 Northland Drive, Suite 410
Austin, TX   78731
(512) 454-1195

MTX Day Care Services, Inc.
523 W. 1st Avenue
Corsicana, TX   75110
(214) 872-5231

Child Care Answers
1499 Regal Row, Suite 400
Dallas, TX   75247
(214) 631-CARE (2273)

YWCA of El Paso
1918 Texas Avenue
El Paso, TX   79901
(915) 533-2311

Initiatives for Children, Inc.
5433 Westheimer, Suite 620
Houston, TX   77056
(713) 840-1255

Children's Enterprises, Inc.
3305 66th Street, Suite 1
Lubbock, TX   79413
(806) 796-0734

Kid Care
115 Plaza De Armas, Suite 240
San Antonio, TX   78205
(512) 227-HELP (4357)

Local Child Care Provider Associations

Professional Home Child Care
  Association
2802 Magnolia
Amarillo, TX   79107

Arlington Professional FDCA
4910 Crest Drive
Arlington, TX   76011
(817) 478-0386

Austin FDCPA
7701 Navarro Place
Austin, TX   78749
(512) 282-6061

Child Care Partnership
1820 Regal Row, Suite 100
Dallas, TX   75235
(214) 638-5454

Dallas Independent Home CCA
813 Ryan Road
Dallas, TX   75224
(214) 374-7443

Family Childcare Association
4707 Twinpost
Dallas, TX   75234
(214) 934-2669

El Paso Professional HCCA
11055 Johnney Miller
El Paso, TX   79936
(915) 598-0455

North Tarrant County Professional DCA
6500 Riddle Drive
Fort Worth, TX   76180
(817) 498-4705

Alliance for Better Child Care
12511 Campos Drive
Houston, TX   77065
(713) 955-6562

Houston Registered FDCHA
2910 Barbee
Houston, TX   77004
(713) 529-2184

Texas Professional Home Child Care
   Association
15135 Forest Lodge Drive
Houston, TX   77070
(713) 376-5425

Irving Independent HCCA
2115 Himes
Irving, TX   75060
(214) 986-7681

Day Care Association of Lubbock
1706 23rd Street, Suite 101
Lubbock, TX   79411
(806) 765-9981

Mesquite Home CCA
2415 Lagoon
Mesquite, TX   75045
(903) 270-0092

Plano Independent Home CCA
2525 Eucalyptus
Plano, TX   75075
(214) 964-3598

Mid-Cities Registered HCCP
1724 Sammy Henderson Street
Rockport, TX   78382-6614
No phone number listed.

Allied Professional HCCA
1826 Oaklawn
Sugarland, TX   77478
(713) 494-6841

Utah

Countywide Referral Agencies

Children First
5215 Greenpine Drive
Murray, UT   84123
(801) 268-9492

Children's Service Society
576 E. South Temple
Salt Lake City, UT   84102
(801) 537-1044

Local Child Care Provider Associations

Utah State University FDCP
UMC 6800
Logan, UT   84335
(801) 750-2169

Professional FCC Association
2047 N. 450 West
Salt Lake City, UT   84015
No phone number listed.

Vermont

Statewide Referral Agency

Vermont Association of Child Care
   Resource & Referral Agencies
Early Childhood Programs
Vermont College
Montpelier, VT   05602
(802) 828-8765

Countywide Referral Agencies

Child Care Resource & Referral of
   Chittenden County
179 S. Winnoski Avenue
Burlington, VT   05401
(802) 863-3367

Child Care Information Service
Vermont College
Montpelier, VT   05602
(802) 828-8771

Local Child Care Provider Associations

Central Vermont Community Action
   Council
15 Ayers Street
Barre, VT   05641
(802) 479-1053

BECA
P.O. Box 342
Bennington, VT   05201
(802) 447-3778

Windham CCA
P.O. Box 6005
Brattleboro, VT   05301
(802) 254-5332

Virginia

Statewide Referral Agency

Virginia Child Care Resource &
   Referral Network
3701 Pender Drive
Fairfax, VA   22030
(703) 218-3730

Countywide Referral Agencies

Next Door Child Care Program
7511 Fordson Road
Alexandria, VA   22306
(703) 765-0925

Virginia Tech Resource & Referral
  Service
201 Church Street
Blacksburg, VA   24061-0537
(703) 231-3213

CVCDA/Office for Children & Youth
810 E. High Street
Charlottesville, VA   22902
(804) 977-4260

Fairfax County Office for Children
3701 Pender Drive, 5th Floor
Fairfax, VA   22030
(703) 359-5860

Kare Line Child Care Resource &
  Referral
1010 Miller Park Square
Lynchburg, VA   24501
(804) 846-4630

Planning Council
130 W. Plume Street
Norfolk, VA   23510
(804) 627-3993

Memorial Child Guidance Clinic
5001 W. Broad Street, Suite 217
Richmond, VA   23230
(804) 282-5993

Child Caring Connection
109 Cary Street, Suite 201
Williamsburg, VA   23185
(804) 229-7940

Local Child Care Provider Associations

Charlottesville CCP Organization
P.O. Box 911
Charlottesville, VA   22902
(804) 971-3400

Fairfax County Office for Children
3701 Pender Drive, 5th Floor
Fairfax, VA   22030
(703) 218-3850

Infant/Toddler FDC System
10560 Main Street, Suite 403
Fairfax, VA   22030
(703) 352-3449

Peninsula DCP Unlimited
1912 Sommerville Drive
Hampton, VA   23663
(804) 851-5790

FDCPA of Tidewater/Peninsula
2842 Stanhope Road
Norfolk, VA   23504
(804) 625-2818

Tidewater CCA
2115 High Street
Portsmouth, VA   23703
(804) 397-2984

Professional CCPA of Virginia
8033 Queen Scott Drive
Richmond, VA   23235
(804) 276-7370

FDCA of Newington Forest
8111 Willowdale Court
Springfield, VA   22153
(703) 455-4596

North Virginia FDCA
P.O. Box 1371
Springfield, VA   22151
(703) 750-6677

Southern Virginia FDCA
107 S. Witchduck Road, Suite 194
Virginia Beach, VA   23462
(804) 463-6681

Virginia Independent CCHA
P.O. Box 2852
Virginia Beach, VA   23450-2852
(804) 468-2643

Council for Children's Services
109 Cary Street
Williamsburg, VA   23185
(804) 253-2499

Washington

Statewide Referral Agency

Washington State Child Care Resource
   & Referral Network
P.O. Box 1241
Tacoma, WA   98401
(206) 383-1735

Countywide Referral Agencies

Child & Family Resource & Referral
15015 Main Street, Suite 206
Bellevue, WA   98007
(206) 865-9350

Volunteers of America/Child Care
   Resource & Referral Network
2802 Broadway
Everett, WA   98201
(206) 258-4213

Daycare Placement Services
P.O. Box 435
Issaquah, WA   98027
(206) 391-9549

Child Care Action Council
P.O. Box 446
Olympia, WA   98507-0446
(206) 754-0810

Child Care Support Services Resource
   & Referral
720 W. Court
Pasco, WA   99301
(509) 547-1718

Washington State University Child Care
   Resource & Referral
103 Commons Hall
Washington State University
Pullman, WA   99164-3610
(509) 335-7625

Child Care Resource & Referral
1313 N.E. 134th Street
Vancouver, WA   98685
(206) 574-6826

Local Child Care Provider Association

Washington State FCC Association
P.O. Box 84207
Seattle, WA   98124-5507
(206) 467-1152

West Virginia

Countywide Referral Agency

Central Child Care of
  West Virginia, Inc.
1205 Quarrier Street
Charleston, WV   25361
(304) 340-3667

Local Child Care Provider Associations

Region Three DCA
P.O. Box 1332
Clarksburg, WV   26301
(304) 624-9416

Hinton FDCPA
Pluto Star Route, Box 20
Hinton, WV   25951
(304) 466-4707

Wisconsin

Statewide Referral Agency

Wisconsin Child Care Improvement
  Society
P.O. Box 369
Hayward, WI   54843
(715) 634-3905

Countywide Referral Agencies

Child Care Information & Referral
  Service, Inc.
P.O. Box 4521
Appleton, WI   54915
(414) 734-0966

Community Action Resource & Referral
  of Walworth County
910 E. Geneva Street, P.O. Box 362
Delavan, WI   53115
(414) 728-8780

Partners in Care Resource & Referral
P.O. Box 242
Depere, WI   54115
(414) 432-7706

Child Care Partnership Resource &
  Referral
P.O. Box 45
Independence, WI   54747
(715) 985-2391

Resource & Referral Center
8600 Sheridan Road
Kenosha, WI 53140
(414) 697-2529

Dane County Community Coordinated
  Child Care
3200 Monroe Street
Madison, WI 53711
(608) 238-7338

Community Coordinated Child Care of
  Milwaukee County, Inc.
2001 W. Vliet Street
Milwaukee, WI 53205
(414) 933-KIDS (5437)

Child Care Resource & Referral of
  Racine
5420 21st Street
Racine, WI 53406
(414) 554-4698

Family Connections Resource &
  Referral
310 Bluff Avenue
Sheboygan, WI 53081
(414) 457-1999

Child Care Resource & Referral Center
  of Wood County
122 8th Street, S.
Wisconsin Rapids, WI 54494
(715) 423-4114

Local Child Care Provider Associations

H.E.A.R.T. FDC, Inc.
3625 Sunnyview Road
Appleton, WI 54914
(608) 733-5834

"Children Are Our Specialty"
FDC Support Group
705 High Street
Clinton, WI 53525
No phone number listed.

ECCO—Eau Clare County
(715) 874-6201
(715) 835-4775

WWECA—Pierce & Saint Croix
  Counties
137 Cairns
Ellsworth, WI 54011
No phone number listed.

Central City FDC System
203 Wisconsin Avenue
Madison, WI 53703
(608) 255-0330

Satellite FCC Inc.
3200 Monroe Street
Madison, WI 53711
(608) 233-4752

Wisconsin FDCA
c/o WECA/AEYC
3510 Monroe Street
Madison, WI   53711
(608) 231-3090

4-C of Milwaukee County
2014 W. McKinley Avenue, Room 102
Milwaukee, WI   53205
(414) 933-5999

Milwaukee FDCPA
2030 N. Buffum Street
Milwaukee, WI   53212
(414) 562-4952

Satellite Child Care
2433 S. 11th Street
Milwaukee, WI   53215
(414) 671-0298

Neenah Support Group
1027 Gregory Street
Neenah, WI   54956
No phone number listed.

Dodge County Support Group
1013 Wilbur Street
Watertown, WI   53094
No phone number listed.

Wyoming

Countywide Referral Agency

Day Care Resource & Referral Service
625 S. Beverly
Casper, WY   82609
(307) 472-5535

Local Child Care Provider Associations

Children's Nutrition Services
1144 Oakcrest
Casper, WY   82601
No phone number listed.

Laramie Support Group
2458 N. 9th
Sp. 47
Laramie, WY   82070
(207) 742-2017

☎

CHAPTER 5

HEALTH

This chapter contains a wide variety of organizations dealing with health issues. Check the Table of Contents or the Index to locate listings for a specific illness.

If nothing in the Table of Contents or the Index sounds pertinent, call organizations in the GENERAL INFORMATION AND REFERRAL SERVICES list at the beginning of this chapter. If you think a local government agency might offer the information you need, check under Health Department in the government offices section of your local telephone directory. Alternatively, check the STATE CHILD AND MATERNITY HEALTH DEPARTMENTS listed at the very end of this chapter.

SEE ALSO

the INFANT CARE section of Chapter 2 for organizations that specialize in the health needs of infants.

Chapter 9, Adolescence, describes organizations that help with the health problems associated with sexually transmitted diseases and addictions.

The MAIL ORDER CATALOGS section of Chapter 12, under Books, lists merchants who supply books offering health advice. Check under Health and Safety for merchants who sell health-promoting products.

The SELF-HELP CLEARINGHOUSES section of Chapter 13 lists agencies that make referrals to local support groups dealing with an emotional problem or with a special-needs child.

☎ ☎ ☎ ☎ ☎ ☎ ☎ ☎ ☎ ☎ ☎ ☎ ☎ ☎ ☎ ☎ ☎ ☎ ☎ ☎

GENERAL HEALTH INFORMATION AND REFERRAL SERVICES

If the health-related information you need is not covered in this chapter, or in other chapters, then you should call the National Health Information Center. It offers a referral service that helps consumers find the appropriate health-care specialists and information providers.

National Health Information Center
P.O. Box 1133
Washington, DC   20013-1133
(301) 565-4167
(800) 336-4797

National Information Center for Orphan
   Drugs & Rare Diseases
P.O. Box 1133
Washington, DC   20013-1133
(800) 456-3505

© This institute at the National Institutes of Health disseminates publications and makes referrals on many health-related subjects concerning children:

National Organization for Rare
   Disorders
P.O. Box 8923
New Fairfield, CT   06812
(203) 746-6518
(800) 999-6673
(800) 447-6673

National Institute of Child Health &
   Human Development
National Institutes of Health
9000 Rockville Pike
Bethesda, MD   20892
(301) 496-5133

© The following groups will also assist with referrals:

© Although many rare disorders affecting children are covered in this chapter, you may require information on another disease. These groups can help:

American Academy of Family
   Physicians
8880 Ward Parkway
Kansas City, MO   64114-2797
(816) 333-9700

American Academy of Pediatrics
P.O. Box 927
Elk Grove Village, IL   60007
(708) 228-5005
(800) 433-9016
(800) 421-0589 (in Illinois)

American Medical Association
515 N. State Street
Chicago, IL   60610
(312) 464-5000

Center for Medical Consumers
237 Thompson Street
New York, NY   10012
(212) 674-7105

National Center for Education in
   Maternal & Child Health
38th and R Streets, N.W.
Washington, DC   20057
(202) 625-8400

National Council on Patient
   Information and Education
1625 I Street, N.W., Suite 1010
Washington, DC   20006
(202) 347-6711

National Library of Medicine
8600 Rockville Pike
Bethesda, MD   20894
(301) 496-6095 (reference questions)
(301) 496-6308 (public information)

© If a surgeon suggests your child
needs an operation, the following office
provides a free service to help consumers find local surgeons for a second
opinion:

National Second Surgical Opinion
   Program
Health Care Financing Administration
330 Independence Avenue, S.W.
Room 4235
Washington, DC   20201
(800) 638-6833
(800) 492-6603 (in Maryland)

© If you need information over the
phone or wish to receive brochures on
health fraud and quackery, call:

Consumer Health Information
(800) 821-6671

DISEASES AND DISORDERS

ALLERGIES, ASTHMA, AND LUNG DISORDERS

American Academy of Allergy & Immunology
611 East Wells Street
Milwaukee, WI   53202
(414) 272-6071
(800) 822-ASMA (2762)
This professional society of physicians makes referrals to local allergists, distributes pamphlets about allergies, and publishes a quarterly newsletter for consumers, *Asthma and Allergies Advocate.*

American Allergy Association
P.O. Box 7273
Menlo Park, CA   94026
(415) 322-1663
This association of allergy patients offers free information on diet, environmental factors, and other subjects of interest to allergy sufferers. They publish an annual handbook, *Living with Allergies* ($15.00), which offers advice on how to avoid allergy problems.

American College of Allergy & Immunology
800 E. Northwest Highway, Suite 1080
Palatine, IL   60067
(708) 359-2800
(800) 842-7777
A professional society of physicians and researchers that makes referrals to the public and offers brochures.

American Lung Association
1740 Broadway
New York, NY   10019
(212) 315-8700
The American Lung Association is involved with numerous lung diseases and conditions, of which asthma is only one. They offer phone information, referrals, and publications.

Asthma & Allergy Foundation of America
1717 Massachusetts Avenue, Suite 305
Washington, DC   20036
(202) 265-0265
The Foundation provides free information by phone and will send educational materials to consumers. They publish *Consumer Advisory Service Bulletins.*

Lung Line
1400 Jackson Street
Denver, CO   80206
(303) 355-LUNG (5864)
(800) 222-LUNG (5864)
This hotline is staffed by health professionals who will answer questions regarding asthma and other respiratory problems.

Mothers of Asthmatics
10875 Main Street, Suite 210
Fairfax, VA   22030
(703) 385-4403
Mothers of Asthmatics offers educational materials and programs to allergy sufferers and families with asthma. Their newsletter, *MA REPORT,* is published monthly.

National Institute of Allergy &
  Infectious Diseases
Office of Communications
9000 Rockville Pike, Building 31
Room 7A32
Bethesda, MD   20892
(301) 496-5717
Responds to inquiries from consumers and professionals, provides information and publications, and conducts and supports research on allergies.

BLOOD DISORDERS

General Organizations

American Society of Hematology
6900 Grove Road
Thorofare, NJ   08086
(609) 845-0003
(800) 257-8290
This professional society of physicians makes referrals to the public regarding blood disorders.

American Society of Pediatric
  Hematology
c/o Carl Pochedly, M.D.
Wyler Children's Hospital
5841 S. Maryland Avenue
Chicago, IL   60637
(312) 702-6808
Although primarily a society for physicians and researchers, this group will make referrals to the public.

Children's Blood Foundation
424 E. 62nd Street, Room 1045
New York, NY   10021
(212) 644-5790
Works to educate the public about blood disorders in children. Offers comprehensive treatment programs in the New York Hospital—Cornell Medical Center.

Fanconi Anemia

Fanconi Anemia Research Fund, Inc.
66 Club Road, Suite 300
Eugene, OR 97401
(503) 344-6307
The Fund shares information concerning this rare disorder among parents of affected children and offers support to affected families. The *FA Family Newsletter* is published annually.

Hemochromatosis/Iron Overload Diseases

Hemochromatosis Research Foundation, Inc.
P.O. Box 8569
Albany, NY 12208
(518) 489-0972
This group helps identify families with the disorder through screening and offers educational materials, counseling, and physician referrals. Publications include *Some Facts About . . . Hemochromatosis* and *Hereditary Hemochromatosis—A Publication for Patients.*

Iron Overload Diseases Association, Inc.
224 Datura Street, Suite 311
West Palm Beach, FL 33401
(305) 659-5616
Offers information and sponsors screening programs. Publications include *Overload, An Ironic Disease* and *Iron Overload Alert.*

Hemophilia

Canadian Hemophilia Society
344 Dupont Street, Suite 206
Toronto, Ontario M5R 3R4
Canada
(416) 922-2132
The Society helps hemophiliacs live a normal life and attain their fullest potential. It offers referrals to treatment centers, vocational training, and counseling, and publishes fact sheets, audiovisual aids, and a newsletter, *Hemophilia Today.*

National Hemophilia Foundation
The Soho Building
110 Greene Street, Suite 406
New York, NY 10012
(212) 219-8180
The National Hemophilia Foundation works to improve the quality of life for everyone affected by hemophilia and related bleeding disorders. The Foundation offers referral services and will send a publications and audiovisuals catalog.

Hereditary Hemorrhagic Telangiectasia

Hereditary Hemorrhagic Telangiectasia Foundation, Inc.
Biochemistry Department
University of Massachusetts
Amherst, MA 01003
(413) 545-2048

The Foundation disseminates information about new forms of treatment on the disease and provides a network of support for affected individuals and their families. A brochure is available.

Histiocytosis-X

Histiocytosis-X Association of America
609 New York Road
Glassboro, NJ   08028
(609) 881-4911
(800) 548-2758
This group offers information, referrals, and support services to affected persons and their families. A bimonthly newsletter is published.

Sickle Cell Disease

National Association for Sickle Cell Disease, Inc.
4221 Wilshire Boulevard, Suite 360
Los Angeles, CA   90010-3503
(213) 936-7205
(800) 421-8453
The Association distributes educational materials to increase awareness of the impact of sickle cell disease. Publications include *HELP, a Guide to Sickle Cell Disease Programs and Services.* A catalog of publications and audiovisual materials is available.

Sickle Cell Disease Branch
National Heart, Lung, & Blood Institute
Federal Building
7550 Wisconsin Avenue, Room 504D
Bethesda, MD   20014
(301) 496-6931
This government office provides limited referral and information services to the public.

Thalassemia

Cooley's Anemia Foundation, Inc.
105 E. 22nd Street
New York, NY   10010
(212) 598-0911
(800) 221-3571
(800) 522-7222 (in NY)
The Foundation promotes research, gives away free blood and transfusion paraphernalia, and disseminates information about Cooley's anemia and allied diseases. It operates the Thalassemia Action Group, a network of young adults who suffer from the disease. Publications include *Cooley's Anemia—A Psychosocial Directory, Cooley's Anemia A Medical Review,* and *Cooley's Anemia—Prevention Through Understanding and Testing.* Audiovisuals and a newsletter, *Lifeline,* are available.

Thrombocytopenia Absent Radius Syndrome

Thrombocytopenia Absent Radius Syndrome Association
312 Sherwood Drive, RD 1
Linwood, NJ   08221
(609) 927-0418
This support group for families suffering from TARS publishes a brochure and newsletter.

BONE PROBLEMS

General Organizations

American Academy of Orthopaedic Surgeons
222 S. Prospect Avenue
Park Ridge, IL   60068
(708) 823-7186
(800) 346-AAOS (2267)
This professional society offers referrals to the public.

Conservative Orthopedics International Association (COIA)
1811 Monroe
Dearborn, MI   48124
(313) 563-0360
COIA is a three-thousand-member group of physicians that promotes preventive, rehabilitative, nonoperative, and noninvasive treatments. Offers referrals to the public.

Pediatric Orthopaedic Society of North America (POSNA)
222 S. Prospect Avenue
Park Ridge, IL   60068
(708) 698-1628
POSNA's main purpose is to offer education to its members but will make limited referrals to the public.

Arthrogryposis Multiplex Congenita

National Support Group for Arthrogryposis Multiplex Congenita
P.O. Box 5192
Sonora, CA   95379
(209) 928-3688
This group maintains a list of physicians with a special interest in the causes and treatment of AMC. It promotes the exchange of information about therapy, surgeries, and available services. Publications include *What is Arthrogryposis?* and a newsletter, *Avenues.*

Freeman-Sheldon Syndrome

Freeman-Sheldon Parent Support Group
509 E. Northmont Way
Salt Lake City, UT   84103
(801) 364-7060
Provides emotional support to families affected by Freeman-Sheldon Syndrome, also known as Whistling Face

Syndrome and Cranio-Carpal-Tarsal-Dysplasia. Families share information about coping, treatments, and relevant medical literature.

Osteogenesis Imperfecta

Osteogenesis Imperfecta
  Foundation, Inc.
P.O. Box 14807
Clearwater, FL   34629-4807
(813) 855-7077
The Foundation is the only national voluntary organization dedicated to meeting the needs of individuals with brittle bone disorder. It makes available literature and videos and offers a network for parents across the country.

Paget's Disease

Paget's Disease Foundation, Inc.
165 Cadman Plaza E.
Brooklyn, NY   11201
(718) 596-1043
The Foundation provides free educational materials to patients and medical professionals. Publications include *Question and Answer Booklet, Understanding Paget's Disease,* a referral list of physicians, and reprints of articles about Paget's disease.

Scoliosis

National Scoliosis Foundation, Inc.
93 Concord Avenue
Belmont, MA   02178
(617) 489-0888
The Foundation alerts the public to the potentially serious health problems associated with abnormal spinal curvatures and develops programs leading to early detection and treatment. It provides literature, audiovisuals, and help with implementing or improving statewide screening programs in schools. Publications include *Background Information for Volunteers and Schools* and *One in Every 10 Persons Has Scoliosis.* Audiovisuals include *Growing Straighter and Stronger.*

Scoliosis Association
P.O. Box 51353
Raleigh, NC   27609
(919) 846-2639
The Scoliosis Association provides support and nonmedical information to patients, their families, and the community. Publications include *Scoliosis Fact Sheet* and *Scoliosis, An Annotated Bibliography.* Audiovisuals include *Scoliosis Screening for Early Detection* and *Watch That Curve.* They also publish a newsletter, *Backtalk.*

CANCER

```
SEE ALSO

the TERMINALLY ILL AND HOSPITALIZED CHILDREN section of this chapter.
```

General Organizations

**AMC Cancer Information
& Counseling Line**
(800) 525-3777
Answers questions about detection,
symptoms, treatment, and prevention of
cancer.

American Cancer Society
1599 Clifton Road, N.E.
Atlanta, GA   30329
(404) 320-3333
The American Cancer Society provides
educational materials and referrals for
most forms of cancer. Catalogs of publications and audiovisuals are available.

**Bone Marrow Transplant Family
Support Network**
P.O. Box 845
Avon, CT   06001
(203) 667-4548
The Network matches people considering or undergoing transplant with others who have had a similar experience
and can offer telephone support. Par-

ents of children with cancer are among
the members.

Canadian Cancer Society
77 Bloor Street W., Suite 1702
Toronto, Ontario   M5S 3A1
Canada
(416) 961-7223
The Society offers emotional support
programs and services including transportation, drugs, and medical supplies
supplementing those provided by the
government. The Society has divisions
in each of the ten Canadian provinces.
It publishes extensive brochures and
has produced a large number of films.

National Cancer Care Foundation
1180 Avenue of the Americas
New York, NY   10036
(212) 221-3300
The National Cancer Care Foundation
helps cancer patients and their families
cope with the impact of cancer by
providing a program of psychological,
social, and educational services. A publications catalog is available.

National Cancer Institute (NCI)
Office of Cancer Communications
9000 Rockville Pike
Building 31, Room 10A30
Bethesda, MD   20892
(301) 496-5583
(800) 4-CANCER (422-6237)
NCI responds to inquiries from the general public and professionals on all cancer subjects. It disseminates many publications on cancer and makes referrals to doctors using the most advanced therapies. Pamphlets especially for children include *What Happened to You Happened to Me* and *Youth Looks at Cancer*.

National Foundation for Cancer
   Research
(800) 321-CURE (2873)
Offers information over the phone about current cancer research.

Brain Tumor

Association for Brain Tumor Research
3725 N. Talman Avenue
Chicago, IL   60618
(312) 286-5571
The Association provides educational materials regarding brain tumors and their treatment, maintains a listing of brain tumor support groups, and makes referrals to community resources. They publish a newsletter, *The Message Line*.

National Brain Tumor Foundation
323 Geary Street, Suite 510
San Francisco, CA   94102
(415) 296-0404
Offers referrals concerning brain tumors.

Childhood Cancer

Candlelighters Childhood Cancer
   Foundation
1901 Pennsylvania Avenue, N.W.
Suite 1011
Washington, DC   20006
(202) 659-5136
The Foundation offers publications and counseling to children who have cancer and to their parents.

Make Today Count, Inc.
101 1/2 S. Union Street
Alexandria, VA   22314-3323
(703) 548-9674
An organization for cancer patients and their families in which groups discuss problems and fears. Encouraging a positive outlook and open communication eases emotional trauma. The group makes referrals and runs a speakers' bureau. It publishes a newsletter and the book, *Make Today Count—Until Tomorrow Comes*.

Parents of Kids with Cancer/Parents' Advocacy for Kids with Cancer
81 Eastside Circle
Petaluma, CA   94954
(707) 763-7967
This group offers support to parents whose children suffer from cancer.

Gastrointestinal Polyposis

Familial Polyposis Registry
Cleveland Clinic Foundation
Department of Colorectal Surgery
Cleveland, OH   44106
(216) 444-6470
(800) 321-5398
The Registry educates medical professionals about familial polyposis and teaches the public about colon cancer prevention. A booklet for patients and the *Familial Polyposis Newsletter* are available.

G.I. Polyposis & Colon Cancer Registry
600 N. Wolfe Street
Johns Hopkins Hospital
Baltimore, MD   21205
(301) 955-3875
This network of hereditary colon cancer registries is dedicated to finding families with the heritable conditions, alerting them to risks, communicating with their physicians, and educating the public. Publications include *Family Studies in Genetic Disorders* and a newsletter, *G.I. Polyposis and Related Conditions.*

Intestinal Multiple Polyposis & Colorectal Cancer (IMPACC)
1006-101 Brinker Drive
Hagerstown, MD   21740
(301) 791-7526
IMPACC is a support group for persons and families with hereditary colon cancer.

Leukemia

Leukemia Society of America, Inc.
733 3rd Avenue
New York, NY   10017
(212) 573-8484
The Leukemia Society of America provides financial aid to patients. A publications and audiovisuals catalog is available upon request. They publish a newsletter, *Society News.*

CARDIOVASCULAR DISEASE

American College of Cardiology
9111 Old Georgetown Road
Bethesda, MD   20814
(301) 897-5400
This professional society offers referrals to the public.

American Heart Association (AHA)
7320 Greenville Avenue
Dallas, TX   75231
(214) 706-1179

The AHA offers several publications aimed at children on the value of exercise and proper diet to prevent heart disease in later life.

Council on Cardiovascular Disease in the Young
American Heart Association National Center
7320 Greenville Avenue
Dallas, TX   75231
(214) 373-6300
The Council works to reduce the incidence of mortality and disability among children with cardiovascular disease. Publications include *Safeguarding Your*
Health During Pregnancy, Innocent Heart Murmurs, If Your Child Has a Congenital Heart Defect, Your Child and Rheumatic Fever, and *Abnormalities of Heart Rhythm—A Guide for Parents.*

High Blood Pressure Information Center
120/80 National Institutes of Health
Bethesda, MD   20892
(301) 496-1809
The Center provides information and disseminates publications on high blood pressure in children and adults.

CHROMOSOMAL ABNORMALITIES

```
┌─────────────────────────────────────────────────┐
│                   SEE ALSO                        │
│                                                   │
│  the MENTAL HEALTH and also the SPECIAL NEEDS,    │
│  HANDICAPS, AND LEARNING DISABILI-                │
│  TIES sections of this chapter.                   │
│                                                   │
└─────────────────────────────────────────────────┘
```

Cri-Du-Chat Syndrome

5p-Society
11609 Oakmont
Overland Park, KS   66210
(913) 469-8900
The Society is a support organization for families who have a child with 5p-Syndrome (also known as Cri-du-Chat and Cat Cry Syndrome). Publications
include the *North American 5p- Syndrome Listing* and the *5p- Newsletter.*

Down Syndrome

Association for Children with Down Syndrome, Inc. (ACDS)
2616 Martin Avenue
Bellmore, NY   11710
(516) 221-4700

ACDS works to provide children with Down syndrome a preschool environment that will aid their ability to participate in mainstream schooling, and to provide continued resources to the older child with Down syndrome. A catalog of publications and audiovisuals is available upon request.

National Association for Down Syndrome (NADS)
P.O. Box 4542
Oak Brook, IL   60521
(708) 325-9112
NADS disseminates free information, provides family support, and sustains local parents groups. The Association offers a list of publications, audiovisuals, and publishes the *NADS Newsletter.*

National Down Syndrome Congress
1800 Dempster Street
Park Ridge, IL   60068-1146
(312) 823-7550
(800) 232-NDSC (6372)
The Congress serves as a clearinghouse for Down syndrome information and makes referrals to local chapters and resources. Publications include two pamphlets: *Down Syndrome* and *Facts About Down Syndrome,* and a newsletter, *Down Syndrome News.*

National Down Syndrome Society (NDSS)
666 Broadway
New York, NY   10012
(212) 460-9330
(800) 221-4602
NDSS provides services for families and individuals affected by Down syndrome. A catalog of publications and audiovisuals is available, as is a newsletter, *National Down Syndrome Society Update.*

Parents of Down Syndrome Children
c/o Montgomery County Association for Retarded Citizens
11600 Nebel Street
Rockville, MD   20852
(301) 984-5792
The Association makes referrals and will provide a *Parent Information Kit.*

Fragile X Syndrome

National Fragile X Foundation (NFXF)
1441 York Street, Suite 215
Denver, CO   80206
(303) 333-6155
(800) 688-8765
NFXF teaches professionals, parents, and the public about diagnosis and treatment of the Fragile X Syndrome and other forms of X-linked mental retardation. The Foundation makes referrals to local support groups for parents.

Fragile X Support, Inc.
1380 Huntington Drive
Mundelein, IL   60060
(312) 680-3317
Fragile X Support assists parents whenever possible by helping them enhance the lives of children with this syndrome. Publications include a brochure, *Fragile X Syndrome.*

Laurence-Moon-Biedl Syndrome

Laurence-Moon-Biedl Syndrome Support Network
122 Rolling Road
Lexington Park, MD   20653
(301) 863-5658
The Network provides information and support to individuals and families affected by LMBS (also called Bardet-Biedl Syndrome). Publications include a brochure describing LMBS and the LMBS Network and a bibliography of articles written about LMBS (1960 to the present). The newsletter *LMBS Network News* is published quarterly.

Monosomy 9P

Support Group for Monosomy 9P
43304 Kipton Nickle Plate Road
La Grange, OH   44050
(216) 775-4255
This support group provides nonclinical information, promotes research on the ninth chromosome, makes referrals, and distributes reports from medical journals.

Prader-Willi Syndrome

Prader-Willi Syndrome Association
6490 Excelsior Boulevard, Room E-102
St. Louis Park, MN   55426
(612) 926-1947
The Association is a support group for both parents and professionals. A catalog of publications and audiovisuals is available.

Trisomy 18/Trisomy 13

Support Organization for Trisomy 18, 13 & Related Disorders
5030 Cole
Pocatello, ID   83202
(208) 237-8782
This group publishes *Trisomy 18: A Book for Families* and a newsletter, *S.O.F.T. Touch.*

Turner's Syndrome

Turner's Syndrome Society
York University Administrative Studies Building
4700 Keele Street, Room 006
Downsview, Ontario   M3J 1P3
Canada
(416) 736-5023

The Society provides support services, referrals, and publishes a booklet entitled *The X's and O's of Turner's Syndrome* and a video documentary.

Turner's Syndrome Society of the United States
3539 Tonkawood Road
Minnetonka, MN   55345-1440
(612) 938-3118
This group offers a referral service, and publishes pamphlets and a newsletter.

CONNECTIVE TISSUE DISORDERS

Ehlers-Danlos Syndrome

Ehlers-Danlos National Foundation
P.O. Box 1212
Southgate, MI   48195
(313) 282-0180
The Foundation provides emotional support and information to those with Ehlers-Danlos syndrome and their families. They publish a newsletter, *Loose Connections.*

Marfan Syndrome

National Marfan Foundation
382 Main Street
Port Washington, NY   11050
(516) 883-8712
The National Marfan Foundation offers information, support, and referrals to physicians and the public. Publications include *The Marfan Syndrome* (2nd

ed.), a children's picture book entitled *How John Was Unique,* and a newsletter, *Connective Issues.*

Pseudoxantoma Elasticum

National Association for PXE
P.O. Box 6925
Albany, NY   12203-1958
(518) 482-3647
This group offers limited information and referral services.

CRANIOFACIAL DISORDERS

General Organizations

National Association for the Craniofacially Handicapped
P.O. Box 11082
Chattanooga, TN   37401
(615) 266-1632
NACH provides information and referrals and assists persons with severe craniofacial deformities with their expenses when they travel for treatment. A list of publications and audiovisuals is available.

National Foundation for Facial Reconstruction
550 1st Avenue
New York, NY   10016
(212) 340-5400
The Foundation supports facilities for the treatment and rehabilitation of patients with facial disfigurements.

Cleft Lip/Cleft Palate

AboutFace—The Craniofacial Family
    Society
123 Edward Street, Suite 1405
Toronto, Ontario   M5G 1E2
Canada
(416) 593-1488
AboutFace was founded to support individuals born with or who have acquired facial abnormalities. One of the main objectives of the organization is to link families with similar concerns. The organization publishes a newsletter, *AboutFace.*

American Cleft Palate—Craniofacial
    Association (ACPA)
1218 Grandview Avenue
Pittsburgh, PA   15211
(412) 481-1376
(800) 24-CLEFT (242-5338)
(800) 23-CLEFT (in Pennsylvania)
The Association educates patients, their families, and the general public about sources of treatment and support for those with cleft palates. A publications catalog is available. The *ACPA Newsletter* is published three times a year.

Canadian Cleft Lip & Palate Family
    Association
180 Dundas Street W., Suite 1508
Toronto, Ontario   M5G 1X8
Canada
(416) 598-2311

This group provides nonmedical support to families of children with a cleft lip and palate. The group offers brochures, referrals, and loans films.

Cleft Palate Parents' Council
28 Cambria Road
Syosset, NY   11791
(516) 679-5135
(516) 931-4252
The Council is a support group for parents.

Hemifacial Microsomia/Goldenhar
    Syndrome Family Support Network
6 Country Way
Philadelphia, PA   19115
(215) 677-4787
The Network offers information about major craniofacial centers in the United States and provides information on issues such as feeding problems, developmental delays due to prolonged hospitalizations, hearing problems, and society's reaction to facial anomalies.

Let's Face It
Box 711
Concord, MA   07142
(508) 371-3186
Let's Face It helps parents through its support network.

National Cleft Palate Association
1218 Grandview Avenue
Pittsburgh, PA   15211
(412) 481-1376
The association is a support group for
parents.

Prescription Parents, Inc.
P.O. Box 426
West Roxbury, MA   02132
(617) 527-0878
Prescription Parents provides support
and assistance to parents of children
born with cleft lip or palate. Discussion
groups, professional speakers, publications, and advocacy are offered. This organization publishes *Concerning Cleft
Lip and Cleft Palate* ($9.95), *Caring for
Your Newborn* ($1.95), *Hearing and Be-
havior: Children Born with Cleft Palate*
($1.95), and audiotapes.

DENTISTRY

American Academy of Pediatric
   Dentistry
211 E. Chicago Avenue, Suite 1036
Chicago, IL   60611
(312) 337-2169
This professional society of dentists
who specialize in treating children offers information and referrals over the
phone. They publish a few brochures of
interest to parents.

American Dental Association
211 E. Chicago Avenue
Chicago, IL   60611
(312) 440-2500
(800) 621-8099
The Association offers referrals. A publications catalog is available.

American Society of Dentistry for
   Children
211 E. Chicago Avenue, Suite 1430
Chicago, IL   60611
(312) 943-1244
The Society, a professional group for
dentists, offers information and referrals to the public.

National Foundation for Ectodermal
   Dysplasias
219 E. Main Street, Box 114
Mascoutah, IL   62258
(618) 566-2020
The Foundation offers support services
to the public and health professionals.
Referrals for treatment are made, and a
scientific advisory board is available to
provide diagnostic information and to
assist with treatment when necessary. A
treatment fund aids families with the
ongoing expense of dental care. Publications include *A Dental Guide to the
Ectodermal Dysplasias, A Family Guide
to the Ectodermal Dysplasias,* and *The
Ectodermal Dysplasias.* They publish a
newsletter, *The Educator.*

National Institute of Dental Research
Office of Planning, Evaluation, &
   Communications
9000 Rockville Pike
Building 31, Room 2C35
Bethesda, MD   20892
(301) 496-4261 (publications)
(301) 496-2883 (audiovisuals)
This government office provides information, publications, and audiovisuals that focus on improving dental health. Materials are targeted to consumers, educators, and health-care professionals.

DIGESTIVE DISORDERS

General Organizations

American Digestive Disease Society
7720 Wisconsin Avenue
Bethesda, MD   20814
(301) 223-0179
This group of physicians offers referrals and education regarding all digestive diseases. They operate a hotline in the evenings from 7:30 to 9:00 P.M. called Gutline. The group publishes brochures, dietary plans for various types of patients, and a newsletter.

Digestive Disease National Coalition
   (DDNC)
511 Capitol Court, N.E., Suite 300
Washington, DC   20002
(202) 544-7499

The Coalition informs the public about the relationship of digestive diseases to nutrition, acts as an advocate for research legislation, and promotes funding for research and education.

National Digestive Diseases Information
   Clearinghouse
Box NDDIC
9000 Rockville Pike
Bethesda, MD   20892
(301) 468-6344
This government-sponsored information and referral service publishes fact sheets, brochures, and summaries of research regarding many digestive problems. In addition, they publish the *Directory of Digestive Diseases Organizations.*

Celiac Disease

American Celiac Society (ACS)
45 Gifford Avenue
Jersey City, NJ   07304
(201) 432-1207
ACS provides educational materials on gluten-free diets to patients, physicians, nutritionists, and others. The society will refer you to local physicians and to a local gluten intolerance group. A publications catalog is available.

Celiac Sprue Association/United States
of America, Inc.
P.O. Box 31700
Omaha, NE   68131-0700
(402) 558-0600
CSA/USA provides information and referral services for persons with celiac
sprue (gluten sensitive enteropathy).
The Association offers a series of low-
cost brochures on gluten-free diets,
gluten-free commercial foods, and related topics, and also publishes a book,
*On the Celiac Condition: A Handbook
for Celiacs and Their Families,* and a
newsletter, *Lifeline.*

Gluten Intolerance Group of North
America
P.O. Box 23053
Seattle, WA   98102-0353
(206) 325-6980
This support group offers counseling,
referrals, and publications which include diet instructions, fact sheets,
gluten-free bread recipes, a cookbook,
and the *GIG Newsletter.*

Ileitis/Colitis

National Foundation for Ileitis &
Colitis, Inc.
444 Park Avenue S., 11th Floor
New York, NY   10016-7374
(212) 685-3440
(800) 343-3637

The Foundation makes referrals and
publishes *People, Not Patients: A
Source Book For Living With IBD,*
other books, audiovisuals, and two
newsletters. A catalog is available.

EATING DISORDERS

Anorexia/Bulimia

American Anorexia/Bulimia Association
133 Cedar Lane
Teaneck, NJ   07666
(201) 836-1800
This information clearinghouse helps
parents, support groups, and children
suffering from eating disorders, and
also publishes a newsletter.

Anorexia Nervosa & Related Eating
Disorders (ANRED)
P.O. Box 5102
Eugene, OR   97405
(503) 344-1144
ANRED offers counseling, referrals, and
publications to anorectics and their
families. The organization publishes a
newsletter, *ANRED Alert.*

National Anorexic Aid Society
5796 Karl Road
Columbus, OH   43229
(614) 436-1112
The Society provides educational materials that help in the early detection
and treatment of eating disorders, and
also publishes a newsletter.

National Association of Anorexia
   Nervosa & Associated Disorders
   (ANAD)
Box 7
Highland Park, IL   60035
(708) 831-3438
With chapters in most states, this
group of parents, patients, and health
professionals offers services to children,
makes referrals, loans educational materials, and generally supports parents.
They publish a newsletter, *Working Together.*

Overeating

Overeaters Anonymous
P.O. Box 92870
Los Angeles, CA   90009
(213) 542-8363
An international organization of eighty-
five hundred chapters that approaches
compulsive eating through the AA
twelve-step system. There are special
groups and publications for teenagers.

Take Off Pounds Sensibly (T.O.P.S.)
P.O. Box 07360
4575 5th Street
Milwaukee, WI   53207
(414) 482-4620
A national organization of twelve thousand chapters, T.O.P.S. encourages sen-
sible weight management. Its weekly
meetings for discussion, support, and
competition help people reach and keep
their goals.

Weight Watchers International
Jericho Atrium
500 N. Broadway
Jericho, NY   11753-2196
(516) 939-0400
Weight Watchers offers a carefully
balanced, low-calorie diet, weekly
support groups, exercise, and tips on
how to modify one's life-style to control
weight gain.

HEARING AND SPEECH PROBLEMS

SEE ALSO

the SPECIAL NEEDS, HANDICAPS, AND LEARNING DISABILITIES section of this chapter
for additional organizations serving handicapped children.

General Organizations

Alexander Graham Bell Association for the Deaf
3417 Volta Place, N.W.
Washington, DC   20007
(202) 337-5220
The Association helps hearing-impaired persons function independently. A subgroup, The International Parents' Organization, comprises parents of hearing-impaired children who have formed local groups. This subgroup promotes early diagnosis, appropriate amplification, and development of speech and listening skills in children. Information, referrals, and a catalog of publications are available, including *Our Kids Magazine* and a newsletter, *Newsounds.*

American Society for Deaf Children
814 Thayer Street
Silver Spring, MD   20910
(301) 585-5400
The Society provides information and support to parents and families with deaf or hearing-impaired children. It offers assistance with educational or legal problems related to the rearing of a hearing-impaired child. Publications include *Summer Camp Directory for Deaf Children,* sign language materials, and a newsletter, *The Endeavor.* A publications catalog is available.

Center for Genetic & Acquired Deafness
St. Christopher's Hospital for Children
Section of Medical Genetics
5th Street and Lehigh Avenue
Philadelphia, PA   19133
(215) 427-4430
(215) 427-4433 (TDD)
The Center assists parents with educational planning and medical treatment for hearing-impaired children.

Children of Deaf Adults (CDA)
Box 30715
Santa Barbara, CA   93130
(805) 682-0997
CDA is a support group for hearing children of deaf parents. They publish a newsletter, *CODA.*

Hear Center
301 E. Del Mar Boulevard
Pasadena, CA   91101
(818) 681-4641
The Center specializes in the early identification of deafness and in providing help as early as possible. Services include counseling, dispensing hearing aids, speech therapy, and testing. Publications include *Conquering Childhood Deafness* and *Effectiveness of Early Detection and Auditory Stimulation on the Speech and Language of Hearing Impaired Children.*

Junior National Association for the Deaf
445 N. Pennsylvania Avenue, Suite 804
Indianapolis, IN   46204
(317) 638-1715
The one hundred twenty local groups of
the Association offer information and
support services to hearing-impaired
teenagers.

National Association of the Deaf (NAD)
814 Thayer Avenue
Silver Spring, MD   20910
(301) 587-1788
NAD works to help the deaf achieve
their maximum potential through increased independence, productivity, and
acceptance into the community. The
NAD Legal Defense Fund protects the
legal rights of deaf persons. Its youth
program, affiliated with the Junior National Association for the Deaf, sponsors
camps for teens and younger children,
workshops, and training. The NAD Public Information Center maintains a
reading library with an extensive collection of deafness-related materials. NAD
is one of the largest publishers of deafness-related books and materials in the
world. A publications catalog is available. NAD publishes a newsletter, the
Broadcaster, and a magazine, the *Deaf
American.*

National Foundation for Children's
   Hearing Education and Research
928 McLean Avenue
Yonkers, NY   10704
(914) 237-2676
This small group of parents and others
concerned with childhood deafness offers limited information and referrals.

National Information Center on
   Deafness (NICD)
Gallaudet University
800 Florida Avenue, N.E.
Washington, DC   20002
(202) 651-5051
(202) 651-5052 (TDD)
NICD is an information clearinghouse
on all aspects of hearing loss, including
such topics as education, communication, and technology. NICD provides
fact sheets, resource listings, reading
lists, and other publications that address frequently asked questions. A publications catalog is available.

Self-Help for Hard of Hearing People
   (SHHH)
7800 Wisconsin Avenue
Bethesda, MD   20814
(301) 657-2248
(301) 657-2249 (TDD)
SHHH has two hundred thirty local
groups that offer support and information to hard-of-hearing people, their
relatives, and friends. A publications
catalog is available upon request.

TRIPOD
955 N. Alfred Street
Los Angeles, CA 90069
(213) 656-4904
(800) 352-8888 (voice and TDD)
(800) 346-8888 (voice and TDD in
   California)
TRIPOD provides support services for
hearing-impaired individuals and their
families. The group offers a preschool
program, educational videos, parent forums, sign-language classes, and specialized day-care. TRIPOD's toll-free
hotline answers questions about rearing
and educating a hearing-impaired child.

Speech and Hearing

**American Speech, Language & Hearing
   Association**
10801 Rockville Pike
Rockville, MD 20852
(301) 897-5700
(800) 638-TALK (8255) (voice and
   TDD)
This Society for professionals providing
speech, language, and hearing therapy
offers information and referrals to the
public.

**National Association for Hearing &
   Speech Action (NAHSA)**
10801 Rockville Pike
Rockville, MD 20852
(301) 897-8682
(800) 638-TALK (8255) (voice and TDD)

NAHSA provides information and referral services to all people with communication disorders, and offers a catalog
of publications and products.

Stuttering

Compulsive Stutterers Anonymous
Box 1406
Park Ridge, IL 60068
(708) 272-3712
Group meetings are based on the
twelve-step program developed by AA
and are for those who seek to free
themselves from stuttering. Guidelines
for founding a new group are available.

International Foundation for Stutterers
P.O. Box 462
Belle Mead, NJ 08502
(201) 359-6469
This support group for stutterers offers
referrals to local self-help groups.

National Center for Stuttering
200 E. 33rd Street
New York, NY 10016
(212) 532-1460
(800) 221-2483
Provides information to parents whose
young child shows early signs of stuttering. Also helps older children and
adults. Publications are available.

Tinnitus

American Tinnitus Association (ATA)
P.O. Box 5
Portland, OR   97297
(503) 248-9985
ATA supports research and educational
activities relating to the cure of tinnitus and other defects or diseases of the
ear. Publications include brochures and
a newsletter, *Tinnitus Today.*

IMMUNIZATION

Dissatisfied Parents Together
128 Branch Road
Vienna, VA   22180
(703) 938-3783
This group offers referrals and information to parents who believe a child of
theirs has been adversely affected by a
vaccine.

IMMUNOLOGIC DISORDERS

General Organizations

American Association of Immunologists
9650 Rockville Pike
Bethesda, MD   20014
(301) 530-7178
This professional society offers referral
services to the public.

AIDS

AIDS Hotline
101 W. Read Street, Suite 825
Baltimore, MD   21202
(800) 638-6252
This hotline offers referrals when adults
and children need testing and counseling.

American Association of Blood Banks
1117 N. 19th Street, Suite 600
Arlington, VA   22209
(703) 528-8200
Provides information on the risk from
blood banks of Acquired Immune Deficiency Syndrome and other diseases.

Foundation for Children with AIDS
77 B Warren Street
Brighton, MA   02135
(617) 783-7300
The Foundation offers information and
referrals for the parents of children
stricken with AIDS.

Gay Men's Health Crisis
129 W. 20th Street
New York, NY   10011
(212) 337-3519 (administration)
(212) 807-6655 (AIDS hotline)
This group answers questions by phone,
makes referrals, and sends out free
brochures, including *Medical Answers
About AIDS* and *Women Need to Know
About AIDS.*

Hemophilia & AIDS/HIV Network for the Dissemination of Information (HANDI)
National Hemophilia Foundation
110 Greene Street, Suite 406
New York, NY   10012
(212) 431-8541
(212) 431-3081
HANDI maintains a very large resource collection of educational materials on hemophilia and AIDS. It will answer questions and make referrals. The group's interests include AIDS prevention, living with hemophilia and AIDS, and treatments for these diseases. Publications include the *HANDI Quarterly,* the *Article Reprint Exchange,* and various bibliographies, resource packets, and fact sheets.

Mothers of A.I.D.S. Patients
P.O. Box 3132
San Diego, CA   92103
(619) 544-0430
This mutual support group for mothers whose children have AIDS publishes a newsletter, provides phone support, and helps other groups get established.

National AIDS Information Clearinghouse
P.O. Box 6003
Rockville, MD   20850
(301) 762-5111
(800) 458-5231

Operated by The Centers for Disease Control (CDC), the Clearinghouse is a major information service for health professionals and the general public. It can refer you to relevant organizations, supply information about hard-to-find educational materials, and provide single or bulk copies of key publications. It maintains databases that list organizations providing AIDS-related services and educational materials.

National AIDS Network
2033 M Street, N.W., Suite 800
Washington, DC   20036
(202) 293-2437
The Network provides information and makes referrals for anyone with AIDS. In addition, it runs Grandma's House, a shelter for children with AIDS.

National Pediatric HIV Resource Center
Children's Hospital of New Jersey
15 S. 9th Street
Newark, NJ   07107
(201) 268-8251
Information and referrals are offered to families who have a child infected with the HIV virus.

Pediatric AIDS Coalition
1331 Pennsylvania Avenue, N.W.
Suite 721-N
Washington, DC   20004
(202) 662-7460

The Coalition works to educate the public about AIDS dangers to children and to help children who are afflicted with the disease.

Public Health Service AIDS Hotline
(800) 342-AIDS (2437)
(800) 243-7889 (voice and TDD)

Ryan White National Fund
c/o Athletes & Entertainers for Kids
Nissan Motor Corp.
P.O. Box 191
Gardena, CA   90248
(213) 276-5437
The Fund helps children with catastrophic illnesses, especially AIDS. It offers educational services, emergency financial help, counseling, and free medical assistance to children and their families.

Immune Deficiency

Chronic Fatigue & Immune Dysfunction Syndrome Society
P.O. Box 230108
Portland, OR   97223
(503) 684-5261
The Society publishes a patient guide and distributes audiovisual materials.

Immune Deficiency Foundation
P.O. Box 586
Columbia, MD   21045
(301) 461-3127

The Foundation disseminates information concerning research and treatment of immune deficiency diseases. Publications include *Immune Deficiency Diseases: An Overview,* the *IDF Newsletter,* and audiovisuals.

Sjogren's Syndrome

Sjogren's Syndrome Foundation, Inc.
382 Main Street
Port Washington, NY   11050
(516) 767-2866
The Sjogren's Syndrome Foundation helps patients and their families cope with the problems and frustrations of living with this chronic disease. It publishes a newsletter called *The Moisture Seekers.*

Systemic Lupus Erythematosus

American Lupus Society
23751 Madison Street
Torrance, CA   90505
(213) 373-1335
(800) 331-1802
The Society provides patients and their families with educational materials and support. A publications catalog is available, as is a newletter, *The Quarterly.*

Lupus Foundation of America
1717 Massachusetts Avenue, N.W.
Washington, DC   20036
(202) 328-4550
(800) 558-0121

The Lupus Foundation refers the public to physicians and to its more than one hundred local chapters nationwide. Publications include *Lupus Erythematosus: A Handbook for Physicians, Patients, and Their Families,* pamphlets, and a newsletter, *Lupus News.*

JOINT DISEASES

Arthritis

American Juvenile Arthritis Organization/Arthritis Foundation
1314 Spring Street, N.W.
Atlanta, GA   30309
(404) 872-7100
The Organization serves as an advocate for children with rheumatic diseases and their families. A publications and audiovisuals catalog is available on request, and several newletters are also published.

National Arthritis and Musculoskeletal and Skin Diseases
Information Clearinghouse
Box AMS9000
Rockville Pike
Bethesda, MD   20892
(301) 495-4484
This government office answers questions, makes referrals, and will send a publications list of materials on arthritis.

Lyme Disease

Lyme Borreliosis Foundation
P.O. Box 462
Tolland, CT   06084
(203) 871-9789
The Foundation and its seventy-five local groups work to educate health professionals and the public about Lyme disease. An information clearinghouse and referral service is available. The Foundation publishes pamphlets and a newsletter, *Lyme Lights.*

KIDNEY DISORDERS

American Association of Kidney Patients
1 Davis Boulevard, Suite LL1
Tampa, FL   33606
(813) 251-0725
The Association supports patients and their families by providing information on dialysis and transplants. Publications include *Living With Renal Failure, Transplant Kidneys, Don't Bury Them,* and a newsletter, *Renalife.*

Kidney Information Clearinghouse
Box NKUDIC
Bethesda, MD   20892
(301) 468-6345
This government office provides referrals and distributes literature on kidney treatments.

National Institute of Diabetes &
Digestive & Kidney Diseases
Office of Health Research Reports
9000 Rockville Pike
Building 31, Room 9A52
Bethesda, MD   20892
(301) 496-3583
This government office disseminates
information to consumers and professionals regarding diabetes, digestive
disorders, and kidney diseases.

National Kidney Foundation
2 Park Avenue, Suite 908
New York, NY   10016
(212) 889-2210
(800) 622-9010
The National Kidney Foundation provides patient publications, professional
materials, transportation to facilities, a
drug bank, and referrals. A catalog of
their many publications and audiovisuals is available.

Polycystic Kidney Research (PKR)
Foundation
922 Walnut Street
Kansas City, MO   64106
(816) 421-1869
The PKR Foundation promotes research
into the cause and cure of polycystic
kidney disease. Publications include
*Polycystic Kidney Disease?; Your Diet
and Polycystic Kidney Disease;* and a
newsletter, *PKR Progress.*

LIVER DISORDERS

American Liver Foundation
998 Pompton Avenue
Cedar Grove, NJ   07009
(201) 857-2626
(800) 223-0179
The Foundation fights more than one
hundred liver diseases by promoting research, education, and patient self-help
groups. A publications and audiovisuals
catalog is available, as are two newsletters that report on research break-
throughs, *Progress* and *Liver Update.*

Children's Liver Foundation
14245 Ventura Boulevard, Suite 201
Sherman Oaks, CA   91423
(818) 906-3021
The Foundation provides family support, education, and advocacy for children with liver disease. Catalogs of its
publications and audiovisuals are available, as well as a newsletter, *CLF Lifeline.*

METABOLIC DISORDERS

General Organizations

Inherited Metabolic Disease (IMD)
Clinic
Children's Hospital/University of
Colorado Health Sciences Center
Box B153
Denver, CO   80218
(303) 861-6847

The IMD Clinic is one of the leading centers for treatment of inherited metabolic diseases in the United States. The Clinic publishes a newsletter, *Inherited Metabolic Diseases,* and a booklet, *Living with PKU.*

National Foundation for Jewish Genetic
　Diseases, Inc.
250 Park Avenue, Suite 1000
New York, NY　10017
(212) 753-5155
The Foundation supplies educational materials and conducts professional symposia.

Albinism/Hypopigmentation

National Organization for Albinism &
　Hypopigmentation (NOAH)
1500 Locust Street, Suite 1816
Philadelphia, PA　19102-4316
(215) 545-2322
(800) 473-2310
NOAH sponsors research and provides information and support to individuals and their families. Publications include bulletins, brochures, and the newsletter *NOAH News.*

Cystic Fibrosis

Cystic Fibrosis Foundation
6931 Arlington Road, Room 200
Bethesda, MD　20814
(301) 951-4422
(800) FIGHT CF (344-4823)

The Foundation offers support services and referrals. A list of publications and audiovisuals is available, and a newsletter, *Commitment.*

Cystinosis

Cystinosis Foundation
17 Lake
Piedmont, CA　94611
(415) 834-7897
The Foundation acts as a support group for parents of children with cystinosis. It publishes fact sheets, a pamphlet called *Facts about Cystinosis,* and a newsletter, *Help Us Grow.*

Diabetes

American Diabetes Association, Inc.
P.O. Box 25757
Alexandria, VA　22314
(703) 549-1500
(800) ADA-DISC (232-3472)
The American Diabetes Association has over eight hundred local chapters working to improve the well-being of all people with diabetes and their families. It offers books, numerous other publications, and a free catalog.

Joslin Diabetes Center
1 Joslin Place
Boston, MA　02215
(617) 732-2400
Although primarily a research organization, the Center also sponsors two

camps for diabetic children. Information on diet and living with diabetes is available in the *Joslin Magazine*.

Juvenile Diabetes Foundation International
432 Park Avenue S., 16th Floor
New York, NY   10016
(212) 889-7575
(800) 223-1138
The Foundation, which has more than one hundred fifty local groups, supports parents and their diabetic children through counseling, discussion groups, and referrals. Publications include the magazine *Diabetes Countdown* and a variety of pamphlets and audiovisuals.

National Diabetes Information Clearinghouse
Box NDIC
Bethesda, MD   20892
(301) 468-2162
This office of the government disseminates information to patients and professionals.

National Institute of Diabetes & Digestive & Kidney Diseases
Office of Health Research Reports
9000 Rockville Pike
Building 31, Room 9A52
Bethesda, MD   20892
(301) 496-3583
This government office responds to inquiries from consumers and professionals.

Dysautonomia

Dysautonomia Foundation, Inc.
370 Lexington Avenue
New York, NY   10017
(212) 889-5222
The Foundation provides information about familial dysautonomia (also called Riley-Day Syndrome) to parents and physicians. Patients can receive treatment at the Dysautonomia Treatment and Evaluation Center at New York University Medical Center. Publications include a treatment manual called *Caring for the Child with Familial Dysautonomia,* several brochures, and audiovisuals.

Galactosemia

Parents of Galactosemic Children, Inc.
1 Ash Court
New York, NY   10956
(914) 638-6350
The major American support group for parents with children suffering from this metabolic disorder.

Gaucher Disease

National Gaucher Foundation
1424 K Street, N.W., 4th Floor
Washington, DC   20005
(202) 393-2777
The Foundation provides information to patients and publishes pamphlets, audiovisuals, and the *Gaucher's Disease Registry Newsletter.*

Glycogen Storage Disease

Association for Glycogen Storage
  Diseases
Box 896
Durant, IA   52747
(319) 785-6038
The Association offers referrals, a list of
publications, and a newsletter, *The Ray.*

Leukodystrophy

United Leukodystrophy Foundation
2304 Highland Drive
Sycamore, IL   60178
(815) 895-3211
This group offers information and coordinates a communication network
among affected families. Publications
include *Facts About Leukodystrophy*
and reprints from medical journals.

Lowe's Syndrome

Lowe's Syndrome Association
222 Lincoln Street
West Lafayette, IN   47906
(317) 743-3634
The Association helps families with
Lowe's Syndrome (also known as
Oculo-Cerebro-Renal Syndrome)
through a program of education and research. Publications include *Care Today, Cure Tomorrow*, and *Living With
Lowe's Syndrome.*

Malignant Hyperthermia

Malignant Hyperthermia Association of
  the United States
P.O. Box 191
Westport, CT   06820
(203) 655-3007
(203) 634-4917 (medic alert hotline)
The Association provides information
and referrals to MH susceptible families
and their physicians. Publications include *Malignant Hyperthermia—The
Anesthesiologist's Nightmare, Preventing Malignant Hyperthermia,* and a
newsletter, *The Communicator.*

Maple Syrup Urine Disease

Maple Syrup Urine Disease Family
  Support Group
RR #2, Box 24-A
Flemingsburg, KY   41041
(606) 849-4679
This Group offers information on
branched-chain ketonuria and publishes
a newsletter, *Maple Syrup Urine Disease Newsletter.*

Mucolipidosis/Mucopolysaccharidosis

Mucolipidosis IV Foundation
6 Concord Drive
Monsey, NY   10952
(914) 425-0639

The Foundation works to improve diagnostic measures, develop a carrier screening test and treatment, and find a cure.

National Mucopolysaccharidosis Society
17 Kraemer Street
Hicksville, NY   11801
(516) 931-6338
The Society serves parents through support, networking, physician referrals, professional and public education. Publications include *What is MPS?* and a newsletter, *Courage.*

Zain Hansen M.P.S. Foundation
1200 Fernwood Drive
P.O. Box 4768
Arcata, CA   95521
(707) 822-5421
This group distributes funds and other assistance to children and their parents, offers referrals, and operates a medical equipment exchange bank. Publications include *Directory of Medical Professionals Experienced in MPS* and *Directory of MPS Research Programs.*

Organic Acidemia

Organic Acidemia Association
1532 S. 87th Street
Kansas City, KS   66111
(913) 422-7080
Offers referrals and a membership roster for networking purposes.

Phenylketonuria

PKU Parents
8 Myrtle Lane
San Anselmo, CA   94960
(415) 457-4632
PKU is a support group for parents of children with PKU.

Porphyria

American Porphyria Foundation
P.O. Box 1075
Santa Rosa Beach, FL   32459
(904) 654-4754
The Foundation offers information and referrals, supports seventeen local chapters, lends books and audiovisuals, and publishes several brochures for patients.

Tay-Sachs Disease

National Tay-Sachs & Allied Diseases Association
385 Elliot Street
Newton, MA   02164
(617) 964-5508
The Association provides public and professional education, services to families, referrals, quality-control testing, and research funding. Publications include *One Day at a Time, Prevent a Tragedy, What Every Family Should Know,* and the newsletter *Breakthrough.*

Williams Syndrome

Williams Syndrome Association
1611 Clayton Spur Court
Ellisville, MO 63011
(314) 227-4411
The Association offers information, referrals, and publications to families with Williams syndrome children.

Wilson's Disease

Wilson's Disease Association
P.O. Box 75324
Washington, DC 20013
(703) 636-3003
The Association provides aid and support to persons who have Wilson or Menkes's syndrome. It offers medical referrals, limited financial aid, and a network of affected persons for mutual support. Publications include a series of brochures, a directory of members, and a newsletter.

NEUROLOGICAL DISORDERS

General Organizations

American Academy of Neurology
221 University Avenue, S.E., Suite 335
Minneapolis, MN 55414
(612) 623-8115
This professional society of physicians offers referrals to the public.

American Association of Neurological Surgeons
22 S. Washington Street, Suite 100
Park Ridge, IL 60068
(708) 692-9500
A professional society offering referrals to the public.

Child Neurology Society
475 Cleveland Avenue, N., Suite 225
St. Paul, MN 55104-5051
(612) 625-7466
The Society comprises physicians with a specialty in child neurology. It offers referrals.

National Institute of Neurological Disorders and Stroke
Office of Scientific and Health Reports
9000 Rockville Pike
Building 31, Room 8A06
Bethesda, MD 20892
(301) 496-5924
This government office offers information and referrals to consumers and professionals.

Acoustic Neuroma

Acoustic Neuroma Association
P.O. Box 398
Carlisle, PA 17013
(717) 249-4783
The Association offers support and information to persons who have experienced acoustic neuromas or other

tumors affecting the cranial nerves. Publications include booklets and a newsletter, *Notes.*

Angelman Syndrome

Angelman Research Group (ARG)
University of Florida
Division of Genetics
Department of Pediatrics
Box J-296, JHMHC
Gainesville, FL 32610-0296
(904) 392-4104
ARG provides information about Angelman syndrome to parents and professionals, encourages networking among families, and pursues research. Its publications include a newsletter, a bibliography, and a directory.

Ataxia

Friedrich's Ataxia Group in America, Inc.
P.O. Box 11116
Oakland, CA 94611
(415) 655-0833
This support group aids persons with ataxia and their families, raises funds for research, and disseminates brochures on the disease.

National Ataxia Foundation
600 Twelve Oaks Center
15500 Wayzata Boulevard
Wayzata, MN 55391
(612) 473-7666

The Foundation offers information and referrals to families of children suffering from all types of ataxia and closely related disorders such as hereditary spastic paraplegia and Charcot-Marie-Tooth syndrome. Publications include *Hereditary Ataxia (HA): The Facts* and a newsletter, *Generations.*

Batten Disease

Batten Disease Support & Research Association
6707 197th Street E.
Spanaway, WA 98387
(206) 847-2926
Provides support, information, and publications to families affected by Batten disease.

Children's Brain Diseases Foundation
Parnussus Heights Medical Building
350 Parnassus Avenue, Suite 900
San Fransisco, CA 94117
(415) 566-5402
The Foundation provides referrals for the public.

Epilepsy

Epilepsy Concern Service Group
1282 Wynnewood Drive
West Palm Beach, FL 33417
(407) 683-0044

This support group, formed by epileptics, offers help to anyone seeking to join or form a self-help group in their area.

Epilepsy Foundation of America
4351 Garden City Drive
Landover, MD   20785
(301) 459-3700
(800) EFA-1000 (332-1000)
The Epilepsy Foundation, with its nearly ninety affiliates, works to improve the lives of epilepsy patients through a broad range of educational, research, and advocacy programs. The National Epilepsy Library and Resource Center offers information on the latest research findings. A pharmacy service is offered to members. A catalog of publications and audiovisuals is available. They publish a newsletter, *National Spokesman.*

Guillain-Barré Syndrome

Guillain-Barré Syndrome Support Group International
P.O. Box 262
Wynnewood, PA   19096
(215) 896-6855
This group has over one hundred chapters that offer support and information to patients of Guillain-Barré Syndrome, also known as Acute Idiopathic Polyneuritis. Publications include *Guil-*

lian-Barré Syndrome, an Overview for the Layperson.

Head Injury

National Head Injury Foundation (NHIF)
333 Turnpike Road
Southboro, MA   01772
(508) 485-9950
(800) 444-NHIF (6443)
With over three hundred fifty local chapters, the NHIF works to educate the public about head injuries and aid the injured. Publications include *National Directory of Head Injury Rehabilitation Services,* a *Catalogue of Educational Materials,* various brochures, and a newsletter.

Phoenix Project
P.O. Box 84151
Seattle, WA   98124
(206) 329-1371
This small group offers information and referrals to survivors of head injury. Publications include *From the Ashes: A Head Injury Self-Advocacy Guide.*

Huntington Disease

Hereditary Disease Foundation (HDF)
1427 7th Street, Suite 2
Santa Monica, CA   90401
(213) 458-4183

Although primarily a foundation that funds research on Huntington disease and other neurological illnesses, the HDF also offers information, referrals, and publications to the public. Their catalog will be sent upon request.

Huntington's Disease Society of America
140 W. 22nd Street
New York, NY   10011-2420
(212) 242-1968
(800) 345-HDSA (4372)
The Society has over one hundred chapters devoted to helping patients with Huntington disease and their families. The Society's information and referral services tap a nationwide network of physicians, scientists, social workers, and other professionals. A catalog of publications and audiovisuals is available, and a newsletter, *The Marker*.

Huntington Society of Canada
13 Water Street N., Suite 3
Cambridge, Ontario   N1R 5T8
Canada
(519) 622-1002
The Society offers family support and education programs to assist patients stricken with Huntington disease. They publish a newsletter and a variety of brochures.

Hydrocephalus

National Hydrocephalus Foundation
Route 1 River Road, Box 210A
Joliet, IL   60436
(815) 467-6548
The Foundation informs individuals with hydrocephalus and their families about relevant services. It maintains a reference library for members and offers publications and audiovisuals to the public.

Joseph Diseases

International Joseph Diseases Foundation, Inc.
P.O. Box 2550
Livermore, CA   94550
The Foundation supports research and helps patients find medical, social, and genetic counseling services. Publications include *Fact Sheet—Joseph Diseases*.

Narcolepsy

American Narcolepsy Association
P.O. Box 1187
San Carlos, CA   94070
(415) 591-7979
(800) 222-6085
(800) 222-6086 (in California)
The Association helps improve the lives of persons with narcolepsy. A list of publications and audiovisuals is avail-

able upon request, as is a newsletter called *Eye Opener.*

Narcolepsy & Cataplexy Foundation of America
Mail Box #22
1410 York Avenue, Suite 2D
New York, NY   10021
(212) 628-6315
Offers information, referrals, and a series of brochures.

Neurofibromatosis

National Neurofibromatosis Foundation, Inc.
141 5th Avenue, Suite 7-S
New York, NY   10010
(212) 460-8980
(800) 323-7938
The Foundation provides patients with information about neurofibromatosis and helps them find medical, social, and genetic counseling. Publications include *Neurofibromatosis: A Handbook for Parents; Neurofibromatosis: Information for Kids; Neurofibromatosis: Information for Patients and Families;* and two newsletters.

Neurofibromatosis, Inc.
3401 Woodridge Court
Mitchellville, MD   20721-8878
(301) 577-8984

This group provides educational, support, clinical, and resource programs, and publishes brochures and the newsletter *Neurofibromatosis Ink.*

Reflex Sympathetic Dystrophy Syndrome

Reflex Sympathetic Dystrophy Syndrome Association
822 Wayside Lane
Haddonfield, NJ   08033
(215) 928-5444
(609) 428-6980
The Association supports research and provides information on physician seminars and patient services. Publications include *Reflex Sympathetic Dystrophy Syndrome: Help Us Stop the Pain.*

Rett Syndrome

International Rett Syndrome Association
8511 Rose Marie Drive
Fort Washington, MD   20744
(301) 248-7031
The Association disseminates information regarding the cause, identification, treatment, and prevention of Rett syndrome. Publications include *The Parent Idea Book, Educational and Therapeutic Intervention in Rett Syndrome,* and a brochure called *What Is Rett Syndrome?*

Reye's Syndrome

National Reye's Syndrome Foundation
426 N. Lewis, P.O. Box 829
Bryan, OH   43506
(419) 636-2679
(800) 233-7393 (24-hour hotline)
(800) 231-7393 (in Ohio)
The Foundation and its forty state groups and one hundred fifty local chapters offer referrals, counseling, and financial aid to families with children suffering from Reye's syndrome.

Spasmodic Torticollis

National Spasmodic Torticollis Association
P.O. Box 873
Royal Oak, MI   48068-0873
(313) 775-1367
(313) 547-2189
Educates the general public and physicians about spasmodic torticollis. Publications include *Fact Sheet: Spasmodic Torticollis, Physician Referral Directory,* and a newsletter.

Spina Bifida

Spina Bifida Association of America
1700 Rockville Pike, Suite 540
Rockville, MD   20852
(301) 770-7222
(800) 621-3141

The Association and its ninety local chapters encourage the care, treatment, education, and vocational development of persons with spina bifida. A list of publications and audiovisuals is available. They publish a newsletter, *Insights.*

Spina Bifida Association of Canada
633 Wellington Crescent
Winnipeg, Manitoba   R3M OA8
Canada
(204) 452-7580
The Spina Bifida Association of Canada, with nearly twenty-five chapters, sells three different information kits—for teachers, parents, and teens. In addition, the Association has several audio-visual programs, booklets, and a newsletter, *Podium.*

Sturge-Weber Syndrome

Sturge-Weber Foundation
P.O. Box 460931
Aurora, CO   80013
(303) 693-2986
(800) 627-5482
The Foundation serves as an information clearinghouse and support network to patients with Sturge-Weber syndrome. They publish brochures and a newsletter.

Tourette Syndrome

Tourette Syndrome Association
42-40 Bell Boulevard
Bayside, NY   11361
(718) 224-2999
(800) 237-0717
The Association has sixty local groups
nationwide that offer information, referrals, and support to patients and their
families. Publications include *Medical
Letter: Summary of Recent Literature*
and a newsletter.

Tuberous Sclerosis

**National Tuberous Sclerosis Association
   (NTSA)**
4351 Garden City Drive, Suite 660
Landover, MD   20785
(301) 459-9888
(800) 225-NTSA (6872)
NTSA offers information and referrals
designed to help patients of tuberous
sclerosis medically, psychologically, and
socially. Publications include *Parent
Booklet* and a brochure called *Tuberous
Sclerosis*. Audiovisuals include *Parents
Ask About TS*.

**Tuberous Sclerosis Association of
   America, Inc.**
1305 Middleborough Row
Middleboro, MA   02370
(508) 947-8893

The Association supports research and
helps patients, families, and health professionals. Publications include
brochures, research bulletins, and a
newsletter, *T.S.A.A.*

NEUROMUSCULAR DISORDERS

General Organizations

**Amyotrophic Lateral Sclerosis (ALS)
   Association**
21021 Ventura Boulevard, Suite 321
Woodland Hills, CA   91364
(818) 340-7500
(800) 340-2060
The Association and its 135 local
groups support research investigating
ALS, also known as Lou Gehrig's
disease. They offer patient services,
public and professional education, and
referrals. Publications include
*Managing Amyotrophic Lateral
Sclerosis (MALS) Manuals, What is
Amyotrophic Lateral Sclerosis?,* and
Home Care. They publish a newsletter
called *Link.*

**International Research Council of
   Neuromuscular Disorders**
1434 Pleasantville Road
Lancaster, OH   43130
(419) 629-3391
This small group of health professionals
offers information and referrals regarding neuromuscular diseases.

Charcot-Marie-Tooth Disease/Peroneal Muscular Atrophy

SEE ALSO

the National Ataxia Foundation, above in the NEUROLOGICAL DISORDERS section under Ataxia.

Charcot-Marie-Tooth Association (CMTA)
c/o Crozer Mills Enterprise Center
600 Upland Avenue
Upland, PA   19015
(215) 499-7486
CMTA offers support and referrals to patients of Charcot-Marie-Tooth disease, also known as Peroneal Muscular Atrophy. It publishes pamphlets, videotapes, and a newsletter, *The CMTA Report.*

Charcot-Marie-Tooth Disease International
1 Springbank Drive
St. Catharines, Ontario   L2S 2K1
Canada
(416) 687-3630
This group provides information, psychological and genetic counseling, and funds for the education of patients.

Dystonia

Benign Essential Blepharospasm Research Foundation, Inc.
P.O. Box 12468
Beaumont, TX   77706
(409) 832-0788
The Foundation is an international clearinghouse for information on facial dystonia. Publications include *Benign Essential Blepharospasm, Meige's and Other Related Disorders.* An audiovisuals catalog is available upon request. The Foundation publishes a newsletter.

Dystonia Medical Research Foundation
8383 Wilshire Boulevard, Suite 800
Beverly Hills, CA   90210
(213) 852-1630
The Foundation funds research, and offers support and referral services to families with a dystonia patient. Various pamphlets are available, as is a newsletter, *Dystonia Dialogue.*

**Dystonia Medical Research
   Foundation-Canada**
777 Hornby Street
Vancouver, British Columbia   V6Z 1S4
Canada
(604) 661-4886
This group is the Canadian affiliate of
the Dystonia Medical Research Foundation.

Multiple Sclerosis

National Multiple Sclerosis Society
205 E. 42nd Street
New York, NY   10017
(212) 986-3240
(800) 624-8236
The Society serves patients through
counseling, advocacy, referrals, and
equipment loans. A publications and
audiovisuals catalog is available upon
request. They publish a newsletter, *In-
side MS.*

Muscular Dystrophy

Muscular Dystrophy Association
810 Seventh Avenue
New York, NY   10019
(212) 586-0808
The Muscular Dystrophy Association
and its more than one hundred sixty
local affiliates offer comprehensive
patient and community services. Its
clinics provide diagnostic services, therapeutic and rehabilitative followup care,
and genetic, vocational, and social service counseling to patients and their
families. Other services include repair
of orthopedic appliances and transportation aid. A catalog of publications
and audiovisuals is available upon request. Also published is the *MDA News-
magazine.*

Myasthenia Gravis

Myasthenia Gravis Foundation (MGF)
53 W. Jackson Boulevard, Suite 1352
Chicago, IL   60604
(312) 427-6252
(800) 541-5454
The Foundation is dedicated to the detection, treatment, and cure of myasthenia gravis. MGF programs include
public and professional information and
education, services to patients, and a
reduced-cost prescription service. Publications include *Facts About MG For
Patients and Families* and *Myasthenia
Gravis—The Disease: A Case History.*

Myoclonus

Myoclonus Families United
1564 E. 34th Street
Brooklyn, NY   11234
(718) 252-2133
This small support group offers physician referrals and information. Publications include a self-help directory.

National Myoclonus Foundation
845 3rd Avenue, 14th Floor
New York, NY   10022
(212) 758-5656
The National Myoclonus Foundation
acts as an information clearinghouse
for people with this rare disorder.

Spinal Muscular Atrophy

Families of Spinal Muscular Atrophy
  (FSMA)
P.O. Box 1465
Highland Park, IL   60035
(708) 432-5551
FSMA provides patient support and promotes public awareness of the following
diseases: Werdnig-Hoffmann, Kugelberg-
Welander, benign congenital hypotonia,
and Aran-Duchenne-Type spinal muscular atrophy. FSMA serves as a referral
service, resource library, and parent
network, and also lends books and therapy equipment.

ORGAN TRANSPLANTS

American Council on Transplantation
700 N. Fairfax Street, Suite 505
Alexandria, VA   22314
(703) 836-4301
(800) ACT-GIVE (228-4483)
The Council offers information, referrals, and financial assistance to children
requiring a transplant.

American Transplant Association (ATA)
P.O. Box 822123
Dallas, TX   75382
(214) 339-7900
ATA helps transplant patients with re-
ferrals and financial aid.

Children's Transplant Association
P.O. Box 53699
Dallas, TX   75253
(214) 287-8484
The Association provides financial assistance to children for medical care,
transportation, and recovery. It runs
residences for patients and families in
Minneapolis, Minnesota, and Shreveport, Louisiana.

United Network for Organ Sharing
  (UNOS)
1100 Boulders Parkway, Suite 500
Richmond, VA   23225
(804) 330-8500
(800) 24-DONOR (243-6667)
UNOS has been established by law as
the official information clearinghouse
for organs used in American transplants.
The Network matches up patients who
need transplants with available organs,
and helps patients with the logistics of
preparing for surgery.

SHORT STATURE

Human Growth Foundation (HGF)
P.O. Box 3090
Falls Church, VA   22043
(703) 883-1773
(800) 451-6434
HGF is composed of parents of children who suffer growth problems. It operates nearly fifty local groups that offer support and information. HGF publishes a brochure called the *Growth Series* and newsletter, *Fourth Friday.*

Little People of America, Inc.
P.O. Box 9897
Washington, DC   20016
(301) 589-0730
Little People of America is dedicated to helping people of short stature and their families through fellowship, moral support, social programs, and the exchange of ideas and information. The LPA Medical Advisory Board helps members become better informed about their particular type of short stature. Publications include *Little People in America: A Social Dimension* and *My Child Is a Dwarf.* They publish a newsletter, *LPA Today.*

Parents of Dwarfed Children (PACT)
11524 Colt Terrace
Silver Spring, MD   20902
(301) 649-3275

PACT serves parents of short-statured children who have recently learned that their child has a form of dwarfism. They offer emotional support, factual information about medical services, educational programs, and introductions to local support groups.

SKIN DISORDERS

General Organizations

American Academy of Dermatology
P.O. Box 3116
Evanston, IL   60201-3116
(708) 869-3954
This professional society of physicians offers referrals to the public.

Acne

Acne Research Institute
1236 Somerset Lane
Newport Beach, CA   92260
(714) 722-1805
This group of physicians and researchers offers limited information and referrals to the public. The Institute publishes one brochure for consumers called *Let's Talk Cosmetics and Acne— A Treatable Disease.*

Congenital Port Wine Stain

National Congenital Port Wine Stain
  Foundation
125 E. 63rd Street
New York, NY   10021
(212) 755-3820
The Foundation serves the needs of individuals with a port wine stain. The
group sponsors and conducts counseling and self-help programs. Publications include a brochure called *The
National Foundation.*

Epidermolysis Bullosa

Dystrophic Epidermolysis Bullosa
  Research Association of America, Inc.
  (D.E.B.R.A.)
141 5th Avenue, Suite 7-South
New York, NY   10010
(212) 995-2220
D.E.B.R.A. provides information for patients and health professionals, and assists patients in finding medical care,
social services, and genetic counseling.
Publications include *Coping with Epidermolysis Bullosa in the Classroom:
An Informed and Sensitive Home/
School Partnership Makes the Difference; Facts About D.E.B.R.A.; Researchers Seek Cause of Enigmatic
Blistering Disorder;* and *Thin-Skinned
Kids.* A newsletter, *EB Currents,* is also
published.

Ichthyosis

Foundation for Ichthyosis & Related
  Skin Types (FIRST)
P.O. Box 20921
Raleigh, NC   27619-0921
(919) 782-5728
FIRST educates its members and the
public regarding medical, psychological,
and social aspects of ichthyosis. Publi-
cations include *Ichthyosis—An
Overview; Ichthyosis—The Genetics of
Its Inheritance;* and a newsletter,
Ichthyosis Focus.

Lice

National Pediculosis Association
P.O. Box 149
Newton, MA   02161
(617) 449-6487
The Association works to prevent lice
infestations and improper use of pesticides. Publications include *The Latest
Greatest Coloring Book about Lice,* developed for children in grades K–3, and
various lice-checking tools.

Psoriasis

National Psoriasis Foundation
6443 S.W. Beaverton Highway
Suite 210
Portland, OR   97221
(503) 297-1545

The Foundation offers referrals to physicians and support groups, distributes literature in schools and libraries, and funds research. A list of publications and audiovisuals is available. Their newsletter called *Bulletin* includes a question-and-answer column written by a physician.

Psoriasis Research Institute
600 Town and Country Village
Palo Alto, CA   94301
(415) 326-1848
The Institute offers counseling, biofeedback and other innovative treatments, as well as education for physicians and patients. Publications include research papers, brochures, and a newsletter.

Scleroderma

Scleroderma Federation, Inc.
1725 York Avenue, Room 29F
New York, NY   10128
(212) 427-7040
The Federation helps organize scleroderma support groups and provides telephone consultation for persons affected by scleroderma. Publications include *About Scleroderma* and *Understanding and Managing Scleroderma.*

United Scleroderma Foundation, Inc.
P.O. Box 350
Watsonville, CA   95077-0350
(408) 728-2202
(800) 722-HOPE (4673)

The United Scleroderma Foundation offers scleroderma patients and their families emotional and educational support. A publications catalog is available upon request. The Foundation publishes the *USF Newsletter.*

SLEEP DISORDERS

American Sleep Disorders Association
604 2nd Street, S.W.
Rochester, MN   55902
(507) 287-6006
Though primarily a scientific organization for professionals working in the field of sleep disorders, the Association will answer questions and make referrals on a limited basis.

National Association of Apnea Professionals (NAAP)
P.O. Box 4031
Waianae, HI   96792
(602) 239-4740
Apnea manifests itself in suspension of breathing for fifteen to twenty seconds, primarily during sleep. It is usually found in infants. NAAP, though an organization for sleep and health-care professionals, does offer information and referrals to the public. NAAP collects clinical and technical data on apnea and other sleep disorders.

VISUAL DISORDERS

SEE ALSO

the SPECIAL NEEDS, HANDICAPS, AND LEARNING DISABILITIES section of this chapter for additional organizations serving handicapped children.

General Organizations

American Academy of Ophthalmology
655 Beach Street
San Francisco, CA   94109
(415) 561-8500
This professional society offers referrals to the public.

American Council of the Blind (ACB)
1010 Vermont Avenue, N.W.
Suite 1100
Washington, DC   20005
(202) 393-3666
(800) 424-8666
ACB offers information and referrals on all aspects of blindness, legal consultation and representation to consumer advocates working on issues related to visual handicaps, and employment opportunity information. It offers an extensive list of publications in Braille, large print, and cassette formats available free or at a small charge. News and information are shared by members through the use of action-memo tapes,

a radio program, and a magazine, the *Braille Forum.*

American Council of the Blind Parents
14400 Cedar Road, Apt. 108
University Heights, OH   44121
(216) 381-1822
(800) 424-8666
This small affiliate of the American Council of the Blind comprises visually impaired parents and parents of visually impaired children. The Council offers a forum for discussing parent-child relationships and publishes a newsletter in large print called *Reflections.*

American Foundation for the Blind
15 W. 16th Street
New York, NY   10011
(212) 620-2000
(800) AF-BLIND (232-5463)
The Foundation works with more than one thousand schools and other organizations to provide programs for the blind. It creates *Talking Books,* operates a huge lending library in Braille,

and publishes numerous books, directories, and other materials. A list is available upon request. Also published is a newsletter, *AFB News*.

Association for Education & Rehabilitation of the Blind & Visually Impaired
206 N. Washington Street, Suite 320
Alexandria, VA 22314
(703) 548-1884
This group of educators and parents provides information and referrals to help give the blind a chance to become happy, contributing members of society.

Blind Children's Fund
230 Central Street
Auburndale, MA 02166-2399
(617) 332-4014
The Fund disseminates information and materials for blind infants and children up to the age of seven, their parents, and the professionals who work with them. A catalog of publications and audiovisuals is available, as is a newsletter, *VIP*.

Braille Institute
741 N. Vermont Avenue
Los Angeles, CA 90029
(213) 480-7580
The Institute publishes many books and educational materials in Braille. It operates divisions for preschoolers and students.

Helen Keller National Center for Deaf-Blind Youths & Adults
111 Middle Neck Road
Sands Point, NY 11050
(516) 944-8900
The Center is mainly devoted to the training of professionals who work with blind children and adults. It offers an information and referral service to parents.

National Association for Parents of the Visually Impaired (NAPVI)
P.O. Box 180806
Camden, NY 13316
(315) 245-3442
(800) 562-6265
NAPVI includes parents, professionals, and other persons dedicated to supporting the parents of visually impaired children. The Association provides bibliographies and lists of camps and other organizations that serve visually impaired children. Publications include *Take Charge! A Resource Guide for Parents of the Visually Impaired*. A list of publications and audiovisuals is available, as is a newsletter called *Awareness*.

National Association for Visually Handicapped
22 W. 21st Street
New York, NY 10010
(212) 889-3141

The Association provides referrals, counseling, and guidance to the partially sighted and their families. Informational booklets and brochures, large-print books for pleasure-reading, textbooks, and testing materials are available for adults and children. Ask for the NAVH publications catalog. Also published is a newsletter for children, *In-Focus,* and one for adults, *Seeing Clearly.*

National Children's Eye Care
   Foundation
1 Clinic Center, A3-108
9500 Euclid Ave.
Cleveland, OH   44195
(216) 444-0488
The Foundation sponsors an education campaign to inform parents, teachers, and children about the importance of eye care and early detection of eye problems. Brochures and a newsletter are also offered.

Ohio State University
Topaz Memorial Library of Vision
338 W. 10th Avenue
Columbus, OH   43210
(614) 422-1888
The Library provides reference and duplicating facilities. Its collection of over six thousand books, journals, pamphlets, bibliographies, and reports fo-

cuses on optometry and ophthalmology, optics, learning disabilities, visual physiology and perception, and pathology of the eye.

Recording for the Blind (RFB)
20 Roszel Road
Princeton, NJ   08540
(609) 452-0606
(800) 221-4792
RFB lends recorded educational books to borrowers who cannot read standard printed material. The RFB library contains 70,000 titles. Services are available to persons with a certified visual, physical, or specific learning disability that substantially limits reading.

Vision Foundation, Inc.
818 Mount Auburn Street
Watertown, MA   02172
(617) 926-4232
(800) 852-3029 (in Massachusetts)
Vision Foundation offers self-help programs for visually impaired and newly blind persons and those with progressively degenerative eye diseases. It maintains an information center. The Foundation produces a large-print and cassette newsletter called *Vision Resource Update*. It also publishes a vision resource list, a brochure titled *All About Vision,* and a book, *Coping with Sight Loss: The Vision Resource Book.*

Cataracts

Parents & Cataract Kids
179 Hunter's Lane
Devon, PA 19333
(215) 293-1917
(215) 721-9131
Parents and Cataract Kids offers referrals and support to families with children affected by cataracts. Publications include *Agencies to Contact for Your Visually Impaired Child, Understanding Congenital Cataracts,* and a newsletter called *In-Sight.*

Retinitis Pigmentosa

Association for Macular Diseases
210 E. 64th Street
New York, NY 10021
(212) 605-3719

The Association provides an information hotline, referrals, counseling programs, and support groups for children and adults suffering degenerative eye disease. It also publishes a newsletter.

RP Foundation Fighting Blindness
1401 Mount Royal Avenue, 4th Floor
Baltimore, MD 21217
(301) 225-9400
(301) 255-9409 (TDD)
(800) 638-2300
The Foundation studies retinitis pigmentosa, Usher syndrome, macular degeneration, and other retinal degenerative conditions. A catalog of publications and audiovisuals is available, as is a newsletter called *Fighting Blindness News.*

TERMINALLY ILL AND HOSPITALIZED CHILDREN

SEE ALSO

the Cancer and AIDS listings of this chapter and the LOSS OF A CHILD section in Chapter 7.

Association for the Care of Children's
  Health (ACCH)
7910 Woodmont Avenue, Suite 300
Bethesda, MD   20814
(301) 654-6549
ACCH comprises health professionals
and parents and is dedicated to enhancing the health and quality of life of
chronically ill and hospitalized children
and their families. It publishes a number of books and pamphlets as well as a
newsletter.

Brass Ring Society
314 S. Main
Ottawa, KS   66067
(913) 242-1666
The Society runs programs for terminally ill children, among them, a make-
a-wish project with participation by
airlines, hotels, and other services.

Children's Hospice International
1101 King Street, Suite 131
Alexandria, VA   22314
(703) 684-0330
(800) 242-4453
This group organizes support systems
for the families of seriously ill children
and families who have lost a child
through accident or violence. In addition, it serves as a clearinghouse for information and publishes audiocassette
tapes.

Children's Wish Foundation
  International
8215 Roswell Road, Bldg. 200
Suite 100
Atlanta, GA   30350
(404) 393-9474
This organization was established to
fulfill the wishes of seriously ill children younger than eighteen.

Coordinating Center for Home &
  Community Care, Inc. (CCHCC)
P.O. Box 613
Brightview Business Center
Millersville, MD   21108
(301) 987-1048 (Baltimore/Annapolis
  area)
(301) 621-7830 (Washington, DC, area)
CCHCC, through safe at-home treatment, provides chronically ill children
with an alternative to lengthy hospital
stays. The Center makes use of medical
facilities in the Baltimore/Washington
area, organizes discharge, and helps set
up and monitor quality care in the
home. In addition, it hosts workshops,
pinpoints home-care needs, offers technical assistance, and distributes educational pamphlets.

MAGIC Foundation
770 Alexandria Drive
Naperville, IL   60565
(708) 369-1605
(708) 383-0808

This group helps chronically ill children and their families through its networking activities. Families of children with similar medical disorders are brought together to share feelings and exchange information. MAGIC also serves as a medical information resource, offers educational seminars, and provides financial assistance where needed.

Mail for Tots
P.O. Box 8699
Boston, MA   02114
(617) 242-3538
Volunteers send letters of good cheer to very ill and handicapped children.

Make-a-Wish Foundation of America
4601 N. 16th Street, Suite 205
Phoenix, AZ   85016
(602) 234-0960
The Foundation grants wishes to terminally ill children younger than eighteen, attending to all logistical and financial arrangements. It publishes a quarterly newsletter, a number of free brochures, and several audiovisuals, including *Real People.*

National Hospice Organization
1901 N. Fort Myer Drive, Suite 307
Arlington, VA   22209
(703) 243-5900
This organization of agencies and individuals promotes hospice care, operates as an advocate, monitors legislation, provides hospice training, encourages medical institutions to teach hospice practices, and runs a reference library. It will make referrals over the telephone.

**Sick Kids Need Involved People, Inc.
  (SKIP)**
216 Newport Drive
Severna Park, MD   21146
(301) 261-2602
SKIP offers help, information, and education to families of children requiring specialized medical care. It fosters home-care for children relying on medical technology.

ALTERNATIVE AND HOLISTIC MEDICINE

American Holistic Medical Association
2002 Eastlake Avenue, E.
Seattle, WA   98102
(206) 322-6842
This professional society of physicians and students involved in holistic medicine will make referrals to the public. It publishes brochures and two books: *Nutritional Guidelines* and *Fitness Guidelines*.

Committee for Freedom of Choice in Medicine
1180 Walnut Avenue
Chula Vista, CA   92011
(619) 429-8200
(800) 227-4473

Keeps the public, physicians, and healers apprised of new techniques in alternative medicine. It makes referrals to consumers looking for a physician in their local area, and also publishes books, pamphlets, cassette tapes, and a magazine, *Choice*.

Touch for Health Foundation
1174 N. Lake Avenue
Pasadena, CA   91104
(818) 794-1181
Works to inform the public about health-promoting techniques involving kinesiology and acupressure. Publishes books, brochures, and a guide to practitioners called the *Touch for Health Directory*.

NUTRITION

If you need information on breastfeeding, infant formula, and the nutritional needs of infants, see Chapter 2 under INFANT CARE. For all other nutritional information, see below.

Some local health departments at the town, county, city, and state levels have offices that supply nutritional advice and literature to the public. If the national organizations listed below do not answer your questions satisfactorily, check the government offices section of your local telephone directory under Health Department. For referrals to local health offices, you can also check the STATE CHILD AND MATERNITY HEALTH DEPARTMENTS section at the end of this chapter.

If your questions concern the food served in schools, see School Food Services under the NUTRITION section.

SEE ALSO

the DISEASES AND DISORDERS section of this chapter under Allergies, Asthma, and Lung Diseases; Digestive Disorders (includes Celiac Disease and Ileitis/ Colitis); and Eating Disorders (includes Anorexia/Bulimia and Overeating).

General Information

American Association of Nutritional Consultants
1641 E. Sunset Road, Room B-117
Las Vegas, NV   89119
(702) 361-1132
The Association makes referrals on a limited basis.

American College of Nutrition
345 Central Park Avenue, Suite 207
Scarsdale, NY   10583
(914) 723-4247
This small group of professionals will refer you to physicians and nutritionists in your area.

American Dietetic Association
216 W. Jackson Boulevard, Suite 800
Chicago, IL   60606
(312) 899-0040
By far the largest organization of its type, this association of dietetic professionals can refer you to experts all over the country.

American Home Economics Association (AHEA)
1555 King Street
Alexandria, VA   22314
(703) 704-4600
AHEA offers referrals in response to questions about food and nutrition.

American Nutritionists Association (ANA)
6710 Bradley Boulevard
Bethesda, MD   20817
(301) 365-1622
This Association informs the public about proper nutrition and will provide referrals.

American School Food Service
  Association (ASFSA)
1600 Duke Street, 7th Floor
Alexandria, VA   22314
(800) 877-8822 (legislation hotline)
(800) 654-5425 (public relations)
Though primarily for food service personnel, ASFSA will provide information
on school food programs, nutrition, and
relevant legislation.

Beech-Nut Nutrition Hotline
Gerber Products Company
Johnson & Johnson Baby Products
(800) 523-6633
(800) 443-7237
(800) 526-3967

Child Nutrition Forum
1319 F Street, N.W., Suite 530
Washington, DC   20004
(202) 393-5060
This coalition of nutrition organizations
is a good source of information on
school lunches and government-funded
food programs for children.

Children's Nutrition Research Center
Baylor College of Medicine
1100 Bates Street
Houston, TX   77030
(713) 799-6006
Although not geared toward answering
questions from the public, this Center
may be helpful if you have very specific
questions about a nutritional problem.

Cooking for Survival
  Consciousness (CSC)
Box 26762
Elkins Park, PA   19117
(215) 635-1022
CSC distributes information about
cooking and good health, with particular attention to preventive health care,
diseases caused by diet, alternative
means of nourishment, malnutrition,
and low-meat diets. The organization
hosts banquets, tastings, and cooking
classes and publishes a guide/directory
and a journal.

Feingold Association of the United
  States (FAUS)
P.O. Box 6550
Alexandria, VA   22306
(703) 768-FAUS (3287)
Based on a nutritional program created
by Ben F. Feingold, this organization
believes that many symptoms, such as
sleep problems, aggression, overactivity,
and learning disabilities are often food-
related. This group offers educational
services for children and adults. FAUS
publishes pamphlets, books, and a
newsletter called *Pure Facts*.

Food & Drug Administration (FDA)
Office of Consumer Affairs
5600 Fishers Lane
Rockville, MD   20857
(301) 443-3170

The FDA answers consumers' inquiries and supplies information and publications concerning foods, drugs, and pharmaceuticals.

Food & Nutrition Information Center
National Agriculture Library, Room 304
10301 Baltimore Road
Beltsville, MD   20705-2351
(301) 504-5719
The Center answers questions and disseminates information, publications, and audiovisual materials on such topics as nutrition, food service management, food technology, and nutrition for adolescents, particularly teenage mothers. Publications are geared toward professionals, educators, and consumers.

Food Research & Action Center
National Anti-Hunger Coalition
1319 F Street, N.W., Suite 500
Washington, DC   20004
(202) 393-5060
Call or write for information on federal programs for low-income families to buy food and receive advice on good nutrition.

Human Nutrition Information Center
U.S. Department of Agriculture
Federal Building
6505 Belcrest Road
Hyattsville, MD   20782
(301) 436-8498
(301) 436-8617

The Center surveys the food consumption and food management practices of households and individuals and summarizes the data in reports. In addition, it publishes data on the nutritive content of food. The agency distributes information needed to improve the nutritional quality of American diets, and provides guidance to help people make the best use of food.

International Vitamin A Consultative Group (INVACG)
c/o International Life Sciences Institute
1126 16th Street, N.W.
Washington, DC   20036
(202) 659-9024
INVACG offers information on how to reduce the occurence of Vitamin A deficiency among human beings.

National Agricultural Library
National Agricultural Library Building
10301 Baltimore Boulevard
Beltsville, MD   20705
(301) 344-3755 (information desk)
Provides reference services to the public.

National Child Nutrition Project
1501 Cherry Street, 3rd Floor
Philadelphia, PA   19102
(215) 496-9003
Offers technical assistance to those concerned with federal health and nutrition programs for children in and out of school. Also offers educational materials for parents.

National Dairy Council
6300 North River Road
Rosemont, IL 60018
(708) 696-1020
Offers information about nutrition research, particularly concerning the nutritional value of dairy products.

Natural Foods Associates
P.O. Box 210
Atlanta, TX 75551
(214) 796-3612
Comprising consumers and professionals, this group offers books and magazines concerning natural foods and organic farming.

Nutrition Education Association
P.O. Box 20301
3647 Glen Haven
Houston, TX 77225
(713) 665-2946
This large group seeks to educate the public through providing a nutrition home study course, publications about fighting cancer through nutrition, and other materials.

Nutrition for Optimal Health
 Association (NOHA)
P.O. Box 380
Winnetka, IL 60093
(312) 835-5030
NOHA distributes information on the scientific basis of good nutrition, gives

cooking classes, and hosts educational seminars. It also maintains a tape library and publishes a cookbook, *Cooking for the Health of It,* and a rotation diet for allergies called *Enjoy Nutritious Variety.*

Oley Foundation
Albany Medical Center
214 Hun Memorial
Albany, NY 12208
(518) 445-5079
(800) 776-6539
The Foundation assists families who have a member on parenteral and/or enteral nutrition at home. It provides networking and a newsletter.

Price-Pottenger Nutrition Foundation
P.O. Box 2614
LaMesa, CA 92041
(619) 582-4168
Named after a physician and a dentist, this group maintains a library and resource file, and offers pamphlets, reprints of magazine articles, books, and videotapes on nutrition.

Society for Nutrition Education
1700 Broadway, Suite 300
Oakland, CA 94612
(415) 444-7133
The Society produces and sells educational publications and films.

173

Vitamin Information Bureau (VIB)
c/o Lifetime Learning
505 Chicago
Evanston, IL   60202
(708) 866-7770

Provides information on the role of vitamins in proper nutrition.

SCHOOL FOOD SERVICES
LISTED BY STATE

If you have questions about the nutritional value of food served in schools, the following offices will help you.

Alabama

Division of Federal Administrative
   Services
Gordon Persons Building
50 N. Ripley Street
Montgomery, AL 36130-3901
(205) 242-8225

Alaska

Department of Education
Food & Nutrition Service
P.O. Box F
Juneau, AK   99811-0500
(907) 465-2865

Arizona

Department of Education
Food & Nutrition Program
1535 W. Jefferson Street
Phoenix, AZ   85007
(602) 542-3362

Arkansas

Department of Education
Child Nutrition
Executive Building, Suite 404
2020 W. 3rd Street
Little Rock, AR   72205
(501) 371-2466

Child Nutrition Programs
P.O. Box 1437, Slot 705
Little Rock, AR   72203-9064
(501) 682-8867

California

Department of Education
Child Nutrition & Food Distribution
   Divisions
P.O. Box 944272
Sacramento, CA   94244-2720
(916) 445-0850

Colorado

Department of Education
Child Nutrition/Transportation Unit
201 E. Colfax Avenue, Room 209
Denver, CO   80203
(303) 866-6661

Department of Health
Child & Adult Care Food Program
Nutrition Section
4210 E. 11th Avenue
Denver, CO   80220
(303) 331-8349

Connecticut

Department of Education
Child Nutrition Programs
P.O. Box 2219
Hartford, CT   06145-2219
(203) 566-3195

Delaware

Department of Public Instruction
School Food Service
P.O. Box 1402
Dover, DE   19903
(302) 736-4718

District of Columbia

DC Public Schools
Food Service Branch
3535 V Street, N.E.
Washington, DC   20018
(202) 576-7400

Florida

Department of Education
Child Nutrition Programs
804 Florida Education Center
Tallahassee, FL   32399
(904) 359-6297

Georgia

Department of Education
School & Community Nutrition
   Division
Twin Towers E., Suite 1658
205 Butler Street, S.E.
Atlanta, GA   30334
(404) 651-9442

Hawaii

Department of Education
School Food Services
1106 Koko Head Avenue
Honolulu, HI   96816
(808) 732-5868

Idaho

Department of Education
Food Services Section
Len B. Jordan Building, Room 213
650 W. State Street
Boise, ID   83720
(208) 334-3106

Illinois

State Board of Education
Department of Child Nutrition
100 N. 1st Street
Springfield, IL   62777
(217) 782-2491

Indiana

Department of Education
Division of School Food & Nutrition
   Programs
State House, Room 229
Indianapolis, IN   46204
(317) 269-9540

Iowa

Department of Education
Food & Nutrition Bureau
Grimes State Office Building
Des Moines, IA   50319-0146
(515) 281-5356

Kansas

Department of Education
School Food Services
State Education Building
120 E. 10th Street
Topeka, KS   66612-1103
(913) 296-2276

Kentucky

Department of Education
Division of School Food Services
Capital Plaza Tower, 6th Floor
Frankfort, KY   40601
(502) 564-4770

Louisiana

Department of Education
Food & Nutrition Services
P.O. Box 94064
Baton Rouge, LA   70804-9064
(504) 342-3720

Maine

Department of Educational & Cultural
   Services
School Nutrition Programs
State House, Station 136
Augusta, ME   04333
(207) 289-5315

Department of Human Services
Bureau of Child & Family Services
State House, Station 11
Augusta, ME   04333
(207) 289-5060

Maryland

Department of Education
Nutrition & Transportation Services
   Office
Maryland State Education Building
200 W. Baltimore Street
Baltimore, MD   21201
(301) 333-2600

Massachusetts

Department of Education
Bureau of Nutrition Services
1385 Hancock Street, 2nd Floor
Quincy, MA   02169-5183
(617) 770-7248

Michigan

Department of Education
Food & Nutrition Services
P.O. Box 30008
Lansing, MI   48909
(517) 373-3314

Minnesota

Department of Education
Child Nutrition Section
Capitol Square Building, Room 951
550 Cedar Street
St. Paul, MN   55101
(612) 296-6986

Mississippi

Department of Education
Division of Child Nutrition
P.O. Box 771
Jackson, MS   39205-0771
(601) 359-2509

Missouri

Department of Elementary & Secondary
   Education
School Food Service
P.O. Box 480
Jefferson City, MO   65102
(314) 751-3526

Department of Health
Food & Nutrition Service
1730 E. Elm Street
Jefferson City, MO   65102
(314) 751-6204

Montana

Office of Public Instruction
Division of School Food Services
Capitol Building, Room 106
Helena, MT   59620
(406) 444-2501

Nebraska

Department of Education
Child Nutrition Programs
301 Centennial Mall S.
Lincoln, NE   68509
(402) 471-3567

Nevada

Department of Education
Child Nutrition Programs
Capitol Complex
Carson City, NV   89710
(702) 885-3117

New Hampshire

Department of Education
Bureau of Food & Nutrition Services
State Office Park S.
101 Pleasant Street
Concord, NH   03301
(603) 271-3646

New Jersey

Department of Education
Bureau of Child Nutrition Programs
Administrative Services
CN 500
Trenton, NJ   08625
(609) 984-1439

School Nutrition & Summer Food
   Services
(609) 984-0692

New Mexico

Department of Education
School Food Services
Education Building
300 Don Gaspar Avenue
Santa Fe, NM   87501-2786
(505) 827-6627

Health & Environment Department
Family Nutrition Section
P.O. Box 968
Santa Fe, NM   87504-0968
(505) 827-0020

New York

Office of Elementary & Secondary
   Education
Bureau of School Food Management
   & Nutrition
Education Building Annex, Room 761
Albany, NY   12234-0001
(518) 474-1765

U.S. Department of Agriculture
New York Summer & Child Care Office
252 7th Avenue, Section 5R
New York, NY   10001-7305
(212) 620-6307

North Carolina

Department of Public Education
Child Nutrition Division Services
217 W. Jones Street
Raleigh, NC   27603-1336
(919) 733-7162

North Dakota

Department of Public Instruction
Child Nutrition & Food Distribution
   Programs
State Capitol
Bismarck, ND   58505
(701) 224-2294

Ohio

Department of Education
School Food Services Division
Ohio Departments Building, Room 713
65 S. Front Street
Columbus, OH   43266-0308
(614) 466-2945

Oklahoma

Department of Education
Child Nutrition Programs
Oliver Hodge Memorial
   Education Building, Room 310
2500 N. Lincoln Boulevard
Oklahoma City, OK   73105-4599
(405) 521-3327

Department of Human Services
Food & Nutrition Services Unit
P.O. Box 25352
Oklahoma City, OK   73125
(405) 521-3581

Oregon

Department of Education
School Nutrition Programs &
   Commodity Distribution
700 Pringle Parkway, S.E.
Salem, OR   97310-0290
(503) 378-3579

Pennsylvania

Department of Education
Child Nutrition Program
P.O. Box 911
Harrisburg, PA   17126-0333
(717) 787-3186

Rhode Island

Department of Education
Office of School Food Services
Roger Williams Building
22 Hayes Street
Providence, RI   02908-5092
(401) 277-2712

South Carolina

Department of Education
Office of School Food Services
Rutledge Building, Room 304
1429 Senate Street
Columbia, SC   29201
(803) 734-8195

South Dakota

Department of Education & Cultural
   Affairs
Child & Adult Nutrition Services
Richard F. Kneip Building
700 Governors Drive
Pierre, SD   57501-2293
(605) 773-3413

H E A L T H

Tennessee

Department of Education
Child Nutrition Programs
Cordell Hull Building, Room 208
436 6th Avenue N.
Nashville, TN   37219-5338
(615) 741-2927

Department of Human Services
Community Services
Citizens Plaza Building, 14th Floor
400 Deadrick Street
Nashville, TN   37219
(615) 741-4953

Texas

Education Agency
School Lunch & Child Nutrition
   Programs
William B. Travis Building
1701 N. Congress Avenue
Austin, TX   78701-1494
(512) 463-8979

Department of Human Services
Food Service Division
P.O. Box 149030, Mail Code 65W
Austin, TX   78714-9030
(512) 450-3370

Utah

Office of Education
Child Nutrition Programs
250 E. 500 South Street
Salt Lake City, UT   84111
(801) 538-7682

Vermont

Department of Education
Child Nutrition Programs
State Office Building
120 State Street
Montpelier, VT   05602-2703
(802) 828-2447

Virginia

Department of Education
School Lunch Program
P. O. Box 6Q
Richmond, VA   23216-2060
(804) 225-2038

Washington

Department of Public Instruction
School Food Services
Mail Stop FG-11
Olympia, WA   98504
(206) 753-3580

West Virginia

Department of Education
Child Nutrition Programs
State Office Building 6
Room B-248
1900 Washington Streeet E.
Charleston, WV   25305
(304) 348-2708

Wisconsin

Department of Public Instruction
Food & Nutrition Service
P.O. Box 7841
Madison, WI   53707
(608) 266-3509

Wyoming

Department of Education
School Food Services
Hathaway Building, Room 284
2300 Capitol Avenue
Cheyenne, WY   82002
(307) 777-6282

Department of Health & Social Services
Division of Health & Medical Services
Hathaway Building, Room 456
2300 Capitol Avenue
Cheyenne, WY   82002
(307) 777-7494

Puerto Rico

Department of Education
School Lunchroom Division
P.O. Box 759
Hato Rey, PR   00919
(809) 754-0790

SCHOOL HEALTH

American School Health Association
7263 State Route 43
Kent, OH   44240
(216) 678-1601
This Association of school health professionals offers information, makes re ferrals, and publishes *A Pocketguide to Health and Health Problems in School Physical Activities.*

National Association of School
   Nurses, Inc.
Lamplighter Lane
P.O. Box 1300
Scarborough, ME   04074
(207) 883-2117
An association for professionals dedicated to promoting the health of schoolchildren. It will answer questions and make referrals on topics related to school health.

National School Health Education
   Committee
c/o American College of Preventive
   Medicine
1015 15th Street, N.W., Suite 403
Washington, DC   20005
(202) 789-0003

This professional society offers limited information and referrals.

MENTAL HEALTH

Aside from the national organizations listed below that help with mental health problems, the State Mental Health offices at the end of the MENTAL HEALTH section are a good source of referrals to help in your community.

SEE ALSO

the SPECIAL NEEDS, HANDICAPS, AND LEARNING DISABILITIES section of this chapter, which lists additional groups that help children suffering from mental problems.

Chapter 9, Adolescence, describes organizations working with juvenile delinquents and other troubled children.

The SELF-HELP CLEARINGHOUSES section of Chapter 13 lists services that refer you to local support groups helping with mental health problems.

AUTISM

Autism Services Center (ASC)
Douglas Education Building
10th Avenue and Bruce Street
Huntington, WV   25701
(304) 525-8014

The Autism Services Center helps those who care for and about autistic people of all ages. In addition to information and referral services for parents, the ASC offers limited direct services such as a summer camp program, monitored employment, apartment living, and training for independent living. The Center distributes a reading list of approximately twenty-five books, monographs, fact sheets, and periodicals on the care and teaching of autistic individuals.

Autism Society of America
1234 Massachusetts Avenue, N.W.
Suite 1017
Washington, DC   20005
(202) 783-0125
The Autism Society of America offers an information and referral service to help parents understand autism and develop skills for dealing with autistic children. The Society helps find Federal and State programs and education services, camps, group homes, and other residential services, diagnostic and evaluation centers, community services, sources of funds, and names of other parents in a general geographic area with the same problems. The Society distributes pamphlets, books, parent handbooks, and publishes a newsletter called *Advocate*.

Behavior Research Institute, Inc. (BRI)
240 Laban Street
Providence, RI   02909
(401) 944-1186
A residential school/treatment center for children and adults with severe be-

havior disorders, including autism, BRI administers individualized behavior modification and special education programs from its facility in Providence and group homes in nearby Massachusetts. The Institute offers information services and distributes films, videotapes, and brochures.

Institute for Child Behavior Research (ICBR)
4182 Adams Avenue
San Diego, CA   92116
(714) 281-7165
The Institute serves as an information clearinghouse on the treatment of autism and other learning and behavior problems. It will answer questions, provide consultation, and make referrals. It publishes a quarterly newsletter on autism, a diagnostic checklist for diagnosing children with severe behavior disorders, plus books, bibliographies, critical reviews, reprints, and videotapes. A publications list is available.

National Autism Hotline
Autism Services Center
Douglass Education Building
10th Avenue and Bruce Street
Huntington, WV   25701
(304) 525-8014
This hotline disseminates information on the treatment of autism and coping strategies for parents.

New York State Society for Autistic
  Children
10 Colvin Avenue, Suite 203
Albany, NY   12206
(518) 459-1418
The Society helps those concerned with
the well-being of autistic children and
can provide a directory of appropriate
services.

Princeton Child Development Institute
300 Cold Soil Road
Princeton, NJ   08540
(609) 924-6280

The Institute provides education, treatment of autistic children, and training
of family members as therapists. It also
takes an interest in behavioral disorders, childhood psychoses, applied behavior analysis, and computer-assisted
instructional programs for autistic and
developmentally-delayed children. The
Institute publishes abstracts, articles,
brochures, bibliographies, and reprints.

COMPULSIVE BEHAVIORS

SEE ALSO

the Phobias and Anxiety Disorders listings in this chapter.

Kleptomaniacs/Shoplifters Anonymous
114 W. 70th Street
New York, NY   10023
(212) 724-4067
A self-help group for people with compulsive stealing problems.

Obsessive-Compulsive Anonymous
P.O. Box 215
New Hyde Park, NY   11040
(516) 741-4901
The group uses the twelve-step method
pioneered by Alcoholics Anonymous to

help people suffering from obsessive-
compulsive behavior.

Obsessive-Compulsive (O.C.)
  Foundation, Inc.
P.O. Box 9573
New Haven, CT   06535
(203) 772-0565
(203) 772-0575
O.C. provides information and referrals
to those suffering from obsessive-
compulsive behaviors.

Shoplifters Anonymous
Metroplitan-Mt. Sinai Hospital
900 S. 8th Street, Room 156
Minneapolis, MN 55404
(612) 925-4860
A self-help group for shoplifters who want to stop. Will provide guidelines for starting a group.

DEPRESSION

**Depression & Related Affective
    Disorders Association, Inc.**
Johns Hopkins Hospital, Meyer 4-181
1601 N. Wolfe Street
Baltimore, MD 21205
(301) 987-5756
(301) 955-4647
(301) 955-3246
The Association is a group of patients, professionals, and families who are concerned about clinical and manic depression. It offers education, support services, and treatment. Publications include an annotated bibliography, a handbook for developing and maintaining affective disorder support groups, and a number of brochures. A newsletter called *Smooth Sailing* is published quarterly.

Depressives Anonymous
329 E. 62nd Street
New York, NY 10021
(212) 689-2600
Serves people whose anxiety and depression lead to adverse behavioral problems. The group's meetings, with professional participation, seek to help change one's approach to life. It publishes a newsletter and provides guidelines for starting new groups.

**Manic & Depressive Support Group,
    Inc. (M.D.S.G.)**
P.O. Box 1747
Madison Square Station
New York, NY 10159
(212) 533-6374
A support group organized for manic-depressives and depressives, their friends and families, M.D.S.G runs rap sessions, holds lectures, publishes a newsletter, and helps new groups get started.

**National Depressive & Manic-Depressive
    Association**
Merchandise Mart, Box 3395
Chicago, IL 60654
(312) 939-2442
An association of nearly one hundred fifty self help groups for depressives, manic-depressives, and their families. It educates the public on the biochemical causes of depression, runs an annual conference, and provides guidelines for starting a group.

National Foundation for Depressive
  Illness, Inc.
P.O. Box 2257
New York, NY   10116
(212) 620-0098
(800) 248-4344

Provides referrals to support groups for
depressed persons.

SUICIDE AND DESTRUCTIVE BEHAVIOR

SEE ALSO

the JUVENILE DELINQUENCY section in Chapter 9.

American Association of Suicidology
2459 S. Ash Street
Denver, CO   80222
(303) 692-0985
The Association is a clearinghouse for
information on suicide. It makes referrals to hotlines and support groups
throughout the country, provides
guidelines for setting up prevention
programs within the schools, and will
mail free pamphlets.

Institute for Studies of Destructive
  Behaviors
1041 S. Menlo Avenue
Los Angeles, CA   90006
(213) 386-5111
The Institute provides a twenty-four-
hour hotline, counseling and special
youth services, substance-abuse pro-

grams, and a residential program for
ex-offenders. The Institute researches
destructive behaviors, prevention strategies, and physiological causes of depression. It publishes a bibliography of
books and journal articles about suicide
and a monthly newsletter, *Intervention*.

National Adolescent Suicide Hotline
(800) 621-4000 (24-hour hotline)
Used by teenagers considering suicide,
the Hotline may also be used by their
parents.

National Committee on Youth Suicide
  Prevention
825 Washington Street
Norwood, MA   02062
(617) 769-5686
The Committee is a volunteer network
of parents and professionals who offer

advice on preventing suicide among the young.

Teen Suicide Prevention Taskforce
P.O. Box 76463
Washington, DC   20013
(214) 642-6000
The Taskforce publishes *Teen Suicide Prevention,* maintains a list of speakers and relevant publications, and assists suicide prevention programs.

Toughlove
See the JUVENILE DELINQUENCY section of Chapter 9.

Youth Suicide National Center
204 E. 2nd Avenue, Suite 203
San Mateo, CA   94401
(415) 347-3961

Consultants at the Center will help community and state educational institutions set up suicide prevention programs. They offer a catalog of publications on suicide.

Wisconsin Clearinghouse
P.O. Box 1468
Madison, WI   53701
(608) 263-2797
(800) 262-6243 (health information)
The Clearinghouse has a free catalog of publications on mental health and substance abuse. In addition, for one dollar, this source will send a pamphlet called *Adolescence and Depression: Dealing with the Crisis of Suicide.*

MENTAL HEALTH AND MENTAL RETARDATION

SEE ALSO

the Center for Infant Study in the INFANT CARE section of Chapter 2.

American Association on Mental Retardation
1719 Kalorama Road, N.W.
Washington, DC   20009
(202) 387-1968

The Association disseminates information on the cause, treatment, and prevention of mental retardation.

Association for Children with
  Retarded Mental Development, Inc.
162 5th Avenue, 11th Floor
New York, NY   10010
(212) 741-0100
Runs a number of programs for developmentally and mentally disabled children and young adults, including family support, rehabilitation, job placement, and social centers. In addition, it operates group homes, offers training and conferences, and publishes a newsletter.

Association for Retarded Citizens of the
  United States (ARC)
P.O. Box 6109
Arlington, TX   76005
(817) 640-0204
ARC is a national organization of over 160,000 volunteers, parents, educators, and professionals dedicated to the welfare of retarded persons. The group informs the public about prevention of mental retardation and the needs and potentials of retarded persons. It develops employment opportunities and improved residential services, and provides counseling and guidance. ARC publishes a wide variety of materials on child development, education, day-care, employment, community organizations, and vocational rehabilitation.

Bethesda Lutheran Home (BLH)
Bethesda Lutheran Home
  Foundation, Inc.
700 Hoffmann Drive
Watertown, WI   53094
(414) 261-3050
BLH offers respite care for the mentally retarded, maintaining fourteen group homes and a main campus. In addition, it offers family counseling and outreach seminars. Their Christian Resource Center supplies information on facilities and resources for the mentally retarded nationwide.

Canadian Association for Community
  Living (CACL)
G. Allan Roeher Institute
Kinsmen Building
York University Campus
4700 Keele Street
Downsview, ON   M3J 1P3
Canada
(416) 661-9611
With over four hundred chapters, CACL heads up the effort to ensure that people with mental handicaps can live, learn, and work in normal environments within the community. CACL aids parents trying to integrate their mentally handicapped children into the traditional school system. It publishes bulletins, books, and audiovisual materials on such issues as deinstitutionalization, education, and recreational activities.

National Clearinghouse on Family
  Support & Children's Mental Health
Portland State University
P.O. Box 751
Portland, OR   97207-0751
(800) 628-1696
The Clearinghouse assists families of
children with serious emotional disorders and also aids mental-health care
professionals. It runs a toll-free telephone service, produces fact sheets on
pertinent issues, and maintains a state-
by-state resource file and a computerized database of information.

National Institutes of Mental Health
  (NIMH)
Public Inquiries
5600 Fishers Lane, Room 15C-05
Rockville, MD   20857
(301) 443-4513
NIMH gathers information on mental
illness and responds to inquiries from
the public. A list of NIMH publications,
several of which are in Spanish, is
available. NIMH puts out fliers and

pamphlets such as *Caring about Kids*
and *Plain Talk*. Single copies are free.

National Mental Health Association
  (NMHA)
1021 Prince Street
Alexandria, VA   22314-2971
(703) 684-7722
NMHA provides information, offers
emotional support and guidance for
families, and helps school systems develop programs for children with mental illnesses. It also lobbies for Federal
mental health legislation and stimulates
funding for research. Its publications
catalog lists pamphlets and booklets on
all aspects of mental health and mental
illnesses. *Focus,* its newsletter, comes
out quarterly.

President's Committee on Mental
  Retardation
330 Independence Avenue, S.W.
Washington, DC   20201
(202) 619-0634
Responds to inquiries and serves as an
advocate for mentally retarded persons.

PHOBIAS AND ANXIETY DISORDERS

SEE ALSO

Compulsive Disorders under the MENTAL HEALTH section of this chapter.

Agoraphobics in Motion (A.I.M.)
605 W. Eleven Mile Road
Royal Oak, MI   48067
(313) 547-0400
The eighteen self-help groups within this organization use discussion sessions, relaxation therapies, and field trips to help relieve the problems arising from anxiety, panic, and fear.

Anxiety Disorder Association of
   America
6000 Executive Boulevard, Suite 200
Rockville, MD   20852-3883
No phone number listed.
This organization is for patients, families, and professionals concerned with phobias and associated disabilities. It publishes the *National Treatment Directory* and a bimonthly newsletter.

Council on Anxiety Disorders
P.O. Box 17011
Winston-Salem, NC   27116
(919) 722-7760
The self-help groups within the Council work to overcome anxiety, panic, fear, obsessive-compulsive behavior, and post-traumatic problems through mutual support, advocacy, and education.

Phobia Society of America
133 Rollins Avenue, Suite 4B
Rockville, MD   20852
(301) 231-9350

Offers information and referrals for people who suffer from phobia and panic attacks.

PSYCHIATRIC DISORDERS AND SOCIAL DISABILITY

American Academy of Child &
   Adolescent Psychiatry
3615 Wisconsin Avenue, N.W.
Washington, DC   20016
(202) 966-7300
The Academy provides diagnosis, research, and treatment of mental illnesses affecting children, adolescents, and their families. It operates as a clearinghouse for information, lobbies government agencies to influence public policy, and runs workshops. The Academy publishes *Facts for Families,* a fact sheet on mental illnesses affecting youngsters; *The Journal of the American Academy of Child and Adolescent Psychiatry;* and a quarterly newsletter for members only.

Canadian Friends of Schizophrenics
95 Barber Green Road, Suite 309
Don Mills, ON   M3C 3E9
Canada
(416) 445-8204
Comprising more than sixty chapters throughout Canada, Friends provides support, information, and advocacy for families and friends of schizophrenics. They publish a newsletter and guidelines for starting new groups.

Emotions Anonymous
P.O. Box 4245
St. Paul, MN   55104
(612) 647-9712
The fifteen hundred chapters of this national organization each meet to provide members with support and hope using a twelve-step process toward emotional well-being. The umbrella organization publishes a quarterly newsletter, runs a pen pal service, and provides group start-up guidelines.

**Information Exchange on Young Adult
   Chronic Patients, Inc. (TIE)**
P.O. Box 1945
New City, NY   10956
(914) 634-0050
TIE comprises young adult chronic patients eighteen to thirty-five who have required mental health services for at least two years or suffer from a psychiatric disorder or social disability. TIE provides information, sponsors research on mental illness, and provides consultation and training.

National Alliance for the Mentally Ill
2101 Willson Boulevard, Apartment 302
Arlington, VA   22201-3008
(703) 524-7600
This national network of nearly one thousand self-help groups is for families of those suffering from severe mental illness. It provides information and emotional support, publishes a newsletter, and supplies guidelines for founding a group.

**National Mental Health Consumer
   Self-Help Clearinghouse**
311 S. Juniper Street, Room 902
Philadelphia, PA   19107
(215) 735-2481
The Clearinghouse helps found self-help groups for mental health patients by providing technical assistance, referrals, and information on a range of topics including fundraising and drop-in centers.

Parents Involved Network
311 S. Juniper Street, Room 902
Philadelphia, PA   19107
(215) 735-2465
Groups within this network help parents of children with severe emotional problems. They provide a forum for discussion, exchange of information, and suggestions for coping.

Reassurance to Each (REACH)
328 E. Hennepin Avenue
Minneapolis, MN   55414
(612) 331-6840
(800) 862-1799 (in Minnesota)
REACH self-help groups, for friends and families of the mentally ill, supply information and emotional support. They also provide guidelines for starting new groups.

Recovery, Inc.
802 N. Dearborn Street
Chicago, IL   60610
(312) 337-5661
The nearly one thousand chapters of
Recovery teach techniques to control
will, temperament, fear, and nervous-
ness. Recovery publishes a newsletter
and group-development guidelines.

Young Emotions Anonymous
P.O. Box 4245
St. Paul, MN   55104
(612) 647-9712
This program run by Emotions Anonymous is for teenagers who need to develop a well-balanced emotional state.

STATE MENTAL HEALTH OFFICES

Alabama

Department of Mental Health & Mental
   Retardation
P.O. Box 3710
Montgomery, AL   36193-5001
(205) 271-9208

Alaska

Division of Mental Health &
   Developmental Disabilities
P.O. Box H-04
Juneau, AK   99811-0620
(907) 465-3370

Arizona

Office of Community Behavioral Health
   Services
Birch Hall
411 N. 24th Street
Phoenix, AZ   85008
(602) 220-6478

Arkansas

Division of Mental Health Services
4313 W. Markham Street
Little Rock, AR   72205-4096
(501) 686-9164

California

Department of Mental Health
Gregory Bateson Building, Room 151
1600 9th Street
Sacramento, CA   95814
(916) 323-8173

Colorado

Division of Mental Health
Fort Logan Mental Health Center
2nd Floor
3520 W. Oxford Avenue
Denver, CO   80236
(303) 762-4073

Connecticut

Department of Mental Health
90 Washington Street
Hartford, CT   06106
(203) 566-3650
(203) 566-3651

Delaware

Division of Alcoholism, Drug Abuse &
  Mental Health
C. T. Building
Delaware State Hospital
1901 N. DuPont Highway
New Castle, DE   19720
(302) 421-6107

District of Columbia

Commission on Mental Health Services
A Building, Room 105
2700 Martin Luther King Avenue S.E.
Washington, DC   20032
(202) 373-7166

Florida

Alcohol, Drug Abuse & Mental Health
  Program Office
Building VI, Room 183
1317 Winewood Boulevard
Tallahassee, FL   32301
(904) 488-8304

Georgia

Division of Mental Health, Mental
  Retardation & Substance Abuse
878 Peachtree Street N.E., Suite 304
Atlanta, GA   30309-3999
(404) 894-6307

Hawaii

Mental Health Division
P.O. Box 3378
Honolulu, HI   96801
(808) 548-6335

Idaho

Bureau of Mental Health
450 W. State Street
Boise, ID   83720
(208) 334-5531

Illinois

Department of Mental Health &
  Developmental Disabilities
401 S. Spring Street
Springfield, IL   62706
(217) 782-7179

Indiana

Department of Mental Health
117 E. Washington Street
Indianapolis, IN   46204-3647
(317) 232-7844

Iowa

Division of Mental Health, Mental
  Retardation, & Developmental
  Disabilities
Hoover State Office Building, 5th Floor
1300 E. Walnut Street
Des Moines, IA   50319
(515) 281-6003

Kansas

Mental Health & Retardation Services
Docking State Office Building
5th Floor
915 Harrison Street
Topeka, KS   66612
(913) 296-3471

Kentucky

Division of Mental Health
Health Services Building
275 E. Main Street
Frankfort, KY   40621
(502) 564-4448

Louisiana

Office of Mental Health
P.O. Box 3776
Baton Rouge, LA   70821
(504) 342-6717

Maine

Bureau of Mental Health
State House, Station 40
Augusta, ME   04333
(207) 289-4230

Maryland

Mental Hygiene Administration
Herbert R. O'Conor State Office
  Building
Room 416-A
201 W. Preston Street
Baltimore, MD   21201
(301) 225-6611

Massachusetts

Department of Mental Health
Hoffman Building
160 N. Washington Street
Boston, MA   02114
(617) 727-5600

Michigan

Department of Mental Health
Lewis Cass Building, 5th Floor
320 S. Walnut Street
Lansing, MI   48913
(517) 373-3500

Minnesota

Mental Health Division
444 Lafayette Road
St. Paul, MN   55155-3828
(612) 296-4497

Mississippi

Department of Mental Health
1101 Robert E. Lee Building
239 N. Lamar Street
Jackson, MS   39201
(601) 359-1288

Missouri

Department of Mental Health
P.O. Box 687
Jefferson City, MO   65102
(314) 751-3070

Montana

Mental Health Bureau
1539 11th Avenue
Helena, MT   59620
(406) 444-3639

Nebraska

Office of Community Mental Health
P.O. Box 94728
Lincoln, NE   68509
(402) 471-2851

Nevada

Division of Mental Hygiene/Mental
  Retardation
Capitol Complex
Carson City, NV   89710
(702) 885-5943

New Hampshire

Mental Health Services
State Office Park S.
105 Pleasant Street
Concord, NH   03301-6523
(603) 271-5041
(800) 852-3345 (in New Hampshire)

New Jersey

Division of Mental Health & Hospitals
13 Roszel Road
Princeton, NJ   08540
(609) 987-0888

New Mexico

Mental Health Bureau
P.O. Box 968
Santa Fe, NM   87503
(505) 827-2647

New York

Mental Health Office
44 Holland Avenue
Albany, NY   12229
(518) 474-4403

North Carolina

Division of Mental Health, Mental
  Retardation & Substance Abuse
  Services
Albemarle Building, Room 1112
325 N. Salisbury Street
Raleigh, NC   27611
(919) 733-7011

North Dakota

Division of Mental Health Services
State Capitol
Bismarck, ND   58505
(701) 224-2766

Ohio

Department of Mental Health
State Office Tower, Room 1180
30 E. Broad Street
Columbus, OH   43226-0414
(614) 466-2337

Oklahoma

Department of Mental Health
P.O. Box 53277, Capitol Station
Oklahoma City, OK   73152
(405) 271-7474

Pennsylvania

Office of Mental Health
P.O. Box 2675
Harrisburg, PA   17105
(717) 787-6443

Rhode Island

Division of Mental Health &
   Community Support Services
Aime J. Forand Building
600 New London Avenue
Cranston, RI   02920
(401) 464-2350

South Carolina

Department of Mental Health
P.O. Box 485
Columbia, SC   29202
(803) 734-7780

Tennessee

Department of Mental Health & Mental
   Retardation
Doctors Building, 6th Floor
706 Church Street
Nashville, TN   37219-5393
(615) 741-3107

Texas

Division of Mental Health Services
P.O. Box 12668
Austin, TX   78711-2668
(512) 465-4510

Utah

Division of Mental Health
P.O. Box 45500
Salt Lake City, UT   84145
(801) 538-4270

Vermont

Department of Mental Health
Waterbury Office Complex
103 S. Main Street
Waterbury, VT   05676
(802) 241-2610

Virginia

Department of Mental Health,
   Mental Retardation & Substance
   Abuse Services
P.O. Box 1797
Richmond, VA   23214
(804) 786-3921

Washington

Mental Health Division
Mail Stop OB-42F
Olympia, WA   98504
(206) 753-5414

West Virginia

Office of Behavioral Health Services
State Office Building 3, Room 451

1800 Washington Street E.
Charleston, WV   25305
(304) 348-0627

Wisconsin

Office of Mental Health
P.O. Box 7851
Madison, WI   53707
(608) 266-3249

Wyoming

Mental Health Program
Hathaway Building, Room 358
2300 Capitol Avenue
Cheyenne, WY   82002-0710
(307) 777-7115

SPECIAL NEEDS, HANDICAPS, AND LEARNING DISABILITIES

GENERAL ORGANIZATIONS

Administration on Developmental
   Disabilities
Hubert H. Humphrey Building
200 Independence Avenue, S.W.
Room 351-D
Washington, DC   20201
(202) 245-2888
This office answers questions, sends
out publications on developmental disabilities, and publishes a directory of
services that train people with handicapping conditions.

American Psychological Association
   (APA)
1200 17th Street, N.W.
Washington, DC   20036
(202) 955-7710
The APA is the largest professional
organization for psychologists in the

SEE ALSO

the MENTAL HEALTH section of this chapter, which lists additional groups aiding special needs children.

The DISEASES AND DISORDERS section of this chapter under Hearing and Speech Problems and Visual Disorders lists organizations serving children with these impairments.

The STATE CHILD AND MATERNITY HEALTH DEPARTMENTS section at the end of this chapter lists referral services for children with special needs, handicaps, and learning disabilities.

The Breastfeeding and Infant Nutrition listings of Chapter 2 include organizations that help children whose disabilities are due to the formula they drank as infants.

The SELF-HELP CLEARINGHOUSES section of Chapter 13 lists offices that can refer you to local mutual aid groups.

The ERIC Clearinghouse on Handicapped and Gifted Children, listed in the GIFTED CHILDREN section of Chapter 8, provides information on programs for the handicapped.

Peterson's Summer Opportunities for Kids and Teenagers, described in the OTHER SUMMER OPPORTUNITIES section of Chapter 11, lists programs for handicapped children.

United States. Among its many services, the APA provides information and referrals to the public on learning disabilities, mental health, and many other topics. The PsycINFO database produced by the APA is the most comprehensive index to psychological literature available today.

Case Western Reserve University
Mental Development Center
11130 Bellflower Road
Cleveland, OH 44106
(216) 368-3540
The Center conducts research and provides mental health services to the developmentally disabled and learning impaired of all ages. Information and referrals are available by phone.

Center for Hyperactive Child
Information, Inc. (CHCI)
P.O. Box 66272
Washington, DC   20035-6272
(703) 920-7495
CHCI provides information on the medical and educational requirements of hyperactive children to parents, teachers, and others.

Center on Human Policy
Syracuse University
724 Comstock Avenue
Syracuse, NY   13244-4230
(315) 443-3851
The Center works to assure that disabled persons are incorporated in educational, vocational, rehabilitative, and residential services. It serves as a clearinghouse of information for parents and professionals on issues such as research, deinstitutionalization, cost of services, and resources.

Clearinghouse on the Handicapped
330 C Street, S.W., Room 3132
Washington, DC   20202
(202) 732-1245
The Clearinghouse answers questions, provides information on government services for the disabled, and sends out several publications.

Coordinating Council for Handicapped
Children (CCHC)
20 E. Jackson Boulevard, Room 900
Chicago, IL   60604
(312) 939-3513
(312) 939-3519 (TDD)
CCHC runs weekly training classes and community workshops on special education rights of disabled children, including a training project which helps parents become group leaders within their communities. It offers two manuals, *How to Organize an Effective Parent/Advocacy Group and Move Bureaucracies* and *How to Get Services by Being Assertive*, plus booklets and fact sheets on special education rights, tax benefits, and special services.

Devereux Foundation
P.O. Box 400
Devon, PA   19333
(215) 964-3000
(800) 345-1292
The Foundation is a national organization of day and residential treatment centers for mentally, emotionally, and developmentally handicapped children and adults. It answers questions, provides consultation, hosts seminars, and publishes catalogs, reprints, periodicals, and films.

Disabilities Research & Information
  Coalition
3530 Stone Way N.
Seattle, WA   98103
(206) 548-0215
The Coalition supplies disabled people
and their families with information on
many issues directly affecting their
lives. It also publishes a magazine.

Early Childhood Intervention
  Clearinghouse
830 S. Spring Street
Springfield, IL   62704
(217) 785-1364
(800) 852-4302 (in Illinois)
The Clearinghouse offers resource materials on young children with special
needs and their families, answers telephone inquiries, and provides reason-
ably priced services to Illinois residents.
It publishes a quarterly newsletter entitled *Early Intervention.*

Easter Seal Society for Disabled
  Children & Adults, Inc.
The Children's Center
2800 13th Street, N.W.
Washington, DC   20009
(202) 232-2342
The Society serves children from birth
to age three having moderate to severe
physical and/or mental handicaps. The
program offers diagnostic, educational,
and prescriptive services that include

parent training, occupational, physical,
and speech-language therapy.

Information, Protection, & Advocacy
  Center for Handicapped Individuals,
  Inc. (IPACHI)
300 I Street, N.E., Suite 202
Washington, DC   20002
(202) 547-8081
(202) 547-6556 (TTY)
IPACHI protects the legal and human
rights of persons with developmental
disabilities and/or mental illnesses and
connects handicapped individuals with
available resources and services. It publishes *Access Washington, A Guide to
Metropolitan Washington for the Physically Disabled,* the *Directory of Services
for Handicapping Conditions,* and an
annual directory of summer programs
for handicapped children.

Institute for Basic Research in
  Developmental Disabilities (IBR)
1050 Forest Hill Road
Staten Island, NY   10314
(718) 494-0600
IBR performs research in autism,
Alzheimer's, epilepsy, fragile X syndrome, and the fundamental scientific
issues underlying all developmental disabilities. Findings are published in
medical and professional journals, and
reprints of these reports are available
from IBR.

Institutes for the Achievement of Human Potential
8801 Stenton Avenue
Philadelphia, PA   19118
(215) 233-2050
The Institute serves children and parents of children who have suffered brain damage causing extreme disabilities, as well as children who seem to be underachieving. It studies teaching methods, counsels parents, offers educational courses, and runs a number of schools.

Intervention with Parents & Children Together, Inc. (PACT)
106 E. Chase Street
Baltimore, MD   21202
(301) 539-7228
PACT provides evaluation and treatment for infants from birth through age two having possible or diagnosed developmental problems. PACT's other services include day-care and therapeutic play groups, parent support and education, and programs for developmentally delayed parents and parents at risk for abuse. It puts out a newsletter, designed for parents and service providers, four times a year.

Life Services for the Handicapped, Inc.
25 E. 21st Street
New York, NY   10010
(212) 420-1500
Life Services was established to aid physically handicapped individuals when their families can no longer care for them. Its Discretionary Trust and Life Service program enables parents, children, and other relatives to leave resources to the disabled without risking loss of public entitlements. The organization works in conjunction with existing community rehabilitation services.

National Association of Developmental Disabilities Councils (NADDC)
1234 Massachusetts Avenue, N.W.
Suite 103
Washington, DC   20005
(202) 347-1234
NADDC serves as an information clearinghouse on developmental disabilities and educates the public about the needs of the disabled. It publishes a newsletter, reports, and monographs.

National Center for Youth with Disabilities (NCYD)
University of Minnesota
Box 72
UMHC Harvard Street at E. River Road
Minneapolis, MN   55455-9940
(612) 626-2825
(800) 333-6293
NCYD offers information to individuals and programs providing services to youth suffering from chronic illnesses or disabilities. The Center runs a com-

puter-based reference library of educational materials and information on training and education resources, model programs and projects, and consultants. NCYD publishes a quarterly newsletter and annotated bibliographies on topics such as educational and vocational decision-making skills, substance abuse, transition from pediatric to adult health care, and sexuality and disability.

National Easter Seal Society
70 E. Lake Street
Chicago, IL   60601
(312) 726-6200
(312) 726-4258 (TDD)
The Society's extensive facilities, programs, and affiliates provide rehabilitation services to persons with disabilities and their families. A list of publications is available.

National Foundation of Dentistry for the Handicapped (NFDH)
1600 Stout Street
Suite 1420
Denver, CO   80202
(303) 573-0264
Established to promote dentistry and dental hygiene for the handicapped, the Foundation's "Campaign of Concern" currently services nearly forty thousand people. The group trains health workers and the disabled, makes referrals to dentists, matches the indigent with volunteer dentists, and runs a portable

dental system for the homebound. It publishes a number of manuals, including *Guidelines for Using Fluorides Among Handicapped Persons,* as well as other audiovisual and written materials.

National Information Center for Children & Youth with Handicaps (NICCYH)
P.O. Box 1492
Washington, DC   20013
(703) 893-6061
(703) 893-8614 (TDD)
(800) 999-5599
NICCYH helps parents, teachers, and others working with disabled children and youth. The Center provides informational kits and publications, answers inquiries, makes referrals, and offers technical assistance. The *NICCYH News Digest* comes out three times a year.

National Information Clearinghouse for Infants with Disabilities & Life-Threatening Conditions
1244 Blossom Street, 5th Floor
Columbia, SC   29208
(803) 777-4435
(800) 922-9234
(800) 922-1107 (in South Carolina)
The Clearinghouse offers free information on services for infants with disabilities and life-threatening conditions. It makes referrals to services that offer diagnosis and treatment, early intervention, parent support and training,

financial and legal assistance, education, respite care, and special-needs adoption.

Pathfinder Resources, Inc.
2324 University Avenue West, Suite 105
St. Paul, MN   55114
(612) 647-6905
Pathfinder helps children with chronic conditions by informing parents and professionals of the options available. Pathfinder publishes a quarterly newsletter in conjunction with the Maternal and Child Health Bureau.

Pediatric Projects, Inc.
P.O. Box 571555
Tarzana, CA   91357
(818) 705-3660
Pediatric Projects distributes books and toys for children and teens to help them understand health-care procedures and to accept disabled individuals. A list is available.

Rehabilitation Institute
Division of Development & Corporate
   Relations
Learning Resources Center (LRC)
261 Mack Boulevard
5th Floor, West End
Detroit, MI   48201
(313) 745-9860
LRC provides information on all aspects of physical disability and rehabilitation. It helps professionals, persons with dis-

abilities, and families of the disabled. Its Patient Education Library contains journals, books, and leaflets on such subjects as self-care management, legislation, architectural barriers, ways to prevent future health complications, and travel. The Media Center provides information on patient and family educational needs through audiocassettes, videotapes, and films. The Medical Library, for the professional, has a collection of current information on physical medicine and rehabilitation. In addition, LRC publishes bibliographies and brochures, answers inquiries, provides reference and literature-searching services, and makes referrals to other sources of information.

Sibling Information Network
Connecticut University Affiliated
   Program on Developmental
   Disabilities
991 Main Street
East Hartford, CT   06108
(203) 282-7050
The Network, comprising siblings, parents, health professionals, and educators, helps people concerned with the needs of families of disabled persons. It operates as an information clearinghouse, giving members access to audiovisual aids, bibliographies, membership directories, research assistance, and sibling program resources, and also publishes a quarterly newsletter.

University of Alabama at Birmingham
Sparks Center for Developmental &
    Learning Disorders
P.O. Box 313, University Station
Birmingham, AL   35294
(205) 934-5471
The Sparks Center educates and trains
professionals who work with developmentally disabled invididuals, provides
services for the disabled, and promotes
basic research in human development.
It responds to inquiries, makes referrals, provides technical assistance to
agencies and consumer organizations,
distributes information on current research, and runs workshops. It publishes abstracts, articles, reviews, and
reprints.

Utah State University
Developmental Center for Handicapped
    Persons
Logan, UT   84322-6800
(801) 750-1980
The Center trains personnel needed to
provide services to the developmentally
disabled. It also offers advisory and consulting services, supplies information
on current research, evaluates special
education programs, hosts seminars
and workshops, and makes referrals.
The Center publishes research and
training papers, a journal, articles, critical reviews, annual reports, and
reprints.

CEREBRAL PALSY

American Academy for Cerebral Palsy
    & Developmental Medicine
P.O. Box 11086
Richmond, VA   23230-1086
(804) 282-0036
This organization of health-care
providers offers referrals to the public.

Canadian Cerebral Palsy Association
    (CCPA)
40 Dundas Street W., Suite 222
Toronto, Ontario   M5G 2C2
Canada
(416) 979-7923
CCPA works to integrate persons with
cerebral palsy into society through a
variety of educational activities. It helps
form support groups, distributes information, and makes referrals.

United Cerebral Palsy Associations, Inc.
7 Penn Plaza, Suite 804
New York, NY   10001
(212) 268-6655
(800) USA-1UCP (872-1827)
This federation has approximately two
hundred state and local affiliates in the
United States. Support services, information, and referrals are available free
to the public. A publications catalog is
available.

DYSLEXIA

National Institute of Dyslexia
P.O. Box 10487
Rockville, MD   20850
(301) 424-8263
The Institute operates a preschool and elementary school, conducts research on classroom strategies, and distributes information to the community at large. It publishes fact sheets, reports, and a newsletter.

Orton Dyslexia Society
724 York Road
Baltimore, MD   21204
(301) 296-0232
(800) ABC-D123 (222-3123)
The Orton Dyslexia Society promotes research, shares knowledge, and encourages appropriate teaching. A publications catalog is available. The Society's newsletter *Perspectives on Dyslexia* is published quarterly.

SPECIAL EDUCATION

American Council on Rural Special
   Education
Miller Hall 359
Western Washington University
Bellingham, WA   98225
(206) 676-3576
Established to improve services to handicapped students and agencies working with them and to enlarge edu-cational opportunities, the Council also offers professional development and job training, makes referrals, and dis-tributes information.

Kids on the Block, Inc.
9385-C Gerwig Lane
Columbia, MD   21046
(301) 290-9095
(800) 368-KIDS (5437)
"Kids" is an instructional method used in the classroom to teach children about disabilities and differences through a one-to-one dialog with pup-pets. Kids on the Block, a coalition of nearly one thousand community-based programs, ensures laws are followed giving disabled children the opportunity to be educated with nondisabled chil-dren.

LEARNING DISABILITIES

Adventures in Movement for the
   Handicapped, Inc. (AIM)
945 Danbury Road
Dayton, OH   45420
(513) 294-4611
AIM helps individuals with visual or hearing handicaps, emotional, or learn-ing disabilities achieve their highest po-tential through specialized exercise movements. AIM distributes a book en-titled *Adventures in Movement,* a film called *Maybe Tomorrow,* and a free brochure.

Association for Children & Adults with
   Learning Disabilities (ACLD)
4156 Library Road
Pittsburgh, PA   15234
(412) 341-1515
ACLD offers free information and referrals to anyone. It publishes a newsletter, *ACLD Newsbriefs,* and distributes
books, abstracts, and indexes of information about learning disabilities.

Children with Attention Deficit
   Disorder (C.H.A.D.D.)
1859 Pine Island Road, Suite 185
Plantation, FL   33322
(305) 384-6869
(305) 792-8100
C.H.A.D.D. consists of nearly sixty chapters dedicated to supplying parents,
teachers, and concerned professionals
with information and support. A
newsletter is published as are guidelines on starting self-help groups.

Council for Exceptional Children (CEC)
1920 Association Drive
Reston, VA   22091
(703) 620-3660
The CEC provides a wide variety of educational, informational, and support
services for persons concerned with the
education of exceptional children. The
Council maintains an information center on the education of handicapped
children, including those with learning
disabilities, and also publishes materials

and a publications catalog. Due to the
wide range of materials available from
this group, specify your interest in
learning disabilities when you contact
them.

Council for Learning Disabilities (CLD)
P.O. Box 40303
Overland Park, KS   66204
(405) 325-4842
CLD improves the quality of education
and general well-being of people with
learning disabilities through teacher education programs and special education. It will answer questions and make
referrals. In addition, it publishes
Learning Disabilities Quarterly and a
biannual newsletter.

Feingold Association of the United
   States
See General Information in the
NUTRITION section of this chapter.

International Imagery Association (IIA)
22 Edgecliff Terrace
Yonkers, NY   10705
(914) 476-1208
(914) 423-5291
IIA encourages the use of imagery
research in the treatment of learning
disabilities, pain, neuroses, and psycho-
somatic disorders. It provides consultation, advice, and makes referrals. Its
publications include newsletters and a
bibliography, as well as reports, journal
articles, and critical reviews.

Learning Disabilities Association of
America (LDA)
4156 Library Road
Pittsburgh, PA   15234
(412) 341-8077
LDA, an organization of parents and
professionals with over 775 chapters,
serves individuals with learning disabilities by educating the public about the
learning disabled and promoting research, treatment, education, and employment. It makes referrals, publishes
a number of news bulletins and a bimonthly newsletter, and hosts an annual conference. LDA's library includes
educational brochures, research reports,
technical and general purpose books,
and teaching handbooks, over five hundred of which are available through
mail order.

Learning Disabilities Network
LD Information Clearinghouse
30 Pond Park Road
Hingham, MA   02043
(617) 740-2327
The Network provides educational and
support services for learning-disabled
persons, their families, and concerned
professionals. It answers questions,
makes referrals, supplies information
on current research, and publishes the
Educational Therapy Guidebook.

National Center for Learning
Disabilities (NCLD)
99 Park Avenue, 6th Floor
New York, NY   10016
(212) 687-7211
NCLD publishes a guide listing state-
by-state resources for the learning disabled, an annual report, and a
magazine sent to those who make inquiries in writing.

University of Missouri at Kansas City
School of Education
Division of Reading & Special
Education
Educational Building
52nd and Holmes Streets
Kansas City, MO   64110
(816) 276-1545
The School of Education studies reading instruction and education, basic
skill development, testing, language and
dialect, instructional methods, tutoring
materials, learning disabilities, and behavioral disorders. It responds to inquiries and makes referrals.

PARENT SUPPORT GROUPS

CAPP National Resource Parent Center
Federation for Children with Special
Needs
95 Berkeley Street, Suite 104
Boston, MA   02116
(617) 482-2915

CAPP helps parents acquire the skills and knowledge needed to assume a greater role in caring for their handicapped children and to work with health professionals in developing programs and policies.

Coalition for Handicapped Americans Information Network (CHAIN)
933 High Street, Suite 106
Worthington, OH   43085
(614) 431-1307
CHAIN, a coalition of parents, disabled persons, and professional organizations, offers information, support, and networking for parent training programs and local parent and family support services. It also provides assistance for parents of recently diagnosed disabled infants and children.

Fetal Alcohol Syndrome Network
158 Rosemont Avenue
Coatesville, PA   19320
(215) 384-1133
The Network confronts the symptoms of fetal alcohol syndrome, including behavioral problems, mental retardation, and learning disabilities. Most members are foster or adoptive parents, though birth parents are welcome. It publishes a newsletter.

Parent Educational Advocacy Training Center (PEATC)
228 S. Pitt Street, Suite 300
Alexandria, VA   22314
(703) 836-2953
(703) 836-3026 (TDD)
(800) 869-6782 (in Maryland, Virginia, and West Virginia)
The Center encourages teamwork between parents of exceptional children and their schools by teaching parents to be effective advocates. The Center publishes a quarterly newsletter and the book *Negotiating the Special Education Maze: A Guide for Parents and Teachers.*

Parentele
5538 N. Pennsylvania Street
Indianapolis, IN   46220
(317) 259-1654
Parentele, a national coalition of volunteer parents and friends of persons with disabilities, offers comprehensive information on issues affecting the lives of people needing special health care. The quarterly newsletter *Crisscross* contains articles about programs and services as well as organization activities.

Parents Helping Parents (PHP)—
A Family Resource Center for Children with Special Needs
535 Race Street, Suite 220
San Jose, CA   95126
(408) 288-5010

PHP is a coalition of volunteer parents, professionals, and counselors concerned with the problems of special-needs families. The organization is divided into groups focusing on a particular disability, including Autism, Cleft Lip/Palate, Intensive Care Nursery Support Parent (ICNSP), Parents of Down Syndrome (PODS), and SODC (Siblings of Disabled Children). PHP publishes a quarterly newsletter.

Pilot Parent Partnerships

2150 E. Highland, Room 105
Phoenix, AZ   85016
(602) 468-3001

Pilot Parent Partnerships links parents of disabled children with trained parent volunteers who can empathize with their feelings and problems. The Partnership makes referrals, maintains a resource directory and lending library, offers workshops for parents, and puts out a bimonthly newsletter.

SPECIAL PRODUCTS

ABLEDATA

Newington Children's Hospital
181 E. Cedar Street
Newington, CT   06111
(203) 667-5405 (voice and TDD)
(800) 344-5405 (voice and TDD)

ABLEDATA, run by the Adaptive Equipment Center of Newington Children's Hospital, maintains an up-to-date database listing over fifteen thousand commercially available products made by nearly two thousand manufacturers. The database offers detailed descriptions of products used for every facet of independent living, including communication, personal care, recreation, and transportation.

Activating Children Through Technology (ACTT)

Western Illinois University
27 Horrabin Hall
Macomb, IL   61455
(309) 298-1014

ACTT offers a microcomputer program that helps children from birth through age six debilitated by serious structural and functional handicaps. ACTT publishes a quarterly newsletter and sells ACTT curriculum, ACTT Starter Kit, software, and other special-education materials.

Children for Special Education Technology

1920 Association Drive
Reston, VA   22091
(703) 620-3660
(800) 873-TALK (8255)

Provides information on helping handicapped children using technology.

National Support Center for Persons
with Disabilities (NSCPD)
P.O. Box 2150
Atlanta, GA 30055
(404) 988-2676
(800) 426-2133 (voice and TDD)
IBM Corporation founded NSCPD to
teach health-care professionals, educators, and individuals how technology
can improve the quality of life for the
disabled person in the school, home,
and at work. Though NSCPD does not
diagnose or prescribe, it provides information on how computers can aid people with vision and hearing problems,
speech impairments, learning disabilities, mental retardation, and mobility
problems. It makes referrals to sources
that can supply more details.

SPORTS

Achilles Track Club (ATC)
356 W. 34th Street
New York, NY 10001
(212) 967-6496
A club for disabled runners aided by
volunteer coaches. Coaching by mail is
available for those outside the New
York City area.

American Blind Bowling Association
67 Bame Avenue
Buffalo, NY 14215
(716) 836-1472

Though an association for those eighteen and older, it will answer questions
and make referrals.

American Blind Skiing Foundation
610 S. William Street
Mt. Prospect, IL 60056
(708) 255-1739
Volunteer instructors teach the blind
skier cross-country skiing, the giant
slalom, and downhill skiing, and ac-
company them to ski areas in Michigan,
Wisconsin, and Colorado.

American Deaf Volleyball Association
300 Roxborough Street
Rochester, NY 14619
(716) 475-6838
Offers camps, programs, and training
for hearing-impaired children and
adults.

American Hearing Impaired Hockey
Association
1143 W. Lake Street
Chicago, IL 60607
(312) 829-2250
For hearing-impaired males age eleven
to twenty-six, the Association runs the
Stan Mikita Hockey School on an annual basis.

American Wheelchair Bowling
Association
N54 W15858 Larkspur Lane
Menomonee Falls, WI 53051
(414) 781-6876

The Association offers information and makes referrals for those confined to a wheelchair who have an interest in bowling. It also hosts competitions, bestows awards, and maintains a hall of fame. It publishes the book *Wheelchair Bowling*.

Blind Outdoor Leisure Development (BOLD)
P.O. Box 6
Aspen, CO   81612
(303) 925-7567
BOLD helps found skiing, skating, camping, biking, fishing, and many other outdoor activity clubs for blind people.

Blind Sports
1939 16th Avenue
San Francisco, CA   94116
(415) 681-1939
Fosters sports leagues for children and adults, runs charitable programs, helps supply equipment, and publishes rule books for sports for the blind.

Handicapped Scuba Association
116 W. El Portal, Suite 104
San Clemente, CA   92672
(714) 498-6128
Trains instructors, sponsors trips and lectures, and promotes scuba diving for the handicapped.

National Amputee Golf Association
P.O. Box 1228
Amherst, NH   03031
(603) 673-1135
Runs prosthetic seminars, sponsors tournaments, and awards scholarships to promote golf for amputees.

National Deaf Bowling Association
9244 E. Mansfield Avenue
Denver, CO   80237
(303) 771-9018
Sponsors tournaments and distributes awards.

National Deaf Women's Bowling Association
33 August Road
Simsbury, CT   06070
(203) 651-8234
Information and referrals are offered by this group.

National Foundation for Happy Horsemanship for the Handicapped
P.O. Box 195
Rockland, DE   19732
(302) 658-4567
The Foundation lets the handicapped participate in horse riding by offering clinics and rehabilitation programs. It also maintains a library and speakers' bureau.

National Foundation of Wheelchair
Tennis
940 Calle Amanecer, Suite B
San Clemente, CA   92672
(714) 361-6811
Runs a Junior Wheelchair Sports Camp
for children seven to eighteen who are
disabled. Publishes educational manuals
and videotapes.

National Handicapped Sports (NHS)
1145 19th Street, N.W., Suite 717
Washington, DC   20036
(301) 652-7505
NHS helps the handicapped participate
in athletics, focusing particularly on
skiing, aerobics, and general fitness. It
produces videotapes and manuals for
aerobic exercise and the *Adaptive Ski
Manual*.

National Sports Center for the Disabled
(NSCD)
P.O. Box 36
Winter Park, CO   80482
(303) 726-5514
NSCD offers recreational opportunities
for disabled persons in the Colorado
Rockies. The program challenges disabled persons to do what was thought
to be undoable in skiing, rafting, climbing, and many other activities. NSCD
publishes a biannual newsletter and
brochure on handicapped skiing.

National Wheelchair Athletic
Association
1604 E. Pikes Peak Avenue
Colorado Springs, CO   80909
(719) 635-9300
Holds regional track and field, swimming, weightlifting, and other tournaments for wheelchair athletes. It
publishes a number of rule books.

National Wheelchair Basketball
Association
110 Seaton Building
University of Kentucky
Lexington, KY   40506
(606) 257-1623
Runs basketball tournaments and
presents awards for wheelchair-bound
athletes, and also publishes an annual
directory and a rule book.

National Wheelchair Softball
Association
1616 Todd Court
Hastings, MN   55033
(612) 437-1792
Hosts tournaments and runs seminars.

Ski for Light
1455 W. Lake Street
Minneapolis, MN   55408
(612) 827-3232
Offers information and referrals to encourage cross-country skiing and other
athletic endeavors for visually impaired
and disabled people.

Special Olympics International
1350 New York Avenue, N.W., Suite 500
Washington, DC   20005
(202) 628-3630
For the mentally retarded ages eight
and up, the Special Olympics conducts
training and competition in more than
twenty sports. Every four years there is
international competition in the Summer and Winter Special Olympic
Games.

U.S. Amputee Athletic Association
P.O. Box 560686
Charlotte, NC   28256
(704) 598-0407
Helps athletes participate in competitions in air weapons, basketball, bicycling,
lawn bowling, Ping Pong, swimming,
track and field, and weightlifting.

U.S. Association for Blind Athletes
33 N. Institute
Brown Hall, Suite 015
Colorado Springs, CO   80903
(719) 630-0422
Hosts competitions for blind athletes,
including national championships, and
publishes *Directory of Organization
Representatives* and a rule book.

U.S. Blind Golfer's Association
300 Cirondelet Street
New Orleans, LA   70130
(504) 522-3203
Offers information and referrals.

U.S. Cerebral Palsy Athletic Association
   (USCPAA)
34518 Warren Road, Suite 264
Westland, MI   48185
(313) 425-8961
USCPAA offers athletes with cerebral
palsy competitions in many different
sports, and publishes *USCPAA Classification and Rules Manual* as well as informational pamphlets.

U.S. Deaf Skiers Association
8980 Rossman Highway
Diamondale, MI   48821
(517) 646-6811 (TDD)
Hosts competitions and selects and
trains deaf skiers for international competition.

Wheelchair Motorcycle Association
101 Torrey Street
Brockton, MA   02401
(508) 583-8614
The Association raises funding and
oversees research and testing of off-
road cycles for the disabled. It also
provides consultation, informative literature, and an audiovisual program.

TRAVEL

Handicapped Travel Club
211-A Creekside
McHenry, IL   60050
(312) 253-1931

For both disabled and ablebodied people who travel in recreational vehicles to explore the United States. Publishes a newsletter and a membership directory.

Travel Information Service (TIS)
Moss Rehabilitation Hospital
1200 W. Tabor Road
Philadelphia, PA   19141-3099
(215) 456-9000
(215) 456-9602 (TDD)

TIS maintains files on travel for the disabled, including such topics as accessibility, accomodations, cruises, restaurants, and transportation within the United States and abroad. TIS will make referrals to travel agencies, airlines, and other groups offering special services to disabled people. A nominal fee is requested to cover handling expenses for information sent through the mail.

REHABILITATION

American Occupational Therapy
   Association, Inc. (AOTA)
1383 Piccard Drive, Suite 301
Rockville, MD   20850-4375
(301) 948-9626
(800) THE-AOTA (843-2682)
A professional association for occupational therapists, AOTA maintains a thirty-five-hundred-volume library and will provide research information on relevant topics.

American Physical Therapy Association
1111 Fairfax Street
Alexandria, VA   22314
(703) 684-2782
This professional association offers consulting and referral services.

Canadian Rehabilitation Council for the
   Disabled (CRCD)
45 Sheppard Avenue E., Suite 801
Willowdale, ON   M2N 5W9
Canada
(416) 250-7490
CRCD offers referrals, film and publications lists, a bimonthly newsletter, and a quarterly journal.

National Rehabilitation Information
   Center (NARIC)
8455 Colesville Road, Suite 935
Silver Spring, MD   20910-3319
(301) 588-9284
(800) 346-2742
NARIC offers information and referrals on disability and rehabilitation. Anyone

visiting the Center has access to all the library's resources. NARIC also publishes a newsletter on disability and rehabilitation.

Rehabilitation Services Administration
Mary E. Switzer Building
330 C Street, S.W.
Washington, DC   20202
(202) 732-1282

The Administration oversees federally funded vocational rehabilitation programs for physically and mentally disabled individuals. It will answer questions and make referrals for professionals and the general public.

PHARMACEUTICALS

When the pediatrician prescribes an unfamiliar drug for a child, we often want detailed information about its effectiveness, potential side effects, and effects when taken with other medications. If you have questions your first step should be a call to the pediatrician or local pharmacist. In the unusual circumstance that they do not satisfy your need for information, the organizations listed below may be able to help.

Another excellent source of drug information is the *Physicians' Desk Reference,* a book available at many libraries.

Below, the first part of this section, General Information Sources, describes the major trade and professional organizations concerned with pharmaceuticals. The second part, Pharmaceutical Companies, lists the firms that manufacture most of the pharmaceuticals in the United States.

GENERAL INFORMATION SOURCES

American Pharmaceutical Association (APhA)
2215 Constitution Avenue, N.W.
Washington, DC   20037
(202) 628-4410 (Library)
(202) 429-7538 (Education Services)

APhA is the largest professional society of pharmacists in the United States. Although primarily for professional pharmacists, the society's library will answer limited questions from the general public.

American Society of Hospital
  Pharmacists International
4630 Montgomery Avenue
Bethesda, MD   20814
(301) 657-3000
This professional society produces the
International Pharmaceutical Abstracts,
a database of technical information. If
you require this type of information,
the Association will tell you who can
provide a search of their database.

Canadian Pharmaceutical Association
1785 Alta Vista Drive, 2nd Floor
Ottawa, Ontario   K1G 3Y6
Canada
(613) 523-7877
This professional society will answer
limited questions from the public concerning all aspects of pharmaceuticals.

Generic Pharmaceutical Industry
  Association (GPIA)
200 Madison Avenue, Suite 2404
New York, NY   10016
(212) 683-1881
The GPIA is a national association of
independent manufacturers and distrib-
utors of generic prescription pharmaceuticals. It provides educational and
technical information to physicians,
pharmacists, and consumers about
generic pharmaceuticals.

Pharmaceutical Manufacturers
  Association (PMA)
1100 15th Street, N.W., Suite 900
Washington, DC   20005
(202) 835-3400
The PMA is a trade association of more
than one hundred firms that discover,
develop, and produce prescription
drugs. The Association's members produce most of the prescription drugs
used in the United States. The group
answers questions from the public and
publishes consumer-oriented materials
on drug use and abuse and on other aspects of drug use and health.

PHARMACEUTICAL COMPANIES

Most of the pharmaceuticals sold in the
United States are manufactured by these
firms:

Abbott Laboratories
Abbott Park
North Chicago, IL   60064
(708) 937-6100

Adria Laboratories
P.O. Box 16529
Columbus, OH   43216-6269
(614) 764-8100

Alcon Laboratories, Inc.
6201 S. Freeway
P.O. Box 6600
Fort Worth, TX   76134
(817) 293-0450

Allergan, Inc.
2525 Dupont Drive
Irvine, CA   92713
(714) 752-4500

Altana Inc.
60 Baylis Road
Melville, NY   11747
(516) 454-7677

Alza Corporation
950 Page Mill Road
P.O. Box 10950
Palo Alto, CA   94303-0802
(415) 494-5000

American Home Products Corporation
685 3rd Avenue
New York, NY   10017
(212) 878-5000

Anaquest
2005 W. Beltline Highway
Madison, WI   53713-2318
(608) 273-0019

B. F. Ascher & Company, Inc.
15501 W. 109th Street
Lenexa, KS   66219
(913) 888-1880

Astra Pharmaceutical Products, Inc.
50 Otis Street
Westboro, MA   01581
(508) 366-1100

Barnes-Hind, Inc.
810 Kifer Road
Sunnyvale, CA   94086
(408) 736-5462

Beecham Laboratories
501 5th Avenue
Bristol, TN   37620
(615) 764-5141

Berlex Laboratories, Inc.
300 Fairfield Road
Wayne, NJ   07470
(201) 694-4100

Boehringer Ingelheim
   Pharmaceuticals, Inc.
900 Ridgebury Road
Ridgefield, CT   06877
(203) 798-9988

Boots Company (USA) Inc.
300 Tri State International, Suite 200
Lincolnshire, IL   60015
(312) 405-7400

Bristol-Myers Company
345 Park Avenue
New York, NY   10154
(212) 546-4000

Bristol-Myers U.S. Pharmaceuticals &
   Nutritional Group
2400 W. Lloyd Expressway
Evansville, IN   47721
(812) 429-5000

Burroughs Wellcome Co.
3030 Cornwallis Road
Research Triangle Park, NC   27709
(919) 248-3000

Carter-Wallace, Inc.
767 5th Avenue
New York, NY   10153
(212) 758-4500

Central Pharmaceuticals, Inc.
120 E. 3rd Street
Seymour, IN   47274
(812) 522-3915

Ciba-Geigy Corporation
Pharmaceuticals Division
556 Morris Avenue
Summit, NJ   07901
(201) 277-5000

Colgate-Hoyt Laboratories
1 Colgate Way
Canton, MA   02021
(617) 821-2880

Connaught Laboratories, Inc.
Route 611, P.O. Box 187
Swiftwater, PA   18370
(717) 839-7187

Critikon, Inc.
4110 George Road
P.O. Box 22800
Tampa, FL   33630-2800
(813) 887-2000

Cutter Biological
4th and Parker Streets
P.O. Box 1986
Berkeley, CA   94701
(415) 420-5000

E. I. Du Pont de Nemours & Company
1007 Market Street
Wilmington, DE   19898
(302) 774-1000

Erbamont N.V.
Soundview Plaza
1266 Main Street
Stamford, CT   06902
(203) 967-4882

Ethicon, Inc.
Route 22
Somerville, NJ   08876
(201) 218-0707

Ferndale Laboratories, Inc.
780 W. Eight Mile Road
Ferndale, MI   48220
(313) 548-0900

Fisons Corporation
Jefferson Road
Rochester, NY   14603
(716) 475-9000

E. Fougera & Company
60 Baylis Road
Melville, NY   11747
(516) 454-7677

Genetech, Inc.
460 Point San Bruno Boulevard
South San Francisco, CA   94080
(415) 266-1000

Glaxo Inc.
5 Moore Drive, Box 13408
Research Triangle Park, NC   27709
(919) 248-2100

Hoechst-Roussel Pharmaceuticals Inc.
Route 202-206 N.
Somerville, NJ   08876-1258
(201) 231-2000

Hoffman-La Roche Inc.
340 Kingsland Street
Nutley, NJ   07110
(201) 235-5000

ICI Pharmaceuticals Groups
Route 202 and New Murphy Road
P.O. Box 751
Wilmington, DE   19897
(302) 575-3000

IOLAB Corporation
500 IOLAB Drive
Claremont, CA   91711
(714) 624-2020

Janssen Pharmaceutica, Inc.
40 Kingsbridge Road
Piscataway, NJ   08854
(201) 524-9591

Johnson & Johnson
1 Johnson & Johnson Plaza
New Brunswick, NJ   08933
(201) 524-0400

Knoll Pharmaceuticals
30 N. Jefferson Road
Whippany, NJ   07981
(201) 887-8300

Lederle Laboratories
1 Cyanamid Plaza
Wayne, NJ   07470
(201) 507-7300

Eli Lilly & Company
Lilly Corporate Center
Indianapolis, IN   46285
(317) 276-2000

Marion Laboratories, Inc.
9300 Ward Parkway
P.O. Box 8480
Kansas City, MO   64114
(816) 966-4000

McNeil Pharmaceutical
Spring House, PA   19477
(215) 628-5000

Merck & Co., Inc.
126 E. Lincoln Avenue
P.O. Box 2000
Rahway, NJ   07065
(201) 574-4000

Merck Sharp & Dohme
Sumneytown Pike
West Point, PA   19486
(215) 661-5000

Merrell Dow Pharmaceuticals Inc.
10123 Alliance Road
P.O. Box 429553
Cincinnati, OH   45242
(513) 948-9111

Miles Laboratories, Inc.
1127 Myrtle Street
P.O. Box 340
Elkhart, IN   46515
(219) 264-8111

Miles Pharmaceuticals
400 Morgan Lane
West Haven, CT   06516
(203) 937-2000

Organon Inc.
375 Mt. Pleasant Avenue
West Orange, NJ   07052
(201) 325-4500

Ortho Diagnostic Systems, Inc.
Route 202
Raritan, NJ   08869
(201) 218-8000

Ortho Pharmaceutical Corp.
U.S. Route 202 S.
Raritan, NJ   08869
(201) 218-6000

Parke-Davis
201 Tabor Road
Morris Plains, NJ   07950
(201) 540-2000

Penick Corporation
158 Mount Olivet Avenue
Newark, NJ   07114
(201) 621-2806

Pfizer Inc.
235 E. 42nd Street
New York, NY   10017
(212) 573-2323

Pharmacia Inc.
800 Centennial Avenue
P.O. Box 1327
Piscataway, NJ   08855-1327
(201) 457-8000

The Procter & Gamble Company
P.O. Box 599
Cincinnati, OH   45201
(513) 983-1100

The Purdue Frederick Company
100 Connecticut Avenue
Norwalk, CT   06856
(203) 853-0123

Reed & Carnrick
1 New England Avenue
Piscataway, NJ   08854
(201) 981-0070

Reid-Rowell, Inc.
901 Sawyer Road
Marietta, GA   30062
(404) 578-9000

A. H. Robins Company
1407 Cummings Drive
Richmond, VA   23261
(804) 257-2000

Roerig
235 E. 42nd Street
New York, NY   10017
(212) 573-2323

Rorer Central Research
800 Business Center Drive
Horsham, PA   19044
(215) 956-5000

Rorer International Pharmaceuticals
1300 Office Center Drive
Fort Washington, PA   19034
(215) 283-6000

Rorer Pharmaceutical Corporation
500 Virginia Drive
Fort Washington, PA   19034
(215) 628 6000

Ross Laboratories
625 Cleveland Avenue
Columbus, OH   43216
(614) 227-3333

Roxane Laboratories, Inc.
1809 Wilson Road
P.O. Box 16532
Columbus, OH   43216
(614) 276-4000

Sandoz Pharmaceuticals Corporation
59 Route 10
East Hanover, NJ   07936
(201) 503-7500

Savage Laboratories
60 Baylis Road
Melville, NY   11747
(516) 454-7677

Schering-Plough Corporation
1 Giralda Farms
P.O. Box 1000
Madison, NJ   07940-1000
(201) 822-7000

Schwarz Pharma Kremers Urban Company
P.O. Box 2038
Milwaukee, WI   53201
(414) 354-4300

Searle Pharmaceuticals
P.O. Box 5110
Chicago, IL   60680
(708) 982-7000

Smith Kline & French Laboratories
1500 Spring Garden Street
P.O. Box 7929
Philadelphia, PA   19101
(215) 751-4000

SmithKline Beecham Corporation
1 Franklin Plaza
P.O. Box 7929
Philadelphia, PA   19101
(215) 751-4000

Squibb Corporation
Route 206 and Provinceline Road
P.O. Box 4000
Princeton, NJ   08543-4000
(609) 921-4000

Sterling Drug Inc.
90 Park Avenue
New York, NY   10016
(212) 907-2000

Surgikos, Inc.
2500 Arbrook Boulevard
P.O. Box 130
Arlington, TX   76010
(817) 465-3141

Survival Technology, Inc.
8101 Glenbrook Road
Bethesda, MD   20814
(301) 656-5600

Syntex Corporation
3401 Hillview Avenue
P.O. Box 10850
Palo Alto, CA   94303
(415) 855-5050

Therakos, Inc.
201 Brandywine Parkway
West Chester, PA   19380
(215) 430-7900

3M Pharmaceuticals
3M Center
Building 270-3A-01
St. Paul, MN   55144
(612) 733-5045

Upjohn Company
7000 Portage Road
Kalamazoo, MI   49001
(616) 323-4000

Vistakon, Inc.
1325 San Marco Boulevard
Jacksonville, FL   32207
(904) 396-2491

Wallace Laboratories
Half-Acre Road, P.O. Box 1001
Cranbury, NJ   08512-0181
(609) 655-6000

Warner-Lambert Company
201 Tabor Road
Morris Plains, NJ   07950
(201) 540-2000

Westwood Pharmaceuticals Inc.
100 Forest Avenue
Buffalo, NY 14213
(716) 887-3400

Winthrop Pharmaceuticals
90 Park Avenue
New York, NY 10016
(212) 907-2000

Wyeth-Ayerst Laboratories
P.O. Box 8299
Philadelphia, PA 19101
(215) 971-5400

Zimmer, Inc.
727 N. Detroit Street
P.O. Box 708
Warsaw, IN 46580
(219) 267-6131

STATE CHILD AND MATERNITY HEALTH DEPARTMENTS

To find local information about child health and other health matters, look in your local telephone directory for the state, city, county, or town health departments. Alternatively, the offices listed below should refer you to the local office you need.

This section includes the departments of health for all fifty states, the District of Columbia, and Puerto Rico. In addition, health offices concerned with maternity, children, families, and special health needs are listed within each state. No address is listed for those departments having the same address as the main department of health.

Alabama

Department of Public Health
434 Monroe Street, Room 381
Montgomery, AL 36130-1701
(205) 261-5052

Family Health Services
(205) 261-5025

Division of Rehabilitative & Crippled
Children's Services
2129 E. South Boulevard
Montgomery, AL 36111
(205) 281-8780

Alaska

Department of Health & Social Services
P.O. Box H-06
Juneau, AK   99811-0601
(907) 465-3030

Family Health Section
1231 Gamble Street
Anchorage, AK   99501
No phone number listed.

Arizona

Department of Health Services
1740 W. Adams Street
Phoenix, AZ   85007
(602) 542-1024

Division of Family Health Services
(602) 255-1223

Maternal & Child Health
Room 200
(602) 255-1870

Office of Children's Rehabilitative
  Services
Room 205
(602) 255-1860

Arkansas

Department of Health
State Health Building
4815 W. Markham Street
Little Rock, AR   72205-3867
(501) 661-2112

Section of Maternal & Child Health
(501) 661-2251

Arkansas Children's Medical Services
Department of Human Services
P.O. Box 1437
Little Rock, AR   72203
(501) 664-4117
(501) 682-2277

California

Department of Health Services
714 P Street, Room 1253
Sacramento, CA   95814
(916) 445-1248

Children's Services
Room 323
(916) 322-2090

Family Health Division
Room 350
(916) 322-9451

Maternal & Child Health Branch
Room 740
(916) 323-3096

Colorado

Department of Health
4210 E. 11th Avenue
Denver, CO   80220
(303) 331-4602

Family Health Services
(303) 331-8359

Handicapped Children's Program
(303) 331-8404

Connecticut

Department of Health Services
150 Washington Street
Hartford, CT   06106
(203) 566-2038

Health Services for Handicapped,
Children's Section
(203) 566-2057

Maternal & Child Health
(203) 566-5601

Delaware

Community Health Services
P.O. Box 637
Dover, DE   19903
(302) 736-4701

Handicapped Children's Services
(302) 736-4786

Maternal & Child Health Services
(302) 736-4785

District of Columbia

Public Health Commission
Universal North Building, Room 825
1875 Connecticut Avenue N.W.
Washington, DC   20009
(202) 673-7700

Bureau of Maternal & Child Health
Room 806
(202) 673-6665
(202) 673-6672

Handicapped and Crippled Children's
    Services
D.C. General Hospital
Building 10
19th and Massachusetts Avenue S.E.
Washington, DC   20003
(202) 675-5214

Florida

Department of Health & Rehabilitative
    Services
Building 11, Room 204
1317 Winewood Boulevard
Tallahassee, FL   32301
(904) 487-1321
(904) 392-4026

Children's Medical Services
Building V, Room 127
1323 Winewood Boulevard
Tallahassee, FL   32301
(904) 487-2690

Georgia

Division of Public Health
878 Peachtree Street N.E., Suite 201
Atlanta, GA   30309
(404) 894-7505

Children's Medical Services
(404) 894-6608

Family Health Services Section
Suite 217
(404) 894-6622

Hawaii

Department of Health
P.O. Box 3378
Honolulu, HI   96801
(808) 548-6505

Children with Special Health Needs
741 Sunset Avenue
Honolulu, HI   96816
(808) 732-3197

Family Health Services Division
3652 Kilauea Avenue
Honolulu, HI   96816
(808) 548-6574

Maternal & Child Health Branch
741-A Sunset Avenue
Honolulu, HI   96816
(808) 548-6576

Idaho

Division of Health
Towers Building, 4th Floor
450 W. State Street
Boise, ID   83720
(208) 334-5930

Bureau of Maternal & Child Health
(208) 334-5967

Children's Special Health Programs
(208) 334-5963

Illinois

Department of Public Health
535 W. Jefferson Street
Springfield, IL   62761
(217) 782-4977

Division of Family Health
(217) 782-4736

Division of Services for Crippled
   Children
University of Illinois at Chicago
2040 Hill Meadows Drive, Suite A
Springfield, IL   62702-4698
(217) 793-2340

Indiana

State Board of Health
P.O. Box 1964
Indianapolis, IN   46206-1964
(317) 633-8400

Division of Maternal & Child Health
and Bureau of Family Health
Services
(317) 633-8449

Division of Services for Crippled
Children
238 S. Meridian Street, 5th Floor
Indianapolis, IN   46225
(317) 232-4283

Iowa

Department of Public Health
Lucas State Office Building
E. 12th and Walnut Streets
Des Moines, IA   50319-0075
(515) 281-5605

Division of Family & Community
Health
(515) 281-4910

Iowa Child Health Specialty Clinics
Hospital School Building, Room 241
Iowa City, IA   52242
(319) 353-4431

Kansas

Division of Health
Landon State Office Building
900 S.W. Jackson
Topeka, KS   66612-1290
(913) 296-1343

Crippled Children's Services
(913) 296-1313

Department of Health & Environment
(913) 296-1300

Kentucky

Department for Health Services
Health Services Building, 1st Floor
275 E. Main Street
Frankfort, KY   40621
(502) 564-3970

Division of Maternal & Child Health
(502) 564-4830

Commission for Handicapped Children
983 Eastern Parkway
1405 E. Burnett Avenue
Louisville, KY   40217
(502) 588-3264

Louisiana

Office of Public Health
P.O. Box 60630
New Orleans, LA   70160
(504) 568-5052

Handicapped Children's Services
(504) 568-5055

Maternal & Child Health Services
(504) 568-5070

HEALTH

Maine

Bureau of Health
State House
Station 11
Augusta, ME   04333
(207) 289-3201

Division of Maternal & Child Health
   and Handicapped Children's Program
(207) 289-3311

Maryland

Department of Health & Mental
   Hygiene
Herbert R. O'Conor State Office
   Building
201 W. Preston Street
Baltimore, MD   21201
(301) 225-6500

Division of Crippled Children, Mental
   Retardation & Developmental
   Disabilities Administration
4th Floor
(301) 225-5580

Division of Infant, Child, & Adolescent
   Health Services
(301) 225-6748

Division of Maternal Health, Family
   Planning, & Hereditary Disorders
3rd Floor
(301) 225-6721

Massachusetts

Department of Public Health
150 Tremont Street
Boston, MA   02111
(617) 727-0201

Bureau of Child & Adolescent Health
   Programs
(617) 727-3372

Maternal & Child Health Section
(617) 727-0940

Services for Children with Special
   Health Care Needs
(617) 727-5812

Michigan

Department of Public Health
P.O. Box 30195
Lansing, MI   48909
(517) 335-8024

Bureau of Community Health Services
P.O. Box 30035
(517) 335-8900

Division of Services to Crippled
   Children
P.O. Box 30035
(517) 373-3416

Minnesota

Department of Health
P.O. Box 9441
Minneapolis, MN   55440
(612) 623-5460

Division of Maternal & Child Health
(612) 623-5166

Mississippi

Department of Health
P.O. Box 1700
Jackson, MS   39215-1700
(601) 960-7634

Bureau of Health Services
(601) 960-7463

Children's Medical Program
(601) 982-6571

Missouri

Department of Health
P.O. Box 570
Jefferson City, MO   65102
(314) 751-6001

Division of Maternal, Child, & Family
  Health and Crippled Children's
  Services
(314) 751-6174

Montana

Department of Health & Environmental
  Sciences
Cogswell Building, Room C108
Helena, MT   59620
(406) 444-2544

Maternal & Child Health Bureau
(406) 444-4740

Nebraska

Department of Health
P.O. Box 95007
Lincoln, NE   68509
(402) 471-2133

Bureau of Medical Services & Grants
(402) 471-3980

Department of Social Services
P.O. Box 95026
Lincoln, NE   68509
(402) 471-3121 (ext. 180)

Nevada

Health Division
Capitol Complex
Carson City, NV   89710
(702) 885-4740

Family Health Services
Kinkhead Building, #200, Room 205
505 E. King Street
Carson City, NV   89710
(702) 885-4885

New Hampshire

Division of Public Health Services
Health & Human Services Building
6 Hazen Drive
Concord, NH   03301-6527
(603) 271-4501

Bureau of Maternal & Child Health
(603) 271-4516

Bureau of Special Medical Services
(603) 271-4596

Office of Family & Community Health
(603) 271-4726

New Jersey

Department of Health
CN 360
Trenton, NJ   08625-0360
(609) 292-7837

Maternal & Child Health Services and
   Special Child Health Services
CN 364
(609) 292-5676

New Mexico

Public Health Division
P.O. Box 968
Santa Fe, NM   87504-0968
(505) 827-0020

Maternal & Child Health Bureau
(505) 827-2350

New York

Health Department
Corning Tower, Room 1408
Empire State Plaza
Albany, NY   12237
(518) 474-2011

Bureau of Child & Adolescent Health
Room 780
(518) 474-2084

Center for Community Health
Room 831
(518) 474-3368

Division of Family Health
Tower Building, Room 890
(518) 473-7922

North Carolina

Division of Health Services
P.O. Box 2091
Raleigh, NC   27602
(919) 733-3446

Maternal & Child Care Section
(919) 733-3816

Maternal & Child Health Branch
(919) 733-7791

Developmental Disabilities Branch
(919) 733-7437

North Dakota

Department of Health
State Capitol
Bismarck, ND   58505
(701) 224-2372

Crippled Children's Services
(701) 224-2436

Division of Maternal & Child Health
(701) 224-2493

Ohio

Department of Health
246 N. High Street
Columbus, OH   43226
(614) 466-3543

Bureau for Children with Medical
  Handicaps
(614) 466-1652

Bureau of Maternal & Child Health
(614) 466-5332

Oklahoma

Department of Health
P.O. Box 53551
Oklahoma City, OK   73152
(405) 271-4200

Maternal & Child Health Medical
  Services
(405) 271-4476

Children's Medical Services
4001 N. Lincoln Boulevard, 4th Floor
Oklahoma City, OK   73105
(405) 521-3902

Oregon

Health Division
P.O. Box 231
Portland, OR   97207
(503) 229-5032

Health Services Division
1400 S.W. 5th Avenue
Portland, OR   97201
(503) 229-6380

Crippled Children's Division
Oregon Health Sciences University
P.O. Box 574
Portland, OR   97207
(503) 225-8362

Pennsylvania

Department of Health
P.O. Box 90
Harrisburg, PA   17108
(717) 787-6436

Division of Maternal & Child Health
(717) 787-7443

Children's Rehabilitative Services
Division of Rehabilitation
714 Health and Welfare Building
Harrisburg, PA   17108
(717) 783-5436

Rhode Island

Department of Health
Cannon Building, Room 401
75 Davis Street
Providence, RI   02908
(401) 277-2231

Division of Family Health and Services
   for Handicapped Children
Room 302
(401) 277-2312

South Carolina

Department of Health & Environmental
   Control
R. J. Aycock Building
2600 Bull Street
Columbia, SC   29201
(803) 734-4880

Bureau of Maternal & Child Health
(803) 734-4670

Division of Children's Health &
   Rehabilitative Services
(803) 734-4610

South Dakota

Department of Health
Joe Foss Building
523 E. Capitol Avenue
Pierre, SD   57501
(605) 773-3361

Division of Health Services
(605) 773-3737

Maternal & Child Health & Crippled
   Children's Services
(605) 773-3737

Tennessee

Department of Health & Environment
Cordell Hull Building, Room 347
436 6th Avenue N.
Nashville, TN   37219-5402
(615) 741-3111

Maternal & Child Health Section or
   Crippled Children's Program
100 9th Avenue N.
Nashville, TN   37219-5405
(615) 741-7353

Texas

Department of Health
1100 W. 49th Street
Austin, TX   78756-3199
(512) 458-7375

Chronically Ill & Disabled Children
   Services
(512) 458-7355

Maternal & Child Health
(512) 458-7700

Utah

Department of Health
288 N. 1460 West
Salt Lake City, UT   84116-0700
(801) 538-6111

Division of Family Health Services
P.O. Box 16650
Salt Lake City, UT   84116-0650
(801) 538-6161

Handicapped Children's Services
   Division
P.O. Box 16650
Salt Lake City, UT   84116-0650
(801) 538-6165

Maternal & Infant Health Bureau
44 Medical Drive
Salt Lake City, UT   84113
(801) 538-4084

Vermont

Department of Health
P.O. Box 70
Burlington, VT   05402
(802) 863-7280

Medical Services Division and Services
   for Handicapped Children
(802) 863-7347

Virginia

Department of Health
James Madison Building, Room 400
109 Governor Street
Richmond, VA   23219
(804) 786-3561

Bureau of Crippled Children
(804) 786-3691

Bureau of Maternal & Child Health
(804) 786-7367

Office of Family Health Services
Room 600
(804) 785-5214

Washington

Division of Public Health
Mail Stop ET-11, P.O. Box 9709
Olympia, WA   98504-9709
(206) 753-5936
(800) 551-0562 (in Washington)

Bureau of Parent-Child Health Services
Airport Building 3, MS-LC-11A
Olympia, WA   98504
(206) 753-7021

Office of Parent & Child Health
Airport Building 3, MS-LC-11A
Olympia, WA   98504
(206) 753-6953

West Virginia

Department of Health
State Office Building 3, Room 206
1800 Washington Street E.
Charleston, WV   25305
(304) 348-2971

Division of Children's Services
1116 Quarrier Street
Charleston, WV   25301
(304) 348-6330

Division of Maternal & Child Health
1143 Dunbar Avenue
Dunbar, WV   25064
(304) 768-6295

Wisconsin

Division of Health
P.O. Box 309
Madison, WI   53701-0309
(608) 266-1511

Maternal & Child Health Unit
(608) 266-2670

Bureau for Children with Physical
    Needs
Department of Public Instruction
P.O. Box 7841
Madison, WI   53707
(608) 266-3886

Wyoming

Division of Health & Medical Services
Hathaway Building, 4th Floor
2300 Capitol Avenue
Cheyenne, WY   82002-0710
(307) 777-6464

Family Health Services and Children's
    Health Services
(307) 777-7941

Puerto Rico

Department of Health
Call Box 70184
San Juan, PR   00936
(809) 250-7227

Family Services
(809) 763-6210

☎

CHAPTER 6

SAFETY

Children have an astonishing ability to put themselves in harm's way. Fortunately, many advisory services and products are available to make a child's world much safer.

The first part of this chapter, POISON CONTROL CENTERS, lists the major, twenty-four-hour poison control centers nationwide. The remainder of this chapter has sections covering GENERAL SAFETY INFORMATION, AIR TRAVEL SAFETY, AUTOMOBILE SAFETY, FIRE SAFETY, FOOD SAFETY, GUN SAFETY, HOME SAFETY, SCHOOL SAFETY, SWIMMING AND BOATING SAFETY, RECREATIONAL SAFETY, AND ENVIRONMENTAL SAFETY.

SEE ALSO

the MAIL ORDER CATALOGS section in Chapter 12, under Health and Safety, for catalogs of safety products designed to protect children.

The SUDDEN INFANT DEATH SYNDROME (SIDS) section of Chapter 7 describes organizations offering preventive help to parents.

☎ ☎

POISON CONTROL CENTERS

A poison control center provides information on poisonous or potentially poisonous substances, including pesticides, industrial and household chemicals, drugs, foods, and plants, as well as information on animal and insect bites and stings. Most of the centers listed below are available twenty-four hours a day. They most frequently answer questions concerning childhood poisoning and drug overdoses. When you call, a nurse, pharmacist, or physician is almost always available to provide information on treatment and tell you what to do. If you are traveling with your child, it is best to call the poison center nearest to you. In the unusual event that you get a busy signal, call another center immediately.

Alabama

Alabama Poison Center
809 University Boulevard E.
Tuscaloosa, AL   35401
(205) 345-0600
(800) 462-0800 (in Alabama)

**Children's Hospital of Alabama Poison
   Control Center**
1600 7th Avenue S.
Birmingham, AL   35233
(205) 933-4050
(205) 933-9201
(205) 933-9202
(800) 292-6678 (in Alabama)

Alaska

Anchorage Poison Center
Providence Hospital
P.O. Box 196604

3200 Providence Drive
Anchorage, AK   99519-0604
(907) 261-3193
(800) 478-3193

Arizona

**Arizona Poison & Drug Information
   Center**
University of Arizona
Arizona Health Sciences Center
Tucson, AZ   85724
(602) 626-6016
(800) 362-0101 (in Arizona)

Samaritan Regional Poison Center
Good Samaritan Medical Center
1130 E. McDowell Road
Phoenix, AZ   85006
(602) 253-3334

Arkansas

Statewide Poison Control Drug
  Information Center
University of Arkansas for Medical
  Sciences
College of Pharmacy
4301 W. Markham Street
Little Rock, AR   72205
(501) 666-5532
(800) 482-8948 (in Arkansas)

California

Central-Coast Counties Regional Poison
  Control Center
Santa Clara Valley Medical Center
1751 S. Bascom Avenue
San Jose, CA   95128
(408) 299-5112
(800) 662-9886

Fresno Regional Poison Control Center
Fresno Community Hospital & Medical
  Center
Fresno and R Streets
Fresno, CA   93715
(209) 445-1222
(800) 346-5922

Los Angeles County Medical Association
  Regional Poison Information Center
1925 Wilshire Boulevard
Los Angeles, CA   90057

(213) 484-5151 (for the general public)
(213) 644-2121 (for doctors and
  hospitals)

San Diego Regional Poison Center
University of California
San Diego Medical Center
225 Dickinson Street
San Diego, CA   92103
(619) 294-6000

San Francisco Bay Area Regional
  Poison Center
San Francisco General Hospital
1001 Potrero Avenue, Room 1E86
San Francisco, CA   94110
(415) 476-6600
(800) 523-2222

UCDMC Regional Poison Control
  Center
2315 Stockton Boulevard
Sacramento, CA   95817
(916) 453-3692 (for emergencies)
(916) 453-3414 (for business
  information)

University of California Poison Control
  Center
Irvine Medical Center
101 City Drive S., Route 78
Orange, CA   92668
(714) 634-5988

Colorado

Rocky Mountain Poison Center
645 Bannock Street
Denver, CO   80204-4507
(303) 629-1123
(800) 332-3073 (in Colorado)
(800) 525-5042 (in Montana)
(800) 442-2702 (in Wyoming)

Connecticut

Connecticut Poison Control Center
University of Connecticut Health Center
Farmington, CT   06032
(203) 674-3456
(203) 674-3457

Delaware

Poison Information Center
Medical Center of South Delaware
Wilmington Division
501 W. 14th Street
Wilmington, DE   19899
(302) 655-3389

District of Columbia

National Capital Poison Center
Georgetown University Hospital
3800 Reservoir Road, N.W.
Washington, DC   20007
(202) 625-3333

Florida

Florida Poison Information Center
Tampa General Hospital
P.O. Box 1289
Tampa, FL   33601
(813) 253-4444
(800) 282-3171

St. Vincent's Medical Center
1800 Barrs Street
Jacksonville, FL   32203
(904) 378-7500
(904) 378-7499 (TTY)

Tallahassee Memorial Regional Medical Center
1300 Miccosukee Road
Tallahassee, FL   32308
(904) 681-5411

Georgia

Georgia Poison Control Center
Grady Memorial Hospital
80 Butler Street, S.E.
Atlanta, GA   30335
(404) 589-4400
(404) 525-3323 (TTY)
(800) 282-5846 (in Georgia)

Regional Poison Control Center
Medical Center of Central Georgia
777 Hemlock Street
Macon, GA   31201
(912) 744-1427
(912) 744-1146
(912) 744-1000

Savannah Regional Poison Control
  Center
Department of Emergency Medicine
Memorial Medical Center
Savannah, GA   31403
(912) 355-5228

Hawaii

Hawaii Poison Center
Kapiolani-Children's Medical Center
1319 Punahou Street
Honolulu, HI   96826
(808) 941-4411
(800) 362-3585

Idaho

Idaho Poison Center
St. Alphonsus Regional Medical Center
1055 N. Curtis Road
Boise, ID   83704
(208) 378-2707
(800) 632-8000

Illinois

Central & Southern Illinois
Regional Poison Resource Center
St. John's Hospital
800 E. Carpenter Street
Springfield, IL   62769
(217) 753-3330
(800) 252-2022

Chicago & Northeastern Illinois
  Regional Poison Control Center
Rush-Presbyterian-St. Luke's Medical
  Center
1753 W. Congress Parkway
Chicago, IL   60612
(312) 942-5969
(800) 942-5969 (in Illinois)

Indiana

Indiana Poison Center
Methodist Hospital of Indiana
1701 N. Senate Boulevard
Indianapolis, IN   46206
(317) 929-2323
(317) 630-6666 (TTY)
(800) 382-9097 (in Indiana)

Iowa

Variety Club Poison & Drug
  Information Center
Iowa Methodist Medical Center
1200 Pleasant Street
Des Moines, IA   50309
(515) 283-6254
(800) 362-2327

University of Iowa Hospitals
Clinics Poison Control Center
Iowa City, IA   52242
(319) 356-2922
(800) 272-6477

Kansas

Mid-America Poison Center
University of Kansas Medical Center
39th and Rainbow Boulevard
Kansas City, KS   66103
(913) 588-6633
(800) 332-6633 (in Kansas)

Wesley Medical Center
550 N. Hillside Avenue
Wichita, KS   67214
(316) 688-2277

Kentucky

Kentucky Regional Poison Center
  of Kosair Children's Hospital
P.O. Box 35070
Louisville, KY   40232-5070
(502) 589-8222
(800) 722-5725 (in Kentucky)

Louisiana

Louisiana Regional Poison Control
  Center
Louisiana State University School of
  Medicine
1501 Kings Highway
Shreveport, LA   71130-3932
(318) 425-1524
(800) 535-0525 (in Louisiana)

Maine

Maine Poison Control Center
Maine Medical Center
22 Bramhall Street
Portland, ME   04102
(207) 871-2381
(800) 442-6305 (in Maine)

Maryland

Maryland Poison Center
University of Maryland School of
  Pharmacy
20 N. Pine Street
Baltimore, MD   21201
(301) 528-7701
(800) 492-2414 (in Maryland)

Massachusetts

Massachusetts Poison Control System
300 Longwood Avenue
Boston, MA   02115
(617) 232-2120
(617) 277-3323 (TTY)
(800) 682-9211 (in Massachusetts)

Michigan

Blodgett Regional Poison Center
Blodgett Memorial Center
1840 Wealthy Street, S.E.
Grand Rapids, MI   49506
(616) 774-7851
(800) 632-2727 (in Michigan)

Great Lakes Poison Center
Bronson Methodist Hospital
252 E. Lovell Street
Kalamazoo, MI   49007
(616) 383-6409
(800) 442-4112 (within area code 616)

Poison Control Center
Children's Hospital of Michigan
3901 Beaubien Boulevard
Detroit, MI   48201
(313) 745-5711
(800) 462-6642 (in Michigan)

Minnesota

Hennepin Regional Poison Center
Hennepin County Medical Center
701 Park Avenue
Minneapolis, MN   55415
(612) 347-3141
(612) 347-6219 (TTY)

Minnesota Regional Poison Center
St. Paul-Ramsey Medical Center
640 Jackson Street
St. Paul, MN   55101
(612) 221-2113
(800) 222-1222 (in Minnesota)

Mississippi

Regional Poison Control Center
University Medical Center
2500 N. State Street
Jackson, MI   39216
(601) 354-7660

Missouri

Cardinal Glennon Children's Hospital
Regional Poison Center
1465 S. Grand Boulevard
St. Louis, MO   63104
(314) 772-5200
(800) 392-9111 (in Missouri)

Children's Mercy Hospital
24th and Gillham Road
Kansas City, MO   64108
(816) 234-3000

Nebraska

Mid-Plains Poison Control Center
Children's Memorial Hospital
8301 Dodge Street
Omaha, NE   68114
(402) 390-5400
(800) 642-9999 (in Nebraska)
(800) 228-9515 (in Colorado, Iowa,
    Kansas, Missouri, South Dakota,
    Wyoming)

New Hampshire

New Hampshire Poison Information
    Center
2 Maynard Street
Hanover, NH   03756
(603) 646-5000
(800) 562-8236 (in New Hampshire)

New Jersey

New Jersey Poison Information &
    Education System
Newark Beth Israel Medical Center
201 Lyons Avenue
Newark, NJ   07112
(201) 923-0764
(201) 926-7443 (administration)
(201) 926-8008 (TTY)
(800) 962-1253 (in New Jersey)

New Mexico

New Mexico Poison & Drug
    Information Center
University of New Mexico
Albuquerque, NM   87131
(505) 843-2551
(505) 277-4261 (administration)
(800) 432-6866 (in New Mexico)

New York

Central New York Poison Control
    Center
Upstate Medical Center
750 E. Adams Street
Syracuse, NY   13210
(315) 476-4766
(800) 252-5655 (except Onondaga
    County)

Ellis Hospital Poison Center
1101 Nott Street
Schenectady, NY   12308
(518) 382-4039
(518) 382-4309

Finger Lakes Regional Poison Center
LIFE LINE
University of Rochester Medical Center
Box 777
Rochester, NY   14620
(716) 275-5151
(716) 275-2700 (TTY)
(716) 275-4354 (office of director)

Hudson Valley Regional Poison Center
Nyack Hospital
N. Midland Avenue
Nyack, NY   10960
(914) 353-1000

Long Island Regional Poison Control
    Center
Nassau County Medical Center
2201 Hempstead Turnpike
East Meadow, NY   11554
(516) 542-2324
(516) 542-2325
(516) 542-2323 (TTY)

New York City Poison Center
455 1st Avenue, Room 123
New York, NY   10016
(212) 340-4494
(212) 764-7667

Western New York Poison Control
   Center at Children's Hospital of
   Buffalo
219 Bryant Street
Buffalo, NY   14222
(716) 878-7654
(716) 878-7655

North Carolina

Catawba Memorial Hospital Poison
   Control Center
Fairgrove Church Road
Hickory, NC   28602
(704) 322-6649

Duke University Poison Control Center
Duke University Medical Center
Durham, NC   27710
(919) 684-8111
(800) 672-1697 (in North Carolina)

Mercy Hospital Poison Control Center
2001 Vail Avenue
Charlotte, NC   28207
(704) 379-5827

Moses H. Cone Memorial Hospital Triad
   Poison Center
1200 N. Elm Street
Greensboro, NC   27401-1020
(919) 379-4105
(800) 722-2222 (in North Carolina)

Western NC Poison Control Center
Memorial Mission Hospital
509 Biltmore Avenue
Asheville, NC   28801
(704) 255-4490
(800) 542-4225

North Dakota

North Dakota Poison Information
   Center
St. Luke's Hospitals
5th Street N. and Mills Avenue
Fargo, ND   58122
(701) 280-5575
(800) 732-2200 (in North Dakota)

Ohio

Akron Regional Poison Control Center
Children's Hospital Medical Center of
   Akron
281 Locust Street
Akron, OH   44308
(216) 379-8562
(800) 362-9922

Central Ohio Poison Control Center
Children's Hospital
700 Children's Drive
Columbus, OH   43205
(614) 228-1323
(800) 682-7625 (in Ohio)

Greater Cleveland Poison Control
Center
2101 Adelbert Road
Cleveland, OH   44106
(216) 231-4455

Lorain Community Hospital
3700 Kolbe Road
Lorain, OH   44053
(216) 282-2220
(800) 821-8972

Mahoning Valley Poison Center
St. Elizabeth Hospital Medical Center
1044 Belmont Avenue
Youngstown, OH   44501
(216) 746-2222
(216) 746-5510 (TTY)

Poison Information Center
Medical College of Ohio Hospital
3000 Arlington Avenue
Toledo, OH   43614
(419) 381-3897

Regional Poison Control System &
Drug & Poison Information Center
University of Cincinnati Medical Center
231 Bethesda Avenue
M.L. 144
Cincinnati, OH   45267-0144
(513) 558-5111
(800) 872-5111 (regional)

Western Ohio Poison & Drug
Information Center
Children's Medical Center
1 Children's Plaza
Dayton, OH   45404-1815
(513) 222-2227
(800) 762-0727 (in Ohio)

Oklahoma

Oklahoma Poison Control Center
Oklahoma Children's Memorial Hospital
P.O. Box 26307
940 N.E. 10th
Oklahoma City, OK   73126
(405) 271-5454
(800) 522-4611 (in Oklahoma)

Oregon

Oregon Poison Center
Oregon Health Sciences University
3181 S.W. Sam Jackson Park Road
Portland, OR   97201
(503) 225-8968
(800) 452-7165

Pennsylvania

Capital Area Poison Center
University Hospital
Milton S. Hershey Medical Center
University Drive
Hershey, PA   17033
(717) 531-6111
(717) 531-6039

Delaware Valley Regional Poison
  Control Center
1 Children's Center
34th & Civic Center Boulevard
Philadelphia, PA   19104
(215) 386-2100 (in emergencies)
(215) 386-2066 (administration)

Keystone Region Poison Center
Mercy Hospital
2500 7th Avenue
Altoona, PA   16603
(814) 946-3711

Lehigh Valley Poison Center
Allentown Hospital
17th and Chew Streets
Allentown, PA   18102
(215) 433-2311

Pittsburgh Poison Center
1 Children's Place
3705 5th Avenue at De Soto Street
Pittsburgh, PA   15213
(412) 681-6669 (in emergencies)
(412) 647-5600
    (administration/consultation)

Northwest Regional Poison Center
Saint Vincent Health Center
232 W. 25th Street
Erie, PA   16544
(814) 452-3232
(800) 822-3232

Susquehanna Poison Center
Geisinger Medical Center
N. Academy Avenue
Danville, PA   17821
(717) 271-6116

Rhode Island

Rhode Island Poison Center
Rhode Island Hospital
593 Eddy Street
Providence, RI   02902
(401) 277-5727
(401) 277-8062 (TTY)

South Carolina

Palmetto Poison Center
University of South Carolina College of
    Pharmacy
Columbia, SC   29208
(803) 765-7359
(800) 922-1117 (in South Carolina)

South Dakota

McKennen Hospital Poison Center
P.O. Box 5045
800 E. 21st Street
Sioux Falls, SD   57117-5045
(605) 336-3894
(800) 952-0123
(800) 843-0505

St. Luke Midland Poison Control
  Center
305 South State Street
Aberdeen, SD   57401
(605) 622-5678
(800) 592-1889

Tennessee

Southern Poison Center, Inc.
848 Adams Avenue
Memphis, TN   38103
(901) 528-6048

T.C. Thompson Children's Hospital
910 Blackford Street
Chattanooga, TN   37403
(615) 778-6100

University of Tennessee Memorial
  Research Center & Hospital
1924 Alcoa Highway
Knoxville, TN   37920
(615) 544-9400

Texas

El Paso Poison Control Center
R.E. Thomason General Hospital
4815 Alameda Avenue
El Paso, TX   79905
(915) 533-1244

North Central Texas Poison Center
P.O. Box 35926
Dallas, TX   75235
(214) 590-5000
(817) 336-6611
(800) 441-0040 (in Texas)

Texas State Poison Center
University of Texas Medical Branch
8th and Mechanic Streets
Galveston, TX   77550
(409) 765-1420
(512) 478-4490 (Austin)
(713) 654-1701 (Houston)
(800) 392-8548 (in Texas)

Utah

Intermountain Regional Poison Control
  Center
50 N. Medical Drive, Building 428
Salt Lake City, UT   84132
(801) 581-2151
(800) 662-0062 (in Utah)

Vermont

Vermont Poison Center
Medical Center Hospital of Vermont
Colchester Avenue
Burlington, VT   05401
(802) 658-3456 (for information)
(802) 656-2721 (for educational
  programs)

Virginia

Blue Ridge Poison Center
University of Virginia Hospital
Charlottesville, VA   22908
(804) 924-5543
(800) 552-3723 (in Virginia, for doctors)
(800) 222-5927 (TTY in Virginia)
(800) 446-9876 (TTY for doctors)

Central Virginia Poison Center
Medical College of Virginia
Box 522
MCV Station
Richmond, VA   23298
(804) 786-9123 (24-hour hotline; call
   collect)
(804) 786-4780 (administration)

Southwest Virginia Poison Center
Roanoke Memorial Hospitals
P.O. Box 13367
Belleview at Jefferson Street
Roanoke, VA   24033
(703) 981-7336

Tidewater Poison Center
150 Kingsley Lane
Norfolk, VA   23505
(804) 489-5288
(800) 552-6337

Washington

Central Washington Poison Center
Yakima Valley Memorial Hospital
2811 Tieton Drive
Yakima, WA   98902
(509) 248-4400
(800) 572-9176 (in Washington)

Mary Bridge Poison Center
Mary Bridge Children's Hospital
P.O. Box 5299
311 S. L Street
Tacoma, WA   98405-0987
(206) 594-1414
(800) 542-6319 (in Washington)

Seattle Poison Center
Children's Hospital & Medical Center
P.O. Box C5371
4800 Sand Point Way, N.E.
Seattle, WA   98105-0371
(206) 526-2121
(800) 732-6985 (in Washington)

Spokane Poison Center
S. 715 Cowley, Suite 132
Spokane, WA   99202
(509) 747-1077 (TTY)
(800) 572-5842 (in Washington)
(800) 541-5624 (in N. Idaho and W.
   Montana)

West Virginia

West Virginia Poison Center
West Virginia University School of
   Pharmacy
3110 McCorkle Avenue, S.E.
Charleston, WV   25304
(304) 348-4211
(800) 642-3625 (in West Virginia)

Wisconsin

Green Bay Poison Control Center
St. Vincent Hospital
P.O. Box 13508
Green Bay, WI   54307-3508
(414) 433-8100

Milwaukee Poison Center
Children's Hospital of Wisconsin
P.O. Box 1997
1700 W. Wisconsin Avenue
Milwaukee, WI   53201
(414) 931-4114

University of Wisconsin Hospital
Regional Poison Control Center
600 Highland Avenue
Madison, WI   53792
(608) 262-3702

Wyoming

Wyoming Poison Center
Hathaway Building, Room 527
Cheyenne, WY   82001
(800) 442-2702

GENERAL SAFETY INFORMATION

Consumer Product Safety Commission
Washington, DC   20207
(800) 638-2772
(800) 638-8720 (TTY)
This government agency advises which toys and children's furniture have been recalled or are considered hazardous. You can call the agency to report an injury due to a product that you feel is unsafe. Its concerns include hazardous consumer products, flammable fabrics, poison prevention packaging, children's hazards, electrical safety, athletic products, power equipment safety, home insulation safety, toy safety. Aside from answering questions over the phone, the Commission will send lists of products that were recalled. Publications include *Crib-Safety—Keep Them on the Safe Side; A Toy and Sports Equipment Safety Guide; Toys—a Fact Sheet;* and *Playground Equipment Guide.* The CPSC also offers a free booklet, *The Super Sitter,* written for baby-sitters, that outlines their responsibilities for children's safety.

Danny Foundation
P.O. Box 680
Alamo, CA   94507
(415) 833-2669
(800) 83-DANNY (833-2669)

The Foundation, named for the founder's son who strangled when his T-shirt strap caught on a crib slat, provides the public with information on the safety of cribs and nursery goods in general. In addition, it conducts research, runs a library and speakers' bureau, and publishes a newsletter and the brochure *Is Your Crib Safe?*

National Child Safety Council (NCSC)
4065 Page Avenue, P.O. Box 1368
Jackson, MI   49204-1368
(517) 764-6070
(800) 222-1464
NCSC provides safety educational materials to law enforcement agencies, schools, and individuals. The Council will supply pamphlets, manuals, posters, and folders, and loans films on bicycle safety, child safety, drug education, and crime prevention. Materials are geared to children's various levels of understanding and experience.

National Consumers League (NCL)
815 15th Street, N.W., Suite 516
Washington, DC   20005
(202) 639-8140
NCL offers information and referrals on air safety, the environment, food and drug safety, and other issues. The League will send a list of its publications.

National Hazards Control Institute
Division of Coeval, Inc.
P.O. Box 667
Easton, PA   18044-0667
(215) 258-7045
The Institute offers a catalog of publications, audiovisual programs, seminars, and services on occupational hazards.

National Head & Spinal Cord Injury
   Prevention Program (NHSCIPP)
22 S. Washington Street
Park Ridge, IL   60068
(312) 692-9500
The American Association of Neurological Surgeons and the Congress of Neurological Surgeons created NHSCIPP as a public service to provide prevention education throughout the United States and Canada. The group educates young people about personal vulnerability and risk taking, anatomical, emotional, and social consequences of head and spine injuries, and proper bystander behavior when head or spinal cord injury is suspected.

National Injury Information
   Clearinghouse
Consumer Product Safety Commission
5401 Westbard Avenue, Room 625
Washington, DC   20207
(301) 492-6424

This agency operates as a clearinghouse for information on injuries. You can call or write to see if other people have had similar problems with non–brand-name products.

National Safety Council
444 N. Michigan Avenue
Chicago, IL   60611
(312) 527-4800
The National Safety Council, the largest safety organization in the United States, has numerous activities, including a child safety club, home study courses in safety, and transportation safety services. Educational programs are directed at groups such as the elderly, youth, bicycle riders, farm workers, drivers, and boaters. The Council has an extensive publications catalog. Hundreds of posters, brochures, and booklets on all aspects of safety, accident prevention, and prevention of occupational illnesses are available. Manuals on such topics as alcohol, fire, accident prevention, and family safety are offered. Special publications evaluate a wide range of consumer activities. Data sheets on accidents, toxic substances, and employee safety are available. Educational films and slide shows can be purchased. The Council publishes forty-four newsletters and eight magazines.

Occupational Safety & Health
   Administration (OSHA)
Office of Information & Consumer
   Affairs
200 Constitution Avenue, N.W.
Room N-3637
Washington, DC   20001
(202) 523-8148
(202) 523-8151 (Publications)
OSHA answers questions from professionals and the general public. It distributes publications on health and safety issues as they relate to the workplace, including environmental exposures during pregnancy.

Safe Kids Are No Accident
111 Michigan Avenue, N.W.
Washington, DC   20010
(202) 338-7227
(202) 939-4993
Sponsored by the National Safety Council and Johnson & Johnson, this service provides educational materials that will prevent injuries among children.

Safety Society
1900 Association Drive
Reston, VA   22091
(703) 476-3431
The Safety Society sponsors educational programs in traffic safety, emergency preparedness, injury control, and sports safety. It distributes a limited number of publications.

AIR TRAVEL SAFETY

Air Line Pilots Association
1625 Massachusetts Avenue, N.W.
Washington, DC   20036
(202) 797-4000

Although mainly providing information to pilots, the Association will answer limited questions and make referrals regarding the safety of airplanes and air travel.

AUTOMOBILE SAFETY

American Academy of Pediatrics
P.O. Box 927
Elk Grove Village, IL   60009
(708) 228-5005
This organization of physicians offers a free booklet called *A Family Shopping Guide to Infant-Child Safety Seats.*

American Automobile Association (AAA)
8111 Gatehouse Road
Falls Church, VA 22047
(703) 222-6466 (Library)
AAA will answer questions, make referrals, and provide photocopies of magazine articles on many automotive subjects, including safety.

American Driver & Traffic Safety Education Association (ADTSEA)
123 N. Pitt Street, Suite 511
Alexandria, VA   22314
(703) 836-4748
ADTSEA is a national professional organization for driver education teachers and others concerned with driver, pedestrian, and traffic safety education. It has affiliates in most states. A publications list is available outlining pamphlets, teaching materials, leaflets, and cassettes offered.

American Seat Belt Council, Inc.
P.O. Drawer F
Jamesburg, NJ   08831
(201) 521-4441
This group offers films and brochures regarding the safe use of seat belts.

Center for Auto Safety
2001 S Street, N.W., Suite 410
Washington, DC   20009
(202) 328-7700
The Center disseminates information about design and assembly defects in new cars and other safety issues. Publications include *The Car Book, The Lemon Book,* and a newsletter, *Lemon Times.*

Highway Users Federation for Safety & Mobility
1776 Massachusetts Avenue, N.W.
Washington, DC   20036
(202) 857-1200
This group promotes highway safety through education. Although mainly serving groups and government agencies, the Federation will answer questions and make referrals for the general public.

Mothers Against Drunk Driving (M.A.D.D.)
511 E. John Carpenter Freeway
Irving, TX   75062
(214) 744-6233
This national organization of nearly four hundred chapters is dedicated to promoting public awareness that drunk driving is criminal behavior.

Motorcycle Safety Foundation (MSF)
Information Resource Center
P.O. Box 5044
Costa Mesa, CA   92628
(714) 241-9922
The Foundation, sponsored by several motorcycle manufacturers, works to reduce motorcycle accidents and injuries. It will answer questions and make referrals over the phone. Publications include a magazine, *Safe Cycling,* and brochures.

National Head Injury Foundation
333 Turnpike Road
Southborough, MA   01772
(508) 485-9950
(800) 444-NHIF (6443)
This group publishes a book called *Safety Belts in School Buses* which costs four dollars.

National Highway Traffic Safety Administration
Traffic Safety Programs
400 7th Street, S.W.
Washington, DC   20590
(202) 366-1755
(202) 366-0123
(800) 424-9393
This office publishes consumer materials concerning motorcycle safety, driver education, driver licensing, alcohol and other drugs in relation to highway safety, occupant protection (safety-belt

and child-seat use), emergency medical services, pedestrian safety, police traffic services, and pupil transportation safety. They publish *How You Can Fight Drunk Drivers*—available at no cost. A list of other publications will be sent on request.

Remove Intoxicated Drivers (R.I.D.)
P.O. Box 520
Schenectady, NY   12301
(518) 372-0034
The 155 chapters of R.I.D. are organized to educate the public, to influ-

ence legislation and public policy about drunk driving, and to aid victims of drunk drivers.

Students Against Drunk Driving (S.A.D.D.)
P.O. Box 800
Marlboro, MA   01752
(617) 481-3568
With over sixteen thousand chapters, S.A.D.D. seeks to educate peers about the inherent dangers of drinking and driving and provides counseling where needed. It publishes a newsletter and guidelines for starting new groups.

FIRE SAFETY

Burn Institute
3737 5th Avenue, Suite 206
San Diego, CA   92103
(619) 291-4764
The Institute offers burn prevention information to people of all ages. Private educational sessions are also provided for fire-setting children and their parents. Publications include consumer guides for fire safety, coloring books and storybooks for children, and brochures such as *Fire Escape Planning; Gasoline Dangers; How to Make Your Home and Family Safe from Fire;* and *Scald Prevention in the Home.*

International Association of Fire Chiefs, Inc.
1329 18th Street, N.W.
Washington, DC   20036
(202) 833-3420
Although primarily a professional association, this group will answer questions, make referrals, and provide free pamphlets on fire prevention.

National Burn Victim Foundation
308 Main Street
Orange, NJ   07050
(201) 731-3112

The Foundation conducts burn prevention programs in schools, provides counseling for young burn victims and their families, and helps determine if burning is from abuse or accident.

National Fire Protection Association (NFPA)
Batterymarch Park
Quincy, MA   02269
(617) 770-3000
NFPA provides technical assistance in fire safety and conducts a wide-ranging public education program which includes providing information on fire prevention. NFPA develops curricula for use in kindergarten through junior high school. It publishes a large number of materials directed at specific audiences. A catalog describing materials on fire prevention for use with children is available.

National Institute for Burn Medicine (NIBM)
909 E. Ann Street
Ann Arbor, MI   48104
(313) 769-9000
The NIBM sponsors the education of medical professionals and the public regarding the prevention and treatment of burns. It distributes free educational pamphlets on burns and their prevention.

FOOD SAFETY

Consumer Information Center
P.O. Box 100
Pueblo, CO   81002
The Center offers a free booklet, *The Safe Food Book: Your Kitchen Guide* (item #526V) and a free brochure, *Safe Food to Go.*

Food & Drug Administration (FDA)
Office of Consumer Affairs
5600 Fishers Lane
Rockville, MD   20857-HFE-88

The FDA monitors and provides information on food labels and additives as well as drugs, cosmetics, and other areas of concern.

Food Safety & Inspection Service
Information Division
Department of Agriculture
14th Street and Independence Avenue, S.W.
Washington, DC   20250
(202) 447-9113

This agency answers questions by phone, offers consumer education, and distributes publications on such sub- jects as how to keep food safe to eat. A publications list is available.

GUN SAFETY

Center to Prevent Handgun Violence
1225 Eye Street, N.W., Suite 1100
Washington, DC   20005
(202) 289-7319
The Center was founded to inform the public about the degree of handgun vi- olence in America, expose the risks and responsibilities of owning a handgun, and teach how to handle guns safely.

National Council for a Responsible Firearms Policy
7216 Stafford Road
Alexandria, VA   22307
(703) 765-2472
This group will answer questions re- garding the safe use and storage of firearms.

HOME SAFETY

American Trauma Society (ATS)
1400 Mercantile Lane, Suite 188
Landover, MD   20785
(301) 925-8811
(800) 556-7890
ATS answers questions and makes re- ferrals on how to reduce suffering, death, and disability from injury. It dis- tributes films, reprints of articles, emergency first-aid glove-compartment cards, and other publications.

Art & Crafts Materials Institute (ACMI)
715 Boylston Street
Boston, MA   02116
(617) 266-6800
ACMI, an association of manufacturers of art materials, conducts a certification program to insure that art materials are nontoxic or properly labeled. ACMI answers questions over the phone and distributes brochures that describe sim- ple tests for school art materials. A list of Institute-certified products is also available.

Art Hazards Information Center

5 Beekman Street
New York, NY   10038
(212) 227-6220
An ongoing study conducted by the Center for Safety in the Arts to determine what, if any, chemical hazards are present in arts and crafts supplies. The Center sponsors courses and workshops and publishes the AHIC Newsletter as well as various books, pamphlets, and fact sheets.

Council on Family Health

420 Lexington Avenue
New York, NY   10017
(212) 210-8836
The Council conducts education programs on family and home health and safety needs. Publications include *Health Emergency Chart; The Care and Safety of Young Children; Child's Mind, Child's Body;* and *Ten Guides to Proper Medicine Use.* Some publications are free, others have a small charge. A list is available.

Federal Bureau of Investigation (FBI)

Office of Congressional and Public
   Affairs
10th Street at Pennsylvania Avenue,
   S.W., Room 6236
Washington, DC   20535
Write for a free brochure called *Crime Resistance—A Way to Protect Your Family Against Crime.*

Phonefriend

American Association of University
   Women
P.O. Box 735
State College, PA   16804
(814) 865-1751
For twenty dollars (which includes shipping), you can receive guidelines for establishing a call-in phone program for latchkey children in your area.

Project Latchkey

National Parents Teachers Association
700 N. Rush Street
Chicago, IL   60611-9894
(312) 787-0977
If your child needs to spend time at home without your supervision—often called a latchkey child—you'll want to get a copy of the National PTA's brochure on how to make your home safer. This group will also refer you to local organizations that help parents maintain safety for their latchkey children.

National Burglar & Fire Alarm Association, Inc. (NBFAA)

7101 Wisconsin Avenue, Suite 1390
Bethesda, MD   20814
(301) 907-3202
NBFAA acts as a clearinghouse for information on all types of alarms.

SCHOOL SAFETY

National Alliance for Safe Schools
  (NASS)
4903 Edgemoor Lane, Apt. 403
Bethesda, MD   20814
(301) 654-2774
Dedicated to helping administrators
and staffs make their schools safe,
secure environments, the Alliance offers
discipline and crime prevention models

in public schools. It will help evaluate
a school district's security measures,
research means for preventing particular problems, and provide technical
analysis of security hardware. It runs
a speakers' bureau, maintains a two-
thousand-volume library and a computerized bibliographic database, and
conducts workshops.

SWIMMING AND BOATING SAFETY

Aquatic Injury Safety Group (AISG)
1555 Penobscot Building
Detroit, MI   48226
(313) 963-1600
(800) 342-0330
AISG offers NO DIVING signs to pools and
swimming facilities, provides information about swimming safety, and generally seeks to educate the community at
large about safe diving.

Boat/U.S. Foundation for Boating
  Safety
Reference Resource Center
880 S. Pickett Street
Alexandria, VA   22304
(703) 823-9550
(800) 336-BOAT (2628)

The Foundation answers questions
about boating safety and offers a variety
of publications, including *Boating and
Drinking, Weather,* and *Hypothermia.*

Coast Guard
Office of Navigation Safety & Waterway
  Services
Auxiliary, Boating, & Consumer Affairs
  Division
Commandant (G-NAB), U.S. Coast
  Guard
Washington, DC   20593
(202) 267-1077
This office will answer questions and
make referrals concerning recreational
boating safety.

National Safe Boating Council (NSBC)
U.S. Coast Guard G-BBS-4
2100 2nd Street, S.W.
Washington, DC   20593
(202) 267-1060
NSBC offers referrals and information regarding recreational boating safety. The Council produces a packet of materials for National Safe Boating Week, which includes a press kit, poster, and bumper sticker.

National Water Safety Congress
   (NWSC)
77 Forsyth Street, S.W.
Atlanta, GA   30335-6801
(404) 331-4834
The Congress promotes swimming, boating, and scuba safety. Although it primarily serves government agencies, the group will answer questions and make referrals to the public. The NWSC distributes water safety course materials, films, safety program descriptions, and a newsletter, *Water Safety Journal.*

United States Lifesaving Association
   (USLA)
Chicago Park District
425 E. 14th Boulevard
Chicago, IL   60605
(312) 294-2332
A professional organization dedicated to enhancing public safety. Among its many interests, USLA conducts swimming programs for underprivileged and inner-city children. Annually it publishes *Beach Directories* and *Emergency Services Directory.*

RECREATIONAL SAFETY

American Ski Federation (ASF)
207 Constitution Avenue, N.E.
Washington, DC   20002
(202) 543-1595
The ASF, a trade association for the ski industry, offers limited information on skiing safety and makes referrals for the public.

Bicycle Federation (BF)
1818 R Street, N.W.
Washington, DC   20009
(202) 332-6986
BF promotes bicycling as a means of transportation and recreation. It provides information on bicycle safety, among other subjects.

National Center for Catastrophic Sports Injury Research
University of North Carolina
311 Woollen
Chapel Hill, NC   27514
(919) 962-2021
The Center offers data on severe sports injuries, particularly those resulting from football.

Opticians Association of America (OAA)
P.O. Box 10110
Fairfax, VA   22030
(703) 691-8355
The OAA offers information and referrals regarding safety and sports eyewear, among other subjects.

Outdoor Power Equipment Institute, Inc. (OPEI)
1901 L Street, N.W., Suite 700
Washington, DC   20036
(202) 296-3484
OPEI is a trade association comprising lawn and garden equipment manufacturers. It will answer questions and make referrals regarding outdoor power equipment safety.

Sporting Goods Manufacturers Association (SGMA)
200 Castlewood Drive
North Palm Beach, FL   33408
(407) 842-4100
This trade association will answer questions and make referrals regarding sporting goods product standards and safety, among other subjects.

ENVIRONMENTAL SAFETY

NATIONAL ORGANIZATIONS

Alliance to End Childhood Lead Poisoning
P.O. Box 33246
Washington, DC   20033-0246
(202) 543-1147
The Alliance informs the public about the risks and remedies of lead poisoning.

Asbestos Institute
1130 Sherbrooke Street W., Suite 410
Montreal, Quebec   H3A 2M8
Canada
(514) 844-3956
The Institute will answer questions over the phone regarding asbestos safety and its use in various products. A list is available of their publications, primarily technical in nature.

Canadian Centre for Occupational
   Health & Safety
250 Main Street E.
Hamilton, Ontario   L8N 1H6
Canada
(416) 572-2981
(800) 263-8276 (helpline)
The Centre, made up of government,
management, and labor representatives,
offers information to Canadians about
chemicals, chemical products, occupational diseases, and safety. In addition,
it publishes technical materials and
runs a twenty-four-hour computer information service as well as the toll-free
helpline.

Chemical Manufacturers Association
   (CMA)
2501 M Street, N.W.
Washington, DC   20037
(202) 887-1100
(800) 262-8200 (Chemical Referral
   Center)
CMA is a trade organization representing many of the chemical firms in the
United States. It provides information
on safety and environmental protection
issues, among many other subjects.

National Institute of Occupational
   Safety & Health Information
   (NIOSH)
Center for Disease Control
4676 Columbia Parkway
Cincinnati, OH   45226
(513) 533-8236

From NIOSH you can receive a list of
nearly three hundred products that
contain carcinogens.

Consumer Information Center
P.O. Box 100
Pueblo, CO   81002
Publishes a variety of brochures on environmental safety, including *A Citi-
zen's Guide to Radon* (item #139V,
costs $1), *Lead and Your Drinking Wa-
ter* (item #432V, costs $.50), and *Re-
moval of Radon from Household Water*
(item #433V, costs $.50).

Hazardous Materials Transportation
   Office
Research & Special Programs
   Administration
U.S. Department of Transportation
400 7th Street, S.W.
Washington, DC   20590
(202) 366-0656
This office advises shippers, governmental agencies, and the general public on
all phases of transportation of hazardous materials, such as explosives, ra-
dioactive materials, poisons, and gases.

National Pesticide Telecommunications
   Network (NPTN)
3601 4th Street
Lubbock, TX   79430
(806) 743-3091
(800) 858-7378

NPTN provides a variety of information about pesticide products, recognition and management of pesticide poisonings, emergency treatment information, safety information, health and environmental effects, and cleanup and disposal procedures. The Network publishes a brochure describing its services. A hotline responds to inquiries from emergency rooms, doctors, and the general public.

Nuclear Regulatory Commission
Office of Governmental & Public Affairs
U.S. Nuclear Regulatory Commission
Washington, DC   20555
(202) 492-7715
This agency regulates the nuclear industry and the storage, handling, and packaging of nuclear materials during transport. It will answer questions and make referrals for the public.

STATE AGENCIES FOR ENVIRONMENTAL PROTECTION AND POLLUTION CONTROL

This section lists departments of environmental affairs in all fifty states and the District of Columbia and Puerto Rico. If a separate office exists for pollution control, that telephone number or address is also listed.

Alabama

Air Division
State Capitol
Montgomery, AL   36130
(205) 271-7861

Department of Environmental
  Management
1751 Congressman William L.
  Dickinson Drive
Montgomery, AL   36130
(205) 271-7700

Alaska

Department of Environmental
  Conservation
P.O. Box O
Juneau, AK   99811-1800
(907) 465-2600

Air Quality Management Section
(907) 465-2666

Arizona

Department of Environmental Quality
2005 N. Central Avenue
Phoenix, AZ   85004
(602) 257-2300

Office of Air Quality
(602) 257-2308

Arkansas

Department of Pollution Control &
  Ecology
P.O. Box 9583
Little Rock, AR 72219
(501) 562-7444

California

Environmental Affairs Agency
1102 Q Street
Sacramento, CA 95814
(916) 322-4203

Air Resources Board
(916) 445-4383

Colorado

Air Quality Control Commission
4210 E. 11th Avenue
Denver, CO 80220
(303) 331-8500

Department of Natural Resources
State Centennial Building, Room 718
1313 Sherman Street
Denver, CO 80203
(303) 866-3311

Connecticut

Department of Environmental
  Protection
State Office Building, Room 1134
165 Capitol Avenue
Hartford, CT 06106
(203) 566-4030

Air Compliance Section
Room 144
(203) 566-4030

Delaware

Department of Natural Resources &
  Environmental Control
P.O. Box 1401
Dover, DE 19903
(302) 736-4764

Air Resources Section
(302) 736-4791

District of Columbia

Environmental Control Division
5010 Overlook Drive, S.W
Washington, DC 20032
(202) 783-3180

Florida

Department of Environmental
  Regulation
Twin Towers Building, Room 618
2600 Blair Stone Road
Tallahassee, FL 32399-2400
(904) 488-4805

Division of Air Resources Management
(904) 488-1344

Georgia

Department of Natural Resources
205 Butler Street, Suite 1252
Atlanta, GA   30334
(404) 656-3500

Air Quality Control Section
(405) 656-6900

Hawaii

Environmental Protection & Health
   Services Division
P.O. Box 3378
Honolulu, HI   96801
(808) 548-6455

Office of Environmental Quality Control
465 S. King Street, Room 104
Honolulu, HI   96813
(808) 548-6915

Idaho

Division of Environmental Quality
Towers Building, 5th Floor
450 W. State Street
Boise, ID   83720
(208) 334-5840

Bureau of Air Quality
(208) 334-5898

Illinois

Environmental Protection Agency
2200 Churchill Road
Springfield, IL   62706
(217) 782-3397

Division of Air Pollution Control
(217) 782-7326

Indiana

Department of Environmental
   Management
105 S. Meridian Street
Indianapolis, IN   46225
(317) 232-3210

Office of Air Management
P.O. Box 6015
Indianapolis, IN   46206-6015
(317) 232-8222

Iowa

Division of Environmental Protection
Wallace State Office Building
E. 9th and Grand Avenue
Des Moines, IA   50319-0034
(515) 281-6284

Air Quality & Solid Waste Protection
   Bureau
(515) 281-8852

Kansas

Division of Environment
Building 740, Forbes Field
Topeka, KS   66620
(913) 296-1535

Bureau of Air Quality & Radiation
  Control
(913) 296-1542

Kentucky

Department of Environmental
  Protection
Fort Boone Plaza
18 Reilly Road
Frankfort, KY   40601
(502) 564-2150

Division for Air Quality
(502) 564-3382

Louisiana

Department of Environmental Quality
P.O. Box 44066
Baton Rouge, LA   70804
(504) 342-1266

Air Quality Division
(504) 342-1206

Maine

Department of Environmental
  Protection
State House
Station 17
Augusta, ME   04333
(207) 289-2811

Bureau of Air Quality Control
(207) 289-2437

Maryland

Department of the Environment
2500 Broening Highway
Baltimore, MD   21224
(301) 631-3084

Air Management Administration
(301) 631-3255

Massachusetts

Division of Air Quality Control
1 Winter Street, 8th Floor
Boston, MA   02108
(617) 292-5593

Executive Office of Environmental
  Affairs
Leverett Saltonstall State Office
  Building
100 Cambridge Street, Room 2000
Boston, MA   02202
(617) 727-9800

Michigan

Division of Environmental Protection
P.O. Box 30028
Lansing, MI   48909
(517) 373-7917

Air Quality Division
(517) 373-7023

Minnesota

Division of Air Quality
Pollution Control Agency
520 Lafayette Road
St. Paul, MN   55155
(612) 296-7331

Environmental Quality Board
Centennial Office Building
658 Cedar Street, Room 300
St. Paul, MN   55155
(612) 296-2603

Mississippi

Bureau of Pollution Control
P.O. Box 10385
Jackson, MS   39209
(601) 961-5171

Missouri

Division of Environmental Quality
P.O. Box 176
Jefferson City, MO   65102
(314) 751-4810

Air Pollution Control Program
(314) 751-4817

Montana

Environmental Sciences Division
Cogswell Building
Capitol Station
Helena, MT   59620
(406) 444-3948

Air Quality Bureau
(406) 444-3454

Nebraska

Department of Environmental Control
P.O. Box 98922
Lincoln, NE   68509-8922
(402) 471-2186

Nevada

Division of Environmental Protection
Capitol Complex
Carson City, NV   89710
(702) 885-4670

New Hampshire

Department of Environmental Services
Health & Human Services Building
6 Hazen Drive
Concord, NH   03301
(603) 271-3503

Division of Air Resources
Caller Box 2033
Concord, NH   03301
(603) 271-1370

New Jersey

Department of Environmental
   Protection
CN 402
Trenton, NJ   08625
(609) 292-2885

Air Division
CN 027
(609) 292-5383

New Mexico

Environmental Improvement Division
Harold Runnels Building
1190 St. Francis Drive
Santa Fe, NM   87503
(505) 827-2850

Air Quality Bureau
(505) 827-0042

New York

Environmental Conservation
   Department
50 Wolf Road
Albany, NY   12233-0001
(518) 457-3446

Division of Air Resources
(518) 457-7231

North Carolina

Division of Environmental Management
P.O. Box 27687
Raleigh, NC   27611
(919) 733-7015

Air Quality Section
(919) 733-3340

North Dakota

Environmental Health Section
P.O. Box 5520
Bismarck, ND   58502-5520
(701) 224-2374

Division of Environmental Engineering
(701) 224-2348

Ohio

Ohio Environmental Protection Agency
P.O. Box 1049
Columbus, OH   43266-0149
(614) 644-2782

Division of Air Pollution Control
(614) 644-2270

Oklahoma

Department of Pollution Control
P.O. Box 53504
Oklahoma City, OK   73152
(405) 271-4677

Air Quality Service
P.O. Box 53551
(405) 271-5220

Oregon

Department of Environmental Quality
Executive Building
811 S.W. 6th Street
Portland, OR   97204-1390
(503) 229-5300

Air Quality Division
(503) 229-5397

Pennsylvania

Department of Environmental
   Resources
P.O. Box 2063
Harrisburg, PA   17120
(717) 787-2814

Bureau of Air Quality Control
P.O. Box 2357
(717) 787-9702

Rhode Island

Department of Environmental
   Management
83 Park Street
Providence, RI   02903
(401) 277-3434

Division of Air & Hazardous Materials
291 Promenade Street
Providence, RI   02908-5767
(401) 277-2797

South Carolina

Division of Environmental Quality
   Control
J. Marion Sims Building, Room 415
2600 Bull Street
Columbia, SC   29201
(803) 734-5360

Bureau of Air Quality Control
(803) 734-4750

South Dakota

Department of Water & Natural
   Resources
Joe Foss Building, Room 209
523 E. Capitol Avenue
Pierre, SD   57501
(605) 773-3151

Division of Air Quality & Solid Waste
Room 416
(605) 773-3153

Tennessee

Air Pollution Control Division
Customs House, 4th Floor
701 Broadway
Nashville, TN 37219-5403
(615) 741-3931

Department of Health & Environment
Cordell Hull Building, Room 347
436 6th Avenue N.
Nashville, TN 37219-5402
(615) 741-3111

Texas

Air Control Board
6330 Highway 290 E.
Austin, TX 78723
(512) 451-5711

Environmental & Consumer Health
  Protection
1100 W. 49th Street
Austin, TX 78756
(512) 458-7541

Utah

Division of Environmental Health
P.O. Box 16690
Salt Lake City, UT 84116-0690
(801) 538-6121

Bureau of Air Quality
(801) 538-6108

Vermont

Natural Resources Agency
Waterbury Office Complex
Center Building
103 S. Main Street
Waterbury, VT 05676
(802) 244-7347

Air Pollution Control Division
(802) 244-8731

Virginia

Council on the Environment
202 N. 9th Street, Room 903
Richmond, VA 23219
(804) 786-4500

State Air Pollution Control Board
P.O. Box 10089
Richmond, VA 23240
(804) 786-2378

Washington

Department of Ecology
St. Martins College
Mail Stop PV-11
Olympia, WA 98504
(206) 459-6168

Air Program Division
(206) 459-6256

West Virginia

Air Pollution Control Commission
1558 Washington Street E.
Charleston, WV   25311
(304) 348-3286

Department of Natural Resources
State Office Building 3, Room 669
1800 Washington Street E.
Charleston, WV   25305
(304) 348-2754

Wisconsin

Department of Natural Resources
P.O. Box 7921
Madison, WI   53707
(608) 266-2121

Bureau of Air Management
(608) 266-0603

Wyoming

Department of Environmental Quality
Herschler Building, 4th Floor
122 W. 25th Street
Cheyenne, WY   82002
(307) 777-7938

Air Quality Division
(307) 777-7391

Puerto Rico

Environmental Quality Board
P.O. Box 11488
Santurce, PR   00910
(809) 725-5140 (ext. 214)

Air Quality Bureau
(809) 725-5140 (ext. 222)

CHAPTER 7

GRIEF AND MOURNING

No loss is as painful as the loss of a child. The organizations in the first part of this chapter, LOSS OF A CHILD, work to ease the grief of parents and others. The second section, SUDDEN INFANT DEATH SYNDROME (SIDS), lists groups helping parents whose child is lost through SIDS.

SEE ALSO

the CANCER and TERMINALLY ILL AND HOSPITALIZED CHILDREN sections in Chapter 5 for additional organizations that help with grief and mourning.

The SELF-HELP CLEARINGHOUSES section of Chapter 13 lists local mutual support groups that help with grief.

☎ ☎

LOSS OF A CHILD

Aiding Mothers & Fathers Experiencing
  Neonatal Death (A.M.E.N.D.)
4324 Berrywich Terrace
St. Louis, MO   63128
(314) 487-7582

A.M.E.N.D. is a free counseling service for parents who have experienced the loss of an infant through miscarriage, stillbirth, or neonatal death.

Association for Recognizing the Life of
Stillborns
11128 W. Frost Avenue
Littleton, CO   80127
(303) 978-9517
For a fee this small organization offers
a Certificate of Life for parents who
have suffered a miscarriage or early
death of an infant.

Compassionate Friends
P.O. Box 3696
Oak Brook, IL   60522
(312) 990-0010
This self-help group is open to any parent who has suffered the loss of a child.
They provide written materials and
"telephone friends" who can help you
through the grieving process.

Good Grief
Inland Empire Perinatal Center
411 Medical Center Building
Spokane, WA   99204
(509) 624-3182
This support group, facilitated by
nurses and mental health counselors, is
for parents who have lost an infant
through miscarriage, stillbirth, or infant death.

Good Grief Program
Judge Baker Guidance Center
295 Longwood Avenue
Boston, MA   02115
(617) 232-8390

The Good Grief Program uses schools
and community groups as bases of support for groups of children and adolescents (preschool through high school)
attempting to cope with death and dy-
ing of friends, classmates, teachers, but
not family members. The Program
helps prevent suicides and eases the bereavement process through advisory
and consulting services. Publications
include *Good Grief: Helping Groups of
Children When a Friend Dies* and a
video or film called *The Death of a
Friend.*

Grief Recovery Institute
8306 Wilshire Boulevard
Los Angeles, CA   90211
(213) 650-1234
(800) 445-4808 (hotline, 8:00 A.M.–
5:00 P.M.)
The National Grief Recovery Hotline
seeks to ease the isolation of those suffering from a loss and to assist them in
coping with their grief.

Heartbeat
2015 Devon Street
Colorado Springs, CO   80909
(719) 596-2575
A self-help group for those trying to
cope with the loss of a friend or family
member through suicide. Will provide
guidelines for starting a group.

Helping Other Parents in Normal Grieving (HOPING)

Edward W. Sparrow Hospital
1215 E. Michigan Avenue
Lansing, MI   48909-7980
(517) 483-3873

HOPING is a mutual-help group of parents who have experienced a miscarriage, stillbirth, or otherwise lost an infant. Programs include direct aid for the bereaved parent and community education. The HOPING newsletter is published monthly.

National Perinatal Bereavement Alliance (NPBA)

13557 Wendy Lane
Saratoga, CA   95070
(408) 867-6266

NPBA is made up of caregivers who offer support to families bereaved by the loss of a child through miscarriage, stillbirth, or newborn death. NPBA principally assists care providers through emotional support and by serving as a clearinghouse for information about perinatal bereavement concepts, resources, and services.

Parents Experiencing Perinatal Death (PEPD)

P.O. Box 38445
Germantown, TN   38138
(901) 372-5102

PEPD offers emotional support and information to parents whose babies have died from premature death, stillbirth, or newborn death. It runs a twenty-four-hour telephone hotline and monthly discussion groups. It provides information on grieving, burial, autopsies, and other legal and medical details. PEPD publishes a pamphlet for bereaved parents in the Memphis area and has created a bibliography of articles, books, and booklets.

Parents of Murdered Children

100 E. 8th Street, Apt. B-41
Cincinnati, OH   45202
(513) 721-5683

This group helps parents and other relatives of children who die violently. It provides information about grieving and publishes a newsletter, *Survivors*.

Parents of Near-Drowners (P.O.N.D.)

14911 National Avenue, Suite 1B
Los Gatos, CA   95032-2632
(408) 358-2661

For parents who have lost a child through drowning or whose child has come close to drowning, this group provides emotional support, works to prevent drowning, supplies information, makes referrals, and publishes a newsletter.

Pen-Grandparents

P.O. Box 3304
Jasper, AL   35502
(205) 384-3053

Pen-Grandparents provides a correspondence network for bereaved grandparents.

Pen-Parents
P.O. Box 8738
Reno, NV   89507-9998
Pen-Parents offers a newsletter and correspondence network for parents suffering from miscarriage or infant loss.

Pregnancy & Infant Loss Center
1421 E. Wayzata Boulevard, Room 40
Wayzata, MN   55391
(612) 473-9372
The Center helps parents who have suffered miscarriage, stillbirth, or infant death by offering referrals and distributing information packets. It publishes the *Loving Arms Newsletter*.

Reach Out to the Parents of an Unknown Child, Inc.
555 N. Country Road
St. James, NY   11780
(516) 862-6743
Reach Out is a support group of parents who have lost a child through miscarriage, stillbirth, or early infant death. It provides phone contact with trained members who have experienced a similar loss.

Resolve Through Sharing
La Crosse Lutheran Hospital
1910 South Avenue
La Crosse, WI   54601
(608) 785-0530
Offers support services to parents who have had a miscarriage or a stillbirth.

SHARE
St. Elizabeth's Hospital
211 S. 3rd Street
Belleville, IL   62222
(618) 234-2415 (ext. 1430)
SHARE helps parents of miscarriages and stillbirths with information and support services. It publishes *SHARE Newsletter*, brochures, and *Thumpy's Story*, a children's book on grief.

Unite, Inc.
c/o Jeanes Hospital
7600 Central Avenue
Philadelphia, PA   19111
(215) 728-2082
(215) 728-3777
Unite sponsors group meetings, an annual conference, a newsletter, and telephone support for parents who have lost a child through miscarriage, stillbirth, or infant death.

SUDDEN INFANT DEATH SYNDROME (SIDS)

American Sudden Infant Death
   Syndrome Institute (ASIDSI)
275 Carpenter Drive, N.E.
Atlanta, GA   30328
(404) 843-1030
(800) 847-SIDS (7437) (in Georgia)
For professional health-care providers
and families suffering the loss of a child
through SIDS, the Institute seeks to
improve infant health care through education, increased clinical services, and
emotional support. In addition, it conducts research into causes and cures,
offers seminars, and runs a speakers'
bureau.

Association of SIDS Program
   Professionals
Massachusetts Center for SIDS
Boston City Hospital
818 Harrison Avenue
Boston, MA   02118
(617) 534-7437
Limited referrals are offered by this
group.

California SIDS Program
2151 Berkeley Way
Annex 4-400
Berkeley, CA   94704
(800) 369-SIDS (7437)
Primarily for Californians.

Canadian Foundation for the Study of
   Infant Deaths
P.O. Box 190
Station R
Toronto, Ontario M4G 3Z9
Canada
(416) 488-3260
(800) 263-1430 (in Canada)
The Foundation provides information
and counseling to families stricken by
SIDS. The group also publishes a num-
ber of brochures.

Colorado SIDS Program, Inc.
1330 Leyden Street, Suite 134
Denver, CO   80220
(303) 320-7771
(800) 332-1018 (in Colorado)
The Program offers information and
counseling to families who have lost a
baby to SIDS. It runs monthly meetings, makes referrals to other local
community resources, and publishes
New Beginnings, a bimonthly newsletter.

Guild for Infant Survival
9178 Nadine River Circle
Fountain Valley, CA   92708
(714) 968-7623
(800) 247-4370

This guild of twenty organizations seeks to prevent Sudden Infant Death Syndrome (SIDS), offers support to the families of SIDS victims, and educates the public about SIDS. It publishes a newsletter, *SIDS Parent.*

Minnesota Sudden Infant Death Center (SIDS Center)
Children's Medical Center
2526 Chicago Avenue S.
Minneapolis, MN   55404
(612) 863-6285
Primarily for residents of Minnesota.

National Center for the Prevention of Sudden Infant Death Syndrome
330 N. Charles Street
Baltimore, MD   21201
(301) 547-0300
(800) 638-SIDS (7437)
Provides advice and referrals over the telephone.

National Sudden Infant Death Syndrome Clearinghouse
8201 Greensboro Drive, Suite 600
McLean, VA   22102
(703) 821-8955

This Clearinghouse offers information and educational materials on SIDS, apnea, and related issues. It responds to inquiries; supplies fact sheets, catalogs, and brochures; and maintains a list of local groups, programs, and individuals involved with SIDS. It also publishes a newsletter called *Information Exchange.*

National Sudden Infant Death Syndrome Foundation
10500 Little Patuxent Parkway
Suite 420
Columbia, MD   21044
(301) 964-8000
(800) 221-7437
The Foundation's eighty chapters strive to eliminate SIDS and related disorders. Through parent-to-parent contact, assistance is given to families whose infants have died from sudden infant death syndrome. The Foundation also distributes pamphlets and booklets and publishes two newsletters, *The Leaflet* and *Parent Cable.*

─────── ☎ ───────

C H A P T E R   8

EDUCATION

Deciding how to educate your child is never easy. The organizations in this chapter will answer questions on a wide range of education issues. These groups also help parents find local schools and choose the best school for their child.

For help with a specific issue, see these sections: PRESCHOOL AND ELEMENTARY SCHOOL EDUCATION; PRIVATE AND ALTERNATIVE EDUCATION; GIFTED CHILDREN; FINANCIAL AID; INTERNATIONAL EXCHANGE PROGRAMS; BILINGUALISM; MINORITY AND UNDERPRIVILEGED CHILDREN; DISCIPLINE IN SCHOOLS; DROPOUT PREVENTION; READING AND LITERACY; TELEVISION VIEWING; and TESTING.

If none of these sections seems useful, try calling some of the groups listed at the beginning of this chapter under GENERAL ORGANIZATIONS. See especially the ERIC Clearinghouses; the National Education Association; and the National PTA. They offer referrals on a huge range of educational subjects.

For help finding information about specific schools in a certain location, particularly public schools, see the last two sections: STATE OFFICES OF THE NATIONAL PTA and STATE EDUCATION AGENCIES.

SEE ALSO

the SPECIAL NEEDS, HANDICAPS, AND LEARNING DISABILITIES section of Chapter 5 for help with the education of special-needs children.

The MAIL ORDER CATALOGS section in Chapter 12 lists merchants offering many educational products.

☎ ☎ ☎ ☎ ☎ ☎ ☎ ☎ ☎ ☎ ☎ ☎ ☎ ☎ ☎ ☎ ☎ ☎ ☎ ☎

GENERAL ORGANIZATIONS

**Association for Childhood Education
International (ACEI)**
11141 Georgia Avenue, Suite 200
Wheaton, MD   20902
(301) 942-2443
(800) 423-3563
The fifteen thousand members of ACEI
support equal educational opportunity
for all children and a raised level of
teacher training and administrator preparedness. To this end they conduct
workshops and disseminate information. A catalog of publications and audiovisual materials is available.

Council for Basic Education (CBE)
725 15th Street, N.W.
Washington, DC   20005
(202) 347-4171
The Council oversees and analyzes research in education and promotes the
teaching of liberal arts such as geogra-
phy, English, science, and foreign languages. It runs a speakers' bureau,
Writing to Learn workshops, and several other programs.

Designs for Change (DFC)
220 S. State Street, Suite 1900
Chicago, IL   60604
(312) 922-0317
DFC's research considers ways to improve public schooling on the local
level. The group helps parents, teachers, administrators, and students implement change, provides consultations
and training, distributes information,
makes referrals, and maintains a resource library.

Education Development Center (EDC)
55 Chapel Street
Newton, MA   02160
(617) 969-7100
The Center brings teachers, researchers, officials, curriculum specialists, and others to pool their ideas and
experience regarding educational improvement.

**ERIC Clearinghouse for Science,
Mathematics, & Environmental
Education**
Ohio State University
1200 Chambers Road, Room 310
Columbus, OH   43212-1792
(614) 292-6717
The Clearinghouse prepares teaching
materials, trains instructors, develops
educational programs, and performs research in the teaching of science, mathematics, and environmental studies.

ERIC Clearinghouse for Social
  Studies/Social Science Education
Indiana University
Social Studies Development Center
2805 E. 10th Street, Suite 120
Bloomington, IN   47405-2373
(812) 855-3838
The Development Center focuses on all
aspects of teaching and learning social
studies including developing curricula
on current issues such as ethnic studies, applying theory to practice, and
examining the content of classroom
materials.

ERIC Clearinghouse on Higher
  Education
George Washington University
1 Dupont Circle, N.W., Suite 630
Washington, DC   20036-1183
(202) 296-2597
The Clearinghouse provides information
on colleges and universities including
programs such as professional and
continuing education, legal issues,
finance, and institutional research. All
the ERIC Clearinghouses are excellent
government-sponsored information
centers that gladly help the public.

ERIC Clearinghouse on Urban
  Education
Teachers College
Columbia University
Institute for Urban & Minority
  Education

Main Hall, Room 300, Box 40
525 W. 120th Street
New York, NY   10027-9998
(212) 678-3433
The Clearinghouse takes a special interest in the problems of urban education,
minority experiences, and urban social
services.

Institute for Responsive Education
  (IRE)
605 Commonwealth Avenue
Boston, MA   02215
(617) 353-3309
Through its research, writings, and
training programs, the Institute promotes parent participation in the
educational process. It publishes the
journal *Equity and Choice* three times
a year.

Institute of Child Development (ICD)
University of Minnesota
51 E. River Road
Minneapolis, MN   55455
(612) 624-2568
The Institute conducts research and
training in the perceptual, cognitive,
language, and social development of
children. Although designed mainly for
researchers and academics, this group
will answer questions and make
referrals to anyone.

International Association for Better Basic Education (IABBE)
19125 S.W. Glenco Place
Dunnellon, FL   32630
(904) 489-9468
An association for anyone interested in improving basic education, the focus is on such issues as speech and spelling, reading, basic math, and handwriting. IABBE publishes a newsletter and a periodical.

International Listening Association (ILA)
c/o Dr. Charles Roberts
Box 90340
McNeese State University
Lake Charles, LA   70609
(318) 475-5120
The Association provides information and publications on effective listening and its affects on educational, cultural, and race relations. ILA maintains a library, hosts seminars and workshops, and publishes an annual newsletter, studies, and reports.

Media Center for Children (MCC)
3 W. 29th Street
New York, NY   10001
(212) 679-9620
MCC is a nonprofit media evaluation and programming resource dedicated to identifying quality films and videotapes for children. While MCC services are intended primarily for librarians, teachers, programmers of media, and filmmakers, it offers information to anyone. Publications include *More Films Kids Like, What to Do When the Lights Go On,* and annotated film lists.

National Association for Year-Round Education
P.O. Box 11386
San Diego, CA   92111
(619) 276-5296
This is an organization for those who see year-round schooling as a means to improve educational standards, meet family life-styles, and provide optimum economic benefits. It maintains a library of research articles, newspaper clippings, and publishes a directory and several periodicals.

National Association of Partners in Education (NAPE)
601 Wythe Street, Suite 200
Alexandria, VA   22314
(703) 836-4880
Dedicated to encouraging volunteer participation in school systems, the Association helps schools start and enhance volunteer programs, emphasizing basic skills, English as a second language, and special education. NAPE encourages businesses and private citizens, particularly older people, to become involved in local schools.

National Association of Secondary
  School Principals (NASSP)
1904 Association Drive
Reston, VA   22091
(703) 860-0200
This association of secondary school
principals and administrators runs the
National Association of Student Councils, the National Honor Society, and
the National Junior Honor Society. It
publishes a number of journals and
newsletters, including *Leadership for
Student Activities,* a magazine for student leaders.

National Coalition of Title I/Chapter I
  Parents (NCTCP)
Edmonds School Building
9th and D Streets, N.W., Room 201
Washington, DC   20002
(202) 547-9286
Title I gives parents of disadvantaged
children the authority to establish advisory councils that coordinate with
other local agencies in planning, running, and evaluating programs for their
children. The Coalition supports complete community involvement and runs
training conferences where information
and experiences are exchanged among
administrators, teachers, parents, and
other concerned persons.

National Conference on Parent
  Involvement (NCPI)
579 W. Iroquois
Pontiac, MI   48053
(313) 334-5887
This conference is held each year to
bring together parents, teachers, and
other supporters of parent involvement
in the schools.

National Congress for Educational
  Excellence
11524 E. Ricks Circle
Dallas, TX   75230
(214) 368-3449
Committed to the basics in education,
the Congress supports an increase in
the teaching of basic skills in the
school curriculum. It counsels parents
on their rights within the educational
structure.

National Education Association (NEA)
1201 16th Street, N.W.
Washington, DC   20036
(202) 833-4000
NEA, comprised of educators, school
support staff, administrators, and teaching students, can provide information
and referrals on a wide range of education issues. One of its current programs
is the Health Information Network,
which fosters comprehensive health education, helping teachers help students

avoid smoking, drug and alcohol abuse, and other destructive behaviors.

National PTA—National Congress of
    Parents & Teachers
700 N. Rush Street
Chicago, IL   60611
(312) 787-0977
An enormous organization of over six million parents, teachers, students, and administrators, National PTA offers information and referrals on a wide range of educational matters. It publishes a number of journals, newsletters, and pamphlets on important child-related topics. Send a self-addressed, stamped envelope for their catalog of many extremely useful brochures.

The Network, Inc. (TNI)
290 S. Main Street
Andover, MA   01810
(508) 470-1080
The Network takes an interest in a broad array of educational issues, running, for example: writing programs for talented children and for adults with limited proficiency; nutrition-education programs; programs for developing computer-based curricula; and school-evaluation programs. It conducts research, provides technical assistance, and distributes information.

Quest International
P.O. Box 566, 537 Jones Road
Granville, OH   43023
(614) 522-6400
Quest helps junior and senior high school students and their parents and teachers develop necessary social skills such as interpersonal communication, enhanced self-esteem, and abstention from substance abuse. The group hosts workshops, provides services for children, and runs a speakers' bureau.

U.S.A. Toy Library Association
2719 Broadway Avenue
Evanston, IL   60201
(312) 864-8240
A group of parents and child-care professionals who promote the value of toys in child development and child-parent relationships, the Association works to increase the use of toys in libraries and day-care centers and will make referrals to the public.

Women's Educational Equity Act
    Publishing Center
Education Development Center, Inc.
55 Chapel Street, Suite 256
Newton, MA   02160
(617) 969-7100
(800) 225-3088
The Center distributes materials that assist schools and colleges in implementing physical education programs fair to both girls and boys.

PRESCHOOL AND ELEMENTARY SCHOOL EDUCATION

American Montessori Society
150 5th Avenue, Suite 203
New York, NY 10011
(212) 924-3209
Montessori education is based on the
concept that young children instinc-
tively love and need purposeful work.
The Montessori environment is based
on controlled freedom in which the
child can pursue his or her own interests with the teacher as an aid and an
observer. The Society establishes educational standards, accredits schools,
provides information and referrals,
maintains an archive, offers technical
assistance in setting up schools, and
runs educational workshops. It publishes a *School Directory* annually.

Department of Child Development &
   Family Studies
Purdue University
West Lafayette, IN 47907
(317) 494-2932
The specialists in this department will
answer questions and offer consultations regarding early childhood education, family studies, parent education,
and marriage and family therapy.

Elementary School Center (ESC)
2 E. 103rd Street
New York, NY 10029
(212) 289-5929
ESC serves as a clearinghouse of information, runs a speakers' bureau, and
publishes books and monographs on elementary education and children.

ERIC Clearinghouse on Elementary &
   Early Childhood Education
University of Illinois
College of Education
805 W. Pennsylvania Avenue
Urbana, IL 61801-4897
(217) 333-1386
The College of Education provides
information to everyone on childhood
development from birth through early
adolescence. Subjects include the influence of prenatal and parenting environments, and learning theory and practice.
It trains teachers and runs educational
and community programs for children.

High/Scope Educational Research
   Foundation
600 N. River Street
Ypsilanti, MI 48197
(313) 485-2000

The Foundation performs research, offers curriculum development, and consultations in early childhood education and child development. It publishes a newsletter, *High/Scope ReSource,* and distributes books and a catalog of audiovisual materials on early childhood education.

Institute for Childhood Resources
210 Columbus Avenue, Room 611
San Francisco, CA   94133
(415) 864-1169
The Institute runs programs and workshops for parents and professionals in child care, play, and parenting. It offers consultation to anyone involved in childhood education and publishes such books as *The Whole Child: A Sourcebook.*

National Association for the Education of Young Children
1834 Connecticut Avenue, N.W.
Washington, DC   20009
(202) 232-8777
(800) 424-2460
The Association is made up of over seventy thousand teachers, directors, and other interested persons involved with day-care programs, play groups and elementary schools. It offers referrals regarding educational services and resources for young children and publishes books, posters, and pamphlets.

National Association of Elementary School Principals (NAESP)
1615 Duke Street
Alexandria, VA   22314
(703) 684-3345
This professional group offers referrals to the public.

National Head Start Association
1220 King Street, Suite 200
Alexandria, VA   22314
(703) 739-0875
The Association assists local Head Start Programs and provides seminars and training in early childhood education.

New England Association for the Education of Young Children
c/o Edgar Klugman
35 Pilgrim Road
Wheelock College
Boston, MA   02215
(617) 734-5200
This group answers questions and distributes publications concerning early childhood education.

Parent Cooperative Pre-Schools International (PCPI)
P.O. Box 90410
Indianapolis, IN   46290
(317) 849-0992
PCPI offers information and educational materials to those interested in parent-run, nonprofit nursery schools. The Co-

operative makes referrals and publishes a newsletter, an annual directory, and a number of handbooks. Call them for the district office number for your locality.

Southern Association on Children Under Six (SACUS)
Box 5403, Brady Station
Little Rock, AR   72215
(501) 227-6404

SACUS will answer questions regarding day care, nursery education, kindergarten education, and standards for the care and education of children under six. The Association distributes books and publishes a journal called *Dimensions*.

PRIVATE AND ALTERNATIVE EDUCATION

PRIVATE SCHOOLS

Committee on Boarding Schools (CBS)
75 Federal Street
Boston, MA   02110
(617) 723-6900
CBS provides information and referrals to the public about boarding schools. It publishes the *Boarding Schools Directory*, the annual *Summer Programs*, and a video on boarding schools.

Council for American Private Education (CAPE)
1625 I Street, N.W., Suite 412
Washington, DC   20006
(202) 659-0016
This coalition of several national organizations representing private schools offers referrals to the public. Periodically it publishes *Private Schools of the United States*.

RELIGIOUS SCHOOLS

Christian

Association of Christian Schools International (ACSI)
P.O. Box 4097
Whittier, CA   90607-4097
(213) 694-4791
Formed to provide representation for Christian schools in conflicts with the government, the Association also oversees student activities such as piano festivals, science fairs, and sporting events. It conducts training seminars, offers reduced purchasing rates for supplies and materials, runs a library of

curriculum materials as well as a placement service.

Christian Schools International (CSI)
3350 E. Paris Avenue, S.E.
Grand Rapids, MI   49512
(616) 957-1070
CSI helps develop and administer curricula for Reformed Christian elementary and secondary schools. It maintains an extensive library and publishes an annual directory of international Christian schools.

Evangelical Lutheran Education Association (ELEA)
Wartburg College
Waverly, IA   50677
(319) 352-8290
The Association is for congregations running Lutheran schools from preschool through junior high. It provides a forum to exchange ideas, runs a testing service and interschool events, sponsors an accreditation program, and maintains a reference library.

National Catholic Educational Association (NCEA)
1077 30th Street, N.W., Suite 100
Washington, DC   20007
(202) 337-6232
Comprising individuals and educational institutions from kindergarten through graduate school, the Association serves as a clearinghouse of information. It publishes directories and manuals, books and reports, pamphlets, papers, and audio- and videocassettes.

Parents for Quality Education (PQE)
P.O. Box 50025
Pasadena, CA   91105
(818) 798-1124
Part of Christian Educators Association International, the parents, teachers, administrators, and others affiliated with PQE run workshops, maintain a speakers' bureau, and offer referrals.

Jewish

Central Organization for Jewish Education (COJE)
770 Eastern Parkway
Brooklyn, NY   11213
(718) 774-4000
Dedicated to promoting Jewish education and religious practice, COJE develops school curricula, runs a center for research on Hasidic history and philosophy, maintains a 125,000-volume library, and publishes several journals, books, and pamphlets.

Coalition for the Advancement of Jewish Education (CAJE)
261 W. 35th Street, Room 12A
New York, NY   10001
(212) 268-4210
For those interested in any aspect of Jewish education, the Coalition runs a

network providing information to teachers, administrators, and youth workers. It publishes a magazine, several journals and periodicals, and an annual directory.

Jewish Education Service of North America

730 Broadway
New York, NY   10003-9540
(212) 529-2000

The Service publishes the *Jewish Education Directory* every three years. In addition, it oversees research on Jewish education, runs a licensing board and a fellowship program, and provides a teacher placement service.

Solomon Schechter Day School Association

155 5th Avenue
New York, NY   10010
(212) 260-8450

The Association, comprising sixty-eight Jewish day schools, provides information, coordinates school accreditation, helps found new schools, develops curricula, and places teachers. Annually it publishes a free directory of its affiliated schools.

United Parents-Teachers Association of Jewish Schools

426 W. 58th Street
New York, NY   10019
(212) 245-8200

The Association is dedicated to involving parents in Jewish education by encouraging them to organize events for families. It runs seminars, lectures, and film showings on social issues; sponsors outreach programs; and publishes booklets on holidays and education.

HOME SCHOOLING

Calvert School

Tuscany Road, Dept. MOS
Baltimore, MD   21210
(301) 243-6030

Calvert provides a complete curriculum for home-teaching from kindergarten through eighth grade. The school's catalog is free.

Center for Early Learning

P.O. Box 250
Amherst, NH   03031
(603) 882-8688

The Center has developed a home-study course for preschoolers to first-graders. A free brochure is available.

Home Education Press

P.O. Box 1083
Tonasket, WA   98855
(509) 486-1351

The free catalog from Home Education Press lists books for parents who are considering home education as an alternative to public education.

Moby Dick Academy (MDA)
Box 236
Ocean Park, WA   98640
(206) 665-4577
The Academy supports home schooling as a viable educational alternative and furthers parents' rights to choose the best educational environment for their children. It distributes information, including a curriculum; publishes a newsletter where parents can exchange information; runs Family Learning Centers, conferences, workshops, a museum, and speakers' service; and makes referrals.

National Association for Legal Support of Alternative Schools (NALSAS)
P.O. Box 2823
Santa Fe, NM   87501
(505) 471-6928
The Association, with over six thousand members, promotes educational alternatives through research, dissemination of information, and legal counsel. It runs a seven-hundred volume library and a speakers' bureau.

National Coalition of Alternative Community Schools (NCACS)
58 Schoolhouse Road
Summertown, TN   38483
(615) 964-3670
The Coalition serves as a clearinghouse of information on alternative schools. It offers consultation on establishing school, home curricula, and learning exchanges. Periodically, it publishes the *National Directory of Alternative Schools.*

Oak Meadow
P.O. Box 712
Blacksburg, VA   24060
(703) 552-3263
Oak Meadow offers a home curriculum, which can also be used as a supplement to school courses, for kindergarten through high school. In addition, it offers a correspondence program.

EDUCATIONAL FREEDOM

Americans for Choice in Education (ACE)
940 W. Port Plaza, Suite 264
St. Louis, MO   63146
(314) 878-0400
ACE is an organization for those who believe there is too much governmental control of the schools and feel they should be able to choose their children's school without loss of tax benefits. It provides parents with information on law and strategy.

Citizens for Educational Reform
927 S. Walter Reed Drive, Room 1
Arlington, VA   22204
(703) 486-8311
This organization opposes compulsory attendance in public schools, encour-

ages parents to let policymakers know how they would like their education tax dollars spent, and insists parents have the right to choose the form of education best for their children. It publishes semiannual and bimonthly periodicals.

Council for Educational Freedom in America (CEFA)
14517 Colonels Choice
Upper Marlboro, MD   20772-2811
(301) 627-4686
For parents, teachers, and administrators who feel that the establishment of schools, school curricula, and funding should be determined by them rather

than by state-controlled standards, the Council sponsors seminars for community leaders and publishes a quarterly and a newsletter.

Parents Rights Organization
12571 Northwinds Drive
St. Louis, MO   63146
(314) 434-4171
This organization works to ensure a parent's legal right to freely choose a child's form of education. Their publications, conferences, workshops and research are all directed to this end. The *Parents Rights Newsletter* is issued quarterly.

GIFTED CHILDREN

SEE ALSO

in the HOBBIES section of Chapter 11 under Pen Pals, Gifted Children's Pen Pals International.

In the CHILDREN'S CLUBS section of Chapter 11 under General Clubs, see the National Beta Club, which is for gifted children.

The *Educational Opportunity Guide,* listed in the OTHER SUMMER OPPORTUNITIES section of Chapter 11, describes programs for academically and artistically gifted children.

NATIONAL ORGANIZATIONS

American Association for Gifted Children (AAGC)
c/o Talent Identification Program
10 W. Duke Building
Duke University
Durham, NC   27706
(919) 684-3847
The Association helps gifted children achieve their potential and employ their gifts in helping others. It offers advice, referrals, and publishes guides for parents, teachers, and others working with gifted children.

The Association for the Gifted (TAG)
P.O. Box 115
Sewell, NJ   08080
(212) 319-9220
TAG is an association for parents and teachers of the gifted that works toward establishing programs for gifted children.

Association for Gifted & Talented Students (AGTS)
Northwestern State University
Natchitoches, LA   71301
(318) 357-4572
AGTS offers parents and educators information about current research on gifted children. The Association runs a speakers' bureau and publishes the bimonthly *Gifted-Talented Digest*.

ERIC Clearinghouse on Handicapped & Gifted Children
Council for Exceptional Children
1920 Association Drive
Reston, VA   22091-1589
(703) 620-3660
The Clearinghouse provides information on education and development for both the gifted and the handicapped. An excellent source of help.

Gifted Child Society (GCS)
190 Rock Road
Glen Rock, NJ   07452
(201) 444-6530
GCS acts as an advocate and sponsors the Saturday Workshop Program and Summer Super Stars, which educate and support gifted children. The Society also provides technical assistance for local groups, trains teachers, and assists parents raising gifted children. It runs a speakers' bureau, workshops, discussion groups, and competitions. GCS also publishes a directory and such books as *How to Help Your Gifted Child.*

National Association for Creative Children & Adults (NACCA)
8080 Springvalley Drive
Cincinnati, OH   45236
(513) 631-1777
NACCA researches creativity and applies its findings to helping people excel. It answers questions concerning personal

development, commonsense problem solving, self-discovery, and giftedness. Publications include *The Creative Child and Adult Quarterly; It's Happening to Creative Children and Adults;* and *Crossroads of Talent.* A publications list is available.

National Association for Gifted Children (NAGC)
4175 Lovell Road, Suite 140
Circle Pines, MN   55014
(612) 784-3475
For librarians, teachers, administrators, and parents who seek to develop pro-grams for the gifted to fulfill their potential, the Association disseminates information, sponsors a training institute, and publishes a number of quarterlies, including the *Gifted Child Quarterly.*

National Foundation for Gifted & Creative Children
395 Diamond Hill Road
Warwick, RI   02886
(401) 738-0937
The Foundation is an advocacy group for gifted and creative children. It advises, consults, and provides an information packet for parents.

STATE PROGRAMS FOR GIFTED CHILDREN

These offices can refer you to the programs available for gifted children in your state.

Alabama

Program for Exceptional Children
Department of Education
1020 Monticello Court
Montgomery, AL   36117
(205) 242-8049

Alaska

Gifted & Talented Education
Department of Special Services
P.O. Box F
Juneau, AK   99811-9981
(907) 465-2970

Arizona

Gifted Department Program Specialist
Department of Education
1535 W. Jefferson Street
Phoenix, AZ   85007
(602) 542-5393

Arkansas

Programs for Gifted/Talented
Arch-Ford Education Building
Room 105-C
4 Capitol Mall
Little Rock, AR   72201
(501) 682-4224

California

Gifted/Talented Education
Department of Education
P.O. Box 944272
Sacramento, CA   94244-2720
(916) 323-6148
(916) 323-4781

Colorado

Gifted/Talented Education
Department of Education
201 E. Colfax Avenue
Denver, CO   80203
(303) 866-6849

Connecticut

Gifted/Talented Programs
Department of Education
25 Industrial Park Road
Middletown, CT   06457
(203) 638-4247
(203) 638-4114

Delaware

Gifted/Talented Programs
Department of Public Instruction
Townsend Building, P.O. Box 1402
Dover, DE   19903
(302) 736-4667

District of Columbia

Gifted/Talented Program
Nalle School
50th and C Streets, S.E.
Washington, DC   20019
(202) 767-7177

Florida

Bureau of Exceptional Children
Department of Education
654 Florida Education Centre
Tallahassee, FL   32399-0400
(904) 488-3103

Georgia

Gifted Education
Division of General Instruction
Department of Education
1952 Twin Towers E.
Atlanta, GA   30334-5040
(404) 656-2586
(404) 656-5812
(404) 656-2414

Hawaii

Gifted/Talented Education Specialist
Office of Instructional Services
189 Lunalilo Home Road
Honolulu, HI   96825
(808) 395-9590

Idaho

Department of Education
Len B. Jordan Office Building
650 W. State Street
Boise, ID   83720
(208) 334-3940

Illinois

Curriculum Improvement Section
  N-242
State Board of Education
100 N. 1st Street
Springfield, IL   62777
(217) 782-2826

Indiana

Gifted/Talented Program Manager
Department of Education
State House, Room 229
Indianapolis, IN   46204
(317) 232-9163

Iowa

Gifted Education Consultant
Department of Education
Grimes State Office Building
Des Moines, IA   50319-0146
(515) 281-3198

Kansas

Gifted/Talented Education Program
Department of Education
State Education Building

120 E. 10th Street
Topeka, KS   66612
(913) 296-3743

Kentucky

Gifted/Talented Education Program
Department of Education
Capital Plaza Tower, Room 1831
Frankfort, KY   40601
(502) 564-2106

Louisiana

Gifted/Talented Programs
Department of Education
P.O. Box 94064
Baton Rouge, LA   70804-9064
(504) 342-3635

Maine

Gifted/Talented Programs Consultant
Department of Educational & Cultural
  Services
State House, Station 23
Augusta, ME   04333
(207) 289-5952

Maryland

Gifted/Talented Division Specialist
Department of Education
Maryland State Education Building
200 W. Baltimore Street
Baltimore, MD   21201
(301) 333-2663

Massachusetts

Gifted/Talented
Bureau of Curriculum Service
Department of Education
1385 Hancock Street
Quincy, MA   02169
(617) 770-7237

Michigan

Gifted/Talented Coordinator
Department of Education
P.O. Box 30008
Lansing, MI   48909
(517) 373-3279

Gifted/Talented Specialist
(517) 373-4213

Minnesota

Gifted Education
Department of Education
Capitol Square Building
550 Cedar Street
St. Paul, MN   55101
(612) 296-4072

Mississippi

Gifted/Talented Consultant
Bureau of Special Service
Department of Education
P.O. Box 771
Jackson, MS   39205-0771
(601) 359-3498

Missouri

Gifted Education Director
Department of Elementary & Secondary
   Education
P.O. Box 480
Jefferson City, MO   65102
(314) 751-2453

Montana

Gifted/Talented Program Specialist
Office of Public Instruction
State Capitol
Helena, MT   59620
(406) 444-4422

Nebraska

Gifted/Talented Program Supervisor
Department of Education
P.O. Box 94987
Lincoln, NE   68509
(402) 471-4337

Nevada

Gifted/Talented Program Consultant
Special Education Branch
Department of Education
400 W. King Street
Capitol Complex
Carson City, NV   89710
(702) 687-3136

New Hampshire

Gifted Education Administrator
Department of Education
State Office Park S.
101 Pleasant Street
Concord, NH   03301
(603) 271-3452

New Jersey

Gifted/Talented Specialist
Division of General Academic Education
Department of Education
CN 500
Trenton, NJ   08625-0500
(609) 984-6287

New Mexico

Gifted/Talented Special Education
   Director
Department of Education
Education Building
300 Don Gaspar Avenue
Santa Fe, NM   87501-2786
(505) 827-6541

New York

Gifted Education Coordinator
Department of Education
Education Building Annex
Room 212 EB
Albany, NY   12234
(518) 474-5966

North Carolina

Gifted Education Consultant
Division for Exceptional Children
Department of Public Instruction
Education Building
116 W. Edenton Street
Raleigh, NC   27603-1712
(919) 733-3004

North Dakota

Gifted/Talented Education
Department of Public Instruction
State Capitol
Bismarck, ND   58505
(701) 224-2277

Ohio

Gifted Education Consultant
Division of Special Education
933 High Street
Worthington, OH   43085
(614) 466-2650

Oklahoma

Gifted/Talented Section Director
Department of Education
Oliver Hodge Memorial Education
   Building
2500 N. Lincoln Boulevard
Oklahoma City, OK   73105
(405) 521-4287

Oregon

Gifted/Talented Specialist
Department of Education
700 Pringle Parkway S.E.
Salem, OR 97310
(503) 378-3879

Pennsylvania

Gifted/Talented Program
Bureau of Special Education
Department of Education
333 Market Street
Harrisburg, PA 17126-0333
(717) 787-6913

Rhode Island

Gifted/Talented Education Specialist
Department of Education
Roger Williams Building
22 Hayes Street
Providence, RI 02908
(401) 277-6523

South Carolina

Gifted Program Coordinator
Department of Education
Rutledge Building, Room 802
1429 Senate Street
Columbia, SC 29201
(803) 734-8385

South Dakota

Gifted Programs Director
Special Education Section
Department of Education
Richard F. Kneip Building
700 Governors Drive
Pierre, SD 57501
(605) 773-3678

Tennessee

Gifted/Talented Programs & Services
  Consultant
Department of Education
Cordell Hull Building, Room 132-A
436 6th Avenue N.
Nashville, TN 37219
(615) 741-2851

Texas

Gifted/Talented Director
Education Agency
William B. Travis Building
1701 N. Congress Avenue
Austin, TX 78701
(512) 463-9455

Utah

Gifted/Talented Specialist
Office of Education
250 E. 500 South
Salt Lake City, UT 84111
(801) 538-7765

Vermont

Gifted Education Consultant
Department of Education
State Office Building
120 State Street
Montpelier, VT   05602
(802) 828-3111

Virginia

Gifted Programs Supervisor
Department of Education
P. O. Box 6Q
Richmond, VA   23216-2060
(804) 225-2070

Washington

Gifted Programs Coordinator
Department of Public Instruction
Mail Stop FG-11
Olympia, WA   98504
(206) 753-8310
(206) 753-2858

West Virginia

Gifted Programs Coordinator
Office of Special Education
Department of Education

State Office Building 6, Room B-304
1900 Washington Streeet E.
Charleston, WV   25305
(304) 348-2696

Wisconsin

Gifted/Talented Program Consultant
Department of Public Instruction
P.O. Box 7841
Madison, WI   53707
(608) 266-3560

Wyoming

Gifted/Talented Coordinator
Department of Education
Hathaway Building
2300 Capitol Avenue
Cheyenne, WY   82002
(307) 777-6226

Puerto Rico

Gifted Education Consultant
Department of Education
Office of External Resources
Hato Rey, PR   00924
(809) 765-1475

FINANCIAL AID

SEE ALSO

the MINORITY AND UNDERPRIVILEGED CHILDREN section of this chapter and the HERITAGE section of Chapter 11 for more organizations that offer scholarships or make referrals to sources of financial aid.

Asparagus Club (AC)
c/o Cecil Bragg
Nabisco Biscuit Co.
100 DeForest Avenue
East Hanover, NJ   07936
(201) 503-2000
This group of food industry managers annually presents fifty-five scholarships worth $750 each to students planning to enter the food industry.

Chinese-American Educational Foundation (CAEF)
12 Chipping Campden Drive
South Barrington, IL   60010
(312) 991-2961
The churches, organizations, and individuals within the Foundation bestow scholarships on college students and awards to high school graduates. The recipients must be of Chinese descent.

Citizens' Scholarship Foundation of America (CSFA)
1505 Riverview Road
St. Peter, MN   56082
(507) 931-1682
The Foundation started Dollars for Scholars, a community self-help movement, involving everyone from local businesses to students, in an effort to raise monies for further education. The monies go to both average and outstanding students pursuing traditional academic routes as well as vocational and technical training.

Harry S. Truman Scholarship Foundation (HSTSF)
712 Jackson Place, N.W.
Washington, DC   20006
(202) 395-4831

Approximately ninety-two students each year become Truman scholars, giving top students opportunities to ready themselves for a government service career.

Hungarian Central Committee for Books & Education (HCCBE)
P.O. Box 110025
Cleveland, OH   44111
(216) 671-0669
The Committee raises money for needy students of Hungarian descent through an assortment of charitable programs.

National Hispanic Scholarship Fund (NHSF)
P.O. Box 728
Novato, CA   94948
(415) 892-9971
The Fund, with a budget of two million dollars, bestows scholarships on graduate and undergraduate students of Hispanic heritage.

National Rehabilitation & Service Foundation (NRSF)
RVA Building, Room 219
2470 Cardinal Loop
Del Valle, TX   78617
(512) 389-2288
The Regular Veterans Association raises money from RVA outposts for scholarships in certain academic areas.

Southeastern Regional Office National Scholarship Service & Fund for Negro Students (NSSFNS)
965 Martin Luther King, Jr. Drive
Atlanta, GA   30314
(404) 577-3990
Primarily dedicated to raising funds for scholarships for black, other minority, and low-income students, the Fund also runs a free consultation and referral service, trains students on how to get through a college interview, and conducts workshops for admissions and guidance counselors.

United Negro College Fund (UNCF)
500 E. 62nd Street
New York, NY   10021
(212) 326-1118
The Fund raises money for black private educational institutions, advises member schools on a broad range of topics, runs college fairs for high school students, manages scholarship programs, and hosts a summer program for premed students.

United Student Aid (USA) Funds
8115 Knue Road
P.O. Box 50437
Indianapolis, IN   46250
(317) 849-6510

With its operating budget of sixty-four million dollars, this organization provides financial aid and low-cost loans to students and their parents. Nearly twenty thousand lending firms and educational institutions participate in these programs.

INTERNATIONAL EXCHANGE PROGRAMS

SEE ALSO

the HERITAGE section in Chapter 11, which lists cultural organizations, some of which sponsor exchange programs for students of certain ethnic backgrounds.

AFS Intercultural Programs
313 E. 43rd Street
New York, NY   10017
(212) 949-4242
An exchange program for students of ages sixteen to eighteen to promote international understanding. Students live in a family setting.

American Council for International Studies (ACIS)
19 Bay State Road
Boston, MA   02215
(617) 236-2051
The Council organizes international travel for teachers and their students as well as exchange programs for both students and teachers who wish to study abroad. It publishes a newsletter and a number of books.

American Institute for Foreign Study Scholarship Foundation (AIFSSF)
140 Greenwich Avenue
Greenwich, CT   06830
(203) 625-0755
The Institute runs an exchange program for foreign students to live with American families. Host families receive scholarships for young people to study and travel abroad.

American Study Program for
   Educational & Cultural Training
   (ASPECT)
26 3rd Street, 5th Floor
San Francisco, CA   94103
(415) 777-4348
(800) US-YOUTH (879-6884)
Runs a student exchange program to
encourage intercultural understanding.

British American Educational
   Foundation (BAEF)
211 E. 43rd Street, Suite 301
New York, NY   10017
(212) 772-3890
An exchange program for American senior high school graduates to spend a
year in an independent British boarding
school before going on to college.

Council on International Educational
   Exchange (CIEE)
205 E. 42nd Street
New York, NY   10017
(212) 661-1414
With a tremendous budget of over $120
million, the Council sponsors international study programs, work camps, and
exchange programs for American students and helps foreign students and
teachers with summer study, travel,
and residences. It supplies information
on international student travel, makes
low-cost travel arrangements, issues the
International Student Identity Card,

books students on flights and for tours,
and arranges for summer jobs abroad.
In New York, it provides inexpensive
travel lodgings for students. Among its
publications are the *Student Travel
Guide,* published annually, and periodic
papers such as the *Teenager's Guide to
Study, Travel and Adventure Abroad.*

Council on Standards for International
   Educational Travel
1906 Association Drive
Reston, VA   22091
(703) 860-5317
The Council comprises educational and
international exchange organizations. It
provides information on international
educational travel for students, parents,
teachers, and administrators. Annually,
it publishes the directory *Advisory List
of International Educational Travel and
Exchange Programs.*

Educational Foundation for Foreign
   Study
1 Memorial Drive
Cambridge, MA   02142
(617) 494-0122
This organization of volunteers in
North and South America, Europe, and
Asia sponsors exchange programs and
gives scholarships. Students live within
a family unit and attend a local high
school. It publishes the pamphlet called
Student Exchange in Your School.

Interexchange
356 W. 34th Street, 2nd Floor
New York, NY   10001
(212) 947-9533
Provides services to American and foreign exchange students, runs a summer job exchange, and an intercultural child-care program. Its publication, *Visit USA,* provides information about exchange programs.

International Cultural Centers for
  Youth (ICCY)
P.O. Box 20336
Columbus Circle Station
New York, NY   10023
(212) 581-2279
This is an interfaith group that offers youth exchange programs.

Open Door Student Exchange (ODSE)
250 Fulton Avenue
P.O. Box 71
Hempstead, NY   11551
(516) 486-7330
A homestay international exchange program for high school students in the United States, Europe, the Middle East, Asia, Australia, and Canada.

Spanish Heritage-Herencia Española
  (SHE)
116-53 Queens Boulevard
Forest Hills, NY   11375
(718) 268-7565
An exchange program for high school students from the United States and Spain, Mexico, Colombia, and the Dominican Republic. There is a three-week group program led by an American teacher; a nonclass, four-week summer-stay program; and a five-week summer-study program. The group also sponsors tours of American high schools and universities and provides placement services.

Youth for Understanding (YFU)
3501 Newark Street, N.W.
Washington, DC   20016
(202) 966-6808
For students and adults wishing to learn more about other cultures, the organization runs a number of exchange programs organized by age and length of stay. YFU offers orientation, placement, insurance, counseling, and language assistance as well as scholarship programs.

BILINGUALISM

Intercultural Development Research Association (IDRA)
5835 Callaghan Road, Suite 350
San Antonio, TX   78228
(512) 684-8180
The Association is involved in research, training, and assisting those interested in bilingual education. In addition, it sponsors workshops and seminars, evaluates and makes recommendations on existing programs within schools, and maintains a library of relevant publications.

National Association for Bilingual Education (NABE)
Union Center Plaza
810 1st Street, N.E., 3rd Floor
Washington, DC   20002
(202) 898-1829

Organized to support bilingual education and equal opportunity, the Association conducts research, educates parents, and hosts conferences and workshops.

National Institute for Multicultural Education (NIME)
844 Grecian, N.W.
Albuquerque, NM   87107
(505) 344-6898
The Institute is dedicated to equal opportunity in education for bilingual school-age children. It runs educational programs and provides advocacy and training. It maintains a seven-thousand-volume library of material on bilingual and equal education, and provides reference services.

MINORITY AND UNDERPRIVILEGED CHILDREN

American Indian Research & Development (AIRD)
2424 Springer Drive, Suite 200
Norman, OK   73069
(405) 364-0656

AIRD promotes the quality of education for gifted Native American students through training and technical advice for education agencies, tribes, and other organizations.

Aspira Association
1112 16th Street, N.W., Suite 340
Washington, DC   20036
(202) 835-3600
Founded to promote education within
the Hispanic community, Aspira counsels high school and college students,
runs workshops and discussion groups,
helps students applying for college admission, and encourages careers in
health care within the Hispanic community.

A Better Chance (ABC)
419 Boylston Street
Boston, MA   02116
(617) 421-0950
ABC oversees placement of talented,
motivated minority students in excellent public and private schools, counsels students on higher education,
encourages leadership roles, and conducts research. Financial aid is available
from schools within the organization.

ERIC Clearinghouse on Rural
  Education & Small Schools
Appalachia Educational Laboratory
1031 Quarrier Street
P.O. Box 1348
Charleston, WV   25325 1348
(800) 624-9120
(800) 344-6646 (in West Virginia)
The Laboratory serves as a clearinghouse for information on the social,
cultural, and economic impact on edu-

cational programs for migrants, Native
Americans, and Mexican Americans
with particular emphasis on small
schools.

LULAC National Educational Service
  Centers (LNESC)
777 N. Capital Street, N.E., Suite 305
Washington, DC   20002
(202) 408-0060
LULAC (League of United Latin American Citizens) helps Hispanic students
pursue higher education. This service
offers counseling in education, financial
aid, and career decisions. In addition, it
offers an annual three-day conference
to build leadership skills and runs a
scholarship program.

National Association for Chicano
  Studies (NACS)
14 E. Cuche LaPoundre
Colorado Springs, CO   80903
(719) 389-6642
NACS offers information and referrals
to people with an academic interest in
Hispanic studies.

National Coalition of Advocates for
  Students (NCAS)
100 Boylston Street, Suite 737
Boston, MA   02116
(617) 357-8507
A coalition of organizations dedicated
to poor, minority, handicapped, and En-

glish-language deficient students, NCAS operates as a clearinghouse for the exchange of information and experiences. It publishes periodicals, bibilographies, and books such as *Barriers to Excellence: Our Children at Risk*.

Sociedad Honoraria Hispanica (SHH)
Glenbrook North High School
2300 Shermer Road
Northbrook, IL   60062
(312) 743-0409

SHH awards superior secondary-school students of Spanish scholarships and trips to Spain and Mexico.

Southern Education Foundation (SEF)
135 Auburn Avenue, N.E., 2nd Floor
Atlanta, GA   30308
(404) 523-0001
SEF was founded to improve and increase educational opportunities for southern school children, particularly minorities. It offers information and referrals.

DISCIPLINE IN SCHOOLS

**End Violence Against the Next
   Generation (EVAN-G)**
977 Keeler Avenue
Berkeley, CA 94708-1498
(415) 527-0454
The professionals comprising this organization are dedicated to eradicating corporal punishment from educational institutions. They provide counseling, run a speakers' bureau, and publish a quarterly and a number of brochures and books on corporal punishment.

**National Center for the Study of
   Corporal Punishment & Alternatives
   in the Schools (NCSCPAS)**
253 Ritter Annex
Temple University
Philadelphia, PA   19122
(215) 787-6091

The Center studies the psychological and educational nature of discipline in schools. It conducts research on post-traumatic stress and supplies legal aid and expert testimony. In addition, it runs workshops, maintains a speakers' bureau, and a large collection of articles on child abuse.

**National Coalition to Abolish Corporal
   Punishment**
155 W. Main Street, Room 100-B
Columbus, OH   43215
(614) 221-8829
This group supports legislative initiative against corporal punishment. Endorsed by such organizations as the American

Bar Association and the National PTA, it publishes a number of educational pamphlets.

National Coalition to Abolish Corporal Punishment in Schools (NCACPS)
6350 Frantz Road, Suite D
Dublin, OH   43017
(614) 766-6688
Made up of both state and national organizations such as the American Medical Association and the National Committee for Prevention of Child Abuse, the coalition seeks to end corporal punishment in the schools. It offers information and referrals to parents.

Parents & Teachers Against Violence in Education
560 S. Hartz Avenue, Suite 408
Danville, CA   94526
(415) 831-1661
Dedicated to the proposition that all children have the right to education free of violence and fear, this organization fights against corporal punishment and psychological and sexual abuse. It provides information and help to parents and teachers and supports grass-roots work in this field, and also publishes *Understanding Corporal Punishment of Schoolchildren.*

DROPOUT PREVENTION

SEE ALSO

Chapter 9, Adolescence.

National Dropout Prevention Center (NDPC)
205 Martin Street
Clemson University
Clemson, SC   29634
(803) 656-2599

The Center operates as a clearinghouse for information on dropout prevention and at-risk youth. It publishes the periodical *Directory of Contacts in Dropout Prevention,* and *National Dropout Prevention Newsletter,* a quarterly.

National Dropout Prevention Network
(NDPN)
1517 L Street
Sacramento, CA   95814
(916) 443-0786
The Network provides advice regarding
the dropout problem to parents and educators.

National Foundation for the
Improvement of Education (NFIE)
1201 16th Street, N.W.
Washington, DC   20036
(202) 822-7840
The Foundation publishes *Blueprint for
Success: Community Mobilization for
Dropout Prevention.*

READING AND LITERACY

American Reading Council (ARC)
45 John Street, Suite 908
New York, NY   10038
(212) 619-6044
ARC provides information on successful
literacy programs and helps groups that
wish to found or improve a literacy program.

Barbara Bush Foundation for Family
Literacy (BBFFL)
1002 Wisconsin Avenue, N.W.
Washington, DC   20007
(202) 338-2006
The Foundation sponsors programs that
bring parents and children together,
encouraging a positive home attitude to
learning. It provides grants, seed
money, and trains volunteers and
teachers. It publishes *First Teachers: A
Family Literacy Handbook for Parents,
Policy Makers, and Literacy Providers.*

Center for the Study of Children's
Literature
Simmons College
300 The Fenway
Boston, MA   02115
(617) 738-2258
The Center offers a community education program in the field of children's
literature, answers questions, and offers
advice to researchers in children's
books.

Contact Literacy Center (CLC)
P.O. Box 81826
Lincoln, NE   68501
(402) 464-0602
(800) 228-8813
CLC functions as a clearinghouse for
information and maintains a computerized list of literacy resources.

Council on Interracial Books for
  Children, Inc. (CIBC)
1841 Broadway
New York, NY   10023
(212) 757-5339
CIBC works to counteract racist, sexist,
and ageist stereotypes and bias in literature and instructional materials for
children. The group offers advisory and
consulting services. It publishes books,
learning materials, and a newsletter, *Interracial Books for Children Bulletin*. A
catalog of publications is available free.

ERIC Clearinghouse on Reading &
  Communication Skills
Indiana University
Smith Research Center
2805 E. 10th Street, Suite 150
Bloomington, IN   47405-2373
(812) 855-5847
The Center studies and researches reading, English, and communication skills
at all grade levels through college. It
trains instructors, prepares teaching
materials, develops tests, and offers information to the public.

International Reading Association
  (IRA)
800 Barksdale Road
P.O. Box 8139
Newark, DE   19714-8139
(302) 731-1600
IRA distributes information on reading
research, adult literacy, literature for
teenagers, computers and reading, and

early childhood and literacy development. It publishes several journals and
an annual directory.

Reading Is Fundamental (RIF)
600 Maryland Avenue, S.W., Suite 500
Washington, DC   20560
(202) 287-3220
This organization of volunteer groups
works to interest children in reading. It
runs reading motivation programs, encourages parents to have children read
at home, and sponsors a book distribution program.

Reading Reform Foundation (RRF)
949 Market Street, Suite 436
Tacoma, WA   98402
(206) 572-9966
RRF believes that phonetics should
form the basis of reading instruction. It
offers information, hosts workshops,
and publishes periodicals and newsletters that support this view.

PUBLICATIONS FOR READING AND LITERACY

Bulletin of the Center for Children's
  Books
University of Chicago Press
Journals Division
P.O. Box 37005
Chicago, IL   60637
(312) 962-7600
The Bulletin publishes nearly sixty book
reviews each month.

Five Owls
2004 Sheridan Avenue S.
Minneapolis, MN   55405-2354
(612) 377-2004
Each bimonthly, sixteen-page issue
of this journal contains reviews of
outstanding new books, a list of recommended books, interviews with well-
known authors, and an essay on a topic
in children's literature.

Horn Book Magazine
31 St. James Street
Boston, MA   02116-4167
(617) 482-5198

Accompanying over seventy reviews in
each bimonthly publication are insight-
ful, in-depth essays on different facets
of children's literature.

Parents' Choice
Parents' Choice Foundation
P.O. Box 185
Waban, MA   02168
(617) 965-5913
This quarterly publication reviews children's books, videos, games, music,
televisions programs, toys, and software.

TELEVISION VIEWING

Action for Children's Television (ACT)
20 University Road
Cambridge, MA   02138
(617) 876-6620
ACT strives for diversity in children's
television and to eliminate commercial-
ism geared at young viewers. Among its
numerous publications are the *TV-
Smart Book for Kids* and *The ACT
Guide to Children's Television: How to
Treat TV with TLC,* plus books for
teenagers, children with special needs,
and bibliographies.

American Family Association
P.O. Drawer 2440
Tupelo, MS   38803
(601) 844-5036
The Association promotes a "biblical,"
ethical society, targeting television as a
particular affront and urging the public
to protest "violence, immorality, pro-
fanity, and vulgarity."

Black Awareness in Television (BAIT)
13217 Livernois
Detroit, MI   48238
(313) 931-3427

BAIT develops programs for television, theater, radio, and video featuring black actors, producers, writers, and directors. It seeks greater exposure on television for black-produced programs, sponsors several theater companies, and backs the "September is Black Reading Month" project.

National Coalition on Television
   Violence (NCTV)
P.O. Box 2157
Champaign, IL   61825
(217) 384-1920
NCTV seeks to lessen the amount of violence in television and movies. It conducts seminars on school nonviolence programs as well as on violent enter-

tainment; offers ratings for music, movies, and television; reviews toys; and provides information on sports violence and aggression.

Society for the Eradication of
   Television
Box 10491
Oakland, CA   94610-0491
(415) 530-2056
Members do not have a working television in their homes and encourage others to dispose of theirs. The group believes television-watching wastes time, prevents personal communication, hampers one's inner life, and causes debilitative addiction. They offer information and publish a newsletter.

TESTING

American College Testing Program
   (ACT)
Box 168
Iowa City, IA   52243
(319) 337-1000
This source has developed the ACT Assessment Program and the Student Needs Analysis Service to help students determine academic direction and financial needs. In addition, the Program provides academic institutions with information used in admissions,

placement, and counseling. It runs a twenty-five-thousand-volume library.

The College Board (TCB)
45 Columbus Avenue
New York, NY   10023
(212) 713-8000
The College Board provides testing for students moving from high school to college; supplies tests to college administrators to help determine placement; and conducts research. Its Educational

Equality Project is a ten-year study on the quality and equality of secondary education. It publishes several periodicals and an annual directory of members.

Educational Records Bureau (ERB)
3 E. 80th Street
New York, NY   10021
(212) 535-0307
Through organized testing programs, results compilation, and research, the Bureau helps member schools evaluate their students' academic achievements. ERB publishes its research findings, trains administrators and teachers, maintains a databank of scores, and helps schools review test results and implement appropriate changes.

Educational Testing Service (ETS)
Rosedale Road
Princeton, NJ   08541
(609) 921-9000
ETS creates tests and offers affiliated services to educational institutions, government agencies, and other organizations; advises on proper testing and measurement; conducts research; offers a summer testing training program; and runs a fifteen-thousand-volume library.

ERIC Clearinghouse on Tests, Measurement, & Evaluation
American Institutes for Research (AIR)

Washington Research Center
3333 K Street N.W.
Washington, DC   20007-3893
(202) 342-5060
AIR prepares tests, determines methods of evaluation and interpretation of test results, and studies testing in general. This government-sponsored program answers questions from the public.

National Center for Fair & Open Testing
342 Broadway
Cambridge, MA   02139
(617) 864-4810
The Center works against prejudice on standardized aptitude and intelligence tests and certification exams by eliminating questions with a racial, sexual, or cultural bias. It runs seminars and workshops, a speakers' bureau, and a thousand-volume library. It publishes a quarterly and a number of books including the *Standardized Testing Reform Sourcebook.*

Secondary School Admission Test Board (SSATB)
20 Nassau Street, Suite 314
Princeton, NJ   08542
(609) 683-4440
The Board provides secondary school entrance exams for six hundred private schools in the United States and abroad. It also offers affiliated services

and training for admission counselors. Annually, it publishes the *SSATB Network Directory* listing nearly seven

hundred consultants, organizations, and schools, and over eleven hundred admissions officers.

STATE OFFICES OF THE NATIONAL PTA

These state offices are a good source for referrals to local PTAs for information about the quality of local schools and for help with many other questions regarding education.

Alabama

Alabama Congress of Parents &
  Teachers, Inc.
207 N. Jackson
Montgomery, AL   36104
(205) 834-2501

Alaska

Alaska Congress of Parents &
  Teachers, Inc.
P.O. Box 201496
Anchorage, AK   99520-1496
(907) 279-9345

Arizona

Arizona Congress of Parents &
  Teachers, Inc.
2721 N. 7th Avenue
Phoenix, AZ   85007
(602) 279-1811

Arkansas

Arkansas Congress of Parents &
  Teachers, Inc.
P.O. Box 687
North Little Rock, AR   72115
(501) 753-5247

California

California Congress of Parents,
  Teachers, & Students, Inc.
P.O. Box 15015
Los Angeles, CA   90015
(213) 620-1100

Colorado

Colorado Congress of Parents,
  Teachers, & Students, Inc.
7251 W. 38th Avenue
Wheat Ridge, CO   80033
(303) 422-2213

Connecticut

The Parent-Teacher Association of
  Connecticut, Inc.
Wilbur Cross Commons
Building 11
60 Connelly Parkway
Hamden, CT   06514
(203) 281-6617

Delaware

Delaware Congress of Parents &
  Teachers, Inc.
92 S. Gerald Drive
Newark, DE   19713
(302) 737-4646

District of Columbia

DC Congress of Parents &
  Teachers, Inc.
J.O. Wilson Elementary School
660 K Street, N.E.
Washington, DC   20002-3530
(202) 543-0333

Florida

Florida Congress of Parents &
  Teachers, Inc.
1747 Orlando Central Parkway
Orlando, FL   32809
(407) 855-7604

Georgia

Georgia Congress of Parents &
  Teachers, Inc.
114 Baker Street, S.E.
Atlanta, GA   30308
(404) 659-0214

Hawaii

Hawaii Congress of Parents, Teachers,
  & Students, Inc.
120 Puhili Street
Hilo, HI   96720
(808) 961-5432

Idaho

Idaho Congress of Parents &
  Teachers, Inc.
620 N. 6th Street
Boise, ID   83702-5553
(208) 344-0851

Illinois

Illinois Congress of Parents &
  Teachers, Inc.
901 S. Spring Street
Springfield, IL   62704
(217) 528-9617

Indiana

Indiana Congress of Parents &
  Teachers, Inc.
2150 Lafayette Road
Indianapolis, IN   46222
(317) 635-1733

Iowa

Iowa Congress of Parents &
    Teachers, Inc.
610 Merle Hay Towers
Des Moines, IA   50310
(515) 276-1019

Kansas

Kansas Congress of Parents &
    Teachers, Inc.
715 S.W. 10th Street
Topeka, KS   66612
(913) 234-5782

Kentucky

Kentucky Congress of Parents &
    Teachers, Inc.
P.O. Box 654
Frankfort, KY   40602-0654
(502) 564-4378

Louisiana

Louisiana Parent-Teacher Association
P.O. Drawer 25363
University Station
Baton Rouge, LA   70894-5515
(504) 343-0386

Maine

Maine Congress of Parents &
    Teachers, Inc.
173 Main Avenue
Farmingdale, ME   04345
No phone number listed.

Maryland

Maryland Congress of Parents &
    Teachers, Inc.
13 S. Carrollton Avenue
Baltimore, MD   21223
(301) 685-0865

Massachusetts

Massachusetts Parent-Teacher-Student
    Association
c/o Arlington High School
869 Massachusetts Avenue
Arlington, MA   02174
(617) 646-6771

Michigan

Michigan Congress of Parents,
    Teachers, & Students
1011 N. Washington Avenue
Lansing, MI   48906
(517) 485-4345

Minnesota

Minnesota Congress of Parents,
    Teachers, & Students
1910 W. County Road B, Suite 105
Roseville, MN   55113-5494
(612) 631-1736

Mississippi

Mississippi Congress of Parents &
    Teachers, Inc.
P.O. Box 1937
Jackson, MS   39215
(601) 352-7383

Missouri

Missouri Congress of Parents &
  Teachers, Inc.
2101 Burlington Street
Columbia, MO   65202-1997
(314) 474-8631

Montana

Montana Congress of Parents &
  Teachers, Inc.
P.O. Box 859
Kalispell, MT   59903-0859
(406) 257-1783

Nebraska

Nebraska Congress of Parents &
  Teachers, Inc.
4600 Valley Road, Room 402
Lincoln, NE   68510-4889
(402) 488-2036

Nevada

Nevada Parent-Teacher Association
1315 Hiawatha Road
Las Vegas, NV   89108
(702) 646-5437

New Hampshire

New Hampshire Congress of Parents &
  Teachers, Inc.
33 Mt. Vernon Road
Amherst, NH   03031
(603) 673-4234

New Jersey

New Jersey Congress of Parents &
  Teachers, Inc.
900 Berkeley Avenue
Trenton, NJ   08618
(609) 393-6709

New Mexico

New Mexico Congress of Parents &
  Teachers, Inc.
P.O. Box 6609
Las Cruces, NM   88006
(505) 382-7083

New York

New York State Congress of Parents &
  Teachers, Inc.
119 Washington Avenue
Albany, NY   12210
(518) 462-5326

North Carolina

North Carolina Congress of Parents &
  Teachers, Inc.
3501 Glenwood Avenue
Raleigh, NC   27612-4934
(919) 787-0534

North Dakota

North Dakota Congress of Parents &
  Teachers, Inc.
810 Divide Avenue
Bismarck, ND   58501
(701) 223-3578

Ohio

Ohio Congress of Parents &
   Teachers, Inc.
427 E. Town Street
Columbus, OH   43215
(614) 221-4844

Oklahoma

Oklahoma Congress of Parents &
   Teachers, Inc.
Moore Schools Administrative Annex
224 S.E. 4th Street
Moore, OK   73160
(405) 799-0026

Oregon

Oregon Congress of Parents &
   Teachers, Inc.
531 S.E. 14th Street
Portland, OR   97214
(503) 234-3928

Pennsylvania

Pennsylvania Congress of Parents &
   Teachers, Inc.
P.O. Box 4384
Harrisburg, PA   17111
(717) 564-8985

Rhode Island

Rhode Island Congress of Parents &
   Teachers, Inc.
1703 Broad Street
Cranston, RI   02905
(401) 785-1970

South Carolina

South Carolina Congress of Parents &
   Teachers, Inc.
1826 Henderson Street
Columbia, SC   29201
(803) 765-0806

South Dakota

South Dakota Congress of Parents &
   Teachers, Inc.
411 E. Capitol
Pierre, SD   57501
(605) 224-0144

Tennessee

Tennessee Congress of Parents &
   Teachers, Inc.
1905 Acklen Avenue
Nashville, TN   37212
(615) 383-9740

Texas

Texas Congress of Parents &
   Teachers, Inc.
408 W. 11th Street
Austin, TX   78701
(512) 476-6769

Utah

Utah Congress of Parents &
   Teachers, Inc.
1037 E. South Temple
Salt Lake City, UT   84102
(801) 359-3875

Vermont

Vermont Congress of Parents &
  Teachers, Inc.
P.O. Box 5
Washington, VT   05675
(802) 883-2226

Virginia

Virginia Congress of Parents &
  Teachers, Inc.
3810 Augusta Avenue
Richmond, VA   23230
(804) 355-2816

Washington

Washington Congress of Parents &
  Teachers, Inc.
2003 65th Avenue, W.
Tacoma, WA   98466-6215
(206) 565-2153

West Virginia

West Virginia Congress of Parents &
  Teachers, Inc.
P.O. Box 130
Barboursville, WV   25504
(304) 736-4089

Wisconsin

Wisconsin Congress of Parents &
  Teachers, Inc.
4797 Hayes Road, Suite 2
Madison, WI   53704
(608) 244-1455

Wyoming

Wyoming Congress of Parents &
  Teachers, Inc.
P.O. Box 3524
Jackson, WY   83001-3524
(307) 733-5302

STATE EDUCATION AGENCIES

These education offices in each state government will answer questions and make referrals on a wide range of questions concerning the public schools in their state.

Alabama

Department of Education
State Office Building, Room 483
501 Dexter Avenue
Montgomery, AL   36130
(205) 261-5156

Alaska

Department of Education
P.O. Box F
Juneau, AK   99811
(907) 465-2800

Arizona

Department of Education
1535 W. Jefferson Street
Phoenix, AZ   85007
(602) 542-4361

Arkansas

Department of Education
Arch-Ford Education Building
Room 304-A, 4 Capitol Mall
Little Rock, AR   72201
(501) 682-4202

California

Department of Education
P.O. Box 944272
Sacramento, CA   94244-2720
(916) 445-2700

Colorado

Department of Education
201 E. Colfax Avenue
Denver, CO   80203
(303) 866-6806

Connecticut

Department of Education
P.O. Box 2219
Hartford, CT   06145
(203) 566-5061

Delaware

Department of Public Instruction
P.O. Box 1402
Dover, DE   19903
(302) 736-4601

District of Columbia

DC Public Schools
Presidential Building, Room 1209
415 12th Street N.W.
Washington, DC   20004
(202) 724-4222

Florida

Department of Education
The Capitol
Plaza Level 08
Tallahassee, FL   32399-0400
(904) 487-1785

Georgia

Department of Education
Floyd Memorial Building
Twin Towers E.
205 Butler Street S.E.
Atlanta, GA   30334
(404) 656-2800

Hawaii

Department of Education
P.O. Box 2360
Honolulu, HI   96804
(808) 548-6405

Idaho

Department of Education
Len B. Jordan Building, Room 200
650 W. State Street
Boise, ID 83720
(208) 334-3301

Illinois

State Board of Education
100 N. 1st Street
Springfield, IL 62777
(217) 782-2221

Indiana

Department of Education
State House, Room 229
Indianapolis, IN 46204-2798
(317) 232-6610

Iowa

Department of Education
Grimes State Office Building
Des Moines, IA 50319-0146
(515) 281-5294

Kansas

Department of Education
State Education Building
120 E. 10th Street
Topeka, KS 66612
(913) 296-3201

Kentucky

Department of Education
Capital Plaza Tower, 1st Floor
Frankfort, KY 40601
(502) 564-4770

Louisiana

Department of Education
P.O. Box 94064
Baton Rouge, LA 70804-9064
(504) 342-3602

Maine

Department of Educational & Cultural
 Services
State House, Station 23
Augusta, ME 04333
(207) 289-5800

Maryland

Department of Education
Maryland State Education Building
200 W. Baltimore Street
Baltimore, MD 21201
(301) 333-2100

Massachusetts

Department of Education
1385 Hancock Street
Quincy, MA 02169
(617) 770-7300

Michigan

Department of Education
P.O. Box 30008
Lansing, MI   48909
(517) 373-3357

Minnesota

Department of Education
Capitol Square Building
550 Cedar Street
St. Paul, MN   55101
(612) 296-2358

Mississippi

Department of Education
P.O. Box 771
Jackson, MS   39205
(601) 359-3513

Missouri

Department of Elementary & Secondary
   Education
P.O. Box 480
Jefferson City, MO   65102
(314) 751-4446

Montana

Office of Public Instruction
Capitol Building, Room 106
Helena, MT   59620
(406) 444-3654

Nebraska

Department of Education
P.O. Box 94987
Lincoln, NE   68509
(402) 471-2465

Nevada

Department of Education
Capitol Complex
Carson City, NV   89710
(702) 885-3100

New Hampshire

Department of Education
State Office Park S.
101 Pleasant Street
Concord, NH   03301
(603) 271-3144

New Jersey

Department of Education
CN 500
Trenton, NJ   08625
(609) 292-4450

New Mexico

Department of Education
Education Building
300 Don Gaspar Avenue
Santa Fe, NM   87501-2786
(505) 827-6635

New York

Office of Elementary & Secondary
 Education
Education Building Annex, Room 875
Albany, NY   12234
(518) 474-4688

North Carolina

Department of Public Education
116 W. Edenton Street
Raleigh, NC   27603-1712
(919) 733-3813

North Dakota

Department of Public Instruction
State Capitol
Bismarck, ND   58505-0164
(701) 224-2260

Ohio

Department of Education
Ohio Departments Building, Room 808
65 S. Front Street
Columbus, OH   43215
(614) 466-3304

Oklahoma

Department of Education
Oliver Hodge Memorial Education
Building, Room 121
2500 N. Lincoln Boulevard
Oklahoma City, OK   73105-4599
(405) 521-3301

Oregon

Department of Education
700 Pringle Parkway S.E.
Salem, OR   97310-0290
(503) 378-3573

Pennsylvania

Department of Education
Harristown Building 2, 10th Floor
333 Market Street
Harrisburg, PA   17126-0333
(717) 787-5820

Rhode Island

Department of Education
Roger Williams Building
22 Hayes Street
Providence, RI   02908
(401) 277-2031

South Carolina

Department of Education
Rutledge Building, Room 1006
1429 Senate Street
Columbia, SC   29201
(803) 734-8492

South Dakota

Division of Education
Richard F. Kneip Building
700 Governors Drive
Pierre, SD   57501-2293
(605) 773-3243

Tennessee

Department of Education
Cordell Hull Building, Room 100
436 6th Avenue N.
Nashville, TN   37219
(615) 741-2731

Texas

Education Agency
William B. Travis Building, Room 2-104
1701 N. Congress Avenue
Austin, TX   78701
(512) 463-8985

Utah

Office of Education
250 E. 500 South
Salt Lake City, UT   84111
(801) 538-7500

Vermont

Department of Education
State Office Building
120 State Street
Montpelier, VT   05602
(802) 828-3135

Virginia

Department of Education
P.O. Box 6Q
Richmond, VA   23216-2060
(804) 225-2023

Washington

Department of Public Instruction
Mail Stop FG-11
Olympia, WA   98504
(206) 753-6717

West Virginia

Department of Education
State Office Building 6, Room B-358
1900 Washington Street E.
Charleston, WV   25305
(304) 348-2681

Wisconsin

Department of Public Instruction
P.O. Box 7841
Madison, WI   53707
(608) 266-1771

Wyoming

Department of Education
Hathaway Building, 2nd Floor
2300 Capitol Avenue
Cheyenne, WY   82002
(307) 777-7673

Puerto Rico

Department of Education
P.O. Box 759
Hato Rey, PR   00919
(809) 754-1100

CHAPTER 9

ADOLESCENCE

Adolescence has been described as a dark tunnel that all children must enter. Fortunately, many organizations help parents through this potentially troubling period. For general information regarding adolescents, see the first section of this chapter, GENERAL ORGANIZATIONS.

Long before children enter adolescence parents consider teaching them sex education. The SEX section of this chapter describes organizations and specific publications and videos that teach about the dangers of teenage pregnancy and sexually transmitted diseases. In addition, some materials answer young children's questions about sex and teach them how to recognize and refuse the unwelcome advances of adults.

Virtually all children will be encouraged to take drugs or alcohol before or during their adolescence. The ADDICTIONS section of this chapter lists many organizations that offer preventive help and make referrals to treatment centers. In addition to drugs and alcohol, this section covers addictions to tobacco, gambling, and sex. The first part describes national organizations. The second part lists state offices that make local referrals and distribute published materials.

The organizations in the JUVENILE DELINQUENCY section are ready to help if your teenager develops serious behavioral problems. Finally, if your child runs away from home, see the RUNAWAYS section.

SEE ALSO

the MENTAL HEALTH section in Chapter 5, particularly under Suicide and Destructive Behavior, if your child is deeply troubled.

GENERAL ORGANIZATIONS

American Academy of Child and
   Adolescent Psychiatry (AACAP)
3615 Wisconsin Avenue, N.W.
Washington, DC   20016
(202) 966-7300
(800) 333-7636
AACAP is a professional society that offers referrals to the public.

Carnegie Council on Adolescent
   Development
2400 N Street, N.W., 6th Floor
Washington, DC   20037-1153
(202) 429-7979
The Council can provide information and referrals regarding the special problems of adolescent development, including dropping out of school, substance abuse, teenage pregnancy and suicide, and criminality. It has a special task force for the "Education of Young Adolescents" and publishes a book entitled *Turning Points: Preparing American Youth for the 21st Century.*

Center for Early Adolescence
University of North Carolina at Chapel
   Hill
Carr Mill Mall, Suite 211
Carrboro, NC   27510
(919) 966-1148
The Center operates as a clearinghouse for adolescent problems and conducts workshops on early adolescence, covering such topics as development and schooling, after-school programs, and parenting. A publications catalog is available upon request.

Society for Adolescent Medicine
19401 E. 40 Highway, Suite 120
Independence, MO   64055
(816) 795-TEEN (8336)
The Society conducts research on normal development and adolescent diseases. It will make referrals.

SEX

This section has three parts: Sex Education; Pregnancy; and Sexually Transmitted Diseases (STDs). Some of the organizations below are listed in only one of these parts yet can help parents on all three topics.

SEE ALSO

the CHILD ABUSE AND NEGLECT section in Chapter 10 for additional organizations that help teach children how to recognize and refuse the unwanted sexual advances of adults or older children.

SEX EDUCATION

American Association of Sex Educators,
   Counselors, and Therapists
   (AASECT)
435 N. Michigan Avenue, Suite 1717
Chicago, IL   60611
(312) 644-0828
AASECT is devoted to training and educating professionals in the field of sex education. It publishes a bibliography of sex education audiovisual materials for all grade levels and other materials.

Birth Control Institute, Inc.
1242 W. Lincoln Avenue, Suite 7-10
Anaheim, CA   92805
(714) 956-4630
The Institute offers education and medical services related to family planning, including birth control, venereal disease testing, pregnancy testing, vasectomy, abortion, and sexuality. It offers brochures concerning sex education.

Center for Population Options
1012 14th Street, N.W., Suite 1200
Washington, DC   20005
(202) 347-5700
The Center publishes resource guides, fact sheets, and reports on adolescent pregnancy, birth control, and HIV transference.

Children's Defense Fund (CDF)
122 C Street, N.W., Suite 400
Washington, DC   20001
(202) 682-8787

SEX

The Fund's mission is to help children avoid having children. It publishes bi-monthly reports to this end.

Concern for Health Options: Information, Care and Education (CHOICE)

125 S. 9th Street, Suite 603
Philadelphia, PA 19107
(215) 592-7644 (Administration)
(215) 592-0550 (Hotline)
CHOICE is a consumer advocate organization concerned with reproductive health care, sexuality education, AIDS, maternity care, and child care. It offers a hotline for parents and teens, and publications for teens about sexuality and for parents about talking to children about sex.

Institute for Family Research & Education

Syracuse University
Slocum Hall, Room 110
Syracuse, NY 13210
(315) 423-4584
The Institute prepares parents to be the sex educators of their own children. Its main goal is preventing teenage pregnancy. The Institute answers questions over the phone and distributes sex education publications.

International Council of Sex Education & Parenthood (ICSEP)

5010 Wisconsin Avenue, N.W., Suite 307
Washington, DC 20016
(202) 364-2310
ICSEP offers information and consulting on the entire spectrum of family health concerns, including child rearing, sex education, sex therapy, family planning, marital relationships, and adolescent problems. A newsletter, *ICSEP News & Views,* is published.

Parents Too Soon

State of Illinois Center
100 W. Randolph Street
Chicago, IL 60601
(312) 917-5926
(800) 4-CALL-US (422-5587)
   (confidential hotline)
Parents Too Soon, an in-state program, seeks to eliminate unwanted teenage pregnancy by offering information, referrals, and information booklets.

Sex Education Coalition (SEC)

20001 O Street, N.W.
Washington, DC 20036
(202) 457-0605
The Coalition offers such publications as *Tips for Parents: Talking with Your Children About Sexuality; What is Sex Ed Really?;* and *Practical Approaches to Sexuality Education Programs,* a handbook of guidelines for developing sex-education programs.

Sex Information & Education Council
of the United States, Inc. (SIECUS)
130 W. 42nd Street, Suite 2500
New York, NY   10036
(212) 819-9770
SIECUS offers family life and sexual information for professionals of all disci-

plines as well as the general public. Its publications include an advocacy guide, *Winning the Battle for Sex Education,* and a guide for parents of small children called *Oh No, What Do I Do Now?*

PREGNANCY

SEE ALSO

the PREGNANCY AND CHILDBIRTH section of Chapter 2.

Birthright, Inc.
686 N. Broad Street
Woodbury, NJ   08096
(609) 848-1818
(800) 848-LOVE (5683)
Birthright, a nondenominational, pro-life group, provides emergency pregnancy services for any girl or woman with an unplanned pregnancy.
Birthright provides pregnancy testing, housing, medical care, counseling, education placement, legal assistance, and adoption referral.

National Organization on Adolescent
Pregnancy & Parenting, Inc.
(NOAPP)
P.O. Box 2365
Reston, VA   22090
(703) 435-3948

NOAPP concerns itself with problems connected with adolescent sexuality, pregnancy, and parenting. It makes referrals and publishes a quarterly newsletter which reviews a wide range of information.

New Jersey Network on Adolescent
Pregnancy (NJNAP)
Rutgers University School of Social
Work
Center for Community Education
75 Easton Avenue
New Brunswick, NJ   08903
(201) 932-8636
NJNAP serves as an information clearinghouse on adolescent pregnancy, prevention, teen parenting, and related issues primarily in New Jersey. It pub-

lishes a six-hundred-page directory of state resources.

North Carolina Coalition on Adolescent Pregnancy
1300 Baxter Street, Suite 171
Charlotte, NC   28204
(704) 335-1313
Offers free information and referrals.

Office of Adolescent Pregnancy Programs
DHHS HHH Building
200 Independence Avenue, S.W.
Room 736E
Washington, DC   20201
(202) 245-7473
The Adolescent Family Life program provides information on services for pregnant adolescents and adolescent parents. This agency will answer questions and make referrals over the phone.

Planned Parenthood Federation of America
810 7th Avenue
New York, NY   10019
(212) 541-7800
This Federation of 188 organizations operates over eight hundred family planning clinics that provide contraceptive services, gynecological services, pregnancy testing and counseling, venereal disease diagnosis, sex education, and other services. The Federation's educational efforts are directed at specific problems such as unwanted pregnancies among adolescents. Its publication topics include contraceptive methods, fertility, teenage sexuality, and sexuality education. Materials include pamphlets, flip charts, posters, a comic book, slides, film strips, and films. A publications catalog is available.

Salvation Army
132 W. 14th Street
New York, NY   10011
(212) 807-4200
Among its many community and social service programs, the Salvation Army runs homes for unwed mothers, hospitals, and clinics. It will make referrals.

School-Age Pregnancy & Prevention Clearinghouse
P.O. Box 149030
Austin, TX   78714-9030
(512) 450-4154
This office provides advice and referrals over the phone.

SEXUALLY TRANSMITTED DISEASES (STDs)

AIDS Hotline
Department of Mental Health & Hygiene
101 W. Read Street, Suite 825
Baltimore, MD   21201
(800) 638-6252 (hotline)
The hotline provides information and makes referrals.

American Council for Healthful Living (ACHL)
439 Main Street
Orange, NJ 07050
(201) 674-7476
The ACHL runs a number of educational programs on such topics as wellness and venereal diseases. The Council will answer questions and make referrals regarding sexually transmitted diseases (STDs). It also publishes pamphlets, posters, and a slide-cassette show about venereal diseases.

American Foundation for the Prevention of Venereal Disease
799 Broadway, Suite 638
New York, NY 10003
(212) 759-2069
The Foundation supplies information on STDs, emphasizing hygiene and prevention.

American Social Health Association (ASHA)
P.O. Box 13827
Research Triangle Park, NC 27709
(919) 361-2742
(800) 227-8922 (VD hotline)
ASHA's venereal disease hotline is a national, toll-free information and referral program providing referrals to five thousand local clinics throughout the United States. Single copies of many pamphlets on venereal diseases and herpes are available free. A list of publications is available.

Blacks Educating Blacks About Sexual Health Issues (BEBASHI)
1528 Walnut Street, Suite 1414
Philadelphia, PA 19102
(215) 546-4140
BEBASHI's counseling, speakers' bureau, phone support, and workshops are directed toward educating African-Americans and Latinos about sexual health problems, particularly AIDS.

Council of Chief State School Officers
Hall of States
400 N. Capitol Street, Suite 379
Washington, DC 20020
(202) 393-8159
(202) 393-8161
Among its many activities, the Council runs programs on AIDS education and maintains an AIDS electronic bulletin board.

Public Health Service
AIDS Hotlines
(800) 342-AIDS (2437)
(800) 243-7889 (for the hearing impaired)
(800) 344-7432 (for Spanish speakers)
Offers information on most AIDS-related subjects.

Sexually Transmitted Diseases (STD) Hotline
(800) 227-8922 (Monday–Friday, 8:00 A.M.–8:00 P.M.)

The Hotline provides information on STDs and makes referrals for medical help.

BROCHURES, BOOKS, AND VIDEOS ABOUT SEXUALLY TRANSMITTED DISEASES

Abbott Laboratories
Public Affairs, Department 383
1 Abbott Park Road
Abbott Park, IL 60064
(800) 323-9100
Send a self-addressed, stamped envelope to receive a free copy of the following pamphlets: *More than Love is Sweeping the Country; Hepatitis: Everything from A to D;* and *AIDS: The New Epidemic.*

American Academy of Dermatology
1567 Maple Avenue
P.O. Box 3116
Evanston, IL 60204-3116
Mail a self-addressed, stamped envelope for a free copy of *Facts About Herpes Simplex* or *A Dermatologist Talks About Warts.*

American Alliance for Health, Physical Education, Recreation & Dance
P.O. Box 704
Waldorf, MD 20601
No phone number listed.
American Alliance publishes two student guides: *STD: A Guide for Today's Young Adults* and *AIDS: What Young Adults Should Know,* both by William L. Yarber.

American College of Obstetricians & Gynecologists
Distribution Center, Suite 300 E.
600 Maryland Avenue, S.W.
Washington, DC 20024-2588
(202) 638-5577
From the ACOG you can request the following pamphlets: *Sexually Transmitted Diseases; Vaginitis: Causes and Treatments; Genital Herpes; Chlamydial Infections; Genital Warts (Condyloma);* and *Pelvic Inflammatory Disease (PID).* Most of these pamphlets are also in Spanish or French.

American Foundation for the Prevention of Venereal Disease, Inc.
799 Broadway, Suite 638
New York, NY 10003
(212) 759-2069
The booklet *Sexually Transmitted Disease (STD) Prevention for Everyone* costs $1 and is written in English, Spanish, or French.

American Medical Association
Order Department
515 N. State Street
Chicago, IL 60610
(800) 621-8335
The booklet *Sexually Transmitted Disease* is available for $1.

Burroughs-Wellcome Company

Research Triangle Park, NC   27709
(919) 248-3000
(800) 234-1124 (Genital Self-
   Examination Hotline)
Call Burroughs-Wellcome's Hotline for
a free copy of the brochures: *Herpes
Alert; Important Information Concerning Genital Herpes;* or *Genital Self Examination (GSE) Guide.*

Center for Health Information

P.O. Box 4636
Foster City, CA   94404
(415) 435-6669
The Center's 128-page book *Play Safe:
How to Avoid Getting Sexually Transmitted Diseases* by Bea Mandel and By-
ron Mandel costs $4.95 plus shipping.

Centers for Disease Control

Center for Prevention Services
Technical Information Services (E-06)
1600 Clifton Road
Atlanta, GA   30333
(404) 639-1819
Call or write for a free copy of the
booklet *Resource List for Information
Materials on Sexually Transmitted Diseases,* which provides information on
education sources for patients and the
general public.

Consumer Information Center

Pueblo, CO   81009
No phone number listed.

The Center offers the following publications free: *Contraception: Comparing
the Options* (Dept. 534V) and *AIDS and
the Education of Our Children: A Guide
for Parents and Teachers* (Dept. 507V).
Be sure your request indicates the correct department.

Coronet/MTI Film & Video

108 Wilmot Road
Deerfield, IL   60015-5196
(312) 940-1260
(800) 621-2131
Coronet/MTI sells or rents videos and
films for teens. Titles include *A Very
Delicate Matter* (on gonorrhea) and
*AIDS: Acquired Immune Deficiency
Syndrome* (narrated by Ally Sheedy),
plus nearly a dozen others on pertinent
sexual-education topics.

Food & Drug Administration

5600 Fishers Lane (HFE-88)
Rockville, MD   20857
(301) 443-3170
The pamphlet *What the Experts Know
About AIDS* is free.

Herpes Resource Center/A.S.H.A.

P.O. Box 13827
Research Triangle Park, NC   27709
(919) 361-2742
(919) 361-2120 (herpes hotline)
The Resource Center publishes a quarterly, a bibliography, a pamphlet, a
book, an audiocassette, and a film, all

bearing pertinent, helpful information about herpes.

March of Dimes
Birth Defects Foundation
1275 Mamaroneck Avenue
White Plains, NY   10605
(914) 428-7100
The March of Dimes puts out the brochure *Sexually Transmitted Disease,* which discusses birth defects in infants. It is free, though donations are welcome.

Montreal Health Press, Inc.
P.O. Box 1000
Station La Cité
Montreal, Quebec   H2W 2N1
Canada
(514) 272-5441
The Press publishes *A Book About Sexually Transmitted Diseases.* The softcover edition costs $2.

National AIDS Information Clearinghouse
P.O. Box 6003
Rockville, MD   20850
(800) 458-5231
Any number of publications, posters, and fact sheets are available free from the Clearinghouse. Publications include *Understanding AIDS* (#33); *How You Won't Get AIDS* (#49); *AIDS and You* (#56); and *AIDS Prevention Guide* (#122), which is a folder with fact

sheets for adults who work with teens. Some of the posters available are: *You Won't Get AIDS* (#55); *There's a Simple Way to Prevent AIDS* (#141); *How Much Do Your Children Know About AIDS?* (#143); and *It Might Take More than Motherwit to Tell My Children What to Do About AIDS* (#144).

National P.T.A.
700 N. Rush Street
Chicago, IL   60611-2571
(312) 787-0977
The P.T.A. publishes several booklets for parents. Titles include: *How to Talk to Your Child About Sex; How to Talk to Your Preteen and Teen About Sex;* and *How to Talk to Your Teens and Children About AIDS.* Single copies are free when you send a self-addressed, appropriately stamped envelope.

Network Publications
ETR Associates
1700 Mission Street
Suite 203, P.O. Box 1830
Santa Cruz, CA   95061-1830
(408) 429-9822
Call ETR to receive information about their catalogs *Prevention of Child Sexual Abuse* and *Reproductive Health Materials.*

O.D.N. Productions, Inc.
74 Varick Street, Suite 304
New York, NY   10013
(212) 431-8923

O.D.N. produces *The Subject is AIDS*, a short film for teens, and a package called the *Child Sexual Abuse Prevention Package*, which contains two films and an audiocassette geared for children. A one-week rental runs $60 plus a $10 handling fee.

R A J Publications
P.O. Box 150720
Lakewood, CO   90215
(303) 237-5110
R A J publishes *A Self-Defense Manual on Herpes; Roses Have Thorns* (on STDs); and *Choices* (on contraception). Each booklet costs $1.50.

STD PROGRAMS OF STATE HEALTH DEPARTMENTS

Most of these offices distribute free materials that educate children about the dangers of STDs and make referrals to health centers for people who require testing or treatment.

Alabama

Department of Public Health
Division of STD Control, Room 665
464 Monroe Street
Montgomery, AL   36130
(205) 242-5017

Alaska

Department of Health & Social Services
Section of Epidemiology
STD Control
P.O. Box 240249
Juneau, AK   99524-0249
(907) 561-4406

Arizona

Department of Health Services
STD Control Program
3008 N. 3rd Street, Suite 208
Phoenix, AZ   85012
(602) 230-5904

Arkansas

Department of Health
AIDS/STD Program
4815 W. Markham Street, Slot 33
Little Rock, AR   72205
(501) 661-2408

California

Department of Health Services
STD Control Program
P.O. Box 2230
Sacramento, CA   95814
(916) 322-2087

Colorado

Department of Health
STD/AIDS Control Program
4210 E. 11th Avenue
Denver, CO   80220
(303) 331-8322

Connecticut

Department of Health Services
STD Control Program
150 Washington Street
Hartford, CT   06106
(203) 566-4492

Delaware

Bureau of Disease Prevention
STD Control Program
P.O. Box 637
Dover, DE   19903
(302) 736-4745

District of Columbia

Public Health Commission
STD Control Program
717 14th Street, N.W., 9th Floor
Washington, DC   20005
(202) 727-9583

Florida

Department of Health & Rehabilitative
   Services
STD Control Program
1317 Winewood Boulevard
Tallahassee, FL   32399-0700
(904) 487-3684

Georgia

Division of Public Health
STD Control Program, Suite 206
2799 Lawrenceville Highway
Decatur, GA   30033
(404) 730-1424

Hawaii

Department of Health
STD/HIV Prevention Program
3627 Kilauea Avenue, Suite 304
Honolulu, HI   96816-2399
(808) 541-2664

Idaho

Bureau of Preventive Medicine
STD Program
450 W. State Street
Boise, ID   83720
(208) 334-5944

Illinois

Department of Public Health
STD Program
525 W. Jefferson Street
Springfield, IL   62761
(217) 782-2747

Indiana

State Board of Health
VD Control Section
P.O. Box 1964
Indianapolis, IN   46206-1964
(317) 633-0856

Iowa

Division of Disease Prevention
STD Control Program
Lucas State Office Building
321 E. 12th Street
1st Floor, East Wing
Des Moines, IA   50319-0075
(515) 281-4936

Kansas

Department of Health & Environment
STD Control Program
109 S.W. 9th Street, Suite 605
Topeka, KS   66612-1271
(913) 296-5597

Kentucky

Department for Health Services
STD Program
275 E. Main Street
Frankfort, KY   40621
(502) 564-4804

Louisiana

Department of Health & Hospitals
VD Control Section
P.O. Box 60630
New Orleans, LA   70603
(504) 568-5275

Maine

Department of Human Services
STD Control Program
State House, Station 11
Augusta, ME   04333
(207) 289-2046

Maryland

Department of Health & Mental
  Hygiene
STD Control Division
Herbert R. O'Conor State Office
  Building
201 W. Preston Street, 3rd Floor
Baltimore, MD   21201
(301) 225-6684

Massachusetts

Department of Public Health
STD Control Program/CDC
305 South Street
Jamaica Plain, MA   02130
(617) 522-3700 (ext. 414 or 410)

Michigan

Department of Public Health
VD Division
P.O. Box 30035
Lansing, MI   48909
(517) 335-8167

Minnesota

Department of Health
AIDS/STD Control Section
P.O. Box 9441
Minneapolis, MN   55440
(612) 623-5203

Mississippi

Department of Health
STD Control Program
P.O. Box 1700
Jackson, MS   39215-1700
(601) 960-7714

Missouri

Department of Health
STD Control Program
P.O. Box 570
Jefferson City, MO   65101
(314) 751-6141
(314) 751-6151

Montana

Department of Health & Environmental
  Sciences
STD Control Section
Cogswell Building
Helena, MT   59620
(406) 444-4740

Nebraska

Department of Health
STD Control Program
P.O. Box 95007
Lincoln, NE   68509
(402) 471-2937

Nevada

Department of Human Resources
STD/AIDS Control Program
505 E. King Street, Room 200
Carson City, NV   89710
(702) 885-4800

New Hampshire

Division of Public Health Services
Bureau of Disease Control
STD Control Program
Health & Human Services Building
6 Hazen Drive
Concord, NH   03301-6527
(603) 271-4490

New Jersey

Department of Health
Division of Epidemiology & Disease
  Control
STD Program
CN 369
Trenton, NJ   08625-0369
(609) 588-7526

New Mexico

Public Health Division
STD Program
Harold Runnels Building, Room S-1150
1190 St. Francis Drive
Santa Fe, NM   87503
(505) 988-6560

New York

Health Department
STD Control Section
Corning Tower, Room 649
Empire State Plaza
Albany, NY   12237
(518) 474-3598

North Carolina

Department of Environment, Health &
   Natural Resources
STD Control Branch
P.O. Box 27687
Raleigh, NC   27611-7687
(919) 733-3039

North Dakota

Department of Health
Division of Disease Control
STD Program
State Capitol
Bismarck, ND   58505-0200
(701) 224-2378

Ohio

Department of Health
STD Program
131 N. High Street
Columbus, OH   43215
(614) 466-2446

Oklahoma

Department of Health
VD Control Program
P.O. Box 53551
Oklahoma City, OK   73152
(405) 271-4061

Oregon

Health Division
STD Program
P.O. Box 231
Portland, OR   97201
(503) 229-5819

Pennsylvania

Department of Health
Division of Acute Infectious Diseases
STD Control
P.O. Box 90
Harrisburg, PA   17108
(717) 787-3981

Rhode Island

Department of Health
Epidemiology—STD Control
Cannon Building, Room 105
3 Capital Hill
Providence, RI   02908
(401) 277-2362

South Carolina

Department of Health & Environmental
    Control
STD Control Division
Robert Mills Building
2600 Bull Street
Columbia, SC   29201
(803) 734-4110

South Dakota

Department of Health
Communicable Disease Program
STD Control Section
Joe Foss Building
523 E. Capitol Avenue
Pierre, SD   57501-3182
(605) 773-3364

Tennessee

Department of Health & Environment
STD Control
C2-200 Cordell Hull Building
Nashville, TN   37219-5402
(615) 741-7387

Texas

Department of Health
STD Control Division
1100 W. 49th Street, Room G-406
Austin, TX   78756
(512) 458-7225

Utah

Department of Health
Bureau of Epidemiology
STD Control Section
288 N. 1460 West
Salt Lake City, UT   84116-0660
(801) 538-6191

Vermont

Department of Health
STD Control Section
P.O. Box 70
Burlington, VT   05401
(802) 863-7245

Virginia

Department of Health
Bureau of STD/AIDS
109 Governor Street, Room 722
Richmond, VA   23219
(804) 786-6267

Washington

Division of Public Health
Office of STD Services
Mail Stop LP-13, Building 14
Air Industrial Park
Olympia, WA   98504
(206) 753-5810

West Virginia

Division of Health & Human Resources
STD Program/AIDS Prevention Program
State Office Building 3
1900 Kanawha Boulevard E.
Charleston, WV   25303
(304) 348-2950

Wisconsin

Division of Health
STD Control Program
P.O. Box 309
Madison, WI   53701-0309
(608) 266-7365

Wyoming

Division of Health & Medical Services
STD Program
Hathaway Building, 4th Floor
2300 Capitol Avenue
Cheyenne, WY   82001
(307) 777-7935

Puerto Rico

University of Puerto Rico
Medical Sciences Campus
STD Control Program
Call Box STD
Capara Heights Station
San Juan, PR   00922
(809) 754-8123
(809) 754-8118

ADDICTIONS

SEE ALSO

the MENTAL HEALTH section in Chapter 5 under Compulsive Behavior.

NATIONAL ORGANIZATIONS

Al-Anon Family Group Headquarters
P.O. Box 862
Midtown Station
New York, NY   10018

(212) 302-7240
(800) 356-9996
A large organization for the relatives
and friends of someone with an alcohol

problem, Al-Anon includes Alateen, for twelve- to twenty-year-olds who are suffering from someone else's alcoholism, usually a parent's. Al-Anon publishes numerous magazines, pamphlets, and books.

Alcoholics Anonymous (AA) World Services
P.O. Box 459
Grand Central Station
New York, NY   10163
(212) 686-1100
A huge, self-help organization famous around the world. There is a local AA group in most towns in the United States. If none is listed in your local phone book, call the phone number above. This national headquarters will send you its catalog of pamphlets, books, and other materials.

Alcohol Research Information Service
1106 E. Oakland
Lansing, MI   48906
(517) 485-9900
This Service is an information clearing-house that distributes pamphlets and teaching materials for grades one through twelve.

American Council for Drug Education
204 Monroe Street
Rockville, MD   20850
(301) 294-0600

The Council supplies parents and educators with numerous brochures, films, and teaching aids concerning the risks of drug abuse.

Cocaine Helpline
(800) COCAINE (262-2463)
This hotline, open twenty-four hours a day, is answered by former cocaine addicts. It refers cocaine users and their parents to treatment centers around the country.

Community Intervention, Inc.
529 S. 70th Street, Suite 570
Minneapolis, MN   55415
(612) 332-6537
(800) 328-0417
This group offers free publications such as *Adolescent Drug and Alcohol Use: Signs and Symptoms*. It also publishes a free newspaper on drug and alcohol use among teenagers.

Families Anonymous
(818) 989-7841
A national organization of over five hundred groups for families and friends of people with substance abuse or behavioral problems. Group meetings are based on the twelve-step program developed by Alcoholics Anonymous.

Gam-Anon Family Groups
P.O. Box 157
Whitestone, NY   11357
(718) 352-1671 (Tuesday & Thursday,
    9:00–11:00 A.M.)
An international group comprising
nearly four hundred chapters for
families and friends of compulsive gamblers. Meetings offer emotional support
and friendship. They publish a newsletter and provide group start-up guidelines. Separate Gam-a-teen groups exist
for teenagers.

Hazelden Educational Materials, Inc.
Box 176
Pleasant Valley Road
Center City, MN   55012
(800) 328-9000
This company has a free catalog of edu-
cational materials designed to prevent
drug and alcohol abuse.

Just Say No Foundation
1777 North California Boulevard
Suite 210
Walnut Creek, CA   94596
(415) 939-6666
(800) 258-2766
Helps form "Just Say No" Clubs which
give seven- to fourteen-year-olds the
peer support groups they may need to
resist drugs.

Narcotics Education, Inc.
12501 Old Columbia Pike
Silver Spring, MD   21740
(301) 680-6740
(800) 548-8700
This nonprofit group supplies classroom materials that help kids reject
drugs. The magazines published are
targeted for specific age groups from
grades 4–12. Call for their free catalog.

**National Clearinghouse for Alcohol &
    Drug Information**
P.O. Box 2345
Rockville, MD   20847-2345
(301) 468-2600
(800) 729-6686
(800) 662-HELP (4357)
This federal information center can
refer you to programs that seek to prevent teenagers from abusing alcohol
and drugs. It makes available
videotapes, posters, fact sheets, and
other literature.

**National Council on Alcoholism &
    Drug Dependence, Inc.**
12 W. 21st Street, 7th Floor
New York, NY   10010
(212) 206-6770
(800) NCA-CALL (622-2255)
The Council educates the professional
community and the public about alcoholism and drug abuse. It publishes
catalogs, books, and brochures.

National Drug Information Center
Families in Action
3845 N. Druid Hills Road, Suite 300
Decatur, GA   30033
(404) 325-5799
Families in Action educates parents and community leaders about the health consequences of drug abuse among children and adolescents. The Center provides information on all aspects of drug and alcohol abuse, parent/child relationships, parent drug prevention groups, and drug paraphernalia. Publications include a journal called *Drug Abuse Update*.

National Federation of Parents for
  Drug-Free Youth
1423 N. Jefferson
Springfield, MO   65802
(417) 836-3709
The more than eight thousand local chapters of this organization are devoted to helping parents with their children's drug and alcohol abuse. The national headquarters makes available brochures such as *What Parents Must Learn About Teens and Cocaine* and various training manuals to help prevent abuse.

National Parent's Resource Institute for
  Drug Education, Inc.
50 Hurt Plaza, Suite 210
Atlanta, GA   30303
(404) 577-4500
(800) 241-9746

This group, called PRIDE, can refer parents to local drug treatment programs for children. If you have a touch tone phone you can hear their free informational tapes about drugs when you call. PRIDE publishes books, research summaries, pamphlets, audio and video cassettes, and journal articles.

Office for Substance Abuse Prevention
  (OSAP)
Alcohol, Drug Abuse, & Mental Health
  Administration
5600 Fishers Lane, Room 9A54
Rockville, MD   20857
(301) 443-0365
OSAP answers questions from consumers and professionals, gathers and publishes drug and alcohol abuse prevention information, and runs workshops on preventing drug and alcohol abuse.

Office on Smoking & Health
Public Information Branch
Parklawn Building
5600 Fishers Lane, Room 1-10
Rockville, MD   20857
(301) 443-5287
This office responds to inquiries from consumers and professionals, offers bibliographic and reference services to researchers and others, and publishes and distributes a number of materials on smoking and health.

Overcomers Outreach, Inc.
2290 W. Whittier Boulevard, Suite A/D
La Habra, CA   90631
(213) 697-3994
This is a national organization of over
685 affiliated self-help groups for addicts such as alcoholics and compulsive
gamblers.

Rational Recovery Systems
P.O. Box 800
Lotus, CA   95651
(916) 621-4374
A secular organization of over sixty
chapters for people with chemical de-
pendencies. Group meetings are run by
members with professional assistance.
Also offered are a newsletter and guidelines for starting a group.

School Challenge Campaign
(800) 541-8787
(800) 624-0100
Parents, school officials, and organizations can recieve free information and
brochures on how to set up an antidrug
program in local communities or
schools. This program is sponsored by
the Department of Education.

Sexaholics Anonymous
P.O. Box 300
Simi Valley, CA   93062
(818) 704-9854
An organization of over seven hundred
chapters for people troubled by sexually
self-destructive attitudes and life-styles.
The groups provide mutual help in
gaining and keeping sexual sobriety.
They offer telephone support, a newsletter, and guidelines for forming groups.

Smokers Anonymous World Services
2118 Greenwich Street
San Francisco, CA   94123
(415) 922-8575
This organization, comprising more
than two hundred fifty chapters, offers
group meetings based on the twelve-
step program developed by AA, adapted
for those who want to quit smoking.
The service offers a newsletter and
technical assistance for establishing
new groups.

Stop Teenage Addiction to Tobacco (STAT)
121 Lyman Street, Suite 210
Springfield, MA   01103
(413) 732-STAT (7828)
STAT seeks to control factors influenc-
ing young people to smoke, particularly
tobacco company advertising and poor
enforcement of laws prohibiting tobacco sales to minors. It publishes *The
Tobacco and Youth Reporter,* which
works to increase public awareness
about tobacco addiction in young people. It also publishes statistics, a poster
on advertising deception, and an extensive analysis of cigarette advertising.

Target—Helping Students Cope with
Alcohol & Drugs
P.O. Box 20626
11724 Plaza Circle
Kansas City, MO   64195
(818) 464-5400
(800) 366-6667

Target offers information and referrals
to all. It produces a monthly newsletter
for high schools, low-cost videos,
brochures, and an interactive software
package, and also offers leadership
training.

STATE AND LOCAL ORGANIZATIONS

Most of the offices listed below make referrals and distribute written materials on how
to prevent drug abuse. These may include pamphlets, journal reports, fact sheets, federal
government publications, books, and manuals. These materials are designed for children
and adults. In addition, some offices lend films and videotapes.

Alabama

Alabama Dracon Clearinghouse
Alabama Department of Mental Health
& Mental Retardation
P.O. Box 3710
Montgomery, AL   36193-5001
(205) 271-9248

Bureau of Mental Illness & Substance
Abuse
(205) 271-9253

Mobile Bay Area Partnership for Youth
305A Glenwood Street
Mobile, AL   36606
(205) 473-3673

Alaska

Alaska Council on Prevention of
Alcohol & Drug Abuse, Inc.
7521 Old Seward Highway
Anchorage, AK   99518
(907) 349-6602

Office of Alcoholism & Drug Abuse
Pouch H-05F
Juneau, AK   99811
(907) 586-6201

Arizona

Office of Community Behavioral Health
Services
Birch Hall
411 N. 24th Street
Phoenix, AZ   85008
(602) 220-6478

Arkansas

Office of Alcohol & Drug Abuse Prevention
P.O. Box 1434
Little Rock, AR   72203
(501) 682-6650

California

Department of Alcohol & Drug Programs
111 Capitol Mall
Sacramento, CA   95814
(916) 445-0834

Los Angeles County Drug Abuse Program Office (DAPO)
849 S. Broadway, 11th Floor
Los Angeles, CA   90014
(213) 974-7176

Orange County Drug Abuse Services
Health Care Agency/Drug Abuse Administration
Prevention Services
515 N. Sycamore Street, Room 113
Santa Ana, CA   92701
(714) 834-2011

Prevention Resource Center
Santa Barbara Health Care Services
Drug Program Office
300 N. Antonio Road
Santa Barbara, CA   93110
(805) 964-8255

San Luis Obispo County Drug Program
2180 Johnson Avenue
San Luis Obispo, CA   93408
(805) 544-4722

Colorado

Alcohol & Drug Abuse Division
4210 E. 11th Avenue
Denver, CO   80220
(303) 331-8201

Connecticut

Connecticut Alcohol & Drug Abuse Commission
999 Asylum Avenue
Hartford, CT   06105
(203) 566-4145

Delaware

Division of Alcoholism, Drug Abuse & Mental Health
C. T. Building
Delaware State Hospital
1901 N. DuPont Highway
New Castle, DE   19720
(302) 421-6107

YMCA of Delaware Resource Center
11th and Washington Streets
Wilmington, DE   19801
(302) 571-6975

District of Columbia

Alcohol & Drug Abuse Services
  Administration
1300 1st Street, N.E., Room 319
Washington, DC   20002
(202) 727-1762

Job Corps
Department of Labor
601 D Street, N.W.
Washington, DC   20013
(202) 588-0288

Washington Area Council on
  Alcoholism & Drug Abuse, Inc.
Information & Referral Department
1232 M Street, N.W.
Washington, DC   20005
(202) 783-1300

Florida

Alcohol & Drug Abuse Program
Building VI, Room 156
Tallahassee, FL   32399-0700
(904) 488-0900

Georgia

Division of Mental Health, Mental
  Retardation & Substance Abuse
878 Peachtree Street, N.E., Suite 319
Atlanta, GA   30309
(404) 894-4785

Middle Georgia Council on Drugs
538 1st Street
Macon, GA   31201
(912) 743-4611

Hawaii

Alcohol & Drug Abuse Branch
P.O. Box 3378
Honolulu, HI   96801-9984
(808) 548-4280

Idaho

Bureau of Social Services
Towers Building, 10th Floor
450 W. State Street
Boise, ID   83720
(208) 334-5934

Illinois

AH Training & Development
  Systems, Inc.
Prevention Resource Center
901 S. 2nd Street
Springfield, IL   62704
(217) 525-3456

Illinois Department of Alcoholism &
  Substance Abuse
State of Illinois Center, Suite 5-600
100 W. Randolph Street
Chicago, IL   60601
(312) 917-3840

Indiana

Division of Addiction Services
117 E. Washington Street
Indianapolis, IN   46204-3647
(317) 232-7816

Greater Indianapolis Council on
  Alcoholism, Inc.
2511 E. 46th Street
Building S
Indianapolis, IN   46205
(317) 542-7128

Iowa

Iowa Substance Abuse Information
  Center
500 1st Street, S.E.
Cedar Rapids, IA   52401
(319) 398-5133

Substance Abuse Division
Lucas State Office Building, 4th Floor
E. 12th and Walnut Streets
Des Moines, IA   50319
(515) 281-3641

Kansas

Alcohol & Drug Abuse Services
Biddle Building, 2nd Floor
300 S.W. Oakley
Topeka, KS   66606
(913) 296-3925

Kentucky

Division of Substance Abuse
Health Services Building
275 E. Main Street
Frankfort, KY   40621
(502) 564-2880
(502) 269-1871

Louisiana

Alexandria/Pineville Alcohol & Drug
  Abuse Clinic
P.O. Box 1060
Pineville, LA   71361-1060
(318) 487-5191

Bossier/Shreveport Substance Abuse
  Clinic
707 Benton Road, Suite 100
Bossier City, LA   71111
(318) 227-5166

Office of Prevention & Recovery from
  Alcohol & Drug Abuse
Louisiana Department of Health &
  Human Resources
2744-B Wooddale Boulevard
Baton Rouge, LA   70805
(504) 922-0721
(504) 922-0730

Substance Abuse Prevention Education
  (SAPE)
Louisiana Department of Education
P.O. Box 94064
Baton Rouge, LA   70804-9064
(504) 342-5430

Maine

Department of Educational & Cultural
  Services
Division of Alcohol & Drug Education
  Services Resource Center
State House, Station 57
Augusta, ME   04333
(207) 289-3876

Department of Human Services
Office of Alcoholism & Drug Abuse
  Prevention
State House, Station 11
Augusta, ME   04333
(207) 289-2781

Maryland

Alcohol & Drug Abuse Administration
Herbert R. O'Conor State Office
  Building
201 W. Preston Street
Baltimore, MD   21201
(301) 225-6441

Central Maryland Alcohol & Drug
  Abuse Prevention Resource Center
Baltimore City Area Health Education
  Center, Inc.
2105 N. Charles Street
Baltimore, MD   21218
(301) 752-3430

Lower Shore Prevention Resource
  Center
Salisbury State College
Holloway Hall 336
Salisbury, MD   21801
(301) 543-6309

Massachusetts

Division of Alcoholism & Drug
  Rehabilitation
150 Tremont Street
Boston, MA   02111
(617) 727-8614

Michigan

Office of Substance Abuse Services
P.O. Box 30035
Lansing, MI   48909
(517) 335-8809

Minnesota

Chemical Dependency Program
  Division
Space Center Building
444 Lafayette Street
St. Paul, MN   55155
(612) 296-1288

Minnesota Prevention Resource Center
2829 Verndale Avenue
Anoka, MN   55303
(612) 427-5310

Mississippi

Division of Alcohol & Drug Abuse
1101 Robert E. Lee Building
239 N. Lamar Street
Jackson, MS   39201
(601) 354-1288

Mississippi Department of Mental
   Health
Division of Alcohol & Drug Abuse
1500 Woolfolk State Office Building
Jackson, MS   39201
(601) 352-1297

Missouri

Division of Alcohol & Drug Abuse
P.O. Box 687
Jefferson City, MO   65102
(314) 751-4942

Montana

Treatment Services Division
1539 11th Avenue
Helena, MT   59620
(406) 444-3904

Nebraska

Alcohol & Drug Information
   Clearinghouse
Alcoholism Council of Nebraska
215 Centennial Mall S., Room 412
Lincoln, NE   68508
(402) 474-0930

Division on Alcoholism & Drug Abuse
P.O. Box 94728
Lincoln, NE   68509-4728
(402) 471-2851

Nevada

Bureau of Alcohol & Drug Abuse
Capitol Complex
Carson City, NV   89710
(702) 885-4790

New Hampshire

Alcohol/Drug Abuse Prevention Project
   of Solve, Inc.
P.O. Box 157
Atkinson, NH   03811
(603) 898-1516

New Hampshire Office of Alcohol &
   Drug Abuse Prevention
State Office Building
17 Water Street
Claremont, NH   03743
(603) 542-6484

New Hampshire Office of Alcohol &
   Drug Abuse Prevention
Waldron Towers
Green Street
Dover, NH   03820
(603) 749-7326

Office of Alcohol & Drug Abuse
   Prevention
Health & Human Services Building
6 Hazen Drive
Concord, NH   03301-6525
(603) 271-4627
(800) 852-3345 (in New Hampshire)

New Jersey

Alcohol, Narcotic & Drug Abuse
   Division
129 E. Hanover Street
Trenton, NJ   08608
(609) 292-5760

Institute for Human Development
   Prevention Unit
1315 Pacific Avenue
Atlantic City, NJ   08401
(609) 345-4035

New Jersey Substance Abuse
   Information Clearinghouse/South
Cooper Hospital University Medical
   Center
Cooper Medical Arts Building
300 Broadway
Camden, NJ   08103
(609) 342-3272

Paterson Counseling Center, Inc.
356 Shunpike Road
Chatham, NJ   07928
(201) 523-8316

Regional Curriculum Services
   Unit—South
New Jersey Department of Education
Tanyard and Salina Roads
Sewell, NJ   08080
(609) 853-6200

New York
Substance Abuse Services Division
P.O. Box 8200
Albany, NY   12203
(518) 457-2061

North Carolina
Alcohol & Drug Services
Division of Mental Health, Mental
   Retardation & Substance Abuse
   Services
North Carolina Department of Human
   Resources
325 N. Salisbury Street
Raleigh, NC   27611
(919) 733-4670

Drug Information Center
Drug Action of Wake County, Inc.
2809 Industrial Drive
Raleigh, NC   27609
(919) 832-4453

Edgecombe-Nash Mental Health, Mental
   Rehabilitation, Substance Abuse
   Services
P.O. Box 4047
Rocky Mount, NC   27803-4047
(919) 977-0151

North Dakota

Division of Alcoholism & Drug Abuse
Professional Building
1839 E. Capitol Avenue
Bismarck, ND   58501
(701) 224-2769

Ohio

Bureau on Alcohol Abuse & Alcoholism
  Recovery
P.O. Box 118
Columbus, OH   43266-0586
(614) 466-3445

Oklahoma

Department of Mental Health
P.O. Box 53277
Capitol Station
Oklahoma City, OK   73152
(405) 271-7474

Oregon

Office of Alcohol & Drug Abuse
  Programs
Capitol Mall
1178 Chemeketa Street, N.E.
Salem, OR   97310
(503) 378-2163

Oregon Drug & Alcohol Information
  Center
Metrolab—A Service of HealthLink
235 N. Graham
Portland, OR   97227
(503) 280-3673
(800) 452-7032 (in Oregon, ext. 3673)

Pennsylvania

Office of Drug & Alcohol Programs
Health and Welfare Building, Room 929
6th and Commonwealth Avenue
Harrisburg, PA   17120
(717) 787-9761
(800) 932-0912

Rhode Island

Division of Substance Abuse
Substance Abuse Administration
  Building
Rhode Island Medical Center
Cranston, RI   02920
(401) 464-2091

South Carolina

The Drugstore Information
  Clearinghouse
South Carolina Commission on Alcohol
  & Drug Abuse (SCCADA)
3700 Forest Drive
Columbia, SC   29204
(803) 734-9559
(803) 734-9520

Marion/Dillon Commission on Alcohol
  & Drug Abuse
P.O. Box 1011
103 Court Street
Marion, SC   29571
(803) 423-5610

South Dakota

Division of Alcohol & Drug Abuse
Joe Foss Building, Room 125
523 E. Capitol Avenue
Pierre, SD   57501-3182
(605) 773-3123

Northeast Prevention Resource Center
South Dakota Human Services Agency
Community Mental Health Center
P.O. Box 1030
900 Skyline Drive
Watertown, SD   57201
(605) 886-7522

Tennessee

Division of Alcohol & Drug Abuse
  Services
Doctors Building, 4th Floor
706 Church Street
Nashville, TN   37219
(615) 741-1921

Texas

Commission on Alcohol & Drug Abuse
1705 Guadalupe Street
Austin, TX   78701-1214
(512) 463-5510

Corpus Christi Drug Abuse
  Council, Inc.
P.O. Box 2725
Corpus Christi, TX   78401
(512) 882-9979

Utah

Substance Abuse Division
P.O. Box 45500
Salt Lake City, UT   84145-0500
(801) 538-3939

Vermont

Office of Alcohol & Drug Abuse
  Programs
Waterbury Office Complex
103 S. Main Street
Waterbury, VT   05676
(802) 241-2170

Virginia

Office of Substance Abuse Services
P.O. Box 1797
Richmond, VA   23214
(804) 786-3906

Washington

Bureau of Alcohol & Substance Abuse
Mail Stop OB-44W
Olympia, WA   98504
(206) 753-5866

West Virginia

Division on Alcoholism & Drug Abuse
State Office Building 3, Room 451
1800 Washington Street E.
Charleston, WV   25305
(304) 348-2276

Wisconsin

Office of Alcohol & Drug Abuse
P.O. Box 7851
Madison, WI   53707-7851
(608) 266-2717

Wisconsin Clearinghouse
University of Wisconsin Hospital &
   Clinics
P.O. Box 1468
Madison, WI   53701
(608) 263-2797

Wyoming

Office of Substance Abuse Programs
Hathaway Building, Room 350
2300 Capitol Avenue
Cheyenne, WY   82002-0710
(307) 777-6945

Puerto Rico

Department of Drug Addiction Services
P.O. Box 21414
Rio Piedras, PR   00928-1414
(809) 764-3795
(809) 763-7575

JUVENILE DELINQUENCY

The first part of this section, Social Service Organizations, lists groups that provide direct help or referrals to troubled teens and their parents. The second part, Research Organizations, describes libraries and academic research groups that study criminality and criminal justice. The third part, State Offices of Juvenile Delinquency, lists state agencies that handle such problems.

SOCIAL SERVICE ORGANIZATIONS

**American Association for Counseling &
   Development (AACD)**
5999 Stevenson Avenue
Alexandria, VA   22304
(703) 823-9800

AACD works to improve counseling and rehabilitation programs for adult and juvenile offenders. The group will answer questions and make referrals.

SEE ALSO

the LEGAL MATTERS section of Chapter 10 for organizations that represent children.

The DROPOUT PREVENTION section of Chapter 8 lists groups that help prevent troubled youth from leaving school.

American Correctional Association (ACA)
4321 Hartwick Road, Suite L-208
College Park, MD   20740
(301) 699-7600
Although primarily concerned with the well-being and education of adult prisoners, ACA will also provide information and referrals regarding juvenile delinquency.

American Youth Work Center
1346 Connecticut Avenue, N.W., Room 925
Washington, DC   20036
(202) 785-0764
This resource organization for youth service agencies and youth workers will help parents find suitable work programs for their troubled children. The Center distributes *The National Directory of Runaway Programs; Adolescent Life Stress as a Predictor of Alcohol Abuse and/or Runaway Behavior; Reaching Troubled Youth;* and other publications. A price list is available.

Because I Love You
P.O. Box 35175
Los Angeles, CA   90035-9998
(213) 659-5289
(213) 322-0224
This is a self-help group focusing on parents of children with behavioral problems such as substance abuse and delinquency.

Fortune Society
39 W. 19th Street
New York, NY   10011
(212) 206-7070
In addition to its work with adult offenders, the Society counsels troubled youth ages sixteen to nineteen. It publishes a newsletter called *The Fortune News.*

Juvenile Justice & Delinquency Prevention
National Criminal Justice Reference Service (NCJRS)
Box 6000
Rockville, MD   20850

(301) 251-5500

(800) 638-8736 (Juvenile Justice
Clearinghouse)

(800) 851-3420 (National Institute of
Justice)

The Juvenile Justice and Delinquency Prevention program serves as a national clearinghouse for information on delinquency. This program answers questions over the phone, makes referrals, and distributes numerous publications.

Men's Rights Association
17854 Lyons
Forest Lake, MN   55025
(612) 464-7887

Among the many concerns of this group is the reduction of juvenile delinquency that sometimes accompanies divorce. The Association provides information, referrals, counseling, and offers free publications.

National Association of Juvenile Correctional Agencies
36 Locksley Lane
Springfield, IL   62704
(217) 787-0690

This group is concerned with prevention of juvenile delinquency and treatment of offenders. Although its services are primarily for professionals in juvenile correction, the Association will answer questions and make referrals for the public.

National Council for Therapy & Rehabilitation Through Horticulture (NCTRH)
9220 Wightman Road, Suite 300
Gaithersburg, MD   20878
(301) 948-3010

NCTRH promotes the use of horticulture and related activities as a therapeutic and rehabilitation method for the handicapped, mentally retarded, emotionally disturbed, and delinquent. The Council maintains listings of allied programs throughout the country.

National Council on Crime & Delinquency (NCCD)
77 Maiden Lane, 4th Floor
San Francisco, CA   94108
(415) 956-5651

NCCD offers information on alternatives to incarceration for violent and nonviolent juvenile offenders. It maintains MODELS, a nationwide database of over five hundred programs designed to deal with juveniles in trouble with the law without institutionalization. Although the Council mainly works with government agencies, it will answer questions by phone and make referrals for the public. Publications include *Alternatives to Imprisoning Young Offenders* and a directory called *Noteworthy Programs*.

Partners, Inc.
701 S. Logan, Suite 109
Denver, CO   80209
(303) 777-7000
Partners recruits, trains, and supervises community volunteers who are matched one-to-one with troubled juveniles diverted from the criminal justice system. Partners is expanding these rehabilitative operations nationwide. The group offers information and referrals to the public.

Prison Families Anonymous
Christ Presbyterian Church
353 Fulton Avenue, Room 11
Hempstead, NY   11550
(516) 538-6065
An organization of self-help groups for friends and families of someone who is imprisoned or embroiled in the criminal or juvenile justice systems. The groups provide information and referrals, telephone support, and peer counseling.

Salvation Army
National Headquarters
799 Bloomfield Avenue
Verona, NJ   07044
(201) 239-0606
Among its many activities, the Salvation Army conducts preventive work with juvenile delinquents. The national headquarters can advise what services they offer in your area.

TOUGHLOVE
P.O. Box 1069
Doylestown, PA   18901
(215) 348-7090
(800) 333-1069
This self-help program for families helps problem teenagers and their parents through counseling. The TOUGHLOVE Support Network maintains an informal listing of more than fourteen hundred groups throughout the nation and worldwide. The national headquarters provides advisory, consulting, and referral services. Publications include *TOUGHLOVE: A Self-Help Manual,* one for parents, one for kids, and *TOUGHLOVE Cocaine.*

United Neighborhood Centers of America, Inc. (UNCA)
1319 F Street, N.W., Suite 603
Washington, DC   20004
(202) 393-3929
UNCA is an umbrella organization and advocate for three hundred sixty settlement houses and neighborhood centers operating throughout the United States. It offers information and referrals regarding juvenile delinquency prevention. A publications list is available.

University of Alabama
Brewer-Porch Children's Center
P.O. Box 870156
Tuscaloosa, AL   35487-0156
(205) 348-7236

The Center develops treatment and education programs for children and teenagers with behavioral problems. It will answer questions, make referrals, and provide telephone counseling. In addition, it runs a short-term residential treatment shelter for school-age children with adjustment problems. Services are free and available to anyone. The Center also publishes research reports, handbooks, and brochures.

Volunteers in Prevention, Probation, Prisons, Inc.
527 N. Main Street
Royal Oak, MI   48067
(313) 398-8550
(313) 398-8551
This organization sponsors volunteer programs in all areas of juvenile and criminal justice. It will answer questions, make referrals, and provide consultations and onsite training. It also offers books, reports, pamphlets, tapes, and films.

RESEARCH ORGANIZATIONS

Note: While the primary goal of these institutions is to help professionals conduct research on criminal behavior and related fields, most offer help to parents researching a specific issue or problem concerning juvenile delinquency. Often a fee is involved when extended assistance is required.

Behavioral Research Institute (BRI)
2305 Canyon Boulevard
Boulder, CO   80302
(303) 444-1682
The Institute conducts academic research on social problem behavior with an emphasis on juveniles. The group will answer questions but will not make referrals to counseling programs. BRI publishes reports, journal articles, and research summaries. A publications list is available on request.

Colorado Department of Social Services Library
1575 Sherman Street
Denver, CO   80203
(303) 866-4086
The Library has a collection of over eleven thousand books and other materials in the areas of public assistance, child psychiatry, juvenile delinquency, and adoption. Full library services are available.

Illinois Department of Mental Health
Institute for Juvenile Research
Research Library
907 S. Wolcott Avenue
Chicago, IL 60612
(312) 996-1733
The Institute runs several major programs, including consultations devoted
to the mental health of juveniles. It
evaluates treatment programs for problem children such as juvenile delinquents, sex offenders, and those with
self-destructive patterns. Its library consists of nearly nine thousand books,
journals, periodicals, and government
publications. It publishes staff-written
articles and books, and will answer
questions, provide consultation, make
referrals, and compile statistics.

Indiana Criminal Justice Institute
101 W. Ohio, Suite 1030
Indianapolis, IN 46204
(703) 643-1689
The Institute maintains a microfiche
collection of nearly fifty thousand
criminal justice publications; publishes
reports, articles, reviews, and data compilations; and provides full library services. It responds to inquiries, provides
consultations, makes referrals, helps
with research, and analyzes data.

New York State Division of Criminal
Justice Services (DCJS)
Executive Park Tower
Stuyvesant Plaza
Albany, NY 12203
(518) 457-6113
The DCJS library, offering limited research services, includes over twenty
thousand law and criminal justice
books, microfiche reports, periodicals, a
police training video/film collection,
and several computerized database systems.

Southern Illinois University at
Carbondale
Center for the Study of Crime,
Delinquency, & Corrections
Carbondale, IL 62901
(618) 453-5701
The Center offers research-oriented in-
formation and consulting services on
delinquency.

Southwest Texas State University
Institute of Criminal Justice Studies
(ICJS)
San Marcos, TX 78666-4610
(512) 245-3030
ICJS studies the prevention and control
of violent crime and delinquency. It
answers questions, makes referrals,
provides consulting services, conducts
research, and hosts seminars.

University of Pennsylvania
Sellin Center for Studies in
   Criminology & Criminal Law
37th and Spruce Streets, 4th Floor
Philadelphia, PA   19104
(215) 898-7411
(215) 898-3098 (Library)
The Center conducts research in delinquency, criminology, and penology and will answer questions on a limited basis. It runs a library.

University of Toronto
Centre of Criminology
John P. Robarts Research Library
130 St. George Street, Room 8001
Toronto, Ontario   M5S 1A1
Canada
(416) 978-7124
The Centre is a research and teaching division within the University of Toronto focusing on aspects of criminology such as sociology of law, sentencing, corrections, alternatives to imprisonment, young offenders, and public attitudes to crime within Canadian society. It will make referrals and provide information on current research. It maintains a library.

STATE OFFICES OF JUVENILE DELINQUENCY

These offices will make referrals to programs that help troubled juveniles in each state.

Alabama

Department of Youth Services
P.O. Box 66
Mt. Meigs, AL   36057
(205) 272-9100 (ext. 102)

Alaska

Division of Family & Youth Services
Pouch H-05
Juneau, AK   99811
(907) 465-3170

Arizona

Juvenile/Community Services Division
1601 W. Jefferson Street, Room 468
Phoenix, AZ   85007
(602) 542-5306

Arkansas

Division of Children & Family Services
P.O. Box 1437
Little Rock, AR   72203-1437
(501) 682-8772

California

Youth Authority Department
4241 Williamsbourgh Drive
Sacramento, CA 95823
(916) 427-4816

Colorado

Division of Youth Services
4255 S. Knox Court
Denver, CO 80236
(303) 762-4695

Connecticut

Department of Children & Youth
   Services
170 Sigourney Street
Hartford, CT 06105
(203) 566-3536

Delaware

Division of Youth Rehabilitative
   Services
Centre & Faulkland Roads
Wilmington, DE 19805
(302) 995-8334

District of Columbia

Youth Services Administration
817 14th Street, N.W., Suite 510
Washington, DC 20005
(202) 727-9411

Florida

Children, Youth & Families Program
   Office
Building VIII
1317 Winewood Boulevard
Tallahassee, FL 32399
(904) 488-8763

Georgia

Division of Youth Services
878 Peachtree Street, N.E., Suite 817
Atlanta, GA 30309
(404) 894-5922

Hawaii

State Law Enforcement Planning
   Agency
426 Queen Street, Room 201
Honolulu, HI 96813
(808) 548-3800

Idaho

Youth Rehabilitation Services
Towers Building, 10th Floor
450 W. State Street
Boise, ID 83720
(208) 334-5698

Illinois

Juvenile Division
P.O. Box 19277
Springfield, IL 62794-9277
(217) 522-2666

Indiana

Department of Correction
State Office Building, Room 804
100 N. Senate Avenue
Indianapolis, IN   46204
(317) 232-5711

Iowa

Bureau of Adult, Children & Family
  Services
Hoover State Office Building, 5th Floor
1300 E. Walnut Street
Des Moines, IA   50319-0114
(515) 281-5521

Kansas

Juvenile Offender Programs
Smith-Wilson Building
300 S.W. Oakley
Topeka, KS   66606
(913) 296-4648

Kentucky

Juvenile Justice Unit
417 High Street, 3rd Floor
Frankfort, KY   40601
(502) 564-3251

Louisiana

Office of Juvenile Services
P.O. Box 94304
Capitol Station
Baton Rouge, LA   70804
(504) 342-6001

Maine

Department of Corrections
State House
Station 111
Augusta, ME   04333
(207) 289-2711

Maryland

Juvenile Services Agency
321 Fallsway
Baltimore, MD   21202
(301) 333-6751

Massachusetts

Department of Youth Services
Fort Point Place
27-43 Wormwood Street, Room 400
Boston, MA   02210
(617) 727-7575

Michigan

Delinquency Services Division
P.O. Box 30037
Lansing, MI   48909
(517) 373-8225

Minnesota

Office of Juvenile Release
Bigelow Building, Room 300
450 N. Syndicate Street
St. Paul, MN   55104
(612) 642-0274

Mississippi

Department of Youth Services
301 N. Lamar Street, Suite 410
Jackson, MS   39201
(601) 359-1066

Missouri

Division of Youth Services
P.O. Box 447
Jefferson City, MO   65102
(314) 751-3324

Montana

Community Corrections Bureau
1539 11th Avenue
Helena, MT   59620
(406) 444-4912

Nebraska

Department of Correctional Services
P.O. Box 94661
Lincoln, NE   68509
(402) 471-2654

Nevada

Youth Services Division
Capitol Complex
Carson City, NV   89710
(702) 885-5982

New Hampshire

Bureau of Secure Care for Children
Health & Human Services Building
6 Hazen Drive
Concord, NH   03301
(603) 271-4478
(603) 271-4451

New Jersey

Division of Juvenile Services
CN 863
Trenton, NJ   08625
(609) 292-5858

New Mexico

Office of Juvenile Justice Programs
1422 Paseo de Peralta
Santa Fe, NM   87501
(505) 827-5072

New York

Youth Division
84 Holland Avenue
Albany, NY   12208
(518) 473-8437

North Carolina

Division of Youth Services
Dobbin Building
705 Palmer Drive
Raleigh, NC   27603
(919) 733-3011

North Dakota

Division of Juvenile Services
State Capitol, 10th Floor
Bismarck, ND   58505
(701) 224-2471

Ohio

Department of Youth Services
51 N. High Street
Columbus, OH   43226-0582
(614) 466-8783

Oklahoma

Division of Children & Youth Services
P.O. Box 25352
Oklahoma City, OK   73125
(405) 521-4440

Oregon

Office of Correctional Services
198 Commercial Street, S.E.
Salem, OR   97310-0450
(503) 378-4507

Pennsylvania

Office of State Facilities for Delinquent
  Youth
P.O. Box 2675
Harrisburg, PA   17105-2675
(717) 787-8834

Rhode Island

Department for Children & Their
  Families
Building 7
610 Mt. Pleasant Avenue
Providence, RI   02908
(401) 457-4750

South Carolina

Department of Youth Services
P.O. Box 7367
Columbia, SC   29202
(803) 734-1420

South Dakota

Board of Charities & Corrections
Joe Foss Building
523 E. Capitol Avenue
Pierre, SD   57501
(605) 773-3478

Tennessee

Youth Services Division
Rachel Jackson Building, 2nd Floor
320 6th Avenue N.
Nashville, TN   37219
(615) 741-3069

Texas

Youth Commission
P.O. Box 9999
Austin, TX   78766
(512) 452-8111

Utah

Division of Youth Corrections
P.O. Box 45500
Salt Lake City, UT   84145-0500
(801) 538-4330

Vermont

Division of Social Services
Osgood Building
Waterbury Office Complex
103 S. Main Street
Waterbury, VT   05676
(802) 241-2131

Virginia

Division of Youth Services
P.O. Box 26963
Richmond, VA   23261
(804) 674-3221

Washington

Division of Juvenile Rehabilitation
Mail Stop OB-32
Olympia, WA   98504
(206) 753-7402

West Virginia

Youth & Community Operations
State Office Building 4
112 California Avenue
Charleston, WV   25305
(304) 348-2036

Wisconsin

Office of Justice Assistance
30 W. Mifflin Street
Madison, WI   53702
(608) 266-7488

Wyoming

Board of Charities & Reform
Herschler Building, 1st Floor
122 W. 25th Street
Cheyenne, WY   82002
(307) 777-7479

Puerto Rico

Correctional Administration
G.P.O. Box 71308
San Juan, PR   00936
(809) 766-4700

RUNAWAYS

SEE ALSO

the MISSING CHILDREN section in Chapter 10.

Covenant House
P.O. Box 731
Times Square Station
New York, NY   10108
(212) 330-0469
(800) 999-9999 (24-hour hotline)
Covenant House cares for and shelters
nearly one thousand homeless or runaway children a day.

Division of Runaway Youth Programs
Department of Health & Human
 Services
P.O. Box 1182
Washington, DC   20013
(202) 755-7800
Call or write for a free copy of the na-
tional directory of runaway youth pro-
grams.

National Network of Runaway & Youth
 Services
1400 I Street, N.W., Suite 330

Washington, DC   20005
(202) 682-4114
Particularly for teenagers twelve to seventeen years old, the Network helps off-
set problems caused by substance
abuse, delinquency, and adolescent
pregnancy. It provides counseling, residential services, and a phone network.

National Runaway Switchboard &
 Suicide Hotline
(800) 621-4000 (24-hour hotline)
The Hotline is used by children on the
run and those considering suicide, and
by their parents.

Runaway Hotline
(800) 231-6946
(800) 392-3352 (in Texas)
This Hotline is used by children on the
run and by their parents.

CHAPTER 10

MISSING CHILDREN, ABUSE, AND LEGAL MATTERS

This chapter has three sections. The MISSING CHILDREN section lists organizations that help parents teach their children how not to get kidnapped and can help parents locate a child who is already missing. The CHILD ABUSE AND NEGLECT section lists sources that help prevent or stop the abuse of children, including hotlines parents can call if they are in danger of harming their children. Finally, the LEGAL MATTERS section lists a wide range of groups devoted to children's rights, divorce, custody matters, child support, the rights of single parents, grandparents, and others.

SEE ALSO

the STATE CONSUMER PROTECTION AGENCIES section in Chapter 12 for offices that help protect the rights of consumers.

☎ ☎

MISSING CHILDREN

If your child is missing, call the local police immediately. However, you should also call some of the organizations listed below to increase the chances that your child will be found quickly.

This section has three parts. The first part, National Government Clearinghouses, lists two organizations (one in Canada, one in the United States) that *every parent of a missing child should call.* The second part, Independent Organizations, lists nongovernmental groups that provide a wide range of services and information to parents of missing children. Finally, the third part, State Clearinghouses for Missing Children, lists the statewide sources that *every parent of a missing child should also call* for the state in which they live.

Many of these national and state offices also offer materials that help teach children to avoid abduction.

SEE ALSO

the RUNAWAYS section of Chapter 9.

The MAIL ORDER CATALOGS section of Chapter 12 under Health and Safety describes tags and other products that help identify your child.

The SELF-HELP CLEARINGHOUSES section of Chapter 13 lists groups that will help you find a local support group comprising other parents of missing children.

NATIONAL GOVERNMENT CLEARINGHOUSES

Canada

Royal Canadian Mounted Police
Missing Children Registry
(613) 993-1525

United States

National Center for Missing & Exploited Children
2101 Wilson Boulevard, Suite 550
Arlington, VA   22201
(703) 235-3900
(703) 235-3535

(800) 843-5678 (hotline)
(800) 826-7653 (TDD)
If your child is missing, or to report sighting a missing child in the U.S., call this group's hotline. It offers assistance and information to parents and organizations searching for missing children. The group also publishes brochures and books such as the *Parental Kidnapping Handbook* and the *Directory of Support Services and Resources for Missing and Exploited Children, Education and Prevention Guidelines.*

INDEPENDENT ORGANIZATIONS

All the groups listed below offer referrals, information, and services to help find missing children. Those for which no description appears are local groups that should be contacted if you live in their region.

Adam Walsh Child Resource Center
770 City Drive S., Suite 3100
Orange, CA   92668
(714) 740-2660
Started by the parents of a six-year-old boy who was kidnapped from a department store and later found dead, the AWCRC offers information and referral services to parents, fingerprinting programs, and safety education for children.

Adam Walsh Child Resource Center
3111 S. Dixie Highway, Suite 244
West Palm Beach, FL   33405
(407) 833-9080

Adam Walsh Child Resource Center
c/o Cooperative Extension
249 Highland Avenue
Rochester, NY   14620
(716) 461-1000 (ext. 56)

Adam Walsh Child Resource Center
410 1600 Hampton Street Building
Columbia, SC   29202
(803) 254-2326

America's Children Held Hostage
30 Stepney Lane
Brentwood, NY   11717
(516) 231-6240

California Child Abduction
Child Abduction Recovery &
   Enforcement Council
1950 Sunwest Boulevard, Suite 200
San Bernadino, CA   92415
(714) 383-3631

California Foundation for the
   Protection of Children
828 Moraga Drive
Los Angeles, CA   90049
(213) 471-6761

Canadian Centre for Missing Children
& Victims of Violence
Provincial Court House, 3rd Floor
1-A Sir Winston Churchill Square
Edmonton, Alberta   T5J 0R2
Canada
(403) 422-4698

Child Find of America
P.O. Box 277
New Paltz, NY   12501
(914) 255-1848
(800) A-WAY-OUT (292-9688)
(800) I-AM-LOST (426-5678)
An international organization that helps
parents locate lost and missing children, its first toll-free number is for
mediation and help for parents; the second toll-free number is for use by lost
children and others who identify them.
Child Find provides registration facilities, a pictorial register, advocacy, and
seminars to increase public awareness,
and also issues a newsletter.

Child Find, Alberta
809 Manning Road, N.E.
Calgary, Alberta   T2E 7M9
Canada
(403) 273-1717

Child Find, Manitoba
P.O. Box 3189
Winnipeg, Manitoba   R3C 4E7
Canada
(204) 831-5678

Child Find, New Brunswick
364 Brunswick Street
Fredericton, New Brunswick   E3A 1S9
Canada
(506) 459-7250

Child Find, Nova Scotia
2756 Gladstone Street
Halifax, Nova Scotia   B3K 4W5
Canada
(902) 453-6633

Child Find, Ontario
345 Lakeshore Road E., Suite 314
Oakville, Ontario   L6J 1J5
Canada
(416) 842-5353

Child Find, Quebec
828 Decaree
St. Laurent, Quebec   H4L 3L9
Canada
(514) 747-4000
(800) 363-2687 (in Quebec)

Child Find, Saskatchewan
2120 St. George Avenue
Saskatoon, Saskatchewan   S7M 0K7
Canada
(306) 934-0700

Child Find of Utah, Inc.
5755 Hansen Circle
Murray, UT   84107
(801) 261-4134

Childkeyppers International
P.O. Box 6456
Lake Worth, FL   33466
(305) 586-6695
Childkeyppers runs a fingerprinting program for children, supplemented by implanting identifiers in their teeth. In addition, they have created an album called "Safety Key for Safety Wise Kids."

Children's Rights of America
12551 Indian Rocks Road, Suite 9
Largo, FL   34644
(813) 593-0090
This small group offers information services to parents of missing children, helps locate missing kids, and offers an outreach program for runaway teenagers. The group publishes several brochures.

Children's Rights of PA, Inc.
P.O. Box 4362
Allentown, PA   18105
(215) 437-2971

Children's Rights of PA, Inc.
P.O. Box 270
Dalton, PA   18414
(717) 563 2628

Childseekers
P.O. Box 6065
Rutland, VT   05701-6065
(802) 773-5988

Citizens to Amend Title 18
P.O. Box 936
Newhall, CA   91321
(805) 259-4435
This group represents parents who have been awarded custody but whose child has been kidnapped by the noncustodial parent. The group seeks to change Title 18, Section 1201A, of the U.S. Code, which lets parental kidnappers of children under eighteen avoid charges. The group offers information to custodial parents.

Exploited Children's Help Organization
720 W. Jefferson Street
Louisville, KY   40202
(502) 585-3246

Family & Friends of Missing Persons & Violent Crime Victims
P.O. Box 27529
Seattle, WA   98125
(206) 362-1081

Find-Me, Inc.
P.O. Box 1612
La Grange, GA   30241
(404) 884-7419
Find-Me counsels families and advises the public about the missing persons phenomenon. The group offers free consultations, referrals, and brochures.

Find the Children
11811 W. Olympic Boulevard
Los Angeles, CA   90064
(213) 477-6721
This group helps parents find children through media exposure and investigation. It offers referral services for parents looking for attorneys, investigators, and counseling services, and publishes *Find the Children,* an annual directory of missing children that includes photographs.

Find the Kids
3047 St. Mary's Avenue
Omaha, NE   68105
(402) 346-8822

Friends of Child Find—Montana
737 S. Billings Boulevard
No. Zero
Billings, MT   59101
(406) 259-6999

Hide & Seek Foundation
P.O. Box 17226
3300 Market Street, #14
Salem, OR   97305
(503) 585-7909

Hug-A-Tree & Survive
c/o Jacqueline Heet
6465 Lance Way
San Diego, CA   92120
(619) 286-7536

This group teaches children what to do if they become lost. "Hug-a-Tree" means kids should stay where they are and wait for help. It instructs kids what type of help will come for them, how to protect themselves, and how to help searchers find them.

I.D. Resource Center of Albuquerque
2719 San Mateo, N.E.
Albuquerque, NM   87110
(505) 883-0983

Illinois Task Force on Parental Child Abduction
645 N. Wood Street
Chicago, IL   60600
(312) 421-3551

Kansas Missing Children Foundation
P.O. Box 8232
Wichita, KS   67208-0232
(316) 684-4888

Kevin Collins Foundation for Missing Children
P.O. Box 590473
San Francisco, CA   94159
(415) 771-8477
(800) 272-0012
The Foundation runs the Child Abduction Response Team, seeks to heighten public awareness of the problem of kidnapping, and offers prevention programs.

Medical Network for Missing Children
67 Pleasant Ridge Road
Harrison, NY   10528
(914) 967-6854
The Network helps identify missing children by physical characteristics such as scars and dental work. It has a medical-dental questionnaire form that parents of missing children should fill out. The Network keeps an archive of medical-dental records of missing kids, and publishes *Safety Advice for Parents and Children.*

**Missing & Exploited Children's
   Association**
P.O. Box 608
Lutherville, MD   21093
(301) 667-0718

Missing Children Help Center
410 Ware Boulevard, Suite 400
Tampa, FL   33619
(813) 623-5437
This is a referral organization that helps to reunite missing kids with their parents. Use the toll-free number (800) USA-KIDS (872-5437) to report your missing child or the sighting of a missing child. A database of fingerprints of missing children is maintained by the Center, plus a list of state search agencies, and national statistics on missing children. It serves as an advocate for child protection laws, seeks to use the media to distribute pictures of missing children, and fosters community awareness.

Missing Children, Inc.
4200 Wisconsin Avenue, N.W.,
   Suite 201
Washington, DC   20016
(202) 686-1791
Missing Children conducts educational programs on abduction prevention, provides information and referrals for victim assistance, and supports legislation on missing children issues.

Missing Children—Minnesota
901 Humboldt Avenue N.
Minneapolis, MN   55411
(612) 572-0456

Missing Children of America (MCA)
P.O. Box 670-949
Chugiak, AK   99567
(907) 248-7300
MCA assists parents in compiling an identification package including fingerprints, medical records, and physical characteristics that help law enforcement agencies find missing children. The organization has a computer file of missing children, and publishes a newsletter as well as child identification packages and brochures on how to protect your children.

Missing Children's Project in CA
1084 Avon Avenue
San Leandro, CA 94579
(415) 483-3576 (24-hour hotline)

Missing Children's Resource Center
1221 22nd Street
San Diego, CA 92102
(619) 456-0804

National Child Safety Council (NCSC)
Missing Children Division
P.O. Box 1368
Jackson, MI 49204-1368
(517) 764-6070
(800) 222-1464 (24-hour hotline)
The NCSC accepts calls regarding missing children, maintains a national database of pictures and bios, and reports cases to the appropriate agencies.

National Missing Children's Locate Center
P.O. Box 1324
Gresham, OR 97030
(503) 665-8544
(800) 443-2751 (ext. 15)
Helps find children nationwide.

Nationwide Patrol
P.O. Box 2629
Wilkes-Barre, PA 18703
(717) 825-7250
Helps parents of missing children by producing fliers and organizing search parties.

North Carolina Center for Missing Children & Child Victimization
P.O. Box 27687
Raleigh, NC 27611
(919) 733-7974
(800) 522-KIDS (5437)

Operation Lookout
National Center for Missing Youth
P.O. Box 231
Mountlake Terrace, WA 98043
(206) 362-7375
(800) 782-7335
Lookout helps find children nationwide.

Oregon Child Custody Protection Association
3555 N.E. Dunlap Avenue
Albany, OR 97321
(503) 928-3448

Protect Your Child
P.O. Box 414
San Lorenzo, CA 94580
(415) 276-2350

Roberta Jo Society
Box 916
Circleville, OH 43113
(614) 474-5020
Founded by the father of a three-year-old who disappeared in 1980, this group offers referrals and publishes a newsletter that contains safety tips for parents.

Savannah Friends of Child Find
711 Highland Drive
Savannah, GA   31406
(912) 355-6425

Search Reports, Inc.—Central Registry
   of the Missing
396 Route 17 N.
Hasbrouck Heights, NJ   07604-3002
(201) 288-4445
This organization provides detailed information on runaway or missing individuals to law enforcement, security,
medical, and social service agencies.
Parents of missing children are also
helped. Search Reports publishes *The
National Missing Persons Report.*

Services for the Missing
P.O. Box 26
Gibbsboro, NJ   08026
(609) 783-3101

Society for Young Victims
Spooner Building
54 Broadway
Newport, RI   02840
(401) 847-5083
The Society helps parents search for
missing children by offering advice, distributing photographs and fliers, and
making referrals. It publishes a
monthly newsletter and other materials
for parents.

Society for Young Victims
927 N. Plum Grove Road, Suite A
Schaumberg, IL   60173
(312) 490-0076

Society for Young Victims
P.O. Box 187
Billerica, MA   01866
(508) 663-4394

Society for Young Victims
5 Washington Street
Manchester, MA   01944
(617) 526-1080

Stop Taking Our Children (S.T.O.C.)
1510 Glen Ayr Drive, #6
Lakewood, CO   80215
(303) 798-1824
(303) 238-1504 (hotline)

Sun Bay Recovery—International
   Missing Children's Division
P.O. Box 704
Largo, FL   34649
(813) 595-7881
Providing search guidelines and counseling (with a fee based on ability to
pay), Sun Bay protects children from
abusive and exploitative environments,
aids cooperation between government
and law enforcement groups, and runs
a referral service.

Tucson Missing Children Program
900 Pima County Courts Building
111 W. Congress Street
Tucson, AZ 85701
(602) 792-8411

Vanished Children's Alliance
300 Orchard City Drive, Suite 151
Campbell, CA 95008
(408) 378-5678

Vanished Children's Alliance
5716 E. 24th Place
Tulsa, OK 74114
(918) 622-7640

Youth Works
311 N. Washington
Bismarck, ND 58501
(701) 255-6909

STATE CLEARINGHOUSES FOR MISSING CHILDREN

Alaska, Hawaii, Idaho, Maine, New Mexico, Utah, West Virginia, and Wisconsin do not have a central clearinghouse where missing children should be reported. In these eight states, you should call your local police and the nearest office of the state police. For the states listed below, however, call your local police *and* the appropriate statewide clearinghouse:

Alabama

Department of Public Safety
Missing Children Bureau
(205) 261-4207
(800) 228-7688 (in Alabama)

Arizona

Department of Public Safety
Criminal Investigation Research Unit
(602) 223-2158

Arkansas

Office of the Attorney General
(501) 371-5028
(800) 482-8982 (in Arkansas)

California

State Department of Justice
(916) 739-5114
(800) 222-3463

Colorado

Bureau of Investigation
(303) 239-4251

Connecticut

State Police
(203) 238-6688
(800) 367-5678 (in Connecticut)

Delaware

State Police
(302) 736-5883

District of Columbia

Metropolitan Police Department
MP/Youth Division
(202) 576-6771

Florida

Department of Law Enforcement
(904) 488-5224
(800) 342-0821 (in Florida)

Georgia

Bureau of Investigation
(404) 244-2554
(800) 282-6564 (in Georgia)

Illinois

Illinois State Police
I-SEARCH
(217) 782-5227
(800) 843-5763 (in Illinois)

Indiana

State Police
Records Division
(317) 232-8310

Iowa

Department of Public Safety
(515) 281-7963
(515) 281-3561
(800) 346-5507 (in Iowa)

Kansas

Bureau of Investigation
(913) 232-6000
(800) 572-7463 (in Kansas)

Kentucky

State Police
Missing Child Information Center
(502) 227-8799
(800) 222-5555 (in Kentucky)

Louisiana

State Police
(504) 925-6189

Department of Health & Human
Services
(504) 342-4049

Maryland

Center for Missing Children
State Police
(301) 799-0190 (through 0195)
(301) 621-1010
(301) 621-1011
(800) 637-5437

Massachusetts

State Police
(800) 447-5269
(800) 622-5999 (in Massachusetts)

Michigan

State Police
(517) 337-6171

Minnesota

State Clearinghouse
(612) 642-0610

Mississippi

State Highway Patrol
(601) 987-1599

Missouri

State Highway Patrol
(314) 751-3313 (ext. 178)

Montana

Department of Justice
(406) 444-3817

Nebraska

State Highway Patrol
(402) 479-4019

Nevada

Office of the Attorney General
(702) 885-4170

New Hampshire

State Police
(603) 271-3636
(800) 525-5555 (in New Hampshire)

Department of Human Services
(603) 271-4699

New Jersey

State Police
(609) 882-2000

New York

Division of Criminal Justice Services
(DCJS)
(518) 457-6326
(800) 346-3543 (in New York)

State Police
(518) 457-6811

North Carolina

Division of Victim & Justice Services
(919) 733-7974
(800) 522-5437 (in North Carolina)

North Dakota

North Dakota Clearinghouse for
   Missing Children
(701) 224-2121
(800) 472-2121 (in North Dakota)

Ohio

Department of Education
(614) 466-6837

Oklahoma

State Bureau of Investigation
(405) 848-6724

Oregon

Oregon State Police
(503) 378-3720
(800) 282-7155 (in Oregon)

Pennsylvania

State Police/Missing Persons Unit
(717) 783-5524
(717) 783-5527

Rhode Island

State Police
(401) 647-3311 (ext. 237)
(800) 544-1144 (in Rhode Island)

South Carolina

Law-Enforcement Division
(803) 737-9080
(800) 322-4453 (in South Carolina)

South Dakota

Attorney General's Office
(605) 773-4614

Tennessee

Bureau of Investigation
(615) 741-0430

Texas

Department of Public Safety
(512) 465-2814
(800) 346-3243 (in Texas)

Vermont

Office of the Attorney General
(802) 828-3171

Virginia

State Police
(804) 674-2026
(800) 822-4453 (in Virginia)

Washington

Crime Information Center (WACIC)
(206) 753-3960
(800) 543-5678 (in Washington)

Wyoming

Office of the Attorney General
(307) 777-7537

CHILD ABUSE AND NEGLECT

The first part of this section, National Organizations, lists groups that help abusive parents and children who are abused. The second part, State Child Welfare Agencies, lists offices that can refer you to help in your own community.

SEE ALSO

under SEX in the Sex Education listings of Chapter 9 for additional groups that teach children to recognize and refuse the sexual advances of others.

The DISCIPLINE IN SCHOOLS section of Chapter 8 describes groups offering information about abusive punishment in schools.

The SELF-HELP CLEARINGHOUSES section of Chapter 13 lists groups that will help you find a local support group of other child abusers.

NATIONAL ORGANIZATIONS

Abusive Men Exploring New Directions (AMEND)
P.O. Box 61281
Denver, CO   80206
(303) 830-7887
AMEND intervenes in men's violence through education, group counseling, and a twenty-four-hour crisis line. It offers referral and counseling services and publishes brochures and the *AMEND Manual for Helpers.*

Administration for Children, Youth, & Families
330 C Street, S.W., Room 2056
P.O. Box 1182
Washington, DC   20013
(202) 245-0347
The Administration answers questions and will make referrals concerning child abuse and domestic violence, daycare and Head Start programs.

American Association for Protecting
  Children
c/o American Humane Association
9725 E. Hampden Avenue
Denver, CO   80231
(303) 695-0811
(800) 2-ASK-AHA (227-5242)
This office runs the National Resource
Center on Child Abuse and Neglect, an
information and referral service. It publishes various newsletters, pamphlets,
and books.

Believe the Children
P.O. Box 1358
Manhattan Beach, CA   90266
(213) 379-3514
A self-help group for parents whose
children have been exploited or abused
by nonfamily members, this office provides guidelines for establishing a local
group and also publishes a newsletter.

Center for Child Protection & Family
  Support (CCPFS)
714 G Street, S.E.
Washington, DC   20003
(202) 544-3144
CCPFS provides referral, advisory, and
consulting services free of charge. It
works to protect inner-city and other
disadvantaged children from all forms
of abuse and victimization, whether
physical, sexual, emotional, institutional, or medical in nature.

Chesapeake Institute, Inc.
10605 Concord Street, Suite 105
Kensington, MD   20895
(301) 949-5000
The Institute deals exclusively with
child sexual victimization. It provides a
long-term treatment program for victims and their families, makes referrals,
and provides advisory and consulting
services.

Child Abuse Institute of Research
P.O. Box 1217
Cincinnati, OH   45201
(606) 441-7409
The Institute investigates the causes of
child abuse, explores prevention methods, and offers counseling to abusers to
help them stop.

Child Abuse Listening & Mediation
  (CALM)
P.O. Box 90754
Santa Barbara, CA   93190
(805) 965-2376
(800) 569-2255 (24-hour listening
  hotline)
CALM offers an 800 hotline in English
and Spanish for parents who feel they
are in danger of taking their frustrations out on their children. CALM also
offers educational and counseling services to high-risk parents. They publish
two newsletters, *CALMWORD* and
Chronicle.

Child Help USA
(800) 422-4453 (24-hour hotline)
Child Help runs the National Child
Abuse Hotline, offers crisis intervention
and counseling, makes referrals, and
publishes a free pamphlet and a $2 in-
formation guide.

Child Welfare League of America
440 1st Street, N.W., Suite 310
Washington, DC   20001-2085
(202) 638-2952
The nearly seven hundred children's
and family service agencies that form
this League offer many services to parents and children. The League makes
referrals to child-abuse agencies, maintains a reference library, and provides
information.

Clearinghouse on Child Abuse &
   Neglect Information
National Center on Child Abuse &
   Neglect
P.O. Box 1182
Washington, DC   20013
(703) 821-2086
This major government agency on child
abuse and neglect maintains a database
of eight thousand documents concerning child mistreatment, descriptions of
over three thousand programs serving
child abuse and neglect victims, descriptions of over one hundred ongoing
research projects in the field, descriptions of about five hundred audiovisual

items, and about three thousand ex-
cerpts from current state and territorial
child abuse and neglect laws. The
Clearinghouse will answer questions,
make referrals, and offers a catalog of
National Center on Child Abuse and
Neglect publications.

Families of Sex Offenders Anonymous
208 W. Walk
West Haven, CT   06516
(203) 931-0015
This is a self-help group for friends and
families of those with harmful sexual
obsessions. The twelve-step program
sees people through their grief. Also offered is a newsletter.

Institute for the Community as
   Extended Family
P.O. 952
San Jose, CA   95108
(408) 280-5055
The Institute comprises more than one
hundred sixty chapters and trains professionals working with child abuse and
family violence victims. It offers counseling and makes referrals.

International Society for Prevention of
   Child Abuse & Neglect
1205 Oneida Street
Denver, CO   80220
(303) 321-3963
The Society sponsors forums and con-
gresses that seek to relieve problems of

Molesters Anonymous
1269 N. E Street
San Bernardino, CA   92405
(714) 355-1100
These self-help groups (with start-up by a professional) are for men who molest children and wish to stop. They work through thought-control techniques and a buddy system. Group guidelines are available for $12.95.

National Center for the Prevention & Control of Rape (NCPCR)
5600 Fishers Lane
Rockville, MD   20857
(301) 443-1910
This government-sponsored agency supports research on the causes of rape and sexual assault, mental health consequences of such acts of violence, treatment of victims (both adults and children), and effectiveness of programs designed to prevent and reduce such assaults. The Center answers questions, makes referrals, and will send a free list of its publications.

National Center for the Prosecution of Child Abuse (NCPCA)
1033 N. Fairfax Street, Suite 200
Alexandria, VA   22314
(703) 739-0321

NCPCA helps in the prosecution of child-abuse criminals. It publishes a monthly newsletter and the *National Directory of Child Abuse Prosecutors.*

National Committee for Prevention of Child Abuse
332 S. Michigan Avenue, Suite 950
Chicago, IL   60604
(312) 663-3520
The Committee conducts research into the causes and prevention of child abuse, serves as an advocate to eliminate abuse, and provides information and referrals.

National Exchange Club Foundation for the Prevention of Child Abuse
3050 Central Avenue
Toledo, OH   43606
(419) 535-3232
The Foundation offers abusive parents counseling that teaches nonviolent coping and child-rearing methods.

Office for Victims of Crime
National Victims Resource Center
Box 6000-AHG
Rockville, MD   20850
(301) 251 5525
The National Victims Resource Center serves as a clearinghouse for information, services, and programs and maintains an enormous library of books and reports on crime and abuse of children.

Office for Victims of Crime
U.S. Department of Justice
633 Indiana Avenue, N.W., Room 1352
Washington, DC   20531
(202) 724-5947
(800) 627-6872
The Office for Victims of Crime provides information, makes referrals, and assists in setting up local programs to aid victims.

Parents Against Molesters
P.O. Box 3557
Portsmouth, VA   23701
(804) 465-1582
This group of molestation victims and their families offers referrals and publishes a newsletter and a brochure.

Parents Anonymous
6733 S. Sepulveda Boulevard, Suite 270
Los Angeles, CA   90045
(213) 410-9732
(800) 352-0386
(800) 421-0353
A national organization of nearly fifteen hundred groups, Parents Anonymous runs self-help meetings facilitated by a professional for those parents worried that they may abuse their children. There are also separate children's support groups.

Parents United
P.O. Box 952
San Jose, CA   95108
(408) 280-5055
(408) 279-1957 (24-hour hotline)
Parents United is for people victimized by sexual abuse. The organization runs weekly meetings and self-help therapy groups, makes referrals for counseling, and brings abused children together for mutual support.

Sexual Abuse Prevention Program
c/o Illusion Theater
528 Hennepin Avenue
Minneapolis, MN   55403
(612) 339-4944
The Program offers publications and theater performances designed to prevent child abuse. Publications include *Touch Study Cards; Touch and Sexual Abuse: How to Talk to Your Kids About It;* and *Child Sexual Abuse Prevention Education: Taking the First Steps.* Also offered are two videos: *Touch* and *No Easy Answers.*

Victims of Child Abuse Laws
   (V.O.C.A.L.)
7485 E. Kenyon Avenue
Denver, CO   80237
(800) 84-VOCAL (848-6225)

Founded to protect those unjustly accused of abusing a child, the forty-one chapters of V.O.C.A.L. work to protect children from wrong-doers within children's legal services. There is a newsletter and guidelines for founding a chapter.

Village of Childhelp
P.O. Box 247
Beaumont, CA   92223
(714) 845-3155
The Village offers a caring, loving home to abused children and provides long-term counseling for children and parents.

Wyandotte House/Neutral Ground
Wyandotte House, Inc.
632 Tauromee
Kansas City, KS   66101
(913) 342-9332
This organization offers a safe home and crisis intervention for children who have been abused or neglected.

Youth Haven, Inc.
P.O. Box 7007
Naples, FL   33941
(813) 774-2904
(813) 774-2698
Youth Haven provides long-term and temporary care and shelter for abused, neglected, and troubled children through the age of eighteen.

STATE CHILD WELFARE AGENCIES

These offices provide information and help concerning child protection, youth advocacy, foster care, emergency funding, and services for children of all ages. Call your state office for referrals to local sources of help regarding any child-abuse problem.

Alabama

Division of Family & Children's Services
James E. Folsom Administrative Building
Room 503
64 N. Union Street
Montgomery, AL   36130-1801
(205) 261-3409

Alaska

Division of Family & Youth Services
Pouch H-05
Juneau, AK   99811
(907) 465-3170

Arizona

Child Protective Services Section
4020 N. 20th Street, Suite 105
Phoenix, AZ   85016
(602) 266-0282

Division of Family Support
P.O. Box 6123
Phoenix, AZ   85005
(602) 255-3596

Arkansas

Division of Children & Family Services
P.O. Box 1437
Little Rock, AR   72203-1437
(501) 682-8772

California

Family & Children Services Branch
744 P Street
MS 9-101
Sacramento, CA   95814
(916) 445-7653

Office of Child Abuse Prevention
(916) 323-2888

Colorado

Division of Child Welfare Services
State Social Services Building, 2nd
   Floor

1575 Sherman Street
Denver, CO   80203-1714
(303) 866-5957

Connecticut

Department of Children & Youth
   Services
170 Sigourney Street
Hartford, CT   06105
(203) 566-3536

Delaware

Division of Child Protective Services
First State Executive Plaza
330 E. 30th Street
Wilmington, DE   19802
(302) 571-6410

District Of Columbia

Family Services Administration
Randall School Building, Room 116
1st and I Streets, S.W.
Washington, DC   20024
(202) 727-5947

Florida

Children, Youth & Families Program
   Office
Building VIII
1317 Winewood Boulevard
Tallahassee, FL   32399
(904) 488-8763

Georgia

Division of Family & Children Services
878 Peachtree Street, N.E., Suite 406
Atlanta, GA   30309
(404) 894-5505

Hawaii

Office of Children & Youth
P.O. Box 3044
Honolulu, HI   96802
(808) 548-7582
(808) 548-7583

Idaho

Family & Children's Services
Towers Building
450 W. State Street
Boise, ID   83720
(208) 334-5688

Illinois

Department of Children & Family
  Services
406 E. Monroe Street
Springfield, IL   62701
(217) 785-2509

Indiana

Child Welfare/Social Services Division
141 S. Meridian Street, 6th Floor
Indianapolis, IN   46225
(317) 232-4420

Iowa

Bureau of Adult, Children & Family
  Services
Hoover State Office Building, 5th Floor
1300 E. Walnut Street
Des Moines, IA   50319-0114
(515) 281-5521

Kansas

Youth Services
Smith-Wilson Building
300 S.W. Oakley
Topeka, KS   66606
(913) 296-3282

Kentucky

Division of Family Services
Human Resources Building, 6th
  Floor W.
275 E. Main Street
Frankfort, KY   40621
(502) 564-6852

Louisiana

Division of Children, Youth & Family
  Services
P.O. Box 3318
Baton Rouge, LA   70821
(504) 342-2297

Maine

Division of Child & Family Services
State House
Station 11
Augusta, ME   04333
(207) 289-5060

Maryland

Office for Children & Youth
State Office Building, Room 1502
301 W. Preston Street
Baltimore, MD   21201
(301) 225-4160

Massachusetts

Office for Children
10 West Street
Boston, MA   02111
(617) 727-8900

Michigan

Office of Children & Youth Services
P.O. Box 30037
Lansing, MI   48909
(517) 373-0093

Minnesota

Division of Children Services
Human Services Building
444 Lafayette Road
St. Paul, MN   55155
(612) 296-5690

Mississippi

Bureau of Family & Children's Services
P.O. Box 352
Jackson, MS   39205
(601) 354-0341

Missouri

Division of Family Services
P.O. Box 88
Jefferson City, MO   65103
(314) 751-4247

Montana

Department of Family Services
P.O. Box 8005
Helena, MT   59601
(406) 444-5900

Nebraska

Center for Children & Youth
P.O. Box 4585
Lincoln, NE   68504-0585
(402) 471-3305

Nevada

Social Service Division
Capitol Complex
Carson City, NV   89710
(702) 885-4766

New Hampshire

Department of Health & Human
   Services
6 Hazen Drive
Concord, NH   03301
(603) 271-4456

New Jersey

Division of Youth & Family Services
1 S. Montgomery Street
Trenton, NJ   08625
(609) 292-6920

New Mexico

Social Services Division
P.O. Box 2348
Santa Fe, NM   87504
(505) 827-4372

New York

Division of Family & Children's
   Services
Ten Eyck Building, 9th Floor
40 N. Pearl Street
Albany, NY   12243
(518) 474-9607

North Carolina

Youth Advocacy & Involvement Office
Elks Building, 1st Floor
121 W. Jones Street
Raleigh, NC   27603-1334
(919) 733-9296

North Dakota

Children & Family Services Division
State Capitol
Bismarck, ND   58505
(701) 224-4811

Ohio

Division of Family & Children Services
State Office Tower, 30th Floor
30 E. Broad Street
Columbus, OH   43226-0423
(614) 466-9824

Oklahoma

Child Welfare Services
P.O. Box 25352
Oklahoma City, OK   73152
(405) 521-3777

Oregon

Children's Services Division
198 Commercial Street, S.E.
Salem, OR   97310
(503) 378-4374

Pennsylvania

Office of Children, Youth, & Families
P.O. Box 2675
Harrisburg, PA   17105
(717) 787-4756

Rhode Island

Department for Children & Their
  Families
Building 7
610 Mt. Pleasant Avenue
Providence, RI   02908
(401) 457-4750

South Carolina

Office of Children, Family & Adult
  Services
P.O. Box 1520
Columbia, SC   29202-1520
(803) 734-6182

South Dakota

Child Protection Services
Richard F. Kneip Building
700 Governors Drive
Pierre, SD   57501
(605) 773-3227

Tennessee

Child Protective Services
Citizens Plaza Building
400 Deaderick Street
Nashville, TN   37219
(615) 741-5939

Commission on Children & Youth
1510 Parkway Towers
404 James Robertson Parkway
Nashville, TN   37217
(615) 741-2633

Texas

Services to Families & Children
P.O. Box 2960
Austin, TX   78769
(512) 450-3020

Utah

Division of Family Services
P.O. Box 45500
Salt Lake City, UT   84115-0500
(801) 538-4100

Vermont

Division of Social Services
Osgood Building
Waterbury Office Complex
103 S. Main Street
Waterbury, VT   05676
(802) 241-2131

Virginia

Bureau of Child Welfare Services
Blair Building
8007 Discovery Drive
Richmond, VA   23229-8699
(804) 662-9695

Washington

Division of Children & Family Services
Mail Stop OB-41
Olympia, WA   98504
(206) 753-7002

West Virginia

Families & Children Unit
State Office Building 6, Room B-850
1900 Washington Street E.
Charleston, WV   25305
(304) 348-7980

Wisconsin

Bureau for Children, Youth & Families
Wilson Street State Office Building,
   Room 465
1 W. Wilson Street
Madison, WI   53707
(608) 266-3036

Wyoming

Bureau of Family Services
Hathaway Building, Room 318
2300 Capitol Avenue
Cheyenne, WY   82002-0710
(307) 777-6285

Puerto Rico

Department of Social Services
P.O. Box 11398
Santurce, PR   00910
(809) 721-4624
(809) 722-7400

LEGAL MATTERS

This section lists groups concerned with children's rights, custody fights, divorce, and the rights of single parents, grandparents, and others.

America's Society of Separated &
   Divorced Men (ASDM)
575 Keep Street
Elgin, IL   60120
(312) 695-2200
ASDM supports father's rights to their children, fights unreasonable child support, alimony, and custody rulings. The group also offers counseling and makes referrals.

Association for Children for
   Enforcement of Support (ACES)
723 Phillips Avenue, Suite 216
Toledo, OH   43612
(419) 476-2511
(800) 537-7072
A national organization of more than two hundred sixty groups, ACES provides information and emotional sustenance for parents having trouble collecting child-support payments. They also publish a newsletter.

Child Support Network
8807 Colesville Road
Silver Spring, MD   20910
(310) 588-9354
The Network provides information, primarily to divorced women, about child support and other legal matters. It also publishes a newsletter, *Child Support Network News.*

Children's Defense Fund (CDF)
122 C Street, N.W., Suite 400
Washington, DC   20001
(202) 628-8787
CDF is a national advocacy program that works for: the right to an education for all children; the protection of children's right to privacy of records kept on them; the right to treatment for institutionalized children; the right to adequate health care for children; and the right of children to receive fair and humane services under the juvenile justice system. CDF's information services are available to everyone at no cost, and a list of publications is available.

Children's Foundation
815 15th Street, N.W., Room 928
Washington, DC   20005
(202) 347-3300
The Foundation distributes fact sheets on child-support collection problems.

Children's Healthcare Is a Legal Duty (CHILD)
P.O. Box 2604
Sioux City, IA   51106
(712) 948-3295
This organization of lawyers, doctors, and others works to protect children's rights to receive medical care despite the efforts of certain groups to deny medical care based on religious convictions. It offers information and referrals.

Children's Rights Group
693 Mission Street
San Francisco, CA   94105
(415) 495-7283
Offers information on how to increase children's services in local communities. The Group runs training programs and advises parents wanting federally funded nutrition programs in their areas.

Children's Rights Project
American Civil Liberties Union
132 W. 43rd Street
New York, NY   10036
(212) 944-9800
A good source of information on all public policy matters and litigation concerning children and families.

Committee for Mother & Child Rights, Inc.
Route 1, Box 256A
Clearbrook, VA   22624
(703) 722-3652

The Committee's thirty national chapters supply information for mothers regarding disputed custody due to divorce. Also provided are a telephone network and guidelines for starting a group.

Custody Action for Lesbian Mothers
   Inc. (CALM)
P.O. Box 281
Narberth, PA   19072
(215) 667-7508
CALM offers litigation support services for lesbian mothers, including free custody litigation in the Delaware Valley, and national consultation. The group also assists gay fathers, and publishes a brochure.

Defense for Children
   International—United States
210 Forsyth Street
New York, NY   10002
(212) 353-0951
This group of lawyers, physicians, and child-care professionals offers a referral service to parents regarding the rights of child victims of sexual abuse, kidnapping, and other crimes. It also publishes a variety of brochures, reports on rights, and newsletters.

Fathers Are Forever
P.O. Box 4804
Panorama City, CA   91412
(818) 846-2219
(800) 248-DADS (3237)

A good source of information on mediation, joint custody matters, and visitation for fathers, grandparents, stepparents, and others who do not have custody of children.

Gay & Lesbian Advocates & Defenders
   (GLAD)
P.O. Box 218
Boston, MA   02112
(617) 426-1350
Focusing on the New England states, GLAD is active in legal defense of lesbians and gay males denied their rights by reason of their sexual preferences. The rights of child custody and visitation are among the many areas this group covers.

Grandparents'-Children's Rights, Inc.
5728 Bayonne Avenue
Haslett, MI   48840
(517) 339-8663
This group provides information and advocacy for grandparents denied the right to see their grandchildren. In addition, it encourages grandparents to form groups to discuss issues, work for legal change, and swap information.

Institute for Child Advocacy
Building 31, 4th Floor
Cleveland, OH   44114-4131
(216) 431-6070
The Institute makes referrals, offers advice, and is involved in advocacy for

children who are in the care or custody of the state or in some way at risk. It also publishes a book called *The Child Advocate.*

Joint Custody Association
10606 Wilkins Avenue
Los Angeles, CA   90024
(213) 475-5352
The Association distributes information on family law and judicial decisions. It helps divorcing couples work out joint custody agreements.

League for Human Rights in Divorce
P.O. Box 985
Southampton, NY   11968
(516) 283-5010
The League is concerned with single parents' rights, children's rights, the relationship of children with divorced parents, and parents undergoing divorce. Free referrals and counseling services are available to divorcing parents and to children of divorced parents.

Legal Services for Children, Inc.
149 9th Street
San Francisco, CA   94103
(415) 863-3762
This organization is a free and comprehensive law office just for minors in San Francisco. Representation, legal ad-

vice, and referrals are provided in any kind of juvenile court matter. This group provides advice on establishing similar service for minors elsewhere.

Mothers Without Custody
P.O. Box 56762
Houston, TX   77256
(713) 840-1622
Offers information and referrals to mothers who live apart from their minor children because of court custody decisions or kidnapping. Publishes a newsletter called *Mother-to-Mother.*

National Association of Counsel for Children
1205 Oneida Street
Denver, CO   80220
(303) 321-3963
The Counsel educates and provides support for those acting as, or training to become, child advocates. It will offer information and make referrals.

National Center for Juvenile Justice
701 Forbes Avenue
Pittsburgh, PA   15219
(412) 227-6950
The Center is concerned with the legal aspects of juvenile delinquency, among other subjects. It will answer limited questions from the public and will make referrals.

National Center for Youth Law
1663 Mission Street, 5th Floor
San Francisco, CA   94103
(415) 543-3307
The seven full-time lawyers in this organization are dedicated to helping
other attorneys around the country
who represent poor youth. These specialists advise on such legal matters as
foster care, housing discrimination
against families, juvenile courts, child
abuse and neglect hearings, employment of youth, and the rights of parents.

National Child Support Advocacy
    Coalition (NCSAC)
P.O. Box 4629
Alexandria, VA   22308
(703) 799-5659
NCSAC works toward enforcement and
collection of child support; provides
networking services for independent
support groups nationally; helps new
groups form; distributes a quarterly
newsletter; and runs an annual conference.

National Child Support Enforcement
    Reference Center
Office of Child Support Enforcement
U.S. Department of Health & Human
    Services
6110 Executive Boulevard, Room 820
Rockville, MD   20852
(301) 443-5106

This office, though primarily designed
to help local governments, officials, and
judges, will answer the public's questions regarding child-support enforcement practices. It publishes *Child
Support Report* (a monthly newsletter)
and *Abstracts of Child Support Techniques.*

National Council for Children's Rights
721 2nd Street, N.E.
Washington, DC   20002
(202) 547-6227
Composed of parent groups who disseminate information and advocate legal reform in child custody laws, the
Council sponsors conferences, makes
referrals, and publishes a newsletter.

National Council of Juvenile & Family
    Court Judges
University of Nevada
P.O. Box 8970
Reno, NV   89507
(702) 784-6012
Although it mainly serves judges, the
Council will respond to anyone's requests for information concerning juvenile justice, courts, and the law. This
group maintains KINDEX, a computerized index to legal periodical literature
concerning children. In addition, it
publishes various law-related materials.

National Legal Resource Center for
Child Advocacy & Protection
American Bar Association
Young Lawyers Division
1800 M Street, N.W.
Washington, DC   20036
(202) 331-2255
This information clearinghouse is used
primarily by attorneys, judges, and
other legal professionals. However, the
Center will help others if time permits.
It offers information on most legal issues concerning children; publishes two
legal journals concerning children's
rights and law; and provides a catalog
of other publications.

National Organization for Women
(NOW)
1000 16th Street, N.W., Suite 700
Washington, DC   20036
(202) 331-0066
NOW will offer advice and referrals to
women who suffer from discrimination
and inequality. Parents in particular
may be interested in information regarding maternity and parental leave
from work.

Organization for the Enforcement of
Child Support
119 Nicodemus Road
Reisterstown, MD   21136
(301) 833-2458
This office helps advise parents of their
rights regarding child support, and

refers parents to local organizations. It
publishes a quarterly newsletter, *The
Pied Piper.*

Parent's & Children's Equality (PACE)
2054 Loma Linda Way S.
Clearwater, FL   33575
(813) 461-3806
PACE works to help children who suffer
during divorce and custody battles. It
offers help in locating children who are
kidnapped by parents and makes referrals for parents who need legal advice
or divorce counseling.

Parents Sharing Custody
P.O. Box 9286
Marina Del Ray, CA   90295
(213) 273-9042
This group offers counseling and parent
education for parents who share
custody after divorce. It works to protect the right of children to have access
to both parents.

Women's Research & Education
Institute (WREI)
1700 18th Street, N.W.
Washington, DC   20009
(202) 328-7070
WREI offers information and referrals
to women who have been denied equal-
ity. Some of its recent publications are
*Family and Medical Leave: Who Pays
for the Lack of It* and the *Directory of
Selected Research and Policy Centers
Working on Women's Issues.*

☎

CHAPTER 11

RECREATION

When it is time for children to play, their fancy ranges over a tremendous variety of activities. This chapter reflects that variety. The first section, SPORTS, lists organizations that provide information on everything from Archery to Wrestling. The HOBBIES section covers everything from Amateur Radio to Treasure Hunting. PETS AND ANIMALS includes both organizations devoted to pet care and those that educate children about wildlife preservation. The CHILDREN'S CLUBS section describes organizations children might wish to join, from general groups like the Scouts, to less well-known groups focusing on specific interests.

In the HERITAGE section you will find groups promoting the culture of many nationalities, and ethnic and racial backgrounds. These groups help children discover their "roots" or satisfy their curiosity about the world. The MONEY HANDLING AND ENTREPRENEUR-SHIP section describes banks, organizations, and products that teach young children about money and show older children how to start a business. Teenagers who seek summer employment will find referral services in the JOBS section. If you want to send a child to camp, the CAMPS section describes the country's major referral agencies. Older children interested in helping others will find the VOLUNTEERING section useful. OTHER SUMMER OPPORTUNITIES lists directories of numerous learning and work programs for teenagers. Finally, the VACATIONS AND TRAVEL section provides a list of travel agencies that specialize in children as well as a list of the tourist offices in all fifty states.

SPORTS

Included here are General Organizations, followed by specific ones for: Archery, Baseball, Basketball, Baton Twirling and Cheerleading, Bicycling, Billiards, Boating, Bowling, Boxing, Camping, Cricket, Croquet, Fencing, Field Hockey, Fishing, Football, Frisbee Throwing, Golf, Gymnastics, Handball, Hiking, Horsemanship, Ice Hockey, Ice Skating, Lacrosse, Martial Arts, Orienteering, Racquet Sports, Riflery, Rodeo, Roller Skating, Running and Walking, Scuba Diving, Skiing, Soccer, Softball, Surfing, Swimming and Diving, Tennis, Track and Field, Volleyball, Water Polo, Water Skiing, Weightlifting, and Wrestling and Arm Wrestling.

SEE ALSO

the SPECIAL NEEDS, HANDICAPS, AND LEARNING DISABILITIES section of Chapter 5 under Sports for organizations serving handicapped or retarded children.

The RECREATIONAL SAFETY section of Chapter 6 describes groups concerned with sporting safety.

GENERAL ORGANIZATIONS

Amateur Athletic Union (AAU)
Carrier Youth Sports Programs
3400 W. 86th Street
P.O. Box 68207
Indianapolis, IN   46268
(317) 872-2900
The AAU sponsors training and competition for nearly two dozen different sports. Each summer it holds the Junior Olympic Games. It publishes an annual directory of AAU officials, a newsletter, and *Sports Manuals.*

American Alliance for Health, Physical Education, Recreation, & Dance
1900 Association Drive
Reston, VA   22091
(703) 476-3400
An organization for students, educators, and instructors of athletics, dance, and recreation, the Alliance maintains an information and referral service. It publishes *Fitting In,* a monthly newsletter for eleven- and twelve-year-olds on fitness and nutrition.

American Fitness Association
6700 E. Pacific Coast Highway,
  Suite 299
Long Beach, CA   90803
(213) 596-6036
This Association of physicians, psychologists, and other exercise professionals offers clinics, seminars, and makes referrals to the public. It publishes a number of directories and periodicals, including *Who's Who in Sports and Fitness*.

American Sports Education Institute
200 Castlewood Drive
North Palm Beach, FL   33408
(407) 842-3600
The nearly forty thousand members of the Institute, through their United States Sports Boosters Clubs of America, promotes and sponsors amateur sports in many local communities. Call the national office for information on Booster Clubs in a particular community.

Direction in Sports
117 W. 9th Street, Suite 520
Los Angeles, CA   90015
(213) 627-9861
Direction in Sports offers programs based on the belief that the teaching and coaching of one's peers can counteract destructive behavior, low self-esteem, and can stimulate academic achievement in our children.

Institute for Athletics & Education
Harold Washington College
30 E. Lake
Chicago, IL   60601
(312) 984-2837
The Institute offers parents, students, and coaches educational seminars on topics such as scholarships, eligibility, and recruiting in an effort to give the high school and college athlete a wide range of educational and athletic opportunities.

**National Association for Girls &
  Women in Sport**
1900 Association Drive
Reston, VA   22091
(703) 476-3450
Comprising educators, instructors, and students, the Association offers referrals to parents. It publishes the handbook *Black Women in Sports*.

**National Association for Sport &
  Physical Education**
1900 Association Drive
Reston, VA   22091
(703) 476-3410
The Association's media resource center provides information to the public on the value of physical education and sports participation, conducts research in sports-related areas, and offers sports training seminars and competitions.

National Association of Police Athletic
  Leagues
200 Castlewood Drive
North Palm Beach, FL   33408
(407) 844-1823
To overcome the often destructive
environment of the inner city, Police
Athletic Leagues offer coeducational
instruction and competition in a variety
of sports from baseball to Tae Kwan Do.
To see if a League is available locally,
consult your telephone directory or call
the national office.

President's Council on Physical Fitness
  & Sports
450 5th Street, N.W., Suite 7103
Washington, DC   20001
(202) 272-3421
Established to promote an interest in
overall physical fitness, the Council
sponsors the Physical Fitness Award
program for ages six to seventeen.

United States Athletes Association
  (USAA)
3735 Lakeland Avenue N., Suite 230
Minneapolis, MN   55422
(612) 522-5844
The USAA encourages participation in
sports as an alternative to substance
abuse and as a means to teach leadership, direction, and problem-solving to
junior high, high school, and college
students.

United States Olympic Committee
1750 E. Boulder Street
Colorado Springs, CO   80909
(719) 632-5551
The Committee is the governing group
which represents the United States at
the Olympics.

Women's Sports Foundation
342 Madison Avenue, Suite 728
New York, NY   10173
(212) 972-9170
Promotes the participation of women in
sports and helps enforce Title IX
programs. Serves as a clearinghouse for
information, presents awards for
outstanding achievement, and publishes
the *College Scholarship Guide* annually.

YMCA Youth Sports
YMCA of the USA
101 N. Wacker Drive
Chicago, IL   60606
(312) 977-0031
(800) USA-YMCA (872-9622)
The YMCA conducts sports programs
for both elementary and secondary
school children. Check your local telephone directory for local programs or
call the toll-free number for referrals.

ARCHERY

American Archery Council
604 Forest Avenue
Park Rapids, MN   56470
(218) 732-3879

The Council publishes the *ABC's of Archery,* the *ABC's of Bowhunting,* and a quarterly newsletter.

Federation of Canadian Archers
333 River Road
Ottawa, Ontario   K1L 8H9
Canada
(613) 748-5604

Fred Bear Sports Club
R.R. 4
4600 S.W. 41st Boulevard
Gainesville, FL   32601
(904) 376-2327
This forty-thousand-member club is concerned with outdoor ecology, wildlife management, and cooperation with chase, fish, and game laws. It runs a museum and publishes several quarterlies, videotapes, and books, including *Fred Bear's World of Archery.*

Junior Olympic Archery Development
1750 E. Boulder Street
Colorado Springs, CO   80909
(719) 578-4576
Part of the National Archery Association, Junior Olympic Archery Development encourages youthful participation in the sport.

National Field Archery Association
31407 Outer 1-10
Redlands, CA   92373
(714) 794-2133

The Association runs schools and tournaments and supports the preservation of game and the natural environment. It has a special committee on youth, a Junior Bowhunter Program, and publishes a bimonthly magazine.

BASEBALL

All American Amateur Baseball Association
340 Walker Drive
Zanesville, OH   43701
(614) 453-7349
The Association was established to organize and promote amateur baseball. Their Limited Division allows players up to the age of twenty-one.

American Amateur Baseball Congress
215 E. Green
Marshall, MI   49068
(616) 781-2002
The Congress serves as an information clearinghouse and a governing body for amateur baseball in the United States, Canada, and Puerto Rico. Annually, it sponsors tournaments at various age levels.

American Baseball Coaches Association
P.O. Box 3545
Omaha, NE   68103-0545
(402) 733-0374
The Association runs clinics and publishes quarterlies, books, and visual materials on baseball.

American League
350 Park Avenue
New York, NY   10022
(212) 371-7600
One of the two major professional leagues.

American Legion Baseball
P.O. Box 1055
Indianapolis, IN   46206
(317) 635-8411
Organizes teams for teenagers supported primarily by local service organizations and business.

Babe Ruth Baseball
P.O. Box 5000
1770 Brunswick Avenue
Trenton, NJ   08638
(609) 695-1434
Baseball programs for children from six to eighteen, including annual "World Series" games and workshops, are organized by this group.

Baseball Canada/Canadian Federation of Amateur Baseball
333 River Road
Ottawa, Ontario   K1L 8H9
Canada
(613) 748-5606

Dixie Youth Baseball, Inc.
P.O. Box 22
Lookout Mountain, TN   37350
(615) 821-6811

Three separate leagues operate under the auspices of Dixie Youth Baseball, each with age categories. There is also a softball league for girls.

George Khoury Association of Baseball Leagues
5400 Meramec Bottom Road
St. Louis, MO   63128
(314) 849-8900
Supervised softball and baseball leagues for girls and boys age seven and up, supported by churches and community groups.

Little League Baseball Incorporated
P.O. Box 3485
Williamsport, PA   17701
(717) 326-1921
Little League has a worldwide network of leagues for children between the ages of six and eighteen.

National Amateur Baseball Federation
12406 Keynote Lane
Bowie, MD   20715
(301) 262-0770
Sponsors age-level tournaments and runs clinics.

National Association of Leagues, Umpires & Scorers
Box 1420
Wichita, KS   67201
(316) 267-7333
Holds an annual tournament and publishes *Official Baseball Rules* annually.

National Baseball Hall of Fame &
    Museum
Box 590
Cooperstown, NY   13326
(607) 547-9988
This is the most famous baseball museum in the world.

National League
350 Park Avenue
New York, NY   10022
(212) 371-7300
This is the office of one of the two major professional leagues.

Pony Baseball
P.O. Box 225
Washington, PA   15301
(412) 225-1060
Pony Baseball has six baseball leagues divided by age group. It also has a softball league for girls.

U.S. Baseball Federation
2160 Greenwood Avenue
Trenton, NJ   08609
(609) 586-2381

In non-Olympic years, the Federation chooses sixty-four young men, age seventeen to eighteen, for an Olympic Festival Team, sixteen of whom become part of the Junior National Team which participates in international competition.

BASKETBALL

Amateur Basketball Association of the
    U.S.A.
1750 E. Boulder Street
Colorado Springs, CO   80909
(719) 632-7687
The Association is for graduating high school seniors and college athletes who wish to play on national teams. It maintains a library of basketball films.

International Association of Approved
    Basketball Officials
P.O. Box 661
West Hartford, CT   06107
(203) 232-7530
This group offers referrals to the public.

BATON TWIRLING AND CHEERLEADING

SEE ALSO

Pop Warner Football in the FOOTBALL section.

International Cheerleading Foundation
10660 Barkley
Overland Park, KS   66212
(913) 649-3666
The Foundation serves as a competition sponsor, offers advice to members, and runs workshops. It publishes the *Encyclopedia of Cheerleading,* and videocassettes, manuals, and books, including *You Can Become a Cheerleader.*

United States Twirling Association
P.O. Box 24488
Seattle, WA   98124
(206) 623-5623
For baton twirlers, their coaches and judges, the Association sets up rules and guidelines, runs tournaments, and hosts clinics and workshops. It publishes periodicals, rulebooks, and manuals.

BICYCLING

American Bicycle Association
P.O. Box 718
Chandler, AZ   85244
(602) 961-1903
To encourage off-road bicycling, the Association oversees local and national competitions.

American Freestyle Association
15561 Product Lane, Suite D-8
Huntington Beach, CA   92649
(714) 898-7694

Offers information on the sport of freestyle bicycling and oversees competitions.

Bicycle Federation of America
1818 R Street, N.W.
Washington, DC   20009
(202) 332-6986
The Federation serves as a clearinghouse of information, helps local groups form bicycling programs, fosters the growth and safety of recreational biking, runs training programs, and has a five-thousand-volume library on pertinent topics. It publishes a monthly newsletter, a brochure, and the *Pro Bike Directory.*

Canadian Cycling Association
333 River Road
Ottawa, Ontario   K1L 8H9
Canada
(613) 748-5629

League of American Wheelmen
6707 Whitestone Road, Suite 209
Baltimore, MD   21207
(301) 944-3399
Dedicated to safe bicycling, the League runs the Effective Cycling Program to teach cyclers safe use of the roads. Annually, it publishes *Bicycle USA Almanac.*

National Bicycle League, Inc.
P.O. Box 729
Dublin, OH   43017
(614) 766-1625
Specifically for BMX racers, the League runs competitions, gives out awards, and maintains records. It publishes a rule book.

National Off-Road Bicycling Association (NORBA)
P.O. Box 1901
Chandler, AZ   85224
(602) 961-0635
NORBA is specifically for off-road cyclers.

U.S. Junior National Cycling Program
1750 E. Boulder Street
Colorado Springs, CO   80909
(719) 578-4581
Part of the U.S. Cycling Federation and geared specifically for younger athletes,

the Program sponsors competitions and selects a junior national team for international meets.

BILLIARDS

Billiard Congress of America
1901 Broadway, Suite 310
Iowa City, IA   52240
(319) 351-2112
The Congress operates as a clearinghouse of information, establishes rules and guidelines, and hosts an annual billiards championship.

Professional Pool Players Association
422 N. Broad Street
Elizabeth, NJ   07206
(201) 355-1302
The Association sponsors a Junior World Championship and offers information regarding pocket billiards.

BOATING

SEE ALSO

the SWIMMING AND BOATING SAFETY section in Chapter 6.

American Canoe Association
P.O. Box 1190
Newington, VA   22122
(703) 550-7523

The Association serves as the rule-making body for canoeing and kayaking within the United States. It offers information, a book and film service, sponsors contests, runs training programs, and distributes awards. It publishes several periodicals with pertinent articles.

American Sailing Association
13922 Marquess Way
Marina Del Ray, CA   90292
(213) 822-7171
With over forty thousand students, schools, and instructors as members, the Association promotes safety and international standards in sail training. It publishes several periodicals, an instructional videotape, and manuals.

American Sail Training Association
21 Algonquin Drive
Middletown, RI   02890
(401) 846-1775
This office gives referrals to sailing instruction programs for youth, sponsors Tall Ship events, and offers awards and scholarships.

Boat Owner's Association of the United States
880 S. Pickett Street
Alexandria, VA   22304
(703) 823-9550
Serves as a clearinghouse of information, with a fifteen-thousand-volume reference library, and operates as an advocate and consumer-protection service.

Canadian Amateur Rowing Association
333 River Road
Ottawa, Ontario   K1L 8H9
Canada
(613) 748-5656

Canadian Canoe Association
333 River Road
Ottawa, Ontario   K1L 8H9
Canada
(613) 748-5623

International Windsurfer Class Association
2030 E. Gladwick Street
Compton, CA   90220
(213) 608-1651
Offers information, referrals, and brochures about the sport of windsurfing.

National Organization for River Sports
314 N. 20th Street
P.O. Box 6847
Colorado Springs, CO   80934
(719) 473-2466
This is a clearinghouse for information on safety, conservation, equipment, and government regulations on canoeing, kayaking, and rafting.

Scholastic Rowing Association of America
120 United States Avenue
Gibbsboro, NJ   08026
(609) 784-3878

Sponsors rowing competitions and serves as an information clearinghouse for youth and children's rowing.

United States Board Sailing Association
P.O. Box 978
Hood River, OR   97031
The Association offers information on board sailing for both amateurs and racers.

United States Canoe Association
606 Ross Street
Middletown, OH   45044
(513) 422-3739
The Association establishes safety standards, researches design elements, and offers training in paddling and water safety. It publishes an annual directory.

U.S. Rowing Association
201 S. Capitol Avenue, Suite 400
Indianapolis, IN   46225
(317) 237-5656
Serving as a governing body for standards, rules, and competition, the Association publishes the *Rowing Directory*.

BOWLING

American Bowling Congress (ABC)
5301 S. 76th Street
Greendale, WI   53129
(414) 421-6400
An organization with over three million members from the United States, Canada, and Puerto Rico, the Congress establishes rules, runs tournaments, certifies equipment, and offers referrals.

Canadian 5 Pin Bowlers' Association
200 Isabella Street, No. 505
Ottawa, Ontario   K1S 1V7
Canada
(613) 230-6394

National Bowling Association
377 Park Avenue S., 7th Floor
New York, NY   10016
(212) 689-8308
The Association promotes bowling for both adults and youth, sponsors bowling tournaments and fundraisers (for the United Negro College Fund and sickle-cell anemia), and distributes awards and scholarships.

National Bowling Council
1919 Pennsylvania Avenue, N.W.,
   Suite 504
Washington, DC   20006
(202) 659-9080
Hosts the National Collegiate Bowling Championship.

**National Bowling Hall of Fame &
   Museum**
111 Stadium Plaza
St. Louis, MO   63102
(314) 231-6340
This is the major bowling museum in the United States.

National Duckpin Bowling Congress
4609 Horizon Circle
Baltimore, MD   21208
(301) 636-BOWL (2695)
The governing body for duckpin bowling, the Congress runs workshops,
hosts tournaments, and gives awards.

Women's International Bowling
  Congress, Inc.
5301 S. 76th Street
Greendale, WI   53129
(414) 421-9000
This group supports bowling for
women, establishes team rules and regulations, conducts workshops, and runs
a hall of fame, museum, and archives.
The Congress also publishes brochures,
handbooks, pamphlets, and an annual
report.

Young American Bowling Alliance
  (YABA)
5301 S. 76th Street
Greendale, WI   53129
(414) 421-4700
Tenpin leagues for persons twenty-one
years old and younger and pee wee
leagues for three- to seven-year-olds. It
gives out certificates, jackets, rings, and
emblems, fosters tournaments, distributes awards, and conducts both the
National Junior Bowling Championships and the National Collegiate
Bowling Championships. Triannually,
the Alliance publishes *New YABA*

World, with articles on youthful
bowlers. It also distributes rule books,
teaching aids, videotapes, posters, and
other promotional literature.

BOXING

American Association for the
  Improvement of Boxing
86 Fletcher Avenue
Mt. Vernon, NY   10552
(914) 664-4571
Tries to minimize the hazards of boxing
by establishing rules and a national
governing body. In addition, it promotes boxing instruction in high
school and college, conducts research
on equipment, distributes information,
and gives a college scholarship to an
outstanding high school senior.

Golden Gloves Association
  of America, Inc.
c/o Jim Beasley
1503 Linda Lane
Hutchinson, KS   67502
(316) 662-3311
The Association comprises organizations that host boxing matches. It runs
an annual tournament.

International Amateur Boxing
  Association
135 Westervelt Place
Cresskill, NJ   07626
(201) 567-3117

The Association oversees international boxing competition in the Olympic and Pan American games, sponsors seminars, clinics, and competitions. It has a special committee on youth and publishes an annual directory, a medical handbook, and other brochures.

Knights Boxing Team—International
560 Campbell Hill
Marietta, GA   30061
(404) 426-7883
(404) 233-8050 (training camp)

Knights encourages boxing as a healthy substitute for substance abuse and crime for boys age twelve and up.

U.S. Amateur Boxing Federation
1750 E. Boulder Street
Colorado Springs, CO   80909
(719) 578-4506
The Federation runs competitions, organized by age group, which peak in the Junior Olympics and the national Olympic team. It publishes informational materials including *U.S.A. Amateur Boxing Federation—Official Rules.*

CAMPING

SEE ALSO

the Hiking section in this chapter.

North American Family Campers Association
P.O. Box 266
Lunenburg, MA   01462
(508) 345-7267
The Association provides information on camping equipment, areas, good practices, and conservation.

CRICKET

U.S. Cricket Association
c/o Art Hazelwood
City of Alexandria
Office of Internal Audit
P.O. Box 178
Alexandria, VA   22314
(703) 838-4918
Primarily for adults, this group offers limited information for children.

CROQUET

U.S. Croquet Association
500 Avenue of the Champions
Palm Beach Gardens, FL   33418
(407) 627-3999
The Association runs tournaments and picks members for the national team. In addition, it offers training programs and publishes a newsletter listing events and competition results.

FENCING

Canadian Fencing Association
333 River Road
Ottawa, Ontario   K1L 8H9
Canada
(613) 748-5633

U.S. Fencing Association
1750 E. Boulder Street
Colorado Springs, CO   80909
(719) 578-4511
The Association organizes age-level fencing instruction and competition and selects a team for international tournaments. It publishes rule books, educational pamphlets, a quarterly magazine, and a semiannual directory.

U.S. Fencing Coaches Association
P.O. Box 274
New York, NY   10159
(212) 532-2557

This association of professionals and enthusiasts conducts research and offers training programs.

FIELD HOCKEY

Canadian Field Hockey Association & Canadian Women's Field Hockey Association
333 River Road
Ottawa, Ontario   K1L 8H9
Canada
(613) 748-5634

U.S.A. Field Hockey Association of America, Inc.
1750 E. Boulder Street
Colorado Springs, CO   80909
(719) 578-4567
The Association runs tournaments to select members for international competitions, serves as a governing body, runs exhibition games and clinics, produces films and training materials, and certifies coaches. It publishes the *USA Field Hockey—Club Directory* annually as well as a number of coaching and umpiring manuals and a newsletter.

U.S.A. Junior Field Hockey Association
1750 E. Boulder Street
Colorado Springs, CO   80909
(719) 578-4567
As part of the U.S.A. Field Hockey Association, the Junior Association encour-

ages safe, enjoyable, and inexpensive participation in field hockey among children ages five to thirteen.

FISHING

American Bass Association
886 Trotters Trail
Wetumpka, AL   36092
(205) 567-6035
The Association runs the National Youth Program of fishing programs for children, including those who are disabled and underprivileged. In addition, it offers information on conservation and sponsors fishing contests.

American Casting Association
1739 Praise Boulevard
Fenton, MO   63026
(314) 225-9443
The Association has a special committee to promote youth involvement, establishes rules for and runs tournaments, and offers training clinics.

American Fishing Tackle Manufacturers Association
1250 Grove Avenue, Suite 300
Barrington, IL   60010
(312) 381-9490
Offers information and referrals to manufacturers of fishing gear.

North American Fishing Club
P.O. Box 35861
Minneapolis, MN   55435
(612) 941-6936
(800) 843-6232
Offers information on fishing outfitters, fishing guides, and on how to improve fishing skills.

U.S. Bass Fishing Association
2090 S. Grand Avenue
Santa Ana, CA   92705
(714) 556-2116
Sponsors tournaments, offers referrals, and publishes *U.S. Bass.*

FOOTBALL

American Football Coaches Association
7758 Wallace Road, Suite 1
Orlando, FL   32819
(407) 351-6113
The Association runs training programs and publishes an annual directory and a summer manual.

Canadian Amateur Football Association
333 River Road
Ottawa, Ontario   K1L 8H9
Canada
(613) 748-5636

National Football Foundation & Hall of Fame
1865 Palmer Avenue
Larchmont, NY   10538
(914) 834-0478

The Foundation runs a twelve-hundred-volume library, a hall of fame, and a scholarship program for athletes who wish to pursue graduate work or medical studies. It publishes informational booklets, including material on college-level athletics.

National Football League
410 Park Avenue
New York, NY   10022
(212) 758-1500
This is headquarters of the major professional football league in the United States.

Pop Warner Football
1315 Walnut Street, Suite 1632
Philadelphia, PA   19107
(215) 735-1450
This office is for youth leagues with teams arranged by both age and weight. There are at least eight levels of play, culminating in regional and national championships. The organization publishes several periodicals and rule books for football, cheerleading, and flag football.

FRISBEE THROWING

International Frisbee Disc Association
P.O. Box 970
San Gabriel, CA   91776
(213) 287-2257
Offers information and referrals to frisbee players.

U.S. Disc Sports Association
1144 E. Garfield Street
Davenport, IA   52803
(319) 324-8043
Offers referrals, keeps records, and publishes *U.S. Disc Club Directory.*

GOLF

All-American Collegiate Golf Foundation
555 Madison Avenue, 12th Floor
New York, NY   10022
(212) 751-5170
The Foundation encourages participation in golf by donating monies to youth charities and providing scholarship funds.

American Junior Golf Association
2415 Steeplechase Lane
Roswell, GA   30076
(404) 998-4653
Promotes participation in competitive golf by girls and boys under the age of eighteen.

Golf Coaches Association of America
Athletic Dept.
USAF Academy
USAF Academy, CO   80840
(303) 472-2280
Establishes guidelines for amateur, collegiate golf, and oversees golf tournaments. Offers referrals to the public.

19th Hole International
Box 1, 2620 Senate Drive
Lansing, MI 48912
(517) 484-5107
Among its many programs, this organization helps establish junior golf programs.

Professional Golfers' Association of
 America
P.O. Box 109601
Palm Beach Gardens, FL 33410-9601
(407) 624-8400
The Association sponsors many golf tournaments, including the PGA Junior Championship, runs training clinics for coaches and students, accredits college programs, and maintains a library of films. It publishes *PGA Magazine* monthly.

U.S. Golf Association
Liberty Corner Road
Far Hills, NJ 07931
(201) 234-2300
The Association maintains a large reference library, sponsors national championships, encourages research, operates as a governing body, and runs a museum. It publishes *Rules of Golf* and other handbooks and manuals on all aspects of golf.

GYMNASTICS

Canadian Gymnastics Federation
333 River Road
Ottawa, Ontario K1L 8H9
Canada
(613) 748-5654

U.S. Gymnastics Federation
201 S. Capitol, Suite 300
Indianapolis, IN 46225
(317) 237-5050
The Federation offers a competitive gymnastics program for five different skill levels, chooses members for a national team, and encourages recreational participation. It publishes a quarterly, a bimonthly magazine, and several handbooks, including *National Compulsory Routines* and *Men's Rules for Competition.*

U.S. Gymnastics National Training
 Center
6855 Hillsdale Court
Indianapolis, IN 46250
(317) 841-1101
The Center will provide limited information and make referrals.

U.S. Gymnastics Safety Association
Washington Office
P.O. Box 465
Vienna, VA 22180
(703) 476-6660
Offers safety information.

U.S. Sports Acrobatics Federation
1434 Country Park
Katy, TX   77450
(713) 578-8671
The Federation serves as an information clearinghouse, providing research materials, other literature, and coaching aids in order to encourage acrobatics participation in the United States. It runs children's services, hosts competitions and provides videotapes of them, and conducts clinics. It publishes a rules book and several bibliographies.

HANDBALL

United States Handball Association
930 N. Benton Ave.
Tucson, AZ   85711
(602) 795-0434

Although mainly for intercollegiate players, the Association oversees tournaments for children and teenagers. It publishes *Annual Guide and Directory* and a bimonthly magazine, *Handball.*

U.S. Team Handball Federation
1750 E. Boulder Street
Colorado Springs, CO   80909
(719) 578-4582
The Federation runs the program sending an American team to the Olympics, establishes play guidelines and standards, and offers referrals.

HIKING

SEE ALSO

the Camping listing in this chapter.

American Hiking Society
1015 31st Street, N.W.
Washington, DC   20007
(703) 385-3252
The Society informs the public about available hiking trails and their proper use. It publishes *Pathways Across*

America, a newsletter on long-distance trails.

Appalachian Mountain Club
5 Joy Street
Boston, MA   02108
(617) 523-0636

The Club runs one of the largest reference libraries on mountaineering in the country, maintains over a thousand miles of trails in the Northeast, plus shelters and a pine hut network. It offers information on conservation, search and rescue, and voluntary care of the environment. It publishes maps, trail guides, and other literature useful to hikers.

Mountaineers
300 3rd Avenue
Seattle, WA   98119
(206) 284-6310
For those age fourteen and over, primarily in the northwestern part of the country, Mountaineers runs hiking, climbing, skiing, and camping excursions and conducts seminars in safe climbing.

HORSEMANSHIP

American Horse Shows Association
220 E. 42nd Street, Suite 409
New York, NY   10017
(212) 972-2472
The Association oversees the rules and regulations of horseback riding and hosts competitions on both junior and adult levels. It publishes educational pamphlets, a rule book, and a monthly magazine called *Horse Show*.

American Vaulting Association
20066 Glen Brae Drive
Saratoga, CA   95070
(408) 867-0402
Vaulting is a sport in which gymnastic moves are performed while riding a horse. The Association offers publications, a video library, runs competitions, and makes referrals.

Camp Horsemanship Association
P.O. Box 188
Lansing, MI   49064
(616) 674-8074
The Association runs instructor certification programs, riding programs, and offers information and referrals to ensure that children and other students receive safe training. It publishes a membership directory on an annual basis.

Harness Horse Youth Foundation
105 W. N. College Street
P.O. Box 266
Yellow Springs, OH   45387
(513) 767-1975
The Foundation works to increase youths participation in harness racing by offering 4-H programs, training camps, internships, and a scholarship program to help further the careers of participants. Annually, it publishes the *Directory to Equine Schools and Colleges*.

Horsemanship Safety Association
120 Ohio Avenue
Madison, WI   53704
(608) 244-8547
The Association teaches proper horsemanship to instructors and students. It
offers lessons for both children and
adults, provides certification for instructors, maintains a library, and
publishes a number of manuals and
a quarterly newsletter.

Pony of the Americas Club, Inc.
5240 Elmwood Avenue
Indianapolis, IN   46203
(317) 788-0107
Each year, nearly fifty member clubs
run three hundred horse shows on a
state, regional, and international level.
In addition, they offer training, information on breeding, and referrals for
young pony enthusiasts.

United States Dressage Federation
P.O. Box 80668
Lincoln, NE   68501
(402) 474-7632
The Federation makes referrals and has
a special committee for the younger
rider. Annually, it publishes the *Calendar of Recognized Competitions.*

United States Pony Clubs, Inc.
893 S. Matlack Street, Suite 210
West Chester, PA   19382-4913
(215) 436-0300

These clubs work to build character
and leadership through participation in
equestrian activities. They sponsor competitions for riders under twenty-one
years of age, run an overseas exchange
program, and publish the *Pony Club
Handbook.*

ICE HOCKEY

Amateur Hockey Association of the United States
2997 Broadmoor Valley Road
Colorado Springs, CO   80906
(719) 576-4990
Overseeing competition rules and regulations, the Association has seven levels
of teams for boys, five for girls, and
chooses a team for international tournaments. It publishes a monthly
magazine, an *Official Guide,* the *Official
Playing Rules Book,* and other instructional materials.

Canadian Amateur Hockey Association
333 River Road
Ottawa, Ontario   K1L 8H9
Canada
(613) 748-5617

Hockey Canada
333 River Road
Ottawa, Ontario   K1L 8H9
Canada
(613) 746-3153

Hockey Hall of Fame & Museum
Exhibition Place
Toronto, Ontario   M6K 3C3
Canada
(416) 595-1345

Hockey North America
1950 Old Gallows Road, Suite 530
Vienna, VA   22180
(703) 356-2300
(800) 446-2539
This is a for-profit league that encourages youth participation.

National Hockey League
960 Sun Life Building
1155 Metcalfe Street
Montreal, Quebec   H3B 2W2
Canada
(514) 871-9220
This is the main, professional hockey
league in North America.

ICE SKATING

Amateur Skating Union of the United
States
1033 Shady Lane
Glen Ellen,   IL 60137
(312) 469-2107
(800) 634-4766
For anyone from age six on who wants
to participate in speed skating, the
Union publishes a handbook and an annual directory.

Canadian Amateur Speed Skating
Association
333 River Road
Ottawa, Ontario   K1L 8H9
Canada
(613) 748-5669

Canadian Figure Skating Association
333 River Road
Ottawa, Ontario   K1L 8H9
Canada
(613) 748-5635

Ice Skating Institute of America
1000 Skokie Boulevard
Wilmette, IL   60091
(312) 256-5060
Established by rink managers and operators to ensure quality programs for
recreational skaters of any age, this
group oversees competency testing,
holds educational seminars, and sponsors competitions.

U.S. Figure Skating Association
20 1st Street
Colorado Springs, CO   80906
(719) 635-5200
The Association oversees rules and regulations of amateur figure skating,
manages competitions, and selects team
members for international tournaments. It offers information and referrals, and publishes an annual rulebook
and the magazine *Skating*.

U.S. International Speed Skating
  Association
17060 Patricia Lane
Brookfield, WI   53005
(800) 872-1423
Through seminars and summer camps,
the Association assists skaters work
toward the Olympic games.

LACROSSE

Lacrosse Foundation
Newton H. White, Jr. Athletic Center
Homewood
Baltimore, MD   21218
(301) 235-6882
Primarily an organization for college-
level lacrosse, the Foundation can an-
swer questions and make referrals.

U.S. Lacrosse Coaches Association
3 Roman Lane
West Islip, NY   11795
(516) 587-1748
This group offers referrals to the public.

MARTIAL ARTS

American Amateur Karate Federation
1930 Wilshire Boulevard, Suite 1208
Los Angeles, CA   90057
(213) 283-8261
The Federation governs the rules and
standards of karate as practiced in the
United States, runs a summer training
program, oversees competitions, and

answers questions from the public. It
publishes an annual directory and a
number of other periodicals.

Judo Canada
333 River Road
Ottawa, Ontario   K1L 8H9
Canada
(613) 748-5640

United States Aikido Federation
98 State Street
Northampton, MA   01060
(413) 586-7122
The Federation establishes standards,
registers all skill levels with the International Aikido Federation, trains instructors, and runs summer camps. It
publishes the *Aikido Guide* annually.

United States Judo Association
19 N. Union Boulevard
Colorado Springs, CO   80909
(719) 633-7750
Through its National Judo Institute, the
Association trains instructors and students and runs a summer camp. It also
has a scholarship program, hosts a national annual tournament, and publishes a number of quarterlies and
handbooks.

United States Judo Federation
50 W. San Fernando, Suite 804
Cranford, NJ   95113
(201) 298-7551

The Federation has a special committee for "Junior Development" and trains instructors and students in the safe practice of judo. It publishes a handbook, a procedure book, and the *High School and College Training Manual.*

United States Tae Kwon Do Union
1750 E. Boulder Street
Colorado Springs, CO 80909
(719) 578-4632
This group runs an instructional and competitive program for youth ranging in age from two to seventeen. The high point is a Junior Olympics.

USA Karate Federation Junior Olympics
The USA Karate Federation
1300 Kenmore Boulevard
Akron, OH 44314
(216) 753-3114

RACQUET SPORTS

The Federation runs a competitive program, organized by skill and age level, which peaks in a Junior Olympics.

ORIENTEERING

Canadian Orienteering Federation
333 River Road
Ottawa, Ontario K1L 8H9
Canada
(613) 748-5649

U.S. Orienteering Federation
P.O. Box 1444
Forest Park, GA 30051
(404) 363-2110
To promote the skills of compass and map reading, the Federation helps found clubs, hosts competitions, selects teams for international competition, and publishes a newsletter.

SEE ALSO

the Tennis listings in this chapter.

American Amateur Racquetball Association (AARA)
815 N. Weber, Suite 101
Colorado Springs, CO 80903
(719) 635-5396

Provides children's services, hosts competitions, and maintains an archives. It publishes the *Official AARA Rules.*

American Platform Tennis Association
Box 901
Upper Montclair, NJ   07043
(201) 744-1190
Publishes a newsletter, an informational booklet, a rulebook, and a tournament schedule.

Canadian Badminton Association
333 River Road
Ottawa, ON   K1L 8H9
Canada
(613) 748-5605

Canadian Racquetball Association
333 River Road
Ottawa, Ontario   K1L 8H9
Canada
(613) 748-5653

Canadian Squash Racquets Association
333 River Road
Ottawa, Ontario   K1L 8H9
Canada
(613) 748-5672

Canadian Table Tennis Association
333 River Road
Ottawa, Ontario   K1L 8H9
Canada
(613) 748-5675

National Paddleball Association
P.O. Box 91
Portage, MI   49081
(616) 323-0011

The Association provides play guidelines and makes recommendations on equipment.

U.S. Badminton Association
501 W. 6th Street
Papillion, NE   68046
(402) 592-7309
The Association establishes rules for badminton in the United States, helps set up clubs, and runs tournaments. It publishes *Badminton U.S.A.*, a quarterly magazine.

U.S. Paddle Tennis Association
189 Seeley Street
Brooklyn, NY   11218
(718) 788-2094
The Association establishes play guidelines and standards, runs clinics and demonstrations, and sponsors tournaments.

U.S. Paddle Tennis Association
Box 30
Culver City, CA   90232
(213) 625-1511
This is a branch office of above.

U.S. Squash Racquets Association
P.O. Box 1216
Bala-Cynwyd, PA   19004
(215) 667-4006
As a governing body for squash rules and regulations, the Association answers questions and makes referrals. It

also publishes a directory of squash courts in the United States.

U.S. Table Tennis Association
1750 E. Boulder Street
Colorado Springs, CO   80909
(719) 578-4583
The Association's youth program is for schools and boys' and girls' clubs. It has a competitive program, organized by age, that culminates in a Junior Olympics. Publications include the monthly *Table Tennis Topics* and instructional booklets and films.

RIFLERY

Amateur Trapshooting Association
601 W. National Road
Vandalia, OH   45377
(513) 898-4638
As a governing body for trapshooting, the Association keeps a reference library and a hall of fame. It also answers questions and makes referrals.

National Rifle Association
1600 Rhode Island Avenue, N.W.
Washington, DC   20036
(202) 828-6291
The Junior Club of the NRA offers education and responsibility courses in using firearms and runs a Junior Olympics competition and camps. In addition, it publishes informational pamphlets and manuals.

RODEO

National High School Rodeo Association, Inc.
12200 Pecos Street, Suite 120
Denver, CO   80234
(303) 452-0820
This group offers information for high school students to participate in rodeo and rodeo competitions. Annually, it publishes a rules manual as well as *20 and 1, A History of High School Rodeo* and *This Is High School Rodeo.*

National Little Britches Rodeo Association
1045 W. Rio Grande
Colorado Springs, CO   80906
(719) 389-0333
For youth ages eight to eighteen interested in rodeo, the Association works to ensure high standards of competition and promote good horsemanship. It publishes a monthly newsletter and a rulebook.

ROLLER SKATING

Artistic Roller Skating Federation
P.O. Box 6579
Lincoln, NE   68501
(402) 483-7551
The Federation runs clinics for coaches and skaters, sponsors competitions, establishes rules and regulations, and maintains an archives containing rule-

books and manuals. It publishes a
newsletter.

**U.S. Amateur Confederation of Roller
  Skating**
4730 South Street
Lincoln, NE   68506
(402) 483-7551

RUNNING AND WALKING

SEE ALSO

the Track and Field listings in this chapter.

**American Running & Fitness
  Association**
9310 Old Georgetown Road
Bethesda, MD   20814
(301) 897-0197
The Association helps increase the
availability of trails, tracks, and other
facilities. It has a two-thousand-volume
reference library and publishes an informational newsletter monthly.

Athletics Congress of the USA
One Hoosier Dome, Suite 140
Indianapolis, IN   46225
(317) 261-0500
A huge organization of track and field
coaches, high school groups, and clubs,
the Congress arranges competitions, of-

This organization oversees rules and
regulations for roller skating competitions and selects members for an international competition team. It publishes
an annual directory.

fers information, and publishes a variety of directories, annuals, and the
Competition Rules for Athletics.

New York Road Runners Club
9 E. 89th Street
New York, NY   10028
(212) 860-4455
This group sponsors numerous races,
offers classes, referrals, maintains a library, and lends films and videotapes.

Road Runners Club of America
c/o Henley Gibble
629 S. Washington Street
Alexandria, VA   22314
The Club offers information on Run for
Your Life, a "fun run" program for

adults and children. It also sponsors races nationwide and publishes a runner's handbook.

Walkways Center
1400 16th Street, Suite 300
Washington, DC   20036
(202) 547-4742

SCUBA DIVING

The Center promotes walking for fitness and offers the Walkways at Your Doorstep project, which works to create paths and walkways in local communities. It also publishes brochures and periodicals.

SEE ALSO

the SWIMMING AND BOATING SAFETY section in Chapter 6.

Recreational Scuba Training Council
567 Joan Street
Land O'lakes, FL   34639
(813) 996-6582
The Council establishes accreditation rules for scuba diving instruction. It will answer questions and make referrals.

SKIING

American Ski Association
1888 Sherman, Suite 500
Denver, CO   80203
(303) 861-1423
(800) 525-SNOW (7669)
The Association organizes trips and social events, and provides emergency aid for recreational and amateur skiers. In

addition, it offers reports on slope conditions and referrals on most ski-related subjects, and publishes the *Ski Directory*.

American Ski Teachers Association
P.O. Box 34
Marshalls Creek, PA   18335
(717) 223-0730
The Association publishes an annual *Directory of Certified Ski Instructors* and *Skiing for Beginners*.

Canadian Ski Association
333 River Road
Ottawa, Ontario   K1L 8H9
Canada
(613) 748-5660

Cross Country Canada
333 River Road
Ottawa, Ontario   K1L 8H9
Canada
(613) 748-5662

Cross Country Ski Areas Association
259 Bolton Road
Winchester, NH   03470
(603) 239-4341
This group of cross-country ski businesses and ski-area operators offers information and referrals to the public.

Eastern Ski Representatives Association
4145 W. Lake Road
Canandaigua, NY   14424
(716) 394-3070
Offers information on skiing in the Eastern United States.

Midwest Ski Areas Association
P.O. Box 20287
Bloomington, MN   55420
(612) 884-9687
Offers information on skiing in the midwestern United States.

National Ski Patrol System, Inc.
133 S. Van Gordon Street
Lakewood, CO   80228
(303) 237-2737
Information on safety and rescue, winter survival, and equipment evaluation is offered by this organization.

New England Ski Representatives
  Association
RD 2
Stowe, VT   05672
(802) 253-8335
This group provides information on skiing in New England.

Pacific Northwest Ski Association
P.O. Box 3448
Kirkland, WA   98083
(206) 822-1770
Information on skiing in the Pacific Northwest is offered by this Association.

Southeastern Ski Representatives
  Association
P.O. Box 183
Rocky Ridge, MD   21778
(301) 631-6474
This office provides information on skiing in the southeastern United States.

Student Ski Association
26 Sagamore Road
Seekonk, MA   02771
(508) 336-8775
Offering low-cost ski trips to college students, the Association publishes *Poor Howard's Guide to Skiing* and *Student Skier,* both annually.

United Ski Industries Association
8377-B Greensboro Drive
McLean, VA   22102
(703) 556-9020

This trade association offers referrals to people looking for ski equipment and services.

United States Ski Association
P.O. Box 100
Park City, UT   84060
(801) 649-9090
Sanctioned as competitive skiing's "official" governing organization by the U.S. Olympic Committee, this Association will answer questions and make referrals on a wide range of subjects. It publishes a directory and a magazine called *Ski Racing.*

U.S. Ski Coaches Association
P.O. Box 1747
Park City, UT   84060
(801) 649-9090
This group oversees rules and regulations of amateur skiing and hosts competitions in Nordic, Alpine, and Freestyle skiing for both the amateur and the recreational skier. It also publishes manuals on skiing, aimed primarily at coaches.

SOCCER

American Youth Soccer Organization (AYSO)
5403 W. 138th Street
Hawthorne, CA   90250
(213) 643-6455
AYSO runs competitions organized by age for those under nineteen and publishes *The ABC's of AYSO—Parents' Handbook.*

Canadian Soccer Association
333 River Road
Ottawa, Ontario   K1L 8H9
Canada
(613) 748-5667

Major Indoor Soccer League
757 3rd Avenue, Suite 2305
New York, NY   10017
(212) 486-7070
An organization that represents professional indoor soccer, the League offers information on its competitions.

National Soccer Coaches Association of America
P.O. Box 5074
Stroudsburg, PA   18630
(717) 421-8720
This group offers referrals to the public.

National Soccer Hall of Fame
58 Market Street
Oneonta, NY   13820
(607) 432-3351
This is a museum for soccer fans.

Soccer Association for Youth (S.A.Y.) Soccer-USA
5945 Ridge Avenue
Cincinnati, OH   45213
(513) 351-7291

S.A.Y. oversees soccer competitions organized by six different age categories, but carefully mixing ability levels to ensure fair play. It publishes *Parents Guide to Soccer* annually as well as a number of periodicals and handbooks.

Soccer Industry Council of America
200 Castlewood Drive
North Palm Beach, FL   33408
(305) 842-4100
This trade association makes referrals to anyone seeking information on soccer equipment.

U.S. Soccer Federation
1750 E. Boulder Street
Colorado Springs, CO   80909
(719) 578-4678
Provides referrals to soccer clubs and teams, and publishes rulebooks.

U.S. Youth Soccer Association
1835 Union Avenue, Suite 190
Memphis, TN   38104
(901) 278-7972
This Association for soccer players ranging in age from five to nineteen runs clinics and competitions, trains and selects players for the national youth soccer team, and publishes the *U.S. Youth Soccer Association—National Directory.* It also publishes handbooks, manuals, videotapes, and a newspaper that includes tips for parents.

SOFTBALL

Amateur Softball Association
2801 N.E. 50th Street
Oklahoma City, OK   73111
(405) 424-5266
This is the main national agency for softball in the United States. It sponsors clinics, competitions, research, and awards; coordinates a Junior Olympics; and maintains a reference library. It also publishes a newsletter, the *Commissioner Directory,* the annual *Official Guide and Rulebook,* and a catalog.

Canadian Amateur Softball Association
333 River Road
Ottawa, Ontario   K1L 8H9
Canada
(613) 746-5735

Cinderella Softball League, Inc.
P.O. Box 1411
Corning, NY   14830
(607) 937-5469
Cinderella runs several leagues for girls up to the age of eighteen, and publishes a rulebook and a newsletter.

National Softball Hall of Fame & Museum
2801 N.E. 50th Street
Oklahoma City, OK   73111
(405) 424-5267
The major softball museum in the United States.

Softball Canada
333 River Road
Ottawa, Ontario   K1L 8H9
Canada
(613) 748-5668

U.S. Slo-Pitch Softball Association
3935 S. Crater Road
Petersburg, VA   23805
(804) 732-4099

SURFING

The Association promotes the growth of amateur slo-pitch softball. It has a wide range of divisions, including one for youth, and also publishes an official rule book, a newsletter, and a softball almanac.

SEE ALSO

the SWIMMING AND BOATING SAFETY section in Chapter 6.

Eastern Surfing Association
11 Adams Point Road
Barrington, RI   02806
(508) 336-6904
Information on surfing and beach ecology on the east coast of the United States is offered by this Association.

National Scholastic Surfing Association
P.O. Box 495
Huntington Beach, CA   92648
(714) 841-3254
For students from sixth grade through college, the Association encourages team competition, maintains a training camp, runs an international exchange program, bestows awards and scholarships, and publishes a newsletter called *Surflines*.

U.S. Surfing Federation
7104 Island Village Drive
Long Beach, CA   90803
(213) 596-7785
Serves as a governing body for amateur surfing and sponsors competitions from which national team members are chosen.

SWIMMING AND DIVING

SEE ALSO

the SWIMMING AND BOATING SAFETY section in Chapter 6.

American Swimming Coaches Association
1 Hall of Fame Drive
Fort Lauderdale, FL   33316
(305) 462-6267
This Association for coaches answers questions and makes referrals to the public, and operates the Swim America program to teach children and adults how to swim. It publishes the yearbook *Journal of Swimming Research* and distributes videotapes.

Canadian Amateur Diving Association
333 River Road
Ottawa, Ontario   K1L 8H9
Canada
(613) 748-5631

Canadian Amateur Swimming Association
333 River Road
Ottawa, Ontario   K1L 8H9
Canada
(613) 748-5673

Canadian Amateur Synchronized Swimming Association
333 River Road
Ottawa, Ontario   K1L 8H9
Canada
(613) 748-5674

International Swimming Hall of Fame
1 Hall of Fame Drive
Fort Lauderdale, FL   33316
(305) 462-6536
This is a museum and reference library devoted to the aquatic arts.

National Interscholastic Swimming Coaches Association of America
c/o Donald R. Allen
Glenbrook South High School
4000 West Lake Avenue
Glenview, IL   60025
(708) 729-2000
Offers information on swimming programs in intermediate and secondary schools.

United States Water Polo
Pan American Plaza, Suite 520
201 South Capitol Avenue
Indianapolis, IN   46254
(317) 237-5599
Runs training clinics for coaches and players, and publishes an annual rulebook.

U.S. Diving, Inc.
201 S. Capitol Avenue, Suite 430
Indianapolis, IN   46225
(317) 237-5252
Runs competitions for divers between the ages of ten and eighteen.

U.S. Swimming, Inc.
1750 E. Boulder Street
Colorado Springs, CO   80909
(719) 578-4578

This office oversees the rules and regulations for amateur swimming; runs instructional programs for anyone five years and older; sponsors competitions; selects members for the national team; and publishes the *United States Swimming Directory* annually.

U.S. Synchronized Swimming, Inc.
201 S. Capitol Avenue, Suite 510
Indianapolis, IN   46225
(317) 237-5700
Hosts competitions for swimmers aged ten and older. Publishes a newsletter, a coaching manual, and a rulebook.

TENNIS

SEE ALSO

the Racquet Sports listings in this chapter.

American Tennis Association
P.O. Box 3277
Silver Spring, MD   20901
(301) 681-4832

This Association for black persons interested in tennis runs special programs for youth and holds an annual tournament. It publishes *Black Tennis Magazine*.

Black Tennis & Sports Foundation
1893 Amsterdam Avenue
New York, NY   10032
(212) 926-5991
The Foundation provides help for black and minority youth interested in pursuing athletics, including tennis, gymnastics, and skating. It organizes tennis teams, competitions, and educational and charitable projects.

Canadian Tennis Association
3111 Steeles Avenue W.
Downsview, Ontario   M3J 3H2
Canada
(416) 655-9777

National Junior Tennis League
c/o USTA Education and Research
707 Alexander Road
Princeton, NJ   08540-6301
(609) 452-2580
(800) 223-0456

The League helps local groups form tennis programs and publishes a number of manuals on how to start a program in your community.

U.S. Tennis Association (USTA)
1212 Avenue of the Americas
New York, NY   10036
(212) 302-3322
USTA oversees the rules and regulations of junior-level tennis and runs a competitive program, organized by age, including the Junior Davis Cup, Junior Federation, and Junior Wightman events. It publishes a wide variety of materials, including two magazines, a yearbook, rules manuals, tennis clinic kits, and the *Official Encyclopedia of Tennis.*

TRACK AND FIELD

SEE ALSO

the Running and Walking section in this chapter.

Athletics Congress of the USA
One Hoosier Dome, Suite 140
Indianapolis, IN   46225
(317) 261-0500

This office oversees the rules and regulations of track and field competition, selects members for the national teams, and runs clinics and camps. It publishes an annual directory, *American Athletics Annual,* and competition rules.

Canadian Track & Field Association
333 River Road
Ottawa, Ontario   K1L 8H9
Canada
(613) 748-5678

U.S. Cross Country Coaches Association
c/o Bill Bergan
Iowa State University
Ames, IA   50011
(515) 294-3723
This small group of coaches offers the public limited referrals.

VOLLEYBALL

Canadian Volleyball Association
333 River Road
Ottawa, Ontario   K1L 8H9
Canada
(613) 748-5681

U.S. Volleyball Association
1750 E. Boulder Street
Colorado Springs, CO   80909
(719) 578-4750
The Association oversees the rules and regulations of volleyball play and sponsors the USA Youth Volleyball Program and USA Junior Olympic Volleyball, both of which have age-level divisions. It publishes *Youth Volleyball* and the *Official U.S. Volleyball Rule Book.*

WATER POLO

Canadian Water Polo Association
333 River Road
Ottawa, Ontario   K1L 8H9
Canada
(613) 748-5682

U.S. Water Polo, Inc.
1750 E. Boulder Street
Colorado Springs, CO   80909
(719) 578-4549
This official governing body of water polo in the United States offers referrals and publishes a rule book.

WATER SKIING

American Water Ski Association
P.O. Box 191
Winter Haven, FL   33880
(813) 324-4341
The Association serves as a governing body for rules and regulations, conducts training programs for instructors, maintains a library, a museum, and a hall of fame. It publishes a directory, educational pamphlets, and a monthly magazine.

Canadian Water Ski Association
333 River Road
Ottawa, Ontario   K1L 8H9
Canada
(613) 748-5683

WEIGHTLIFTING

U.S. Powerlifting Federation

P.O. Box 18485
Pensacola, FL   32523
(904) 477-4863
The Federation runs clinics, medical programs, championships and meets, and has a special committee for youth development.

U.S. Weightlifting Federation

1750 E. Boulder Street
Colorado Springs, CO   80909
(719) 578-4508
The Federation runs national competitions and selects members for the Pan-American and Olympic teams, serves as a governing body for rules and regulations, and offers a videotape series for coaching weightlifting. It publishes a bimonthly newsletter.

WRESTLING AND ARMWRESTLING

American Armwrestling Association

c/o Bob O'Leary
P.O. Box 132
Scranton, PA   18504
(717) 342-4984
The Association sponsors competitions and distributes awards.

Canadian Amateur Wrestling Association

333 River Road
Ottawa, Ontario   K1L 8H9
Canada
(613) 748-5686

National Wrestling Coaches Association

Athletic Department
University of Utah
Salt Lake City, UT   84112
(801) 581-3836
Offers information and referrals regarding high school and college-level wrestling.

U.S.A. Wrestling

225 S. Academy Boulevard
Colorado Springs, CO   80901
(719) 597-8333
(800) 654-4653
(800) 999-USAW (8729)
USA Wrestling has several age-level divisions for regional, national, and international competition and also sponsors clinics and camps. It publishes *International Wrestling Rules,* a series of books on wrestling-related topics, educational pamphlets, and several periodicals.

HOBBIES

This section includes these hobbies: Amateur Radio, Arts and Crafts, Astronomy, Aviation, Ceramics, Coin Collecting, Computers, Dolls and Toys, Environmental Sciences, Games and Word Puzzles, Gardening, Genealogy, Insects, Magic, Models, Music, Pen Pals, Photography, Rock Collecting, Sand Castles, Shell Collecting, Sports Card Collecting, Stamp Collecting, Theater and Film, and Treasure Hunting.

SEE ALSO

the MAIL ORDER CATALOGS section in Chapter 12 under Educational Products, Science and Nature, and Toys and Games for additional items to interest young hobbyists.

AMATEUR RADIO

American Radio Relay League (ARRL)
225 Main Street
Newington, CT   06111
(203) 666-1541
ARRL serves licensed amateur radio operators. It operates the National Traffic System, a nationwide message network. Publications include *Radio Amateur's Handbook* and booklets aimed at beginners.

American Shortwave Listeners Club (ASWLC)
16182 Ballad Lane
Huntington Beach, CA   92649
(714) 846-1685

This group of shortwave and DX radio hobbyists publishes a magazine, *SWL,* and an annual, *Equipment Survey.*

Association of North American Radio Clubs (ANARC)
P.O. Box 143
Falls Church, VA   22046
(703) 534-7443
ANARC acts as an information clearinghouse for radio clubs and those who wish to find and join local clubs. It publishes a list of members and a monthly newsletter.

International Radio Club of America
(IRCA)
P.O. Box 21074
Seattle, WA   98101
(206) 522-2521
This club is for hobbyists who listen to long-distance broadcasts on the AM band. Publications include a newsletter, *DX Monitor,* and various technical manuals.

Longwave Club of America (LWCA)
45 Wildflower Road
Levittown, PA   19057
(215) 945-0543

LWCA serves hobbyists who specialize in longwave transmissions of less than 540 kHz. Publications include *Lowdown* and *Beacon Guide Updaters.*

North American Shortwave Association
(NASWA)
45 Wildflower Road
Levittown, PA   19057
(215) 945-0543
Associated with its sister organization, the Longwave Club of America, NASWA supports hobbyists who specialize in shortwave communications.

ARTS AND CRAFTS

SEE ALSO

Chaselle, Inc., J. L. Hammett Co., and Nasco in Chapter 12 in the MAIL ORDER CATALOGS section under Educational Materials.

American Needlepoint Guild
728 Summerly Drive
Nashville, TN   37209
(615) 352-8174
For anyone interested in the art of needlepoint, the Guild offers correspondence courses and the "Steps to Perfection" instructional program, encourages an interest in the craft's history, and sponsors exhibitions. It

publishes *Needle Pointers* six times a year.

American Needlewoman
P.O. Box 6472
Fort Worth, TX   76115
(800) 433-2231
This source offers a catalog of needlepoint, quilting, and crocheting books, supplies, and kits. It is available for $1.

American Quilter's Society
P.O. Box 3290
Paducah, KY   42001
(502) 898-7903
The Society runs competitions, helps
sell quilts, and offers referrals to quilt-
ers.

American Society of Artists
P.O. Box 1326
Palatine, IL   60078
(312) 991-4748
The Society's Resource Center has a
collection of catalogs, books, and periodicals on arts and crafts.

**Association of Crafts & Creative
  Industries**
1100-H Brandywine Boulevard
P.O. Box 2188
Zanesville, OH   43702
(614) 452-4541
The Association offers information and
referrals about where to buy crafts
supplies, and publishes the annual *ACCI
Directory.*

Barker Enterprises, Inc.
15106 10th Avenue, S.W.
Seattle, WA   98166
(206) 244-1870
The $2 Barker catalog offers everything
you need to make your own candles including Santa and skull molds, dipping
vats, decals, and how-to books.

Berman Leathercraft
25 Melcher Street
Boston, MA   02210-1599
(617) 426-0870
A complete supply of leather-working
materials and tools is offered in the $3
Berman catalog. Available are skins,
tools, buckles, and books as well as
products specifically related to Indian
leather-craft.

Boycan's Craft Supplies
P.O. Box 897
Sharon, PA   16146
Boycan's catalog lists craft supplies and
kits that have been marked down.

Chaselle, Inc.
9645 Gerwig Lane
Columbia, MD   21046
(301) 381-9611
(800) CHASELLE (242-7355)
(800) 492-7840 (in Maryland)
The company's free *Art & Craft Materials* catalog offers a complete supply of
tools for woodworking, sculpting, weav-
ing, etching, and more.

Clotilde Inc.
237 S.W. 28th Street
Fort Lauderdale, FL   33315
(305) 761-8655
The $1 Clotilde catalog lists sewing
supplies and how-to-sew videotapes.

Craftsway Corp.
4118 Lakeside Drive
Richmond, CA   94806
(415) 223-3144
Craftway sells informational publications on needlework and crafts as well as embroidery kits, needlework patterns, and supplies.

Crochet Association International
P.O. Box 131
Dallas, GA   30132
(404) 445-7137
This group provides instructional seminars, fairs, and educational pamphlets.

Dick Blick Art Materials
P.O. Box 1267
Galesburg, IL   61401
(309) 343-6181
Though primarily for art teachers, this four-hundred-page free catalog has everything an artist could want. Most of the supplies are available in small quantities if payment accompanies the order.

Embroiderer's Guild of America
335 W. Broadway, Suite 100
Louisville, KY   40202
(502) 589-6956
The Guild hosts competitions, exhibits, and trips; provides information on embroidery using its extensive reference library; and certifies masters of the craft.

Florida Supply House Catalog
P.O. Box 847
Bradenton, FL   33506
This is a large, seventy-two-page catalog offering craft and hobby supplies.

Grey Owl Indian Craft Co.
113-15 Springfield Boulevard
Queens Village, NY   11429
(718) 464-9300
For the child intrigued with the culture of Native Americans, this $2 catalog is the answer. Here you will find beads, feathers, tomahawk heads, war bonnets, log drums, actual-size tepees, informative books, and music.

H. H. Perkins Co.
10 S. Bradley Road
Woodbridge, CT   06525
(203) 389-9501
(800) 462-6600
The $1 Perkins catalog offers books, kits, and supplies for those interested in chair caning and basket weaving.

Knitting Guild of America
P.O. Box 1606
Knoxville, TN   37901
(615) 524-2401
The Guild runs competitions and distributes awards. It publishes a number of brochures and a journal containing articles on knitting craft and design.

Metropolitan Museum of Art
  and Thomas J. Watson Library
Fifth Avenue & 82nd Street
New York, NY   10028
(212) 879-5500
This is a vast collection of nearly three
hundred thousand books, microfilm,
and microfiche, on art, art history, and
archaeology from Ancient Egypt
through the twentieth century. Though
primarily serving graduate students and
researchers, the library will answer
questions from the public.

National Endowment for the Arts
  Library/Information Center
1100 Pennsylvania Avenue, N.W.
Washington, DC   20506
(202) 682-5485
The National Endowment has a collection of over six thousand books on
crafts and the arts, including dance,
music, literature, and design.

National Gallery of Art Library
Sixth and Constitution Avenue, N.W.
Washington, DC   20565
(202) 842-6511

This library has nearly two hundred
thousand books, periodicals, and micro-
form on art, architecture, and the deco-
rative arts. Though primarily serving
graduate students and researchers, it
will answer questions from the public.

Needle Works
P.O. Box 7052
Pine Bluff, AR   71611
(501) 535-4958
This is a publisher of informational and
pattern handbooks for needleworking
and other crafts.

Pourette Mfg. Co.
6910 Roosevelt Way, N.E.
P.O. Box 15220
Seattle, WA   98115
(206) 525-4488
Everything you could possibly need for
making candles is included in the $2
Pourette catalog. The cost of the catalog is deducted from your first order.
An additional catalog lists soap-making
products.

ASTRONOMY

SEE ALSO

Edmund Scientific and MMI Corporation in the MAIL ORDER CATALOGS section of Chapter 12 under Science and Nature.

Amateur Astronomers, Inc.
Sperry Observatory
Union College
1033 Springfield Avenue
Cranford, NJ   07016
(201) 276-3319
This group offers information and gives referrals by phone. Publications include a newsletter and an annual, *Sperry Observations—Journal of Amateur Astronomers.*

Association of Lunar & Planetary Observers (ALPO)
P.O. Box 16131
San Francisco, CA   94116
(415) 566-5786
ALPO serves amateur astronomers who use telescopes. It publishes a magazine, *ALPO Quarterly,* and an annual, *Solar System Ephemeris.*

Astronomical League (AL)
6235 Omie Circle
Pensacola, FL   32504
(904) 477-8732
The League is a coalition of more than one hundred sixty astronomical organizations. It offers referrals to local societies. Publications include the magazine, *The Reflector.*

Astronomical Society of the Pacific (ASP)
1290 24th Avenue
San Francisco, CA   94122
(415) 661-8660 (administration)
(415) 661-0500 (astronomy news hotline)
ASP includes professional and amateur astronomers. It will answer questions and make referrals by phone. Publications include introductory materials on how to get children started in astronomy and a catalog of educational materials, called *Selectory,* is available free of charge.

Friends United Through Astronomy (FUTA)
8191 Woodland Shore, Lot 12
Brighton, MI   48116
(313) 227-9347

This group of amateur astronomers offers referrals for children who wish to learn about the hobby. Contact them for full details. Publications include *Celestial Observer* and *FUTA Listings*.

Meade Instruments Corp.
1675 Toronto Way
Costa Mesa, CA   92626
(714) 556-2291
Meade will send a catalog of the telescopes and supplies they manufacture.

Planetary Society
65 N. Catalina Avenue
Pasadena, CA   91106-9899
(818) 793-5100
Cofounded by Carl Sagan, this large group offers information and referrals. Contact the Society for a list of books and other publications it distributes.

Sky Publishing Corp.
P.O. Box 9111
Belmont, MA   02238
(617) 864-7360
This company will send its catalog of astronomy-related materials.

Space Camp/Space Academy
The Space & Rocket Center
1 Tranquility Base
Huntsville, AL   35807
(800) 63-SPACE (637-7223)
Through a series of programs for grades 4 through 10, children are introduced to all aspects of space travel including space suits, simulated missions, and rocket propulsion.

Star Blazers
4505 Silver Hollow Drive
Corpus Christi, TX   78413
(512) 850-8637
Star Blazers combines the study of astronomy with explorations of the self, creativity, leadership, and communication. It provides workbooks and guide books for holding group meetings.

Young Astronaut Program
1211 Connecticut Avenue, N.W.,
   Suite 800
Washington, DC   20036
(202) 682-1986
This program was established to stimulate an interest in mathematics, technology, and science among elementary and junior high school students. It helps teachers and students who want to form local groups.

AVIATION

American Aviation Historical Society
2333 Otis Street
Santa Ana, CA   92704
(714) 549-4818
This society is for those interested in aviation history. It has a library of twenty-thousand slides, books, and periodicals on military and aviation history

and relevant biographies. Its book service offers discounts on aviation books.
It publishes a number of periodicals,
monographs, and *Museum and Display
Aircraft of the United States.*

First Flight Society
P.O. Box 1903
Kitty Hawk, NC   27949
(919) 441-2773
The Society promotes aviation past,
present, and future, with a particular
emphasis on the Wright brothers' flight
at Kitty Hawk. It publishes a newsletter
and pamphlets.

COIN COLLECTING

CERAMICS

A.R.T. Studio Clay Co.
1555 Louis Avenue
Elk Grove Village, IL   60007
(312) 593-6060
This ceramic supply house will send a
catalog of their offerings.

Scott Publications
30595 W. Eight Road
Livonia, MI   48152
(313) 477-6650
This firm publishes hobbyist books on
how to make ceramics. They will send a
catalog describing their books.

SEE ALSO

Hobby Surplus Sales under the Models listings of this chapter.

American Numismatic Association
818 N. Cascade Avenue
Colorado Springs, CO   80903-3279
(719) 632-2646
(800) 367-9723
The Association has a junior membership for children ages eleven to seventeen and a junior publication called
First Strike. Its library maintains a collection of over thirty-five thousand
books, periodicals, and auction catalogs

covering coins, tokens, banking, and
more.

**American Numismatic Society Library
    & Museum**
Broadway at 155th Street
New York, NY   10032
(212) 234-3130
This Society has a tremendous collection of more than one hundred thousand books, periodicals, and other

items, plus nearly four hundred reels of microfilm. It publishes a number of periodicals, monographs, and bibliographies.

**Combined Organizations of Numismatic
Error Collectors of America
(CONECA)**
P.O. Box 932
Savannah, GA   31402
(912) 232-8655
For coin collectors, CONECA offers authentication and evaluation services,

provides education and research, hosts competitions, distributes awards, and maintains a museum. It publishes a monthly magazine.

Numismatics International (NI)
P.O. Box 670013
Dallas, TX   75367
(214) 361-7543
NI distributes information to children on coin collecting and runs a twenty-thousand-volume reference library.

COMPUTERS

SEE ALSO

Chaselle, Inc. and Opportunities for Learning, Inc. in the MAIL ORDER CATALOGS section of Chapter 12 under Educational Materials, and see Heath Co. under Science and Nature.

Boston Computer Society
1 Center Plaza
Boston, MA   02108
(617) 367-8080
For both individuals and organizations seeking to learn about computers, the Society runs a resource center, a computer institute, educational programs, and user groups. It publishes *Computer Update* (bimonthly) and *BCS Buying Guide* (semiannual).

Capital PC User Group
51 Monroe Street
Rockville, MD   20850
(301) 656-8372
Capital serves as a clearinghouse for members with IBM PC's and compatibles. The Group offers monthly courses, an annual convention, and publishes *Capital PC Monitor* (monthly) and *Capital PC Membership Directory* (annual).

Computer Book Club
TAB Books
13311 Monterey Avenue
Blue Ridge Summit, PA   17294-0850
(217) 794-2191
(800) 233-1128
Call or write to receive a catalog.

Crab Apple
14 Eleanor Place
Monsey, NY   10952
No phone number listed.
For families who own an Apple, Crab
Apple assists with hardware, software,
and programming and distributes the
latest technological information.
There's a monthly meeting and a
monthly publication called *Crab Apple
Bulletin*.

Family Software Catalog
Evanston Educators
915 Elmwood Avenue
Evanston, IL   60202
(312) 475-2556
(800) 972-5855 (in Illinois)
Games and educational software for
preschoolers and older children are offered in this $2 catalog.

FOG—First Osborne Group
P.O. Box 3474
Daly City, CA   94015
(415) 755-2000

FOG provides information, problem
solving, and public-domain software. It
publishes *Foghorn* and *Foglight*
monthly and runs an annual convention.

Heathkit Catalog
Heath Co.
Benton Harbor, MI   49022
(616) 982-3200
Call or write for the free catalog, which
lists self-study programs, electronic
product kits, and testing equipment.

Learning Gifts
P.O. Box 56-1006
Miami, FL   33256-1006
(305) 252-0455
(800) 874-7588
This free, two-hundred-page catalog
lists a wide range of educational and
entertainment computer software.

National Epson Users Group
Box 8088
State College, PA   16803
(814) 237-5511
For users of Epson printers and computers and MS-DOS systems, this users
group lends support and technical
know-how and keeps a fourteen-hun-
dred-disk library. There's an annual
convention and publication of *The Epson Lifeboat* nine times a year.

PC Hackers
12155 Edgecliff
Los Altos, CA   94022
(415) 941-2796
For both MS-DOS and PC-DOS users,
PC Hackers gives technical advice and
software information, and publishes the
monthly *PC Hackers Newsletter.*

**PC-SIG Library-Personal Computer
   Software**
1030 E. Duane Avenue, Suite D
Sunnyvale, CA   94086
(408) 730-9291
PC-SIG maintains a collection of over
sixteen hundred software packages,
many of them public domain, for the
IBM PC. It is also a clearinghouse for
other programs, fellow hackers, and
clubs.

Public (Software) Library
P.O. Box 35705
Houston, TX   77235-5705
(713) 665-7017
(800) 242-4PSL (4775)
For those with an IBM PC or compatible, this catalog lists public-domain
software of entertainment, educational,
or graphic programs in a wide spectrum of fields. For $2 you receive a
sample monthly newsletter and a list of
more than a thousand programs.

DANCE

National Dance Institute
594 Broadway, Room 805
New York, NY   10012
(212) 226-0083
The Institute helps schools create dance
programs and provides films to teach
and encourage young dancers.

**Professional Dance Teachers
   Association**
P.O. Box 91
Waldwick, NJ   07463
(201) 447-0355
This group of teachers specializes in
ballet, jazz, and modern dance. It offers
information to parents on teachers and
dance schools nationwide.

United Square Dancers of America
8913 Seaton Drive
Huntsville, AL   35802
(205) 881-6044
This large group of dancers and callers
provides pamphlets and makes referrals.

**United States National Institute of
   Dance**
38 S. Arlington Avenue
East Orange, NJ   07019
(201) 673-9225
Offers referrals to parents seeking
dance teachers and dance companies
for their children.

DOLLS AND TOYS

SEE ALSO

Cherry Tree Toys in the Models section of this chapter. Many of the mail order suppliers listed in Chapter 12 under Toys and Games offer additional items of interest.

Antique Toy Collectors Club of America
c/o Robert R. Grew
Carter, Ledyard & Milburn
2 Wall Street, Suite 1500
New York, NY   10005
(212) 238-8803
The Club runs educational and research projects, records the history of toys, and publishes informational pamphlets, a directory, and a newsletter.

Doll Artisan Guild
35 Main Street
P.O. Box 1113
Oneonta, NY   13820-1113
(607) 432-4977
For those interested in antique porcelain doll reproduction and dollmaking, the Guild provides information on the craft, offers seminars and manufacturers' discounts, runs classes and contests, and gives advice when requested. It publishes a bimonthly magazine.

Doll Collectors of America (DCA)
14 Chestnut Road
Westford, MA   01886
(508) 692-8392
DCA collects and distributes information on early dolls, their history, and preservation. It publishes a newsletter and a manual.

Doll Factory
1953 S. Military Trail
West Palm Beach, FL   33415
(407) 967-9772
The $2 catalog shows a range of dolls, including realistic infant dolls, dolls with wooden faces and hands, anatomically correct dolls, and a doll that giggles and gurgles.

Doll Repair Parts, Inc.
9918 Lorain Avenue
Cleveland, OH   44102-4694
(216) 961-3545

Here you'll find everything you need to repair a damaged doll or make a new one. The $1 catalog offers wigs and doll molds, teeth and eyes, as well as books on doll repair and collecting.

Enchanted Doll House
Route 7
Manchester Center, VT 05255-0697
(802) 362-1327
The $2 catalog offers many dolls including character dolls such as the Seven Dwarfs, Robin Hood, and Paddington Bear. In addition, there are Madame Alexander dolls, trains, and other toys and doll accessories.

Ertl Collectors Club
Highway 136 and 20
Dyersville, IA 52040
(319) 875-2000
(800) 553-4886
(800) 942-4618 (in Iowa)
For those interested in die-cast toys, the Club operates as a clearinghouse of information. It publishes the *Collector's Handbook* annually, plus a newsletter and a calendar of activities.

Jan's Small World
3146 Myrtle
Billings, MT 59102
(406) 652-2689
Jan's offers a $3 catalog containing dollhouse accoutrements from tiny

fruits and vegetables to a bearskin rug and wiring supplies.

My Sister's Shoppe
1671 Penfield Road
Rochester, NY 14625
(716) 381-4037
The $2 catalog advertises two dollhouse kits plus decorating pieces such as artificial grass and a Victorian Christmas tree.

Standard Doll Company
23–83 31st Street
Long Island City, NY 11105
(718) 721-7787
The $3 Standard Doll catalog has everything you'll ever need for making your own dolls and sewing clothes for them.

United Federation of Doll Clubs
8-B East Street
P.O. Box 14146
Parkville, MO 64152
(816) 741-1002
This group makes referrals, responds to inquiries, and runs an annual conference with exhibits.

ENVIRONMENTAL SCIENCES

National Geographic Society
Educational Services, Department 88
17th and N Streets
Washington, DC 20036
(202) 857-7378

The Society has many publications, both printed and audiovisual, prepared for a younger audience. Call or write for a catalog.

Youth Environmental Society (YES)
P.O. Box 441
Cranbury, NJ   08512
(609) 655-8030

YES works with youth to develop leadership through environmental action. Its activities include weekend retreats and other programs for high school, college, and community environmentalists. The Society publishes both a newsletter, *Environs,* and the *New Jersey Environmental Directory.*

GAMES AND WORD PUZZLES

SEE ALSO

the MAIL ORDER CATALOGS section of Chapter 12 under Toys and Games.

American Checker Federation (ACF)
3475 Belmont Avenue
Baton Rouge, LA   70808
(504) 344-8429
In addition to its adult programs, ACF sponsors a youth program for checker players ages seven to seventeen.

American Chess Foundation
Box 15
Whitestone, NY   11357
(212) 353-1456
The Foundation promotes chess playing among school-aged children, and provides information and referrals to local programs.

American Crossword Federation
P.O. Box 69
Massapequa Park, NY   11762
(516) 795-8823
For all those lovers of the crossword puzzle, the Federation sponsors competitions, makes customized puzzles, runs a hotline for insoluable clues, and publishes a newsletter and books of crosswords.

American International Checkers
    Society (AICS)
11010 Horde Street
Wheaton, MD   20902
(301) 949-5920

This group sponsors local and state checker competitions.

Atari Game Club
P.O. Box AGC
Half Moon Bay, CA   94019
Write for a membership application and list of publications.

Intellevision Game Club
P.O. Box 4010
Burlingame, CA   94010
No phone number listed.
Write for a membership application and list of publications.

International Backgammon Association
1300 Citrus Circle
Ft. Lauderdale, FL   33315
(305) 527-4033
The Association runs competitions, advises on strategies, and promotes the game of backgammon. It publishes an annual magazine and a monthly list of tournaments.

International Fantasy Gaming Society (IFGS)
2208 Fairfax
Denver, CO   80207
(303) 333-4347
For anyone interested in fantasy and role-play, IFGS organizes a variety of scenarios. In addition, there's an annual convention, the monthly publication *Melee,* and several rulebooks and handbooks.

National Puzzler's League (NPL)
Spring Valley Road
Morristown, NJ   07960
(201) 538-4584
For those intrigued by word puzzles, NPL offers an annual convention and the monthly magazine, *Enigma.*

North American Tiddlywinks Association (NATWA)
10416 Haywood Drive
Silver Spring, MD   20902
(301) 681-9345
Those avid tiddlywinkers who want to play in tournaments should become members. There's a convention every year and a semiannual magazine, *Newswink.*

Puzzle Buffs International (PBI)
1772 State Road
Cuyahoga Falls, OH   44223
(216) 923-2397
PBI offers information about word puzzles and games. The group publishes eight issues of *The World's Largest Crosswords* each year, the quarterly, *Puzzle Buffs,* and runs a semiannual meeting.

Scrabble Crossword Game Players (SCGP)
c/o Williams & Co.
P.O. Box 700
Greenport, NY   11944
(516) 477-0033

This group sponsors Scrabble tournaments throughout the United States and Canada.

U.S. Chess Federation
186 Route 9W
New Windsor, NY   12550
(914) 562-8350
The largest chess group in the United States, the Federation sponsors tournaments, promotes chess in schools, and sells recommended chess books and equipment. Publications include *Chess Life* and *U.S. Chess Scholastic Newsletter*.

U.S. Othello Association
Arnold Kling
11517 Daffodil Lane
Silver Spring, MD   20902
(301) 649-4378
This group promotes Othello competitions.

U.S. Trivia Association (USTA)
8217 S. Hazelwood Drive
Lincoln, NE   68510
(402) 489-7604
The Association runs a radio program, has a Hall of Fame, and an eight-thousand-volume library. USTA's monthly publication is *Trivia Unlimited Magazine*.

World Wide Games
Box 450
Delaware, OH   43015
(614) 369-9631
This group's free catalog lists handmade games that the whole family can play.

GARDENING

American Community Gardening Association (ACGA)
c/o Chicago Botanic Garden
Box 400
Glencoe, IL   60022
(312) 835-0250
ACGA provides information and support for community and business groups interested in community gardening. It sponsors contests, an annual conference, and publishes *Multilogue* on a monthly basis and the *Journal of Community Gardening* on a quarterly basis.

American Horticultural Society (AHS)
P.O. Box 0105
Mt. Vernon, VA   22121
(703) 768-5700
AHS is for both the amateur and the professional gardener. It sponsors a seed exchange and provides information through its Plant Sciences Data Center. Publications include the monthly *American Horticulturist,* various handbooks and calendars.

Arthur Eames Allgrove
Box 459
Wilmington, MA   01887
No phone number listed.
Write for their catalog of gardening
tools.

Brooklyn Botanic Garden
1000 Washington Avenue
Brooklyn, NY   11225-1099
(718) 622-4433
Offers a videocassette called *Get Ready,
Get Set, Grow: A Kid's Guide to Good
Gardening,* which comes with a booklet
for the young gardener and one for the
teaching adult.

Garden Club of America (GCA)
598 Madison Avenue
New York, NY   10022
(212) 753-8287
The GCA is for amateur gardeners and
promotes love of gardening, protection
of our natural environment, and civic
planting. It has a four-thousand-volume
library and puts out a monthly bulletin.

George Park Seed Co.
Huxbury Road
Greenwood, SC   29647-0001
(803) 223-7333
Call or write for their mail-order cata-
log of gardening products.

Hobby Greenhouse Association (HGA)
8 Glen Terrace
Bedford, MA   01730
(617) 275-0377
For those who grow plants using artificial light, the HGA provides information
on such topics as disease and propaga-
tion of seeds. The Association has a
quarterly publication, *Hobby Greenhouse,* and an annual convention.

Indoor Gardening Society of America
   (IGSA)
128 W. 58th Street
New York, NY   10019
(212) 321-6049
Through its publication *The Indoor
Garden* and its activities, IGSA provides
information to the amateur and the
professional on indoor gardening.

National Garden Bureau (NGB)
1311 Butterfield, Suite 310
Downers Grove, IL   60515
(312) 963-6999
The NGB's mission is to provide information about home gardening, particularly seeds, for everyone from the home
gardener to the media. They have a gardening program for children and an annual convention.

National Gardening Association (NGA)
180 Flynn Avenue
Burlington, VT   05401
(802) 863-1308
The NGA provides information and sponsors a seed exchange. It publishes how-to guides such as *The Youth Garden Book,* manuals, the monthly *National Gardening Magazine,* and annual directories for seeds.

National Junior Horticultural Association (NJHA)
441 E. Pine Street
Fremont, MI   49412
(616) 924-5237
NJHA runs educational programs and sponsors contests and projects to encourage younger people to become interested in gardening. It publishes a newsletter and has an annual meeting.

Safer Gardens
P.O. Box 1665
New York, NY   10116
This source produces nontoxic gardening products and puts out a free pamphlet entitled *Safer Gardens and Houseplants.*

W. Atlee Burpee & Co.
Warminster, PA   18974
(800) 333-5808
(800) 362-1991 (in Pennsylvania)
The free catalog *Kinder-Garden* describes a complete kit for the youthful gardener including a premarked plastic mat that guides the planting of flowers and vegetables. There are also small-size gloves and tools.

Women's National Farm & Garden Association
2402 Clearview Drive
Glenshaw, PA   15116
(412) 486-7964
Among its many activities, the Association presents one hundred fifty awards each year to students who wish to pursue the study of animal husbandry, agriculture, horticulture, and/or forestry. In addition, it gives awards to handicapped students of horticulture therapy, provides financial assistance for teachers to attend conservation conferences, and sponsors 4-H competitions. It publishes a directory and several periodicals.

GENEALOGY

Genealogical Data Services
P.O. Box 9
Fence, WI   54120
(715) 336-2010
Genealogical Data Services will provide compilations for genealogical investigators.

Genealogical Institute
P.O. Box 22045
Salt Lake City, UT   84122
(801) 532-3327
The Genealogical Institute publishes
*Immigration Digest, Research News,
Teaching Genealogy,* and various
sourcebooks. In addition, it provides
training, research services, computerized searches, and maintains an extensive reference library.

Institute of Family History & Genealogy
21 Hanson Avenue
Somerville, MA   02143
(617) 666-0877
Formed to promote the study of genealogy with a particular emphasis on the
New England region, this group sponsors courses and lectures, runs a small
library, and publishes *New England Genealogy,* which is a quarterly, plus a
newsletter and a variety of manuals.

INSECTS

American Entomological Society (AES)
1900 Race Street
Philadelphia, PA   19103
(215) 561-3978
For both the professional and the
amateur, AES publishes the latest scientific findings and maintains a fifteen-
thousand-volume library. It publishes
Entomological News and runs a convention, both five times a year.

Butterfly Lovers International (BLI)
1005 Market Street, Room 207
San Francisco, CA   94103
(415) 864-1169
BLI provides information, education,
and works to protect butterfly species
that are endangered.

Young Entomologists' Society (YES)
1915 Peggy Place
Lansing, MI   48910
(517) 887-0499
YES is an information exchange for
anyone interested in insect collecting.
It publishes *YES Quarterly* and the
semiannual directory *YES International
Entomological Resource Guide.*

MAGIC

Abracadabra Magic Shop
P.O. Box 714
Dept. C-534
Middlesex, NJ   08846-0714
(201) 805-0200
Their $1 *Fun Catalog* offers inexpensive
magic tricks and gags. Hot and sour
candy, a squirting lighter, marked
cards, and a floating eyeball are just
some of your choices. In the $3.95
Giant Magic Catalog you will find
more sophisticated magic tricks.

Abracadabra Press
116 Onyx Avenue, P.O. Box 334
Balboa Island, CA   92662
(714) 675-0966

The Press is a publisher of magic
books.

Al's Magic Shop
1205 Pennsylvania Avenue, N.W.
Washington, DC   20004
(202) 789-2800
Al's is a retailer of magic supplies that
offers a catalog.

American Museum of Magic
P.O. Box 5
Marshall, MI   49068
(616) 781-7666
This Museum maintains a collection of
over two hundred fifty thousand magic-
related goods, and puts out a newsletter.

Ash's Magic Catalog
4955 N. Western
Chicago, IL   60625
(312) 271-4030
This $2 catalog has over one hundred
pages to choose from. You'll be able to
push a cigarette through a quarter,
make pennies disappear, or take photographs with a squirting camera.

Hank Lee's Magic Factory
125 Lincoln Street
Boston, MA   02111
(617) 482-8749
(617) 482-8750
This huge, three-hundred-fifty-page catalog sells for $6 and has magic props
for the beginner and the professional.

International Brotherhood of Magicians
(IBM)
P.O. Box 89
Bluffton, OH   45817
(419) 358-8555
IBM membership includes professional
and semiprofessional magicians, assistants, and suppliers. It publishes the
monthly *The Linking Ring* and runs an
annual convention.

Lee Jacobs Productions
P.O. Box 362
Pomeroy, OH   45769-0362
(614) 992-5208
This is a publisher of books on comedy,
magic, and mind-reading as well as
posters of magicians.

Louis Tannen, Inc.
6 W. 32nd Street
New York, NY   10001
(212) 239-8383
Call or write to request their *Catalog of
Magic.*

Magical Youths International (MYI)
61551 Bremen Highway
Mishawaka, IN   46544
(219) 255-4747
For children and all those who still
have the child within them, MYI publishes *Top Hat* six times a year and
Flash Paper semiannually.

Magic, Inc.
5082 N. Lincoln Avenue
Chicago, IL   60625
(312) 334-2855
Call or write to request Magic's catalog of supplies.

Magic Ltd./Lloyd E. Jones
P.O. Box 3186
San Leandro, CA   94578
(415) 531-5490

This source publishes both trade and textbooks for the amateur and professional magician.

Society of American Magicians (SAM)
P.O. Box 368
Mango, FL   33550
(813) 689-9772
SAM offers lectures, workshops, competitions, and an annual convention. It publishes *M-U-M Magazine* monthly.

MODELS

SEE ALSO

Cuisenaire Company of America, Inc. in the MAIL ORDER CATALOGS section of Chapter 12 under Educational Products.

Academy of Model Aeronautics (AMA)
1810 Samuel Morse Drive
Reston, VA   22090
(703) 435-0750
Members receive a model airplane pilot's license allowing them to compete in official competitions. The AMA also runs a museum, publishes *Model Aviation* (monthly) and *Model Aircraft* (biennial), and sponsors an annual meeting.

American Model Soldier Society & American Military Historical Society
1528 El Camino Real
San Carlos, CA   94070
(415) 591-8125
The reference library of more than two thousand historical sources is helpful to collectors and modelers as well as military history buffs.

Century Flying Model Rockets
Dept. 220
P.O. Box 1988
Phoenix, AZ   85001

The Century Model Rocket Catalog lists rocket model kits for both beginner and advance modelers.

Cherry Tree Toys
408 S. Jefferson Street, P.O. Box 369
Belmont, OH   43718
(614) 484-4363
This sixty-page catalog features kits and tools for making dollhouses, trains, and trucks. There are toy wheels, clocks, various size toy people, smokestacks, and more. The catalog costs $1.

Circus Model Builders, International (CMB)
347 Lonsdale Avenue
Dayton, OH   45419
(513) 299-0515
For those eight through fifteen years old with a serious interest in the circus and circus modeling and those sixteen and older who have built models, CMB links members to exchange ideas, help solve problems, and create new models. Models are displayed publicly to honor the circus as an institution.

Estes Industries
1295 H Street
Penrose, CO   81240
(719) 372-6565
Call or write to receive their Model Rocket Catalog.

Hobby Surplus Sales
287 Main Street
P.O. Box 2170J
New Britain, CT   06050
This $2, seventy-page catalog is filled with model cars and planes, boats, and trains. There are engines, scenery, tracks, plus items for coin, stamp, and baseball-card collectors and miniature-dollhouse builders.

H. O. Center of the World
P.O. Box 348
Marion, CT   06444
(203) 628-8948
The $2 H.O. catalog supplies kits, parts, and accessories for more than two hundred trucks and cars.

Lionel Railroader Club
P.O. Box 748
Mt. Clemens, MI   48046
(313) 949-4100
For all those lovers of Lionel trains, the Club serves as a clearinghouse of information on games and products. Its newsletter lists supplies.

Miniature Figure Collectors of America (MFCA)
1988 Foster Drive
Hatfield, PA   19440
(215) 855-2232
MFCA's membership includes collectors, modelers, and sellers of miniature

soldiers. Ask for its list of publications and about its annual exhibition.

Model Car Collectors Association
5113 Sugar Loaf Drive, S.W.
Roanoke, VA   24018
(703) 774-8109
For those who make or collect model cars, the Association runs competitions, publishes a bimonthly journal, and conducts an annual meeting.

National Association of Rocketry
1311 Edgewood Drive
Altoona, WI   54720
(715) 834-8074
This group helps schools set up educational programs and clubs, provides rocket plans, certifies records, and sponsors demonstrations. It publishes a monthly magazine.

Northeastern Scale Models Inc.
P.O. Box 727
Methuen, MA   01844
(508) 688-6019
A $1 catalog provides lumber for do-it-yourself miniature builders. There are mahogany strips, miniature gutters, ship decking, and wooden car parts.

Polk's Model Craft Hobbies
346 Bergen Avenue
Jersey City, NJ   07304
(201) 332-8100
Call or write to receive a catalog.

Teen Association of Model Railroading (TAMR)
1028 Whaley Road, Route 4
New Carlisle, OH   45344
(513) 845-0455
TAMR helps those age thirteen to twenty-one to build and run model railroads. It publishes *HOTBOX* and an annual directory.

Terminal Hobby Shop
5619 W. Florist Avenue
Milwaukee, WI   53218
(414) 527-0770
(800) 347-1147
The eight-hundred-page catalog *The World of HO Scale* costs $13.98 and contains everything you'll need for building a model railroad. In addition, the somewhat less comprehensive catalogs *The World of Large Scale* and *The World of N & Z Scale* each sell for $9.98.

Toy Train Operating Society
25 W. Walnut Street, Suite 308
Pasadena, CA   91103
(818) 578-0673
The Society has a special children's program and a charitable service, runs competitions, sponsors shows, and maintains a reference library about toy trains. It publishes an annual directory and archival reprints.

Valley Plaza Hobbies
12160 Hamlin Street
North Hollywood, CA   91606
No phone number listed.
Write to receive a catalog of their
models.

Western Associated Modelers (WAM)
6073 Sunrise Drive
Lower Lake, CA   95457
(707) 994-6643
For those interested in constructing
model planes, boats, and cars, WAM establishes safety standards and hosts
novice, junior, and senior tournaments.

MUSIC

SEE ALSO

the MAIL ORDER CATALOGS section of Chapter 12 under Audio- and Videotapes.

American Guild of Music (AGM)
5354 Washington Street
Downers Grove, IL   60515
(312) 968-0173
Primarily for those who play stringed
instruments such as the guitar and the
mandolin, the Guild runs competitions,
workshops, exhibits, and an annual
convention. It publishes handbooks for
students and the quarterly *AGM Associ-
ate News.*

Americas Boychoir Federation &
    International Federation of Children's
    Choirs
Shallway Foundation
120 S. 3rd Street
Connellsville, PA   15425
(412) 628-3939

Members of the boys choir are from
North, South, and Central America. The
International Federation has separate
boys and girls choirs and a mixed choir.

Association for Classical Music (AFCM)
130 W. 56th Street
New York, NY   10019
(212) 315-1248
AFCM encourages the appreciation of
classical music and runs a music literacy program for elementary-school children.

Black Music Association (BMA)
307 S. Broad Street
Philadelphia, PA   19107
(215) 732-2460

Working through schools and universities, BMA offers information on black music heritage and how to increase the presence of blacks in music both as performers and as business participants. It publishes *Innervisions* on a monthly basis and runs an annual conference.

Detroit Jazz Center (DJC)
2628 Webb
Detroit, MI   48206
(313) 867-4141
DJC was established as a forum for the exchange of information on jazz and for bringing together all those interested in jazz. It includes everything from business management consulting to arranging concert programs. DJC publishes the monthly newsletter *World Stage* and the annual *Detroit Jazz Center Calendar.*

Drum Corps, International
P.O. Box 548
Lombard, IL   60148
(312) 495-9866
Formed to perpetuate artistic standards in high school and community drum and bugle corps for the young, the Corps makes referrals and hosts competitions.

Fretted Instrument Guild of America
    (FIGA)
2344 S. Oakley Avenue
Chicago, IL   60608
(312) 376-1143

For both the professional and hobbyist of guitars and banjos, FIGA runs workshops, concerts, and exhibits. In addition, it has a collection of musical arrangements, some no longer published. There's an annual convention and several publications.

Guitar Foundation of America (GFA)
P.O. Box 1090A
Garden Grove, CA   92642
No phone number listed.
Membership is for those interested in classical guitar. GFA keeps a library of music and books, runs meetings, and publishes the quarterly newsletter *Soundboard,* the annual *Facsimile Series,* and other periodicals.

International Clarinet Society (ICS)
c/o Dr. David Pino
Department of Music
Southwest Texas State University
San Marcos, TX   78666
(515) 245-2651
To promote fellowship among clarinet players, teachers, and manufacturers throughout the world, ICS keeps a library and archives, sponsors an annual convention, and publishes the quarterly *The Clarinet.*

International Country & Western Music
    Association (ICWMA)
102 E. Exchange Avenue, Suite 302
Fort Worth, TX   76106

ICWMA makes referrals, sponsors an international exchange program, and presents annual awards. There is a quarterly newsletter.

International Rhythm & Blues Association (IRBA)
11616 S. Lafayette Avenue
Chicago, IL   60628
(312) 264-2166
IRBA collects rhythm and blues history and provides scholarships for music students who intend to have a career in rhythm and blues.

International Rock 'n' Roll Music Association (IRMA)
P.O. Box 50111
Nashville, TN   37205
(615) 297-9072
IRMA offers information to all, especially those involved in rock and roll from performers to record companies. It keeps a library of pertinent materials and publishes the annual *Communiqué.*

International Trombone Association (ITA)
c/o Vern Kagarice
School of Music
North Texas State University
Denton, TX   76203
(817) 565-3720
The ITA is for all enthusiasts of the trombone from students to manufacturers. The Association maintains a library

and archives, holds workshops, runs contests, and presents awards.

International Trumpet Guild (ITG)
School of Music
Western Michigan University
Kalamazoo, MI   49008
(616) 387-4700
This network of trumpet players hosts an annual meeting and publishes the quarterly *Journal,* and the biennial *Directory.*

Maple Leaf Club (MLC)
5560 W. 62nd Street
Los Angeles, CA   90056
For lovers of ragtime, MLC offers concerts and the bimonthly publication *Rag Times.*

National Flute Association (NFA)
805 Laguna
Denton, TX   76201
(817) 387-9472
Membership is open to anyone interested in the flute, from the amateur to the professional. NFA offers competitions, conventions, and publications including *The Flutist.*

National Traditional Country Music Association (NTCMA)
P.O. Box 438
Walnut, IA   51577
(712) 366-1136

To preserve traditional bluegrass, folk, and country music, NTCMA sponsors an annual contest and festival, offers children's programs, holds seminars and jam sessions, and publishes *Tradition Magazine* six times a year.

New Orleans Jazz Club (NOJC)
828 Royal Street, Suite 265
New Orleans, LA   70116
(504) 455-6847
To promote Dixieland/New Orleans style jazz, NOJC holds jam sessions, concerts, a radio show, lectures, and educational programs. It publishes *Second Line* on a quarterly basis and holds an annual convention.

Society for Strings (SS)
170 W. 73rd Street, Apt. 10A
New York, NY   10023
(212) 877-8378
Each summer for six weeks, SS runs the Meadowmount School of Music for ages twelve to twenty-five to better the fine art of playing string instruments such as the viola and violin.

Violin Society of America (VSA)
85-07 Abindgon Road
Kew Gardens, NY   11415
(718) 849-1373
Membership is for all those, from students to restorers, in some way affiliated with the world of the violin. There is a biennial competition and a scholar-ship offered to students interested in the arts of violin-making and restoration, and an annual convention. The Society's journal is published two to four times a year.

World Folk Music Association (WFMA)
5428 MacArthur Boulevard, N.W.,
    Suite 204
Washington, DC   20016
(202) 362-2225
WFMA serves as an exchange for information on folk music. It sponsors concerts and seminars and publishes the newsletter *Folk News*.

PEN PALS

Friends Around the World (FAW)
P.O. Box 10266
Merrillville, IN   46411-0266
(219) 884-9327
For anyone interested in an international pen pal, FAW matches correspondents on the basis of general interests, age, and sex.

Gifted Children's Pen Pals International
c/o Dr. Debby Sue van de Vender
166 E. 61st Street
New York, NY   10021
(212) 355-2469
This service is for gifted children ranging in age from four to eighteen. The child must be certified as gifted or entered in a gifted program.

International Pen Friends (IPF)
P.O. Box 290065
Brooklyn, NY 11229
(718) 769-1785
IPF offers programs for youth organizations and schools. Pen pals are matched by common interests, age, and gender and can correspond in English, French, German, Portuguese, or Spanish. Cassette-tape exchanges are available for the blind and handicapped.

League of Friendship
P.O. Box 509
Mt. Vernon, OH 43050
(614) 392-3166
Through its foreign pen pal program, the League fosters international understanding and friendship. It supplies matched correspondents for youth ages twelve through twenty-five.

Science Fiction Pen Pal Club
P.O. Box 2522
Renton, WA 98056
No phone number listed.
This club matches correspondents having an interest in science fiction.

Student Letter Exchange
215 5th Avenue, S.E.
Waseca, MN 56093
(507) 835-3691
Facilitates correspondence for youth ages ten to nineteen within the United States and fifty foreign countries.

World Pen Pals (WPP)
1694 Como Avenue
St. Paul, MN 55108
(612) 647-0191
Through its pen pal program, WPP serves nearly fifty thousand students between the ages of twelve and twenty living in the United States and in one hundred fifty other countries.

PHOTOGRAPHY

Apidea
Associated Photographers International
22231 Mulholland Highway, No. 119
P.O. Box 4055
Woodland Hills, CA 91365
(818) 888-9270
This group's monthly newsletter helps the freelance photographer find clients, has articles on technique, and lists contests.

American Society of Photographers
    (ASP)
P.O. Box 52900
Tulsa, OK 74152
(918) 743-2122
The monthly newsletter features instructional articles on photography.

Competitive Camera
363 7th Avenue
New York, NY 10001
No phone number listed.
A free catalog lists discounted photographic equipment.

47th Street Photo, Inc.
38 E. 19th Street
New York, NY   10003
(212) 260-4415
Call or write for a free catalog of photographic equipment at reasonable prices.

Photographic Society of America (PSA)
3000 United Founders Boulevard,
    Suite 103
Oklahoma City, OK   73112
(405) 843-1437

The *PSA Journal* features articles with practical information for the amateur photographer.

Pictorial Photographers of America
299 W. 12th Street
New York, NY   10014
(212) 242-1117
The monthly newsletter *Light and Shade* focuses on improving technique and is for both the amateur and the professional.

ROCK COLLECTING

SEE ALSO

Learning Things, Inc. in the MAIL ORDER CATALOGS section of Chapter 12 under Science and Nature.

American Federation of Mineralogical
    Societies (AFMS)
920 S.W. 70th Street
Oklahoma City, OK   73193
(405) 631-2674
Membership is for gem hobbyists and novice stone-cutters. AFMS focuses on the earth sciences, in particular geology and mineralogy. Its publication, *American Federation Newsletter,* comes out nine times a year, and the group holds an annual convention.

Gem & Mineral Display Co.
P.O. Box 22145
Phoenix, AZ   85028
No phone number listed.
This company sells stone-cutting equipment.

Gemological Institute of America
1660 Stewart Street
Santa Monica, CA   90404
(213) 829-2991
The quarterly publication *Gems and Gemology* contains articles on gem identification, location, and more.

International Sand Collectors Society
43 Highview Avenue
Old Greenwich, CT   06870
(203) 637-2801
This Society is for those who collect sand, soil, or minerals. It has a museum with more than four hundred samples, and encourages collection and classification.

Mineralogical Society of America (MSA)
1625 I Street, N.W., Suite 414
Washington, DC   20006
(202) 775-4344
For professionals, students, and hobbyists interested in mineralogy, the MSA offers membership, publishes the bimonthly *American Mineralogist,* the quarterlies *Lattice* and *Mineralogical Abstracts,* and holds an annual convention.

Star Diamond Industries
17022 Montanero Avenue
Carson, CA   90746
(213) 325-9696
Call or write for a catalog and a free copy of *Gem-Making as a Hobby.*

The Treasure Chest
Route 40, Box 54
Havre De Grace, MD   21078
(301) 939-4468
The Treasure Chest is a seller of supplies for rock hunting.

SAND CASTLES

International Association of Sand Castle
  Builders
172 N. Pershing Avenue
Akron, OH   44313
(216) 864-6353
For sand castle "engineers," the Association offers advice, support, and sponsors competitions. It also informs the public about dangers to beaches.

SHELL COLLECTING

SEE ALSO

Dover Scientific Co. in the MAIL ORDER CATALOGS section of Chapter 12 under Science and Nature.

American Malacological Union (AMU)
3706 Rice Boulevard
Houston, TX 77005
(713) 668-8252
AMU is for anyone intrigued by mollusks, from the weekend hobbyist to the scientist and curator. There's an annual symposium, the semiannual publication *American Malacological Bulletin,* a newsletter, and an annual publication of AMU's member list.

Benjane Arts
P.O. Box 298
West Hempstead, NY 11552
(516) 483-1330
The $2 charge for the *Sea Shell Catalog,* which pictures some of the shellart for sale, is deductible from your order.

Collector's Cabinet
153 E. 57th Street
New York, NY 10022
(212) 355-2033
For $.50 you'll receive their *Sea Shell Catalog* price list of nearly two thousand species of shell and other marine life.

Conchologists of America (CA)
2644 Kings Highway
Louisville, KY 40205
(502) 458-5719
For both professional and amateur mollusk collectors, CA offers exhibits, field trips, and lectures as well as a quarterly bulletin and annual convention.

Florida Supply House
P.O. Box 847
Bradenton, FL 33506
No phone number listed.
Write for the $1 catalog of shells and shell art.

SPORTS CARD COLLECTING

SEE ALSO

Hobby Surplus Sales in the Models section of this chapter.

Beckett Publications
4887 Alpha Road, Suite 200
Dallas, TX   75244
(214) 991-6657
Call or write for a free copy of the
Beckett Sports Products Catalog.

Donruss Co.
Box 2038
Memphis, TN   38101
(901) 775-2960
Donruss is a maker of baseball cards.

Fleer Corp.
10th and Somerville
Philadelphia, PA   19141
(215) 455-2000
Fleer is a maker of baseball cards.

**Larry Fritsch Baseball Card Collection
   Museum**
10 Chestnut Street
Cooperstown, NY   13326
(607) 547-2174

The Museum houses more than twenty
thousand cards.

Major League Marketing
25 Ford Road
Westport, CT   06880
No phone number listed.
Major League makes Score and Sport-
flic cards.

Metropolitan Museum of Art
Print Study Department
Fifth Avenue and 82nd Street
New York, NY   10028
(212) 535-7710
The Metropolitan's Jefferson Burdick
Collection of baseball cards is one of
the largest in the world.

Topps Chewing Gum Co.
254 36th Street
Brooklyn, NY   11232
(718) 768-8900
Topps makes baseball cards.

STAMP COLLECTING

SEE ALSO

Hobby Surplus Sales under the Models listings of this chapter.

American First Day Cover Society (AFDCS)
1611 Corral Drive
Houston, TX   77090
(713) 444-8327
For those collectors particularly interested in American and foreign first-day covers, AFDCS runs clinics and an annual meeting, oversees research, and publishes *First Days* eight times each year.

American Philatelic Society (APS)
P.O. Box 8000
100 Oakwood Avenue
State College, PA   16803
(814) 237-3803
Membership in APS is for those collectors seeking information on such items as revenue stamps, first-day covers, and postal history. It maintains a large library, runs seminars, and provides a forum for buying and selling stamps. APS publishes *Youth Activities Booklet*, handbooks, monographs, and the monthly *American Philatelist*.

American Topical Association (ATA)
P.O. Box 630
Johnstown, PA   15907
(814) 539-6301
Particularly for collectors seeking stamps by their theme, the ATA has a slide and lecture service, a sales exchange, and holds an annual meeting. It publishes *Topical Time* bimonthly plus several informational handbooks.

Benjamin Franklin Junior Stamp Club
U.S. Postal Service
475 L'Enfant Plaza, Room 5630
Washington, DC   20260
(202) 268-2352
To encourage an interest in stamp collecting, the Postal Service distributes information on stamps and their subjects to younger people. There's a monthly newsletter.

Collectors Club
22 E. 35th Street
New York, NY   10016
(212) 683-0559

The Collectors Club runs competitions, holds lectures, and maintains a library. The *Collectors Club Philatelist* is published six times yearly.

Errors, Freaks & Oddities Collector's Club
1903 Village Road W.
Norwood, MA   02062
(617) 769-6531
For collectors intrigued by errors in production and cancellations, this club is dedicated to finding the causes of errors. It holds auctions occasionally, has an annual meeting, and publishes *EFO Collector* on a monthly basis.

Gross Stamp Co.
860 Broadway
New York, NY   10003
(212) 254-6100
Gross publishes albums, reference texts, and handbooks for the collector.

H. E. Harris & Co., Inc.
P.O. Box 7087
Portsmouth, NH   03801
(603) 433-0400
(800) 822-5556 (for orders)
A great resource for stamp collectors, this venerable company sells American and foreign stamps as well as albums and refill pages. The $1 you pay for the catalog gives you a $5 discount from your first purchase.

Junior Philatelists of America
P.O. Box 701010
San Antonio, TX   78270-1010
(512) 650-0507
Membership in this group is offered to those under age twenty-two to encourage stamp collecting. The organization provides research and a pen pal service. Its monthly publication is the *Philatelic Observer*.

Minkus Publications
41 W. 25th Street
New York, NY   10010
(212) 741-1334
Minkus publishes a journal as well as albums and catalogs.

Philatelic Catalog
U.S. Postal Service
Philatelic Sales Division
Washington, DC   20265-9997
(202) 268-2314
This is a free catalog of stamp collecting materials provided by the U.S. Postal Service. It is issued bimonthly.

Philatelic Foundation
21 E. 40th Street
New York, NY   10016
(212) 889-6483
The Foundation presents slide shows on philately to schools and youth organizations. Members of the Foundation provide authentication and evaluation services.

Scott Publishing Co.
P.O. Box 828
Sidney, OH   45635
No phone number listed.
Scott's free catalog contains the whole gamut of a stamp collector's needs.

U.S. Stamp Information Service
Office of Stamps, Box 764
Washington, DC   20044
(202) 268-2000
This office provides general information on stamp collecting.

THEATER AND FILM

American Alliance for Theatre &
  Education
Theatre Arts Department
Virginia Tech
Blacksburg, VA
(703) 231-7624
This organization is composed of teachers, directors, recreation workers, and parents interested in children's theater. Publishes a quarterly called *Youth Theatre Journal,* as well as educational and curriculum aids for using theater in education.

Clowns of America, Inc.
P.O. Box 570
Lake Jackson, TX   77566-0570
(409) 297-6699
Comprising over one hundred local chapters, Clowns of America is for anyone who wishes to study the art of clowning. The organization's publication, *The New Calliope,* comes out bimonthly.

International Thespian Society
3368 Central Parkway
Cincinnati, OH   45225
(513) 559-1996
For those junior and senior high school students already involved in drama clubs, the Society provides referrals, sponsors festivals, and publishes the quarterly *Dramatics.*

Rainbow Company Children's Theatre
821 Las Vegas Boulevard N.
Las Vegas, NV   89101
(702) 386-6553
Rainbow produces quality theater for a children's audience, trains a core group of young boys and girls and adolescents in theater arts at a professional level, and offers classes in creative dramatics for children ages four to seventeen and for adults.

School Projectionist Club of America
P.O. Box 707
State College, PA   16804
(814) 237-4376
The Club supplies study guides for junior high, high school, and college students interested in use and repair of

audiovisual and television equipment. To receive further information, send a self-addressed, stamped, legal-size envelope.

Young Actors Guild

125 S. 4th Street
Connellsville, PA   15425
(412) 628-3939

For children ages two to sixteen who are interested in the performing arts, the Guild offers training in acting, singing, and dancing.

Young Audiences, Inc.

115 E. 92nd Street
New York, NY   10128
(212) 831-8110

Young Audiences, Inc. provides professional performances of music, dance, and theater in schools. The group offers a variety of publications about performing before young audiences.

TREASURE HUNTING

Circle of Companions (COC)

1 Examino Building
Segundo, CO   81070
No phone number listed.

COC provides a forum for swapping information and experiences of treasure hunting, prospecting, and mining. It maintains a library, store, museum, and holds an annual meeting. COC also publishes the monthly *Adventure Bulletin*, the quarterly *Examino Express*, plus papers, catalogs, and circulars.

Prospectors & Treasure Hunters Guild

23520 Highway 12
Segundo, CO   81070
No phone number listed.

For both the amateur and the professional treasure hunter, the Guild maintains a reference library, answers technical questions, and maps trails. It publishes a monthly newsletter, a number of journals, manuals, bulletins, and handbooks.

Relco Industries

P.O. Box 920839
Houston, TX   77292-0839
(713) 682-2728

Relco offers a free catalog of metal detectors for those seeking lost and hidden treasure.

Treasure Book Headquarters

P.O. Box 328
Conroe, TX   77301
No phone number listed.
Write for a free catalog of Treasure Book's collection.

Treasure Hunter Research and Information Center (THRIC)

P.O. Box 314
Gibson, LA   70356
No phone number listed.

THRIC has a library and a book exchange for aficionados of metal detecting, exploring, and prospecting. In addition, it publishes the quarterly *Treasure Hunting Research Bulletin* and other books on treasure hunting.

PETS AND ANIMALS

A good source of information about pets is a local zoo or a major zoo in a large city. Most zoos employ experts who field questions from the public. Pet store owners, though not necessarily pet experts, usually try to answer their customers' questions. Local humane societies are also helpful. Look in your local telephone yellow pages under Animal and Pet.

This chapter has sections on Birds, Cats, Dogs, Fish and Aquariums, Horses, Marine Animals, Rabbits, Turtles, Lost Pets, Pet Behavior Problems, Pet Products, Boarding and Transportation, and Wildlife Preservation and Humane Societies.

BIRDS

American Birding Association (ABA)
P.O. Box 470
Sonoita, AZ   85637
(800) 634-7736
The ABA will answer questions and make referrals on a wide range of topics.

American Federation of Aviculture (AFA)
3118 W. Thomas Road, Suite 713
Phoenix, AZ   85017
(602) 484-0931
Offers information on the raising and care of birds as a way of conserving bird life. It publishes *Watchbird* every two months.

American Ornithologists' Union (AOU)
National Museum of Natural History
Smithsonian Institution
Washington, DC   20560
(602) 621-1026
The Union answers questions, makes referrals, and distributes the *Handbook of North American Birds,* among other publications.

Audubon Workshop
1501 Paddock Drive
Northbrook, IL   60062
(312) 729-6660
Offers a free color catalog of bird seed, bird feeders, and birdhouses.

Birding Book Society
Pathway Book Clubs
50 Northwestern Drive, P.O. Box 1999
Salem, NH   03079
(603) 898-1200
The Society sells field guides and books on birding, and offers a free catalog.

Bird 'n Hand
40 Pearl Street
Framingham, MA   01701
(508) 879-1552
This source offers a free catalog of birdseed and feeders, including tube and platform feeders and a clear plastic model for the window.

COM-U.S.A.
P.O. Box 122
Elizabethtown, NJ   07207
(201) 353-0669
This group runs monthly information seminars on identifying, classifying, and breeding cage birds. It publishes a monthly newsletter.

Duncraft
33 Fisherbill Road
Penacook, NH   03303
(603) 224-0200
This firm will send a free catalog of birdhouses, feeders, and food.

Hyde Bird Feeder Co.
56 Felton Street, P.O. Box 168
Waltham, MA   02254
(617) 893-6780

A solid stock of bird-watching products including feeders and books are offered in Hyde's free color catalog.

National Audubon Society
950 3rd Avenue
New York, NY   10022
(212) 832-3200 (general information)
(212) 832-6523 (rare bird alert hotline)
The Society's members have a special interest in wildlife and conservation issues. Their publications include *Audubon Adventures,* a magazine for children.

National Wildlife Federation
1412 16th Street, N.W.
Washington, DC   20036
(202) 637-3700
The Federation has four million members who support conservation efforts, and offers information and referrals by phone to parents whose children are interested in birding.

CATS

American Cat Fanciers Association (ACFA)
P.O. Box 203
Point Lookout, MO   65726
(417) 334-5430
For persons interested in raising, breeding, and showing purebred cats, the Association maintains a registry and

licenses cat shows. It publishes a
newsletter and a number of books as
well as *Show and Registration Rules.*

Cat Care Society
5985 W. 11th Avenue
Lakewood, CO   80214
(303) 239-9690
A local cat shelter that is a good source
of information, the Society sells books,
posters, and other cat-related items.

Cornell Feline Health Center
College of Veterinary Medicine
Cornell University
Ithaca, NY   14853
(607) 253-3414
The Center educates veterinarians and
cat owners about the diseases of cats. It
publishes pamphlets.

Friends of Animals, Inc. (FOA)
11 W. 60th Street
New York, NY   10023
(201) 922-2600
(800) 631-2212
FOA offers free information on low-cost
spay/neuter programs nationwide.

Gebhardt-Heriot Foundation for All
   Cats (GHFC)
33 Bruce Court
Cedar Grove, NJ   07009
(201) 857-9236

Dedicated to the care of the cat, GHFC
runs cat-care schools and seminars on
health and nutrition, helps fund research, supports shelters, and works to
enforce humane standards.

DOGS

American Kennel Club (AKC)
51 Madison Avenue
New York, NY   10010
(212) 696-8200
The Club runs a seventeen-thousand-
volume library, an information service,
and a stud registry of nearly thirty-five
million dogs. It hosts competitions and
publishes *The Complete Dog Book.*

Association of Obedience Clubs &
   Judges (AOCJ)
328 Parkside Drive
Suffern, NY   10901
(914) 357-1812
Though primarily for dog trainers and
judges, the Association will provide information on obedience training and
make referrals.

Friends of Animals, Inc. (FOA)
11 W. 60th Street
New York, NY   10023
(201) 247-8077
(800) 631-2212
FOA offers free information on low-cost
spay/neuter programs nationwide.

Ladies Kennel Association of America
465 Edgewood Avenue
St. James, NY 11780
No phone number listed.
The Association promotes purebred breeding, and offers limited advice and referrals.

National Association of Dog Obedience Instructors
2286 E. Steel Road
St. Johns, MI 48879
(517) 224-8683
Though primarily for dog trainers, the Association will make referrals and offer advice on a limited basis.

Owner Handler Association of America (OHA)
R.D. 3, Box 89
Stagecoach Road
Lehighton, PA 18235
(215) 377-0566
OHA fosters an interest in dog handling for purebreds. It hosts seminars, publishes a bimonthly newsletter, and its local chapters offer obedience and handling courses.

United Kennel Club
100 E. Kilgore Road
Kalamazoo, MI 49001-5598
(616) 343-9020
Maintains a library plus a registry of purebred dogs. It sponsors shows and gives awards.

FISH AND AQUARIUMS

Aquarium Club of America
P.O. Box 157
Belprie, OH 45714
(614) 423-9509
Mail-order discount fish and aquarium supplies are offered through this club.

Bio-Marine Supply Co.
Box 285
Venice, CA 90291
No phone number listed.
This Company will provide marine specimens. Write for its catalog.

Goldfish Society of America
P.O. Box 1367
South Gate, CA 90280
(213) 633-6016
Provides information and referrals to anyone interested in goldfish. It publishes the *Goldfish Report* each month.

National Aquarium Society (NAS)
Department of Commerce Building
Room B-037
Washington, DC 20230
(202) 377-2826
NAS runs the National Aquarium, where it conducts educational programs and provides information to the public. Its two publications are the monthly *Tank Talk* and the quarterly *Fish Lines*.

HORSES

SEE ALSO

the Horsemanship and Rodeo listings under the SPORTS section of this chapter.

☎ ☎

American Horse Protection Assn., Inc. (AHPA)
1038 31st Street, N.W.
Washington, DC   20007
(202) 965-0500
AHPA works to protect horses living in the wild, race horses, and others that may be neglected. It publishes a quarterly newsletter.

American Mustang & Burro Association
P.O. Box 216
Liberty Hill, TX   78642-0216
(512) 778-6041
This groups publishes books and posters on protecting America's wild horses.

MARINE ANIMALS

SEE ALSO

the Wildlife Preservation and Humane Societies listings of this chapter.

☎ ☎

Warning: Some of the materials available from the organizations below may have sickening photographs of cruel treatment of marine animals. These publications are *not* designed for children, though may be suitable for teenagers.

Cousteau Society
930 W. 21st Street
Norfolk, VA   23517
(804) 627-1144

Founded by world-famous Jacques Cousteau, the Society sells a calendar, books, a model kit of its boat *Calypso,* and much more.

Friends of the Sea Otter
P.O. Box 221220
Carmel, CA   93922
(408) 625-3290
This group works to save the environment of otters off the coast of California. They sell books and gift items.

Greenpeace USA, Inc.
1611 Connecticut Avenue, N.W.
Washington, DC   20009
(202) 462-1177
This daring and effective organization
works to end the commercial hunting
of whales, sea lions, and other species.
Brochures describing the group's activities are offered.

Seal Rescue Fund
Whale Protection Fund
Center for Environmental Education
624 9th Street, N.W.
Washington, DC   20001
(202) 373-3600
The Center makes available books,
posters, and an information packet on
how to protect seals, and also has materials on whale protection.

Whale Center
3929 Piedmont Avenue
Oakland, CA   94611
(415) 654-6621
A research, conservation, and educational group, the Whale Center sells
books, records, posters, and gifts.

RABBITS

Humans Against Rabbit Exploitation
  (H.A.R.E.)
P.O. Box 1553
Williamsport, PA   17703
(717) 322-3252
Works to prevent the commercial ex-
ploitation of rabbits.

TURTLES

National Turtle & Tortoise Society, Inc.
P.O. Box 2955
Glendale, Arizona 85311-2955
(602) 997-4551
Provides information to hobbyists on
the care and conservation of turtles.

LOST PETS

If your pet is lost, you should look first in your local yellow pages under Animal Shelters
to identify area groups that might recover the animal and offer advice. Placing signs with
a photograph of the animal around the neighborhood can help greatly, especially if you

do it quickly. Some people have their animals tattooed with a local or national registry service. This two-minute procedure does not generally require anesthesia. Unlike collars and tags which can be lost, the tattoo is permanent. If your pet is found, anyone calling the registry will be able to locate you.

The following services will register pets.

Aid-a-Pet
Pet Find, Inc.
P.O. Box 100
Gresham, OR   97030
(800) 243-2738
This firm takes down information on any lost pet that is reported to it, whether the animal is wearing Pet Find's tag or not.

National Dog Registry
P.O. Box 116
Woodstock, NY   12498
(914) 679-2355
This registry of tattooed dogs provides a twenty-four-hour service that reports findings of lost animals to their owners.

Petfinders, Inc.
609 Columbus Avenue
New York, NY   10024-1408
(212) 362-4557
(800) 223-4747
This is a nonprofit organization that provides a tag for your pet. If the animal is injured, Petfinders can act on your behalf and guarantee payment to a veterinarian. If your pet is lost, counsel will be given to you until the animal is found.

PET BEHAVIOR PROBLEMS

Animal Behavior Hotline
(415) 474-4202
This free service of the San Francisco SPCA is staffed by trained animal behaviorists. They can help with problems such as soiling of the house, barking, and aggressive behavior. Sometimes literature about your pet's problem will also be sent.

Tree House Animal Foundation, Inc.
1212 W. Carmen Avenue
Chicago, IL   60640
(312) 784-5488 (pet-care hotline,
    12:00 A.M.–5:00 P.M.)
This group will answer any questions about pet problems over the phone. Animal behavior experts and veterinarians are consulted if needed. The Foundation also has a free catalog of books, pet supplies, and gift items.

PET PRODUCTS

**American Pet Products Manufacturers
    Association**
60 E. 42nd Street
New York, NY   10165
(212) 867-2290

Though membership is for manufacturers, the Association runs a program to promote an interest in pet care. It will make referrals and give advice over the phone.

Gaines Pet Care Booklets
P.O. Box 877
Young America, MN   55399
(312) 222-8792
The dog or cat owner can write or call for a free list of posters and informational booklets.

**Massachusetts Society for the
  Prevention of Cruelty to Animals**
350 S. Huntington Avenue
Boston, MA   02130
(617) 522-7400

BOARDING AND TRANSPORTATION

Send a self-addressed, stamped, #10 envelope to receive a catalog listing instructional aids, posters, and booklets on the care of pets.

Pedigrees, The Pet Catalog
15 Turner Drive, P.O. Box 110
Spencerport, NY   14559-0110
(716) 352-1232
This free catalog lists a whole range of gifts and products for pet owners. There are pet toys and owner's T-shirts, cages and bird treats, leashes, dog booties, beds, and pet carriers.

SEE ALSO

the Dogs listings in this chapter.

American Boarding Kennels Association
455 Galley Road, Room 400A
Colorado Springs, CO   80915
(719) 591-1113
The Association will make referrals and provide information about kennels.

**Independent Pet & Animal
  Transportation Association (IPATA)**
P.O. Box 129
Arvada, CO   80001
No phone number listed.
IPATA assists pet owners in relocating their animals, providing help with documentation, health certification, and flight reservations.

WILDLIFE PRESERVATION AND
HUMANE SOCIETIES

SEE ALSO

the Marine Animals listings in this chapter.

Warning: Some of the materials available from these organizations may have sickening photographs of cruel treatment of animals. These publications are *not* designed for children, though may be suitable for teenagers.

American Anti-Vivisection League
  Society
Suite 204, Noble Plaza
801 Old York Road
Jenkintown, PA   19046-1685
(215) 887-0816
This group educates the public about the cruel and unnecessary use of animals in medical experiments. Write or call for the Society's list of pamphlets, buttons, bumper stickers, T-shirts, and books.

American Humane Association (AHA)
9725 E. Hampden Avenue
Denver, CO   80231
(303) 695-0811
(800) 842-4637
In operation since 1877, the AHA works to prevent cruelty, abuse, and neglect of children and animals. Its free publications catalog describes pamphlets, posters, and other materials.

American Humane Education Society
350 S. Huntington Avenue
Boston, MA   02130
(617) 522-7400
This group works to prevent cruelty to animals. A publications list is available.

American Society for the Prevention of
  Cruelty to Animals (ASPCA)
441 E. 92nd Street
New York, NY   10128
(212) 876-7700
The ASPCA has been sheltering and protecting animals since 1866. Ask for the Society's list of books, pet-care information sheets, buttons, posters, and other items.

American Wildlife Foundation (AWF)
1717 Massachusetts Avenue, N.W.
Washington, DC   20036
(202) 265-8393

AWF helps the governments of African countries fight poaching and killing of wild animals. It makes available posters and the quarterly publication *Wildlife News*.

Elsa Clubs of America
516 S. Lincoln Street, Room 1
Santa Maria, CA   93454
(805) 928-3775
Founded by Joy Adamson, author of books about Elsa the Lion, this group provides educational materials to children concerning wild animals.

International Society for Animal Rights, Inc. (ISAR)
421 S. State Street
Clarks Summit, PA   18411
(717) 586-2200
ISAR makes available educational materials seeking to abolish animal experimentation.

National Wildlife Federation (NWF)
1412 16th Street, N.W.
Washington, DC   20036
(202) 637-3700
NWF works to protect wildlife through legislation and education. Among its many publications are two magazines for children: *Backyard* (preschoolers three to five) and *Ranger Rick* (ages six to twelve).

Wildlife Preservation Trust Intl.
34th Street and Girard Avenue
Philadelphia, PA   19104
(215) 222-3636
This organization works to protect endangered species around the world. It has a low membership fee for anyone under sixteen years of age. Published are brochures, posters, and data sheets on endangered species.

CHILDREN'S CLUBS

Here you will find a variety of organizations whose membership are children. They are organized into these sections: General Clubs; Political and Peace Organizations; Religious Organizations; and Service and Vounteer Organizations.

GENERAL CLUBS

Many of these groups have local chapters throughout the United States. Before calling the national headquarters listed below, try looking in your local telephone directory.

SEE ALSO

the HERITAGE section of this chapter for children's organizations based on nationality or ethnic background.

The Student Career Education Groups listings under JOBS later in this chapter lists career-oriented clubs for older teenagers.

Boys Clubs of America
771 1st Avenue
New York, NY   10017
(212) 351-5900
For both boys and girls ranging in age from seven to eighteen, Boys Clubs offers organized recreational, athletic, and social activities.

Boy Scouts of America
1325 Walnut Hill Lane
Irving, TX   75015-2079
(214) 580-2000
The Boy Scouts, organized into age categories, offers boys and young men organized outdoor activities, develops character, and teaches responsible citizenship.

Camp Fire, Inc.
4601 Madison Avenue
Kansas City, MO   64112-1278
(816) 756-1950
Camp Fire programs teach both girls and boys camping skills, responsible citizenship, and self-reliance.

4-H Youth Development
U.S. Department of Agriculture
Washington, DC   20250
(202) 447-5853
4-H teaches rural and urban children ages nine to nineteen agricultural, technological, and interpersonal skills. It also provides camping and international exchange programs.

Girls Clubs of America
30 E. 33rd Street
New York, NY   10016
(212) 689-3700
Girls Clubs offers girls and young women athletic activities and health and education programs, including AIDS awareness and substance-abuse prevention.

Girl Scouts of the U.S.A.
830 3rd Avenue
New York, NY   10022
(212) 940-7500
Through its camping, international, and other programs, the Girl Scouts helps

girls ages five to seventeen to develop individually and as citizens. Groups are arranged by age.

Jack & Jill of America, Inc.
1065 Gordon, S.W.
Atlanta, GA   30310
(404) 753-8471
For mothers and their children, this group helps develop community social, recreational, and cultural programs.

National Beta Club
151 W. Lee Street, P.O. Box 730
Spartanburg, SC   29304
(803) 583-4553
For children in the fifth through twelfth grades who have outstanding leadership and academic abilities.

National Resource Center
441 W. Michigan Street
Indianapolis, IN   46202
(317) 634-7546
Affiliated with the Girls Clubs of America, the Center functions as an information clearinghouse and offers research, training, and promotional services.

YMCA of the United States
101 N. Wacker Drive
Chicago, IL   60606
(312) 977-0031
(800) USA-YMCA (872-9622)
Local Y's offer a variety of athletic programs, summer camp, and child-care facilities. There are also a number of national programs organized by age.

YWCA of the United States
726 Broadway
New York, NY   10003
(212) 614-2700
Local Y's offer young women of all backgrounds programs to increase self-awareness, health, and fitness in an effort to enhance their sense of worth.

POLITICAL AND PEACE ORGANIZATIONS

American Student Council Association
National Association of Elementary
  School Principles
1516 Duke Street
Alexandria, VA   22314-3483
(703) 684-3345
The Association helps elementary and middle schools set up student councils in which the children elect their own leaders. It publishes handbooks for students and teachers on how to organize a student council.

Amnesty International
Children's Special Edition/Urgent
  Action
P.O. Box 1270
Nederland, CO   80466
(303) 440-0913
Children in the fourth through eighth grades write letters to political leaders asking for action.

Children's Campaign for Nuclear
  Disarmament
14 Everit Street
New Haven, CT   06511
(203) 226-3694
Run by children under the age of eighteen, the Campaign works to halt the
arms race.

Frontlash
815 16th Street, N.W.
Washington, DC   20006
(202) 783-3993
This support group of the AFL-CIO
teaches students of high school and
college age about union values, labor
history, and youth work issues.

Junior Statesmen of America
Junior Statesmen Foundation
650 Bair Island Road, Suite 201
Redwood City, CA   94063
(415) 366-2700
(800) 334-5353
Helps high-school-age children learn
about participation in the democratic
process and teaches leadership skills.

Mobilization for Survival
Youth Task Force
11 Garden Street
Cambridge, MA   02138
(617) 354-0008
For high school students interested in
feminism, an end to racism, military
intervention, and the nuclear arms
buildup.

National Association for the
  Advancement of Colored People
  (NAACP)
Youth & College Division
4805 Mt. Hope Drive
Baltimore, MD   21215-3297
(301) 358-8900 (ext. 9142)
The NAACP works to eradicate the presence of racism in this country. Its
youth councils teach young students
the realities of the political process.

National Teenage Republican
  Headquarters
P.O. Box 1896
Manassas, VA   22110
(703) 368-4214
Trains teenagers to be active in sup-
porting Republican values and election
efforts.

National Traditionalist Caucus
P.O. Box 971
G.P.O.
New York, NY   10116
(212) 685-4689
This Caucus is a conservative, anti-
Communist, patriot organization for
teenagers and college students.

Sparticus Youth League
P.O. Box 3118
Church Street Station
New York, NY   10960
(212) 732-7860
A revolutionary, pro-Socialist group for
children fifteen years old and up.

Students & Youth Against Racism
P.O. Box 1819
Madison Square Station
New York, NY 10159
(212) 741-0633
This national student group works to end racism, homophobia, and sexism.

World Federalist Association
P.O. Box 15250
Washington, DC 20003
(800) HATE-WAR (428-3927)
The Association endorses a strong, fair-minded United Nations as the means to world peace.

Young Democrats of America
c/o National Democratic Committee
430 S. Capitol Street, S.E.
Washington, DC 20003
(202) 863-8000
Promotes the interests of the Democratic Party among high school and college students.

Young Republican National Federation
310 1st Street, S.E.
Washington, DC 20003
(202) 662-1340
Promotes the interests of the Republican Party among high school and college students.

Youth Against War & Fascism
46 W. 21st Street
New York, NY 10010
(212) 355-0352

Works to oppose war, racism, and other forms of discrimination.

YMCA's of the United States
Youth & Government
101 N. Wacker Drive
Chicago, IL 60606
(312) 977-0031
(800) USA-YMCA (872-9622)
Through its model legislatures and conferences, this program exposes high school students to the democratic process.

RELIGIOUS ORGANIZATIONS

Catholic

Cadet Commanderies
Knights of St. John Supreme
   Commandery
6517 Charles Avenue
Parma, OH 44129
(216) 845-0570
Cadet is for Catholic boys and young men between the ages of eight and sixteen, to learn the three virtues of faith, hope, and charity through volunteer service. The Knights also run sports programs.

Columbian Squires
Knights of Columbus Supreme Council
1 Columbus Plaza
New Haven, CT 06507
(203) 772-2130

The Knights of Columbus try to instill leadership skills tempered by spiritual, physical, intellectual, and social development in boys and young men from twelve to eighteen.

Junior Auxiliary

Supreme Ladies' Auxiliary of the
    Knights of St. John
802 W. Franklin
Evansville, IN   47710
(812) 424-4443
For girls ranging in age from eight to sixteen, to develop involvement in Catholic volunteer services.

National Federation for Catholic Youth Ministry

3900-A Hairwood Road, N.E.
Washington, DC   20017
(202) 636-3825
Serves as an umbrella organization for diocesan youth groups and sponsors meetings of youth leaders.

Jewish

B'nai B'rith Youth Organization

1640 Rhode Island Avenue, N.W.
Washington, DC   20036
(202) 857-6633
Encourages leadership skills and offers educational, recreational, and social activities. Groups are organized by age and sex.

Hashomer Hatzair

150 5th Avenue
New York, NY   10011
(212) 242-0532
A Zionist organization for youth ranging in age from nine to twenty-three, the group encourages the life-style of the kibbutz and offers summer camping programs and educational trips to Israel.

Lubavitch Youth Organization

770 Eastern Parkway
Brooklyn, NY   11213
(718) 953-1000
For children over the age of twelve, the Organization's activities seek to revitalize a sense of Jewishness and of Jewish heritage.

National Conference of Synagogue Youth

Union of Orthodox Congregations
    of America
70 W. 36th Street
New York, NY   10018
(212) 244-2011
For youth ages thirteen to eighteen, the Conference offers recreational, social, and educational events encouraging a commitment to a life guided by the Torah. It runs camps, trips to Israel, and a number of programs for the disabled.

Young Judaea/Haschachar
50 W. 58th Street
New York, NY   10019
(212) 303-8263
Sponsored by local Hadassah groups,
Haschachar works to increase awareness of one's Jewishness and provide
education about community service and
about Israel. For youth from the fourth
to twelfth grades, summer camps and a
number of educational trips to Israel
are offered.

Protestant and Nondenominational

Awana Clubs International
1 E. Bode Road
Streamwood, IL   60107
(312) 213-2000
Awana teaches Christian living to nursery school through high-school-age
children both in the United States and
abroad.

Boys' & Girls' Brigades of America
P.O. Box 9863
Baltimore, MD   21284
(301) 391-4331
This group offers Bible training, athletics, and outdoor and social activities to
children ages six to eighteen years old.

**International Society of Christian
    Endeavor**
1221 E. Broad Street
P.O. Box 1110
Columbus, OH   43216
(614) 258-9545
The Society strongly encourages its
members (age six and up) to pursue a
devotional life dedicated to service and
Christian citizenship.

Lutheran Youth Fellowship
Lutheran Church Missouri Synod
1333 S. Kirkwood Road
St. Louis, MO   63122
(314) 965-9000
Its Bible study, religious, and social activities for junior high and high school
students encourage Christian fellowship.

**Presbyterian Church (U.S.A.) Youth
    Club**
100 Witherspoon Street
Louisville, KY   40202-1396
(502) 569-5497
This organization serves as an umbrella
for locally established youth groups. It
publishes a directory.

Salvation Army
799 Bloomfield Avenue
Verona, NJ   07044
(201) 239-0606
The Salvation Army runs many programs for girls and boys organized by
sex and age. It promotes Bible study,

leadership skills, and spiritual and social development.

United Calvinist Youth
P.O. Box 7259
1333 Alger Street, S.E.
Grand Rapids, MI   49510
(616) 241-5616
A number of programs, organized by age, are offered to impart the concept of service and the idea of Christian living. There are also outdoor activity programs.

Young Life
720 W. Monumental Street
P.O. Box 520
Colorado Springs, CO   80901
(719) 473-4262
Offers Bible study, summer camps, and leadership workshops for junior high and high school students in order to spread the gospel of Christ.

SERVICE AND VOLUNTEER ORGANIZATIONS

SEE ALSO

the VOLUNTEERING section of this chapter for additional organizations welcoming those who donate their time.

Big Brothers/Big Sisters of America
230 N. 13th Street
Philadelphia, PA   19108
(215) 567-7000
This program reaches out to school children (usually underprivileged in some way) through a program matching them with an older youth or adult. It offers counseling, referrals, family services, and a variety of other programs.

Interact
Rotary International
1560 Sherman Avenue
1 Rotary Center
Evanston, IL   60201
(312) 866-3294
Rotary clubs for fourteen to eighteen year-olds seek to instill leadership skills, develop a sense of social responsibility, and encourage personal growth. It has a program for disabled youth, and sponsors scout troops.

Junior Civitan International

P.O. Box 130744
Birmingham, AL   35213-0744
(205) 591-8910
The organization, for junior high and high school students, fosters leadership skills, involvement in the democratic process, academic achievement, and personal growth and responsibility.

Junior Optimist Octagon International

4494 Lindell Boulevard
St. Louis, MO   63108
(314) 371-6000
The junior divisions of Optimist International seek to instill leadership skills, self-awareness, involvement in the governmental process, and a sensitivity to the spiritual and cultural aspects of life.

Key Club International

3636 Woodview Trace
Indianapolis, IN   46268
(317) 875-8755
A branch of Kiwanis International for high-school-age students, Key Club encourages service to the community, leadership skills, and good citizenship.

Leo Club Program

300 22nd Street
Oakbrook, IL   60570
(312) 571-5466
A junior division of the Lions Club for youth ages fourteen to twenty-eight, Leo Clubs train youth in community involvement and leadership.

National Grange Junior

National Grange Youth & Young Adults
1616 H Street, N.W.
Washington, DC   20006
(206) 357-9331
With an emphasis on agriculture, the Grange's programs impart an awareness of the importance of service and cooperation to improve the community, build character, and promote leadership abilities.

YMCA Leaders Clubs

40 W. Long Street
Columbus, OH   43215
(614) 224-2225
These clubs train youth ranging in age from twelve to eighteen to participate in community service, social events, and volunteer activities within the Y.

Zenith Clubs

International Training in
   Communication
2519 Woodland Drive
Anaheim, CA   92801
(714) 995-3660
Zenith's educational programs for junior high and high school students encourage communication skills, public speaking, and leadership development.

HERITAGE

All the groups listed below are sources for information and referrals concerning the cultures, countries, and racial or ethnic groups they represent. If your children ask for information on their "roots," or need information on another culture for a school project, these organizations are an excellent place to start your search.

Not all the groups listed below sponsor youth programs. However, most will try to help you find a local youth group. Some of these groups also provide scholarship money for college, medical expenses, student exchange programs, and even summer camp.

AFGHAN

Afghan Youth Council in America
P.O. Box 751
Annandale, VA   22003
(703) 476-8773
This group of noncommunist Afghanis offers assistance to Afghan youth in the United States.

AFRICAN-AMERICAN

**African National People's Empire
   Re-Established**
13902 Robson Street
Detroit, MI   48227
(313) 837-0627
This group works to promote the health and welfare of African peoples.

Afro-Am Publishing Co.
910 South Michigan Avenue, Suite 556
Chicago, IL   60605
(312) 922-1147
(312) 922-1286

This company compiles data on the African-American experience, assembles resource information, produces publications, and distributes educational materials for grades kindergarten through high school. Contact Afro-Am for a list of its many publications.

**Association for the Study of
   Afro-American Life & History**
1407 14th Street, N.W.
Washington, D.C.   20005
(202) 667-2822
Although mainly serving scholars and college students, the Association offers limited information and referrals to younger students interested in African-American culture.

Black World Foundation
P.O. Box 2869
Oakland, CA   94609
(415) 547-6633

An information clearinghouse for the study of black culture in the United States.

National Black Child Development Institute
1463 Rhode Island Avenue, N.W.
Washington, DC   20005
(202) 387-1281
The Institute works to improve the lives of black children in the United States. It offers an information and referral service.

Visions Foundation
P.O. Box 37049
Washington, DC   20013
(202) 287-3360
The Foundation offers educational programs to promote appreciation of black culture in the United States.

ALBANIAN

Free Albania Organization
409 W. Broadway
South Boston, MA   02127
(617) 269-5192
This group works to perpetuate the customs and traditions of Albanians in the United States.

ARAB

National Association of Arab Americans (NAAA)
2033 M Street, N.W., Suite 300
Washington, DC 20036
(202) 467-4800
NAAA and its fifty regional groups work to promote Arab–U.S. understanding and to support Americans of Arab ancestry.

ARMENIAN

Armenian Church Youth Organization of America
Armenian Church of America
630 2nd Avenue
New York, NY   10016
(212) 686-0710
This is the primary group for Armenian youth in the United States.

Armenian Students Association of America
395 Concord Street
Belmont, MA   02178
(617) 484-9548
The Association provides loans and scholarships to college students of Armenian descent.

ASIAN

The Asia Society
725 Park Avenue
New York, NY   10021
(212) 288-6400
The Society offers an information and referral service.

AUSTRALIAN

America-Australia Interaction
   Association
7873 Heritage Drive, Suite 123
Annandale, VA   22003
(703) 750-1234
Educational and cultural programs are
offered to promote relations between
the United States and Australia.

AUSTRIAN

Austrian Forum
Cultural Affairs Section
Austrian Consulate General
11 E. 52nd Street
New York, NY   10022
(212) 759-5165
Acts as a clearinghouse for information
on Austria.

BELGIAN

Belgian American Educational
   Foundation
195 Church Street
New Haven, CT   06510
(203) 777-5765
Promotes Belgian culture through various educational activities.

CAMBODIAN

Khmer Youth Leadership Council
179 E. Robie
St. Paul, MN   55117
(612) 227-9291

The Council serves the children of
Cambodian heritage of ages fourteen
and over.

CHINESE

China Institute in America
125 E. 65th Street
New York, NY   10021
(212) 744-8181
The Institute promotes Chinese culture
in the United States.

Taiwanese Association of America
P.O. Box 3302
Iowa City, IA   52244
(319) 338-9082
Offers cultural information and services
to children.

CROATIAN

Junior Tamburitzans
Croatian Fraternal Union of America
100 Delaney Drive
Pittsburgh, PA   15235
(412) 351-3909
This is the national headquarters of a
fraternal organization that sponsors
Croatian youth activities in local chapters around the country.

CUBAN

Cuban American National Council, Inc.
300 Southwest 12th Avenue, 3rd Floor
Miami, FL   33130-2038
(305) 642-3484

While this group does not directly sponsor youth groups, it does provide referrals and information that can benefit Cuban-American children.

CZECH

American Sokol Organization
6424 W. Cermak Road
Berwyn, IL   60402
(312) 795-6671
This group works to maintain Czech culture and customs in the United States.

Czech Heritage Foundation
P.O. Box 761
Cedar Rapids, IA   52406
(319) 365-0868
Sponsors educational and student exchange programs.

DANISH

Young Vikings of the Danish
   Brotherhood in America
3717 Harney Street
Omaha, NE   68131
(402) 341-5049
This group promotes Danish language and culture.

Danish Brotherhood in America
P.O. Box 31748
Omaha, NE   68131
(402) 341-5049

The one hundred twenty groups of this organization offer cultural information and financial aid for a variety of purposes, including college and camp.

DUTCH

Netherland-America Foundation
1 Rockefeller Plaza, 11th Floor
New York, NY   10020
(212) 246-1429
The Foundation offers referrals and financial help for Americans of Dutch descent.

FINNISH

Finlandia Foundation
6148 Glen Tower
Los Angeles, CA   90068
(213) 462-1683
This group sponsors scholarships and offers cultural information.

FRENCH

Federation of French American Women
240 Highland Avenue
Fall River, MA   02720
(508) 678-1800
The Federation promotes French culture, sponsors French speaking contests, and hosts youth festivals.

French-American Aid for Children
630 5th Avenue, Suite 3053
New York, NY   10111
(212) 632-3650

This group provides financial aid for underpriviledged children in the United States and France.

Union Saint-Jean-Baptiste
Box F, 1 Social Street
Woonsocket, RI   02895
(401) 769-0520
(800) 225-USJB (8752)
This fraternal group of French Roman Catholics offers life insurance, cultural information, and various services to children.

GERMAN

German-American National Congress
4740 N. Western Avenue, 2nd Floor
Chicago, IL   60625
(312) 275-1100
The Congress promotes German culture and customs in the United States.

Hermann Sons Youth Chapters
Order of the Sons of Hermann in Texas
P.O. Box 1941
San Antonio, TX   78297
(512) 226-9261
Based primarily in Texas, this fraternal group promotes German culture.

GREEK

Daughters of Penelope
1707 L Street, N.W., Suite 200
Washington, DC   20036
(202) 785-9284

This group awards scholarships to girls of Greek descent. It is affiliated with Maids of Athena.

Greek Orthodox Young Adult League
27-09 Crescent Street
Astoria, NY   11102
(718) 626-5210
A program that promotes leadership training and religious education.

Sons of Pericles
Maids of Athena
1707 L Street, N.W., Suite 200
Washington, DC   20036
(202) 785-9284
This office promotes the appreciation of Greek culture in children of all ages. Maids of Athena is a sister organization that shares the same address but has a different phone number: (202) 737-7638. These groups aid in many charitable activities.

HISPANIC

Association for Puerto-Rican–Hispanic Culture
83 Park Terrace W.
New York, NY   10034
(212) 942-2338
Promotes Hispanic culture through a variety of cultural events.

HUNGARIAN

American Hungarian Federation
2631 Copley Road
Akron, OH   44321
(216) 666-1313
Promotes Hungarian culture among
youth and adults.

**National Federation of American
 Hungarians**
1450 Grace Avenue
Cleveland, OH   44107
(216) 226-4089
Educates Americans of Hungarian descent about their heritage.

INDIAN

Association of Indian Muslims
P.O. Box 10654
Silver Spring, MD   20904
(301) 730-5456
Offers cultural information and financial information to Muslims living in
the United States.

**National Federation of Asian Indian
 Organizations**
P.O. Box 462
Wakefield Station
Bronx, NY   10466
(203) 329-8010
Represents seventy groups of Indian-
Americans.

IRISH

Ancient Order of Hibernians in America
Junior Division
31 Logan Street
Auburn, NY   13021
(315) 252-3895
This headquarters for over seven hundred lodges nationwide promotes the
study of Irish culture, history, and arts
for children ages nine and up.

Knights of Equity
47 JoAnn Drive
West Seneca, NY   14224
(716) 675-1601
Promotes Irish culture and offers scholarships for high school and college students.

ISRAELI

America Israel Friendship League
134 E. 39th Street
New York, NY   10016
(212) 213-8630
Promotes Israeli culture in the United
States and sponsors a high school exchange program.

ITALIAN

**Italian Catholic Federation Central
 Council**
1801 Van Ness Avenue, Suite 330
San Francisco, CA   94109
(415) 673-8240

The Council provides a number of cultural, religious, and charitable activities, including up to two hundred scholarships per year.

National Italian American Foundation (NAIF)
666 11th Street, N.W., Suite 800
Washington, DC   20001
(202) 638-0220
NAIF offers an information clearinghouse regarding all Italian-American subjects. It provides scholarships to college students.

Order Sons of Italy in America
219 E. Street, N.E.
Washington, DC   20002
(202) 547-2900
This huge organization offers many cultural, educational, and charitable activities.

JAPANESE

Japanese American Citizens League
1765 Sutter Street
San Francisco, CA   94115
(415) 921-5225
The League promotes Japanese culture in the United States.

Japan Society
333 E. 47th Street
New York, NY   10017
(212) 832-1155

The Society works to increase understanding between the United States and Japan through a variety of educational activities and information services.

KOREAN

Korean American Coalition
3921 Wilshire Boulevard, Suite LL100
Los Angeles, CA   90010
(213) 380-6175
This small group offers a limited-information clearinghouse.

LITHUANIAN

Lithuanian-American Community
2713 W. 71st Street
Chicago, IL   60629
(312) 436-0197
This office offers educational services to children of all ages with an interest in Lithuanian culture.

Lithuanian Catholic Federation Ateitis
7235 S. Sacramento
Chicago, IL   60629
(312) 434-2243
This Federation of four organizations helps children of all ages.

NATIVE AMERICAN

Cherokee Nation Youth Leadership Program
P.O. Box 948
Tahlequah, OK   74465
(918) 456-0671

This Program develops leadership and work skills in Cherokee youth of sixteen years and over.

Indian Youth of America
P.O. Box 2786
Sioux City, IA   51106
(712) 252-3230
The educational programs of this group help to increase pride in Indian children of all ages and all tribes.

National Indian Youth Council
318 Elm Street, S.E.
Albuquerque, NM   87102
(505) 247-2251
Offers educational, cultural, and employment information for Indian youth.

National Indian Youth Leadership Project
101 S. Clark Street
Gallup, NM   87301
(505) 863-9521
The Project offers leadership training programs in five states for youth in grades seven through twelve.

NORWEGIAN

Sons of Norway Youth Club
1455 W. Lake Street
Minneapolis, MN   55408
(612) 827-3611
This is a fraternal organization for high school students.

PHILIPPINE

Legionarios del Trabajo in America
Grand Lodge
2154 S. San Joaquin Street
Stockton, CA   95206
(209) 463-6516
This fraternal group offers cultural education and scholarships.

POLISH

Polish National Alliance of the U.S.
Youth Programs
6100 N. Cicero Avenue
Chicago, IL   60646
(312) 286-0500
(800) 621-3723
The Alliance offers sports and arts activities for children in local lodges around the country.

Polish Roman Catholic Union of America
984 N. Milwaukee Avenue
Chicago, IL   60622
(312) 278-3210
(800) 772-8632
Sponsors music, language, and other classes for children of Polish descent.

Polish Union of America
761 Fillmore Avenue
Buffalo, NY   14212
(716) 893-1365
The one hundred twenty local chapters of the Polish Union offer education and other services to children.

PORTUGUESE

Luso-American Fraternal Federation
1951 Webster Street
Oakland, CA   94612
(415) 452-4318
This fraternal group has nearly thirty youth councils that sponsor a variety of activities for youths.

ROMANIAN

American Romanian Orthodox Youth
2522 Grey Tower Road
Jackson, MI   49201
(517) 522-4800
Supports youth groups from Romanian Orthodox parishes.

RUSSIAN

American Carpatho-Russian Youth
American Carpatho-Russian Diocese
312 Garfield Street
Johnstown, PA   15906
(814) 536-4207
This church group of the Eastern Orthodox faith supports youth groups from ages ten and up.

Byelorussian-American Youth Organization
P.O. Box 1123
New Brunswick, NJ   08903
No phone number listed.
Promotes Byelorussian culture.

Tolstoy Foundation
200 Park Avenue S., Room 1612
New York, NY   10003
(212) 677-7770
The Foundation promotes Russian culture in the United States.

SCOTTISH

Council of Scottish Clans & Associations
929 Cooper Avenue
Columbus, GA   31906
(404) 327-2508
The Council is a clearinghouse for information on Scottish culture, educational opportunities, and local groups throughout the United States.

Scottish Heritage U.S.A.
P.O. Box 457
Pinehurst, NC 28374
(919) 295-4448
Promotes Scottish culture in the United States.

SERBIAN

Junior Order of the Serb National Federation
3 Gateway Center
6F1 South
Pittsburgh, PA   15222
(412) 263-2875
Promotes Serbian culture in lodges across the United States.

SLOVAK

Slovak Catholic Sokol
P.O. Box 899
Passaic, NJ   07055
(201) 777-2605
This source is primarily a sponsor of
youth groups and athletic activities for
Catholics of Slovak heritage.

Slovak Gymnastic Union of the U.S.A.
P.O. Box 189
East Orange, NJ   07019
(201) 676-0280
Promotes Slovak culture and sports ac-
tivities.

SWEDISH

Swedish Council of America
2600 Park Avenue
Minneapolis, MN   55407
(612) 871-0593
Promotes Swedish culture in the United
States.

**Swedish Women's Educational
  Association International**
7505 North Avenue
Lemon Grove, CA   92045
(619) 463-0092
Offers information on Swedish culture
to Americans.

TURKISH

**Assembly of Turkish American
  Associations**
1522 Connecticut Avenue, N.W.
Washington, DC   20036
(202) 483-9090
Offers cultural and educational services
to adults and children.

UKRAINIAN

**Association of American Youth of
  Ukrainian Descent**
4004 Roanoke Circle
Minneapolis, MN   55422
(612) 377-4031
Designed for children over seven, this
group promotes the study of Ukrainian
music, arts, language, and history.

League of Ukrainian Catholic Youth
St. Peter and Paul Church
2280 W. 7th Street
Parma, OH   44113
(216) 861-2176
This group works through churches to
sponsor youth activities.

PLAST, Ukrainian Youth Organization
144 2nd Avenue
New York, NY   10003
(212) 475-6960
PLAST promotes physical fitness, character building, and Ukrainian culture.

Ukrainian American Youth
    Association, Inc.
136 2nd Avenue
New York, NY   10003
(212) 477-3084
Offers arts, cultural, and summer camp
programs to children of Ukrainian descent from ages five and up.

WELSH

Welsh National Gymanfa Ganu
    Association
662 Melwood Drive, N.E.
Warren, OH   44483
(216) 372-5885
This federation of Welsh organizations
and churches promotes Welsh culture,
particularly music.

MONEY HANDLING AND ENTREPRENEURSHIP

The number of books, publications, banks, and associations concerned with teaching children about money and starting their own businesses is surprisingly small. This section lists most of them.

BANKS

Many local banks offer special accounts for children. If you do not find one locally that provides the services your children desire, the banks below specialize in serving children and teenagers.

First Children's Bank
c/o First New York Bank for Business
111 E. 57th Street
New York, NY   10022
(212) 644-0670
First Children's Bank, an offshoot of
the First New York Bank for Business,
has a branch at one of the most famous
toy stores in the world: F. A. O.
Schwarz.

Checking and savings accounts require a minimum balance of five hundred dollars to avoid monthly or quarterly fees. College certificates of deposit require a thousand-dollar minimum. Accounts may be opened by mail.

The bank also distributes two free publications: *The Buck Starts Here,* a comic book, and *Saving Money Is Smart,* a coloring book.

Young Americans Bank
250 Steele Street
Denver, CO   80206
(303) 394-4357

By far the most innovative "kid's bank" in the United States, the Young Americans Bank offers a wide variety of services. A twelve-member Youth Advisory Board helps the bank design services customized to interest children. Customers under eighteen years old receive checks and a photo identification card. Separate bank cards are usable at twenty-thousand automated teller machines nationwide through the Mini-Bank and Cirrus networks. A special Mastercard designed for young people is also available.

The bank offers installment loans to children who start a business or just want to buy something they fancy. Student loans, travelers' checks, savings accounts, certificates of deposit, and bank-by-mail services are also available.

The bank is affiliated with the Young Americans Education Foundation, which sponsors a variety of educational programs in economics, financial planning, college financial planning, investing, and entrepreneurship. Children of all ages who live in, or can travel to, the Denver area can participate.

ORGANIZATIONS

Association of Collegiate Entrepreneurs
Center for Entrepreneurship
Wichita State University
1845 N. Fairmont
Wichita, KS   67208
(316) 689-3000

The Association offers a four-day summer camp for college and high school students interested in learning the skills needed to start a business.

Junior Achievement, Inc. (JA)
45 Clubhouse Drive
Colorado Springs, CO   80906
(719) 540-8000

This large nonprofit group of one hundred thousand volunteers seeks to "provide young people with practical economic education programs and experiences in the competitive private enterprise system." JA offers programs for elementary school through high school students in which local business people provide classroom training. Contact your local school or JA directly for details.

Money Management Institute
2700 Sanders Road
Prospect Heights, IL   60070
(708) 564-6291

Among its publications and brochures, the Institute offers a fifty-page booklet called *Children and Money Management.*

Personal Economics Program (PEP)
American Bankers Association
1120 Connecticut Avenue, N.W.
Washington, DC 20036
(202) 663-5394
(202) 663-5425
PEP works through banks nationwide to teach young people about banking and money handling. Publications include a free comic book for ages six through twelve called *Meet the Bank.* Other publications, mainly for teenagers, include *Banking Is the Answer, Managing Your Checking Account,* and *The Bank Book: A Guide to Bank Services.* Videos on similar topics are also available. Contact your local bank or PEP directly.

BOOKS, PUBLICATIONS, KITS, AND SOFTWARE

Kids Mean Business. This newsletter, published bimonthly, offers true stories about business enterprises run by children. The emphasis is on children who not only succeeded at running a business but also made a contribution to society. It can be ordered from Homeland Publications, 1808 Capri, Seabrook, TX 77586, (713) 474-4730 for $8.00 per year.

The owners of Homeland Publications, Bonnie and Noel Drew, have written *Kid Biz* ($9.95), a book which suggests 101 money-making projects for children. In addition, they offer a software package, *Kids Business* ($19.95), in IBM compatible format. The software contains financial worksheets and other programs to supplement *Kid Biz.*

Zillions. This junior version of *Consumer Reports* offers children ages eight to fourteen advice on how to handle money and be an informed consumer. Like its parent publication, *Zillions* includes evaluations of products (conducted by a panel of children). Published bimonthly at $13.95 per year, the magazine is available from Consumer Reports for Kids, Subscription Dept., P.O. Box 51777, Boulder, CO 80321-1777, (800) 786-8001.

The Busine$$ Kit. Geared toward children eight and over, this kit ($49.95) contains an audiotape, a variety of booklets, a calendar, a do-it-yourself business plan, stationery and business cards, and other items to help a child start a business. A toll-free hotline for members who have business questions is part of the package, as is a one-year subscription to the newsletter, *Busines$ Kids/America's Future.* The newsletter can be ordered separately for $9.65 per year. Place orders with Busines$ Kids, P.O. Box 149003, Coral Gables, FL 33114-9003, (800) 852-4544.

Other services offered by Busines$ Kids include a scholarship program and venture capital fund that invests in businesses started by disadvantaged children.

Kids' Business. This kit ($39.95) for children ages four to eleven contains such essentials as company stationery, a checkbook, sale stickers, stamp pad, play money, message and receipt pads, and more. The kit is an educational toy rather than a serious business tool. It is available from: Toys to Grow On, P.O. Box 17, Long Beach, CA 90801, (800) 542-8338.

The Teenager Entrepreneur's Guide, a book by Sarah L. Riehm ($8.95), offers practical information on how to start a business. It is available from Surrey Books, 230 E. Ohio Street, Suite 120, Chicago, IL 60611, (312) 751-7330.

Teach Your Child the Value of Money, a book by Harold and Sandy Moe ($7.95), can be ordered from Harsand Press, N. 8565 Holseth Road, Holman, WI 54636, (608) 526-3848.

It Doesn't Grow on Trees, a book by Jean R. Peterson ($9.95), is available from Betterway Publications, P.O. Box 219, Clozet, VA 22932, (804) 823-5661.

Making Cents: Every Kid's Guide to Money, a book by Elizabeth Wilkinson ($8.95), is published by Little Brown & Co., 34 Beacon Street, Boston, MA 02108, (617) 227-0730.

The Kid's Money Book, a book by Neale S. Godfrey, is published by Checkboard Press, 30 Vese Street, New York, NY 10007, (212) 571-6300.

Federal Reserve Banks. The twelve Federal Reserve Banks around the nation publish a variety of free educational materials, some designed for children and high school students. Of particular value to junior high and senior high school students is a series of comic books published by the Federal Reserve of New York. Titles include: *The Story of Money; The Story of Consumer Credit; Once Upon a Dime; The Story of Foreign Trade and Exchange; The Story of Inflation; The Story of Checks and Electronic Payments;* and *The Story of Banks and Thrifts.* Additional publications include booklets on coins and detecting counterfeit currency, plus videos, slide shows, and other educational tools. To request copies of the comic books and to receive a free copy of the Fed's catalog *Public Information Materials,* contact one of these offices:

Board of Governors of the Federal
  Reserve System
Publications Services
MS—138
Washington, DC   20551
(202) 452-3244

Federal Reserve Bank Atlanta
Public Information Dept.
104 Marietta Street, N.W.
Atlanta, GA   30303-2713
(404) 521-8788

Federal Reserve Bank Boston
Public Services Dept.
P.O. Box 2076
Boston, MA   02106-2076
(617) 973-3459

Federal Reserve Bank Chicago
Public Information Center
230 S. LaSalle Street
Chicago, IL   60690
(312) 322-5111

Federal Reserve Bank Cleveland
Public Affairs Dept.
P.O. Box 6387
Cleveland, OH   44101-1387
(216) 579-3079

Federal Reserve Bank Dallas
Public Affairs Dept.
Station K
Dallas, TX   75222
(214) 651-6289
(214) 651-6266

Federal Reserve Bank Kansas City
Public Affairs Dept.
925 Grand Avenue
Kansas City, MO   64198
(816) 881-2402

Federal Reserve Bank Minneapolis
Public Affairs Dept.
250 Marquette Avenue
Minneapolis, MN   55480
(612) 340-2446

Federal Reserve Bank New York
Public Information Dept.
33 Liberty Street
New York, NY   10045
(212) 720-6134

Federal Reserve Bank Philadelphia
Public Information Dept.
P.O. Box 66
Philadelphia, PA   19105
(215) 574-6115

Federal Reserve Bank Richmond
Public Services Dept.
P.O. Box 27622
Richmond, VA   23261
(804) 697-8109

Federal Reserve Bank St. Louis
Public Information Office
P.O. Box 442
St. Louis, MO   63166
(314) 444-8444 (ext. 545)

Federal Reserve Bank San Francisco
Public Information Dept.
P.O. Box 7702
San Francisco, CA   94120
(415) 974-2163

JOBS

GENERAL INFORMATION

Finding a summer job can be a frustrating experience for teenagers. Some simply end up working at a fast-food restaurant. Others prefer to explore better-paying and more educational jobs.

The Telephone Book. The best place to start a job search is your local telephone book. Some phone directories have a blue-page section listing federal, state, and local government offices. Other directories list these offices under United States, your state's name, or your city or county name. Within these categories check the listings under Employment, Labor, or Youth. Chances are you will find at least one office that helps teens find jobs.

High School Guidance Office. The guidance counselor often maintains a bulletin board or file listing local job opportunities.

Local Business and Youth Organizations. A good source of leads are such groups as the local Chamber of Commerce, Rotary or Lions Club, YM/YWCA, Boys Club, Girls Club, and other similar associations.

Employment Agencies. Check your telephone book under Employment for a list of local agencies that may be looking for teen workers.

The Job Corps. This program offers training, education, and guidance to disadvantaged youth ages sixteen to twenty-two. For more information, call your state labor office listed below.

The Federal Summer Jobs Program. In December of each year, the Office of Personnel Management publishes Announcement No. 414, which is called *Summer Jobs: Opportunities in the Federal Government.* You must be sixteen and over to apply for these competitive jobs, many of which are in cities. To learn of opportunities in your area, call the nearest Federal Information Center listed in the last chapter of this book and ask for the nearest Office of Personnel Management.

Youth Conservation Corps. This work program for youths between fifteen and eighteen offers the chance to work outdoors in national parks, forests, and elsewhere. To learn of opportunities, contact the national office:

National Park Service
Department of the Interior, Room 4415
1100 L Street, N.W.
Washington, DC   20013
(202) 343-5514

STUDENT CAREER EDUCATION GROUPS

Business Professionals of America
5454 Cleveland Avenue
Columbus, OH   43231
(614) 895-7277
This group is for high school students interested in business careers.

Distributive Education Clubs of
   America
1908 Association Drive
Reston, VA   22091
(703) 860-5000
For high school students considering careers in marketing and retailing.

DPMA Club Program
Data Processing Management
   Association
505 Busse Highway
Park Ridge, IL   60068
(312) 825-8124
For all students interested in data processing careers.

Future Business Leaders of America
P.O. Box 17417
Washington, DC   20041
(703) 860-3334
For high school students contemplating business careers.

Future Farmers of America
National FFA Center
P.O. Box 15160
Alexandria, VA   22309
(703) 360-3600
Future Farmers is for high school students preparing for careers in agriculture.

Future Homemakers of America
1910 Reston Drive
Reston, VA   22091
(703) 476-4900
This group is for high school boys and
girls anticipating becoming homemakers.

70001 Training and Employment
   Institute
501 School Street, S.W., Suite 600
Washington, DC   20024
(202) 484-0103
The Institute helps troubled youth and
potential dropouts through career
training.

Technology Student Association
1914 Association Drive
Reston, VA   22091
(703) 860-9000
Promotes technological careers among
junior and senior high school students.

Vocational Industrial Clubs of America
P.O. Box 3000
Leesburg, VA   22075
For high school students thinking
about careers in industry, business, or
technology.

STATE DEPARTMENTS OF LABOR

These offices will help you identify work opportunities in your community.

Alabama

Department of Labor
James E. Folsom Administrative
   Building, Room 651
64 N. Union Street
Montgomery, AL   36130
(205) 261-3460

Alaska

Department of Labor
P.O. Box 21149
Juneau, AK   99802
(907) 465-2700

Arizona

Labor Department
P.O. Box 19070
Phoenix, AZ   85005
(602) 255-4515

Arkansas

Department of Labor
10421 W. Markham
Little Rock, AR   72205
(501) 682-4541

California

Department of Industrial Relations
525 Golden Gate Avenue
San Francisco, CA   94102
(415) 557-3356

Colorado

Department of Labor & Employment
State Centennial Building
1313 Sherman Street
Denver, CO   80203
(303) 866-2782

Connecticut

Department of Employment & Training
(203) 566-1513

Department of Labor
200 Folly Brook Boulevard
Wethersfield, CT   06109
(203) 566-4384

Delaware

Department of Labor
Elbert N. Carvel State Office Building,
6th Floor
820 N. French Street
Wilmington, DE   19801
(302) 571-2710
(302) 571-2861

Florida

Department of Labor & Employment
  Security
Division of Labor, Employment,
  & Training
Atkins Building, Room 300
1320 Executive Center Drive
Tallahassee, FL   32399-0667
(904) 488-7228

Georgia

Department of Labor
148 International Boulevard
Atlanta, GA   30303
(404) 656-3011
(404) 656-3028
(404) 656-5921

Hawaii

Department of Labor & Industrial
  Relations
830 Punchbowl Street
Honolulu, HI   96813
(808) 548-3150
(808) 548-3153

Idaho

Department of Labor & Industrial
  Services
Statehouse Mall
Boise, ID   83720
(208) 334-3950

Illinois

Department of Labor
310 S. Michigan Avenue
Chicago, IL   60604
(217) 782-6206
(312) 793-2800
(800) 654-4620 (in Illinois)

Indiana

Department of Labor
State Office Building, Room 1013
100 N. Senate Avenue
Indianapolis, IN   46204
(317) 232-2663

Iowa

Division of Labor
1000 E. Grand Avenue
Des Moines, IA   50319
(515) 281-3606

Kansas

Division of Employment Standards &
   Labor Relations
1430 S.W. Topeka Boulevard
Topeka, KS   66612-1853
(913) 296-7475

Kentucky

Labor Cabinet
U.S. Highway 127
South Building, Bay 4
Frankfort, KY   40601
(502) 564-3070

Louisiana

Department of Labor
P.O. Box 94094
Baton Rouge, LA   70804-9094
(504) 342-3011

Maine

Department of Labor
P.O. Box 309
Augusta, ME   04330
(207) 289-3788

Maryland

Division of Labor & Industry
501 St. Paul Place
Baltimore, MD   21202
(301) 333-4179
(800) 492-6226 (in Maryland)

Massachusetts

Department of Labor & Industries
Leverett Saltonstall State Office
   Building
100 Cambridge Street
Boston, MA   02202
(617) 727-3454
(617) 727-3969

Michigan

Department of Labor
P.O. Box 30015
Lansing, MI   48909
(517) 373-9600
(517) 373-8871
(517) 699-1324

Minnesota

Department of Labor & Industry
443 Lafayette Road
St. Paul, MN   55101
(612) 296-6490
(612) 296-6529
(612) 297-2826

Mississippi

Employment Security Commission
P.O. Box 1699
Jackson, MS   39125-1699
(601) 961-7400
(601) 354-8711

Missouri

Department of Labor & Industrial
   Relations
P.O. Box 59
Jefferson City, MO   65104
(314) 751-4091
(314) 751-3979

Montana

Department of Labor & Industry
P.O. Box 1728
Helena, MT   59624
(406) 444-3555

Nebraska

Department of Labor
P.O. Box 94600
State House Station
Lincoln, NE   68509-4600
(402) 475-8451

Nevada

Labor Commission
Capitol Complex
Carson City, NV   89710
(702) 885-4850

New Hampshire

Department of Labor
19 Pillsbury Street
Concord, NH   03301
(603) 271-3176
(603) 271-3172

New Jersey

Department of Labor
CN 110
Trenton, NJ   08625-0110
(609) 292-2323
(609) 292-9772
(609) 292-2000

New Mexico

Department of Labor
Aspen Plaza
1596 Pacheco Street
Santa Fe, NM   87502
(505) 827-6875

New York

Labor Department
State Campus, Building 12
Albany, NY   12240
(518) 457-9000
(518) 457-2727

North Carolina

Department of Labor
Labor Building
4 W. Edenton Street
Raleigh, NC   27601
(919) 733-7166
(919) 733-2355

North Dakota

Department of Labor
State Capitol, 5th Floor
Bismarck, ND   58505
(701) 224-2660

Ohio

Department of Industrial Relations
P.O. Box 825
Columbus, OH   43266-0567
(614) 644-2223

Oklahoma

Department of Labor
1315 N. Broadway Place
Oklahoma City, OK   73103
(405) 235-0530

Oregon

Bureau of Labor & Industries
State Office Building
1400 S.W. 5th Avenue
Portland, OR   97201
(503) 229-5737

Pennsylvania

Department of Labor & Industry
Labor & Industry Building, Room 1700
7th and Forster Streets
Harrisburg, PA   17120
(717) 787-3757
(717) 787-3157
(717) 787-8665

Rhode Island

Department of Labor
220 Elmwood Avenue
Providence, RI   02907
(401) 457-1800
(401) 457-1870

South Carolina

Labor Department
P.O. Box 11329
Columbia, SC   29211
(803) 734-9600

South Dakota

Department of Labor
Richard F. Kneip Building
700 Governors Drive
Pierre, SD   57501-2277
(605) 773-3101
(605) 773-3681

Tennessee

Department of Labor
501 Union Building, 2nd Floor
Nashville, TN   37219-5385
(615) 741-2582
(615) 741-3786

Texas

Department of Labor & Standards
P.O. Box 12157
Capitol Station
Austin, TX   78711
(512) 463-3172
(512) 463-3173

Utah

Labor/Anti-Discrimination Division
P.O. Box 510910
Salt Lake City, UT   84151-0910
(801) 530-6800

Vermont

Department of Labor & Industry
State Office Building
120 State Street
Montpelier, VT   05602
(802) 828-2286

Virginia

Department of Labor & Industry
P.O. Box 12064
Richmond, VA   23241
(804) 786-2377
(804) 786-9878
(804) 786-5873

Washington

Department of Labor & Industries
Mail Stop HC-101
Olympia, WA   98504
(206) 753-6307
(206) 753-6308
(206) 753-5173

West Virginia

Department of Labor
State Office Building 3, Room 319
1800 Washington Street E.
Charleston, WV   25305
(304) 348-7890

Wisconsin

Department of Industry, Labor &
    Human Relations
P.O. Box 7946
Madison, WI   53707
(608) 266-7552

Wyoming

Department of Labor & Statistics
Herschler Building, 2nd Floor
122 W. 25th Street
Cheyenne, WY   82002
(307) 777-7261
(307) 777-6380

Puerto Rico

Department of Labor & Human
   Resources
Prudencio Rivera Martinez Building
505 Munoz Rivera Avenue
Hato Rey, PR   00918
(809) 754-2119
(809) 754-5808
(809) 754-2110

CAMPS

If you are searching for an appropriate summer camp, you will find these organizations helpful:

Advisory Council on Camps (ACC)
174 Sylvan Avenue
Leonia, NJ   07605
(201) 592-6667
ACC offers a free referral service to help parents locate a camp, summer school, or other summer activity suitable for their children. Their library contains camp catalogs and other information on camps.

American Camping Association (ACA)
5000 State Road, Room 67 N.
Martinsville, IN   46151
(317) 342-8456
(800) 428-CAMP (2267)

This group of camp owners, counselors, and others publishes an annual book called *Guide to Accredited Camps* that briefly describes twenty-four hundred camps accredited by the ACA.

Association of Jewish Sponsored Camps
130 E. 59th Street
New York, NY   10022
(212) 751-0477
The Association offers a free referral and information service to parents who wish to place their children in a Jewish-sponsored camp in the New York area. This office publishes the annual *Camp Listings*.

Christian Camping International/U.S.A.
   (CCI)
P.O. Box 646
Wheaton, IL   60189
(312) 462-0300
CCI publishes the annual *Guide to Christian Camps and Conference Centers,* a directory of member camps and annual events.

National Camping Association
353 West 56th Street
New York, NY   10019
(212) 246-0052
This large association of camp owners and directors offers limited information to the public.

VOLUNTEERING

SEE ALSO

the CHILDREN'S CLUBS section of this chapter under Service and Volunteer Organizations for additional groups seeking volunteers.

Teenagers who wish to volunteer their time will find thousands of organizations grateful for their help. A local school guidance counselor, local chapters of the Red Cross, YM/YWCA, and other local voluntary groups will be glad to hear from your children. The groups below can also help you find a suitable opportunity:

Amigos De Las Americas
5618 Star Lane
Houston, TX   77057
(713) 782-5290
(800) 231-7796
This program sends youths over age sixteen to Latin America for two to eight weeks to work as health-care assistants.

Four-One-One
7304 Beverly Street
Annandale, VA   22003
(703) 354-6270
The youth arm of this organization acts as a national clearinghouse for volunteerism for children ages four to seventeen. They publish several directories of programs and other materials on volunteerism.

United Way of America
701 N. Fairfax Street
Alexandria, VA   22314
(703) 836-7100
The United Way has twenty-three hundred chapters, some of which use volunteers. You can find a local chapter by checking your local telephone book or by calling the national office in Virginia.

Volunteer—The National Center
1111 N. 19th Street, Suite 500
Arlington, VA   22209
(703) 276-0542
Volunteer and its four hundred local affiliates offer information and referrals to those who wish to donate their time. A catalog of Volunteer's publications is available.

OTHER SUMMER OPPORTUNITIES

Several books describe the many opportunities available to teenagers for educational and work-related activities:

Peterson's Summer Opportunities for Kids and Teenagers, from Peterson's Guides, P.O. Box 2123, Princeton, NJ 08543-2123, (800) 338-3282 or (609) 243-9111. Included are about thirteen hundred programs for children of all ages including summer schools and internships. The book has a section for the handicapped, the gifted, and for programs that offer financial assistance. Some programs offer work opportunities for high school students.

Also available from Peterson's are these useful books: *Summer Employment Directory of the United States* ($14.95), *Internships* ($27.95), and *Directory of Overseas Summer Jobs* ($14.95).

Summer Options for Teenagers, by Cindy Ware, Arco Books, Simon & Schuster, 200 Old Tappan Road, Old Tappan, NJ 07675, (201) 767-5937. The programs listed, both in the United States and abroad, fall into these categories: research, studio and performing arts, outdoor adventure, volunteer positions and internships, and work opportunities.

Educational Opportunity Guide, from Duke University, Talent Identification Program, 1121 West Main Street, Suite 100, Durham, NC 27705, (919) 683-1400. This guide lists programs catering to artistically and academically gifted students, from kindergarten through the twelfth grade.

VACATIONS AND TRAVEL

The first part of this section cites the handful of travel services and books devoted to families with children. The second part lists the free travel information services in each state.

NATIONWIDE TRAVEL INFORMATION AND SERVICES

The travel agents listed below specialize in child travel. Aside from booking flights, hotels, and other conventional services, these companies anticipate and handle the potential difficulties created when traveling with children. The agents find special tours for children and families, set up customized itineraries, offer advice about children flying alone, and much more.

Families Welcome!
21 W. Colony Place, Suite 140
Durham, NC   27705
(919) 968-6744
(800) 326-0724

Rascals in Paradise
650 5th Avenue, Suite 505
San Francisco, CA   94107
(415) 978-9800
(800) U-RASCAL (872-7225)

International Family Adventures
P.O. Box 172
New Canaan, CT   06840
(203) 863-2106

Schilling Travel Service
722 2nd Avenue S.
Minneapolis, MN   55402
(612) 332-1100

The following services specialize in tours for grandparents and grandchildren traveling together.

AARP Travel Service
4801 W. 110th Street
Overland Park, KS   66211
(800) 365-5358

Grandtravel
The Ticket Counter
6900 Wisconsin Avenue, Suite 706
Chevy Chase, MD   20815
(301) 986-0790
(800) 247-7651

If traveling by car, the American Automobile Association (AAA) offers many valuable services including travel planning. Call them at (800) 336-HELP (4357) for details about joining and for the location of your nearest office.

All the major car rental agencies will rent car seats for children. To make a reservation call:

Alamo
(800) 462-5266

Avis
(800) 331-1212

Budget
(800) 527-0700

Hertz
(800) 654-3131

National
(800) 328-4567

The National Child Safety Council and the Department of Transportation offer a free brochure called *Kids and Teens in Flight*. Call them at (800) 222-1464 or (202) 366-2220.

The two books and one magazine listed below are probably the best sources for advice on traveling with children and for suggested destinations that children enjoy.

Super Family Vacations ($12.95), by Martha Shirk and Nancy Klepper, Harper & Row Publishers, 10 East 53rd Street, New York, NY 10022, (212) 207-7000.

Great Vacations With Your Kids ($12.95), by Dorothy Jordon and Marjorie A. Cohen, E. P. Dutton Books, 375 Hudson Street, New York, NY 10013, (212) 366-2000.

Family Travel Times ($35 per year) is an 8–12-page magazine published ten times per year offering advice on how to travel, what to see, and where to stay with children of all ages. A sample copy is $1. The publisher is Travel With Your Children, 80 Eighth Avenue, New York, NY 10011, (212) 206-0688.

STATE TOURISM OFFICES

Alabama

Department of Tourism & Travel
532 S. Perry Street
Montgomery, AL   36104
(205) 261-4169
(800) 252-2262
(800) 392-8096 (in Alabama)

Alaska

Division of Tourism
P.O. Box E
Juneau, AK   99811
(907) 465-2010

Arizona

Office of Tourism
1100 W. Washington Street
Phoenix, AZ   85007
(602) 542-3618

Arkansas

Department of Parks & Tourism
1 Capitol Mall
Little Rock, AR   72201
(501) 371-7777
(800) 643-8383
(800) 828-8974 (in Arkansas)

California

Office of Tourism
1121 L Street, Suite 600
Sacramento, CA   95814
(916) 332-1396
(916) 332-1397
(800) 862-2543

Colorado

Department of Tourism
1625 Broadway, Suite 1700
Denver, CO   80202
(303) 592-5410
(800) 255-5550

Connecticut

Department of Economic
    Development/Vacations
210 Washington Street
Hartford, CT   06106
(203) 566-3948
(800) 243-1685
(800) 842-7492 (in Connecticut)

Delaware

Tourism Office
P.O. Box 1401
Dover, DE   19903
(302) 739-4271
(800) 441-8846
(800) 282-8667 (in Delaware)

District of Columbia

Convention & Visitor's Center
1212 New York Avenue, N.W.
Washington, DC   20005
(202) 789-7000

Florida

Dept. of Commerce
Division of Tourism
107 W. Gaines Street
Tallahassee, FL   32399-2000
(904) 487-1462

Georgia

Tourist Division
Box 1776
Atlanta, GA   30301
(404) 656-3590
(800) 847-4842

Hawaii

Visitors Bureau
Waikiki Business Plaza, Suite 801
2270 Kalakaua Avenue
Honolulu, HI   96815
(808) 923-1811

Idaho

Department of Commerce
Capitol Building, Room 108
Boise, ID   83720
(208) 334-2470
(800) 635-7820

Illinois

Office of Tourism
310 S. Michigan Avenue
Chicago, IL   60604
(312) 793-2094
(800) 545-7300
(800) 359-9299 (in Illinois)

Indiana

Tourism Development Office
1 N. Capitol, Suite 700
Indianapolis, IN   46225-2288
(317) 232-8860
(800) W-WANDER (992-6337)

Iowa

Tourism Office
200 E. Grand Avenue
Des Moines, IA   50309-2882
(515) 281-3679
(800) 345-4692

Kansas

Travel & Tourism Division
400 W. 8th Street, Suite 500
Topeka, KS   66603
(913) 296-2009
(800) 252-6727 (in Kansas)

Kentucky

Department of Travel Development
Capital Plaza Tower, 22nd Floor
Frankfort, KY   40602
(502) 564-4930
(800) 225-8747

Louisiana

Office of Tourism
P.O. Box 94291
Baton Rouge, LA   70804-9291
(504) 342-8119
(800) 334-8626

Maine

Publicity Bureau
P.O. Box 23000
97 Winthrop Street
Hallowell, ME   04347
(207) 289-2423
(800) 533-9595

Maryland

Office of Tourist Development
217 E. Redwood Avenue
Baltimore, MD   21202
(301) 974-3517
(800) 331-1750

Massachusetts

Division of Tourism
100 Cambridge Street, 13th Floor
Boston, MA   02202
(617) 727-3201
(800) 533-6277

Michigan

Travel Bureau
P.O. Box 30226
Lansing, MI   48909
(517) 373-1195
(800) 543-2-YES (543-2937)

Minnesota

Tourist Information Center
375 Jackson Street
Farm Credit Service Building
St. Paul, MN   55101
(612) 296-5029
(800) 328-1461
(800) 652-9747 (in Minnesota)

Mississippi

Division of Tourism
P.O. Box 22825
Jackson, MS   39205
(601) 359-3414
(800) 647-2290

Missouri

Division of Tourism
P.O. Box 1055
Jefferson City, MO   65101
(314) 751-4133

Montana

Promotion Division
1424 9th Avenue
Helena, MT   59620
(406) 444-2654
(800) 541-1447

Nebraska

Division of Travel & Tourism
P.O. Box 94666
Lincoln, NE   68509
(402) 471-3796
(800) 228-4307
(800) 742-7595 (in Nebraska)

Nevada

Commission on Tourism
Capitol Complex
600 E. Williams Street, Suite 207
Carson City, NV   89710
(702) 687-4322
(800) 237-0774

New Hampshire

Office of Vacation Travel
P.O. Box 856
Concord, NH   03301
(603) 271-2343
(603) 271-2666
(800) 258-3608 (in Northeast region,
   but not New Hampshire)

New Jersey

Division of Travel & Tourism
CN 826
Trenton, NJ   08625
(609) 292-2470

New Mexico

Travel Division
Joseph Montoya Building
1100 St. Francis Drive
Santa Fe, NM   87503
(505) 827-0291
(800) 545-2020

New York

Division of Tourism
1 Commerce Plaza
Albany, NY   12245
(518) 474-4116
(800) 225-5697 (in Northeast, except
   Maine)

North Carolina

Travel & Tourism Division
430 N. Salisbury Street
Raleigh, NC   27611
(919) 733-4171
(800) VISIT-NC (847-4862)

North Dakota

Tourism Promotion
Liberty Memorial Building
State Capitol
Bismarck, ND   58505
(701) 224-2525
(800) 437-2077
(800) 472-2100 (in North Dakota)

Ohio

Office of Tourism
P.O. Box 1001
Columbus, OH   43266-0101
(614) 466-8444
(800) BUCKEYE (282-5393)

Oklahoma

Division of Tourism
500 William Rogers Building
Oklahoma City, OK   73105
(405) 521-2409
(800) 652-6552 (in bordering states)
(800) 522-8565 (in Oklahoma)

Oregon

Tourism Division
539 Cottage Street, N.E.
Salem, OR   97310
(503) 378-3451
(800) 547-7842
(800) 233-3306 (in Oregon)

Pennsylvania

Bureau of Travel
439 Forum Building
Harrisburg, PA   17120
(717) 787-5453
(800) 847-4872

Rhode Island

Tourism & Promotion Division
7 Jackson Walkway
Providence, RI   02903
(401) 277-2601
(800) 556-2484 (in New England,
    Middle Atlantic States)

South Carolina

Division of Tourism
1205 Pendleton Street
Columbia, SC   29201
(803) 734-0122

South Dakota

Division of Tourism
Capital Lake Plaza
711 Wells Avenue
Pierre, SD   57501
(605) 773-3301
(800) 952-2217
(800) 843-1930 (in South Dakota)

Tennessee

Tourist Department
P.O. Box 23170
Nashville, TN   37202
(615) 741-7994

Texas

Tourist Development
P.O. Box 12008
Capitol Station
Austin, TX   78711
(512) 426-9191
(800) 888-8839

Utah

Travel Council
Council Hall
Capitol Hill
Salt Lake City, UT   84114
(801) 538-1030

Vermont

Travel Division
134 State Street
Montpelier, VT   05602
(802) 828-3236

Virginia

Division of Tourism
202 N. 9th Street, Suite 500
Richmond, VA   23239
(804) 786-4484
(800) 847-4882

Washington

Tourism Division
101 General Administration Building
Olympia, WA   98504
(206) 586-2088
(800) 544-1800

West Virginia

Travel West Virginia
State Capitol
Charleston, WV   25305
(304) 348-2286
(800) CALL-WVA (225-5982)

Wisconsin

Division of Tourism
P.O. Box 7970
Madison, WI   53707
(608) 266-2161
(800) 432-8747
(800) 372-2737 (in Wisconsin and
    bordering states)

Wyoming

Travel Commission
I-25 and College Drive
Cheyenne, WY   82002
(307) 777-7777
(800) 225-5996

Puerto Rico

Tourism Company
P.O. Box 4435
Old San Juan Station
San Juan, PR   00905
(809) 721-2400

CHAPTER 12

CONSUMER GOODS

These days there's a seemingly endless supply of products for children. Yet, sometimes you can't find a particular item conveniently. The three sections in this chapter will help you negotiate through this maze of products. The first section, MAIL ORDER CATALOGS, describes some of the best sources to buy virtually anything you and your child could desire. The second section, MANUFACTURERS OF TOYS, FURNITURE, AND ACCESSORIES, helps you locate manufacturers if you need product information, repairs, or a replacement part. The last section, STATE CONSUMER PROTECTION AGENCIES, will help you determine if a particular store or manufacturer has consumer complaints filed against it.

SEE ALSO

the GENERAL SAFETY INFORMATION section in Chapter 6, particularly the Consumer Product Safety Commission, for information about safety recalls and safety problems associated with specific products or brands.

The HOBBIES and the PETS AND ANIMALS sections in Chapter 11 also list mail order catalogs.

☎ ☎ ☎ ☎ ☎ ☎ ☎ ☎ ☎ ☎ ☎ ☎ ☎ ☎ ☎ ☎ ☎ ☎ ☎ ☎

MAIL ORDER CATALOGS

Almost every product your child will ever need can be purchased through the mail. Although many catalogs described below carry a price tag, some firms will gladly send you a free copy. Call to find out.

This section has the following categories: Audio- and Videotapes, Baby Supplies, Books, Children's Wear, Educational Products, Furniture and Furnishings, Gifts, Health and Safety, Maternity and Nursing Clothes, Science and Nature, Swing Sets and Playhouses, and Toys and Games.

AUDIO- AND VIDEOTAPES

SEE ALSO

mail order merchants in the Books, Educational Products, and Toys and Games listings of this chapter.

Alcazar Records
P.O. Box 429, S. Main Street
Waterbury, VT   05676
(802) 244-8657
(800) 541-9904
Request the free children's catalog to receive a comprehensive listing of tapes, records, and compact discs. Mister Rogers is here as well as Raffi, Pete Seeger, and Linda Arnold, *Sesame Street* book-cassette sets, story-telling tapes, and children's videos.

Audio-Forum
96 Broad Street
Guilford, CT   06437
(203) 453-9794
(800) 243-1234
This source carries audio- and videotapes for your child (or an adult) to learn a foreign language, typing, reading music, and much more on his or her own. Popular board games in a variety of foreign languages are also available. There is a free brochure.

Children's Recordings
P.O. Box 1343
Eugene, OR   97440
(503) 485-1634
The free catalog from Children's
Recordings includes stories and music.
You can get a recording of Claire
Bloom reading *The Tale of Peter Rabbit*
or Jack Nicholson reading *How the
Camel Got His Hump.*

Educational Record Center, Inc.
Building 400, Suite 400
1575 Northside Drive, N.W.
Atlanta, GA   30318-4928
(404) 352-8282
(800) 438-1637 (orders)
The Center's $1 catalog offers over five
hundred films, videos, cassettes, and
records of the most popular children's
musicians and perennial movie favorites
such as *The Wizard of Oz.* There are
"greatest hits," Christmas collections,
and spoken recordings of classic stories.

Little Ears
P.O. Box 56168
Tucson, AZ   85703
(602) 888-2830
The free catalog lists what Little Ears
has selected as the fifty topnotch music
and story recordings for children. All
are on sale at 10–20 percent less than
the suggested retail price.

Music for Little People
P.O. Box 1460
Redway, CA   95560
(800) 346-4445
Records and tapes, including Raffi, Pete
Seeger, and Riders in the Sky are listed
in this free catalog alongside an unusual selection of musical instruments.
You can choose a kazoo, a lap harp, a
half-size guitar, a three-quarter-size
ukulele, a West African mbira, or something else that may suit your fancy.

BABY SUPPLIES

A-Plus Products, Inc.
P.O. Box 4057
Santa Monica, CA   90405
(213) 399-1177
(800) 359-9955
A-Plus offers a free color brochure of
helpful items for infants and younger
children, including bath cushions, rattles, a baby-food storage shelf, and an
inflatable potty.

Baby & Company, Inc.
P.O. Box 906
New Monmouth, NJ   07748
(201) 671-7777
Products for babies and toddlers such
as wooden toys, a lambskin comforter,
and a baby rain poncho are sold by this
firm. The $1 charge for a catalog is de-
ductible from your first order.

Baby Biz
P.O. Box 404
Eldorado Springs, CO   80025
(303) 499-2469
This company has a range of handy items for beginning parents. The free brochure advertises breast pumps and snowsuits, diaper covers and car window sunshades.

Baby Dreams
P.O. Box 3338
Gaithersburg, MD   20878
(800) 638-5965
Calico and cotton-blend diaper bags, changing pads, and pillows are carried by this firm, as well as quilted covers for booster seats, car seats, and strollers. The $1 catalog charge is deductible from your first order.

Baby Name-a-Grams Designer Birth Announcements
P.O. Box 8465, Dept. DD90
St. Louis, MO   63132
(314) 966-BABY (2229)
The free brochure and sample depict a unique birth announcement for your baby. Your child's name is transformed into any number of calligraphic sketches such as a kangaroo or a baby carriage.

Best Selection, Inc.
2626 Live Oak Highway
Yuba City, CA   95991
(916) 673-9798

The $2 catalog pictures a wide selection of baby supplies from portable bottle warmers to baby hammocks, breast pumps, safety gates, and bath aids.

Chaselle, Inc.
9645 Gerwig Lane
Columbia, MD   21046
(301) 381-9611
(800) CHASELLE (242-7355)
(800) 492-7840 (in Maryland)
Baby products for day-care centers or your home are offered by Chaselle. The free catalog advertises baby furniture, teething rings, and a rocking horse.

Children's Corner
520 Monument Square
Racine, WI   53403
(800) 445-7033
Included in the free brochure are a baby monitor, a portable playpen, and a wipe warmer.

Courier Health Care, Inc.
P.O. Box 1210
Agona Hills, CA   91301
(818) 991-1931
(800) 543-5387
This source offers plenty of items for the expectant mother and new parent, including nursing bras, a scale with a wall-mounted readout, a childproof medicine box, baby slings, and diaper covers. The catalog costs $1.

Diap-Air

P.O. Box 103
Upton, NY   11973
Sells diaper covers. The brochure is free.

Diaperaps

P.O. Box 3050
Granada Hills, CA   91344
(818) 886-7377
(800) 477-3425
Sells diaper covers. The brochure is free.

Direct-To-You Baby Products

4599 Peardale Drive
Las Vegas, NV   89117
(702) 364-1979
The $.50 catalog advertises practical and fun items for your baby. Included are a set of miniature knee pads, a natural lambskin, a black-and-white hanging mobile, and a toilet lid lock. Instructional and entertainment videos are also available.

Family Clubhouse

6 Chiles Avenue
Asheville, NC   28803
(704) 254-9236
This source sells biodegradable disposable diapers, diaper covers, bath products, bibs and dishes, no-skid socks, and cotton baby clothes. The $1 catalog clearly displays colors and fabrics.

Hazelwood

P.O. Box 4455
Panorama City, CA   91412-4455
(818) 891-1693
The free catalog advertises diaper covers and airbrushed T-shirts.

Infant Wonders

14431 Chase Street, Suite E-181
Panorama City, CA   91402
(818) 892-6407
These products are designed specifically for the newborn: black-and-white crib sheets, mobiles, and soft toys. When you send for the brochure, be sure to include a #10, self-addressed, stamped envelope.

Livonia

10 Main Street, P.O. Box 495
Chester, NY   10918-9989
(914) 469-2449
Primarily a maker of white leather baby shoes with the name in gold on one sole, the birthdate on the other, Livonia also carries bibs, bathrobes, rattles, aprons, and slippers.

Moonflower Birthing Supply

P.O. Box 128
Louisville, CO   80027
(303) 665-2120
In addition to birthing supplies, Moonflower carries products for parents, infants, and older children, including diaper covers and breast pumps, food

grinders, and backpack child carriers. Books are also available. Send two first-class stamps to receive your brochure.

Natural Elements
145 Lee Street
Santa Cruz, CA 95060
(408) 425-5448
Natural Elements supplies you with baby needs such as diaper covers and baby carriers, lullaby tapes and soaps all made from natural materials. Also available are health remedies such as cough syrup and colic tablets.

One Step Ahead
P.O. Box 46
Deerfield, IL 60015
(800) 274-8440
This company sells a vast array of baby products from strollers to biodegradable, disposable diapers. It emphasizes the latest inventions and improvements. The catalog is $2.

Rainbows & Lollipops, Inc.
13276 Paxton Street
Pacoima, CA 91331
(818) 897-7330
From baby carriers to toilet-training supplies, this $1 catalog contains a full range of baby goods, including diaper bags, car seats, cabinet locks, and stove-knob covers.

Right Start Catalog
5334 Sterling Center Drive
Westlake Village, CA 91361
(800) 548-8531
The $2 fee for the catalog is refunded when you place an order. Right Start carries the latest inventions and the old standbys in everything from trough-shaped changing pads to old-fashioned wooden high chairs.

Sweet Dreems, Inc.
130 E. Wilson Bridge Road, Suite 205
Worthington, OH 43085
(614) 431-0496
(800) 662-6542
Sweet Dreems sells a device that calms babies by imitating the vibration and sound of a car traveling along the highway. A brochure is free.

Tendercare Diapers
R-Med International
5555 71st Street, Suite 8300
Tulsa, OK 74136
(918) 491-9140
(800) 34 IM DRY (344-6379)
Tendercare makes disposable diapers with cellulose fibers and a plastic outer shell rather than the absorbent gels used by other brands. A free price list is available.

BOOKS

Baby-Go-to-Sleep Center
P.O. Box 1332
Florence, AL   35631
(800) 537-7748
A free color catalog of approximately
one hundred old children's classics and
contemporary gems provides a nice
blend of expensive illustrated editions
and inexpensive versions.

Be Healthy Inc.
51 Saltrock Road
Baltic, CT   06330
(203) 822-8573
(800) 433-5523
Offers a free catalog of books, audio-
and videotapes, and products for expectant and new parents.

Bellerophon Books
36 Anapaca Street
Santa Barbara, CA   93101
(805) 965-7034
An excellent collection of cut-out and
coloring books that help your child explore the worlds of history and culture.
The catalog is free.

Better Beginnings Catalog
345 N. Main Street
W. Hartford, CT   06117
(203) 236-4907
(800) 274-0068

The $1 catalog lists books and record-
ings for young children and babies, as
well as handbooks for their parents.

Birth & Life Bookstore
7001 Alonzo Avenue, N.W.
P.O. Box 70625
Seattle, WA   98107-0625
(206) 789-4444
(800) 736-0631 (orders)
The owner of this excellent bookstore,
Lynn Moen, reads all the books she
sells and can discuss them intelligently.
Her thirty-two-page catalog called *Imprints* offers reviews and descriptions to
help parents make an informed choice
when ordering by mail. The free catalog
includes books, videos, and audiotapes
on most maternity, childbirth, and parenting subjects.

Books of Wonder
132 7th Avenue
New York, NY   10011
(212) 989-3270
New York's largest bookstore for children carries new, old, and rare books.
There are two catalogs: one for new
books, one for old and rare books. They
cost $3 each. In addition, a monthly
newsletter is sent out to anyone on the
store's mailing list.

Children's Book & Music Center
2500 Santa Monica Boulevard
Santa Monica, CA   90404
(213) 829-0215
(800) 443-1856
This free, eighty-page, well-organized
catalog lists books, videos, musical instruments, tapes, and records for infants and children through the age of
nine.

Children's Small Press Collection
719 N. 4th Avenue
Ann Arbor, MI   48104
(313) 668-8056
(800) 221-8056
Books published by over one hundred
small presses, from picture books and
cookbooks to books on how to cope
with divorce and death, are listed in the
free catalog.

Child's Collection
155 Avenue of the Americas, 14th Floor
New York, NY   10013
(212) 691-7266
A selection of the finest new and old
books, chosen with loving care. Their
fifty-page catalog is available at no cost.

Chinaberry Book Service
2830 Via Orange Way, Suite B
Spring Valley, CA   92078-1521
(619) 670-5200
(800) 777-5205

Chinaberry's free, hundred-page catalog
contains detailed, informed descriptions
of each book from board books for tiny
children to storybooks for older children. There are also music and story
cassettes and books for parents.

Consumer Information Center
P.O. Box 100
Pueblo, CO   81002
No phone number listed.
The United States Government provides
free booklets on several hundred topics.
Be sure to request *Plain Talk About
Raising Children* and the free catalog of
booklets.

Dover Publications, Inc.
31 E. 2nd Street
Mineola, NY   11501-3582
(212) 255-3755
(516) 294-7000
Dover offers books of magic tricks,
science activities, paper-doll books, coloring books, low-priced editions, and
inexpensive posters. Be sure to ask for
the juvenile books catalog. It's free.

Geode Educational Options
P.O. Box 106
West Chester, PA   19381
(215) 692-0413
Geode provides games and books to
help children develop creativity and cooperative skills. In addition, the com-

pany sells noncompetitive board games. A catalog is available at no charge.

Gleanings
60 Priorway Drive
Novelty, OH   44072
(216) 321-0214
This free catalog of children's books contains a section of "classics" and sections based on reading-skill level.

Gryphon House
P.O. Box 275
Mt. Rainier, MD   20712
(301) 779-6200
(800) 638-0928
Over two hundred thoughtfully chosen books for preschoolers are presented in this illustrated catalog. There are books of poetry, books for special occasions, books for overcoming difficult experiences, story and picture books. Be sure to ask for the free Early Childhood Catalog.

International Childbirth Education Association (ICEA)
P.O. Box 20048
Minneapolis, MN   55420
(612) 854-8660
(800) 624-4934
ICEA will send you a free catalog of the five hundred books they sell regarding pregnancy, birth, and newborns. The titles are for both consumers and professionals.

Learn Me Bookstore
175 Ash Street
St. Paul, MN   55126
(612) 490-1805
A $1 catalog lists books, games, and records bearing a social message such as portraying women in nontraditional roles. The parenting books they offer also incorporate fathers and ethnic peoples.

Los Angeles Birthing Institute
4529 Angeles Crest Highway, Suite 209
La Canada, CA   91011
(818) 952-6310
This source carries classic children's books and books on pregnancy, birth, and parenting. The catalog is free.

Parentbooks
201 Harbord Street
Toronto, Ontario   M5S 1H6
Canada
(416) 537-8334
Parentbooks offers a free brochure listing nearly eighty selected titles concerning maternity, childbirth, and the first few years of life. Patti Kirk, the owner, is happy to suggest books that will meet your needs. The store also offers bibliographies of its books on midwifery, premature babies, child abuse, behavioral problems, and many other topics. Both parents and health professionals are helped.

Parent Teacher Store
2575 Regency Road
Lexington, KY   40503
(606) 277-3555
Serving both parents and teachers, this store offers a free catalog containing books as well as educational toys and games. The focus is on toddlers and older children.

Planned Parenthood Bookstore
2211 E. Madison
Seattle, WA   98112
(206) 328-7715
This store carries books about sexuality, puberty, maternity, childbirth, and child rearing. You can request bibliographies of their books on certain topics, but no general catalog is available.

Practical Parenting
18326 Minnetonka Boulevard
Deephaven, MN   55391
(612) 475-3527
(800) 255-3379
Offers a free catalog of the Practical Parenting books and other titles.

Read It Again
32 Winter Street
Goffstown, NH   03045
No phone number listed.
Offering about one hundred fifty titles, the selection ranges from board books to golden oldies and newer gems for older children. A $1 charge for the catalog is deductible from your first order.

Salad Days
P.O. Box 996
Harpers Ferry, WV   25425
(304) 782-1106
(800) 258-3274
Encompassing long-popular titles, newer favorites, and books for parents, Salad Days provides a thoughtfully selected list of items. The $1 charge for the catalog is refunded when you place an order.

Telltales
P.O. Box 614
Bath, ME   04530
(207) 443-3177
(800) 922-READ (7323)
The $2 catalog beautifully advertises illustrated versions of the classics. The selection of items ranges from books on architecture and science to books that deal with childhood difficulties. Costumes, for book-related play, are also available.

Totline Books
P.O. Box 2255
Everett, WA   98203
(206) 485-3335
(800) 334-4769 (orders)
A free catalog lists activity books for your preschooler.

CHILDREN'S WEAR

Abbie Hasse Catalog
P.O. Box 1078
Cedar Hills, TX   75104
(800) 637-9806
The free catalog pictures clothes for those special occasions including overalls made from raw silk, lace dresses, and tuxedos for tiny people. Also available are lunch boxes and director's chairs emblazoned with your child's name.

After the Stork
1501 12th Street, N.W., P.O. Box 26200
Albuquerque, NM   87104
(505) 243-9100
(800) 333-KIDS (5437)
Cotton clothing that is bright, wearable, and appealing is After the Stork's specialty. The firm carries clothing for children from babies to size sixteen, including sweat suits, T-shirts, long johns, pants, and turtlenecks. The catalog is $1.

Alice in Wholesale Land
140 Linden Street
Oakland, CA   94607
(415) 452-0507
Discounted name brands for children from newborn to size fourteen. The catalog is $2.

Allstar Costume
125 Lincoln Boulevard, Dept. C-300
Middlesex, NJ   08846
(201) 805-0200
Allstar stocks any costume your child might want from tomatoes and dinosaurs to Ninja warriors. Accessories such as masks, wands, and mustaches are also available. The catalog costs $1.

Biobottoms
P.O. Box 6009
Petaluma, CA   94953
(707) 778-7945
(707) 778-7152
Biobottoms specializes in natural-fiber items such as diaper covers in wool, cotton, and nylon as well as a full line of clothing, including rain gear and shoes. Children's furniture accessories are also available. A catalog costs $1.

Brights Creek
Bay Point Place
Hampton, VA   23653
(804) 827-1850
(800) 622-9202
Brights Creek's free catalog pictures everyday and party clothing for infants to size-fourteen teens. There are sweats and corduroys, raincoats and sweaters, shirts and jackets, most made of acrylic or cotton-polyester.

Children's Collection
1717 Post Oak Boulevard
Houston, TX   77056-3882
(713) 622-4415
(713) 622-4350
A free catalog changes with the seasons and is very conscious of what's in and what's out for children who want the latest in party clothes, school clothes, or rain gear.

Children's Shop
P.O. Box 625
Chatham, MA   02633
(508) 945-4811
(800) 426-8716
Free twenty-page catalogs picturing a wide range of clothes are sent out three times a year, depending on the season. Everything is included from stone-washed denim to cotton infantwear, insulated vests and rain ponchos.

Garnet Hill
Main Street, P.O. Box 262
Franconia, NH   03580
(603) 823-5545
(800) 622-6216
Specializing in natural-fiber bedding and clothing, this company's free catalog offers cotton turtlenecks and jumpsuits, a wool sweater coat, silk long underwear, and terrycloth bed sheets.

Good Gear for Little People
Washington, ME   04574
(207) 845-2211
(207) 845-2233
For outdoor wear, this free catalog carries an enormous selection: the Baby Bag for infants, balaclavas, wool button-down sweaters with matching leggings, and snowsuits for toddlers and infants of all sizes. There are also baby monitors, bicycle helmets, and activity books.

Olsen's Mill Direct
1200 Highway 21, P.O. Box 2266
Oshkosh, WI   54903
(414) 685-6688
Creators of the world-famous OshKosh B'Gosh overalls, Olsen's manufactures a whole line of rugged children's wear. Select what you want from a free catalog.

Shoes & Socks, Inc.
1281 Andersen Drive, Suite D
San Rafael, CA   94901
(800) 228-1820
The free catalog features shoes and socks for children from infant to size twelve. You'll have lots to choose from including T-straps, baby booties, and sheepskin slippers.

Soft as a Cloud
1355 Meadowbrook Avenue
Los Angeles, CA   90019
(213) 933-4417
The $1 catalog charge is refunded with your order of cotton or other natural-fiber clothing for your infant or toddler. A wide selection is available.

Soft Shoes
4295 Deming Road
Everson, WA   98247
(206) 592-5748
Send one first-class stamp to receive a brochure listing elk-hide shoes and slippers for the whole family.

Suzo
P.O. Box 186, Pleasant Street
Grafton, VT   05146
(802) 843-2555
The $2 catalog presents a large selection of costumes, including pirate and princess outfits, and mice, pigs, and turtles. These costumes are made of quality materials.

Toad'ly Kids
2428 Patterson Avenue
Roanoke, VA   24016
(703) 981-0233
(800) 621-5809 (orders)

The $2 catalog displays a wide range of clothes from corduroy overalls to a christening robe. Along with turtlenecks and flannel shirts, there are taffeta rompers and sailor suits. A small selection of unusual toys is also available.

Wild Child
1813 Monroe Street
Madison, WI   53711
(608) 251-6445
Play clothes from three months to twelve years. Buy leggings or tank tops in a choice of twenty-four bright, cheerful colors. The catalog is free.

Wooden Soldier
North Hampshire Common
North Conway, NH   03860-0800
(603) 356-7041
(603) 356-6343
For the classic in children's wear, refer to the Wooden Soldier's free catalog. Here you will find mother-daughter or matching sister outfits, sailor suits, and suspender pants.

EDUCATIONAL PRODUCTS

SEE ALSO

Audio- and Videotapes, Science and Nature, and Toys and Games in this chapter for additional products.

The Home Schooling section of PRIVATE AND ALTERNATIVE EDUCATION, Chapter 8, lists sources for learning materials parents can use to educate their children at home as an alternative to regular schools.

The Computers listings under HOBBIES, Chapter 11, offers sources of educational software.

ABC School Supply
6500 Peachtree Industrial Boulevard
P.O. Box 4750
Norcross, GA   30091
(404) 447-5000
Your choice of three free catalogs—*The Preschool Source, Early Learning Materials,* or the four-hundred-page "full" catalog—allows you to choose from an all-encompassing choice of tools for stimulating your child. Everything is included from wooden puzzles to globes.

Chad's Newsalog
50 Business Parkway
Richardson, TX   75081
(214) 680-9787
(800) 262-CHAD (2423)
For $10 you receive twelve monthly installments of the newsletter which sells instructional games and toys, explains their value, and provides other bits of educational information. You can request a free issue at no cost.

Chaselle, Inc.
9645 Gerwig Lane
Columbia, MD   21046
(301) 381-9611
(800) CHASELLE (242-7355)
(800) 492-7840 (in Maryland)
You have a choice of four free catalogs: *Pre-School & Elementary School Materials; Art & Craft Materials; General School & Office Products;* or *Educational Software.* Each offers a complete range of products in its category. Note: There is a $25 minimum order.

Constructive Playthings
1227 E. 119th Street
Grandview, MO   64030-1117
(816) 761-5900

The free *Home Edition* catalog offers puzzles, costumes, train sets, bath toys, and science toys. The $3 *School Edition* carries all this and more, including ethnic dolls and playground equipment.

Cuisenaire Company of America, Inc.
12 Church Street
New Rochelle, NY 10802
(914) 235-0900
(800) 237-3142
The free catalog offers toys and games for learning math concepts as well as science kits, chemistry sets, and models.

Didax Educational Resources
1 Centennial Drive
Peabody, MA 01960
(508) 532-9060
(800) 458-0024
Some toys and handbooks offered in this free catalog are designed especially for home use in teaching reading, science, and math to children from kindergarten to sixth grade.

Educational Activities, Inc.
P.O. Box 87
Baldwin, NY 11510
(516) 223-4666
(800) 645-3739
Educational Activities sells videos and software programs for teaching the three R's, computer skills, science, social studies, and more to all grade

levels through high school. There are also records and cassettes with songs and games for younger children. The brochure is free.

Educational Teaching Aids
199 Carpenter Avenue
Wheeling, IL 60090
(312) 520-2500
The large, $2 catalog advertises everything from construction sets to children's furniture, including wooden puzzles and pictures of trucks and animals. Records and musical instruments are also available.

Environments, Inc.
P.O. Box 1348
Beaufort Industrial Park
Beaufort, SC 29901-1348
(800) EI-CHILD (342-4453)
This free, two-hundred-page catalog offers a wide selection of furniture, toys, and educational products for preschoolers and children in the early grades.

Good Apple
P.O. Box 299
Carthage, IL 62321
(217) 357-3981
(800) 435-7234
Good Apple's free catalog displays activity books and software programs for reading, writing, grammar, math, and creative thought.

J. L. Hammett Co.
30 Hammett Place
Braintree, MA 02184
(617) 848-1000
(800) 672-1932
This huge, five-hundred-page, free catalog is loaded with school supplies, art supplies, toys for tots, sports equipment, tricycles, furniture, and science kits.

Kaplan School Supply Corp.
1310 Lewisville-Clemmons Road
Lewisville, NC 27023
(919) 766-7374
(800) 334-2014
(800) 642-0610 (in North Carolina)
Primarily for day-care centers and preschools, this free catalog makes available to parents furniture, safety products, and toys for infants, toddlers, and older children. Among the offerings are push toys, kitchen sets, playhouses, trucks, swings, and climbing sets.

Leonard Bear Learning, Ltd.
319 S. 7th Street
St. Charles, IL 60174
(312) 377-9322
Leonard Bear and Maynard Bear are teddy bears used to teach children basic concepts and social skills, respectively. Monthly letters from each bear's mother give the child-owner a different assignment for Leonard or Maynard, indirectly becoming a lesson for the child. Call or write for the free brochure.

Nasco
901 Janesville Avenue
Ft. Atkinson, WI 53538
(414) 563-2446
The free *Learning Fun* catalog offers schoolroom merchandise for pre- and elementary schoolers, including cardboard bricks and building blocks. Additional free catalogs with a variety of teaching tools include *Math, Arts & Crafts,* and *Science.*

Opportunities for Learning, Inc.
20417 Nordoff Street
Chatsworth, CA 91311
(818) 341-2535
The free catalog *Materials for Early Education* sells learning software, puzzles, and building sets. Other catalogs available include *Much Ado About Math, The Right Selections for the Gifted* (grades 4–12), and *Materials for the Gifted* (grades K–8). The free, ninety-page *Microcomputer Software* catalog lists programs that will help your younger child with the three R's, and your older child prepare for the ACTs and SATs. Graphics programs are also available.

Zaner-Bloser
1459 King Avenue
P.O. Box 16764-6764
Columbus, OH   43216-6764
(614) 221-5851
(614) 486-0221

Zaner-Bloser helps you pinpoint your child's strongest method of learning—auditory, kinesthetic, or visual. The firm's guides, workbooks, and software help you teach your child based on his or her personal strengths. There is a free catalog available.

FURNITURE AND FURNISHINGS

> ### SEE ALSO
>
> Baby Supplies and Educational Products in this chapter for more catalogs that include furniture.

All But Grown-Ups
P.O. Box 555
Berwick, ME   03901
(800) 448-1550
The free catalog advertises maple furniture including clothes chests, table-and-chair sets, bunk beds, and toy chests. Also available is a bead maze and an easel.

American Art & Graphics, Inc.
P.O. Box 75239
Seattle, WA   98125-0239
(800) 524-3900
For decorating your child's room, you might want to browse through this $1 catalog that has posters of everything from teddy bears to sports cars.

Company Store
500 Company Store Road
La Crosse, WI   54601
(608) 785-1400
(800) 356-9367
The free catalog pictures many accessories for your baby's crib such as flannel sheets and down comforters, and bumper pads, plus merino wool stroller liners. There are also lots of parkas and vests, mittens and gaiters.

Conran's Mail Order
475 Oberlin Avenue S.
Lakewood, NJ   08701-1053
(201) 905-8800
The $2 catalog lists both wood and laminate furniture and decorations for chil-

dren and adults. Available are rugs and shelving, tables-and-chairs, bunk beds, bureaus, wardrobes and lamps.

Country Workshop
95 Rome Street
Newark, NJ   07105
(201) 589-3407
(800) 526-8001
Choose unfinished furniture you can finish yourself or let Country Workshop do it for you. The $1 catalog presents cleverly made cribs and bunk beds, bureaus, stools, and desks.

Crate & Barrel
P.O. Box 3057
Northbrook, IL   60065-3057
(312) 272-3112
Crate & Barrel's $2 catalog carries plastic tables and chairs, lamps, desks, toy boxes, rockers, and easels. The offerings change each season.

Fabrications
P.O. Box 67
East Meadow, NY   11554
(516) 496-8730
To decorate walls, you may want a personalized wall plaque with clothing pegs made in the shape of a ballet shoe, a duck, or a train. The $1 charge for the brochure is refunded when you place an order.

First Class
3305 Macomb Street, N.W.
Washington, DC   20008
(202) 363-3449
The free catalog presents table-and-chair sets, one made of maple, one with oversized pencils as legs; a white wicker rocker; and a Chippendale chair.

Fun Furniture
8451 Beverly Boulevard
Los Angeles, CA   90048
(213) 655-2711
Fun Furniture carries furniture made to look like something else. The $1 catalog includes a toy chest disguised as a taxi, storage shelves resembling palm trees, and a dinosaur-shaped headboard.

H.U.D.D.L.E.
11159 Santa Monica Boulevard
Los Angeles, CA   90025
(213) 836-8001
The $2 catalog offers creative, different children's furniture, most made of modular parts to expand and recombine as your infant becomes a toddler and then a child. Desks, chairs, beds, and bureaus are all available.

Peaceable Kingdom Press
2954 Hillegass Avenue
Berkeley, CA   94705
(415) 654-9989

If you wish to adorn your child's walls with posters by some of our most popular illustrators such as Maurice Sendak or famous characters like Peter Rabbit and Babar, ask for this free catalog.

Pine Specialties
Rt. 2, Box 276
Randleman, NC   27317
A child-size chair, loveseat, rocker, stool, pegboard, toy chest, all made of country-style pine are listed in the $2 catalog.

Sears, Roebuck & Co.
(800) 366-3000
Wooden, metal, or plastic cribs, changing tables, high chairs, and playpens are all available in traditional or contemporary styles. The *Home* and *Style* catalogs cost $5, deductible from your first order; the *Toys* catalog is free.

Shaker Workshops
P.O. Box 1028
Concord, MA   01742
(617) 646-8985
Classic Shaker furniture, including a rocker for a nursing mother and smaller chairs for smaller people, can be bought finished or for home assembly. The $1 catalog also advertises hanging shelves, peg racks, and stools.

Squiggles and Dots
P.O. Box 870
Seminole, OK   74868
(800) 937-KIDS (5437)
From the free catalog you can order chairs with pink udders, a cat-shaped lamp, or a holstein table.

SweetGrass
445 Bishop Street, N.W., Suite A
Atlanta, GA   30318
(404) 875-3754
SweetGrass offers American country-style chairs, beds, and folk art reproductions for adults and rockers, wing chairs, dolls, and doll furniture for children. The catalog is free of charge.

Tabor Inc.
8220 W. 30th Court
Hialeah, FL   33016
(305) 557-1481
The free brochure lists changing tables, dressers, and cribs as well as a child-sized rocker in the shape of a teddy bear.

GIFTS

American Stationery Company, Inc.
100 Park Avenue
Peru, IN   46970
(317) 473-4438
From American Stationery you can order personalized stationery, including a set with colored balloons. The catalog is free.

Disney Catalog

475 Oberlin Avenue S.
Lakewood, NJ   08701-6989
(201) 905-0111
From this $2 catalog you can order an entire array of children's wear, including slippers, coveralls, and bathrobes, all decorated with popular Disney characters. Dolls, films, and book-cassette sets are also available.

Lighter Side

4514 19th Court E., P.O. Box 25600
Bradenton, FL   34203
(813) 747-2356
For that particularly silly, fun gift, pick something from this free catalog. Included are tablecloths for coloring on, a singing statue of Elvis, and a wand for blowing enormous, six-foot bubbles.

Metropolitan Museum of Art

Special Service Office
Middle Village, NY   11381
(718) 326-7050
From the free catalog select an illustrated book, toy, or game based on the museum's own collection. Choices range from a plastic knight and castle to classic editions and beautiful posters.

Museum Books Mail-Order

San Francisco Museum of Modern Art
P.O. Box 182203
Chattanooga, TN   37422
(800) 447-1454

The free catalog presents a selection of artful and clever books and art-related toys that changes each season.

Santa's Elves

Santa Claus, IN   47579
No phone number listed.
Handwritten notes are sent in response to children's Christmas letters to Santa Claus. There is no catalog and no fee, though donations are gladly accepted.

Smithsonian Institution

Dept. 0006
Washington, DC   20073-0006
(202) 357-1826
(703) 455-1700 (orders)
Based on the vast collections of the Smithsonian, this free toy and gift catalog includes such items as astronaut suits, old-fashioned teddy bears, freeze-dried ice cream, and Louisville Slugger baseball bats.

Stocking Fillas

3229 Hubbard Road
Landover, MD   20785
(800) 638-8886
This free catalog presents a great selection of stocking stuffers, such as kazoos, collapsible cups, windup toys, magic candles, and party favors. Most items cost less than $2.

Walt Disney World
Mail Order Dept.
P.O. Box 10,070
Lake Buena Vista, FL   32830-0070
(407) 824-4718
In this free catalog you will find a vast collection of Disney character soft dolls as well as baby dishes, party supplies, and jewelry.

Walter Drake & Sons
68 Drake Building
Colorado Springs, CO   80940
(719) 596-3854
Drake specializes in the inexpensive but personalized gift. From the free catalog select a tote bag, balloon, pencil, or something else and have your child's name embossed on it.

HEALTH AND SAFETY

SEE ALSO

Chapter 5, Health, and Chapter 6, Safety. Some of the organizations in those chapters sell products for specific health and safety problems.

All Points Products
17029 Devonshire Street, Room 169
Northridge, CA   91325
(818) 360-7424
All Points manufactures the Baby Beeper, a tiny pendant necklace that transmits a beep to the parent's receiver when the child wanders too far away or falls into water. Send a #10, self-addressed stamped envelope to receive your catalog.

Allergy Control Products
96 Danbury Road
Ridgefield, CT   06877
(203) 438-9580
(800) 422-DUST (3878)

Products such as mattress and pillow covers, dehumidifiers, air filters, and face masks are available for anyone allergic to house dust or mold spore. The free catalog also advertises an insect-venom extractor.

Baby Safety Specialists, Inc.
2139 N. University Drive, Suite 196
Coral Springs, FL   33071-9966
(305) 341-9072
(800) 537-3412
This free brochure lists several dozen child safety gadgets including cabinet locks, corner cushions for coffee tables, toilet seat straps, and shopping cart safety belts.

Baby Table Bumper Productions
11684 Ventura Boulevard, Room 208
Studio City, CA 91604
(818) 763-2355
Use the "Thumper Bumper" to pad your coffee table and protect your toddler. The flier is free.

Child Safety Catalog
KinderKraft Inc.
P.O. Box 5433
Arlington, VA 22205
(703) 841-1902
This is a free catalog of top-quality safety products. Included are sealable garbage cans, a child-proof medicine box, and safety doorknob covers.

CritiCard, Inc.
445 W. Jackson
Centennial Plaza
Naperville, IL 60540-9990
(312) 357-6866
(800) 331-8801
CritiCard makes identification tags detailing your child's medical history that can be attached to a shoelace. Valuable for emergencies, but the tags are useful only if the hospital is a participant in the CritiCard program. Call or write for a free brochure.

F & H Child Safety Co.
P.O. Box 2228
Evansville, IN 47714
(812) 479-8485

The $1 catalog lists home safety products such as cord shorteners, baby harnesses, a device to keep shoelaces tied, and cabinet locks.

Federal Emergency Management Association
P.O. Box 70274
Washington, DC 20024
(703) 471-7596
"Big Bird Gets Ready for Hurricanes" is a free kit created to help a family, particularly its children, cope with the fear and actuality of major storms. The kit also contains useful advice for parents in handling an emergency.

Lifesaver Charities
P.O. Box 2533
Garden Grove, CA 92640
(714) 530-7100
ID tags containing spaces for a child's name, insurance and allergy information, emergency phone numbers, and parental consent for medical treatment. Send a #10, self-addressed stamped envelope to receive a catalog.

Perfectly Safe
7245 Whipple Avenue, N.W.
North Canton, OH 44720
(216) 494-4366
The $1 catalog advertises safety items such as childproof latches, gates, and socket plugs. Also available is an alarm that sounds when a child falls into the

pool and buttons for automatic-dial phones picturing the person being called.

SelfCare Catalog

P.O. Box 130
Mandeville, LA   70448
(504) 892-8032
(800) 345-3371
SelfCare supplies a whole range of products from blood-pressure monitors and weight scales to ear scopes and travel potty seats. Clothes for exercise and sleep are also listed in the free catalog.

Westags, Inc.

P.O. Box C
Flourtown, PA   19031
(215) 233-5141
(800) 232-2873
These plastic ID tags, in a choice of four colors, can be laced into a child's sneaker. There's enough room on each tag for listing allergies, address, and emergency phone numbers, and, of course, your child's name. The brochure is free.

MATERNITY AND NURSING CLOTHES

Babe too! Patterns

3457 E. K4 Highway
Assaria, KS   67416
(913) 667-5125

Send a #10, self-addressed stamped envelope to receive the catalog of nursing-wear sewing patterns.

Bosom Buddies

P.O. Box 6138
Kingston, NY   12401
(914) 338-2038
The free brochure lists several different styles of nursing bras in cotton or nylon, including sizes F, G, and H. You can also get a sports bra, bra extenders, and nursing pads.

Colten Creations

54C Burk Drive
Silver Bay, MN   55614
(218) 226-3716
Colten creates patterns for nursing clothes you can make yourself. Send a #10, self-addressed stamped envelope to receive your brochure.

Designer Series

P.O. Box 736
N. Hollywood, CA   91609
(818) 763-7315
For $.50 you receive a brochure listing a wide range of nursing bras from size 32A to 46G. Available are a sports bra and a lightweight bra for sleep as well as a stomach supporter a friend once referred to as a "belly bag."

5th Avenue Maternity

P.O. Box 21826
Seattle, WA   98111-3826
(206) 343-7046
(800) 426-3569

A range of maternity clothes for work, casual wear, and dress is available through this $2 catalog, which changes with the seasons. Accessories such as swimsuits, hosiery, and bras are also to be had.

Holly Nicolas Nursing Collection

P.O. Box 7121
Orange, CA   92613-7121
(714) 639-5933

For the price of a #10, self-addressed envelope with two first-class stamps you receive the catalog describing almost a dozen maternity styles for home and office wear. Fabric swatches are included.

Maternity Modes, Inc.

4950 W. Main Street
Skokie, IL   60077
(312) 677-0099

Maternity wear, both formal and casual, is listed in the $1 catalog.

Motherhood

1330 Colorado Avenue
Santa Monica, CA   90404-2142
(213) 450-1011
(800) 227-1903

Two free, seasonal catalogs advertise maternity or nursing clothes. Motherhood has stores across the country that sell a complete range of clothes including shorts and T-shirts, overalls, sundresses, nightgowns, bras, and robes.

Mother Nurture Breastfeeding Apparel & Patterns

103 Woodland Drive, Dept. MOSP
Pittsburgh, PA   15228-1715
(412) 344-5940

Both patterns and ready-to-wear clothes with emphasis on work attire are included in this $2 catalog. Almost three-dozen outfits are available as well as breast shields, pads, and a breast pump.

Mother's Place

6836 Engle Road
P.O. Box 94512
Cleveland, OH   44101-4512
(800) 444-6864

This free catalog carries inexpensive maternity clothes, some appropriate for the office. Available are sweatshirts, underwear, slips, nightgowns, sweaters, and skirts.

Mothers Work

1309 Noble Street, 5th Floor
Philadelphia, PA   19123
(215) 625-9259

This $3 catalog pictures clothes geared especially for the working woman. With the catalog come swatches of the fabric the clothes are made from, including silk, denim, wool gaberdine, and rayon.

Motherwear
P.O. Box 114-SP
Northampton, MA   01061
(413) 586-3488
The free catalog encompasses a wide gamut of items from parenting books to nursing clothes. Here you will find maternity jumpers and sweatshirts, diaper covers, infant shoes, as well as a parenting library.

Page Boy Maternity
8918 Governors Row
Dallas, TX   75247
(214) 951-0055
(800) 225-3103
Page Boy carries a selection of very fashionable maternity clothes including a black velvet dress and a floral silk tu-

nic to be worn over a black dress. The catalog costs $2.50.

Reborn Maternity
564 Columbus Avenue
New York, NY   10024
(212) 362-6965
The $2 catalog presents a strong selection of both formal and casual maternity clothes, including a rayon skirt-and-jacket set for office wear and a striped jumpsuit for play wear.

ReCreations Maternity
P.O. Box 191038
Columbus, OH   43209
(614) 236-1109
(800) 621-2547
Attractive, comfortable maternity clothes are featured in the $3 catalog. There are jumpers and jumpsuits made of cotton, rayon, or linen, and silk dresses. Most items come in solid colors, making mix and match easy.

SCIENCE AND NATURE

SEE ALSO

Educational Products in this chapter for additional science items.
   The HOBBIES section of Chapter 11 also lists catalogs to interest young science and nature enthusiasts.

Discovery Corner
Lawrence Hall of Science
University of California
Berkeley, CA   94720
(415) 624-1016
For an array of fun, science-oriented toys and gifts get this $1 catalog. Among other things there is a crystal-growing kit, a Slinky, and a micro-scope.

Dover Scientific Co.
P.O. Box 6011
Long Island City, NY   11106
(718) 721-0136
The $1 catalog briefly introduces you to the company's Indian artifacts, minerals, and shells. Related books are also available.

Edmund Scientific
101 E. Gloucester Pike
Barrington, NJ   08007
(609) 573-6260
(609) 547-8880
The free, eighty-page catalog offers a terrific spread of choices for your child ranging from glow-in-the-dark necklaces to radiometers, star maps, prisms, telescopes, and telescope parts.

Heath Co.
Benton Harbor, MI   49022
(616) 982-3200
(800) 444-3284
The free catalog contains building kits for every possible electronic gadget: computers, televisions, stereos, and more.

Learning Things, Inc.
68A Broadway, P.O. Box 436
Arlington, MA   02174
(617) 646-0093
The free catalog is full of science and math toys and tools for children and their parents. Included are rock collections, carpentry tools, wall charts, and polyhedral dice.

Merrell Scientific/World of Science
1665 Buffalo Road
Rochester, NY   14624
(716) 426-1540
This huge, two-hundred-page, $2 catalog contains all you'll need to help your child develop an interest in science. Items include Magic Rocks and ant farms, anatomical models and rocket models. You can also choose from a solid library of science and nature books.

MMI Corporation
2950 Wyman Parkway
P.O. Box 19907
Baltimore, MD   21211
(301) 366-1222
There are two free catalogs: one for astronomy and one for geology.

Nasco
901 Janesville Avenue
Ft. Atkinson, WI   53538
(414) 563-2446
Nasco's free *Science* catalog contains nearly three hundred pages of microscopes, dissection kits, butterfly nets, mineral collections, animal cages, and much more.

Small World Toys
P.O. Box 5291
Beverly Hills, CA   90210
No phone number listed.
The free catalog makes engrossing reading. Here are science-related toys for children ages four to twelve, including kits for testing luminosity, skeleton-models for the human body, and a land-rover to be put together with elastic belts and pulleys.

SWING SETS AND PLAYHOUSES

Big Toys
7717 New Market
Olympia, WA   98501
(800) 423-0082
(800) 752-7511 (in Washington state)
Big Toys makes assemble-your-own log construction play sets that can be added on to as your child grows. The catalog is free.

CedarWorks
Rt. 1, Box 640
Rockport, ME   04856
(207) 236-3183
This firm sells swings and climbing sets, in a range of sizes, made from ash and cedar. Add-ons such as trapezes, slides, and rope ladders are sold separately. The catalog is free.

Child Life Play Specialties, Inc.
55 Whitney Street, P.O. Box 6159
Holliston, MA   01746
(508) 429-4639
(800) 462-4445
The $1 catalog, whose cost is deducted from your first order, advertises green-painted swings and climbing sets made from pressure-treated cedar and fir.

Children's Playgrounds Inc.
P.O. Box 1547
Cambridge, MA   02238-9990
(617) 497-1588
This free catalog features indoor play sets made of heavy, red-plastic tubing with lots of add-on pieces and outdoor sets built for heavy-duty use.

Children's Playgrounds Inc.
P.O. Box 370
Unionville, Ontario   L3R 2Z7
Canada
(416) 475-7648
See description above.

Creative Playgrounds Ltd.
P.O. Box 10
McFarland, WI   53558
(608) 838-3326
The free catalog offers pressure-treated pine play sets, some fairly elaborate, as well as a tire swing, a sandbox, and a seesaw.

English Garden Toys
P.O. Box 786
Indianola, PA   15051
(412) 767-5332
(800) 445-5675
These swing-and-climbing sets are fashioned from tubular steel appropriate for both indoor or outdoor use. The free catalog also lists tunnels, seesaws, and plastic sandboxes.

Florida Playground & Steel Co.
4701 S. 50th Street
Tampa, FL   33619
(813) 247-2812
(800) 444-2655
The free catalog advertises long-lasting slides, merry-go-rounds, and swing sets made of galvanized steel.

GYM*N*I Playgrounds, Inc.
P.O. Box 96, Laurel Bend
New Braunfels, TX   78130
(512) 629-6000
(800) 232-3398

Play sets from the simple to the elaborate, made of pressure-treated wood, are available through this free catalog.

Isis Innovations
177 Thornton Drive
Hyannis, MA   02601
(508) 790-5992
(800) 245-5224 (orders)
From this free catalog you can order aerial playhouses and swing-and-climbing sets made of redwood and maple. There are optional add-ons.

Wood Built of Wisconsin, Inc.
P.O. Box 92-SP
Janesville, WI   53547
(608) 754-5050
Buy your own lumber and use Wood Built's hardware and accessories, including precut dowels, cables and mounts, and steel slides to construct a play set. The catalog is free.

Woodplay Incorporated
P.O. Box 27904
Raleigh, NC   27611-7904
(919) 832-2970
Play sets made of redwood and steel with slides and lookout towers, rope ladders, and swings are detailed in this free catalog.

TOYS AND GAMES

SEE ALSO

the Educational Products and Science and Nature sections of this chapter. The Dolls and Toys and Games and Puzzles listings under HOBBIES, Chapter 11, list additional catalogs of interest.

Abilities International
Old Forge Road
Elizabethtown, NY   12932-0398
(518) 873-6456
This $1, thirty-two-page catalog holds a wonderful collection of toys, clothes, and baby supplies. Here you can find a plastic schoolhouse in a shoe, a wooden train, a puppet theater, block sets, games, puzzles, and books.

Action BMX Cycle Co.
255 Wolfner Drive
Fenton, MO   63026
(314) 343-9466
The large $2 catalog lists not only skateboards, scooters, and bicycles but lots of parts and accessories, including clothes and videos.

Afterschool
1401 John Street
Manhattan Beach, CA   90266
(213) 545-1073
This free catalog contains toys such as a model kit for an erupting volcano, an ant farm, and easily cleaned, nylon-covered foam blocks.

Animal Town Game Company
P.O. Box 2002
Santa Barbara, CA   93120
(805) 682-7343
This firm makes tapes, books, and toys that emphasize cooperative behavior while children play and learn. Also available are colored chalk, an umbrella with a duck handle, and a set of small gardening tools. The catalog is free.

Ark Catalog
4245 Crestline Avenue
Fair Oaks, CA   95628
(916) 967-2607
For $1 you can get an enjoyable color catalog of unique wooden toys, including Little Red Riding Hood and the Pied Piper, as well as a tepee pattern, modeling beeswax, a Goldilocks cookie-cutter, and books of folk tales and myths.

Bear-in-Mind
53 Bradford Street
West Concord, MA   01742
(508) 369-1167
Here you'll find close to two hundred
teddy bears of many sizes, from the pe-
tite to the enormous. The $1 catalog
also lists bearfoot slippers and collectors' books.

Big City Kite Co.
1201 Lexington Avenue
New York, NY   10028
(212) 472-2623
This $2 catalog (cost deducted from
your first order) pictures numerous
beautiful and unusual kites. There are
box kites, stunt kites, Japanese carp
wind socks, and simple diamond kites.

Bits & Pieces
1 Puzzle Place, B8016
Stevens Point, WI   54481
(715) 341-3521
(800) JIG-SAWS (544-7297)
A huge variety of puzzles is offered in
this free catalog. Jigsaw puzzles, books
of puzzles, sculpture puzzles, and puzzles for children are all included.

Boomerang Man
1806 N. 3rd Street, Room SP
Monroe, LA   71201-4222
(318) 325-8157

A whole array of exotic boomerangs is
available through this free catalog.
Australian boomerangs of plastic or
plywood, Texas boomerangs, and night-
flying boomerangs are just some of the
many offered.

Childcraft
20 Kilmer Road
Edison, NJ   08818
(800) 367-3255
(800) 631-5657 (orders)
The free Childcraft catalog specializes
in instructional toys such as color-in
flash cards, microscopes, and building
blocks. These are supplemented with
fun things like piñatas, costumes, and
racing-car sets.

Family Pastimes
R. R. 4
Perth, Ontario   K7H 3C6
Canada
No phone number is listed. The $1 cat-
alog offers board games that encourage
cooperation because no one can win
unless the participants help each other.

Fantasy Den
25 Morehouse Avenue
Stratford, CT   06497
(203) 377-2968
The Fantasy Den has a tremendous collection of teddy bears and other stuffed
animals such as wombats and koala

bears. Here you'll find the famous series that includes Amelia Bearheart and Albeart Einstein. The $1.75 catalog also offers posters and bear-making equipment.

F.A.O. Schwarz

P.O. Box 182225
Chattanooga, TN   37422-7225
(800) 426-TOYS (8697)
The $5 catalog, like the New York store, offers the most fabulous, expensive, unusual toys you might ever consider buying.

Fisher-Price

Consumer Affairs
636 Girard Avenue
E. Aurora, NY   14052-1880
(800) 432-5437
The free catalog lists by name and model number all those spare toy parts you need to repair a broken Fisher-Price toy. A picture catalog costs $2.

Gifted Children's Catalog

2922 N. 35th Avenue, Suite 4
Phoenix, AZ   85061-1408
(602) 272-1853
(800) 528-6050
Toys with a gentle approach to educating your child such as pop-up books, star charts, a beginner's chess set, and a leaf press are offered in this $2 catalog.

Gil & Karen's Toy Box

3975 Kim Court
Sebastopol, CA   95472
(707) 823-8128
This source has a free catalog full of wooden toys such as blocks in their own personalized toy box. There are also name, number, and alphabet puzzles, toolboxes, a dollhouse, and a train set.

Ginny Graves

5328 W. 67th Street
Prairie Village, KS   66208
(913) 262-0691
Send a #10, self-addressed stamped envelope to receive information regarding *Discovery Stuff,* which contains fifty-two possible art projects, and *What Can I Do Now Mommy?,* an art-activity book for younger children.

Growing Child

P.O. Box 620
Lafayette, IN   47902
(317) 423-2624
This free catalog offers a great selection of toys, books, and recordings. For children up to age ten there are shape sorters, puzzles, hand puppets, a make-believe kit, blocks, great books both old and new, and recordings by Mister Rogers et al.

Hancock Toy Shop
97 Prospect Street
Jaffrey, NH 03452
(603) 532-7504
The $1 catalog sells handmade wooden toys and children's furniture.

HearthSong
P.O. Box B
Sebastopol, CA 95473
(707) 829-1550
(800) 325-2502
A huge array of interesting and different items for children is offered by this $1 catalog. Here you will find a finger-puppet theater and tiddlywinks, a children's lyre and a popcorn popper for the fireplace, a German dollhouse and wooden-headed dolls.

High Fly Kite Co.
30 West End Avenue
Haddonfield, NJ 08033
(609) 429-6260
Here is a great selection of exotic kites. The free catalog lists box kites, wind socks, Japanese fighting kites, and a tremendous (but expensive) airfoil kite as well as parts and supplies if you want to create your own kite.

Into the Wind/Kites
1408 Pearl Street
Boulder, CO 80302
(303) 449-5356

This large, free catalog boasts of dragon kites in stunning colors, five-foot snowflake kites, stunt kites. In addition, there are gliders, boomerangs, and kite-making supplies.

Johnson & Johnson Child Development Toys
6 Commercial Street
Hicksville, NY 11801-9955
(800) 645-7470
Johnson & Johnson runs a special program for newborns in which every month you receive a toy especially targeted to your child's age and developmental level. Over an eighteen-month period you receive approximately twenty of the best available toys for your baby. Call for free information on the program.

Judy/Instructo
4325 Hiawatha Avenue S.
Minneapolis, MN 55406
(612) 721-5761
(800) 523-1713
Wooden inlay puzzles of maps or the alphabet, many with knobs for younger hands and with fifteen pieces or less, are offered for sale in this free catalog.

Julia & Brandon
791 Roscommon Drive
Vacaville, CA 95688
(707) 446-8838

The free catalog is filled with toys, safety gadgets, and other supplies for your toddler and preschooler. There's a portable Sassy seat, plates for newcomers to the dining table, light-switch extenders, bathtub spout covers, see-through spin tops, easy jigsaw puzzles and wooden puzzles, and picture boards with attachable/removable vinyl figures.

Just for Kids!
75 Paterson Street, P.O. Box 15006
New Brunswick, NJ   08906-5006
(800) 443-5827
This firm offers a free catalog featuring toys and games, party supplies and costumes. Depending on the season (there are three different catalogs), you can purchase wading pools or bunny costumes, holiday cookie cutters and sweatshirts, as well as a log cabin playhouse, a ballerina costume, child-size golf clubs, and an electronic keyboard.

Klutz Flying Apparatus Catalogue
2121 Staunton Court
Palo Alto, CA   94306
(415) 857-0888
The free catalog advertises, along with juggling supplies, a wooden yo-yo, a clock that runs on leftover vegetables, a wand for blowing eight-foot bubbles, and a pink flamingo. There are also how-to books, a book on juggling, one of songs for children to sing along with, and a children's cookbook.

LEGO Shop-at-Home Service
55 Taylor Road, P.O. Box 640
Enfield, CT   06082-3298
(203) 749-0706
(203) 749-2291
LEGO's free catalog offers every possible LEGO set or part you could possibly wish to order.

Pacific Puzzle Company
378 Guemes Island Road
Anacortes, WA   98221
(206) 293-7034
Pacific Puzzle sells wooden puzzles in the shapes of numbers, the alphabet, maps, and animals. The catalog is available at no cost.

Puzzle People, Inc.
22719 Tree Farm Road
Colfax, CA   95713
(916) 637-4823
This firm offers alphabet puzzles, animal puzzles, or map puzzles, plus a few stand-up animal puzzles, all made of wood. Call or write for a free brochure.

Racing Strollers Inc.
P.O. Box 2189
Yakima, WA   98907
(509) 457-0925
(800) 548-7230
The free brochure advertises the Baby Jogger, an all-terrain stroller, and the Walkabout, a smaller-wheeled model.

Sensational Beginnings
P.O. Box 2009, 430 N. Monroe
Monroe, MI   48161
(313) 242-2147
(800) 444-2147
The free catalog contains a great collection of toys for babies and toddlers ranging from black-and-white pictures to big soft blocks, wagons, and tricycles.

Toys Unique
595 N. Westgate
Grand Junction, CO   81505
(303) 242-7092
The $1 retail price list offers an intriguing selection of rocking toys such as swans and dinosaurs, pelicans, and lions. The seats are luxuriously cushioned and the necks padded.

Troll
100 Corporate Drive
Mahwah, NJ   07430
(201) 529-8000
(800) 247-6101 (orders)

Both the *Learn & Play* and the *Family Gifts* catalogs are free. The first has lots of toys, games, and books such as pogo sticks, toy cookware, and costumes. The second catalog supplements this nicely with rattles, crayon-shaped cups, and cassettes.

Wisconsin Wagon Co.
507 Laurel Avenue
Janesville, WI   53545
(609) 754-0026
From the free catalog you can select reproductions of wheelbarrows, scooters, and wagons from 1900–1940 made of oak, steel, and rubber. These are built to last.

Woodmonger
George Baumgardner
111 N. Siwash
Tonasket, WA   98855
(509) 485-3414
The free flier describes a deluxe ecologically sensitive rocking horse made from silver pine of trees left standing in wildfires, not live trees.

MANUFACTURERS OF TOYS, FURNITURE, AND ACCESSORIES

The manufacturer is often your best source for help if you have questions about a toy, children's accessory, or piece of furniture. In addition, if you need a replacement part or a repair on a children's product, the manufacturer often proves the only recourse.

However, in many cases, only the brand name, not the manufacturer, appears on the toy itself. Unless you kept the original box, it is nearly impossible to tell who made the product.

The first section below, Directory of Brand Names, lists hundreds of manufacturer names alongside the brand names. Once you identify a manufacturer, turn to the second section, Directory of Manufacturers, for its phone number and address.

DIRECTORY OF BRAND NAMES

BRAND NAME	MANUFACTURER NAME
Action Lift	Moore Products
Age of Wonder	Jolly Jumper Inc.
Alcazam	Silo Inc.
All Plus Lotion, Cream, Shampoo	A-Plus Products Inc.
Alphabet Blocks Trim Strips	Priss Prints Inc.
Alpine	Child Craft
Ambi	Small World Toys
Ambi Toys	Davis Grabowski Inc.
Ambi Toys	Playspaces International Inc.
Americana	Child Craft
American Widgeon	American Widgeon
Amore Line	Lloyderson Dolls & Toys
Animal Nappers, Animal Packers, Animal Snackers, Animal Splashers, and Animal Zappers	Hoopla
Animal Pockets	Kids Forever Products
Anti Colic Valves	A-Plus Products Inc.
Apollo	Daust Juvenile Products Inc.
Aprica	Aprica U.S.A.
Aqua Learn	Aqua Learn Inc.
Aqua Tech	Pansy Ellen Products Inc.
Aristo Brats	Davida
Artful Badger	Creative Imaging
Astrotemp	Marshall Products
Auto Latches	A-Plus Products Inc.
Avent	Kids Corp. International

BRAND NAME	MANUFACTURER NAME
Babee-Tenda	Baby-Tenda Corporation
Babi Bags	Romar Intl. Babi Bags
Baby B	Nogatco International Inc.
Baby Bana	Pinky Baby Products
Baby Blanky	Unity Products Inc.
Baby Buddies	Happytimes
Baby Buddy	Baby Buddies Inc.
Baby Chef	Marshall Products
Baby Cuddler III	Small Waves Ltd.
Baby-Go-To-Sleep Tapes	Flying Colors Inc.
Baby Jogger	Racing Strollers Inc.
Baby Joy	Tradis Inc.
Baby Lambsdown	Crestwood Industries, Inc.
Baby Loo	G. W. Dmka Inc.
Baby Manners	Davida
Baby-Mate	Baby-Tenda Corp.
Baby's First Choice	TOT Inc./Turn on Toys
Babyshades	Two Little Girls Inc.
Baby Sit	Peg Perego U.S.A. Inc.
Baby Sitter II	A-Plus Products Inc.
Babysnug Super-Bunting	Cherry Tree
Baby Soaps	Chase Holding Co. Inc.
Babys Sof-Sak	MFP Manufacturing
Baby Susan	Pansy Ellen Products Inc.
Baby-Tenda	Baby-Tenda Corp.
Ballons & Glouds Trim Strips	Priss Prints Inc.
Balloon Bears	Jolly Jumper Inc.
Bambino Babys Blanket	Crestwood Industries Inc.
Bambino Basket	Beautiful Bambino Inc.
Bambola	Small World Toys
Barbie	Priss Prints Inc.
BathBag	BooBear Products Inc.
Bath Bumper Products	Kiness & Co.
Bathtime Magic	Discovery Music
Bath Trainer	Century Products Company

BRAND NAME	MANUFACTURER NAME
Batman	Priss Prints Inc.
Beach Ball Bears	Pansy Ellen Products Inc.
Beachcombers (Sandals)	Gerber Products Company
Bearbath Stuffed Animal Cleaner	Bear Care Company
Bedford	Child Craft
Bedtime Originals	Lambs & Ivy
Beeper Finder	B.E.E.P. Inc.
Behavior Board	Behavior Products
Belly Belts	Happytimes
Belted Baby Bags	Sandbox Industries
Belvedere	Child Craft
Berkley	Welsh Company
Best Day's	G. W. Dmka Inc.
Best of Friends	Lloyderson Dolls & Toys
Bib-in-a-Bag	Newborne Company, Inc.
Bionics Pinless Diapers	Nurturtech
Bionics Smarti Pants	Nurturtech
Bottle Bank	Cambium Design Co.
Bottle Bootie	Prince Lionheart
Bottle Lamp	Cambium Design Co.
Bottlenanny	Babyline Products
Bow Wow	A-Plus Products Inc.
Boynton for Babies	Perfect Fit Industries
Bradley	Child Craft
Bright Starts	Pansy Ellen Products Inc.
Buddy Behemoth	Woods by Hartco Inc.
Buena Vista Records	Walt Disney Records
Bug Bonnet	Two Little Girls Inc.
BuggeeBag	BooBear Products Inc.
Burper	Nurturtech
Busy Rider Activity Set	Toy Time Inc.
Bye Bye	Peg Perego U.S.A. Inc.
Cannon	Kids Corp. International
Capri	Welsh Company
Caravan	Welsh Company

BRAND NAME	MANUFACTURER NAME
Caravel	Peg Perego U.S.A. Inc.
Carta-Kid	Great Kid Co.
Cassie's Collection	Noel Joanna Inc.
Catalina	Child Craft
Catch-a-Wink	Century Products Company
Changing Table Pad Covers	Sandbox Industries
Chelsea	Child Craft
Chesapeake, Chesapeake II	Child Craft
Chicco	Artsana of America/Chicco
Child Comfort Cover	Justin Time Productions Inc.
Child Safe	Child Safety Products
Child Safety Alert	B.E.E.P. Inc.
Child's Play Books	Playspaces International Inc.
Child View Mirror	Prince Lionheart
Clippa-Safe	Silver Cross America Inc.
Cloth Latches	A-Plus Products Inc.
CMS Records	Silo Inc.
Collectors Classics	Gund, Inc.
Colorettes	Delby System
Comfi Ride	A-Plus Products Inc.
Comfort Plus	Marshall Products
Comfort Tote	Comfort Products
Comfy Seat	Pansy Ellen Products Inc.
Comfy Tot	Comfort Products
Comfy Wipe Warmer	Wheeler Enterprises
Commander	Century Products Inc.
Commuter	Newborne Company, Inc.
Cool Mickey	Priss Prints Inc.
Coupe Deluxe	Century Products Inc.
Cozy Baby Products	Cozy Baby Products
Cozy Carrier	Cozy Carrier Co. Inc.
Cozy Cushion	Pinky Baby Products
Cradle Art	TOT Inc./Turn on Toys
Crawl Space	Century Products Inc.
Creative Imaging	Creative Imaging

BRAND NAME	MANUFACTURER NAME
Crib Bibs	Sandbox Industries
Crib'n'Bed	Child Craft
Crib Sack	Perfect Fit Industries
Cricket	Welsh Company
Crisis Control Center	Project Marketing Group, Inc.
Cuboids	Samson-McCann
Cuddler Mattress Pad	Small Waves Ltd.
Cuddle Time	Triboro Quilt Mfg. Corp.
Cuddlies (Plush Toys)	Gerber Products Company
Curity	Gerber Childrenswear, Inc.
Cushie Comfort	Comfort Products
Dad Bag	Newborne Company, Inc.
Dance on Video	V.I.E.W. Video Inc.
Day'n Nite	Century Originals
Deb'n Heir	Relative Industries
Delby Dinosaurs	Delby System
Denim Bears	Pansy Ellen Products Inc.
Designer Lites	Pansy Ellen Products Inc.
Diaperaps	Diaperaps
Dinodorables	Delby System
Dino-Soaps	Chase Holding Co. Inc.
Discovery Music	Silo Inc.
Diset	Playspaces International Inc.
Disney Babies	Priss Prints Inc.
Disneyland Records	Walt Disney Records
Dixie Furniture Co.	Henry Link Corporation
Dolly Carrier	Cozy Carrier Co. Inc.
Dollysnug	Cherry Tree
Domani Quattro	Peg Perego U.S.A. Inc.
Double-Feature	Wimmer-Ferguson Child Products, Inc.
Double Guard Auto Booster	Gerry Baby Products Company
Dreamland	Gerber Childrenswear, Inc.
Duette	Peg Perego U.S.A. Inc.
DuffleCool	J. L. Childress Co.
Eat In Your Car	Anacapa Corporation

BRAND NAME	MANUFACTURER NAME
Eat N'Run	Starwares
Electrigard	Child Safety Products
Ellen Miklas Originals	Ellen Miklas Originals
Emmaljunga	Bandaks Emmaljunga Inc.
Encore	Etc. "Environmental Teen Concepts"
Evolution Changing Table	Newborne Company, Inc.
Executive Pony Line	Woods by Hartco Inc.
Express Breast Feeding System	J. L. Childress Co.
Eyes-R-Dry	Prince Lionheart
E-Z Go	Century Products Inc.
Fairfax	Welsh Company
Fantasia	Child Craft
Fashion Dolls—Porcelain	Lloyderson Dolls & Toys
Faucet Friends	A-Plus Products Inc.
Finger Latch	Child Safety Products
Firefly	Welsh Company
First Class	Newborn Company, Inc.
First Meals High Chair	Gerry Baby Products Company
First Years	Kiddie Products Inc.
Fischerform	Small World Toys
Fishrings	A-Plus Products Inc.
Fish Tales	Pansy Ellen Products Inc.
Fits Rite Car Seat Cover	Pansy Ellen Products Inc.
Flap Hats	Flap Happy
Flightmaster	Welsh Company
Flying Colors Books	Flying Colors Inc.
Flying Duck	Diaperaps
Fold'n'Go	Century Products Inc.
Foodfile	A-Plus Products Inc.
Foothold Security Gate	Gerry Baby Products Company
Freedom	Century Products Inc.
Freedom Trainer	G. W. Dmka Inc.
Free Hand	C. J. Leachco, Inc.
Friendly Forest	Priss Prints Inc.
Funtime Bath Arch	Century Originals

BRAND NAME	MANUFACTURER NAME
Gateway	Century Products Inc.
Gautier	Gautier USA
General Mica	General Mica Corp.
Gentle Giraffe	A-Plus Products Inc.
Geuther	Kids Corp. International
Ginny Deer	Delby System
Glenwood	Welsh Company
Glider Rocking Chair Covers	Sandbox Industries
Good Behavior Book	Behavior Products
Good Behavior Game	Behavior Products
Goosefeathers	Goosefeathers
Goosling	Goosefeathers
Gotta Getta Gund	Gund, Inc.
Gowi	Small World Toys
Grab a Seat	Gram Gram, Inc.
Graduate Booster Seat	Pansy Ellen Products Inc.
Gram's Kids	Gram Gram, Inc.
Grand Prix	Welsh Company
Great American Toy Line	Woods by Hartco Inc.
Great Heart	Brass Key Inc.
Growing Up Great Toys	Brass Key Inc.
Growth Chart	Priss Prints Inc.
Guardian Car Seat	Gerry Baby Products Company
Half-Pint Urinal	Baby Motivations Co.
Handy-Holder Bib	Unity Products Inc.
Happy Hopper	Welsh Company
Happy Shade	Chase Holding Co. Inc.
Happy Time Baby Line	Lloyderson Dolls & Toys
Hares-Bears!	Decorate-It!, Inc.
Head-A-Bed	Lear Siegler Seymour Corp./Worldsbest Etc. "Environmental Teen Concepts"
Headboards Collection	
Head's Rite Car Sear Cover	Pansy Ellen Products Inc.
Head's Rite Stroller Cover	Pansy Ellen Products Inc.
Heirloom Pony Line	Woods by Hartco Inc.
Heritage	Welsh Company

BRAND NAME	MANUFACTURER NAME
Herlag	International Products Trading Inc.
Hi & Mitey	Century Products Inc.
High Chair Helper	Toy Time Inc.
Hitch-hiker	Nurturtech
Hug & Tug	Chase Holding Co. Inc.
Hugger	Unity Products Inc.
Huggy Tuggy	Century Originals
Ice Cream Bears	Pansy Ellen Products Inc.
In'n Out Alarm	B.E.E.P. Inc.
Infant Car Seat Covers	Sandbox Industries
Infant Cot	Gram Gram, Inc.
Infantasia Video Mobiles	V.I.E.W. Video Inc.
Infantry	A-Plus Products Inc.
Infant Stim-mobile	Wimmer-Ferguson Child Products, Inc.
Infant Swaddler	Comfort Silkie Company Inc.
Ital Baby	Child Craft
j & m picturshades	J. M. Designs Inc.
Jazz on Video	V.I.E.W. Video Inc.
Jilly Mac	Dianes Designs Inc.
Joe Scruggs	Silo Inc.
Johnny Step Up	Century Products Inc.
Jolly Buggy, Jolly Clowns, Jolly Jumper, Jolly Rider, and Jolly Rider II	Jolly Jumper Inc.
Joy Baby	Joy Baby Inc.
Jumbo Stick-ups Self-Packs	Priss Prints Inc.
Kanga-rocka-roo	Century Products Inc.
Kangouron	Century Originals
Keep Neat	Pansy Ellen Products Inc.
Keepsafe	Lear Siegler Seymour Corp./Worldsbest
Kettler	International Products Trading Inc.
Kiddi Comfort	Comfort Products
Kiddie Corners Foam Pads	Baby Motivations Co.
Kid Kaper	C. J. Leachco, Inc.
Kidsprints	Petco Kidsprints

BRAND NAME	MANUFACTURER NAME
Kimbo Kids Read-Alongs	Kimbo Educational
KinderGund	Gund, Inc.
Kit Right Baby	Sit Right Baby Products (Ckenbe Inc.)
Kiwi	Prodigy Corp.
Kuddler	Cuddly Komfort Affectueux Inc.
Lamby	Lamby Nursery Collection
Lanz of Salzburg	Alison's Design Inc.
Leipold	Kids Corp. International
Le Mans	Welsh Company
Liddlestuff	KLM Woodworks
Light Switch Extension	Baby Motivations Co.
L'il Stuff	Great Kid Co.
Link-Taylor Corp.	Henry Link Corporation
Little Bear Furniture Line	Woods by Hartco Inc.
Little Bow Keeps Shoelace Holder	Marriott Concepts, Inc.
Little Lounger	Pansy Ellen Products Inc.
Little Playmates	Woodkrafter Kits
Little Sleeper	Welsh Company
Little Steps	Steven Mfg. Company
Lost West!	Decorate-It!, Inc.
Lovey Bear	Priss Prints Inc.
Loving Lift	Moore Products
Lull-A-Baby	Small Waves Ltd.
Lullaby Magic, Lullaby Magic II	Discovery Music
Luv Buggy, Luv Bus	Delta Enterprise
Maclaren	Marshall Products
MagMag	Marshall Products
Make-a-Mess	Great Kid Co.
Malibu	Welsh Company
Marimekko Pikko	Perfect Fit Industries
Meal Time High Chair	Gerry Baby Products Company
Melamine Dinosaur Dishes	Anacapa Corporation
Merry Menagerie	Priss Prints Inc.
Mess Kit	Newborne Company, Inc.
Mess Kit, Jr.	Gram Gram, Inc.

BRAND NAME	MANUFACTURER NAME
Mini-Crib	Delta Enterprise
Mite-Hite Crib Mirrors	Baby Motivations Co.
Mommy's Pride & Joy	Lloyderson Dolls & Toys
Monbebe	Silver Cross America Inc.
Monte Carlo	Welsh Company
Mop-Petz	Kamar International Inc.
Morning Magic	Discovery Magic
Mr. Hi-Lo Baby Chair	Metis Corporation
Music for Little People	Boosey & Hawkes
My Chair	Pansey Ellen Products Inc.
My Little Foot Steps	Karbyco International Corp.
My Little Marina	Century Products Company
My Little Shower	Century Products Company
Nanci	Nanci Industries
Nap	Prince Lionheart
Nap Pac	Century Originals
Napper	Snoozy's Room
Naps	Snoozy's Room
Natural Choice	Crystal Medical Products, Inc.
Nature Baby	California Concepts
Netpaks—Tape and Toy Sets	Kimbo Educational
Newborne Changing Center	Newborne Company, Inc.
Newborne Cradle	Newborne Company, Inc.
Newport	Child Craft
Noah's Art	Creative Imaging
No Jo	Noel Joanna Inc.
Olympic Shopper	Peg Perego U.S.A. Inc.
Omagles	Century Products Company
Opera on Video	V.I.E.W. Video Inc.
Organizer	Newborne Company, Inc.
Original Baby Sling	Noel Joanna Inc.
Pacer	Welsh Company
Pacifier Plus	Joy Baby Inc.
Paci-Keeper Pacifier Leash	Marriott Concepts, Inc.
Pack-A-Snack	Newborne Company, Inc.

BRAND NAME	MANUFACTURER NAME
Padded Hangers	Independent Products Co., Inc.
Pak Seat Deluxe	Gram Gram, Inc.
Pak Seat Jr.	Gram Gram, Inc.
Pansyette Infant Bath Aid	Pansy Ellen Product Inc.
Parent Pak	Calle International Inc.
Park Forest	Child Craft
Pastel Playmates	Pansy Ellen Products Inc.
Patch Peddler	Goosefeathers
Patriot	Welsh Company
Pattern-Play	Wimmer-Ferguson Child Products, Inc.
Peek A Boo Penquin	A-Plus Products Inc.
Personalized Name Tunes	Kidselebration, Inc.
Pet Pouch Toy Organizer	Pansy Ellen Products Inc.
Petit Personn	Matt 'n Alli
Petrus	Petrus Imports, Inc.
PillowTote	Snoozy's Room
Pinky	Pinky Baby Products
Playful Bears	Pansy Ellen Products Inc.
Play Pen and Portabed Pad Covers	Sandbox Industries
Play Pieces	First Step Designs Ltd.
Pliko	Peg Perego U.S.A. Inc.
Pocket Blanket	Nurturtech
Pocket Change	Newborne Company, Inc.
Podee Hand-Free Nursing System	Podee, Inc.
Polar Fleece Flap Hats	Flap Happy
Polliwog	Kiness & Co.
Poptops	Two Little Girls Inc.
Port-a-Bath	Century Products Inc.
Porta Pad	Great Kid Co.
Portaplay	TOT Inc./Turn on Toys
Portofino	Peg Perego U.S.A. Inc.
Prairie Tales!	Decorate-It!, Inc.
Pregnancy Pillow Comfort Wedge	Pansy Ellen Products Inc.
Profiles	Child Craft
Protect-A-Babe	Janco

BRAND NAME	MANUFACTURER NAME
Protex-a-Matt	Baby Motivations Co.
Puddle Pads	Americare Products Inc.
Puffy Friends	Jolly Jumper Inc.
Pull Pall	A-Plus Products Inc.
Puppetdears Bath Sponge Puppets	Delby System
Puppet-Go-Round	Century Products Company
Quiltex	Elston's Inc.
Raffi	Silo Inc.
Railnet Deck & Balcony Railing Guards	Railnet Corporation
Rainbow & Stars Trim Strips	Priss Prints Inc.
Rainbow Bag	Snoozy's Room
Rainbow Bears	Jolly Jumper Inc.
Rambler	Welsh Company
Red Star	Gerber Childrenswear, Inc.
Refrigerator Latches	A-Plus Products Inc.
Riddle King Games	Playspaces International Inc.
Ride Rite Car Seat Cover	Pansy Ellen Products Inc.
Ring A Ding Cow	A-Plus Products Inc.
Ring Around	A-Plus Products Inc.
Roadster	Century Products Inc.
Rock & Sleep	Century Products Inc.
Rock-A-Bye Collection	A Child's Gift of Lullabyes
Rocking Chair Covers	Sandbox Industries
Rocky	A-Plus Products Inc.
Roma	Child Craft
Rose Bud	Marcus Bros.
Ruggie Bear	Century Originals
Safe-T-Hug	Janco
Safe-T-Nanny	Babyline Products
Safety Bath Ring with Comfy Seat	Pansy Ellen Products Inc.
Safety Sitter	Tailored Baby
Sani-Stor	Prince Lionheart
Sara's Ride	Sara's Ride, Inc.
Sav-A-Mat	Pansy Ellen Products Inc.
Savoy	Welsh Company

BRAND NAME	MANUFACTURER NAME
Scholar	Newborne Company, Inc.
Seamore	Century Products Inc.
Sea-Nanigans!	Decorate-It!, Inc.
Seat Neat	Prince Lionheart
Seatsaver	Prince Lionheart
Security-Lok	Child Safety Products
See-Sides	TOT Inc./Turn on Toys
Sesame Street	Delta Enterprise
Shade Rite	Pansy Ellen Products Inc.
Sheets and Bumpers	Sandbox Industries
Shelcore	Shelcore Inc.
Sheres	Sherkit/Div., Sheres Industries Inc.
Sherkit	Sherkit/Div. Sheres Industries Inc.
Shoozies Infant Shoehorn	Marriott Concepts, Inc.
Shuttle	Prodigy Corp.
Siebring	Welsh Company
Silgo	Silgo International
Sillytime Magic	Discovery Music
Silver Cross	Silver Cross America Inc.
Simplex Puzzles	Playspaces International Inc.
Sinkadink, The Kids' Sink	Newborne Company, Inc.
Sipper Gripper	Little Kids, Inc.
Sit 'n Play	Peg Perego U.S.A. Inc.
Sit-Tight	Unity Products Inc.
Sleep'n Go	Century Products Inc.
Slumber Pad	Century Products Inc.
Smart Kid Stuff	International Cargo
Smart Starts	Pansy Ellen Products Inc.
Snappy Bibs	Chase Holding Co. Inc.
Sneak-R-Stilts	Woods by Hartco Inc.
Snoo	Snoozy's Room
Snoozanne	Snoozy's Room
Snoozles Inflatable Comfortoys	Talus Corporation
Snuggie Bug	Tailored Baby
Snuggle Wool	Anzam Industries

BRAND NAME	MANUFACTURER NAME
Snug n' Dry	Americare Products Inc.
Soft and Silkie Security Blanket	Comfort Silkie Company, Inc.
Soft Care	Gerber Childrenswear, Inc.
Softer Image	Softer Image
Somerhus	Child Craft
Somerset, Somerset II	Child Craft
Somerset II	Etc. "Environmental Teen Concepts"
Sorrento	Child Craft
Sound Starter	Century Products Inc.
Soupçon	Elston's Inc.
SpaceMobile	TOT Inc./Turn on Toys
Sponge Drops	Delby System
Spongee	A-Plus Products Inc.
Star Coupe	Century Products Inc.
Starlet O'Hara	Delby System
Stay Close	Stay Close Inc.
STE Carseats	Century Products Inc.
Stimulearn	Small World Toys
Stroll 'n Play	Peg Perego U.S.A. Inc.
Stroller Covers	Sandbox Industries
Stuffed Animal "Clean & Care Kit"	Bear Care Company
Suga Pacifier Pets	Marriott Concepts Ltd.
Sunny Bunny	Pansy Ellen Products Inc.
Super Coupe	Century Products Inc.
Super Gate, Super Seat	North States Industries Inc.
Superpark-it Seat	Ancar Enterprises Inc.
Super Swing	Century Products Inc.
Super Yard	North States Industries Inc.
Sweet Cheeks	Lloyderson Dolls & Toys
Sweet Dreamer	Relative Industries
Sweet Tweet	A-Plus Products Inc.
Teddy Bear (Bath Sponge)	Delby System
Teddy Bed	Premarq Inc.
Tenda	Baby-Tenda Corp.
TenderCare Diapers	RMED International

BRAND NAME	MANUFACTURER NAME
Tender Twin	Peg Perego U.S.A. Inc.
3 Bears (Bath Sponge)	Delby System
Tinkling Twins	A-Plus Products Inc.
Toddle Towel	Pinky Baby Products
Toidey Seat & Deflector	Baby Motivations Co.
Tolo Toys	Davis Grabowski Inc.
Tooti Frooti	Comfort Products
Topper	Century Products Inc.
Totbots	A-Plus Products Inc.
Tote-A-Potty	A-Plus Products Inc.
Tote-A-Tot	Comfort Products
Touchball	TOT Inc./Turn on Toys
Touch N Teddy	A-Plus Products Inc.
Touchstone Records	Walt Disney Records
ToyBag	BooBear Products Inc.
Travel Desk Sets	Toy Time Inc.
Travelette (sponge wash cloth)	Delby System
Travelin' Magic	Discovery Music
Travel Tray	Toy Time Inc.
Travel Yard	Delta Enterprise
Trav'l Light Quick Trip Tote	J. L. Childress Co.
Tricolor	A-Plus Products Inc.
Triplette	Peg Perego U.S.A. Inc.
Tub Club Bath Aid	Pansy Ellen Products Inc.
Tub Toy Pockets	Kids Forever Products
Tub Toy Pouch	Pansy Ellen Products Inc.
Turn On Toys	TOT Inc./Turn On Toys
Twin Bedspreads	Sandbox Industries
Twinner	Racing Strollers Inc.
Two Stage Toilet Trainer	Gerry Baby Products Company
Tyke	Elston's Inc.
Unity	California Kids
Upright Head Support Pillow	Tailored Baby
Vanderbilt	Welsh Company
Venezia	Child Craft

BRAND NAME	MANUFACTURER NAME
Victor Costa	Trina for Infants
Victoriana	Child Craft
Voo Zoo!	Decorate-It!, Inc.
Walkabout	Racing Strollers Inc.
Walk 'n Play	Peg Perego U.S.A. Inc.
Walt Disney Records	Walt Disney Records
Warmwipes	Marshall Products
Warwick	Welsh Company
Way to Go	Century Products Inc.
Wee Sing	Silo Inc.
Wee Wear	Elston's Inc.
Wellington	Child Craft
Wellington	Etc. "Environmental Teen Concepts"
Westchester	Child Craft
Wide Top	Gerber Products Company
Widgeon	American Widgeon
Wiggle Wrap	C. J. Leachco Inc.
Woodenworks	Century Originals
Wownow	Two Little Girls Inc.
Yorktowne	Welsh Company
Young-Hinkle Corp.	Henry Link Corporation
Young Times	Stahlwood/Young Times
Young Times International Collection	Stahlwood/Young Times
Yummy Bear	G.E.T. Enterprises Inc.
Zicoli	Zicoli Incorporated
Zittenfield Diaper Bags	Relative Industries
Zoom Spoon	Fun-tional Toys Inc.

DIRECTORY OF MANUFACTURERS

AAMCO Baby Products
1122 W. Washington Boulevard, Room D
Montebello, CA   90640
(213) 727-9144

A Child's Gift of Lullabyes
1508 16th Avenue
South Nashville, TN   37212
(615) 385-0022

Alison's Design Inc.
117 35th Street
Manhattan Beach, CA   90266
(213) 546-4227

Ambassador Corporation
500 Library Street
San Fernando, CA   91340
(818) 365-9861

American Baby Concepts
1 Baby Concepts
Wheatland, IA   52771
(319) 374-1231
(800) 537-7181

American Baby Imports Ltd.
8831 Shirley Avenue
Northridge, CA   91324
(818) 349-6050

American Widgeon
376 Brannan Street
San Francisco, CA   94107
(415) 974-6803

Americare Products Inc.
P.O. Box 1384
Newportville, PA   19056
(800) 336-4353

Anacapa Corporation
25933 Frampton Avenue
Harbor City, CA   90710
(213) 325-9131
(800) 255-9270

Ancar Enterprises Inc.
7511 N.W. 73rd Street, Suite 106
Miami, FL   33166
(305) 888-3173

Ansa Bottle Company Inc.
425 W. Broadway
Muskogee, OK   74402
(918) 687-1664
(800) 527-1096

Anzam Industries
10062 Riverhead Drive
San Diego, CA   92129
(619) 484-9639
(800) 288-7303

A-Plus Products Inc.
2601 Ocean Park, Suite 304
Santa Monica, CA   90405
(213) 399-1177
(800) 359-9955

Aprica U.S.A.
1200 Howell Avenue
Anaheim, CA   92805
(714) 634-0402

Aqua Learn Inc.
932 Parker Street
Berkeley, CA   94710
(415) 841 9188

Artsana of America/Chicco
200 5th Avenue, Room 910
New York, NY   10010
(212) 255-6977

Babies' Alley
339 5th Avenue
New York, NY   10016
(212) 679-4700

Baby & Child
P.O. Box 1506
Centreville, VA   22020
(703) 368-9555

Baby Bag Company
P.O. Box 566
Cumberland, ME   04021
(207) 829-5037

Baby Bjorn of North America Inc.
P.O. Box 1322
Shaker Heights, OH   44120
(216) 662-2922

Baby Buddies Inc.
615 Jasmine Avenue N., Suite I
Tarpon Springs, FL   34689
(813) 934-3359

Babyline Products
80 St. Andrews Avenue
Welland, Ontario   L3B 1E4
Canada
(416) 734-6398

Baby Motivations Co.
16230 Harkey Road
Pearland, TX   77584
(713) 489-8623

Baby Needs Inc.
605 Cameron Street
Burlington, NC   27215
(919) 227-6202
(800) 334-5321

Baby-Tenda Corp.
123 S. Belmont
Kansas City, MO   64123
(816) 231-2300

Baby Trend Inc.
17950 E. Ajax Circle
City of Industry, CA   91748
(818) 965-6788
(800) 328-7363

Baby World Company, Inc.
P.O. Box 219, Pike Street
Grafton, WV   26354
(304) 265-2120
(800) 545-2800

Bandaks Emmaljunga Inc.
737 S. Vinewood
Escondido, CA   92025
(619) 739-8911

Bantam Collections Inc.
131 W. 33rd Street, Room 1703
New York, NY   10001
(212) 564-6750
(800) 647-7784

Bassett Furniture Industries Inc.
P.O. Box 626
Bassett, VA   24055
(703) 629-6000

Bear Care Company
279 S. Beverly Drive, Suite 957
Beverly Hills, CA   90212
(213) 397-4082

Beautiful Bambino Inc.
Route 2, Box 321A
Cambridge, MN   55008
(612) 689-3844

Bébé Chic Inc.
115 River Road, Suite 303
Edgewater, NJ   07020
(201) 941-5414

Behavior Products
18627 Brookhurst Street, Suite 298
Fountain Valley, CA   92708
(714) 826-5711

Binky-Griptight Inc.
519-523 Paterson Avenue
Wallington, NJ   07057
(201) 935-4580
(800) 526-6320

Boobear Products Inc.
P.O. Box 494
Woodmere, NY   11598
(516) 569-0742

Boosey & Hawkes
52 Cooper Square
New York, NY   10003
(212) 979-1090
(800) 645-9582

Brass Key Inc.
2010 48th Avenue
East Tacoma, WA   98424
(206) 922-3812

California Concepts
2234 Gladwick
Compton, CA   90220
(213) 537-0161
(800) 421-5576

Calle International Inc.
P.O. Box 260046
St. Louis, MO   63126
(314) 842-3063

Cambium Design Co.
P.O. Box 2304
Leucadia, CA   92024
(619) 753-7310

Carlson Children's Products, Inc.
P.O. Box 4442
Naperville, IL   60567
(800) 933-3309

Carmel Furniture
126 13th Street
Brooklyn, NY   11215
(718) 499-6038

C & T International, Inc.
12 Caesar Place
Moonachie, NJ   07074
(201) 896-2555

Century Originals
3166 E. Slauson Avenue
Vernon, CA   90058
(213) 581-2299

Century Products Company
9600 Valley View Road
Macedonia, OH   44056
(216) 468-2000
(800) 222-9825

Chase Holding Co. Inc.
8040 Deering Avenue, Room 4
Canoga Park, CA   91304
(818) 703-0898
(800) 992-2119

Cherry Tree
131 Varick Street
New York, NY   10013
(212) 691-1120

Child Craft
P.O. Box 444
E. Market Street
Salem, IN   47167
(812) 883-3111

Child Safe Products Inc.
2509 E. Thousand Oaks
Thousand Oaks, CA   91360
(805) 492-6775

Child Safety Products/BB
  Marketing, Inc.
8825 S. 184th
Kent, WA   98031
(206) 521-9150
(800) 274-2557

C. J. Leachco, Inc.
124 E. 14th Street, Suite 103
Ada, OK   74820
(405) 436-1142

Colgate Mattress/Colgate
  International Ltd.
941 Longfellow Avenue
Bronx, NY   10474
(212) 991-0750

Comfort Products
1421 Champion Drive, Suite 311
Carrollton, TX   75006
(214) 241-4349

Comfort Silkie Company Inc.
P.O. Box AE
Sunland, CA   91040
(818) 352-0601
(800) 266-BABY (2229)

Cosco Inc.
2525 State Street
Columbus, IN   47201
(812) 372-0141

Cozy Baby Products
Empire State Building, Room 5010
New York, NY   10018
(212) 947-2710

Cozy Carrier Co. Inc.
18105 Valley View Road
Eden Prairie, MN   55346
(612) 934-0687

Creative Imaging
P.O. Box 1410
Pacific Palisades, CA   90272
(213) 454-3900
(800) 347-4747

Crestwood Industries, Inc.
13500 Bel-Red Road, Suite 7
Bellevue, WA   98005
(206) 641-1763

Crib Mates/Gu-Di Enterprises
650 Fountain Avenue
Brooklyn, NY   11208
(718) 257-7800
(800) 431-3166

Crystal Medical Products, Inc.
1110 Lake Cook Road
Buffalo Grove, IL   60089
(312) 520-1425
(800) 248-9235

Cuddly Komfort Affectueux Inc.
403 Eardley Road, P.O. Box 364
Aylmer, Quebec   J9H 5E7
Canada
(819) 684-3301

Danara
13 Central Boulevard S.
Hackensack, NJ   07606
(201) 641-4350

Daust Juvenile Products Inc.
401 Marcy Avenue
Brooklyn, NY   11206
(718) 384-3200
(800) 662-3883

Davida
819 Santee Street, Room 712
Los Angeles, CA   90014
(213) 629-2971

Davis Grabowski Inc.
6350 N.E. 4th Avenue
Miami, FL   33138
(305) 751-3667

Decorate-It!, Inc.
6320 Canoga Avenue, Suite 1600
Woodland Hills, CA   91367
(818) 595-1013
(800) 828-3300

Degree Baby Products
23457 Haynes Street
West Hills, CA   91307
(818) 713-0485
(800) 234-9777

Delby System
450 7th Avenue
New York, NY   10123
(212) 594-5036

Delta Enterprise
175 Liberty Avenue
Brooklyn, NY   11212
(718) 385-1000

Dianes Designs, Inc.
1440 Greenbriar Road
Glendale, CA   91207
(818) 243-1909

Diaperaps
110 E. 9th Street, Suite B-629
Los Angeles, CA   90079
(213) 622-8620

Diplomat Juvenile Corp.
118 Railroad Avenue
West Haverstraw, NY   10993
(914) 786-5552
(800) 247-9063

Discovery Music
4130 Greenbush Avenue
Sherman Oaks, CA   91423
(818) 905-9794
(800) 451-5175

Dolly Inc.
320 N. 4th Street
Tipp City, OH   45371
(513) 667-5711

Dream Machine Inc.
7192 Patterson Drive
Garden Grove, CA   92641
(714) 895-4943

Dundee Mills Inc.
111 W. 40th Street
New York, NY   10018
(212) 840-7200

Educational Programs, Inc.
8003 Old York Road
Elkins Park, PA   19117
(215) 635-1700
(800) 523-5341

Ellen Miklas Originals
8960 Townline Road
Kewaskum, WI   53040
(414) 626-4766

Elston's Inc.
110 E. 9th Street, Room 13-665
Los Angeles, CA   90079
(213) 628-2831

Etc. "Environmental Teen Concepts"
A Child Craft Company
501 E. Market Stret
Salem, IN   47167
(812) 883-3111

Evenflo Juvenile Furniture Company
1801 Commerce Drive
Piqua, OH   45356
(513) 773-3971

Evenflo Products Company
771 N. Freedom Street
Ravenna, OH   44266
(216) 296-3465
(800) 356-2229

Fairland Products Inc.
16737 S. Parkside Avenue
Cerritos, CA   90701
(213) 926-3837

First Step Design Ltd.
369 Congress Street
Boston, MA   02210
(617) 527-3043

Fisher-Price
Division of Quaker Oats Co.
636 Girard Avenue
East Aurora, NY   14052
(716) 687-3000
(800) 433-5437

Flap Happy
2322 Walnut Avenue
Venice, CA   90291
(213) 391-1316
(800) 234-3527

Flexible Flyer Company
100 Tubb Avenue
West Point, MS   39773
(601) 494-4732
(800) 521-6233

Flying Colors Inc.
224 N. Court Street
Florence, AL   35631
(205) 760-0025
(800) 537-7748

Fun-tional Toys Inc.
P.O. Box 79205
Lakewood, OH   44107
(216) 228-3172

Gautier USA
1382 W. McNab Road
Fort Lauderdale, FL   33309
(305) 975-3303

General Mica Corp.
1850 N.E. 144th Street
North Miami, FL   33181
(305) 949-7247

Gerber Childrenswear, Inc.
1 Financial Center
Boston, MA   02111
(617) 268-5100
(800) 642-4452

Gerber Products Company
Gerber Division
445 State Street
Fremont, MI   49412
(616) 928-2000

Gerry Baby Products Company
12520 Grant Drive
Denver, CO   80233
(303) 457-0926
(800) 525-2472

G.E.T. Enterprises Inc.
6015 Westline
Houston, TX   77036
(713) 779-4500

Glenna Jean Manufacturing
P.O. Box 2187
Petersburg, VA   23803
(804) 861-0687
(800) 446-6018

Gloria Shavel Inc.
225 5th Avenue
New York, NY   10010
(212) 685-2220

Goosefeathers
5695 Eagle Rock Court
Santa Rosa, CA   95409
(707) 538-8901
(800) 456-5122

Graco Children's Products Inc.
P.O. Box 100, Main Street
Elverson, PA   19520
(215) 286-5951
(800) 523-8498

Gram Gram, Inc.
5567 Kearny Villa Road
San Diego, CA   92123
(619) 292-6015
(800) 621-0852

Great Kid Co.
20 Rugg Road
Allston, MA   02134
(617) 254-0859

Gund, Inc.
P.O. Box H
Edison, NJ   08818
(201) 248-1500

G. W. Dmka Inc.
168 E. Main Street
Prospect Park, NJ   07508
(201) 595-5599

Habermaass Corporation/T.C. Timber
P.O. Box 42
Skaneateles, NY   13152
(315) 685-6660
(800) 468-6873

Happytimes
P.O. Box 6037
San Diego, CA   92106
(619) 226-7661

Hedstrom Corp.
P.O. Box 432
Bedford, PA   15522
(814) 623-9041

Henry Link Corporation
P.O. Box 1249
Lexington, NC   27292
(704) 249-5400

Hoopla
1250 Addison Street, Room 110
Berkeley, CA   94702
(415) 649-8547

House of Hatten, Inc.
2200 Denton Drive, Suite 110
Austin, TX   78758
(512) 837-4467

Infants Specialty Company
7101 E. Slauson Avenue
Commerce, CA   90040
(213) 723-1026
(800) 762-6872

International Cargo
162 Eastern Avenue
Lynn, MA   01902
(617) 598-1400

International Playthings Inc.
120 Riverdale Road
Riverdale, NJ   07457
(201) 831-1400
(800) 631-1272

International Products Trading Inc.
380 Franklin Turnpike
Mahwah, NJ   07430
(201) 529-4500

Janco
P.O. Box 1374
Aptos, CA   95001
(408) 684-1894

J. L. Childress Co.
552 N. Waverly Street
Orange, CA   92667
(714) 997-4534

J. M. Designs Inc.
317-F Highway 70
East Garner, NC   27529
(919) 779-2294

Johnson & Johnson Baby Products Co.
Child Development Products
Grandview Road
Skillman, NJ   08558
(201) 874-1837

Jolly Jumper Inc.
P.O. Box M
Woonsocket, RI   02895
(401) 765-5950
(800) 682-5168

Joy Baby Inc.
300 Harris Avenue, Suite E
Sacramento, CA   95838
(916) 927-8800

Justin Time Productions, Inc.
P.O. Box 1265
Teaneck, NJ   07666
(201) 251-8180

Kaleidoscope Design, Inc.
1755 N. Oak Road
Plymouth, IN   46563
(219) 936-7950
(800) 451-3228

Kamar International Inc.
23639 Hawthorne Boulevard
Torrance, CA   90505
(213) 373-5466
(800) 635-5368

Karbyco International Corp.
103 Willow Way, Suite 1
Cherry Hill, NJ   08034
(609) 429-8747

Kartell USA
P.O. Box 1000
Easley, SC   29641
(803) 271-6932
(800) 845-2517

Kiddie Kingdom
611 S. Anderson Street
Los Angeles, CA   90023
(213) 839-3617

Kiddie Products Inc.
1 Kiddie Drive
Avon, MA   02322
(508) 588-1220
(800) 225-0382

Kids Corp. International
12020 S.W. 114th Place
Miami, FL   33176
(305) 255-0014
(800) 327-5537

Kids Forever Products
P.O. Box 2056
Darien, IL   60559
(312) 985-8052

Kidselebration, Inc.
P.O. Box 2033
New York, NY   10011
(212) 222-7748
(800) KIDS-321 (543-7321)

Kids' Quarters, Inc.
229 Cedar Trail
Winston-Salem, NC   27104
(919) 765-8631

Kimbo Educational
10 N. 3rd Avenue
Long Branch, NJ   07740
(201) 229-4949
(800) 631-2187

Kindergard Corp.
14822 Venture Drive
Dallas, TX   75234
(214) 243-7101
(800) 527-2338

Kinderworks Corporation
P.O. Box 1441
Portsmouth, NH   03801
(603) 436-1441

Kiness & Co.
13901 N.E. 175th Street
Woodinville, WA   98072
(206) 487-3006
(800) 733-3004

KLM Woodwords
103 S. White Oak Road
White Oak, TX   75693
(214) 759-5305
(800) 442-6263

Kolcraft Enterprises, Inc.
1691 Phoenix Boulevard, Suite 250
Atlanta, GA   30349
(404) 991-4676

Kolcraft Products Inc.
3455 W. 31st Place
Chicago, IL   60623
(312) 247-4494

Lambs & Ivy
5978 Bowcraft Street
Los Angeles, CA   90016
(213) 839-5155
(800) 345-2627

Lamby Nursery Collection
P.O. Box 5125
Petaluma, CA   94953
(707) 763-4222
(800) 669-0527

Laura D's Folk Art Furniture, Inc.
106 Gleneida Avenue
Carmel, NY   10512
(914) 228-1440

Lear Siegler Seymour Corp./Worldsbest
885 N. Chestnut Street
Seymour, IN   47274
(812) 522-5130
(800) 457-9881

Lego Systems, Inc.
555 Taylor Road
Enfield, CT   06082
(203) 749-2291
(800) 243-4870

Lewis of London
25 Power Drive
Hauppauge, NY   11788
(516) 582-8300

Life Manufacturing Co. Inc.
20 Meridian Street
East Boston, MA   02128
(617) 569-1200

Lil' Lamb's Keeper
2403 2nd Avenue N.
Birmingham, AL   35203
(205) 322-0464
(800) 472-3736

Little Tikes Company
2180 Barlow Road
Hudson, OH   44236
(216) 650-3000
(800) 321-0183

Lloyderson Dolls & Toys
House of Lloyderson
617 W. Chestnut Street
Lancaster, PA   17603
(717) 291-5867
(800) 222-3655

Mapes Industries Inc.
637 Middle Neck Road
Great Neck, NY   11023
(516) 487-7995

Marcus Bros.
1755 McDonald Avenue
Brooklyn, NY   11230
(718) 645-4565

Marriott Concepts, Inc.
200 W. 900 North
Springville, UT   84663
(801) 226-5353
(800) 999-SUGA (7842)

Marshall Products
Juvenile Division
600 Barclay Boulevard
Lincolnshire, IL   60069
(312) 634-6300
(800) 323-1482

Matchbox Toy (USA) Ltd.
141 W. Commercial Avenue
Moonachie, NJ   07074
(201) 935-2600

Matt 'N Alli
2 Lawson Avenue
East Rockaway, NY   11518
(516) 593-5466
(800) 736-4571

Metis Corporation
394 Bel Marin Keys Boulevard, Suite 6
Novato, CA   94949
(415) 382-0803

MFP Manufacturing
317 W. 13th Street
Hays, KS   67601
(800) 637-2229

Moore Products
596 Teredo Drive
Redwood City, CA   94065
(415) 592-0245

Nanci Industries
P.O. Box 241
Germantown, MD   20878
(301) 948-0008

Nasta International Inc.
200 5th Avenue
New York, NY   10010
(212) 929-8085

N. D. Cass Company
62 Canal Street
Athol, MA   01331
(508) 249-3205

Newborne Company, Inc.
River Road
Worthington, MA   01098
(413) 238-5551
(800) 237-1712

Noel Joanna Inc.
22942 Arroya Vista Rancho
Santa Margarita, CA   92688
(714) 858-9717
(800) 854-8760

Nogatco International Inc.
86 Lackawanna Avenue
West Paterson, NJ   07424
(201) 785-4907
(800) 922-0938

North States Industries Inc.
1200 Mendelssohn Avenue, Suite 210
Minneapolis, MN   55427
(612) 541-9101

Nu-Line Industries
214 Nu-Line Street
Suring, WI   54174
(414) 842-2141
(800) 558-7300

Nurturtech
163 Milton Road
Litchfield, CT   06759
(203) 567-8123

Nutri-Books Corp.
Division of Royal Publications Inc.
790 W. Tennessee Avenue
Denver, CO   80223
(303) 778-8383

**Okla Homer Smith Furniture
Mfg. Co., Inc.**
416 S. 5th Street
Fort Smith, AR   72901
(501) 783-6191

Paidi of North America
Division of World-Wide Trade Corp.
14080 H Sullyfield Circle
Chantilly, VA   22021
(703) 631-8094

Pansy Ellen Products Inc.
1245 Old Alpharetta Road
Alpharetta, GA   30201
(404) 751-0442

Patchkraft, Inc.
89-B Dell Glen Avenue
Lodi, NJ   07644
(201) 340-3300

Peg Perego U.S.A. Inc.
3625 Independence Drive
Fort Wayne, IN   46818
(219) 482-8191

Perfect Fit Industries
Boynton for Babies Division
303 5th Avenue
New York, NY   10016
(212) 679-6656

Petco Kidsprints
12-L Lindscott Road
Woburn, MA   22021
(617) 938-7966
(800) 634-0043

Petrus Imports, Inc.
965 Concord Street
Framingham, MA   01701
(508) 875-8338

Pinky Baby Products
8450 Westpark Drive, Room 104
Houston, TX   77063
(713) 781-9200

Playskool Baby Inc.
1027 Newport Avenue
Pawtucket, RI   02862
(401) 431-8697

Playskool Inc.
1027 Newport Avenue
Pawtucket, RI   02862
(401) 421-5000

Playspaces International Inc.
31-D Union Avenue
Sudbury, MA   01776
(508) 443-7146
(800) 367-3304

Pockets of Learning
31-G Union Avenue
Sudbury, MA   01776
(508) 443-5808
(800) 635-2994

Podee, Inc.
9560 Black Mountain Road
San Diego, CA   92126
(619) 566-3748

Premarq Inc.
P.O. Box 840
Astoria, OR   97103
(503) 861-0386
(800) 423-3833

Prince Lionheart
3070 Skyway Drive, Building 502
Santa Maria, CA   93455
(805) 922-2250
(800) 544-1132

Priss Prints Inc.
3002 Jeremes Landing
Garland, TX   75043
(214) 278-5600

Prodigy Corp.
916 Main Street
Acton, MA   01720
(508) 263-9041

Project Marketing Group, Inc.
4601 N. Dixie Highway
Boca Raton, FL   33431
(407) 392-2792
(800) 426-1456

QRP Inc.
200 Mill Street
Gardener, MA   01440
(508) 632-1269

Quiltex Co. Inc.
112 W. 34th Street
New York, NY   10007
(212) 594-2205
(800) 237-3636

Racing Strollers Inc.
P.O. Box 2189
Yakima, WA   98902
(509) 457-0925
(800) 548-7230 (ext. 4)

Railnet Corporation
3413 Sunset Avenue
Boise, ID   83703
(208) 342-4568

Regent Baby Products Corp.
43-21 52nd Street
Woodside, NY   11377
(718) 458-5855

Relative Industries
500 Library Street
San Francisco, CA   91340
(818) 365-9861

RMED International
P.O. Box 10209
Sedona, AZ   86336
(602) 282-1175
(800) 344-6379

Romar International Babi Bags
112 W. 34th Street
New York, NY   10001
(212) 736-9555

Safe-Strap Co. Inc.
180 Old Tappan Road
Old Tappan, NJ   07675
(201) 767-7450
(800) 356-7796

Safety 1st Inc.
200 Boylston Street
Chestnut Hill, MA   02167
(617) 964-7744
(800) 962-7233

Samson-McCann
638 Ramona Street
Palo Alto, CA   94301
(415) 321-9560

Sandbox Industries
P.O. Box 477
Tenafly, NJ   07670
(201) 567-5696

Sanitoy Inc.
P.O. Box 2167
Fitchburg, MA   01420
(508) 345-7571

Sara's Ride Inc.
2448 Blake Street
Denver, CO   80205
(303) 292-2224

Sassy Inc.
666 Dundee Road
Northbrook, IL   60062
(616) 243-0767

Shelcore Inc.
3474 S. Clinton Avenue
South Plainfield, NJ   07080
(201) 561-7900

Sherkit
Division of Sheres Industries Inc.
10280 Ray Lawson Boulevard
Montreal, Quebec   H1J 1L9
Canada
(514) 351-7910
(800) 361-8989

Siamar International
11844 Rancho Bernardo Road
San Diego, CA   92128
(619) 451-6483

Silgo International
650 Arizona Street
Chula Vista, CA   92011
(619) 420-9920
(800) 365-8182

Silo Inc.
P.O. Box 429
Waterbury, VT   05676
(800) 244-5178

Silver Cross America Inc.
P.O. Box 4377
Highland Park, NJ   08904
(800) 387-5115

Simmons Juvenile Products
613 E. Beacon Avenue
New London, WI   54961
(414) 982-2140

Sit Right Baby Products
Ckenbe Inc.
P.O. Box 3275
Yuba City, CA   95992
(916) 671-3947
(800) 525-9755

Small Waves Ltd.
1145-H Dominguez
Carson, CA   90746
(213) 604-0504

Small World Toys
P.O. Box 5291
Beverly Hills, CA   90291
(213) 645-9680
(800) 421-4153

Snap Ups Kids Ltd.
131 W. 33rd Street, Room 1106
New York, NY   10001
(212) 244-6440

Snoozy's Room
933 Exmoor Way
Sunnyvale, CA   94087
(408) 738-1705

Snugli Inc.
P.O. Box 33538
Denver, CO   80233
(303) 989-2181

Softer Image
1073 Laurie Avenue
San Jose, CA   95125
(408) 978-9755

Spectrum Juvenile Products, Inc.
1974 Ohio Street
Lisle, IL   60532
(312) 852-9585
(800) 343-4945

Stahlwood/Young Times
117 Franklin Park Avenue
Youngsville, NC   27596
(919) 556-8411

Starwares
3600 E. Olympic Boulevard
Los Angeles, CA   90023
(213) 265-2600

Stay Close Inc.
2607 S. Decker Lake Boulevard
West Valley City, UT   84119
(801) 975-9879
(800) 333-1155

Steven Mfg. Company
224 E. 4th Street
Hermann, MO   65041
(314) 486-5494

Strolee of California
21800 Oxnard Street, Suite 700
Woodland Hills, CA   91367
(818) 346-5200

Tabor Inc.
8220 W. 30th Court
Hialeah, FL   33016
(305) 557-1481

Tailored Baby
500 Library Street
San Fernando, CA   91340
(818) 365-9861

Talus Corporation
400 Riverside Street
Portland, ME   04103
(207) 797-9230

Texas Juvenile Products Inc.
3503 Polk Street
Houston, TX   77003
(713) 222-8675

TOT Inc./Turn on Toys
P.O. Box 32239
Washington, DC   20007
(202) 337-1177

Toy Time Inc.
53 Melden Drive
Brunswick, ME   04011
(207) 725-9800

Tracers Furniture Inc.
612 Waverly Avenue
Mamaroneck, NY   10543
(914) 381-5777

Tradis Inc.
18600 N.E. 2nd Avenue
Miami, FL   33179
(305) 653-8141

Triboro Quilt Mfg. Corp.
172 S. Broadway
White Plains, NY   10605
(914) 428-7551

Trina for Infants
P.O. Box 1431
Fall River, MA   02722
(508) 678-7601
(800) 558-BABY (2229)

TRP, Inc.
1766 Bloomsbury Avenue
Ocean, NJ   07712
(201) 922-1410
(800) 524-2622

Two Little Girls Inc.
617 Huntington
San Bruno, CA   94066
(415) 873-2229
(800) 437-2229

Unity Products Inc.
Box 1309, Muir Beach
Sausalito, CA   94965
(415) 388-3202

Velsco Inc.
180 Berry Street
Brooklyn, NY   11211
(718) 782-7959

V.I.E.W. Video Inc.
34 E. 23rd Street
New York, NY   10010
(212) 674-5550

Walt Disney Records
3900 W. Alameda Avenue
Burbank, CA 91505
(818) 567-5301

Welsh Company
1535 S. 8th Street
St. Louis, MO 63104
(314) 231-8822

Wheeler Enterprises
12936 Beethoven Boulevard
Silver Springs, MD 20904
(301) 890-5568

Wimmer-Ferguson Child Products, Inc.
P.O. Box 10427
Denver, CO 80210
(800) 747-2454

Woodkrafter Kits
42A N. Elm Street
Yarmouth, ME 04096
(207) 846-3746
(800) 345-3555

Woods by Hartco Inc.
1280 Glendale Milford Road
Cincinnati, OH 45215
(513) 771-4430
(800) 543-1340

World-Wide Travel Corp.
9629 Lee Highway
Fairfax, VA 22030
(703) 352-1001

Zicoli Incorporated
265 Sunrise Highway
Rockville Centre, NY 11571
(516) 825-8200

STATE CONSUMER PROTECTION AGENCIES

To check for complaints filed against a local company prior to purchasing a product or service, call the Better Business Bureau, listed in your telephone directory. Also call your state consumer protection agency, listed below, for referrals to local or county consumer offices familiar with local firms.

These consumer protection agencies will also tell you how to handle a complaint should you wish to file one.

Alabama

Consumer Protection Division
Office of the Attorney General
11 S. Union Street
Montgomery, AL 36130
(205) 261-7334
(800) 392-5658 (in Alabama)

Alaska

Consumer Protection Section
Office of the Attorney General
1031 W. 4th Avenue, Suite 110
Anchorage, AK 99501
(907) 279-0428

Office of the Attorney General
100 Cushman Street, Suite 400
Fairbanks, AK 99701
(907) 456-8588

Arizona

Financial Fraud Division
Office of the Attorney General
1275 W. Washington Street
Phoenix, AZ 85007
(602) 255-3702
(800) 352-8431 (in Arizona)

Financial Fraud Division
Office of the Attorney General
402 W. Congress Street, Suite 315
Tucson, AZ 85701
(602) 628-5501

Arkansas

Consumer Protection Division
Office of the Attorney General
201 E. Markham Street
Little Rock, AR 72201
(501) 371-2341 (voice and TDD)
(800) 482-8982 (in Arkansas)

California

Department of Consumer Affairs
107 S. Broadway, Room 8020
Los Angeles, CA 90012
(213) 620-4360
(213) 620-2179 (TDD)

Bureau of Automotive Repair
Department of Consumer Affairs
10240 Systems Parkway
Sacramento, CA 95827
(916) 366-5055
(800) 952-5210 (in California for auto
    repair only)

Department of Consumer Affairs
1020 N Street
Sacramento, CA 95814
(916) 445-1254 (consumer information)
(916) 445-0660 (complaint assistance)
(916) 322-1700 (TDD)

Public Inquiry Unit
Office of the Attorney General
1515 K Street, Suite 511
Sacramento, CA 94244

(916) 322-3360
(800) 952-5225 (in California)
(800) 952-5548 (in California TDD)

Colorado

Consumer & Food Specialist
Department of Agriculture
1525 Sherman Street, 4th Floor
Denver, CO   80203
(303) 866-3561

Consumer Protection Unit
Office of the Attorney General
1525 Sherman Street, 3rd Floor
Denver, CO   80203
(303) 866-5167

Connecticut

Antitrust/Consumer Protection
Office of the Attorney General
30 Trinity Street
Hartford, CT   06106
(203) 566-5374

Department of Consumer Protection
State Office Building
165 Capitol Avenue
Hartford, CT   06106
(203) 566-4999
(800) 842-2649 (in Connecticut)

Delaware

Division of Consumer Affairs
Department of Community Affairs
820 N. French Street, 4th Floor
Wilmington, DE   19801
(302) 571-3250

**Economic Crime/Consumer Rights
  Division**
Office of the Attorney General
820 N. French Street
Wilmington, DE   19801
(302) 571-3849

District of Columbia

**Department of Consumer & Regulatory
  Affairs**
614 H Street, N.W.
Washington, DC   20001
(202) 727-7000

Florida

Consumer Protection Division
Office of the Attorney General
401 N.W. 2nd Avenue, Suite 450
Miami, FL   33128
(305) 377-5619

Division of Consumer Services
508 Mayo Building
Tallahassee, FL   32399
(904) 488-2226
(800) 327-3382
(800) 342-2176 (in Florida TDD)

Georgia

Governor's Office of Consumer Affairs
2 Martin Luther King, Jr. Drive, S.E.
East Tower, Plaza Level
Atlanta, GA   30334
(404) 656-7000
(800) 282-5808 (in Georgia)

Hawaii

Office of Consumer Protection
Department of Commerce & Consumer
  Affairs
250 S. King Street, Room 520
Honolulu, HI   96812
(808) 548-2560 (administration)
(808) 548-2540 (complaints)

Idaho

Attorney General's Office
Room 120, State House
Boise, ID   83720
(208) 334-2400

Illinois

Consumer Protection Division
Office of the Attorney General
100 W. Randolph, 12th Floor
Chicago, IL   60601
(312) 917-3580
(312) 793-2852 (TDD)

Department of Citizens Rights
100 W. Randolph, 12th Floor
Chicago, IL   60601
(312) 917-3289
(312) 793-2852 (TDD)

Governor's Office of Citizens Assistance
201 W. Monroe Street
Springfield, IL   62706
(217) 782-0244
(800) 642-3112 (in Illinois)

Indiana

Consumer Protection Division
Office of the Attorney General
219 State House
Indianapolis, IN   46204
(317) 232-6330
(800) 382-5516 (in Indiana)

Iowa

Consumer Protection Division
Office of the Attorney General
1300 E. Walnut Street, 2nd Floor
Des Moines, IA   50319
(515) 281-5926

Kansas

Consumer Protection Division
Office of the Attorney General
Kansas Judicial Center, 2nd Floor
Topeka, KS   66612
(913) 296-3751
(800) 432-2310

STATE CONSUMER PROTECTION AGENCIES

Kentucky

Consumer Protection Division
Office of the Attorney General
209 St. Clair Street
Frankfort, KY 40601
(502) 564-2200
(800) 432-9257 (in Kentucky)

Consumer Protection Division
Office of the Attorney General
514 W. Liberty Street, Suite 139
Louisville, KY 40202
(502) 588-3262

Louisiana

Consumer Protection Section
Office of the Attorney General
State Capitol Building
P.O. Box 94005
Baton Rouge, LA 70804
(504) 342-7013

Office of Agro-Consumer Services
Department of Agriculture
325 Loyola Avenue, Room 317
New Orleans, LA 70112
(504) 568-5472

Maine

Bureau of Consumer Credit Protection
State House, Station 35
Augusta, ME 04333
(207) 289-3731

Consumer & Antitrust Division
Office of the Attorney General
State House, Station 6
Augusta, ME 04333
(207) 289-3716 (9:00 A.M.–1:00 P.M.)

Mediation Consumer Service
Office of the Attorney General
991 Forest Avenue
Portland, ME 04104
(207) 797-8978 (1:00 P.M.–4:00 P.M.)

Maryland

Consumer Protection Division
Office of the Attorney General
7 N. Calvert Street
Baltimore, MD 21202
(301) 528-8662 (9:00 A.M.–1:00 P.M.)
(301) 576-6372 (in Baltimore TDD)
(301) 565-0451 (in Washington TDD)

Licensing & Consumer Services
Motor Vehicle Administration
6601 Ritchie Highway, N.E.
Glen Burnie, MD 21062
(301) 768-7420

Consumer Protection Division
Office of the Attorney General
138 E. Antietam Street, Suite 210
Hagerstown, MD 21740
(301) 791-4780

Consumer Protection Division
Office of the Attorney General
State Office Complex
Route 50 and Cypress Street
Salisbury, MD   21801
(301) 543-6620

Massachusetts

Consumer Affairs & Business
  Regulation
1 Ashburton Place, Room 1411
Boston, MA   02108
(617) 727-7780

Consumer Protection Division
Department of the Attorney General
1 Ashburton Place, 19th Floor
Boston, MA   02108
(617) 727-7780

Consumer Protection Division
Department of the Attorney General
436 Dwight Street
Springfield, MA   01103
(413) 785-1951

Michigan

Bureau of Automotive Regulation
Michigan Department of State
Lansing, MI   48918
(517) 373-7858
(800) 292-4204 (in Michigan)

Consumer Protection Division
Office of the Attorney General
670 Law Building
Lansing, MI   48913
(517) 373-1140

Michigan Consumers Council
414 Hollister Building
106 W. Allegan Street
Lansing, MI   48933
(517) 373-0947
(517) 737-0701 (TDD)

Minnesota

Consumer Services Division
Office of the Attorney General
320 W. 2nd Street
Duluth, MN   55802
(218) 723-4891

Office of Consumer Services
Office of the Attorney General
117 University Avenue
St. Paul, MN   55155
(612) 296-2331

Mississippi

Consumer Protection Division
Office of the Attorney General
P.O. Box 220
Jackson, MS   39205
(601) 354-6018
(601) 359-3680

Regulatory Services
Department of Agriculture &
    Commerce
P.O. Box 1609
Jackson, MS   39215
(601) 359-3648

Missouri

Department of Economic Development
P.O. Box 1157
Jefferson City, MO   65102
(314) 751-4962

Trade Offense Division
Office of the Attorney General
P.O. Box 899
Jefferson City, MO   65102
(314) 751-2616
(800) 392-8222 (in Missouri)

Montana

Consumer Affairs Unit
Department of Commerce
1424 9th Avenue
Helena, MT   59620
(406) 444-4312

Nebraska

Consumer Protection Division
Department of Justice
P.O. Box 94906
Lincoln, NE   68509
(402) 471-2682

Nevada

Consumer Affairs Division
Department of Commerce
201 Nye Building
Capitol Complex
Carson City, NV   89710
(702) 885-4340

Department of Commerce
State Mail Room Complex
Las Vegas, NV   89158
(702) 486-4150

New Hampshire

Consumer Protection & Antitrust
    Division
Office of the Attorney General
State House Annex
Concord, NH   03301
(603) 271-3641

New Jersey

Division of Consumer Affairs
1100 Raymond Boulevard, Room 504
Newark, NJ   07102
(201) 648-4010

Division of Law
Office of the Attorney General
1100 Raymond Boulevard, Room 316
Newark, NJ   07102
(201) 648-4730

Department of the Public Advocate
CN 850
Trenton, NJ   08625
(609) 292-7087
(800) 792-8600 (in New Jersey)

New Mexico

Consumer & Economic Crime Division
Office of the Attorney General
P.O. Drawer 1508
Santa Fe, NM   87504
(505) 827-6910
(800) 432-2070 (in New Mexico)

New York

Bureau of Consumer Frauds &
   Protection
Office of the Attorney General
State Capitol
Albany, NY   12224
(518) 474-5481

State Consumer Protection Board
99 Washington Avenue
Albany, NY   12210
(518) 474-8583

Bureau of Consumer Frauds &
   Protection
Office of the Attorney General
120 Broadway
New York, NY   10271
(212) 341-2300

Consumer Protection Board
250 Broadway, 17th Floor
New York, NY   10007
(212) 587-4482

North Carolina

Consumer Protection Section
Office of the Attorney General
Department of Justice Building
P.O. Box 629
Raleigh, NC   27602
(919) 733-7741

North Dakota

Consumer Fraud Division
Office of the Attorney General
State Capitol Building
Bismarck, ND   58505
(701) 224-3404
(800) 472-2600 (in North Dakota)

Office of the Attorney General
State Capitol Building
Bismarck, ND   58505
(701) 224-2210

Ohio

Consumer's Counsel
137 E. State Street
Columbus, OH   43215
(614) 466-9605 (both voice and TDD)
(800) 282-9448 (in Ohio)

Consumer Frauds & Crimes Section
Office of the Attorney General
30 E. Broad Street
State Office Tower, 15th Floor
Columbus, OH   43266
(614) 466-8831
(614) 466-4986
(614) 466-1393 (TDD)
(800) 282-0515 (in Ohio)

Oklahoma

Assistant Attorney General for
Consumer Affairs
Office of the Attorney General
112 State Capitol Building
Oklahoma City, OK   73105
(405) 521-3921

Department of Consumer Credit
Jim Thorpe Building, Room B-82
Oklahoma City, OK   73105
(405) 521-3653

Oregon

Financial Fraud Section
Department of Justice
Justice Building
Salem, OR   97310
(503) 378-4320

Pennsylvania

Bureau of Consumer Protection
Office of the Attorney General
27 N. 7th Street
Allentown, PA   18101
(215) 821-6990

Bureau of Consumer Protection
Office of the Attorney General
919 State Street, Room 203
Erie, PA   16501
(814) 871-4371

Bureau of Consumer Protection
Office of the Attorney General
Strawberry Square, 14th Floor
Harrisburg, PA   17120
(717) 787-9707
(800) 441-2555 (in Pennsylvania)

Office of Consumer Advocate-Utilities
Office of the Attorney General
Strawberry Square, 14th Floor
Harrisburg, PA   17120
(717) 783-5048

Bureau of Consumer Protection
Office of the Attorney General
1009 State Office Building
1400 W. Spring Garden Street
Philadelphia, PA   19130
(215) 560-2414

Bureau of Consumer Protection
Office of the Attorney General
Manor Building, 4th Floor
564 Forbes Avenue
Pittsburgh, PA   15219
(412) 565-5135

Bureau of Consumer Protection
Office of the Attorney General
State Office Building, Room 358
100 Lackawanna Avenue
Scranton, PA   18503
(717) 963-4913

Rhode Island

Consumer Protection Division
Department of the Attorney General
72 Pine Street
Providence, RI   02903
(401) 277-2104

Rhode Island Consumer's Council
365 Broadway
Providence, RI   02909
(401) 277-2764

South Carolina

Consumer Fraud & Antitrust Section
Office of the Attorney General
P.O. Box 11549
Columbia, SC   29211
(803) 734-3970

Department of Consumer Affairs
P.O. Box 5757
Columbia, SC   29250
(803) 734-9452
(800) 922-1594 (in South Carolina)

South Dakota

Division of Consumer Affairs
Office of the Attorney General
Anderson Building
Pierre, SD   57501
(605) 773-4400

Tennessee

Antitrust & Consumer Protection
   Division
Office of the Attorney General
450 James Robertson Parkway
Nashville, TN   37219
(615) 741-2672

Division of Consumer Affairs
Department of Commerce & Insurance
1808 W. End Building, Suite 105
Nashville, TN   37219
(615) 741-4737
(800) 342-8385 (in Tennessee)

Texas

Consumer Protection Division
Office of the Attorney General
P.O. Box 12548, Capitol Station
Austin, TX   78711
(512) 463-2070

Consumer Protection Division
Office of the Attorney General
Renaissance Place, 7th Floor
714 Jackson Street
Dallas, TX   75202
(214) 742-8944

Consumer Protection Division
Office of the Attorney General
4824 Alberta Street, Suite 160
El Paso, TX   79905
(915) 533-3484

Consumer Protection Division
Office of the Attorney General
1001 Texas Avenue, Suite 700
Houston, TX   77002
(713) 223-5886

Consumer Protection Division
Office of the Attorney General
806 Broadway, Suite 312
Lubbock, TX   79401
(806) 747-5238

Consumer Protection Division
Office of the Attorney General
4309 N. 10th, Suite B
McAllen, TX   78501
(512) 682-4547

Consumer Protection Division
Office of the Attorney General
200 Main Plaza, Suite 400
San Antonio, TX   78205
(512) 225-4191

Utah

Consumer Affairs
Office of the Attorney General
130 State Capitol
Salt Lake City, UT   84114
(801) 533-5319

Division of Consumer Protection
Department of Business Regulation
P.O. Box 45802
Salt Lake City, UT   84145
(801) 530-6601

Vermont

Public Protection Division
Office of the Attorney General
109 State Street
Montpelier, VT   05602
(802) 828-3171

Weights & Measures Division
Department of Agriculture
116 State Street
Montpelier, VT   05602
(802) 828-2436

Virginia

Office of Consumer Affairs
Department of Agriculture & Consumer
   Services
100 N. Washington Street, Suite 412
Falls Church, VA   22046
(703) 532-1613

Division of Consumer Counsel
Office of the Attorney General
Supreme Court Building
101 N. 8th Street
Richmond, VA   23219
(804) 786-2115

Office of Consumer Affairs
Department of Agriculture & Consumer
  Services
Room 101, Washington Building
1100 Bank Street
Richmond, VA   23219
(804) 786-2042
(800) 552-9963 (in Virginia)

Washington

Consumer & Business Fair Practices
  Division
Office of the Attorney General
N. 121 Capitol Way
Olympia, WA   98501
(206) 753-6210

Consumer & Business Fair Practices
  Division
Office of the Attorney General
1366 Dexter Horton Building
Seattle, WA   98104
(206) 464-7744
(800) 551-4636 (in Washington)

Consumer & Business Fair Practices
  Division
Office of the Attorney General
W. 1116 Riverside Avenue
Spokane, WA   99201
(509) 456-3123

Consumer & Business Fair Practices
  Division
Office of the Attorney General
949 Market Street, Suite 380
Tacoma, WA   98402
(206) 593-2904

West Virginia

Consumer Protection Division
Office of the Attorney General
812 Quarrier Street, 6th Floor
Charleston, WV   25301
(304) 348-8986
(800) 368-8808

Weights & Measures
Department of Labor
570 McCorkla Avenue S.W.
St. Albans, WV   25177
(304) 727-5781

Wisconsin

Trade & Consumer Protection
927 Loring Street
Altoona, WI   54720
(715) 839-3848

Trade & Consumer Protection
200 N. Jefferson Street, Suite 146A
Green Bay, WI 54301
(414) 436-4087

Office of Consumer Protection
Department of Justice
P.O. Box 7856
Madison, WI 53707
(608) 266-1852
(800) 362-8189 (in Wisconsin)

Trade & Consumer Protection
P.O. Box 8911
Madison, WI 53708
(608) 266-9836
(800) 362-3020 (in Wisconsin)

Office of Consumer Protection
Department of Justice
819 N. 6th Street, Room 520
Milwaukee, WI 53203
(414) 227-4948

Trade & Consumer Protection
10320 W. Silver Spring Drive
Milwaukee, WI 53225
(414) 438-4844

Wyoming

Office of the Attorney General
123 State Capitol Building
Cheyenne, WY 82002
(307) 777-7841
(307) 777-6286

Puerto Rico

Department of Justice
P.O. Box 192
Old San Juan, PR 00902
(809) 721-2900

Department of Consumer Affairs
P.O. Box 41059
Minillas Station
Santurce, PR 00940
(809) 722-7555

CHAPTER 13

INFORMATION ON ANY TOPIC

As mentioned in Chapter 1, a rule of thumb during research is to *start* with the most specific source of information available. If you are reading this last chapter, it is probably because you have checked the Contents or the Index, skimmed the book, and failed to find an organization that sounds pertinent for your current information need.

This chapter includes resources to help you research most topics. If you would like to identify an expert, an organization, or find written materials on any subject, see THE BEST SOURCES FOR RESEARCH below. The handful of directories and referral services listed should help get you started.

If you believe the information you need is available from a government source, check your local telephone directory. Also see GOVERNMENT REFERRAL SERVICES below. The two sections here list federal and state government referral agencies whose main job is to help the public identify the appropriate office in their government's bureaucracy. If you ever felt these bureaucracies were too large or disorganized to find the right source for information, you may be pleasantly surprised.

The final section of this chapter, SELF-HELP CLEARINGHOUSES, lists referral services that help identify local support groups or other organizations helping with physical, emotional, or family problems.

THE BEST SOURCES FOR RESEARCH

EXPERTS AND DIRECTORIES

The reference books listed below are by far the most useful printed sources that cover many subjects. If your local library does not own a copy, call a larger library in your region or one of the libraries listed below. Reference librarians at large and medium-size libraries usually keep these books close at hand. If your question is short and specific, the librarian may check one of these books while you wait on the phone.

The Encyclopedia of Associations (EA) is the source to consult if you want to talk to an expert on a topic not covered in this book. This annual multivolume set contains information on more than twenty thousand national associations in the United States. Every topic imaginable is covered.

If EA is unavailable locally and if librarians are unwilling to do a search for you over the phone, call the American Society of Association Executives (ASAE). They will help you identify a group that might help. Note that many associations listed in *The Encyclopedia of Associations* are not members of the ASAE and therefore would not be referred if you call.

American Society of Association
    Executives
1575 I Street, N.W.
Washington, DC   20005
(202) 626-2723

Directories in Print. The two volumes in this reference set describe approximately eight thousand specialized directories on numerous subjects. You will find listed such books as *Free and Inexpensive Learning Materials; Directory of Medical Specialists; Pennsylvania Job Bank;* and *Directory of Residential Treatment Facilities for Emotionally Disturbed Children.* Many of the directories listed in *Directories in Print* can be found at large libraries. Virtually all are available for purchase from their publishers.

Research Centers Directory. If you wish to identify a research organization working within the sciences, the humanities, education, the social sciences, and other fields, check *Research Centers Directory* (RCD). The seventy-five hundred groups listed in RCD are affiliated with companies, universities, the government, and other nonprofit organizations. In most cases, you should check RCD only if the *Encyclopedia of Associations* proves unsatisfactory.

REFERENCE SERVICES

Most major public libraries offer a limited reference service to anyone who calls. College libraries and company libraries in your area may also oblige. When calling a library, always ask to speak to a reference librarian. Sometimes a library assistant answers the phone first. Assistants mean well but are not properly trained to offer reference services.

Librarians often juggle several responsibilities at the same time. Be patient when you call. If your question can be answered within a few minutes, the librarian will probably help. Longer requests are beyond the scope of most telephone reference services.

If libraries in your region won't help with a telephone request, call one of the libraries below:

Telephone Reference Service
Correspondence Section
Library of Congress
Washington, DC   20540
(202) 287-5522

Reference-Information Service
Mid-Manhattan Branch
New York Public Library
455 Fifth Avenue
New York, NY   10016
(212) 340-0849

SPECIAL-SUBJECT LIBRARIES

If you seek information not covered in this book and you can't identify an association or government office that will help, a specialized librarian is the next-best source. These directories will guide you:

Directory of Special Libraries and Information Centers. This five-volume set, covering over seventeen thousand sources, is by far the best reference to locate a library with a certain specialty. Included are academic, private, government, and public libraries indexed by subject.

Subject Collections. This volume covers seven thousand special-subject collections found mainly in universities, museums, and public libraries.

An alternative to using these library directories is to call the Special Libraries Association. One of their Information Specialists will help you identify an appropriate library. While this service is valuable, note that only special-subject libraries belonging to the Association will be referred.

Special Libraries Association
1700 18th Street, N.W.
Washington, DC   20009
(202) 234-4700

Another association making library referrals by phone is the Association of College and Research Libraries. This group offers a much smaller number of choices than the Special Libraries Association.

Association of College & Research
   Libraries
American Library Association
50 Huron Street
Chicago, IL   60611
(312) 944-6780

BUYING BOOKS

Subject Guide to Books in Print. Approximately seven hundred fifty thousand books are available in print in the United States. This three-volume set lists these books by subject. If you would like to buy a book on a certain topic, the *Subject Guide to Books in Print* (SGBIP) is the best place to find a book that meets your needs. Most bookstores and libraries own SGBIP.

Another way to identify books on a topic is to call the appropriate organizations listed in *Who To Call.* Many of these groups sell, or will recommend, what they believe are the best books in their specialty.

If you seek a book on subjects concerning parenting and child rearing, you should also consider calling one of the bookstores listed in Chapter 12 in the MAIL ORDER CATALOGS section under Books. See in particular Birth & Life Bookstore and Parentbooks. Both stores offer extensive catalogs of books for parents. Both stores also have knowledgeable owners who will advise you which books will best answer your questions on a particular parenting subject.

GOVERNMENT REFERRAL SERVICES

STATE INFORMATION OFFICES

If you need to identify which office in your state government can answer a particular question, the referral services below will help.

Alabama

(205) 261-2500

Alaska

(907) 465-2111

Arizona

(602) 542-4900

Arkansas

(501) 371-3000

California

(916) 322-9900

Colorado

(303) 866-5000

Connecticut

(203) 566-2211

Delaware

(302) 736-4000

District of Columbia

(202) 727-1000

Florida

(904) 488-1234

Georgia

(404) 656-2000

Hawaii

(808) 548-2211

Idaho

(208) 334-2411

Illinois

(217) 782-2000

Indiana

(317) 232-3140

Iowa

(515) 281-5011

Kansas

(913) 296-0111

Kentucky

(502) 564-2500

Louisiana

(504) 342-6600

Maine

(207) 289-1110

Maryland

(301) 974-2000

Massachusetts

(617) 727-2121

Michigan

(517) 373-1837

Minnesota

(612) 296-6013

Mississippi

(601) 354-7011

Missouri

(314) 751-2000

Montana

(406) 444-2511

Nebraska

(402) 471-2311

Nevada

(702) 885-5000

New Hampshire

(603) 271-1110

New Jersey

(609) 292-2121

New Mexico

(505) 827-4011

New York

(518) 474-2121

North Carolina

(919) 733-1110

North Dakota

(701) 224-2000

Ohio

(614) 466-2000

Oklahoma

(405) 521-2011

Oregon

(503) 378-3131

Pennsylvania

(717) 787-2121

Rhode Island

(401) 277-2000

South Carolina

(803) 734-1000

South Dakota

(605) 773-3011

Tennessee

(615) 741-3011

Texas

(512) 463-4630

Utah

(801) 538-3000

Vermont

(802) 828-1110

Virginia

(804) 786-0000

Washington

(206) 753-5000

West Virginia	Wisconsin	Wyoming
(304) 348-3456	(608) 266-2211	(307) 777-7220

FEDERAL INFORMATION CENTERS

If you need to identify which office in the federal government can answer a particular question, the referral services below will help. If none are located in your state, call the nearest Federal Information Center.

Alabama

Birmingham (205) 322-8591
Mobile (205) 438-1421

Alaska

Anchorage (907) 271-3650

Arizona

Phoenix (602) 261-3313

Arkansas

Little Rock (501) 378-6177

California

Los Angeles (213) 894-3800
Sacramento (916) 551-2380
San Diego (619) 557-6030
San Francisco (415) 556-6600
Santa Ana (714) 836-2386

Colorado

Colorado Springs (719) 471-9491
Denver (303) 844-6575
Pueblo (303) 544-9523

Connecticut

Hartford (203) 527-2617
New Haven (203) 624-4720

Florida

Ft. Lauderdale (305) 522-8531
Jacksonville (904) 354-4756
Miami (305) 536-4155
Orlando (305) 422-1800
St. Petersburg (813) 893-3495
Tampa (813) 229-7911
West Palm Beach (407) 833-7566

Georgia

Atlanta (404) 331-6891

Hawaii

Honolulu (808) 551-1365

Illinois

Chicago (312) 353-4242

Indiana

Gary (219) 883-4110
Indianapolis (317) 269-7373

Iowa

Statewide (800) 532-1556

Kansas

Statewide (800) 432-2934

Kentucky

Louisville (502) 582-6261

Louisiana

New Orleans (504) 589-6696

Maryland

Baltimore (301) 962-4980

Massachusetts

Boston (617) 565-8121

Michigan

Detroit (313) 226-7016
Grand Rapids (616) 451-2628

Minnesota

Minneapolis (612) 370-3333

Missouri

St. Louis (314) 425-4106
All other points (800) 392-7711

Nebraska

Omaha (402) 221-3353
All other points (800) 642-8383

New Jersey

Newark (201) 645-3600
Trenton (609) 396-4400

New Mexico

Albuquerque (505) 766-3091

New York

Albany (518) 463-4421
Buffalo (716) 846-4010
New York (212) 264-4464
Rochester (716) 546-5075
Syracuse (315) 476-8545

North Carolina

Charlotte (704) 376-3600

Ohio

Akron (216) 375-5638
Cincinnati (513) 684-2801
Cleveland (216) 522-4040
Columbus (614) 221-1014
Dayton (513) 223-7377
Toledo (419) 241-3223

Oklahoma

Oklahoma City (405) 231-4868
Tulsa (918) 584-4193

Oregon

Portland (503) 221-2222

Pennsylvania

Philadelphia (215) 597-7042
Pittsburgh (412) 644-3456

Rhode Island

Providence (401) 331-5565

Tennessee

Chattanooga (615) 265-8231
Memphis (901) 521-3285
Nashville (615) 242-5056

Texas

Austin (512) 472-5494
Dallas (214) 767-8585
Fort Worth (817) 334-3624
Houston (713) 229-2552
San Antonio (512) 224-4471

Utah

Salt Lake City (801) 524-5353

Virginia

Norfolk (804) 441-3101
Richmond (804) 643-4928
Roanoke (703) 982-8591

Washington

Seattle (206) 442-0570
Tacoma (206) 383-5230

Wisconsin

Milwaukee (414) 271-2273

SELF-HELP CLEARINGHOUSES

Clearinghouses are excellent sources for referrals to local organizations of all types, particularly those offering support groups for emotional and family concerns such as adoption, alcoholism, bereavement, developmental disability, divorce, foster care, learning dysfunction, remarriage, mental health, parenting, retirement, single life, vocation and career, and more.

NATIONAL

American Self-Help Clearinghouse
St. Clare's-Riverside Medical Center
Denville, NJ   07834
(201) 625-7101
(201) 625-9053 (TDD)
The Center offers referrals to groups nationwide.

National Self-Help Clearinghouse
33 W. 42nd Street, Room 620N
New York, NY   10036
(212) 840-1258
(212) 840-1259
The Clearinghouse runs a data bank and telephone service that makes referrals to self-help groups and clearinghouses nationwide.

Self-Help Center
1600 Dodge Avenue, Room S-122
Evanston, IL   60201
(708) 328-0470
This source makes referrals to local groups nationwide.

STATE AND LOCAL

Arizona

Community Information & Referral Service
1515 East Osborn Road
Phoenix, AZ   85014
(602) 263-8856
This service makes referrals in Central and Northern Arizona.

California

Bay Area Self-Help Clearinghouse
2398 Pine Street
San Francisco, CA   94110
(415) 921-4401
This organization is a regional clearinghouse for eleven counties and over six hundred self-help groups in the Bay Area. The Clearinghouse offers information and referrals, training and consultation for groups and individuals, community education programs, and a quarterly newsletter.

California Self-Help Center
UCLA, 2349 Franz Hall
405 Hilgard Avenue
Los Angeles, CA   90024-1563
(213) 825-1799
(800) 222-LINK (5465) (in California)
The Center helps Californians cope with life-disrupting problems, such as bereavement, illness, parenting, divorce, and addiction. Its toll-free number and computerized data bank can connect callers with over thirty-seven hundred self-help groups throughout California.

Central California Regional Self-Help Center
Merced County Mental Health Department
650 W. 19th Street
Merced, CA   95340
(209) 385-6937
The Center provides research and referral services throughout a thirteen-county region in central California.

Community Resources Information Services (CRIS)
P.O. Box 3953
Santa Barbara, CA   93130
(805) 682-2727
For Santa Barbara County, CRIS offers information and referral services over the phone and publishes a directory of available services. CRIS is the parent organization of CALL-line (Community Assistance Listening Line), a twenty-four-hour crisis-intervention service.

Friends Network
Stanislaus County Special Projects
346 Burney Street
Modesto, CA   95354
(209) 525-7454
Provides referrals and publishes a directory of over seventy groups.

Hotline of San Luis Obispo County, Inc.
P.O. Box 654
San Luis Obispo, CA   93506
(805) 544-6016
The Hotline's staff of trained volunteers offers telephone crisis intervention, information, and referrals all on a twenty-four-hour basis.

Northern California Regional Self-Help Center
5370 Elvas Avenue
Sacramento, CA   95819
(916) 456-2070
The Center offers referrals and publishes the *Tri-County Self-Help Directory, Media Guide for Self-Help Groups,* and the *Self-Help Group Training Manual.*

Northern Region Self-Help Center
Mental Health Association
8912 Volunteer Lane
Sacramento, CA   95826
(916) 368-3100

Southern California Regional Self-Help Center
San Diego Mental Health Association
3958 3rd Avenue
San Diego, CA   92103
(619) 298-3152

Support Group Clearinghouse
Mental Health Association of Merced County
P.O. Box 343
Merced, CA 95341
(209) 723-5111
This office maintains a clearinghouse for over seventy-five support groups in Merced County, operates an information and referral service, and provides support to local groups.

Connecticut

Connecticut Self Help/Mutual Support Network
The Consultation Center of CMHC
19 Howe Street
New Haven, CT   06511
(203) 789-7645
Services include referrals to the public, technical assistance in starting and maintaining groups, and educational workshops. The Network publishes the *Self Help Directory* and the *Connecticut Directory of Self Help/Mutual Support Groups.*

Illinois

The Self-Help Center (SHC)
1600 Dodge Avenue, Suite S-122
Evanston, IL   60201
(312) 328-0470
(800) 322-6274 (in Illinois)
The SHC offers referrals to self-help groups for nearly four hundred physical and emotional problems. The Center maintains a statewide database of two thousand self-help groups and resource listings.

Self-Help Center
Family Service of Champaign County
405 S. State Street
Champaign, IL   61820
(312) 328-0470

Iowa

Self-Help Clearinghouse
Iowa Pilot Parents, Inc.
33 N. 12th Street
Fort Dodge, IA   50501
(515) 576-5870
(800) 383-4777 (in Iowa)

Kansas

Self-Help Network
The Wichita State University
Department of Psychology
Campus Box 34
Wichita, KS   67208-1595
(316) 689-3170

The Network serves as a resource center and clearinghouse for self-help groups throughout Kansas. It publishes the *Directory of Self-Help/ Mutual Support Groups.*

Massachusetts

Massachusetts Clearinghouse of Mutual Help Groups
Massachusetts Cooperative Extension
Division of Home Economics
113 Skinner Hall
University of Massachusetts
Amherst, MA   01003
(413) 545-2313

Michigan

Center for Self Help
Riverwood Center
P.O. Box 547
1485 Highway M-139
Benton Harbor, MI   49022-0547
(616) 925-0594
(800) 336-0341 (in Michigan)
This office operates as a regional self-help clearinghouse for southwestern Michigan and northern Indiana. It provides networking for individuals, groups, professionals and agencies, and publishes the *Directory of Self-Help Groups.*

Michigan Self-Help Clearinghouse
109 W. Michigan Avenue, Suite 900
Lansing, MI   48933
(517) 484-7373
(800) 752-5858 (in Michigan)
The Clearinghouse's computerized database of over seventeen hundred self-help groups is available through its toll-free number. If no appropriate group exists, the caller can be placed on a "seeker" list and be connected with other callers having similar concerns.

Minnesota

First Call for Help
166 E. 4th Street
St. Paul, MN   55104
(612) 291-8427 (administration)
(612) 224-1133

Minnesota Mutual Help Resource Center
Community Care Resources
Wilder Foundation
919 Lafond Avenue
St. Paul, MN   55104
(612) 642-4060
Runs a phone referral service and publishes the *Minnesota Mutual Help Resource Directory,* which lists more than twenty-five hundred mutual-help support groups within Minnesota.

Missouri

Kansas City Association for Mental Health

Westport Allen Center
706 W. 42nd Street
Kansas City, MO   64111
(816) 561-1800 (administration)
(816) 561-HELP (4357) (24-hour
  hotline)
Provides referrals on a round-the-clock basis to locate support groups, agencies, therapists, mental-health centers, and community services.

Nebraska

Self-Help Information Service of Nebraska, Inc.

1601 Euclid Avenue
Lincoln, NE   68502
(402) 476-9668
The Self-Help Information Service disseminates information about mutual self-help throughout the state. It publishes directories and a newsletter.

New Jersey

Self-Help Clearinghouse

St. Clare's-Riverside Medical Center
Pocono Road
Denville, NJ   07834
(201) 625-7101 (information and
  referral services)
(201) 625-9053 (TDD)
(800) 367-6274 (in New Jersey)

The Self-Help Clearinghouse offers referrals in New Jersey. It also sponsors MASHnet, a computerized networking service for persons suffering from rare disorders or conditions for which no self-help group exists. Finally, the Clearinghouse publishes *Self-Help Groups for People with AIDS* (a group development manual).

New York

Brooklyn Self-Help Clearinghouse

30 3rd Avenue
Brooklyn, NY   11217
(718) 834-7341
(718) 834-7373

Chemung/Schuyler Self-Help Clearinghouse

Economic Opportunity Program
207 S. Catherine Street
P.O. Box 690
Montour Falls, NY   14865
(607) 535-2468
(800) 348-0448
The Clearinghouse maintains an up-to-date directory of self-help groups and a Schuyler County Human Services Directory.

Dutchess County Self-Help Clearinghouse

Information Line of United Way
United Way of Dutchess County
P.O. Box 832
Poughkeepsie, NY   12602

(914) 473-1500
(914) 473-1511 (TDD)
The Self-Help Clearinghouse maintains a database of self-help groups in Dutchess Country, and publishes a directory of self-help groups. Through Information Line, callers can also be connected to other services in the community.

Erie County Self-Help Clearinghouse
Mental Health Association of Erie
    County, Inc.
1237 Delaware Avenue
Buffalo, NY   14209
(716) 886-1242
Offers a referral service and publishes a Self-Help Directory.

Fulton County Self-Help Clearinghouse
113 Bleecker Street
Gloversville, NY   12078
(518) 725-4310
Provides referrals to residents of Fulton County, New York.

Greene County Self-Help Clearinghouse
1 Bridge Street
Catskill, NY   12414
(518) 943-9205
Makes referrals to groups within Greene County.

HELPLINE
22 W. 3rd Street
Corning, NY   14830
(607) 936-4114
(800) 346-2211 (in New York)
HELPLINE provides general information and referral services to Steuben County residents and accepts participants for a free county-wide financial counseling program.

HELPLINE Information & Referral
    Service
The Volunteer Center, Inc.
115 E. Jefferson Street
Syracuse, NY   13202
(315) 474-7011
HELPLINE is a twenty-four-hour service staffed by professionals. It makes referrals to more than one hundred fifty area self-help groups and the offices listed in the *Syracuse/Onondaga County Human Services Directory*.

Herkimer County Self-Help
    Clearinghouse
104 N. Washington Street
Herkimer, NY   13350
(315) 866-1310
Herkimer County Self-Help Clearinghouse is a twenty-four-hour listening and referral service. It publishes the *Herkimer County Self-Help Clearinghouse Support Group Directory*.

Long Island Self-Help Clearinghouse (LISHC)
Self-Help Action Center, Inc.
New York Institute of Technology
Central Islip Campus
Central Islip, NY   11722
(516) 348-3030
(516) 348-3031
LISHC provides referral services to self-help groups and mutual support programs for any number of emotional and family concerns. It maintains a library and publishes *People Helping People Directory of Mutual-Support Resources.*

Montgomery County Self-Help Clearinghouse
St. Mary's Hospital
427 Guy Park Avenue
Amsterdam, NY   12010
(518) 842-1900
The Montgomery Clearinghouse offers information about support groups and health education programs for people within Montgomery County and its surrounding areas.

New York City Self-Help Clearinghouse, Inc.
New York City Technical College of the City University of New York
P.O. Box 022812
Brooklyn, NY   11202
(718) 596-6000

The Clearinghouse makes referrals and publishes *Appleshare,* a directory of over seven hundred self-help groups for New York City, national and local hotlines, and clearinghouses across the country.

New York State Self-Help Clearinghouse
New York State Council on Children & Families
Corning Tower, 28th Floor
Empire State Plaza
Albany, NY   12223
(518) 474-6293
Provides referrals to a network of over thirty local self-help clearinghouses that cover thirty-four counties.

Niagara Self-Help Clearinghouse
The Mental Health Association in Niagara County, Inc.
151 East Avenue
Lockport, NY   14094
(716) 433-3780
The Clearinghouse provides referrals to self-help support groups.

Otsego County Self-Help Clearinghouse
OURS Parents' Center
OURS Associates
9 S. Main Street
Oneonta, NY   13820
(607) 432-8623

This office serves as a referral service for Otsego County, listing nearly forty support groups.

Rensselaer County Self-Help Clearinghouse
Commission on Economic Opportunity (CEO) for the Rensselaer County Area, Inc.
2331 5th Avenue
Troy, NY   12180
(518) 272-6012
The CEO offers referrals on many topics but has a special mission to help low-income people become self-sufficient.

Schenectady Self-Help Clearinghouse
Human Services Planning Council
432 State Street, Room 220
Schenectady, NY   12305
(518) 372-3395
(518) 374-2244 (information)
The Schenectady Clearinghouse provides networking to local, state, and national resources. It maintains a library of self-help organizing materials, information on more than one hundred local self-help groups, and publishes directories of state and national clearinghouses.

Self-Help Clearinghouse
Mental Health Association of Rockland County, Inc.
Robert L. Yeager Health Center

Building J, Sanatorium Road
Pomona, NY   10970
(914) 354-0200 (ext. 3609 or 3604)
Offers referral services, promotes networking between groups and professional services, and publishes a directory of self-help groups in Rockland County.

Self-Help Clearinghouse of Cattaraugus County
American Red Cross
Olean Branch of Greater Buffalo Chapter
Olean Service Center
528 N. Barry Street
Olean, NY   14760
(716) 372-5800
Distributes information on self-help groups, provides meeting information on a twenty-four-hour basis, and publishes a self-help newsletter and directory.

Tompkins County Mental Health Association
313 N. Aurora Street
Ithaca, NY   14850
(607) 273-9250
The Association provides advocacy, education, information, and referrals concerning mental-health issues and services.

Westchester Self-Help Clearinghouse
Westchester Community College AA/B
75 Grasslands Road
Valhalla, NY   10595
(914) 347-3620
The Westchester Clearinghouse provides information and referrals to more than two hundred fifty self-help groups in Westchester County. It publishes the *Directory of Self-help Groups in Westchester County.*

North Carolina

Supportworks
1012 Kings Drive, Suite 923
Charlotte, NC   28283
(704) 331-9500
Supportworks serves the greater Mecklenberg region.

Oregon

**NW Regional Self-Help Groups
   Clearinghouse**
718 W. Burnside Avenue
Portland, OR   97209
(503) 222-5555 (information)
(503) 226-9360 (research)
The NW Regional Clearinghouse maintains a database of over thirty-six hundred resources in Multnomah, Clackamas, and Washington Counties in Oregon, and Clark County in Washing-ton. It publishes a monthly resource file, and the following annual directories: *Human Services Directory; Self-Help Groups Directory;* and *Guide to Services & Information for Cancer Patients.*

Pennsylvania

Philadelphia Clearinghouse
c/o Self-Help Institute
462 Monastery Avenue
Philadelphia, PA   19128
(215) 482-4316

Self Help Group Network
710 1/2 South Avenue
Pittsburgh, PA   15221
(412) 247-5400
The Network maintains a computerized database of self-help groups and individuals interested in self-help within southwestern Pennsylvania (the Pittsburgh area). It publishes the *Directory of Self-Help Groups in Southwestern PA.*

**Self-Help Group Network of the
   Pittsburgh Area**
1323 Forbes Avenue
Pittsburgh, PA   15219
(412) 261-5363

**Self-Help Information Network
Exchange of Lackawanna County
(SHINE)**
Voluntary Action Center of
Northeastern Pennsylvania
225 N. Washington Avenue
Park Plaza, Lower Level
Scranton, PA   18503
(717) 961-1234 (24-hour hotline)
SHINE serves as a parent for over one
hundred twenty-five support organizations which fall into four categories:
physical health; mental health; substance abuse; and family concerns such
as parenting, aging, separation/divorce,
and death.

Rhode Island

The Support Group Helpline
Rhode Island Department of Health
Cannon Building
Davis Street
Providence, RI   02908
(401) 277-2231

South Carolina

The Support Group Network
Lexington Medical Center
2720 Sunset Boulevard
West Columbia, SC   29169
(803) 791-9227
The Network makes referrals to mutual
support groups in the Richland/Lexing-
ton County areas and assists in starting

needed support groups in the following
categories: addictions, bereavement,
health problems, disabilities, mental
health, parenting, and life transitions.

Tennessee

Support Group Clearinghouse
Mental Health Association of Knox
County
6712 Kingston Road, Room 203
Knoxville, TN   37919
(615) 584-6736

Texas

Houston Area Self-Help Clearinghouse
Mental Health Association
2211 Norfolk
Houston, TX   77098
(713) 523-8963
The Clearinghouse serves Houston and
Harris counties.

San Antonio Self-Help Clearinghouse
Mental Health Association
1407 N. Main
San Antonio, TX   78212
(512) 826-2288

Self Help Clearinghouse, Dallas
Mental Health Association of Dallas
County
2500 Maple Avenue
Dallas, TX   75201-1998
(214) 871-2420

Texas Self-Help Clearinghouse
Mental Health Association in Texas
1111 W. 24th Street
Austin, TX   78705
(512) 476-0611

Virginia

Self-Help Clearinghouse of Greater
   Washington
100 N. Washington Street, Suite 232
Falls Church, VA   22046
(703) 536-4100
The Clearinghouse runs a referral service and publishes a directory of self-
help groups in the Washington
metropolitan area.

Canada

Canada Council on Social Development
P.O. Box 3505, Station C
Ottawa, Ontario   K1Y 4G1
Canada
(613) 728-1865

Family Life Education Council
233 12th Avenue, S.W.
Calgary, Alberta   T2R 0G9
Canada
(403) 262-1117

Saskatchewan Self-Help Development
   Unit
410 Cumberland Avenue N.
Saskatoon, Saskatchewan   S7N 1M6
Canada
(306) 652-7817

Self-Help Clearinghouse of Metro
40 Orchard View Boulevard, Suite 215
Toronto, Ontario   M4R 1B9
Canada
(416) 487-4355

Self-Help Connection
5739 Inglis Street
Halifax, Nova Scotia   B3H 1K5
Canada
(902) 422-5831

Self-Help Resource Clearinghouse
NorWest Coop & Health Center
103-61 Tyndall Avenue
Winnipeg, Manitoba   R2X 2T4
Canada
(204) 589-5500
(204) 633-5955

INDEX